Microsoft

Core Reference

PROGRAMMING
MICROSOFT®
.NET

Microsoft®
.net

Jeff Prosise

Wintellect®

PUBLISHED BY
Microsoft Press
A Division of Microsoft Corporation
One Microsoft Way
Redmond, Washington 98052-6399

Library of Congress Cataloging-in-Publication Data
Prosise, Jeff.
    Programming Microsoft .NET (core reference) / Jeff Prosise.
        p. cm.
    Includes index.
    ISBN 0-7356-1376-1
    1. Microsoft.net framework.   2. Microsoft software.   3. Internet programming.   I. Title.

  QA76.625 .P76   2002
  005.2'76--dc21   2002016626

Printed and bound in the United States of America.

2 3 4 5 6 7 8 9   QWT   7 6 5 4 3 2

Distributed in Canada by H.B. Fenn and Company Ltd.

A CIP catalogue record for this book is available from the British Library.

Microsoft Press books are available through booksellers and distributors worldwide. For further informa-
tion about international editions, contact your local Microsoft Corporation office or contact Microsoft
Press International directly at fax (425) 936-7329. Visit our Web site at www.microsoft.com/mspress.
Send comments to *mspinput@microsoft.com*.

Acquisitions Editor: Anne Hamilton
Project Editor: John Pierce
Technical Editor: Marc Young

Body Part No. X08-04505

To Abby

Contents at a Glance

Table of Contents

Part 3   ## The Cutting Edge

12   **ADO.NET**   **563**

Acknowledgments

I'd like to take a moment to thank the numerous people who contributed to the production of this book and lent their unselfish support to the person who wrote it.

First, a tip of the hat to John Pierce, wordsmith par excellence, and Marc Young, who is the most thorough technical editor I've ever had the pleasure of working with. Both are veterans of many books and are among the best in the business at what they do. I hate to even think about what this book would look like had it not been for them.

Next, a profound thanks to the colleagues whom I pressed into service to read chapters and provide technical feedback: Francesco Balena, Jason Clark, John Lam, John Robbins, Kenn Scribner, and Dave Webster. I'm especially indebted to Jeffrey Richter for sharing with me his deep knowledge of the .NET Framework.

Special thanks also to the many people inside and outside Microsoft who answered my questions and helped me overcome technical obstacles. The list includes, but is not limited to, Peter Drayton, Rob Howard, Erik Olson, and Brent Rector.

And lest I forget, a heartfelt thanks to Microsoft Press illustrator Rob Nance, who got me out of a jam when I needed comic book covers for the sample programs in Chapter 6. Also to Microsoft's Anne Hamilton, who allowed me the opportunity to write this book and waited patiently for me to deliver, and Claudette Moore, my agent and longtime friend, who pressed me to get this project off the ground.

Finally, to my family: my wife, Lori, and my children, Adam, Amy, and Abby. Writing a book is hard work. This time around I proved that it's harder on the author's family than it is on the author himself. These four endured a lot while I spent endless days and nights laboring over the manuscript, and words can't express how good it feels to know that they're always there for me, rooting for me every step of the way.

Look, kids. I'm done!

Introduction

Yes, it's that time again—time to throw away everything you know and start all over. The era of Microsoft .NET has arrived, and with it comes a promise to change software development as we know it. Microsoft .NET is many things, but first and foremost it's a better way to write software in an Internet-centric world. To benefit from .NET, you'll find it helpful to let go of any preconceived notions and prepare yourself to think about software in a whole new light. That means shedding comfortable clothing such as the Windows API, MFC, and COM, and immersing yourself in new ways of developing and architecting software that are unlike anything you've seen before.

When I began writing this book in July 2001, I had been working with the .NET Framework SDK for more than a year. The .NET Framework was in beta at the time and was still months away from emerging as a released product. When I first laid eyes on it, I expected to see something that resembled COM. What I saw instead was a radical departure from anything Microsoft had done before and a better way to write software. If your company's plans include Web apps, Web services, or other applications that use the Internet as their platform, there simply is no better way to write those applications than to use Microsoft .NET. I would no more consider writing a Web app today with ASP than I would consider using a wrench to drive nails. The first ingredient for a successful software project is picking the right tool for the job. If your job involves Web programming (and maybe even if it doesn't), Microsoft .NET is just the tool that you need.

This book is about Microsoft .NET—what it is, how it works, and how to write software that uses it. Among other things, you'll learn about the common language runtime (CLR) and the highly structured environment that it provides for executing code compiled from C#, Visual Basic .NET, and other languages. You'll learn about the .NET Framework class library (FCL), the stunningly comprehensive class library that provides the API managed applications write to. You'll become acquainted with the programming models embodied in the FCL, including Windows Forms, Web Forms, and XML Web services. And just as important, you'll learn how to make all the pieces work together to write sophisticated applications that leverage the power of Microsoft .NET.

The Journey Ahead

Programming Microsoft .NET tells a story—the story of Microsoft .NET. You can read it from beginning to end and learn in step-wise fashion how to write software that targets the .NET Framework. The book is also structured so that individual chapters stand alone. If you're a seasoned .NET developer who simply wants to learn about multithreading, turn to Chapter 14 for a detailed treatment of threads and thread synchronization. If it's custom ASP.NET server controls that float your boat, go straight to Chapter 8. The information you find there will help you get the job done with a minimum of wasted motion.

If you prefer the beginning-to-end approach, here's what you'll encounter along the way. Part 1 of this book builds the foundation you need for understanding and profiting from subsequent chapters. You'll become acquainted with the Microsoft .NET Framework, which includes the common language runtime and the .NET Framework class library. You'll learn about the framework's type system and about some of the more than 7,000 types included in the FCL. You'll also learn about one of the .NET Framework's most important programming models: Windows Forms. Windows Forms lets you build GUI applications similar to the ones that are so prevalent in Windows today. Later on, in Chapter 15, you'll even learn how to pair Windows Forms with the .NET Framework's remoting subsystem to build rich client apps that link to remote servers.

Part 2 is all about ASP.NET—the portion of the .NET Framework that helps you build Web applications and Web services. Web programming today is a black art built around HTML, DHTML, ASP, COM, and other loosely related technologies. Web programming tomorrow will be a science, thanks to ASP.NET. If you've tried Web programming before and don't like it because you don't like dealing with slow, weakly typed scripting languages and find browser DOMs more trouble than they're worth, ASP.NET might just change your mind. It's a true second-generation technology for building applications that run on the Web. Moreover, it brings compiled code, strong type safety, and (to a degree) browser independence to Web programming. Chapters 5 through 11 cover ASP.NET in detail and impart the skills you need to write cutting-edge ASP.NET Web applications and Web services.

Part 3 rounds out the book with detailed coverage of selected portions of the .NET Framework. Topics include ADO.NET, which provides a database access API for managed applications; XML and all the classes that the FCL provides for dealing with XML data; threading, or how to write multithreaded code and coordinate the actions of concurrently running threads; and remoting, which provides a framework for writing closely coupled distributed applications. Take these chapters to heart and you'll be able to hold your own in conversations at .NET parties.

A Word About Programming Languages

One of the hallmarks of the .NET Framework is that it is language-agnostic. For the first time in history, it matters little what language you choose to write code in because in the end all languages exercise the same set of features in the .NET Framework.

I do all my coding in C#, in part because C# is the only language designed specifically with the .NET Framework in mind, and also, because I'm an old C++ guy, C# feels natural to me. Since I'm a C# programmer, the vast majority of the code samples in this book are written in C#, too. Few of the concepts presented in the book, however, relate only to C#. This book is about programming the .NET Framework, and C# happens to be the vehicle that I use to express my thoughts. If you prefer Visual Basic .NET or COBOL instead, it is my hope that this book will be no less valuable to you. Once you know how to open a connection to a database with ADO.NET, the code for actually doing it is remarkably similar whether it's written in Visual Basic .NET or C#.

Most of the samples in this book were written by hand, without the help of Visual Studio .NET. That's not a knock on Visual Studio .NET; it's evidence of my belief that learning is best accomplished by coding and not by having someone else code for you. Once you understand what goes into a Windows form or a Web form or a Web service, you'll find Visual Studio .NET an able partner in helping to create them. Writing applications the old-fashioned way first will increase your depth of understanding and better prepare you to work in an environment in which tools shoulder part of the load for you.

System Requirements

To compile and run the more than 75 sample programs included in this book, you must have the .NET Framework Software Development Kit (SDK) installed on your machine. The SDK runs on Windows NT 4.0, Windows 2000, Windows XP, and presumably on later versions of Windows as well. The CD that comes with this book includes version 1.0 of the .NET Framework SDK as well as Service Pack 1. When newer versions become available, you can download them by pointing your browser to *http://msdn.microsoft.com/downloads/default.asp?url=/downloads/sample.asp?url=/msdn-files/027/000/976/msdncompositedoc.xml*. We all know that URLs change. If you go to this one and find that it's no longer valid, visit the Microsoft .NET home page at *http://www.microsoft.com/net* for the latest information on where to find the SDK.

Chapters 5 through 11 of this book, which cover ASP.NET, impose another requirement on your system. In addition to being outfitted with the .NET Framework SDK, your PC needs to have Microsoft's Web server, Internet Information Services (IIS), installed. Because ASP.NET requires Windows 2000 or Windows XP, you need one of those operating systems, too. On the Professional editions of these operating systems, IIS isn't part of the default installation. To install IIS, open Add or Remove Programs in Control Panel and select Add/Remove Windows Components. You'll find a check box for IIS. Be sure to install IIS *before* installing the SDK to make sure ASP.NET gets installed, too.

Some of the chapters in this book include sample programs built with Visual Studio .NET and provide Visual Studio .NET–specific instructions. You don't have to have Visual Studio .NET to build code that targets the .NET Framework; the SDK comes with command-line compilers. However, Visual Studio .NET offers a highly integrated development environment that makes writing, testing, and debugging code easier. If you don't already own a copy of Visual Studio .NET, you can purchase one from Microsoft. For more information, visit *http://msdn.microsoft.com/vstudio/howtobuy*.

What's on the CD

Programmers like goodies. The CD that comes with this book contains the following delectable delights:

- All of the book's sample programs, source code included
- A fully searchable electronic version of the book
- The .NET Framework SDK version 1.0 and Service Pack 1

You'll find instructions on the CD for installing the components that come on it. If AutoPlay is enabled on your PC, simply pop the CD in a drive to get started. In addition to being included on the CD, the sample files are available for download from *http://www.microsoft.com/mspress/books/5200.asp*.

Support

If you have comments about this book, questions you want answered, or errors to report, please post them at *http://forum.wintellect.com/pro_ms_net*. I'll check the message board regularly and do my best to respond. Others will monitor message traffic also and jump in as appropriate. If you have a question, chances are someone else has one just like it. The answer may already be posted. If not, by posting your question in a public forum, you enable others to benefit from the answer as well.

I'd like to tell you that this book contains no errors, but of course I'd be lying. I've done everything humanly possible to verify the accuracy of every sentence and every code sample, but errors will inevitably surface. You'll find an up-to-date errata list at *http://www.wintellect.com/about/instructors/prosise/ netbook.asp*. If you don't want to fuss with a long URL, simply go to *http:// www.prosise.com*, and you'll find a link there.

If you'd like to contact Microsoft Press directly about this book or need to resolve packaging problems (such as a defective or missing CD), you can contact them on line at *http://www.microsoft.com/mspress/support*. If you prefer paper mail, the address is:

Microsoft Press
Attn: *Programming Microsoft .NET Editor*
One Microsoft Way
Redmond, WA 98052-6399

Blogs and Other Things That Go Bump in the Night

Ever wonder what it's like to write a book? When I wrote my first one in 1990, I learned that writing a book is an emotional roller coaster filled with peaks and valleys. The peaks are the elation that you feel when you describe a complex technical topic in a way that lifts the veil so that others can understand. The valleys come from thinking of the sheer magnitude of the effort that lies before you. Many is the time I wish I had kept a diary of that period in my life. Although I vividly remember the incredible relief I felt when I packaged up the last chapter and dropped it into a Fedex box (publishers still required printed manuscripts in those days), most of the day-to-day details of that experience escape me.

That's why I documented my experience writing *Programming Microsoft .NET* in my very own book blog. "Blog" is short for "Web log"; it's a diary published on the Internet. People all over the world tracked my progress as I wrote this book by checking my (almost) daily blog entries. If you'd like to relive the experience, you'll find the finished blog at *http://www.wintellect.com/about/ instructors/prosise/blog*.

Finally, a personal note. There's no shortage of Microsoft .NET programming books on the market. I'm humbled that you chose this one, and I sincerely hope your investment in this book pays for itself many times over. Enjoy!

Jeff Prosise
March 13, 2002

Part 1

Essential Concepts

1

Hello, .NET

"A journey of a thousand miles must begin with a single step."
—Sixth century B.C. Chinese philosopher Lao Tzu

Software development today is an industry beset by incompatibilities. Modules written in different languages don't easily integrate. Programs run on separate machines must jump through hoops to talk to each other. Applications developed for different operating systems are built on incompatible APIs, making porting difficult. And as the industry's focus shifts from stand-alone applications and client/server programs to applications that live and run on the Web, new kinds of incompatibilities appear—incompatibilities between programming models that have stood the test of time and models that have evolved without planning or forethought to fill a void that needed filling. Instead of compiled languages, we have scripting languages. Instead of rich graphical user interfaces, we have HTML. And instead of object-oriented programming, we have enterprise-class applications built with mixtures of procedural code, HTML, DHTML, XML, COM, and other unrelated technologies.

Microsoft has a vision of the future that addresses these issues and many more. That vision is embodied in an initiative called Microsoft .NET. Microsoft .NET, or simply .NET as it is more commonly called, is a new way of building and deploying software that leverages standards such as HTTP and XML to make interoperability a reality rather than a dream, and that relies on the Internet to make software services available on an unprecedented scale. An important part of the initiative is the .NET Framework, which is a platform for building and running .NET applications. The framework isn't required for building .NET applications, but it makes the development process eminently easier and less time-consuming. Among its many benefits: it brings object-oriented programming to the Web; it eliminates many of the most common and debilitating kinds of software bugs; and it provides a common API for all languages, meaning the language that you choose at the beginning of a project won't paint you into a corner at the end.

This chapter is your first step on the road to becoming a .NET Framework programmer. In it, you'll become acquainted with the framework's two core components: the common language runtime and the .NET Framework class library. You'll learn about metadata, common intermediate language, managed modules, and assemblies. At the end of the chapter, you'll write your first framework application. The information you come away with will enrich your understanding of the .NET Framework and help you understand what goes on under the hood when you build and run the applications presented in subsequent chapters.

The Microsoft .NET Initiative

The term "Microsoft .NET" refers to a massive effort on Microsoft's part to get away from traditional software development and to build—with help from partners all over the industry—the Internet into a service-oriented software platform. Read the documents that provide an overview of .NET on Microsoft's Web site, and you'll encounter the term "XML Web services" repeatedly. An XML Web service is an application that runs on a Web server and exposes callable API functions, or *Web methods*, to clients on the Internet. XML is part of the name because Web services and Web service clients use XML to exchange data. As XML Web services proliferate, the Internet will become a software platform with an API far richer than any operating system. Today's applications rely primarily on operating system services. Tomorrow's applications will use Web services to validate credit card purchases, check the status of airline flights, and perform other everyday tasks. With luck, your favorite restaurants will make their menus available via a Web service so that you can check the daily specials from the comfort of your computer desk.

Web services aren't something that Microsoft invented, nor are they proprietary to Microsoft .NET. Web services rely on open standards such as HTTP, XML, and SOAP. (SOAP, in case you don't know, is an acronym for Simple Object Access Protocol; it's an Internet standard that describes how applications can interoperate—that is, call methods on each other—using HTTP and other protocols.) Because they're an industry standard and not a Microsoft standard, Web services are already proliferating on the Internet. Significantly, most of the Web services that are available today do not use the .NET Framework and do not run on Windows. Web services are about interoperability. It's relatively simple to write a Web service client that runs on Windows and invokes methods on a Web service running on Linux. In the future, online directories that are themselves Web services will enable companies to advertise their Web services. Need a Web service that exposes real-time stock quotes or shipment tracking information? Microsoft and others are building UDDI (Universal Description, Discovery, and Integration) registries that make such information available on a global scale.

If XML Web services can be written without Microsoft's help, then what does Microsoft .NET bring to the party? Plenty. First, .NET validates the Web service concept by throwing the weight of an industry giant behind it. Second, Microsoft is busy writing Web services of its own, promoting Web service initiatives such as .NET My Services, upgrading its enterprise server products to fit seamlessly into a service-oriented world, and upgrading Visual Studio and other development tools to speak the language of Web services. Third, and perhaps most important, is that Microsoft .NET includes the .NET Framework. You can write Web services using *x*86 assembly language if you want to, but the .NET Framework makes writing Web services so easy that just about anyone can write one. You'll learn all about Web services and the framework's support for them in Chapter 11.

The Microsoft .NET Framework

The .NET Framework is a platform for building and running applications. Its chief components are the common language runtime (CLR, or simply "the runtime") and the .NET Framework class library (FCL). The CLR abstracts operating system services and serves as an execution engine for *managed applications*—applications whose every action is subject to approval by the CLR. The FCL provides the object-oriented API that managed applications write to. When you write .NET Framework applications, you leave behind the Windows API, MFC, ATL, COM, and other tools and technologies you're familiar with, and you use the FCL instead. Sure, you can call a Windows API function or a COM object if you want to, but *you don't want to* because doing so requires transitioning from *managed code* (code run by the CLR) to *unmanaged code* (native machine code that runs without the runtime's help). Such transitions impede performance and can even be vetoed by a system administrator.

Microsoft .NET is chiefly about XML Web services, but the .NET Framework supports other programming models as well. In addition to writing Web services, you can write console applications, GUI applications ("Windows Forms"), Web applications ("Web Forms"), and even Windows services, better known as NT services. The framework also helps you *consume* Web services—that is, write Web service clients. Applications built on the .NET Framework are not, however, required to use Web services.

Next to XML Web services, the portion of the framework with the greatest potential to change the world is ASP.NET. The name comes from Active Server Pages (ASP), which revolutionized Web programming in the 1990s by providing an easy-to-use model for dynamically producing HTML content on Web servers using server-side script. ASP.NET is the next version of ASP, and it provides a compelling new way to write Web applications that's unlike anything that has preceded it. Because ASP.NET is such an important part of the framework, and because the number one question asked by developers in the software industry today is "How do I write applications that run on the Web?," a large portion of this book—all of Part 2, in fact—is devoted to it.

But first things first. The key to understanding the .NET Framework and the various programming models it supports is to understand the common language runtime and the FCL. The next several sections discuss both and introduce other important concepts that are vital for learning how to write Web services and other managed applications.

The Common Language Runtime

If the .NET Framework were a living, breathing human being, the common language runtime would be its heart and soul. Every byte of code that you write for the framework either runs in the CLR or is given permission by the CLR to run outside the CLR. Nothing happens without the CLR's involvement.

The CLR sits atop the operating system and provides a virtual environment for hosting managed applications. When you run a managed executable, the CLR loads the module containing the executable and executes the code inside it. Code that targets the CLR is called managed code, and it consists of instructions written in a pseudo-machine language called *common intermediate language*, or CIL. CIL instructions are just-in-time (JIT) compiled into native machine code (typically *x*86 code) at run time. In most cases, a given method is JIT compiled only one time—the first time it's called—and thereafter cached in memory so that it can be executed again without delay. Code that isn't called is never JIT compiled. While JIT compilation undeniably impacts performance, its negative effects are mitigated by the fact that a method is compiled only once during the application's lifetime and also by the fact that the CLR team at Microsoft has gone to extraordinary lengths to make the JIT compiler as fast and efficient as possible. In theory, JIT compiled code can outperform ordinary code because the JIT compiler can optimize the native code that it generates for the particular version of the host processor that it finds itself running on. JIT compiled code is *not* the same as interpreted code; don't let anyone tell you otherwise.

The benefits of running code in the managed environment of the CLR are legion. For starters, as the JIT compiler converts CIL instructions into native code, it enacts a code verification process that ensures the code is type safe. It's practically impossible to execute an instruction that accesses memory that the instruction isn't authorized to access. You'll never have problems with stray pointers in a managed application because the CLR throws an exception before the stray pointer is used. You can't cast a type to something it's not because that operation isn't type safe. And you can't call a method with a malformed stack frame because the CLR simply won't allow it to happen. In addition to eliminating some of the most common bugs that afflict application programs, code verification security makes it eminently more difficult to write malicious code that intentionally inflicts harm on the host system. In the unlikely event that you don't want code verification security, you can have it turned off by a system administrator.

Code verification security is also the chief enabling technology behind the CLR's ability to host multiple applications in a single process—a feat of magic that it works by dividing the process into virtualized compartments called *application domains*. Windows isolates applications from one another by hosting them in separate processes. An unfortunate side effect of the one-process-per-application model is higher memory consumption. Memory efficiency isn't vital on a stand-alone system that serves one user, but it's paramount on servers set up to handle thousands of users at once. In certain cases (ASP.NET applications and Web services being the prime examples), the CLR doesn't launch a new process for every application; instead, it launches one process or a handful of processes and hosts individual applications in application domains. Application domains are secure like processes because they form boundaries that managed applications can't violate. But application domains are more efficient than processes because one process can host multiple application domains and because libraries can be loaded into application domains and shared by all occupants.

Another benefit of running in a managed environment comes from the fact that resources allocated by managed code are garbage collected. In other words, you allocate memory, but you don't free it; the system frees it for you. The CLR includes a sophisticated garbage collector that tracks references to the objects your code creates and destroys those objects when the memory they occupy is needed elsewhere. The precise algorithms employed by the garbage collector are beyond the scope of this book, but they are documented in detail in Jeffrey Richter's book *Applied Microsoft .NET Framework Programming* (Microsoft Press, 2002).

Thanks to the garbage collector, applications that consist solely of managed code don't leak memory. Garbage collection even improves performance because the memory allocation algorithm employed by the CLR is fast—much faster than the equivalent memory allocation routines in the C runtime. The downside is that when a collection does occur, everything else in that process stops momentarily. Fortunately, garbage collections occur relatively infrequently, dramatically lessening their impact on performance.

Programming Languages

Yet another benefit of running applications in a CLR-hosted environment is that all code reduces to CIL, so the programming language that you choose is little more than a lifestyle choice. The "common" in common language runtime alludes to the fact that the CLR is language-agnostic. In other environments, the language you use to implement an application inevitably affects the application's design and operation. Code written in Visual Basic 6, for example, can't easily spawn threads. To make matters worse, modern programming languages such as Visual Basic and Visual C++ use vastly different APIs, meaning that the knowledge you gain programming Windows with Visual Basic is only marginally helpful if your boss asks you to write a DLL in C++.

With the .NET Framework, all that changes. A language is merely a syntactic device for producing CIL, and with very few exceptions, anything you can do in one language, you can do in all the others, too. Moreover, regardless of what language they're written in, all managed applications use the same API: that of the .NET Framework class library. Porting a Visual Basic 6 application to Visual C++ is only slightly easier than rewriting the application from scratch. But porting a Visual Basic .NET application to C# (or vice versa) is much more reasonable. In the past, language conversion tools have been so imperfect as to be practically useless. In the era of the .NET Framework, someone might write a language converter that really works. Because high-level code ultimately compiles to CIL, the framework even lets you write a class in one language and use it (or derive from it) in another. Now that's language independence!

Microsoft provides CIL compilers for five languages: C#, J#, C++, Visual Basic, and JScript. The .NET Framework Software Development Kit (SDK) even includes a CIL assembler called ILASM, so you can write code in raw CIL if you want to. Third parties provide compilers for other languages, including Perl, Python, Eiffel, and, yes, even COBOL. No matter what language you're most comfortable with, chances are there's a CIL compiler that supports it. And you can sleep better knowing that even if you prefer COBOL, you can do almost anything those snobby C# programmers can do. That, of course, won't prevent them from ribbing you for being a COBOL person, but that's another story.

Managed Modules

When you build a program with the C# compiler, the Visual Basic .NET compiler, or any other compiler capable of generating CIL, the compiler produces a *managed module*. A managed module is simply an executable designed to be run by the CLR. It typically, but not always, has the file name extension EXE, DLL, or NETMODULE. Inside a managed module are four important elements:

- A Windows Portable Executable (PE) file header

- A CLR header containing important information about the module, such as the location of its CIL and metadata

- Metadata describing everything inside the module and its external dependencies

- The CIL instructions generated from the source code

Every managed module contains metadata describing the module's contents. Metadata is *not optional*; every CLR-compliant compiler must produce it. That's important, because it means every managed module is self-describing. Think about it this way. If someone hands you an ordinary EXE or DLL today, can you easily crack it open and figure out what classes are inside and what members those classes contain? No way! If it's a managed module, however, no problem. Metadata is like a COM type library, but with two important differences:

- Type libraries are optional; metadata is not

- Metadata fully describes a module; type libraries sometimes do not

Metadata is important because the CLR must be able to determine what types are present in each managed module that it loads. But it's also important to compilers and other tools that deal with managed executables. Thanks to metadata, Visual Studio .NET can display a context-sensitive list of the methods and properties available when you type the name of a class instance into the program editor, a feature known as IntelliSense. And thanks to metadata, the C# compiler can look inside a DLL containing a class written in Visual Basic .NET and use it as the base class for a derived class written in C#.

Metadata

A module's core metadata is stored in a collection of tables. One table, the TypeDef table, lists all the types defined in the module. ("Type" is a generic term for classes, structs, enumerations, and other forms of data understood by the CLR.) Another table lists the methods implemented by those types, another lists the fields, another lists the properties, and so on. By reading these tables, it's possible to enumerate all the data types defined in the module as well as the members each type includes. Additional tables list external type references (types and type members in other modules that are used by this module), the assemblies containing the external types, and more.

Additional metadata information is stored outside the tables in heaps containing items referenced by table entries. For example, class names and method names are stored in the string heap; string literals are stored in a separate heap called the user-string heap. Together, metadata tables and heaps define everything you (or the CLR) could possibly want to know about a module's contents and external dependencies.

The portion of a managed module that holds the module's CIL is sprinkled with *metadata tokens* that refer to entries in the metadata tables. Each row in each table is identified by a 32-bit metadata token consisting of an 8-bit table index and a 24-bit row index. When a compiler emits the CIL for a method, it also emits a metadata token identifying the row containing information about the method. When the CLR encounters the token, it can consult the table to discover the method's name, visibility, signature, and even its address in memory.

The metadata format is interesting from an academic point of view, but it's rare that an application developer finds use for such knowledge. Most applications don't manipulate metadata directly; they leave that to the CLR and to compilers. Applications that need to read and write metadata can do so by using either of two APIs provided by the .NET Framework. Called the *reflection APIs*, these APIs insulate the developer from the binary metadata format. One is an unmanaged API exposed through COM interfaces. The other is a managed API exposed through classes in the FCL's *System.Reflection* namespace.

Using the reflection APIs to write a tool that lists the types and type members in a managed module is relatively easy. But if inspecting metadata is your goal, you don't have to write a tool because the .NET Framework SDK has one already. Called ILDASM, it uses reflection to reveal the contents of managed executables. Figure 1-1 shows ILDASM displaying ImageView.exe, one of the sample programs in Chapter 4. The tree depicts the one class defined in the module (*MyForm*) and all the members of that class. But here's the cool part. If you start ILDASM with a */ADV* (for "Advanced") switch and select the View/MetaInfo/Show command (or press Ctrl+M, which works regardless of whether you started ILDASM with a */ADV* switch), a window pops up detailing all the rows in all the metadata tables (Figure 1-2). By checking and unchecking items in the View/MetaInfo menu, you can configure ILDASM to display metadata in different ways.

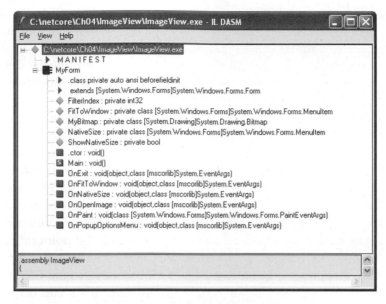

Figure 1-1   The ILDASM view of ImageView.exe.

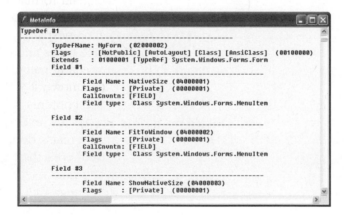

Figure 1-2   Metadata displayed by ILDASM.

Common Intermediate Language

CIL is often described as a pseudo-assembly language because it defines a native instruction set for a processor. In this case, however, the processor is the CLR, not a piece of silicon. You don't have to know CIL to program the .NET Framework any more than you have to know *x*86 assembly language to program Windows. But a rudimentary knowledge of CIL can really pay off when a method in the FCL doesn't behave the way you expect it to and you want to know why. You don't have the source code for the FCL, but you do have the CIL.

In all, CIL includes about 100 different instructions. Some are the typical low-level instructions found in silicon instruction sets, like instructions to add two values together (ADD) and to branch if two values are equal (BEQ). Other instructions work at a higher level and are atypical of those found in hardware instruction sets. For example, NEWOBJ instantiates an object, and THROW throws an exception. Because the CIL instruction set is so rich, code written in high-level languages such as C# and Visual Basic .NET frequently compiles to a surprisingly small number of instructions.

CIL uses a stack-based execution model. Whereas *x*86 processors load values into registers to manipulate them, the CLR loads values onto an evaluation stack. To add two numbers together, you copy them to the stack, call ADD, and retrieve the result from the stack. Copying a value from memory to the stack is called *loading*, and copying from the stack to memory is called *storing*. CIL has several instructions for loading and storing. LDLOC, for example, loads a value onto the stack from a memory location, and STLOC copies it from the stack to memory and removes it from the stack.

For an example of CIL at work, consider the following C# source code, which declares and initializes two variables, adds them together, and stores the sum in a third variable:

```
int a = 3;
int b = 7;
int c = a + b;
```

Here's the CIL that Microsoft's C# compiler produces, with comments added by hand:

```
ldc.i4.3  // Load a 32-bit (i4) 3 onto the stack
stloc.0   // Store it in local variable 0 (a)
ldc.i4.7  // Load a 32-bit (i4) 7 onto the stack
stloc.1   // Store it in local variable 1 (b)
ldloc.0   // Load local variable 0 onto the stack
ldloc.1   // Load local variable 1 onto the stack
add       // Add the two and leave the sum on the stack
stloc.2   // Store the sum in local variable 2 (c)
```

As you can see, the CIL is pretty straightforward. What's not obvious, however, is how the local variables a, b, and c (locals 0, 1, and 2 to the CLR) get allocated. The answer is through metadata. The compiler writes information into the method's metadata noting that three local 32-bit integers are declared. The CLR retrieves the information and allocates memory for the locals before executing the method. If you disassemble the method with ILDASM, the metadata shows up as a compiler directive:

```
.locals init (int32 V_0, // Local variable 0 (a)
              int32 V_1, // Local variable 1 (b)
              int32 V_2) // Local variable 2 (c)
```

This is a great example of why metadata is so important to the CLR. It's used not only to verify type safety, but also to prepare execution contexts. Incidentally, if a C# executable is compiled with a /DEBUG switch, ILDASM will display real variable names instead of placeholders such as V_0.

The .NET Framework SDK contains a document that describes the entire CIL instruction set in excruciating detail. I won't clutter this chapter with a list of all the CIL instructions, but I will provide a table that lists some of the most commonly used instructions and describes them briefly.

Common CIL Instructions

Instruction	Description
BOX	Converts a value type into a reference type
CALL	Calls a method; if the method is virtual, virtualness is ignored
CALLVIRT	Calls a method; if the method is virtual, virtualness is honored
CASTCLASS	Casts an object to another type
LDC	Loads a numeric constant onto the stack
LDARG[A]	Loads an argument or argument address [A] onto the stack
LDELEM	Loads an array element onto the stack
LDLOC[A]	Loads a local variable or local variable address [A] onto the stack
LDSTR	Loads a string literal onto the stack
NEWARR	Creates a new array
NEWOBJ	Creates a new object
RET	Returns from a method call
STARG	Copies a value from the stack to an argument
STELEM	Copies a value from the stack to an array element
STLOC	Transfers a value from the stack to a local variable
THROW	Throws an exception
UNBOX	Converts a reference type into a value type

The same ILDASM utility that lets you view metadata is also a fine CIL disassembler. For a demonstration, start ILDASM and use it to open one of the System.*.dll DLLs in the \%SystemRoot%\Microsoft.NET\Framework\v1.0.*nnnn* directory. These DLLs belong to the .NET Framework class library. After opening the DLL, drill down into its namespaces and classes until you find a method you want to disassemble. Methods are easy to spot because they're marked with magenta rectangles. Double-click the method and you'll see its CIL, complete with compiler directives generated from the method's metadata. Better still, ILDASM is a round-trip disassembler, meaning that you can pass the disassembled code to ILASM and reproduce the CIL that you started with.

When speaking to groups of developers about CIL, I'm often asked about intellectual property issues. If you and I can disassemble the FCL, what's to prevent a competitor from disassembling your company's product? Reverse-engineering CIL isn't trivial, but it's easier than reverse-engineering *x*86 code. And decompilers that generate C# source code from CIL are freely available on the Internet. So how do you protect your IP?

The short answer is—it depends. Code that runs only on servers—XML Web services, for example—isn't exposed to users, so it can't be disassembled unless someone breaches your firewall. Code distributed to end users can be scrambled with third-party code obfuscation utilities. Obfuscators can't guarantee that no one can read your code, but they can make doing so harder. In the final analysis, someone who has physical access to your CIL and wants to reverse-engineer it badly enough will find a way to do it. If it's any consolation, the Java community has grappled with this problem for years. There is no perfect solution other than sticking strictly to server-side apps.

Assemblies

You now know that compilers that target the .NET Framework produce managed modules and that managed modules contain CIL and metadata. But you might be surprised to learn that the CLR is incapable of using managed modules directly. That's because the fundamental unit of security, versioning, and deployment in the .NET Framework is not the managed module but the assembly.

An *assembly* is a collection of one or more files grouped together to form a logical unit. The term "files" in this context generally refers to managed modules, but assemblies can include files that are not managed modules. Most assemblies contain just one file, but assemblies can and sometimes do include multiple files. All the files that make up a multifile assembly must reside in the same directory. When you use the C# compiler to produce a simple EXE, that EXE is not only a managed module, it's an assembly. Most compilers are capable of producing managed modules that aren't assemblies and also of adding other files to the assemblies that they create. The .NET Framework SDK also includes a tool named AL (Assembly Linker) that joins files into assemblies.

Multifile assemblies are commonly used to glue together modules written in different languages and to combine managed modules with ordinary files containing JPEGs and other resources. Multifile assemblies are also used to partition applications into discrete downloadable units, which can be beneficial for code deployed on the Internet. Imagine, for example, that someone with a dial-up connection wants to download a multi-megabyte application housed in a single-file assembly. Downloading the code could take forever. To mitigate the problem, you could divide the code into multiple files and make the files part of the same assembly. Because a module isn't loaded unless it's needed, the user won't incur the cost of downloading the portions of the application that aren't used. If you're smart about how you partition the code, the bulk of the application might not have to be downloaded at all.

How does the CLR know which files belong to an assembly? One of the files in the assembly contains a *manifest*. Physically, the manifest is just more metadata; when a compiler creates a managed module that also happens to be an assembly, it simply writes the manifest into the module's metadata. Logically, the manifest is a road map to the assembly's contents. Its most important elements are

- The assembly's name

- A list of the other files in the assembly, complete with cryptographic hashes of the files' contents

- A list of the data types exported from other files in the assembly and information mapping those data types to the files in which they're defined

- A version number in the format *major.minor.build.revision* (for example, 1.0.3705.0)

The manifest can also include other information such as a company name, description, requested security permissions, and culture string. The latter identifies the assembly's targeted culture (for example, "en-US" for "United States English") and is typically used with so-called "satellite assemblies" that contain only resources. Figure 1-3 depicts a multifile assembly that consists of three managed modules and a JPEG file. Main.exe holds the manifest, and the manifest contains references to the other files. In the eyes of the file system, these are still separate files. But to the CLR, they're one logical entity.

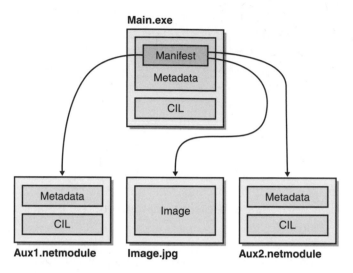

Figure 1-3 Multifile assembly.

In the absence of information directing them to do otherwise, compilers produce assemblies that are weakly named. "Weakly named" means that the assembly is not cryptographically signed and that the CLR uses only the name stored in the assembly manifest (which is nothing more than the assembly's file name without the file name extension) to identify the assembly. But assemblies can be strongly named. A strongly named assembly contains the publisher's public key and a digital signature that's actually a hash of the assembly manifest where the public key is stored.

The digital signature, which is generated with the publisher's private key and can be verified with the public key, makes the assembly's manifest (and, by extension, the assembly itself) tamperproof. A strongly named assembly's identity derives from the assembly name, the public key, the version number, and the culture string, if present. Any difference, no matter how small, is sufficient to distinguish two otherwise identical assemblies.

The SDK's AL utility can be used to create strongly named assemblies. Most language compilers, including the C# and Visual Basic .NET compilers, can also emit strongly named assemblies. It's up to you whether to deploy weakly or strongly named assemblies. The right choice is dictated by the assemblies' intended use. If an assembly is to be deployed in the global assembly cache (GAC)—a global repository used by assemblies designed to be shared by multiple applications—it must be strongly named.

An assembly must also be strongly named if you want to take advantage of version checking. When the CLR loads a weakly named assembly, it does no version checking. That can be good or bad. It's good if you replace an old version of the assembly with a new one (perhaps one that has undergone bug fixes) and want applications that use the assembly to automatically use the new one. It's bad if you've thoroughly tested the application against a specific version of the assembly and someone replaces the old assembly with a new one that's riddled with bugs. That's one symptom of the DLL Hell that Windows developers are all too familiar with. Strong naming can fix that. When the CLR loads a strongly named assembly, it compares the version number in the assembly to the version number that the application doing the loading was compiled against. (That information, not surprisingly, is recorded in the module's metadata.) If the numbers don't match up, the CLR throws an exception.

Strict version checking, of course, has pitfalls of its own. Suppose you elect to use strong naming, but later you find a bug in your assembly. You fix the bug and deploy the revised assembly. But guess what? Applications that use the assembly won't load the new version unless you rebuild them. They'll still load the old version, and if you delete the old version, the applications won't run at all. The solution is to modify the CLR's binding policy. It's relatively simple for an administrator to point the CLR to a new version of a strongly named assembly by editing a configuration file. Of course, if the newer version has bugs, you're right back to square one. That's why you don't let just anyone have administrator privileges.

Working with assemblies sounds pretty complicated—and at times, it is. Fortunately, if you're not building shared assemblies or assemblies that link to other assemblies (other than the FCL, which, by the way, is a set of shared assemblies), most of the issues surrounding naming and binding fall by the wayside. You just run your compiler, copy the resulting assembly to a directory, and run it. Couldn't be much simpler than that.

The .NET Framework Class Library

Windows programmers who code in C tend to rely on the Windows API and functions in third-party DLLs to get their job done. C++ programmers often use class libraries of their own creation or standard class libraries such as MFC. Visual Basic programmers use the Visual Basic API, which is an abstraction of the underlying operating system API.

Using the .NET Framework means you can forget about all these anachronistic APIs. You have a brand new API to learn, that of the .NET Framework class library, which is a library of more than 7,000 types—classes, structs, interfaces, enumerations, and delegates (type-safe wrappers around callback functions)—that are an integral part of the .NET Framework. Some FCL classes contain upward of 100 methods, properties, and other members, so learning the FCL isn't a chore to be taken lightly. The bad news is that it's like learning a brand new operating system. The good news is that every language uses the same API, so if your company decides to switch from Visual Basic to C++ or vice versa, the investment you make in learning the FCL isn't lost.

To make learning and using the FCL more manageable, Microsoft divided the FCL into hierarchical namespaces. The FCL has about 100 namespaces in all. Each namespace holds classes and other types that share a common purpose. For example, much of the window manager portion of the Windows API is encapsulated in the *System.Windows.Forms* namespace. In that namespace you'll find classes that represent windows, dialog boxes, menus, and other elements commonly used in GUI applications. A separate namespace called *System.Collections* holds classes representing hash tables, resizable arrays, and other data containers. Yet another namespace, *System.IO,* contains classes for doing file I/O. You'll find a list of all the namespaces present in the FCL in the .NET Framework SDK's online documentation. Your job as a budding .NET programmer is to learn about those namespaces. Fortunately, the FCL is so vast and so comprehensive that most developers will never have to tackle it all.

The following table lists a few of the FCL's namespaces and briefly describes their contents. The term "et al" refers to a namespace's descendants. For example, *System.Data* et al refers to *System.Data, System.Data.Common, System.Data.OleDb, System.Data.SqlClient,* and *System.Data.SqlTypes.*

A Sampling of FCL Namespaces

Namespace	Contents
System	Core data types and auxiliary classes
System.Collections	Hash tables, resizable arrays, and other containers
System.Data et al	ADO.NET data access classes
System.Drawing	Classes for generating graphical output (GDI+)
System.IO	Classes for performing file and stream I/O
System.Net	Classes that wrap network protocols such as HTTP
System.Reflection et al	Classes for reading and writing metadata
System.Runtime.Remoting et al	Classes for writing distributed applications
System.ServiceProcess	Classes for writing Windows services
System.Threading	Classes for creating and managing threads
System.Web	HTTP support classes
System.Web.Services	Classes for writing Web services
System.Web.Services.Protocols	Classes for writing Web service clients
System.Web.UI	Core classes used by ASP.NET
System.Web.UI.WebControls	ASP.NET server controls
System.Windows.Forms	Classes for GUI applications
System.Xml et al	Classes for reading and writing XML data

The first and most important namespace in the FCL—the one that *every* application uses—is *System*. Among other things, the *System* namespace defines the core data types employed by managed applications: bytes, integers, strings, and so on. When you declare an int in C#, you're actually declaring an instance of *System.Int32*. The C# compiler recognizes int as a shortcut simply because it's easier to write

```
int a = 7;
```

than it is to write

```
System.Int32 a = 7;
```

The *System* namespace is also home for many of the exception types defined in the FCL (for example, *InvalidCastException*) and for useful classes such as *Math*, which contains methods for performing complex mathematical operations; *Random*, which implements a pseudo-random number generator; and *GC*, which provides a programmatic interface to the garbage collector.

Physically, the FCL is housed in a set of DLLs in the \%System-Root%\Microsoft.NET\Framework\v1.0.*nnnn* directory. Each DLL is an assembly that can be loaded on demand by the CLR. Core data types such as Int32 are implemented in Mscorlib.dll; other types are spread among the FCL DLLs. The documentation for each type lists the assembly in which it's defined. That's important, because if a compiler complains about an FCL class being an undefined type, you must point the compiler to the specific assembly that implements the class for you. The C# compiler uses */r[eference]* switches to identify referenced assemblies.

Obviously, no one chapter (or even one book) can hope to cover the FCL in its entirety. You'll become acquainted with many FCL classes as you work your way through this book. Chapter 3 kicks things off by introducing some of the FCL's coolest classes and namespaces. For now, realize that the FCL *is* the .NET Framework API and that it's an extraordinarily comprehensive class library. The more you use it, the more you'll like it, and the more you'll come to appreciate the sheer effort that went into putting it together.

Your First .NET Framework Application

If the information presented thus far in Chapter 1 seems hopelessly abstract, take heart: things are about to get concrete very quickly. It's time to develop your first .NET Framework application. And what better way to start than by writing a managed version of "Hello, world"? To keep it simple, we'll write a console application—one that runs in a command prompt window. That will keep the code as uncluttered as possible and allow us to focus on the issues that matter most.

Hello, World

Figure 1-4 lists the contents of Hello.cs, a C# source code file containing the .NET Framework version of "Hello, world." To compile it, open a command prompt window, go to the directory where Hello.cs is stored, and type the following command:

```
csc /target:exe /out:Hello.exe Hello.cs
```

This command invokes the C# compiler and produces an executable named Hello.exe. The */target* switch, which can be abbreviated */t*, tells the compiler to produce a console application. Because a console application is the default, and because the default EXE file name is the name of the CS file, you can save wear and tear on your fingers by compiling the program with the command

```
csc Hello.cs
```

Once the compilation process is complete, run Hello.exe by typing *hello* at the command prompt. "Hello, world" should appear in the window, as shown in Figure 1-5.

Hello.cs
```
using System;

class MyApp
{
    static void Main ()
    {
        Console.WriteLine ("Hello, world");
    }
}
```

Figure 1-4   "Hello, world" in C#.

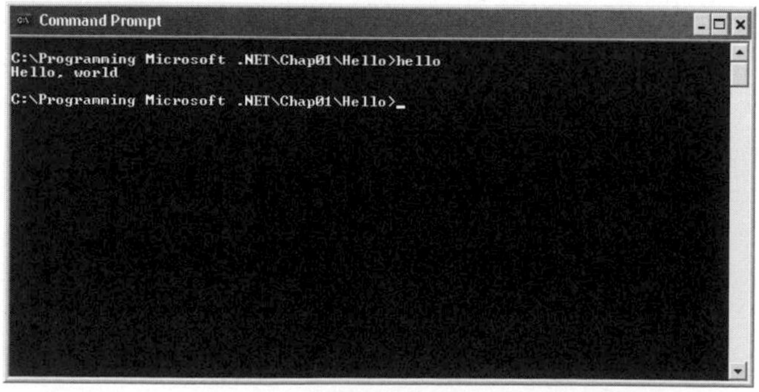

Figure 1-5   Output from Hello.exe.

So what happened when you ran Hello.exe? First, a short *x*86 stub emitted by the compiler transferred control to the CLR. The CLR, in turn, located and called the program's *Main* method, which compiled to three simple CIL instructions. The JIT compiler transformed the instructions into *x*86 machine code and executed them. Had you compiled and run the EXE on another type of machine, the same CIL instructions would have compiled to instructions native to the host processor.

Inside Hello.cs

Let's talk about the code in Figure 1-4. For starters, every application has to have an entry point. For a C# application, the entry point is a static method named *Main*. Every C# application has one. Because C# requires that all methods belong to a type, in Hello.cs, *Main* is a member of *MyApp*. There's nothing magic about the class name; you could name it *Foo* and it would work just the same. If an application contains multiple classes and multiple *Main* methods, a */main* switch tells the C# compiler which class contains the *Main* method that's the entry point.

The one and only statement in *MyApp.Main* is the one that writes "Hello, world" to the console window. If Hello were a standard Windows application written in C or C++, you'd probably use *printf* to write the output. But this isn't a standard Windows application. It's a .NET Framework application, and .NET Framework applications use the FCL to write to console windows. The FCL's *System* namespace features a class named *Console* that represents console windows. Look up *Console* in the FCL reference, and you'll find that it contains a static method named *WriteLine* that writes a line of text to the window (or to wherever standard output happens to point at the time).

The statement

```
using System;
```

at the beginning of the program is a syntactical simplification. Remember that the FCL contains more than 7,000 members divided into approximately 100 namespaces. Without the *using* directive, you'd have to qualify the reference to *Console* by prefacing the class name with the namespace name, as shown here:

```
System.Console.WriteLine ("Hello, world");
```

But with the *using* directive, you can abbreviate the reference by specifying only the class name. It's not a big deal here, but when you write programs containing hundreds, perhaps thousands, of references to FCL classes, you'll appreciate not having to type the namespace names over and over. Most languages support the *using* directive or an equivalent. In Visual Basic .NET, it's called *Imports*.

What happens if two namespaces contain identically named classes and you use both of those classes in your application? Simple: you have to qualify the references one way or another. The following code won't compile because both namespaces contain classes named *ListBox*:

```
using System.Windows.Forms;
using System.Web.UI.WebControls;
  :
ListBox winLB = new ListBox (); // Create a Windows Forms ListBox
ListBox webLB = new ListBox (); // Create a Web Forms ListBox
```

Consequently, you have two choices. The first is to fully qualify the class names:

```
System.Windows.Forms.ListBox winLB =new System.Windows.Forms.ListBox ();
System.Web.UI.WebControls.ListBox webLB =
    new System.Web.UI.WebControls.ListBox ();
```

The second is to use an alternative form of the *using* directive to create aliases for the fully qualified class names:

```
using winListBox = System.Windows.Forms.ListBox;
using webListBox = System.Web.UI.WebControls.ListBox;
  :
winListBox winLB = new winListBox (); // Create a Windows Forms ListBox
webListBox webLB = new webListBox (); // Create a Web Forms ListBox
```

This example is admittedly contrived because you'll probably never use a Web Forms *ListBox* and a Windows Forms *ListBox* in the same program (not for any reason I can think of, anyway). But the principle is valid just the same.

More About the *Main* Method

Hello's *Main* method accepts no parameters and returns no data, but that's just one of four different ways that you can prototype *Main*. All of the following are legitimate:

```
static void Main ()
static int Main ()
static void Main (string[] args)
static int Main (string[] args)
```

The *args* parameter is an array of strings containing the program's command-line arguments. The string at index 0 is the first argument, the string at index 1 is the second, and so on. If you rewrote the program this way:

```
using System;

class MyApp
{
    static void Main (string[] args)
    {
        Console.WriteLine ("Hello, " + args[0]);
    }
}
```

and started it by typing *hello .NET*, the output from the program would be "Hello, .NET." Use the form of *Main* that receives an *args* parameter if you want to accept command-line input in your program.

The modified form of Hello.cs in the previous paragraph has one little problem: if you run it without any command-line parameters, it throws an exception because the 0 in *args*[0] constitutes an invalid array index. To find out how many command-line parameters were entered, read the string array's *Length* property, as in:

```
int count = args.Length;
```

This statement works because an array in the framework is an instance of *System.Array*, and *System.Array* defines a property named *Length*. You can use *Length* to determine the number of items in any array, no matter what type of data the array stores.

Inside Hello.exe

If you'd like to see Hello.exe as the CLR sees it, start ILDASM and open Hello.exe. You'll see the window shown in Figure 1-6. The first red triangle represents the assembly manifest. Double-click it, and you'll see a list of assemblies that this assembly depends on (".assembly extern mscorlib"), as shown in Figure 1-7. You'll also see the assembly name (".assembly Hello") and a list of the modules that make up the assembly. Because Hello.exe is a single-file assembly, it's the only module that appears in the list.

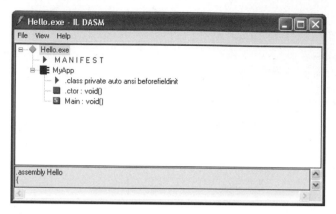

Figure 1-6   ILDASM displaying the contents of Hello.exe.

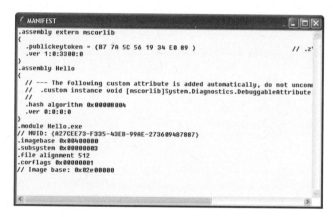

Figure 1-7   Hello.exe's manifest.

ILDASM also reveals that Hello.exe contains a class named *MyApp* and that *MyApp* contains two methods: a constructor (*.ctor*) and *Main*. The constructor was generated automatically by the compiler; it's a default constructor that takes no arguments. The "S" in the box next to *Main* indicates that *Main* is a static method. Double-clicking *Main* displays the CIL generated for that method by the C# compiler. (See Figure 1-8.) The statement

```
.entrypoint
```

isn't CIL but is simply a directive noting that this method is the program's entry point. The entry point's identity came from Hello.exe's CLR header. Next, the statement

```
.maxstack 1
```

is information obtained from the method prologue—data bytes preceding the method in the CIL—indicating that this method requires no more than one slot in the CLR's evaluation stack. The CLR uses this information to size the evaluation stack prior to invoking the method.

Main's CIL consists of just three simple instructions:

- A LDSTR instruction that places "Hello, world" on the evaluation stack
- A CALL instruction that calls *System.Console*'s *WriteLine* method in Mscorlib
- A RET instruction that ends the method

As you can see, it's relatively easy to use ILDASM to figure out how a method works. Early .NET Framework developers spent copious amounts of time figuring out how the FCL works by poring over the CIL for individual methods.

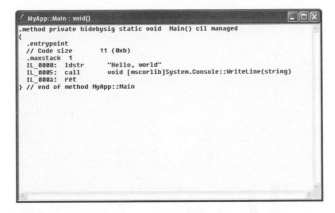

Figure 1-8   The *Main* method disassembled.

The Big Picture

Hello.exe is a far cry from a full-blown Web service or an eBay-style Web app, but it's an important beginning. Why? Because at the CLR level, all applications are created equal. Once you know how to write code that leverages the CLR, learning to write GUI applications, Web applications, and other .NET Framework application types is simply a matter of learning the programming models and getting to know your way around the FCL—which is precisely what the remainder of this book is about.

To summarize what you've learned so far: the .NET Framework is a platform for Web services and other kinds of applications. Applications that target the .NET Framework are managed applications. They're made of CIL and meta-data, and they're JIT compiled at run time and executed by the CLR. Languages such as C# and Visual Basic .NET are syntactic tools for generating CIL. For the first time in programming history, language is unimportant because, at the end of the day, all languages exercise the same set of features in the CLR and FCL.

Ironically, the .NET Framework grew out of an effort by a lot of smart people at Microsoft to make COM programming easier. Little did they know that the solution they'd come up with wasn't to fix what was broken, but to tear it down and start over again. That's what the .NET Framework is: a new beginning. The sooner you can let go of the old ways of writing and executing code, the more quickly you'll adapt to the .NET way.

2
Types and Exceptions

Before you begin drilling down into the Microsoft .NET Framework class library (FCL) and the various programming models that it supports, it's helpful to understand what the FCL is made of. The FCL is a library of "types," which is a generic way of referring to classes, structs, interfaces, enumerations, and delegates. This chapter defines these terms and will make Chapter 3 more meaningful to developers who are new to the .NET Framework. This chapter also introduces some potential pitfalls related to types, including common errors that arise when using types that encapsulate file handles and other resources that aren't managed by the garbage collector.

Understanding the .NET Framework's type system and the differences between the various kinds of data types that it supports is important, but so is understanding how types are loaded, versioned, and deployed. Types are packaged in assemblies. The FCL is a set of many different assemblies, each one of them shared so that any application can use it. Applications, too, are deployed as assemblies. You already know that an assembly is a group of one or more files. You even created a single-file assembly (Hello.exe) in Chapter 1. What you don't know—yet—is how to create assemblies of your own that contain types that can be used by other programs. You'll remedy that in this chapter by building and deploying a multifile, multilanguage assembly, and then building a client that dynamically links to it. In addition to gaining valuable insight into how the FCL works, you'll see what it takes to build class libraries of your own and learn how to use the assembly-based versioning mechanism in the common language runtime (CLR) to avoid DLL Hell—the term used to describe what happens when a fix made to a DLL for the benefit of one application breaks another application (or perhaps breaks the very application that the fix was intended to help).

Finally, you'll learn about exception handling. Applications that use the .NET Framework employ a C++-like *try/catch* mechanism to achieve robustness without having to check the return value from each and every method call. In fact, checking return values does little good because the CLR and FCL don't flag errors by returning error codes; they throw exceptions. A working knowledge of how exception handling works and how languages such as C# expose the CLR's exception handling mechanism is essential to becoming a proficient .NET Framework programmer.

.NET Framework Data Types

The C in FCL stands for "class," but the FCL isn't strictly a class library; it's a library of types. *Types* can mean any of the following:

- Classes
- Structs
- Interfaces
- Enumerations
- Delegates

Understanding what a type is and how one type differs from another is crucial to understanding the FCL. The information in the next several sections will not only enrich your understanding of the FCL, but also help you when the time comes to build data types of your own.

Classes

A class in the .NET Framework is similar to a class in C++: a bundle of code and data that is instantiated to form objects. Classes in traditional object-oriented programming languages such as C++ contain member variables and member functions. Framework classes are richer and can contain the following members:

- Fields, which are analogous to member variables in C++
- Methods, which are analogous to member functions in C++
- Properties, which expose data in the same way fields do but are in fact implemented using accessor (*get* and *set*) methods
- Events, which define the notifications a class is capable of firing

Here, in C#, is a class that implements a *Rectangle* data type:

```csharp
class Rectangle
{
    // Fields
    protected int width = 1;
    protected int height = 1;

    // Properties
    public int Width
    {
        get { return width; }
        set
        {
            if (value > 0)
                width = value;
            else
                throw new ArgumentOutOfRangeException (
                    "Width must be 1 or higher");
        }
    }

    public int Height
    {
        get { return height; }
        set
        {
            if (value > 0)
                height = value;
            else
                throw new ArgumentOutOfRangeException (
                    "Height must be 1 or higher");
        }
    }

    public int Area
    {
        get { return width * height; }
    }

    // Methods (constructors)
    public Rectangle () {}
    public Rectangle (int cx, int cy)
    {
        Width = cx;
        Height = cy;
    }
}
```

Rectangle has seven class members: two fields, three properties, and two methods, which both happen to be constructors—special methods that are called each time an instance of the class is created. The fields are protected, which means that only *Rectangle* and *Rectangle* derivatives can access them. To read or write a *Rectangle* object's width and height, a client must use the *Width* and *Height* properties. Notice that these properties' *set* accessors throw an exception if an illegal value is entered, a protection that couldn't be afforded had *Rectangle*'s width and height been exposed through publicly declared fields. *Area* is a read-only property because it lacks a *set* accessor. A compiler will flag attempts to write to the *Area* property with compilation errors.

Many languages that target the .NET Framework feature a *new* operator for instantiating objects. The following statements create instances of *Rectangle* in C#:

```
Rectangle rect = new Rectangle ();      // Use first constructor
Rectangle rect = new Rectangle (3, 4); // Use second constructor
```

Once the object is created, it might be used like this:

```
rect.Width *= 2;      // Double the rectangle's width
int area = rect.Area; // Get the rectangle's new area
```

Significantly, neither C# nor any other .NET programming language has a *delete* operator. You create objects, but the garbage collector deletes them.

In C#, classes define *reference types*, which are allocated on the garbage-collected heap (which is often called the *managed heap* because it's managed by the garbage collector) and accessed through *references* that abstract underlying pointers. The counterpart to the reference type is the *value type*, which you'll learn about in the next section. Most of the time you don't have to be concerned about the differences between the two, but occasionally the differences become very important and can actually be debilitating to your code if not accounted for. See the section "Boxing and Unboxing" later in this chapter for details.

All classes inherit a virtual method named *Finalize* from *System.Object*, which is the ultimate root class for all data types. *Finalize* is called just before an object is destroyed by the garbage collector. The garbage collector frees the object's memory, but classes that wrap file handles, window handles, and other unmanaged resources ("unmanaged" because they're not freed by the garbage collector) must override *Finalize* and use it to free those resources. This, too, has some important implications for developers. I'll say more later in this chapter in the section entitled "Nondeterministic Destruction."

Incidentally, classes can derive from at most one other class, but they can derive from one class and any number of interfaces. When you read the documentation for FCL classes, don't be surprised if you occasionally see long lists of base "classes," which really aren't classes at all, but interfaces. Also be aware that if you don't specify a base class when declaring a class, your class derives implicitly from *System.Object*. Consequently, you can call *ToString* and other *System.Object* methods on any object.

Structs

Classes are intended to represent complex data types. Because class instances are allocated on the managed heap, some overhead is associated with creating and destroying them. Some types, however, are "simple" types that would benefit from being created on the stack, which lives outside the purview of the garbage collector and offers a high-performance alternative to the managed heap. Bytes and integers are examples of simple data types.

That's why the .NET Framework supports value types as well as reference types. In C#, value types are defined with the *struct* keyword. Value types impose less overhead than reference types because they're allocated on the stack, not the heap. Bytes, integers, and most of the other "primitive" data types that the CLR supports are value types.

Here's an example of a simple value type:

```
struct Point
{
    public int x;
    public int y;

    public Point (int x, int y)
    {
        this.x = x;
        this.y = y;
    }
}
```

Point stores *x* and *y* coordinates in fields exposed directly to clients. It also defines a constructor that can be used to instantiate and initialize a *Point* in one operation. A *Point* can be instantiated in any of the following ways:

```
Point point = new Point (3, 4); // x==3, y==4
Point point = new Point ();      // x==0, y==0
Point point;                     // x==0, y==0
```

Note that even though the first two statements *appear* to create a *Point* object on the heap, in reality the object is created on the stack. If you come from a C++ heritage, get over the notion that *new* always allocates memory on the heap. Also, despite the fact that the third statement creates a *Point* object whose fields hold zeros, C# considers the *Point* to be uninitialized and won't let you use it until you explicitly assign values to *x* and *y*.

Value types are subject to some restrictions that reference types are not. Value types can't derive from other types, although they implicitly derive from *System.ValueType* and can (and often do) derive from interfaces. They also shouldn't wrap unmanaged resources such as file handles because value types have no way to release those resources when they're destroyed. Even though value types inherit a *Finalize* method from *System.Object*, *Finalize* is never called because the garbage collector ignores objects created on the stack.

Interfaces

An interface is a group of zero or more abstract methods—methods that have no default implementation but that are to be implemented in a class or struct. Interfaces can also include properties and events, although methods are far more common.

An interface defines a contract between a type and users of that type. For example, many of the classes in the *System.Collections* namespace derive from an interface named *IEnumerable*. *IEnumerable* defines methods for iterating over the items in a collection. It's because the FCL's collection classes implement *IEnumerable* that C#'s *foreach* keyword can be used with them. At run time, the code generated from *foreach* uses *IEnumerable*'s *GetEnumerator* method to iterate over the collection's contents.

Interfaces are defined with C#'s *interface* keyword:

```
interface ISecret
{
    void Encrypt (byte[] inbuf, out byte[] outbuf, Key key);
    void Unencrypt (byte[] inbuf, out byte[] outbuf, Key key);
}
```

A class or struct that wants to implement an interface simply derives from it and provides concrete implementations of its methods:

```
class Message : ISecret
{
    public void Encrypt (byte[] inbuf, out byte[] outbuf, Key key)
    {
      ...
    }

    public void Unencrypt (byte[] inbuf, out byte[] outbuf, Key key)
    {
      ...
    }
}
```

In C#, the *is* keyword can be used to determine whether an object implements a given interface. If *msg* is an object that implements *ISecret*, then in this example, *is* returns true; otherwise, it returns false:

```
if (msg is ISecret) {
    ISecret secret = (ISecret) msg;
    secret.Encrypt (...);
}
```

The related *as* operator can be used to test an object for an interface and cast it to the interface type with a single statement.

Enumerations

Enumerations in .NET Framework–land are similar to enumerations in C++. They're types that consist of a set of named constants, and in C# they're defined with the *enum* keyword. Here's a simple enumerated type named *Color*:

```
enum Color
{
    Red,
    Green,
    Blue
}
```

With *Color* thusly defined, colors can be represented this way:

```
Color.Red     // Red
Color.Green   // Green
Color.Blue    // Blue
```

Many FCL classes use enumerated types as method parameters. For example, if you use the *Regex* class to parse text and want the parsing to be case-insensitive, you don't pass a numeric value to *Regex*'s constructor; you pass a member of an enumerated type named *RegexOptions*:

```
Regex regex = new Regex (exp, RegexOptions.IgnoreCase);
```

Using words rather than numbers makes your code more readable. Nevertheless, because an enumerated type's members are assigned numeric values (by default, 0 for the first member, 1 for the second, and so on), you can always use a number in place of a member name if you prefer.

The *enum* keyword isn't simply a compiler keyword; it creates a bona fide type that implicitly derives from *System.Enum*. *System.Enum* defines methods that you can use to do some interesting things with enumerated types. For example, you can call *GetNames* on an enumerated type to enumerate the names of all its members. Try *that* in unmanaged C++!

Delegates

Newcomers to the .NET Framework often find delegates confusing. A delegate is a type-safe wrapper around a callback function. It's rather simple to write an unmanaged C++ application that crashes when it performs a callback. It's impossible to write a managed application that does the same, thanks to delegates.

Delegates are most commonly used to define the signatures of callback methods that are used to respond to events. For example, the FCL's *Timer* class (a member of the *System.Timers* namespace) defines an event named *Elapsed* that fires whenever a preprogrammed timer interval elapses. Applications that want to respond to *Elapsed* events pass a *Timer* object a reference to the method they want called when an *Elapsed* event fires. The "reference" that they pass isn't a raw memory address but rather an instance of a delegate that wraps the method's memory address. The *System.Timers* namespace defines a delegate named *ElapsedEventHandler* for precisely that purpose.

If you could steal a look at the *Timer* class's source code, you'd see something like this:

```
public delegate void ElapsedEventHandler (Object sender, ElapsedEventArgs e);

public class Timer
{
    public event ElapsedEventHandler Elapsed;
    .
    .
    .

}
```

Here's how *Timer* fires an *Elapsed* event:

```
if (Elapsed != null) // Make sure somebody's listening
    Elapsed (this, new ElapsedEventArgs (...)); // Fire!
```

And here's how a client might use a *Timer* object to call a method named *UpdateData* every 60 seconds:

```
Timer timer = new Timer (60000);
timer.Elapsed += new ElapsedEventHandler (UpdateData);
    .
    .
    .

void UpdateData (Object sender, ElapsedEventArgs e)
{
    // Callback received!
}
```

As you can see, *UpdateData* conforms to the signature specified by the delegate. To register to receive *Elapsed* events, the client creates a new instance of

ElapsedEventHandler that wraps *UpdateData* (note the reference to *Update-Data* passed to *ElapsedEventHandler*'s constructor) and wires it to *timer*'s *Elapsed* event using the += operator. This paradigm is used over and over in .NET Framework applications. Events and delegates are an important feature of the type system.

In practice, it's instructive to know more about what happens under the hood when a compiler encounters a delegate definition. Suppose the C# compiler encounters code such as this:

```
public delegate void ElapsedEventHandler (Object sender, ElapsedEventArgs e);
```

It responds by generating a class that derives from *System.MulticastDelegate*. The *delegate* keyword is simply an alias for something that in this case looks like this:

```
public class ElapsedEventHandler : MulticastDelegate
{
    public ElapsedEventHandler (object target, int method)
    {
      ...
    }

    public virtual void Invoke (object sender, ElapsedEventArgs e)
    {
      ...
    }
  ...
}
```

The derived class inherits several important members from *MulticastDelegate*, including private fields that identify the method that the delegate wraps and the object instance that implements the method (assuming the method is an instance method rather than a static method). The compiler adds an *Invoke* method that calls the method that the delegate wraps. C# hides the *Invoke* method and lets you invoke a callback method simply by using a delegate's instance name as if it were a method name.

Boxing and Unboxing

The architects of the .NET Framework could have made every type a reference type, but they chose to support value types as well to avoid imposing undue overhead on the use of integers and other primitive data types. But there's a downside to a type system with a split personality. To pass a value type to a method that expects a reference type, you must convert the value type to a reference type. You can't convert a value type to a reference type per se, but you can *box* the value type. Boxing creates a copy of a value type on the managed heap. The opposite of boxing is *unboxing*, which, in C#, duplicates a reference type on the stack. Common intermediate language (CIL) has instructions for performing boxing and unboxing.

Some compilers, the C# and Visual Basic .NET compilers among them, attempt to provide a unified view of the type system by hiding boxing and unboxing under the hood. The following code wouldn't work without boxing because it stores an int in a *Hashtable* object, and *Hashtable* objects store references exclusively:

```
Hashtable table = new Hashtable (); // Create a Hashtable
table.Add ("First", 1);             // Add 1 keyed by "First"
```

Here's the CIL emitted by the C# compiler:

```
newobj      instance void
            [mscorlib]System.Collections.Hashtable::.ctor()
stloc.0
ldloc.0
ldstr       "First"
ldc.i4.1
box         [mscorlib]System.Int32
callvirt    instance void
            [mscorlib]System.Collections.Hashtable::Add(object,
                                                        object)
```

Notice the BOX instruction that converts the integer value 1 to a boxed value type. The compiler emitted this instruction so that you wouldn't have to think about reference types and value types. The string used to key the *Hashtable* entry ("First") doesn't have to be boxed because it's an instance of *System.String*, and *System.String* is a reference type.

Many compilers are happy to box values without being asked to. For example, the following C# code compiles just fine:

```
int val = 1;      // Declare an instance of a value type
object obj = val; // Box it
```

But in C#, unboxing a reference value requires an explicit cast:

```
int val = 1;
object obj = val;
int val2 = obj;      // This won't compile
int val3 = (int) obj; // This will
```

You lose a bit of performance when you box or unbox a value, but in the vast majority of applications, such losses are more than offset by the added efficiency of storing simple data types on the stack rather than in the garbage-collected heap.

Reference Types vs. Value Types

Thanks to boxing and unboxing, the dichotomy between value types and reference types is mostly transparent to the programmer. Sometimes, however, you must know which type you're dealing with; otherwise, subtle differences between the two can impact your application's behavior in ways that you might not expect.

Here's an example. The following code defines a simple reference type (class) named *Point*. It also declares two *Point* references, *p1* and *p2*. The reference *p1* is initialized with a reference to a new *Point* object, and *p2* is initialized by setting it equal to *p1*. Because *p1* and *p2* are little more than pointers in disguise, setting one equal to the other does *not* make a copy of the *Point* object; it merely copies an address. Therefore, modifying one *Point* affects both:

```
class Point
{
    public int x;
    public int y;
}
    .
    .
    .
Point p1 = new Point ();
p1.x = 1;
p1.y = 2;
Point p2 = p1; // Copies the underlying pointer
p2.x = 3;
p2.y = 4;


Console.WriteLine ("p1 = ({0}, {1})", p1.x, p1.y); // Writes "(3, 4)"
Console.WriteLine ("p2 = ({0}, {1})", p2.x, p2.y); // Writes "(3, 4)"
```

The next code fragment is identical to the first, save for the fact that *Point* is now a value type (struct). But because setting one value type equal to another creates a copy of the latter, the results are quite different. Changes made to one *Point* no longer affect the other:

```
struct Point
{
    public int x;
    public int y;
}
    .
    .
    .
Point p1 = new Point ();
p1.x = 1;
p1.y = 2;
Point p2 = p1; // Makes a new copy of the object on the stack
p2.x = 3;
```

```
p2.y = 4;

Console.WriteLine ("p1 = ({0}, {1})", p1.x, p1.y); // Writes "(1, 2)"
Console.WriteLine ("p2 = ({0}, {1})", p2.x, p2.y); // Writes "(3, 4)"
```

Sometimes differences between reference types and value types are even more insidious. For example, if *Point* is a value type, the following code is perfectly legal:

```
Point p;
p.x = 3;
p.y = 4;
```

But if *Point* is a reference type, the very same instruction sequence won't even compile. Why? Because the statement

```
Point p;
```

declares an *instance* of a value type but only a *reference* to a reference type. A reference is like a pointer—it's useless until it's initialized, as in the following:

```
Point p = new Point ();
```

Programmers with C++ experience are especially vulnerable to this error because they see a statement that declares a reference and automatically assume that an object is being created on the stack.

The FCL contains a mixture of value types and reference types. Clearly, it's sometimes important to know which type you're dealing with. How do you know whether a particular FCL type is a value type or a reference type? Simple. If the documentation says it's a class (as in "String Class"), it's a reference type. If the documentation says it's a structure (for example, "DateTime Structure"), it's a value type. Be aware of the difference, and you'll avoid frustrating hours spent in the debugger trying to figure out why code that looks perfectly good produces unpredictable results.

Nondeterministic Destruction

In traditional environments, objects are created and destroyed at precise, deterministic points in time. As an example, consider the following class written in unmanaged C++:

```
class File
{
protected:
    int Handle; // File handle

public:
    File (char* name)
    {
```

```
        // TODO: Open the file and copy the handle to Handle
    }

    ~File ()
    {
        // TODO: Close the file handle
    }
};
```

When you instantiate this class, the class constructor is called:

```
File* pFile = new File ("Readme.txt");
```

And when you delete the object, its destructor is called:

```
delete pFile;
```

If you create the object on the stack instead of the heap, destruction is still deterministic because the class destructor is called the moment the object goes out of scope.

Destruction works differently in the .NET Framework. Remember, you create objects, but you never delete them; the garbage collector deletes them for you. But therein lies a problem. Suppose you write a *File* class in C#:

```
class File
{
    protected IntPtr Handle = IntPtr.Zero;

    public File (string name)
    {
        // TODO: Open the file and copy the handle to Handle
    }

    ~File ()
    {
        // TODO: Close the file handle
    }
}
```

Then you create a class instance like this:

```
File file = new File ("Readme.txt");
```

Now ask yourself a question: when does the file handle get closed?

The short answer is that the handle gets closed when the object is destroyed. But when is the object destroyed? When the garbage collector destroys it. When does the garbage collector destroy it? Ah—there's the key question. You don't know. You can't know because the garbage collector decides on its own when to run, and until the garbage collector runs, the object isn't destroyed and its destructor isn't called. That's called *nondeterministic destruction*, or NDD. Technically, there's no such thing as a destructor in managed code. When you write something that looks like a destructor in C#, the compiler actually overrides the *Finalize* method that your class inherits from *System.Object*. C# simplifies the syntax by letting you write something that looks like a destructor, but that arguably makes matters worse because it implies that it is a destructor, and to unknowing developers, destructors imply deterministic destruction.

Deterministic destruction doesn't exist in framework applications unless your code does something really ugly, like this:

```
GC.Collect ();
```

GC is a class in the *System* namespace that provides a programmatic interface to the garbage collector. *Collect* is a static method that forces a collection. Garbage collecting impedes performance, so now that you know that this method exists, forget about it. The last thing you want to do is write code that simulates deterministic destruction by calling the garbage collector periodically.

NDD is a big deal because failure to account for it can lead to all sorts of run-time errors in your applications. Suppose someone uses your *File* class to open a file. Later on that person uses it to open the same file again. Depending on how the file was opened the first time, it might not open again because the handle is *still open if the garbage collector hasn't run.*

File handles aren't the only problem. Take bitmaps, for instance. The FCL features a handy little class named *Bitmap* (it's in the *System.Drawing* namespace) that encapsulates bitmapped images and understands a wide variety of image file formats. When you create a *Bitmap* object on a Windows machine, the *Bitmap* object calls down to the Windows GDI, creates a GDI bitmap, and stores the GDI bitmap handle in a field. But guess what? Until the garbage collector runs and the *Bitmap* object's *Finalize* method is called, the GDI bitmap remains open. Large GDI bitmaps consume lots of memory, so it's entirely conceivable that after the application has run for a while, it'll start throwing exceptions every time it tries to create a bitmap because of insufficient memory. End users won't appreciate an image viewer utility (like the one you'll build in Chapter 4) that has to be restarted every few minutes.

So what do you do about NDD? Here are two rules for avoiding the NDD blues. The first rule is for programmers who use (rather than write) classes that encapsulate file handles and other unmanaged resources. Most such classes implement a method named *Close* or *Dispose* that releases resources that require deterministic closure. If you use classes that wrap unmanaged resources, call *Close* or *Dispose* on them the moment you're finished using them. Assuming *File* implements a *Close* method that closes the encapsulated file handle, here's the right way to use the *File* class:

```
File file = new File ("Readme.txt");
    .
    .
    .

// Finished using the file, so close it
file.Close ();
```

The second rule, which is actually a *set* of rules, applies to developers who write classes that wrap unmanaged resources. Here's a summary:

■   Implement a protected *Dispose* method (hereafter referred to as the "protected *Dispose*") that takes a Boolean as a parameter. In this method, free any unmanaged resources (such as file handles) that the class encapsulates. If the parameter passed to the protected *Dispose* is true, also call *Close* or *Dispose* (the public *Dispose* inherited from *IDisposable*) on any class members (fields) that wrap unmanaged resources.

■   Implement the .NET Framework's *IDisposable* interface, which contains a single method named *Dispose* that takes no parameters. Implement this version of *Dispose* (the "public *Dispose*") by calling *GC.SuppressFinalize* to prevent the garbage collector from calling *Finalize,* and then calling the protected *Dispose* and passing in true.

■   Override *Finalize. Finalize* is called by the garbage collector when an object is "finalized"—that is, when an object is destroyed. In *Finalize*, call the protected *Dispose* and pass in false. The false parameter is important because it prevents the protected *Dispose* from attempting to call *Close* or the public *Dispose* on any encapsulated class members, which may *already* have been finalized if a garbage collection is in progress.

■   If it makes sense semantically (for example, if the resource that the class encapsulates can be closed in the manner of a file handle), implement a *Close* method that calls the public *Dispose*.

Based on these principles, here's the right way to implement a *File* class:

```
class File : IDisposable
{
    protected IntPtr Handle = IntPtr.Zero;

    public File (string name)
    {
        // TODO: Open the file and copy the handle to Handle.
    }
```

(continued)

```
~File ()
{
    Dispose (false);
}

public void Dispose ()
{
    GC.SuppressFinalize (this);
    Dispose (true);
}

protected virtual void Dispose (bool disposing)
{
    // TODO: Close the file handle.
    if (disposing) {
        // TODO: If the class has members that wrap
        // unmanaged resources, call Close or Dispose on
        // them here.
    }
}

public void Close ()
{
    Dispose ();
}
}
```

Note that the "destructor"—actually, the *Finalize* method—now calls the protected *Dispose* with a false parameter, and that the public *Dispose* calls the protected *Dispose* and passes in true. The call to *GC.SuppressFinalize* is both a performance optimization and a measure to prevent the handle from being closed twice. Because the object has already closed the file handle, there's no need for the garbage collector to call its *Finalize* method. It's still important to override the *Finalize* method to ensure proper disposal if *Close* or *Dispose* isn't called.

Dynamic Linking

When you ran the C# compiler in Chapter 1, you created an assembly named Hello.exe. Hello.exe is as simple as an assembly can be: it contains but one file and it lacks a strong name, meaning that the common language runtime performs no version checking when loading it.

Weakly named, single-file assemblies are fine for the majority of applications. But occasionally developers need more. For example, you might want to write a library of routines that other applications can link to, similar to a dynamic link library (DLL) in Windows. If you do, you'll need to know more about assemblies. Perhaps you'd like to write a library for the private use of your application. Or maybe you've heard that Microsoft .NET solves the infamous DLL Hell problem and you'd like to know how. The next several sections walk you, tutorial-style, through the process of creating, deploying, and dynamically linking to a multifile assembly. During the journey, you'll see firsthand how such assemblies are produced and what they mean to the design and operation of managed applications. And just to prove that the framework is language-agnostic, you'll write half of the assembly in C# and half in Visual Basic .NET.

Creating a Multifile Assembly

The assembly that you're about to create contains two classes: one named *SimpleMath*, written in Visual Basic .NET, and another named *ComplexMath*, written in C#. *SimpleMath* has two methods: *Add* and *Subtract*. *ComplexMath* has one method, *Square*, which takes an input value and returns the square of that value.

Physically, the assembly consists of three files: Simple.netmodule, which holds the *SimpleMath* class; Complex.netmodule, which holds *ComplexMath*; and Math.dll, which houses the assembly manifest. Because the managed modules containing *SimpleMath* and *ComplexMath* belong to the same assembly, clients neither know nor care about the assembly's physical makeup. They simply see one entity—the assembly—that contains the types they're interested in.

Here's how to create the assembly:

1. Create a new text file named Complex.cs and enter the source code shown in Figure 2-1.

2. Compile Complex.cs into a managed module with the command

    ```
    csc /target:module complex.cs
    ```

    The */target* switch tells the C# compiler to generate a managed module that is neither an EXE nor a DLL. Such a module can't be used by itself, but it can be used if it's added to an assembly. Because you didn't specify a file name with a */out* switch, the compiler names the output file Complex.netmodule.

3. In the same directory, create a new text file named Simple.vb. Type in the source code shown in Figure 2-2.

4. Compile Simple.vb with the following command:

    ```
    vbc /target:module simple.vb
    ```

This command produces a managed module named Simple.netmodule, which makes up the Visual Basic .NET half of the assembly's code.

5. Create an assembly that binds the two managed modules together by running the SDK's AL (Assembly Linker) utility as follows:

```
al /target:library /out:Math.dll simple.netmodule
complex.netmodule
```

The resulting file—Math.dll—contains the assembly manifest. Inside the manifest is information identifying Simple.netmodule and Complex.netmodule as members of the assembly. Also encoded in the assembly manifest is the assembly's name: Math.

Complex.cs

```csharp
using System;

public class ComplexMath
{
    public int Square (int a)
    {
        return a * a;
    }
}
```

Figure 2-1   The *ComplexMath* class.

Simple.vb

```vb
Imports System

Public Class SimpleMath
    Function Add (a As Integer, b As Integer) As Integer
        Return a + b
    End Function

    Function Subtract (a As Integer, b As Integer) As Integer
        Return a - b
    End Function
End Class
```

Figure 2-2   The *SimpleMath* class.

You just created the .NET Framework equivalent of a DLL. Now let's write a client to test it with.

Dynamically Linking to an Assembly

Follow these simple steps to create a console client for the Math assembly:

1. In the same directory that Math.dll, Simple.netmodule, and Complex.netmodule reside in, create a new text file named Math-Demo.cs. Then enter the code shown in Figure 2-3.

2. Compile MathDemo.cs with the following command:

    ```
    csc /target:exe /reference:math.dll mathdemo.cs
    ```

    The compiler creates an EXE named MathDemo.exe. The */reference* switch tells the compiler that MathDemo.cs uses types defined in the assembly whose manifest is stored in Math.dll. Without this switch, the compiler would complain that the types are undefined.

    Notice that in step 2, you did *not* have to include a */reference* switch pointing to Simple.netmodule or Complex.netmodule, even though that's where *SimpleMath* and *ComplexMath* are defined. Why? Because both modules are part of the assembly whose manifest is found in Math.dll.

MathDemo.cs
```
using System;

class MyApp
{
    static void Main ()
    {
        SimpleMath simple = new SimpleMath ();
        int sum = simple.Add (2, 2);
        Console.WriteLine ("2 + 2 = {0}", sum);

        ComplexMath complex = new ComplexMath ();
        int square = complex.Square (3);
        Console.WriteLine ("3 squared = {0}", square);
    }
}
```

Figure 2-3   Client for the Math assembly.

Now that you have a client ready, it's time to test CLR-style dynamic linking. Here's a script to serve as a guide:

1. In a command prompt window, run MathDemo.exe. You should see the output shown in Figure 2-4, which proves that MathDemo.exe successfully loaded and used *SimpleMath* and *ComplexMath*.

2. Temporarily rename Complex.netmodule to something like Complex.foo.

3. Run MathDemo again. A dialog box appears informing you that a *FileNotFoundException* occurred. The exception was generated by the CLR when it was unable to find the module containing *ComplexMath*. Click the No button to acknowledge the error and dismiss the dialog box.

4. Restore Complex.netmodule's original name and run MathDemo again to verify that it works.

5. Modify MathDemo.cs by commenting out the final three statements—the ones that use *ComplexMath*. Then rebuild MathDemo.exe by repeating the command you used to build it the first time.

6. Run MathDemo. This time, the only output you should see is "2 + 2 = 4."

7. Temporarily rename Complex.netmodule again. Then run Math-Demo.exe. No exception occurs this time because MathDemo.exe doesn't attempt to instantiate *ComplexMath*. The CLR doesn't load modules that it doesn't need to. Had this code been deployed on the Internet, the CLR wouldn't have attempted to download Complex.netmodule, either.

8. Restore Complex.netmodule's name, uncomment the statements that you commented out in step 5, and rebuild MathDemo.exe one more time.

Figure 2-4   MathDemo output.

You've now seen firsthand how dynamic linking works in the .NET Framework and demonstrated that the CLR loads only the parts of an assembly that it has to. But what if you wanted to install the assembly in a subdirectory of the application directory? Here's how to deploy the assembly in a subdirectory named bin:

1. Create a bin subdirectory in the application directory (the directory where MathDemo.exe is stored).

2. Move Math.dll, Simple.netmodule, and Complex.netmodule to the bin directory. Run MathDemo.exe again. The CLR throws a *FileNot-FoundException* because it can't find the assembly in the application directory.

3. Create a new text file named MathDemo.exe.config in the application directory, and then enter the statements shown in Figure 2-5. MathDemo.exe.config is an XML application configuration file containing configuration data used by the CLR. The *probing* element tells the CLR to look in the bin subdirectory for assemblies containing types referenced by MathDemo.exe. You can include multiple subdirectory names by separating them with semicolons.

4. Run MathDemo again and verify that it works even though the assembly is now stored in the bin directory.

These exercises demonstrate how assemblies containing types used by other applications are typically deployed. Most assemblies are private to a particular application, so they're deployed in the same directory as the application that they serve or in a subdirectory. This model is consistent with the .NET Framework's goal of "XCOPY installs," which is synonymous with simplified install and uninstall procedures. Because MathDemo.exe doesn't rely on any resources outside its own directory tree, removing it from the system is as simple as deleting the application directory and its contents.

MathDemo.exe.config
```
<configuration>
  <runtime>
    <assemblyBinding xmlns="urn:schemas-microsoft-com:asm.v1">
      <probing privatePath="bin" />
    </assemblyBinding>
  </runtime>
</configuration>
```

Figure 2-5   MathDemo.exe's application configuration file.

Versioning an Assembly

If you were to modify Simple.vb or Complex.cs right now and inadvertently introduce an error, the CLR would be happy to load the buggy assembly the next time you run MathDemo.exe. Why? Because the assembly lacks a strong name. The CLR's versioning mechanism doesn't work with weakly named assemblies. If you want to take advantage of CLR versioning, you must assign the assembly a strong name. Strong naming is the key to avoiding DLL Hell.

Use the following procedure to create a strongly named assembly containing the *SimpleMath* and *ComplexMath* classes:

1. Go to the bin subdirectory and run the SDK's SN (Strong Name) utility. The following command generates a "key file" named Keyfile.snk containing public and private keys that can be used for strong naming:

   ```
   sn /k Keyfile.snk
   ```

2. Use AL to create a strongly named assembly that uses the keys found in Keyfile.snk:

   ```
   al /keyfile:keyfile.snk /target:library/out:Math.dll
   /version:1.0.0.0 simple.netmodule complex.netmodule
   ```

   The */keyfile* switch identifies the key file. The */version* switch specifies the version number written to the assembly's manifest. The four values in the version number, from left to right, are the major version number, the minor version number, the build number, and the revision number.

3. Go to MathDemo.exe's application directory and rebuild Math-Demo.cs using the following command:

   ```
   csc /target:exe /reference:bin\math.dll mathdemo.cs
   ```

   This time, MathDemo.exe is bound to the strongly named Math assembly. Moreover, the new build of MathDemo.exe contains metadata noting what version of the assembly it was compiled against.

4. Verify that MathDemo.exe works as before by running it.

So far, so good. You've created a version of MathDemo.exe that is strongly bound to version 1.0.0.0 of a private assembly whose manifest is stored in Math.dll. Now use the following exercises to explore the ramifications:

1. Execute the following command in the bin directory to increment the assembly's version number from 1.0.0.0 to 1.1.0.0:

```
al /keyfile:keyfile.snk /target:library/out:Math.dll
/version:1.1.0.0 simple.netmodule complex.netmodule
```

2. Run MathDemo.exe. Because MathDemo.exe was compiled against version 1.0.0.0 of the assembly, the CLR throws a *FileLoadException*.

3. Restore the assembly's version number to 1.0.0.0 with the following command:

```
al /keyfile:keyfile.snk /target:library /out:Math.dll
/version:1.0.0.0 simple.netmodule complex.netmodule
```

4. Open Complex.cs and change the statement

```
return a * a;
```

to read

```
return a + a;
```

Clearly this is a buggy implementation because the *Square* method now doubles *a* rather than squaring it. But the version number has been reset to 1.0.0.0—the one MathDemo.exe was compiled against. What will the CLR do when you rebuild Complex.netmodule and run MathDemo again?

5. Rebuild Complex.netmodule with the command

```
csc /target:module /out:bin\Complex.netmodule complex.cs
```

Run MathDemo.exe. Once again, the CLR throws an exception. Even though the version number is valid, the CLR knows that Complex.netmodule has changed because Math.dll's manifest contains a cryptographic hash of each of the files in the assembly. When you modified Complex.netmodule, you modified the value it hashes to as well. Before loading Complex.netmodule, the CLR rehashed the file and compared the resulting hash to the hash stored in the assembly manifest. Upon seeing that the two hashes didn't match, the CLR threw an exception.

Now suppose circumstances were reversed and that version 1.0.0.0 contained the buggy *Square* method. In that case, you'd *want* MathDemo.exe to use version 1.1.0.0. You have two options. The first is to recompile MathDemo.exe against version 1.1.0.0 of the assembly. The second is to use a *binding redirect* to tell the CLR to load version 1.1.0.0 of the assembly when

MathDemo asks for version 1.0.0.0. A binding redirect is enacted by modifying Math-Demo.exe.config as follows:

```
<configuration>
  <runtime>
    <assemblyBinding xmlns="urn:schemas-microsoft-com:asm.v1">
      <dependentAssembly>
        <assemblyIdentity name="Math"
          publicKeyToken="cd16a90001d313af" />
        <bindingRedirect oldVersion="1.0.0.0" newVersion="1.1.0.0" />
      </dependentAssembly>
      <probing privatePath="bin" />
    </assemblyBinding>
  </runtime>
</configuration>
```

The new *dependentAssembly* element and its subelements instruct the CLR to resolve requests for Math version 1.0.0.0 by loading version 1.1.0.0 instead. The *publicKeyToken* attribute is a tokenized representation (specifically, a 64-bit hash) of the public key encoded in Math's assembly manifest; it was obtained by running SN with a */T* switch against Math.dll:

```
sn /T math.dll
```

Your assembly's public key token will be different from mine, so if you try this out on your code, be sure to plug your assembly's public key token into Math-Demo.exe.config's *publicKeyToken* attribute.

Now you can have your cake and eat it too. The CLR enacts a strong versioning policy to prevent incorrect versions of the assembly from being loaded, but if you *want* to load another version, a simple configuration change makes it possible.

Sharing an Assembly: The Global Assembly Cache

Suppose that you build the Math assembly with the intention of letting any application, not just MathDemo.exe, use it. If that's your goal, you need to install the assembly where any application can find it. That location is the *global assembly cache* (GAC), which is a repository for shared assemblies. The FCL is several shared assemblies. Only strongly named assemblies can be installed in the GAC. When the CLR attempts to load an assembly, it looks in the GAC even before it looks in the local application directory.

The .NET Framework SDK includes a utility named GacUtil that makes it easy to install and uninstall shared assemblies. To demonstrate, do this:

1.   Create a directory named Shared somewhere on your hard disk. (There's nothing magic about the directory name; call it something

else if you like.) Move the files in MathDemo.exe's bin directory to the Shared directory. Then delete the bin directory.

2. Go to the Shared directory and install the Math assembly in the GAC by executing the following command:

```
gacutil /i math.dll
```

3. Run MathDemo.exe. It should run fine, even though the assembly that it relies on is no longer in a subdirectory of the application directory.

4. Remove the assembly from the GAC by executing this command:

```
gacutil /u math
```

5. Run MathDemo.exe again. This time, the CLR throws an exception because it can't find the Math assembly in the GAC or in a local directory.

That's shared assemblies in a nutshell. They must be strongly named, and the act of installing them in the GAC makes them shared assemblies. The downside to deploying shared assemblies is that doing so violates the spirit of XCOPY installs. Installing a shared assembly on an end user's machine requires version 2 or later of the Windows Installer or a third-party installation program that is GAC-aware because GacUtil comes with the .NET Framework SDK and is not likely to be present on a nondeveloper's PC. Uninstalling a shared assembly requires removing it from the GAC; simply deleting files won't do the trick.

Applying Strong Names Using Attributes

The SDK's AL utility is one way to create strongly named assemblies, but it's not the only way, nor is it the most convenient. An easier way to produce a strongly named assembly is to attribute your code. Here's a modified version of Complex.cs that compiles to a strongly named single-file assembly:

```
using System;
using System.Reflection
[assembly:AssemblyKeyFile ("Keyfile.snk")]
[assembly:AssemblyVersion ("1.0.0.0")]

public class ComplexMath
{
    public int Square (int a)
    {
        return a * a;
    }
}
```

And here's how Simple.vb would look if it, too, were modified to build a strongly named assembly:

```
Imports System
Imports System.Reflection
<Assembly:AssemblyKeyFile ("Keyfile.snk")>
<Assembly:AssemblyVersion ("1.0.0.0")>

Public Class SimpleMath
    Function Add (a As Integer, b As Integer) As Integer
        Return a + b
    End Function

    Function Subtract (a As Integer, b As Integer) As Integer
        Return a - b
    End Function
End Class
```

AssemblyKeyFile and *AssemblyVersion* are *attributes*. Physically, they map to the *AssemblyKeyFileAttribute* and *AssemblyVersionAttribute* classes defined in the FCL's *System.Reflection* namespace. Attributes are mechanisms for declaratively adding information to a module's metadata. These particular attributes create a strongly named assembly by signing the assembly and specifying a version number.

Delayed Signing

Unless an assembly is strongly named, it can't be installed in the GAC and its version number can't be used to bind clients to a particular version of the assembly. Strongly naming an assembly is often referred to as "signing" the assembly because the crux of strong naming is adding a digital signature generated from the assembly manifest and the publisher's private key. And therein lies a problem. In large corporations, private keys are often locked away in vaults or hardware devices where only a privileged few can access them. If you're a rank-and-file programmer developing a strongly named assembly and you don't have access to your company's private key (which is exactly the situation that Microsoft developers find themselves in), how can you fully test the assembly if you can't install it in the GAC or use its version number to do strong versioning?

The answer is delayed signing. Delayed signing embeds the publisher's public key (which is available to everyone) in the assembly and reserves space for a digital signature to be added later. The presence of the public key allows the assembly to be installed in the GAC. It also enables clients to build into their metadata information denoting the specific version of the assembly that they were compiled against. The lack of a digital signature means the assembly is no longer tamperproof, but you can fix that by signing the assembly with the publisher's private key before the assembly ships.

How does delayed signing work? If Public.snk holds the publisher's public key, the following command creates and delay-signs a Math assembly (note the */delaysign* switch):

```
al /keyfile:public.snk /delaysign /target:library /out:Math.dll
/version:1.1.0.0 simple.netmodule complex.netmodule
```

You can also delay-sign using attributes:

```
[assembly:AssemblyKeyFile ("Public.snk")]
[assembly:AssemblyVersion ("1.0.0.0")]
[assembly:DelaySign (true)]
```

In either event, the resultant assembly contains the publisher's public key but lacks the signature generated with the help of the private key. To sign the assembly before releasing it, have someone who has access to the publisher's private key do this:

```
sn /R Math.dll keyfile.snk
```

Using this statement assumes that Keyfile.snk holds the publisher's public and private keys.

One trap to watch for regarding delayed signing is that neither the */delaysign* switch nor the *DelaySign* attribute in and of itself enables the assembly to be installed in the GAC or strongly versioned. To enable both, run the SN utility against the assembly with a */Vr* switch to enable verification skipping:

```
sn /Vr Math.dll
```

After signing the assembly with the publisher's private key, disable verification skipping by running SN with a */Vu* switch:

```
sn /Vu Math.dll
```

Verification skipping enables an assembly to be loaded without verifying that it hasn't been tampered with. After all, verification can't be performed if the assembly lacks the digital signature used for verification. Verification skipping doesn't have to be enabled every time the assembly is built. Enabling it once is sufficient to enable verification skipping until it is explicitly disabled again by running SN with a */Vu* switch.

Exception Handling

When something goes wrong during the execution of an application, the .NET Framework responds by throwing an exception. Some exceptions are thrown by the CLR. For example, if an application attempts to cast an object to a type that it's not, the CLR throws an exception. Others are thrown by the FCL—for example, when an application attempts to open a nonexistent file. The types of exceptions that the .NET Framework throws are legion, so an application that targets the framework better be prepared to handle them.

The beauty of exceptions in the world of managed code is that they're an intrinsic part of the .NET Framework. In the past, languages (and even individual language compilers) have used proprietary means to throw and handle exceptions. You couldn't throw an exception in Visual Basic and catch it in C++. You couldn't even throw an exception in a function compiled with one C++ compiler and catch it in a function compiled with another. Not so in a managed application. The CLR defines how exceptions are thrown and how they're handled. You can throw an exception in any language and catch it in any other. You can even throw exceptions across machines. And to top it off, languages such as C# and Visual Basic .NET make exception handling extraordinarily easy.

Catching Exceptions

C# uses four keywords to expose the CLR's exception handling mechanism: *try*, *catch*, *finally*, and *throw*. The general idea is to enclose code that might throw an exception in a *try* block and to include exception handlers in a *catch* block. Here's an example:

```
try {
    Hashtable table = new Hashtable ();
    table.Add ("First", 1);
    string entry = (string) table["First"]; // Retrieve 1 and cast it
}
catch (InvalidCastException e) {
    Console.WriteLine (e.Message);
}
```

An integer is not a string, so attempting to cast it to one will generate an *InvalidCastException*. That will activate the *InvalidCastException* handler, which in this example writes the message encapsulated in the exception object to the console. To write a more generic *catch* handler that catches any exception thrown by the framework, specify *Exception* as the exception type:

```
catch (Exception e) {
    ...
}
```

And to respond differently to different types of exceptions, simply include a *catch* handler for each type you're interested in:

```
try {
    ...
}
catch (InvalidCastException e) {
    ...
}
catch (FileNotFoundException e) {
    ...
}
catch (Exception e) {
    ...
}
```

The CLR calls the handler that most closely matches the type of exception thrown. In this example, an *InvalidCastException* or *FileNotFoundException* vectors execution to one of the first two *catch* handlers. Any other FCL exception type will activate the final handler. Notice that you don't have to dispose of the *Exception* objects you catch because the garbage collector disposes of them for you.

All of the exception types defined in the FCL derive directly or indirectly from *System.Exception*, which defines a base set of properties common to FCL exception types. Thanks to *System.Exception*, for example, all FCL exception classes contain a *Message* property, which holds an error message describing what went wrong, and a *StackTrace* property, which details the call chain leading up to the exception. Derivative classes frequently add properties of their own. For instance, *FileNotFoundException* includes a *FileName* property that reveals what file caused the exception.

The FCL defines dozens of different exception classes. They're not defined in any one namespace but are spread throughout the FCL's roughly 100 namespaces. To help you get a handle on the different types of exceptions you're liable to encounter, the following table lists some of the most common exception types.

Common FCL Exception Classes

Class	Thrown When
ArgumentNullException	A null reference is illicitly passed as an argument
ArgumentOutOfRangeException	An argument is invalid (out of range)
DivideByZeroException	An attempt is made to divide by 0
IndexOutOfRangeException	An invalid array index is used
InvalidCastException	A type is cast to a type it's not
NullReferenceException	A null reference is dereferenced
OutOfMemoryException	A memory allocation fails because of a lack of memory
WebException	An error occurs during an HTTP request

As in C++, exception handlers can be nested. If method A calls method B and method B throws an exception, the exception handler in method B is called provided a suitable handler exists. If method B lacks a handler for the type of exception that was thrown, the CLR looks for one in method A. If A too lacks a matching exception handler, the exception bubbles upward to the method that called A, then to the method that called the method that called A, and so on.

What does the .NET Framework do with unhandled exceptions? It depends on the application type. When a console application suffers an uncaught exception, the framework terminates the application and writes an error message to the console window. If the application is a Windows Forms application, the framework alerts the user with a message box. For a Web Forms application, the framework displays an error page. Generally speaking, it's far preferable to anticipate exceptions and handle them gracefully than allow your users to witness an unhandled exception.

Guaranteeing Execution

Code in a *finally* block is guaranteed to execute, whether an exception is thrown or not. The *finally* keyword really comes in handy when you're dealing with those pesky classes that wrap file handles and other unmanaged resources. If you write code like

```
File file = new File ("Readme.txt");
    .
    .
    .
file.Close ();
```

you've left a file open if an exception occurs after the file is opened but before *Close* is called. But if you structure your code this way, you're safe:

```
File file = null;
try {
    file = new File ("Readme.txt");
        .
        .
        .
}
catch (FileNotFoundException e) {
    Console.WriteLine (e.Message);
}
finally {
    if (file != null)
        file.Close ();
}
```

Now *Close* is called regardless of whether an exception is thrown.

Be aware that *try* blocks accompanied by *finally* blocks do not have to have *catch* blocks. In the previous example, suppose you want to make sure the file is closed, but you don't really care to handle the exception yourself; you'd rather leave that to a method higher up the call stack. Here's how to go about it:

```
File file = null;
try {
    file = new File ("Readme.txt");
    .
    .
    .
}
finally {
    if (file != null)
        file.Close ();
}
```

This code is perfectly legitimate and in fact demonstrates the proper way to respond to an exception that is best handled by the caller rather than the callee. Class library authors in particular should be diligent about not "eating" exceptions that callers should be aware of.

Throwing Exceptions

Applications can throw exceptions as well as catch them. Look again at the *Width* and *Height* properties in the *Rectangle* class presented earlier in this chapter. If a user of that class passes in an invalid *Width* or *Height* value, the *set* accessor throws an exception. You can also rethrow exceptions thrown to you by using the *throw* keyword with no arguments.

You can use *throw* to throw exception types defined in the FCL, and you can use it to throw custom exception types that you define. Although it's perfectly legal to derive custom exception types from *System.Exception* (and even to declare exception classes that derive directly from *System.Object*), developers are encouraged to derive from *System.ApplicationException* instead, primarily because doing so enables applications to distinguish between exceptions thrown by the framework and exceptions thrown by user code.

That's the theory, anyway. The reality is that the FCL derives some of its own exception classes from *ApplicationException*, meaning that having *ApplicationException* as a base type is not a reliable indicator that the exception wasn't thrown by the framework. Don't believe any documentation that says otherwise.

Next Up: The .NET Framework Class Library

The information presented in this chapter sets the stage for Chapter 3, which introduces the all-important .NET Framework class library. Now when you encounter the term "class" or "struct," you'll know precisely what it means. When you use a class that has a *Close* or *Dispose* method, you'll realize that it probably wraps an unmanaged resource that shouldn't wait to be freed until the garbage collector runs. You'll understand how code that uses types defined in the FCL dynamically links to FCL assemblies. And you'll know how to respond gracefully when the FCL throws an exception.

Without further delay, therefore, let's peel the curtain away from the .NET Framework class library and learn how to use it to write great applications.

3

The .NET Framework Class Library

The .NET Framework class library (FCL) provides the API that managed applications write to. Including more than 7,000 types—classes, structs, interfaces, enumerations, and delegates—the FCL is a rich resource that includes everything from basic types such as *Int32* and *String* to exotic types such as *Regex*, which represents regular expressions, and *Form*, which is the base class for windows in GUI applications. I'll often use the word "classes" to refer to FCL members, but realize that I'm taking literary license and that the FCL is not, as you are well aware after reading Chapter 2, merely a class library.

The FCL is partitioned into approximately 100 hierarchically organized namespaces. *System* is the root for most namespaces. It defines core data types such as *Int32* and *Byte,* as well as utility types such as *Math* and *TimeSpan*. A name such as *System.Data* refers to a namespace that is a child of the *System* namespace. It's not unusual to find namespaces nested several levels deep, as in *System.Runtime.Remoting.Channels.Tcp.*

Segregating FCL types into namespaces adds structure to the .NET Framework class library and makes it easier to find the classes you need as you learn your way around the FCL. Learning is made easier by the fact that namespace names reflect what the types in a namespace are used for. For example, *System.Web.UI.WebControls* contains ASP.NET Web controls, while *System.Collections* is home to the FCL's collection classes—*Hashtable*, *ArrayList*, and others.

This chapter introduces some of the .NET Framework class library's key classes and namespaces. It's not meant to be exhaustive; no chapter can possibly cover the FCL in its entirety. The classes you'll read about here are ones that tend to be used by a broad cross-section of applications. They were chosen not only for their generality, but also because they provide a fair and accurate representation of the breadth, depth, and wide-ranging capabilities of the .NET Framework class library.

File and Stream I/O

Classes in the *System.IO* namespace enable managed applications to perform file I/O and other forms of input and output. The fundamental building block for managed I/O is the stream, which is an abstract representation of byte-oriented data. Streams are represented by the *System.IO.Stream* class. Because *Stream* is abstract, *System.IO* as well as other namespaces include concrete classes derived from *Stream* that represent physical data sources. For example, *System.IO.FileStream* permits files to be accessed as streams; *System.IO.MemoryStream* does the same for blocks of memory. The *System.Net.Sockets* namespace includes a *Stream* derivative named *NetworkStream* that abstracts sockets as streams, and the *System.Security.Cryptography* namespace defines a *CryptoStream* class used to read and write encrypted streams.

Stream classes have methods that you can call to perform input and output, but the .NET Framework offers an additional level of abstraction in the form of readers and writers. The *BinaryReader* and *BinaryWriter* classes provide an easy-to-use interface for performing binary reads and writes on stream objects. *StreamReader* and *StreamWriter*, which derive from the abstract *TextReader* and *TextWriter* classes, support the reading and writing of text.

One of the most common forms of I/O that managed and unmanaged applications alike are called upon to perform is file I/O. The general procedure for reading and writing files in a managed application is as follows:

1. Open the file using a *FileStream* object.

2. For binary reads and writes, wrap instances of *BinaryReader* and *BinaryWriter* around the *FileStream* object and call *BinaryReader* and *BinaryWriter* methods such as *Read* and *Write* to perform input and output.

3. For reads and writes involving text, wrap a *StreamReader* and *StreamWriter* around the *FileStream* object and use *StreamReader* and *StreamWriter* methods such as *ReadLine* and *WriteLine* to perform input and output.

4. Close the *FileStream* object.

That this example deals specifically with file I/O is not to imply that readers and writers are only for files. They're not. Later in this chapter, you'll see a sample program that uses a *StreamReader* object to read text fetched from a

Web page. The fact that readers and writers work with any kind of *Stream* object makes them powerful tools for performing I/O on any stream-oriented media.

System.IO also contains classes for manipulating files and directories. The *File* class provides static methods for opening, creating, copying, moving, and renaming files, as well as for reading and writing file attributes. *FileInfo* boasts the same capabilities, but *FileInfo* exposes its features through instance methods rather than static methods. The *Directory* and *DirectoryInfo* classes provide a programmatic interface to directories, enabling them to be created, deleted, enumerated, and more via simple method calls. Chapter 4's ControlDemo application demonstrates how to use *File* and *Directory* methods to enumerate the files in a directory and obtain information about those files.

Text File I/O

The reading and writing of text files from managed applications is aided and abetted by the *FileStream*, *StreamReader*, and *StreamWriter* classes. Suppose you wanted to write a simple app that dumps text files to the console window—the functional equivalent of the old DOS TYPE command. Here's how to go about it:

```
StreamReader reader = new StreamReader (filename);
for (string line = reader.ReadLine (); line != null;line = reader.ReadLine ())
    Console.WriteLine (line);
reader.Close ();
```

The first line creates a *StreamReader* object that wraps a *FileStream* created from *filename*. The *for* loop uses *StreamReader.ReadLine* to iterate through the lines in the file and *Console.WriteLine* to output them to the console window. The final statement closes the file by closing the *StreamReader*.

That's the general approach, but in real life you have to anticipate the possibility that things might not go strictly according to plan. For example, what if the file name passed to *StreamReader*'s constructor is invalid? Or what if the framework throws an exception before the final statement is executed, causing the file to be left open? Figure 3-1 contains the source code for a managed version of the TYPE command (called LIST to distinguish it from the real TYPE command) that responds gracefully to errors using C# exception handling. The *catch* block traps exceptions thrown when *StreamReader*'s constructor encounters an invalid file name or when I/O errors occur as the file is being read. The *finally* block ensures that the file is closed even if an exception is thrown.

List.cs

```
using System;
using System.IO;

class MyApp
{
    static void Main (string[] args)
    {
        // Make sure a file name was entered on the command line
        if (args.Length == 0) {
            Console.WriteLine ("Error: Missing file name");
            return;
        }

        // Open the file and display its contents
        StreamReader reader = null;

        try {
            reader = new StreamReader (args[0]);
            for (string line = reader.ReadLine (); line != null;
                line = reader.ReadLine ())
                Console.WriteLine (line);
        }
        catch (IOException e) {
            Console.WriteLine (e.Message);
        }
        finally {
            if (reader != null)
                reader.Close ();
        }
    }
}
```

Figure 3-1 A managed application that mimics the TYPE command.

Because the FCL is such a comprehensive class library, passing a file name to *StreamReader*'s constructor isn't the only way to open a text file for reading. Here are some others:

```
// Use File.Open to create a FileStream, and then wrap a
// StreamReader around it
FileStream stream = File.Open (filename, FileMode.Open, FileAccess.Read);
StreamReader reader = new StreamReader (stream);

// Create a FileStream directly, and then wrap a
// StreamReader around it
FileStream stream = new FileStream (filename, FileMode.Open, FileAccess.Read);
```

```
StreamReader reader = new StreamReader (stream);

// Use File.OpenText to create a FileStream and a
// StreamReader in one step
StreamReader reader = File.OpenText (filename);
```

There are other ways, too, but you get the picture. None of these methods for wrapping a *StreamReader* around a file is intrinsically better than the others, but they do demonstrate the numerous ways in which ordinary, everyday tasks can be accomplished using the .NET Framework class library.

*StreamReader*s read from text files; *StreamWriter*s write to them. Suppose you wanted to write *catch* handlers that log exceptions to a text file. Here's a *LogException* method that takes a file name and an *Exception* object as input and uses *StreamWriter* to append the error message in the *Exception* object to the file:

```
void LogException (string filename, Exception ex)
{
    StreamWriter writer = null;
    try {
        writer = new StreamWriter (filename, true);
        writer.WriteLine (ex.Message);
    }
    finally {
        if (writer != null)
            writer.Close ();
    }
}
```

Passing true in the second parameter to *StreamWriter*'s constructor tells the *StreamWriter* to append data if the file exists and to create a new file if it doesn't.

Binary File I/O

BinaryReader and *BinaryWriter* are to binary files as *StreamReader* and *StreamWriter* are to text files. Their key methods are *Read* and *Write*, which do exactly what you would expect them to. To demonstrate, the sample program in Figure 3-2 uses *BinaryReader* and *BinaryWriter* to encrypt and unencrypt files by XORing their contents with passwords entered on the command line. Encrypting a file is as simple as running Scramble.exe from the command line and including a file name and password, in that order, as in:

```
scramble readme.txt imbatman
```

To unencrypt the file, execute the same command again:

```
scramble readme.txt imbatman
```

XOR-encryption is hardly industrial-strength encryption, but it's sufficient to hide file contents from casual intruders. And it's simple enough to not distract from the main point of the application, which is to get a firsthand look at *BinaryReader* and *BinaryWriter*.

Scramble.cs contains two lines of code that merit further explanation:

```
ASCIIEncoding enc = new ASCIIEncoding ();
byte[] keybytes = enc.GetBytes (key);
```

These statements convert the second command-line parameter—a string representing the encryption key—into an array of bytes. Strings in the .NET Framework are instances of *System.String*. *ASCIIEncoding.GetBytes* is a convenient way to convert a *System.String* into a byte array. Scramble XORs the bytes in the file with the bytes in the converted string. Had the program used *UnicodeEncoding.GetBytes* instead, encryption would be less effective because calling *UnicodeEncoding.GetBytes* on strings containing characters from Western alphabets produces a buffer in which every other byte is a 0. XORing a byte with 0 does absolutely nothing, and XOR encryption is weak enough as is without worsening matters by using keys that contain lots of zeros. *ASCIIEncoding* is a member of the *System.Text* namespace, which explains the *using System.Text* directive at the top of the file.

```
Scramble.cs
using System;
using System.IO;
using System.Text;

class MyApp
{
    const int bufsize = 1024;

    static void Main (string[] args)
    {
        // Make sure a file name and encryption key were entered
        if (args.Length < 2) {
            Console.WriteLine ("Syntax: SCRAMBLE filename key");
            return;
        }

        string filename = args[0];
        string key = args[1];
        FileStream stream = null;

        try {
            // Open the file for reading and writing
```

Figure 3-2   A simple file encryption utility.

Scramble.cs *(continued)*

```
        stream = File.Open (filename, FileMode.Open,
            FileAccess.ReadWrite);

        // Wrap a reader and writer around the FileStream
        BinaryReader reader = new BinaryReader (stream);
        BinaryWriter writer = new BinaryWriter (stream);

        // Convert the key into a byte array
        ASCIIEncoding enc = new ASCIIEncoding ();
        byte[] keybytes = enc.GetBytes (key);

        // Allocate an I/O buffer and a key buffer
        byte[] buffer = new byte[bufsize];
        byte[] keybuf = new byte[bufsize + keybytes.Length - 1];

        // Replicate the byte array in the key buffer to create
        // an encryption key whose size equals or exceeds the
        // size of the I/O buffer
        int count = (1024 + keybytes.Length - 1) / keybytes.Length;
        for (int i=0; i<count; i++)
            Array.Copy (keybytes, 0, keybuf, i * keybytes.Length,
                keybytes.Length);

        // Read the file in bufsize blocks, XOR-encrypt each block,
        // and write the encrypted block back to the file
        long lBytesRemaining = stream.Length;

        while (lBytesRemaining > 0) {
            long lPosition = stream.Position;
            int nBytesRequested = (int) System.Math.Min (bufsize,
                lBytesRemaining);
            int nBytesRead = reader.Read (buffer, 0,
                nBytesRequested);

            for (int i=0; i<nBytesRead; i++)
                buffer[i] ^= keybuf[i];

            stream.Seek (lPosition, SeekOrigin.Begin);
            writer.Write (buffer, 0, nBytesRead);
            lBytesRemaining -= nBytesRead;
        }
    }
    catch (Exception e) {
        Console.WriteLine (e.Message);

    }
    finally {
```

Scramble.cs *(continued)*

```
            if (stream != null)
                stream.Close ();
        }
    }
}
```

Collections

The .NET Framework class library's *System.Collections* namespace contains classes that serve as containers for groups, or *collections*, of data. *Hashtable* is one example of a *System.Collections* type. It implements hash tables, which feature lightning-fast lookups. Another example is *ArrayList*, which represents resizable arrays. The presence of these and other types defined in *System.Collections* means you can spend more time writing code that makes your application unique and less time writing tedious infrastructural code.

The following table lists the core collection classes defined in *System.Collections*. Succeeding sections formally introduce the *Hashtable* and *ArrayList* classes. Other collection classes, including *Stack* and *SortedList*, are used in sample programs presented in this chapter and others.

System.Collections Collection Classes

Class	Implements
ArrayList	Resizable arrays
BitArray	Bit arrays
Hashtable	Tables of key/value pairs structured for fast lookups
Queue	First-in, first-out (FIFO) buffers
SortedList	Tables of sorted key/value pairs accessible by key or index
Stack	Last-in, first-out (LIFO) buffers

One characteristic of all the collection classes in *System.Collections* (with the exception of *BitArray*, which stores Boolean values) is that they're weakly typed. In other words, they store instances of *System.Object*. Weak typing enables collections to store virtually any kind of data because all .NET Framework data types derive directly or indirectly from *System.Object*. Unfortunately, weak typing also means that you have to do a lot of casting. For example, if you put a string in a *Hashtable* in C# and then retrieve it, you have to cast it back to a string to call *String* methods on it. If you're morally opposed to casting, you can use the *System.Collections* classes *CollectionBase* and *DictionaryBase* as base classes for strongly typed collections of your own. However, it's very likely that a future version of the .NET Framework will support something called *generics*, which are analogous to C++ templates. If you can stomach a moderate amount of casting for now, building type-safe collection classes should be a lot easier in the future.

Hash Tables

Since the dawn of computing, programmers have searched for ways to optimize data retrieval operations. When it comes to fast lookups, nothing beats the hash table. Hash tables store key/value pairs. When an item is inserted, the key is hashed and the resulting value (modulo the table size) is used as an index into the table, specifying where the item should be stored. When a value is retrieved, the key is hashed again. The resulting index reveals the item's precise location in the table. A well-designed hash table can retrieve items with just one lookup, irrespective of the number of items in the table.

System.Collections.Hashtable is the FCL's hash table data type. The following code uses a *Hashtable* object to build a simple French-English dictionary. The values stored in the table are the French words for the days of the week. The keys are the English words for the same:

```
Hashtable table = new Hashtable ();
table.Add ("Sunday",    "Dimanche");
table.Add ("Monday",    "Lundi");
table.Add ("Tuesday",   "Mardi");
table.Add ("Wednesday", "Mercredi");
table.Add ("Thursday",  "Jeudi");
table.Add ("Friday",    "Vendredi");
table.Add ("Saturday",  "Samedi");
```

With the hash table initialized in this manner, finding the French equivalent of Tuesday requires one simple statement:

```
string word = (string) table["Tuesday"];
```

Items can also be added to a *Hashtable* using string indexes:

```
Hashtable table = new Hashtable ();
table["Sunday"]    = "Dimanche";
table["Monday"]    = "Lundi";
table["Tuesday"]   = "Mardi";
table["Wednesday"] = "Mercredi";
table["Thursday"]  = "Jeudi";
table["Friday"]    = "Vendredi";
table["Saturday"]  = "Samedi";
```

Semantically, there's a difference between adding items with *Add* and adding them with indexers. *Add* throws an exception if the key you pass to it is already in the table. Indexers don't. They simply replace the old value with the new one.

Physically, a *Hashtable* stores items added to it in *System.Collections.DictionaryEntry* objects. Each *DictionaryEntry* object holds a key and a value that are exposed through properties named *Key* and *Value*. Because *Hashtable* implements the FCL's *IDictionary* interface, which in turn derives indirectly from *IEnumerable*, you can use the C# *foreach* command (or the Visual Basic .NET *For Each* command) to enumerate the items in a *Hashtable*. The following code writes all the keys and values stored in a *Hashtable* named *table* to the console window:

```
foreach (DictionaryEntry entry in table)
    Console.WriteLine ("Key={0}, Value={1}\n", entry.Key, entry.Value);
```

Hashtable also has methods for removing items (*Remove*), removing all items (*Clear*), checking for the existence of items (*ContainsKey* and *ContainsValue*), and more. To find out how many items a *Hashtable* contains, read its *Count* property. To enumerate only a *Hashtable*'s keys or values, use its *Keys* or *Values* property.

Two factors control *Hashtable* lookup performance: the *Hashtable*'s size and the uniqueness of the hashes produced from the input keys. A *Hashtable*'s size is dynamic; the table automatically grows as new items are added to it to minimize the chance of collisions. A collision occurs when two different keys hash to identical table indexes. *Hashtable* uses a double hashing algorithm to mitigate the negative effect of collisions on performance, but the best performance comes when there are no collisions at all.

Grow operations are expensive because they force the *Hashtable* to allocate new memory, recompute the table indexes, and copy each item to a new position in the table. By default, a *Hashtable* is sized for 0 items, meaning that many grow operations are required to grow it to a respectable size. If you know in advance approximately how many items you'll be adding to a *Hashtable*, set the table's initial size by passing a count to the class constructor. The following statement creates a *Hashtable* whose size is optimized for 1,000 items:

```
Hashtable table = new Hashtable (1000);
```

Initializing the *Hashtable* size in this manner doesn't affect lookup performance, but it can improve insertion speed by a factor of 2 or more.

When a *Hashtable* grows, it always assumes a size that's a prime number to minimize the likelihood of collisions. (Statistically, if *n* is a random number, *n* modulo *m* is more likely to produce a unique result if *m* is a prime number.) By default, a *Hashtable* expands its memory allocation when the item count exceeds a predetermined percentage of the table size. You can control the percentage by varying the *load factor*. A load factor of 1.0 corresponds to 72 percent, 0.9 corresponds to 65 percent (0.9 × 72), and so on. Valid load factors range from 0.1 to 1.0. The following statement sizes a *Hashtable* for 1,000 items and sets its load factor to 0.8, meaning that the *Hashtable* will grow when the item count reaches approximately 58 percent of the table size:

```
Hashtable table = new Hashtable (1000, 0.8f);
```

The default load factor (1.0) is fine for most applications, so chances are you'll never need to change it.

Maximizing the uniqueness of hash values generated from input keys is also critical to a *Hashtable*'s performance. By default, *Hashtable* hashes an input key by calling the key's *GetHashCode* method, which all objects inherit from *System.Object*. If you key values with instances of a class whose *GetHashCode* method does a poor job of generating unique hash values, do one of the following to optimize performance:

- Override *GetHashCode* in a derived class and provide an implementation that produces unique hash values.

- Create a type that implements *IHashCodeProvider* and pass a reference to an instance of that type to *Hashtable*'s constructor. *Hashtable* will respond by calling the object's *IHashCodeProvider.GetHashCode* method to hash the input keys.

Many FCL data types, including strings, hash just fine and therefore work well as *Hashtable* keys right out of the box.

Hashtable calls a key's *Equals* method—another method inherited from *System.Object*—to compare keys. If you use a custom data type as *Hashtable* keys and the *Equals* method your type inherits from *System.Object* doesn't accurately gauge equality, either override *Equals* in the derived class or pass *Hashtable*'s constructor an *IComparer* interface whose *Compare* method is capable of comparing keys.

Resizable Arrays

The FCL's *System* namespace contains a class named *Array* that models the behavior of static arrays. *System.Collections.ArrayList* encapsulates dynamic arrays—arrays that can be sized and resized as needed. *ArrayList*s are useful when you want to store data in an array but don't know up front how many items you'll be storing.

Creating an *ArrayList* and adding items to it is simplicity itself:

```
ArrayList list = new ArrayList ();
list.Add ("John");
list.Add ("Paul");
list.Add ("George");
list.Add ("Ringo");
```

Add adds an item to the end of the array and grows the array's memory allocation if necessary to accommodate the new item. The related *Insert* method inserts an item into an *ArrayList* at a specified position and moves higher-numbered items upward in the array. *Insert* also grows the array if that's necessary.

If you know approximately how many items you'll be adding to an *Array-List*, you should specify a count at creation time to minimize the number of resizing operations performed. The following code creates an *ArrayList* containing 100,000 integers:

```
ArrayList list = new ArrayList ();
for (int i=0; i<100000; i++)
    list.Add (i);
```

The next code sample does the same, but does it in half the time (10 milliseconds versus 20 milliseconds on the machine I tested it on):

```
ArrayList list = new ArrayList (100000);
for (int i=0; i<100000; i++)
    list.Add (i);
```

To retrieve an item from an *ArrayList*, use a 0-based index:

```
int i = (int) list[0];
```

And to assign a value to an existing array element, do this:

```
list[0] = 999;
```

The *Count* property reveals how many items an *ArrayList* contains. Consequently, one way to iterate through the items in an *ArrayList* is as follows:

```
for (int i=0; i<list.Count; i++)
    Console.WriteLine (list[i]);
```

You can also iterate with *foreach*:

```
foreach (int i in list)
    Console.WriteLine (i);
```

To remove items from an *ArrayList*, call *Remove, RemoveAt, RemoveRange,* or *Clear*. When items are removed, items with higher indexes are automatically shifted down to fill the void. If you delete the item at index 5, for example, the item at index 6 becomes the item at index 5, the item at index 7 becomes the item at index 6, and so on.

Instances of *ArrayList* automatically allocate memory to accommodate new items. They don't automatically release that memory when items are removed. To downsize an *ArrayList* to fit exactly the number of items that it currently contains, call *TrimToSize*. The following example adds 1000 integers to an *ArrayList*, deletes the first 500, and then resizes the array to fit the remaining 500:

```
// Add items
ArrayList list = new ArrayList (1000);
for (int i=0; i<1000; i++)
    list.Add (i);

// Remove items
list.RemoveRange (0, 500);

// Resize the array
list.TrimToSize ();
```

The number of items that an *ArrayList* can hold without allocating additional memory is called its *capacity*. You can find out the capacity of an *ArrayList* from its *Capacity* property. *Capacity* is a get/set property, so you can use it to set the capacity as well as to read it. The ability to increase an *ArrayList*'s capacity on the fly comes in handy if you don't know how many items the array will store when you create it, but you do know approximately how many it will store when you start adding items.

The WordCount Application

WordCount is a console application that provides statistics on word usage in text files. To use it, go to a command prompt and type the command name followed by a file name, as in the following:

```
wordcount readme.txt
```

The output consists of an alphabetically sorted list of words found in the file and the number of times that each word appears. WordCount uses a *StreamReader*, a *Hashtable*, and an *ArrayList* to do its work. For good measure, it also throws in a *SortedList*. Its source code appears in Figure 3-3.

When executed, WordCount opens the input file and reads through it a line at a time with repeated calls to *StreamReader.ReadLine*. It extracts the words from each line by calling a local method named *GetWords*, and it uses each word returned by *GetWords* as a key in the *Hashtable*. If the key doesn't exist—meaning the word hasn't been encountered before—WordCount adds a 1 to the *Hashtable* and keys it with the word. If the key does exist—meaning the word has been encountered before—WordCount reads the associated integer value from the *Hashtable*, increments it by one, and writes it back using the same key. By the time WordCount reaches the end of the file, every word it encountered is represented as a key in the *Hashtable*, and the value associated with each key is a count of the number of times the word appears. Thus, the *Hashtable*'s purpose is twofold:

■   It provides a super-fast way to determine whether a word has been encountered before.

■ It provides a store for the word list and associated occurrence counts.

How do *ArrayList* and *SortedList* fit into the picture? When *GetWords* begins parsing a line of text, it has no idea how many words it will encounter. Because it can't very well store the results in a static array, it uses a dynamic array—an *ArrayList*—instead. After parsing is complete, *GetWords* allocates a static array just large enough to hold the items in the *ArrayList* and copies the *ArrayList* to the static array with *ArrayList.CopyTo*. Then it returns the static array to the caller.

Method *Main* uses a *SortedList* object to sort the word list before writing it to the console window. One simple statement copies the *Hashtable* to the *Sort-edList*; a *foreach* loop extracts items from the *SortedList* and outputs them to the screen. Because the values used to key the items in the *SortedList* are strings, the simple act of inserting them into the *SortedList* sorts them alphabetically.

```
WordCount.cs
using System;
using System.IO;
using System.Collections;

class MyApp
{
    static void Main (string[] args)
    {
        // Make sure a file name was entered on the command line
        if (args.Length == 0) {
            Console.WriteLine ("Error: Missing file name");
            return;
        }

        StreamReader reader = null;
        Hashtable table = new Hashtable ();

        try {
            // Iterate through the file a word at a time, creating

            // an entry in the Hashtable for each unique word found
            // and incrementing the count for each word that's
            // encountered again
            reader = new StreamReader (args[0]);

            for (string line = reader.ReadLine (); line != null;
                line = reader.ReadLine ()) {
                string[] words = GetWords (line);
```

Figure 3-3 WordCount source code.

WordCount.cs   *(continued)*

```
            foreach (string word in words) {
                string iword = word.ToLower ();
                if (table.ContainsKey (iword))
                    table[iword] = (int) table[iword] + 1;
                else
                    table[iword] = 1;
            }
        }

        // Sort the Hashtable entries using a SortedList
        SortedList list = new SortedList (table);

        // Display the results
        Console.WriteLine ("{0} unique words found in {1}",
            table.Count, args[0]);

        foreach (DictionaryEntry entry in list)
            Console.WriteLine ("{0} ({1})",
                entry.Key, entry.Value);
    }
    catch (Exception e) {
        Console.WriteLine (e.Message);
    }
    finally {
        if (reader != null)
            reader.Close ();
    }
}

static string[] GetWords (string line)
{
    // Create an ArrayList to hold the intermediate results
    ArrayList al = new ArrayList ();

    // Parse the words from the line and add them to the ArrayList
    int i = 0;
    string word;
    char[] characters = line.ToCharArray ();

    while ((word = GetNextWord (line, characters, ref i)) != null)
        al.Add (word);

    // Return a static array that is equivalent to the ArrayList
    string[] words = new string[al.Count];
    al.CopyTo (words);
    return words;
}
```

WordCount.cs *(continued)*

```
static string GetNextWord (string line, char[] characters,
    ref int i)
{
    // Find the beginning of the next word
    while (i < characters.Length &&
        !Char.IsLetterOrDigit (characters[i]))
        i++;

    if (i == characters.Length)
        return null;

    int start = i;

    // Find the end of the word
    while (i < characters.Length &&
        Char.IsLetterOrDigit (characters[i]))
        i++;

    // Return the word
    return line.Substring (start, i - start);
}
}
```

Regular Expressions

One of the lesser known but potentially most useful classes in all of the .NET Framework class library is *Regex*, which belongs to the *System.Text.RegularExpressions* namespace. *Regex* represents regular expressions. Regular expressions are a language for parsing and manipulating text. (A full treatment of the language is beyond the scope of this book, but wonderful tutorials are available both in print and on line.) *Regex* supports three basic types of operations:

- Splitting strings into substrings using regular expressions to identify separators

- Searching strings for substrings that match patterns in regular expressions

- Performing search-and-replace operations using regular expressions to identify the text you want to replace

One very practical use for regular expressions is to validate user input. It's trivial, for example, to use a regular expression to verify that a string entered into a credit card field conforms to a pattern that's consistent with credit card numbers—that is, digits possibly separated by hyphens. You'll see an example of such usage in a moment.

Another common use for regular expressions is to do screen scraping. Say you want to write an app that displays stock prices gathered from a real-time (or near real-time) data source. One approach is to send an HTTP request to a Web site such as Nasdaq.com and "screen scrape" the prices from the HTML returned in the response. *Regex* simplifies the task of parsing HTML. The downside to screen scraping, of course, is that your app may cease to work if the format of the data changes. (I know because I once wrote an app that used screen scraping to fetch stock prices, and the *day after* I published it, my data source changed the HTML format of its Web pages.) But unless you can find a data source that provides the information you want as XML, screen scraping might be your only choice.

When you create a *Regex* object, you pass to the class constructor the regular expression to encapsulate:

```
Regex regex = new Regex ("[a-z]");
```

In the language of regular expressions, "[a-z]" means any lowercase letter of the alphabet. You can also pass a second parameter specifying *Regex* options. For example, the statement

```
Regex regex = new Regex ("[a-z]", RegexOptions.IgnoreCase);
```

creates a *Regex* object that matches any letter of the alphabet without regard to case. If the regular expression passed to the *Regex* constructor is invalid, *Regex* throws an *ArgumentException*.

Once a *Regex* object is initialized, you call methods on it to apply the regular expression to strings of text. The following sections describe how to put *Regex* to work in managed applications and offer examples regarding its use.

Splitting Strings

Regex.Split splits strings into constituent parts by using a regular expression to identify separators. Here's an example that divides a path name into drive and directory names:

```
Regex regex = new Regex (@"\\");
string[] parts = regex.Split (@"c:\inetpub\wwwroot\wintellect");
foreach (string part in parts)
    Console.WriteLine (part);
```

And here's the output:

```
c:
inetpub
wwwroot
wintellect
```

Notice the double backslash passed to *Regex*'s constructor. The @ preceding the string literal prevents you from having to escape the backslash for the compiler's sake, but because the backslash is also an escape character in regular expressions, you have to escape a backslash with a backslash to form a valid regular expression.

The fact that *Split* identifies separators using full-blown regular expressions makes for some interesting possibilities. For example, suppose you wanted to extract the text from the following HTML by stripping out everything in angle brackets:

```
<b>Every</b>good<h3>boy</h3>does<b>fine</b>
```

Here's the code to do it:

```
Regex regex = new Regex ("<[^>]*>");
string[] parts =
    regex.Split ("<b>Every</b>good<h3>boy</h3>does<b>fine</b>");
foreach (string part in parts)
    Console.WriteLine (part);
```

And here's the output:

```
Every
good
boy
does
fine
```

The regular expression "<[^>]*>" means anything that begins with an opening angle bracket ("<"), followed by zero or more characters that are *not* closing angle brackets ("[^>]*"), followed by a closing angle bracket (">").

With *Regex.Split* to lend a hand, you could simplify this chapter's Word-Count utility considerably. Rather than having the *GetWords* method manually parse a line of text into words, you could rewrite *GetWords* to split the line using a regular expression that identifies sequences of one or more nonalphanumeric characters as separators. Then you could delete the *GetNextWord* method altogether.

Searching Strings

Perhaps the most common use for *Regex* is to search strings for substrings matching a specified pattern. *Regex* includes three methods for searching strings and identifying the matches: *Match*, *Matches*, and *IsMatch*.

The simplest of the three is *IsMatch*. It provides a simple yes or no answer revealing whether an input string contains a match for the text represented by a regular expression. Here's a sample that checks an input string for HTML anchor tags (<a>):

```
Regex regex = new Regex ("<a[^>]*>", RegexOptions.IgnoreCase);
if (regex.IsMatch (input)) {
    // Input contains an anchor tag
}
else {
    // Input does NOT contain an anchor tag
}
```

Another use for *IsMatch* is to validate user input. The following method returns true if the input string contains 16 digits grouped into fours separated by hyphens, and false if it does not:

```
bool IsValid (string input)
{
    Regex regex = new Regex ("^[0-9]{4}-[0-9]{4}-[0-9]{4}-[0-9]{4}$");
    return regex.IsMatch (input);
}
```

Strings such as "1234-5678-8765-4321" pass the test just fine; strings such as "1234567887654321" and "1234-ABCD-8765-4321" do not. The ^ and $ characters denote the beginning and end of the line, respectively. Without these characters, strings such as "12345-5678-8765-4321" would pass, even though you didn't intend for them to. Regular expressions such as this are often used to perform cursory validations on credit card numbers. If you'd like, you can replace "[0-9]" in a regular expression with "/d". Thus, the expression

```
"^\d{4}-\d{4}-\d{4}-\d{4}$"
```

is equivalent to the one above.

Figure 3-4 contains the source code for a grep-like utility named NetGrep that uses *IsMatch* to parse a file for lines of text containing text matching a regular expression. Both the file name and the regular expression are entered on the command line. The following command lists all the lines in Index.html that contain anchor tags:

```
netgrep index.html "<a[^>]*>"
```

This command displays all lines in Readme.txt that contain numbers consisting of two or more digits:

```
netgrep readme.txt "\d{2,}"
```

In the source code listing, note the format specifier used in the *WriteLine* call. The "D5" in "{0:D5}" specifies that the line number should be formatted as a decimal value with a fixed field width of 5—for example, 00001.

NetGrep.cs

```csharp
using System;
using System.IO;
using System.Text.RegularExpressions;
class MyApp
{
    static void Main (string[] args)
    {
        // Make sure a file name and regular expression were entered
        if (args.Length < 2) {
            Console.WriteLine ("Syntax: NETGREP filename expression");
            return;
        }

        StreamReader reader = null;
        int linenum = 1;

        try {
            // Initialize a Regex object with the regular expression
            // entered on the command line
            Regex regex = new Regex (args[1], RegexOptions.IgnoreCase);

            // Iterate through the file a line at a time and
            // display all lines that contain a pattern matching the
            // regular expression
            reader = new StreamReader (args[0]);
            for (string line = reader.ReadLine (); line != null;
                line = reader.ReadLine (), linenum++) {
                if (regex.IsMatch (line))
                    Console.WriteLine ("{0:D5}: {1}", linenum, line);
            }
        }
        catch (Exception e) {
            Console.WriteLine (e.Message);
        }
        finally {
            if (reader != null)
                reader.Close ();

        }
    }
}
```

Figure 3-4   NetGrep source code.

IsMatch tells you whether a string contains text matching a regular expression, but it doesn't tell you where in the string the match is located or how many matches there are. That's what the *Match* method is for. The following example displays all the *Href*s in Index.html that are followed by URLs enclosed in quotation marks. The metacharacter "\s" in a regular expression denotes whitespace; "\s" followed by an asterisk ("\s*") means any number of consecutive whitespace characters:

```
Regex regex = new Regex ("href\\s*=\\s*\"[^\"]*\"", RegexOptions.IgnoreCase);

StreamReader reader = new StreamReader ("Index.html");

for (string line = reader.ReadLine (); line != null;
    line = reader.ReadLine ()) {
    for (Match m = regex.Match (line); m.Success; m = m.NextMatch ())
        Console.WriteLine (m.Value);
}
```

The *Match* method returns a *Match* object indicating either that a match was found (*Match.Success* == true) or that no match was found (*Match.Success* == false). A *Match* object representing a successful match exposes the text that produced the match through its *Value* property. If *Match.Success* is true and the input string contains additional matches, you can iterate through the remaining matches with *Match.NextMatch.*

If the input string contains (or might contain) multiple matches and you want to enumerate them all, the *Matches* method offers a slightly more elegant way of doing it. The following example is functionally equivalent to the one above:

```
Regex regex = new Regex ("href\\s*=\\s*\"[^\"]*\"", RegexOptions.IgnoreCase);

StreamReader reader = new StreamReader ("Index.html");

for (string line = reader.ReadLine (); line != null;
    line = reader.ReadLine ()) {
    MatchCollection matches = regex.Matches (line);
    foreach (Match match in matches)
        Console.WriteLine (match.Value);
}
```

Matches returns a collection of *Match* objects in a *MatchCollection* whose contents can be iterated over with *foreach.* Each *Match* represents one match in the input string.

Match objects have a property named *Groups* that permits substrings within a match to be identified. Let's say you want to scan an HTML file for *Href*s, and for each *Href* that *Regex* finds, you want to extract the target of that *Href*—for example, the dotnet.html in href="dotnet.html." You can do that by using parentheses to define a group in the regular expression and then use the *Match* object's *Groups* collection to access the group. Here's an example:

```
Regex regex = new Regex ("href\\s*=\\s*\"([^\"]*)\"", RegexOptions.IgnoreCase);

StreamReader reader = new StreamReader ("Index.html");

for (string line = reader.ReadLine (); line != null;
    line = reader.ReadLine ()) {
    MatchCollection matches = regex.Matches (line);
    foreach (Match match in matches)
        Console.WriteLine (match.Groups[1]);
}
```

Notice the parentheses that now surround the part of the regular expression that corresponds to all characters between the quotation signs. That defines those characters as a group. In the *Match* object's *Groups* collection, *Groups*[0] identifies the full text of the match and *Groups*[1] identifies the subset of the match in parentheses. Thus, if Index.html contains the following line:

```
<a href="help.html">Click here for help</a>
```

both *Value* and *Groups*[0] evaluate to the text

```
href="help.html"
```

Groups[1], however, evaluates to

```
help.html
```

Groups can even be nested, meaning that virtually any subset of the text identified by a regular expression (or subset of a subset) can be extracted following a successful match.

Replacing Strings

If you decide to embellish NetGrep with the capability to perform search-and-replace, you'll love *Regex.Replace*, which replaces text matching the regular expression in the *Regex* object with text you pass as an input parameter. The following example replaces all occurrences of "Hello" with "Goodbye" in the string named *input*:

```
Regex regex = new Regex ("Hello");
string output = regex.Replace (input, "Goodbye");
```

The next example strips everything in angle brackets from the input string by replacing expressions in angle brackets with null strings:

```
Regex regex = new Regex ("<[^>]*>");
string output = regex.Replace (input, "");
```

A basic knowledge of regular expressions (and a helping hand from *Regex*) can go a long way when it comes to parsing and manipulating text in .NET Framework applications.

Internet Classes

The FCL's *System.Net* namespace includes classes for performing Internet-related tasks such as submitting HTTP requests to Web servers and resolving names using the Domain Name System (DNS). The daughter namespace *System.Net.Sockets* contains classes for communicating with other machines using TCP/IP sockets. Together, these namespaces provide the foundation for the FCL's Internet programming support. Other namespaces, such as *System.Web* and *System.Web.Mail*, contribute classes of their own to make the .NET Framework a first-rate tool for writing Internet-enabled applications.

Two of the most useful classes in the *System.Net* namespace are *WebRequest* and *WebResponse*, which are abstract base classes that serve as templates for object-oriented wrappers placed around HTTP and other Internet protocols. *System.Net* includes a pair of *WebRequest/WebResponse* derivatives named *HttpWebRequest* and *HttpWebResponse* that make it easy for managed applications to fetch Web pages and other resources available through HTTP. Learning about these classes is a great starting point for exploring the Internet programming support featured in the FCL.

HttpWebRequest and *HttpWebResponse*

HttpWebRequest and *HttpWebResponse* reduce the otherwise complex task of submitting HTTP requests to Web servers and capturing the responses to a few simple lines of code. To submit a request, use the *WebRequest* class's static *Create* method to create a request and then call *GetResponse* on the resulting *HttpWebRequest* object:

```
WebRequest request = WebRequest.Create ("http://www.wintellect.com");
WebResponse response = request.GetResponse ();
```

GetResponse returns an *HttpWebResponse* object encapsulating the response. Calling *GetResponseStream* on *HttpWebResponse* returns a *Stream* object that you can wrap a reader around to read the response. The following code echoes the text of the response to a console window:

```
StreamReader reader = new StreamReader (response.GetResponseStream ());
for (string line = reader.ReadLine (); line != null;
    line = reader.ReadLine ())
    Console.WriteLine (line);
reader.Close ();
```

It's that simple. *HttpWebRequest* also contains methods named *BeginGetResponse* and *EndGetResponse* that you can use to submit asynchronous Web requests, which might be useful if you don't want to wait around for large amounts of data to come back through a slow dial-up connection.

The LinkList application in Figure 3-5 uses the *WebRequest*, *WebResponse*, and *Regex* classses to list a Web page's hyperlinks. Its input is the URL of a Web page; its output is a list of all the URLs accompanying *Hrefs* in the Web page. Fetching the Web page is easy thanks to *WebRequest.GetResponse*. *Regex.Match* simplifies the task of parsing the *Hrefs* out of the response. To see LinkList in action, as shown in Figure 3-6, compile it and type *linklist* followed by a URL at the command prompt:

```
linklist http://www.wintellect.com
```

LinkList also demonstrates that *StreamReader* objects can read from any kind of stream, not just file streams. Specifically, it uses a *StreamReader* to read the contents of the stream returned by *WebResponse*'s *GetResponseStream* method. This is abstraction at its finest and is the primary reason that the FCL's architects decided to use readers and writers to abstract access to streams.

```csharp
LinkList.cs
using System;
using System.IO;
using System.Net;
using System.Text.RegularExpressions;

class MyApp
{
    static void Main (string[] args)
    {
        if (args.Length == 0) {
            Console.WriteLine ("Error: Missing URL");
            return;
        }

        StreamReader reader = null;

        try {
            WebRequest request = WebRequest.Create (args[0]);
            WebResponse response = request.GetResponse ();
            reader = new StreamReader (response.GetResponseStream ());
            string content = reader.ReadToEnd ();

            Regex regex = new Regex ("href\\s*=\\s*\"([^\"]*)\"",
                RegexOptions.IgnoreCase);

            MatchCollection matches = regex.Matches (content);
            foreach (Match match in matches)
```

Figure 3-5 LinkList source code.

LinkList.cs *(continued)*

```
            Console.WriteLine (match.Groups[1]);
        }
        catch (Exception e) {
            Console.WriteLine (e.Message);
        }
        finally {
            if (reader != null)
                reader.Close ();
        }
    }
}
```

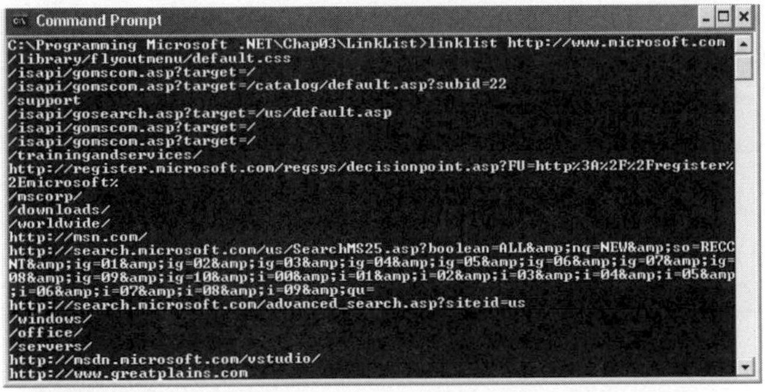

Figure 3-6 LinkList output.

The *System.Web.Mail* Namespace

Want to send e-mail from a .NET Framework application? You could do it the hard way by using sockets to establish a connection to a mail server and then transmit a mail message using Simple Mail Transfer Protocol (SMTP). Or you could do it the easy way and rely on classes in the *System.Web.Mail* namespace. *System.Web.Mail* provides a simple managed interface to SMTP. The core classes are *MailMessage*, which represents e-mail messages; *MailAttachment*, which represents attachments; and *SmtpMail*, which places a friendly wrapper around the host system's SMTP mail service.

Here's how easy it is to send e-mail from a managed application:

```
using System.Web.Mail;
    .
    .
    .
MailMessage message = new MailMessage ();
message.From = "webmaster@wintellect.com";
message.To = "Everyone@wintellect.com";
message.Subject = "Scheduled Power Outage";
message.Body = "Our servers will be down tonight.";
```

(continued)

```
SmtpMail.SmtpServer = "localhost";
SmtpMail.Send (message);
```

Having the capability to send e-mail programmatically can come in handy in countless ways. For example, you might want to send e-mail confirmations to customers who purchase merchandise from your Web site, or you might write your own software to transmit electronic newsletters to clients. Whatever your motivation, it doesn't get much easier than this.

Figure 3-7 contains the source code for a simple e-mail client named Send-Mail, built around the *MailMessage* and *SmtpMail* classes. To spice things up just a bit, and to serve as a preview of things to come, SendMail isn't a console application—it's a Web application. Specifically, it's an ASP.NET Web form. (See Figure 3-8.) Clicking the Send Mail button activates the *OnSend* method, which composes an e-mail message from the user's input and sends it to the recipient. To run the application, copy SendMail.aspx to the \Inetpub\wwwroot directory of a PC that has ASP.NET and Internet Information Services installed on it. Then open a browser and type *http://localhost/sendmail.aspx* in the address bar. Once the Web form appears, fill in the fields and click the Send Mail button to send an e-mail message.

Some machines require a bit of reconfiguring to allow ASP.NET applications to send mail. If SendMail.aspx throws an exception when you click the Send Mail button, here's what to do. First make sure your machine's SMTP service is running. You can do that in the IIS configuration manager or in the Services Control Panel applet. Second, make sure the SMTP service is configured to allow relaying from localhost. To do that, open the IIS configuration manager (you'll find it in Administrative Tools), right-click Default SMTP Virtual Server, select Properties, click the Access tab, click the Relay button, select Only The List Below, and use the Add button to add 127.0.0.1 to the list of computers allowed to relay.

SendMail.aspx

```
<%@ Import Namespace="System.Web.Mail" %>

<html>
  <body>
    <h1>Simple SMTP E-Mail Client</h1>
    <form runat="server">
      <hr>
      <table cellspacing="8">
        <tr>
          <td align="right" valign="bottom">From:</td>
          <td><asp:TextBox ID="Sender" RunAt="server" /></td>
        </tr>
```

Figure 3-7 A Web-based e-mail client.

```
      <tr>
        <td align="right" valign="bottom">To:</td>
        <td><asp:TextBox ID="Receiver" RunAt="server" /></td>
      </tr>
      <tr>
        <td align="right" valign="bottom">Subject:</td>
        <td><asp:TextBox ID="Subject" RunAt="server" /></td>
      </tr>
      <tr>
        <td align="right" valign="top">Message:</td>
        <td><asp:TextBox ID="Body" TextMode="MultiLine" Rows="5"
          Columns="40" RunAt="server" /></td>
      </tr>
    </table>
    <hr>
    <asp:Button Text="Send Mail" OnClick="OnSend" RunAt="server" />
  </form>
  </body>
</html>

<script language="C#" runat="server">
  void OnSend (Object sender, EventArgs e)
  {
      MailMessage message = new MailMessage ();
      message.From = Sender.Text;
      message.To = Receiver.Text;
      message.Subject = Subject.Text;
      message.Body = Body.Text;
      SmtpMail.SmtpServer = "localhost";
      SmtpMail.Send (message);
  }
</script>
```

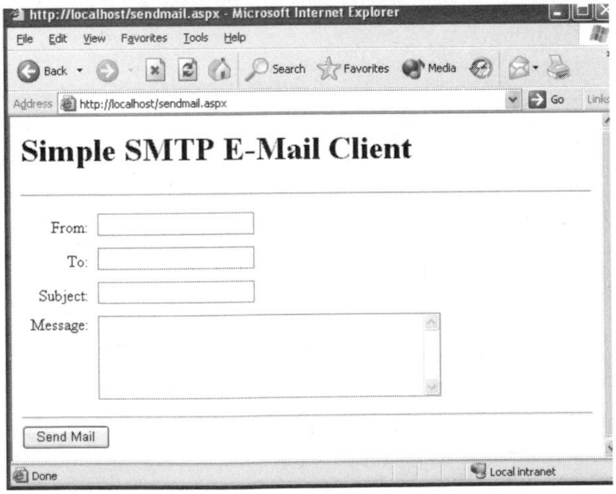

Figure 3-8   The SendMail application.

Data Access

In recent years, Microsoft has promoted an alphabet soup of database access technologies. First was ODBC. Then came DAO, RDO, ADO, and OLE DB, to name just a few. The .NET Framework has its own database API called ADO.NET. The bad news is that despite its name, ADO.NET has little in common with ADO. The good news is that learning the basics of ADO.NET requires all of about 15 minutes.

The classes that make up ADO.NET are found in the *System.Data* namespace and its descendants. Some ADO.NET classes, such as *DataSet*, are generic and work with virtually any kind of database. Others, such as *DataReader*, come in two distinctly different flavors: one for Microsoft SQL Server databases (*SqlDataReader*) and one for all others (*OleDbDataReader*). *Sql* classes belong to the *System.Data.SqlClient* namespace. They use a managed provider (that is, a database access layer that consists solely of managed code) that's optimized to work with Microsoft SQL Server databases. Significantly, *Sql* classes work only with SQL Server. *OleDb* classes, on the other hand, can be used with any database for which an OLE DB provider that is compatible with the .NET Framework is available. They tend to be somewhat slower than *Sql* classes because they're not optimized for any particular database and because they rely on a combination of managed and unmanaged code, but they're also more generic, enabling you to switch databases without having to rewrite your application. *OleDb* classes are defined in the *System.Data.OleDb* namespace.

ADO.NET is covered in detail in Chapter 12. The next several sections of this chapter offer an introductory look at ADO.NET, which will help you understand some of the data-aware sample programs presented in intervening chapters. For readers accustomed to working with traditional database APIs, the sections that follow also provide an educational first look at data access in the era of .NET.

DataReaders

One of the most common tasks that data-aware applications are asked to perform involves executing a query and outputting the results. For managed applications, the *DataReader* class is the perfect tool for the job. *DataReader* objects expose the results of database queries as fast, forward-only, read-only streams of data. *DataReader*s come in two flavors: *SqlDataReader* for SQL Server databases and *OleDbDataReader* for other types of databases. The following example uses *SqlDataReader* to query the Pubs database that comes with Microsoft SQL Server for all the records in the "Titles" table. It then writes the "Title" field of each record to a console window:

```
SqlConnection connection =
    new SqlConnection ("server=localhost;uid=sa;pwd=;database=pubs");
connection.Open ();

SqlCommand command =
    new SqlCommand ("select * from titles", connection);
SqlDataReader reader = command.ExecuteReader ();

while (reader.Read ())
    Console.WriteLine (reader.GetString (1));

connection.Close ();
```

The *SqlConnection* object represents the database connection. *Open* opens a connection, and *Close* closes it. *SqlCommand* encapsulates the query used to extract records from the database. Calling *ExecuteReader* on the *SqlCommand* object executes the command and returns a *SqlDataReader* object. Reading the records returned by the query is as simple as calling *SqlDataReader.Read* repeatedly until it returns null.

I purposely didn't include exception handling code in this sample to keep the code as simple and uncluttered as possible. In the real world, you'll want to use *try/catch/finally* to recover gracefully from errors and to ensure that the database connection is closed even in the face of inopportune exceptions:

```
SqlConnection connection =
    new SqlConnection ("server=localhost;uid=sa;pwd=;database=pubs");

try {
    connection.Open ();

    SqlCommand command =
        new SqlCommand ("select * from titles", connection);
    SqlDataReader reader = command.ExecuteReader ();

    while (reader.Read ())
        Console.WriteLine (reader.GetString (1));
}
catch (SqlException e) {
    Console.WriteLine (e.Message);
}
finally {
    connection.Close ();
}
```

Tailoring this code to work with databases other than Microsoft SQL Server is a simple matter of changing the *Sql* classes to *OleDb* classes and modifying the connection string accordingly.

Inserts, Updates, and Deletes

A *Command* object's *ExecuteReader* method executes a query and returns a *DataReader* encapsulating the results. The complementary *ExecuteNonQuery* method performs inserts, updates, and deletes. The following code uses a SQL INSERT command to add a record to SQL Server's Pubs database:

```
SqlConnection connection =
    new SqlConnection ("server=localhost;uid=sa;pwd=;database=pubs");

try {
    connection.Open ();
    string sqlcmd =
        "insert into titles (title_id, title, type, pub_id, " +
        "price, advance, royalty, ytd_sales, notes, pubdate) " +
        "values ('BU1001', 'Programming Microsoft.NET', " +
        "'Business', '1389', NULL, NULL, NULL, NULL, " +
        "'Learn to program Microsoft.NET', 'Jan 01 2002')";
    SqlCommand command = new SqlCommand (sqlcmd, connection);
    command.ExecuteNonQuery ();
}
catch (SqlException e) {
    Console.WriteLine (e.Message);
}
finally {
    connection.Close ();
}
```

To update or delete a record (or set of records), you simply replace the INSERT command with an UPDATE or DELETE command. Of course, there are other ways to add, modify, and remove records. The full range of options is discussed in Chapter 12.

DataSets and *DataAdapters*

DataSet, which belongs to the *System.Data* namespace, is the centerpiece of ADO.NET. A *DataSet* is an in-memory database capable of holding multiple tables and even of modeling constraints and relationships. Used in combination with *SqlDataAdapter* and *OleDbDataAdapter*, *DataSet* can handle virtually all the needs of modern-day data access applications and is frequently used in lieu of *DataReader* to facilitate random read/write access to back-end databases.

The following code fragment uses *SqlDataAdapter* and *DataSet* to query a database and display the results. It's functionally equivalent to the *SqlData-Reader* example presented earlier:

```
SqlDataAdapter adapter = new SqlDataAdapter (
    "select * from titles",
    "server=localhost;uid=sa;pwd=;database=pubs"
```

```
);

DataSet ds = new DataSet ();
adapter.Fill (ds);

foreach (DataRow row in ds.Tables[0].Rows)
    Console.WriteLine (row[1]);
```

SqlDataAdapter serves as a liaison between *DataSet* objects and physical data sources. In this example it executes a query, but it's capable of performing inserts, updates, and deletes, too. For details, see—you guessed it—Chapter 12.

Reflection

You already know that managed applications are deployed as assemblies, that assemblies contain files that are usually (but not always) managed modules, and that managed modules contain types. You also know that every managed module has metadata inside it that fully describes the types defined in the module, and that assemblies carry additional metadata in their manifests identifying the files that make up the assembly and other pertinent information. And you've seen how ILDASM can be used to inspect the contents of an assembly or managed module. Much of the information that ILDASM displays comes straight from the metadata.

The *System.Reflection* namespace contains types that you can use to access metadata without having to understand the binary metadata format. The term "reflection" means inspecting metadata to get information about an assembly, module, or type. The .NET Framework uses reflection to acquire important information at run time about the assemblies that it loads. Visual Studio .NET uses reflection to obtain IntelliSense data. The managed applications that you write can use reflection, too. Reflection makes the following operations possible:

- Retrieving information about assemblies and modules and the types they contain

- Reading information added to a compiled executable's metadata by custom attributes

- Performing late binding by dynamically instantiating and invoking methods on types

Not every managed application uses reflection or has a need to use reflection, but reflection is something every developer should know about, for two reasons. First, learning about reflection deepens one's understanding of the

.NET Framework. Second, reflection can be extraordinarily useful to certain types of applications. While far from exhaustive, the next few sections provide a working introduction to reflection and should at least enable you to hold your own when the conversation turns to reflection at a .NET party.

Retrieving Information About Assemblies, Modules, and Types

One use for reflection is to gather information at run time about assemblies, managed modules, and the types that assemblies and modules contain. The key classes that expose the functionality of the framework's reflection engine are

- *System.Reflection.Assembly*, which represents assemblies

- *System.Reflection.Module*, which represents managed modules

- *System.Type*, which represents types

The first step in acquiring information from an assembly's metadata is to load the assembly. The following statement uses the static *Assembly.LoadFrom* method to load the assembly whose manifest is stored in Math.dll:

```
Assembly a = Assembly.LoadFrom ("Math.dll");
```

LoadFrom returns a reference to an *Assembly* object representing the loaded assembly. A related method named *Load* takes an assembly name rather than a file name as input. Once an assembly is loaded, you can use *Assembly* methods to retrieve all sorts of interesting information about it. For example, the *GetModules* method returns an array of *Module* objects representing the modules in the assembly. *GetExportedTypes* returns an array of *Type* objects representing the types exported from the assembly (in other words, the assembly's public types). *GetReferencedAssemblies* returns an array of *AssemblyName* objects identifying assemblies used by this assembly. And the *GetName* method returns an *AssemblyName* object that serves as a gateway to still more information encoded in the assembly manifest.

Figure 3-9 contains the source code listing for a console application named AsmInfo that, given the name of a file containing an assembly manifest, uses reflection to display information about the assembly. Included in the output is information indicating whether the assembly is strongly or weakly named, the assembly's version number, the managed modules that it consists of, the types exported from the assembly, and other assemblies containing types that this assembly references. When run on the weakly named version of the Math assembly (Math.dll) presented in Chapter 2, AsmInfo produces the following output:

```
Naming: Weak
Version: 0.0.0.0

Modules
```

```
math.dll
simple.netmodule
complex.netmodule

Exported Types
  SimpleMath
  ComplexMath

Referenced Assemblies
  mscorlib
  Microsoft.VisualBasic
```

You can plainly see the two types exported from the Math assembly (*SimpleMath* and *ComplexMath*) and the modules that make up the assembly (Math.dll, Simple.netmodule, and Complex.netmodule). Mscorlib appears in the list of referenced assemblies because it contains the core data types used by virtually all managed applications. Microsoft.VisualBasic shows up also because one of the modules in the assembly, Simple.netmodule, was written in Visual Basic .NET.

AsmInfo.cs
```csharp
using System;
using System.Reflection;

class MyApp
{
    static void Main (string[] args)
    {
        if (args.Length == 0) {
            Console.WriteLine ("Error: Missing file name");
            return;
        }

        try {
            // Load the assembly identified on the command line
            Assembly a = Assembly.LoadFrom (args[0]);
            AssemblyName an = a.GetName ();

            // Indicate whether the assembly is strongly or
            // weakly named
            byte[] bytes = an.GetPublicKeyToken ();
            if (bytes == null)
                Console.WriteLine ("Naming: Weak");
            else
                Console.WriteLine ("Naming: Strong");

            // Display the assembly's version number
```

Figure 3-9   AsmInfo source code.

```
        Version ver = an.Version;
        Console.WriteLine ("Version: {0}.{1}.{2}.{3}",
            ver.Major, ver.Minor, ver.Build, ver.Revision);

        // List the modules that make up the assembly
        Console.WriteLine ("\nModules");
        Module[] modules = a.GetModules ();
        foreach (Module module in modules)
            Console.WriteLine ("  " + module.Name);

        // List the types exported from the assembly
        Console.WriteLine ("\nExported Types");
        Type[] types = a.GetExportedTypes ();
        foreach (Type type in types)
            Console.WriteLine ("  " + type.Name);

        // List assemblies referenced by the assembly
        Console.WriteLine ("\nReferenced Assemblies");
        AssemblyName[] names = a.GetReferencedAssemblies ();
        foreach (AssemblyName name in names)
            Console.WriteLine ("  " + name.Name);
    }
    catch (Exception e) {
        Console.WriteLine (e.Message);
    }
  }
}
```

If you'd like to know even more about an assembly—specifically, about the modules that it contains—you can use the *Module* objects returned by *Assembly.GetModules*. Calling *GetTypes* on a *Module* object retrieves a list of types defined in the module—all types, not just exported types. The following code sample writes the names of all the types defined in *module* to a console window:

```
Type[] types = module.GetTypes ();
foreach (Type type in types)
    Console.WriteLine (type.FullName);
```

To learn even more about a given type, you can call *GetMembers* on a *Type* object returned by *GetTypes*. *GetMembers* returns an array of *MemberInfo* objects representing the type's individual members. *MemberInfo.MemberType* tells you what kind of member a *MemberInfo* object represents. *Member-Types.Field*, for example, identifies the member as a field, while *Member-Types.Method* identifies it as a method. A *MemberInfo* object's *Name* property exposes the member's name. Using these and other *Type* members, you can drill down as deeply as you want to into a type, even identifying the parameters passed to individual methods (and the methods' return types) if you care to.

Using reflection to inspect the contents of managed executables is probably only interesting if you plan to write diagnostic utilities. But the fact that reflection exists at all leads to some other interesting possibilities, one of which is discussed in the next section.

Custom Attributes

One of the ground-breaking new language features supported by CLR-compliant compilers is the *attribute*. Attributes are a declarative means for adding information to metadata. For example, if you attribute a method this way and compile it without a "DEBUG" symbol defined, the compiler emits a token into the module's metadata noting that *DoValidityCheck* can't be called:

```
[Conditional ("DEBUG")]
public DoValidityCheck ()
{
  ...
}
```

If you later compile a module that calls *DoValidityCheck*, the compiler reads the metadata, sees that *DoValidityCheck* can't be called, and ignores statements that call it.

Attributes are instances of classes derived from *System.Attribute*. The FCL defines several attribute classes, including *System.Diagnostics.ConditionalAttribute*, which defines the behavior of the *Conditional* attribute. You can write attributes of your own by deriving from *Attribute*. The canonical example of a custom attribute is a *CodeRevision* attribute for documenting source code revisions. Revisions noted with source code comments—a traditional method for documenting code revisions—appear only in the source code. Revisions noted with attributes, however, are written into the compiled executable's metadata and can be retrieved through reflection.

Here's the source code for a custom attribute named *CodeRevisionAttribute*:

```
[AttributeUsage (AttributeTargets.All, AllowMultiple=true)]
class CodeRevisionAttribute : Attribute
{
    public string Author;
    public string Date;
    public string Comment;

    public CodeRevisionAttribute (string Author, string Date)
    {
```

(continued)

```
        this.Author = Author;
        this.Date = Date;
    }

}
```

The first statement, *AttributeUsage*, is itself an attribute. The first parameter passed to it, *AttributeTargets.All*, indicates that *CodeRevisionAttribute* can be applied to any element of the source code—to classes, methods, fields, and so on. The second parameter permits multiple *CodeRevisionAttribute*s to be applied to a single element. The remainder of the code is a rather ordinary class declaration. The class constructor defines *CodeRevisionAttribute*'s required parameters. Public fields and properties in an attribute class can be used as optional parameters. Because *CodeRevisionAttribute* defines a public field named *Comment*, for example, you can include a comment string in a code revision attribute simply by prefacing the string with "Comment=."

     Here's an example demonstrating how *CodeRevisionAttribute* might be used:

```
[CodeRevision ("billg", "07-19-2001")]
[CodeRevision ("steveb", "09-30-2001", Comment="Fixed Bill's bugs")]
struct Point
{
    public int x;
    public int y;
    public int z;
}
```

Get the picture? You can attribute any element of your source code by simply declaring a *CodeRevisionAttribute* in square brackets. You don't have to include the word *Attribute* in the attribute name because the compiler is smart enough to do it for you.

     Reflection is important to developers who write (or use) custom attributes because it is through reflection that an application reads information added to its (or someone else's) metadata via custom attributes. The following code sample enumerates the code revision attributes attached to type *Point* and writes them to the console window. Enumeration is made possible by *Member-Info.GetCustomAttributes*, which reads the custom attributes associated with any element that can be identified with a *MemberInfo* object:

```
MemberInfo info = typeof (Point);
object[] attributes = info.GetCustomAttributes (false);

if (attributes.Length > 0) {
    Console.WriteLine ("Code revisions for Point struct");
    foreach (CodeRevisionAttribute attribute in attributes) {
        Console.WriteLine ("\nAuthor: {0}", attribute.Author);
        Console.WriteLine ("Date: {0}", attribute.Date);
```

```
        if (attribute.Comment != null)
            Console.WriteLine ("Comment: {0}", attribute.Comment);
    }
}
```

And here's the output when this code is run against the *Point* struct shown above:

```
Code revisions for Point struct

Author: billg
Date: 07-19-2001

Author: steveb
Date: 09-30-2001
Comment: Fixed Bill's bugs
```

Writing a reporting utility that lists all the code revisions in a compiled executable wouldn't be difficult because types and type members are easily enumerated using the reflection techniques described in the previous section.

Dynamically Loading Types (Late Binding)

A final use for reflection is to dynamically load types and invoke methods on them. "Dynamic loading" means binding to a type at run time rather than compile time. Let's say your source code references a type in another assembly, like this:

```
Rectangle rect = new Rectangle ();
```

Here you're practicing early binding because your compiler inserts data into the resulting executable, noting that a type named *Rectangle* is imported from another assembly. Late binding gives you the ability to use a type without embedding references to it in your metadata. Late binding is accomplished by using reflection.

One use for late binding is to facilitate plug-ins. Suppose you want to enable third-party developers to extend your application by contributing images to the splash screen your app displays when it starts up. Because you don't know in advance what plug-ins might be present at startup, you can't early bind to classes in the plug-ins. But you can late bind to them. If you instruct third-party developers to build classes named *PlugIn*, and if each *PlugIn* class contains a method named *GetImage* that returns an image to the caller, the following code calls *GetImage* on each plug-in represented in the list of assembly names in the *names* array:

```
ArrayList images = new ArrayList ();

foreach (string name in names) {
    Assembly a = Assembly.Load (name);
    Type type = a.GetType ("PlugIn");
    MethodInfo method = type.GetMethod ("GetImage");
    Object obj = Activator.CreateInstance (type);
    Image image = (Image) method.Invoke (obj, null);
    images.Add (image);
}
```

At the end, the *ArrayList* named *images* holds an array of *Image* objects representing the images obtained from the plug-ins.

Visual Basic .NET uses late binding to interact with variables whose declared type is *Object*. Late binding is an important part of the .NET Framework architecture and something you should be aware of even if you don't use it.

The FCL in Review

That does it for a whirlwind tour of the .NET Framework class library. The FCL is a vast resource that's far richer and more comprehensive in scope than the Windows API, MFC, or any other API or class library that Microsoft has ever devised. It's *the API* for managed applications. We've barely scratched the surface in this chapter, but there's much more still to come.

Up to now, all the applications presented in this book save one—Send-Mail—have been console applications. Console applications are just one of five application types that the FCL supports. Now that you're no longer a stranger to the .NET Framework, it's time to branch out and learn how to build other types of applications. Phase 2 of your journey begins in Chapter 4, which introduces the programming model used to write GUI applications for the .NET Framework.

4

Windows Forms

The Microsoft .NET Framework is chiefly a platform for writing Web applications and Web services, but it supports other programming models as well. Chapter 3 spotlighted console applications and even threw in a Web application for good measure. This chapter is about Windows Forms—the programming model used to write GUI applications for the .NET Framework.

On the outside, Windows Forms applications look like ordinary Windows applications. They have windows, and they frequently incorporate common GUI application elements such as menus, controls, and dialog boxes. On the inside, they're managed applications in every sense of the word. They contain common intermediate language (CIL) and metadata, they use the .NET Framework class library (FCL), and they run in the highly managed environment of the common language runtime (CLR).

The chief benefit to writing Windows applications the Windows Forms way is that the framework homogenizes the GUI programming model and eliminates many of the bugs, quirks, and inconsistencies that plague the Windows API. For example, every experienced Windows programmer knows that certain window styles can be applied to a window only when the window is created. Windows Forms largely eliminates such inconsistencies. If you apply a style that's only meaningful at creation time to an existing window, the framework quietly destroys the window and re-creates it with the specified style. In addition, the FCL is much richer than the Windows API, and when you write Windows Forms applications, you have the full power of the FCL at your disposal. More often than not, Windows Forms applications require less code than conventional Windows applications. For example, an application written to the native Windows API requires hundreds of lines of code (or a third-party graphics library) to extract an image from a JPEG file. A Windows Forms application needs just one.

The Windows Forms Programming Model

In Windows Forms, the term "form" is a synonym for window. An application's main window is a form. If the application has other top-level windows, they too are forms. Dialog boxes are also forms. Despite their name, Windows Forms applications don't have to look like forms. They, like traditional Windows applications, exercise full control over what appears in their windows.

Windows Forms applications rely heavily upon classes found in the FCL's *System.Windows.Forms* namespace. That namespace includes classes such as *Form*, which models the behavior of windows, or "forms"; *Menu*, which represents menus; and *Clipboard*, which provides a managed interface to the system's clipboard. The *System.Windows.Forms* namespace also contains numerous classes representing controls, with names like *Button*, *TextBox*, *ListView*, and *MonthCalendar*.

At the heart of nearly every Windows Forms application is a class derived from *System.Windows.Forms.Form*. An instance of the derived class represents the application's main window. It inherits from *Form* scores of properties and methods that make up a rich programmatic interface to forms. Want to know the dimensions of a form's client area? In Windows, you'd call the *GetClientRect* API function. In Windows Forms, you read the form's *ClientRectangle* or *ClientSize* property. Many properties can be written to as well as read. For example, you can change a form's border style by writing to its *BorderStyle* property, resize a form using its *Size* or *ClientSize* property, or change the text in a form's title bar with its *Text* property.

Another important building block of a Windows Forms application is a *System.Windows.Forms* class named *Application*. That class contains a static method named *Run* that drives a Windows Forms application by providing a message pump. You don't see the message pump, of course—the very existence of messages is abstracted away by the .NET Framework. But it's there, and it's one more detail you don't have to worry about because the framework sweats such details for you.

Many Windows Forms applications also rely on classes in the *System.Drawing* namespace. *System.Drawing* contains classes that wrap the Graphics Device Interface+ (GDI+) portion of Windows. Classes such as *Brush* and *Pen* represent logical drawing objects. They define the look of lines, curves, and fills. The *Bitmap* and *Image* classes represent images and are capable of importing images from a variety of file types, including BMP files, GIFs, and JPEGs.

But the most important *System.Drawing* class of all is *Graphics*. *Graphics* is the Windows Forms equivalent of a Windows device context; it's the conduit for graphical output. If you want to draw a line in a Windows form, you call

DrawLine on a *Graphics* object. If you want to draw a string of text, you call *DrawString*. *Graphics* contains a rich assortment of methods and properties that you can use to write graphical output to a form or any other device (such as a printer) that you can associate with a *Graphics* object.

Your First Windows Form

You're a programmer, so when it comes to learning a new platform, nothing speaks to you better than a "Hello, world" application. (Entire companies have been built around "Hello, world" applications.) Figure 4-1 lists the Windows Forms version of "Hello, world." Figure 4-2 shows the resulting application.

Hello.cs
```csharp
using System;
using System.Windows.Forms;
using System.Drawing;

class MyForm : Form
{
    MyForm ()
    {
        Text = "Windows Forms Demo";
    }

    protected override void OnPaint (PaintEventArgs e)
    {
        e.Graphics.DrawString ("Hello, world", Font,
            new SolidBrush (Color.Black), ClientRectangle);
    }

    static void Main ()
    {
        Application.Run (new MyForm ());
    }
}
```

Figure 4-1   Hello.cs source code.

Figure 4-2   The "Hello, world" Windows Forms sample.

In a Windows Forms application, each form is represented by an instance of a class derived from *Form*. In Hello.cs, the derived class is named *MyForm*. *MyForm*'s constructor customizes the form's title bar text by assigning a string to *MyForm*'s *Text* property. *Text* is one of more than 100 properties that *MyForm* inherits from *Form*.

Every Windows programmer knows that windows receive WM_PAINT messages, and that most screen rendering is performed in response to these messages. In Windows Forms, the equivalent of a WM_PAINT message is a virtual *Form* method named *OnPaint*. A derived class can override this method to paint itself in response to WM_PAINT messages.

The *OnPaint* override in *MyForm* (notice the keyword *override*, which tells the C# compiler that you're overriding rather than hiding a virtual method inherited from a base class) writes "Hello, world" to the form's client area—the portion of the form bounded by the window border and title bar. *OnPaint* is passed a *PaintEventArgs* (*System.Windows.Forms.PaintEventArgs*) object, which contains properties named *Graphics* and *ClipRectangle*. The *Graphics* property holds a reference to a *Graphics* object that permits *OnPaint* to draw in the form's client area. *ClipRectangle* contains a reference to a *Rectangle* (*System.Drawing.Rectangle*) object that describes which part of the client area needs repainting.

MyForm.OnPaint uses *Graphics.DrawString* to render its output. The first parameter to *DrawString* is the string itself. The second is a *Font* (*System.Drawing.Font*) object that describes the font in which the text should be rendered. *MyForm.OnPaint* uses the form's default font, a reference to which is stored in the *Form* property named *Font*. The third parameter is a *Brush* (*System.Drawing.Brush*) object specifying the text color. *OnPaint* uses a black *SolidBrush* (*System.Drawing.SolidBrush*) object, resulting in black text. The fourth and final parameter is a formatting rectangle describing where the text should be positioned. *MyForm.OnPaint* uses the form's entire client area, a description of which is found in the *Form* property named *ClientRectangle*, as the formatting rectangle. Because *DrawString* outputs text in the upper left corner of the formatting rectangle by default, "Hello, world" appears in the form's upper left corner.

If you wanted "Hello, world" displayed in the center of the window, you could use an alternate form of *DrawString* that accepts a *StringFormat* object as an input parameter and initialize the *StringFormat*'s *Alignment* and *LineAlignment* properties to center the string horizontally and vertically. Here's the modified version of *OnPaint*:

```
protected override void OnPaint (PaintEventArgs e)
{
    StringFormat format = new StringFormat ();
    format.Alignment = StringAlignment.Center;
    format.LineAlignment = StringAlignment.Center;
    e.Graphics.DrawString ("Hello, world", Font,
        new SolidBrush (Color.Black), ClientRectangle, format);
}
```

The final member of *MyForm* is a static method named *Main*. *Main* is the application's entry point. Displaying the form on the screen is a simple matter of instantiating *MyForm* and passing a reference to the resulting object to *Application.Run*. In Figure 4-1, the statement

```
Application.Run (new MyForm ());
```

instantiates *MyForm* and displays the form.

Once you've entered the code in Figure 4-1 and saved it to a file named Hello.cs, you'll need to compile it. Open a command prompt window, go to the folder where Hello.cs is stored, and type

```
csc /target:winexe hello.cs
```

The */target* switch tells the compiler to produce a GUI Windows application (as opposed to a console application or, say, a DLL). The resulting executable is named Hello.exe.

Drawing in a Form: The GDI+

Writing Windows Forms applications that incorporate rich graphics means getting to know *Graphics* and other classes that expose the Windows GDI+ to managed code. The GDI has existed in Windows since version 1. The GDI+ is an enhanced version of the GDI that's available on any system with Windows XP or the .NET Framework installed.

One of the differences between the GDI and the GDI+ is the latter's support for gradient brushes, cardinal splines, and other drawing aids. But the larger difference lies in their respective programming models. Unlike the GDI, which uses a stateful model, the GDI+ is mostly stateless. A traditional Windows application programs values such as fonts and text colors into a device context. A Windows Forms application doesn't. It passes parameters detailing output characteristics to every *Graphics* method it calls. You saw an example of this in the previous section's sample program, which passed a *Font* object and a *Solid-Brush* object to the *DrawString* method to identify the output font and text color.

Drawing Lines, Curves, and Figures

Font and *SolidBrush* are graphics primitives used to control the output rendered to a form. But they're not the only primitives the GDI+ places at your disposal. Here are some of the others:

GDI+ Graphics Primitives

Class	Description
Bitmap	Represents bitmapped images
Font	Defines font attributes: size, typeface, and so on
HatchBrush	Defines fills performed with hatch patterns
LinearGradientBrush	Defines fills performed with linear gradients
Pen	Defines the appearance of lines and curves
SolidBrush	Defines fills performed with solid colors
TextureBrush	Defines fills performed with bitmaps

Some of these classes are defined in the *System.Drawing* namespace; others belong to *System.Drawing.Drawing2D*. Pens, which are represented by instances of *Pen*, control the appearance of lines and curves. *Font* objects control the appearance of text, while brushes, represented by *HatchBrush*, *Linear-GradientBrush*, *SolidBrush*, and *TextureBrush*, control fills. The following *OnPaint* method draws three different styles of rectangles: one that has no fill, a second that's filled with red, and a third that's filled with a gradient that fades from red to blue:

```
protected override void OnPaint (PaintEventArgs e)
{
    Pen pen = new Pen (Color.Black);

    // Draw an unfilled rectangle
    e.Graphics.DrawRectangle (pen, 10, 10, 390, 90);

    // Draw a rectangle filled with a solid color
    SolidBrush solid = new SolidBrush (Color.Red);
```

```
e.Graphics.FillRectangle (solid, 10, 110, 390, 90);
e.Graphics.DrawRectangle (pen, 10, 110, 390, 90);

// Draw a rectangle filled with a gradient
Rectangle rect = new Rectangle (10, 210, 390, 90);
LinearGradientBrush gradient =
    new LinearGradientBrush (rect, Color.Red,
    Color.Blue, LinearGradientMode.Horizontal);
e.Graphics.FillRectangle (gradient, rect);
e.Graphics.DrawRectangle (pen, rect);
}
```

The output is shown in Figure 4-3. The *Pen* object passed to *DrawRectangle* borders each rectangle with a black line that's 1 unit wide. (By default, 1 unit equals 1 pixel, so the lines in this example are 1 pixel wide.) The brushes passed to *FillRectangle* govern the fills in the rectangles' interiors. Observe that outlines and fills are drawn separately. Veteran Windows developers will find this especially interesting because Windows GDI functions that draw closed figures draw outlines and fills together.

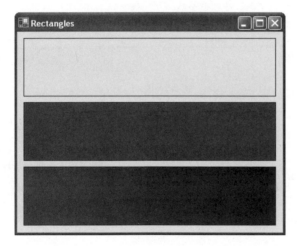

Figure 4-3   Rectangles rendered in a variety of styles.

The *Graphics* class includes a variety of public *Draw* and *Fill* methods that you can use to draw lines, curves, rectangles, ellipses, and other figures. A partial list appears in the following table. The documentation that comes with the .NET Framework SDK contains an excellent dissertation on the GDI+, and it's packed with examples demonstrating how to draw anything from the simplest line to the most complex filled figure.

Graphics Methods for Drawing Lines, Curves, and Figures

Method	Description
DrawArc	Draws an arc
DrawBezier	Draws a Bezier spline
DrawCurve	Draws a cardinal spline
DrawEllipse	Draws a circle or an ellipse
DrawIcon	Draws an icon
DrawImage	Draws an image
DrawLine	Draws a line
DrawPie	Draws a pie-shaped wedge
DrawPolygon	Draws a polygon
DrawString	Draws a string of text
FillEllipse	Draws a filled circle or ellipse
FillPie	Draws a filled pie-shaped wedge
FillPolygon	Draws a filled polygon
FillRectangle	Draws a filled rectangle

Disposing of GDI+ Objects

As you learned in Chapter 2, classes that wrap unmanaged resources such as file handles and database connections require special handling to ensure that their resources are properly released. *Pen*, *Brush*, and other GDI+ classes that represent graphics primitives fall into this category because they wrap GDI+ handles. Failure to close GDI+ handles can result in debilitating resource leaks, especially in applications that run for a very long time. To be safe, you should call *Dispose* on pens, brushes, and other primitives to deterministically dispose of the resources that they encapsulate. Even *Graphics* objects should be disposed of if they're created programmatically rather than obtained from a *PaintEventArgs*.

One way to dispose of GDI+ objects is to call *Dispose* on them manually:

```
Pen pen = new Pen (Color.Black);
    .
    .
    .
pen.Dispose ();
```

Some C# programmers prefer the special form of *using* that automatically generates calls to *Dispose* and encloses them in *finally* blocks. One advantage of this technique is that it ensures *Dispose* is called, even if an exception is thrown:

```
using (Pen pen = new Pen (Color.Black)) {
  .
  .
  .
}
```

And some programmers do neither, banking on the hope that the garbage collector will kick in before the GDI+ runs out of resource space, or that the application won't run long enough for GDI+ resources to grow critically low.

Another approach is to create pens, brushes, and other graphics primitives when an application starts up and to use and reuse them as needed. This dramatically reduces the number of GDI+ resources that an application consumes, and it all but eliminates the need to call *Dispose* on each and every GDI+ object. It also improves performance ever so slightly.

Coordinates and Transformations

When you call *DrawRectangle* and *FillRectangle*, you furnish coordinates specifying the position of the rectangle's upper left corner and distances specifying the rectangle's width and height. By default, distances are measured in pixels. Coordinates specify locations in a two-dimensional coordinate system whose origin lies in the upper left corner of the form and whose x and y axes point to the right and down, respectively. If the default coordinate system or unit of measure is ill-suited to your needs, you can customize them as needed by adding a few simple statements to your program.

The coordinates passed to *Graphics* methods are *world coordinates*. World coordinates undergo two transformations on their way to the screen. They're first translated into *page coordinates*, which denote positions on a logical drawing surface. Later, page coordinates are translated into *device coordinates*, which denote physical positions on the screen.

The GDI+ uses a transformation matrix to convert world coordinates to page coordinates. Transformation matrices are mathematical entities that are used to convert x-y coordinate pairs from one coordinate system to another. They're well established in the world of computer graphics and well documented in computer science literature.

The transformation matrices that the GDI+ uses to perform coordinate conversions are instances of *System.Drawing.Drawing2D.Matrix*. Every *Graphics* object encapsulates a *Matrix* object and exposes it through a property named *Transform*. The default matrix is an *identity matrix*, which is the mathematical term for a transformation matrix that performs no transformation (just as multiplying a number by 1 yields the same number). You can customize the transformation matrix—and hence the way world coordinates are converted to page coordinates—in either of two ways. Option number one is to initialize an instance of *Matrix* with values that produce the desired transformation and assign it to the *Transform* property. That's no problem if you're an expert in linear algebra, but mere mortals will probably prefer option number two, which involves using *Graphics* methods such as *TranslateTransform* and *RotateTransform* to define coordinate transformations. *TranslateTransform* moves, or *translates*, the coordinate system's origin by a specified amount in the x and y directions. *RotateTransform* rotates the x and y axes. By combining the two, you can place the origin anywhere you want it and orient the x and y axes at any angle.

Confused? Then maybe an example will help. The following *OnPaint* method draws a rectangle that's 200 units wide and 100 units tall in a form's upper left corner, as seen in Figure 4-4:

```
protected override void OnPaint (PaintEventArgs e).
{
    SolidBrush brush = new SolidBrush (Color.Red);
    e.Graphics.FillRectangle (brush, 0, 0, 200, 100);
    brush.Dispose ();
}
```

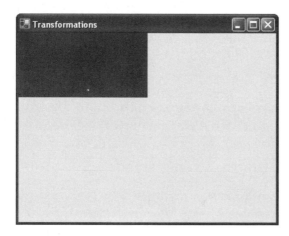

Figure 4-4   Rectangle drawn with no translation or rotation.

The next *OnPaint* method draws the same rectangle, but only after calling *TranslateTransform* to move the origin to (100,100). Because the GDI+ now adds 100 to all x and y values you input, the rectangle moves to the right and down 100 units, as shown in Figure 4-5:

```
protected override void OnPaint (PaintEventArgs e)
{
    SolidBrush brush = new SolidBrush (Color.Red);
    e.Graphics.TranslateTransform (100.0f, 100.0f);
    e.Graphics.FillRectangle (brush, 0, 0, 200, 100);
    brush.Dispose ();
}
```

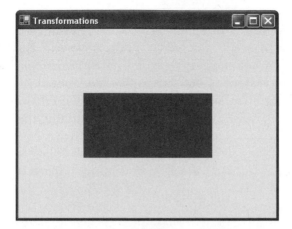

Figure 4-5   Rectangle drawn with translation applied.

The final example uses *RotateTransform* to rotate the *x* and *y* axes 30 degrees counterclockwise after moving the origin, producing the output shown in Figure 4-6:

```
protected override void OnPaint (PaintEventArgs e)
{
    SolidBrush brush = new SolidBrush (Color.Red);
    e.Graphics.TranslateTransform (100.0f, 100.0f);
    e.Graphics.RotateTransform (-30.0f);
    e.Graphics.FillRectangle (brush, 0, 0, 200, 100);
    brush.Dispose ();
}
```

Figure 4-6   Rectangle drawn with translation and rotation applied.

TranslateTransform and *RotateTransform* are powerful tools for positioning the coordinate system and orienting its axes. A related method named *ScaleTransform* lets you scale the coordinate system as well.

Something to keep in mind when you use transforms is that the order in which they're applied affects the output. In the preceding example, the coordinate system was first translated and then rotated. The origin was moved to (100,100) and then rotated 30 degrees. If you rotate first and translate second, the rectangle appears in a different location because the translation occurs along axes that are already rotated. Think of it this way: if you stand in a room, walk a few steps forward and then turn, you end up in a different place than you would had you turned first and *then* started walking. The same principle applies to matrix transformations.

Figure 4-8 lists the source code for a sample program named Clock that draws an analog clock face (see Figure 4-7) that shows the current time of day. The drawing is done with *FillRectangle* and *FillPolygon*, but the transforms are the real story. *TranslateTransform* moves the origin to the center of the form by translating *x* and *y* coordinates by amounts equal to half the form's width and height. *RotateTransform* rotates the coordinate system in preparation for drawing the hour and minute hands and the squares denoting positions on the clock face. *ScaleTransform* scales the output so that the clock face fills the form regardless of the form's size. The coordinates passed to *FillRectangle* and *FillPolygon* assume that the form's client area is exactly 200 units wide and 200 units tall. *ScaleTransform* applies *x* and *y* scaling factors that scale the output by an amount that equals the ratio of the physical client area size to the logical client area size.

So much happens in *MyForm*'s *OnPaint* method that it's easy to miss an important statement in *MyForm*'s constructor:

```
SetStyle (ControlStyles.ResizeRedraw, true);
```

This method call configures the form so that its entire client area is invalidated (and therefore repainted) whenever the form's size changes. This step is essential if you want the clock face to shrink and expand as the form shrinks and expands. If it's not clear to you what effect this statement has on the output, temporarily comment it out and recompile the program. Then resize the form and observe that the clock face doesn't resize until an external stimulus (such as the act of minimizing and restoring the form) forces a repaint to occur.

Figure 4-7   Analog clock drawn with the GDI+.

Clock.cs

```
using System;
using System.Windows.Forms;
using System.Drawing;

class MyForm : Form
{
    MyForm ()
    {
        Text = "Clock";
        SetStyle (ControlStyles.ResizeRedraw, true);
    }

    protected override void OnPaint (PaintEventArgs e)
    {
        SolidBrush red = new SolidBrush (Color.Red);
        SolidBrush white = new SolidBrush (Color.White);
        SolidBrush blue = new SolidBrush (Color.Blue);

        // Initialize the transformation matrix
        InitializeTransform (e.Graphics);

        // Draw squares denoting hours on the clock face
        for (int i=0; i<12; i++) {
            e.Graphics.RotateTransform (30.0f);
            e.Graphics.FillRectangle (white, 85, -5, 10, 10);
        }

        // Get the current time
```

Figure 4-8   Clock source code.

Clock.cs   *(continued)*

```csharp
        DateTime now = DateTime.Now;
        int minute = now.Minute;
        int hour = now.Hour % 12;

        // Reinitialize the transformation matrix
        InitializeTransform (e.Graphics);

        // Draw the hour hand
        e.Graphics.RotateTransform ((hour * 30) + (minute / 2));
        DrawHand (e.Graphics, blue, 40);

        // Reinitialize the transformation matrix
        InitializeTransform (e.Graphics);

        // Draw the minute hand
        e.Graphics.RotateTransform (minute * 6);
        DrawHand (e.Graphics, red, 80);

        // Dispose of the brushes
        red.Dispose ();
        white.Dispose ();
        blue.Dispose ();
    }

    void DrawHand (Graphics g, Brush brush, int length)
    {
        // Draw a hand that points straight up, and let
        // RotateTransform put it in the proper orientation
        Point[] points = new Point[4];
        points[0].X = 0;
        points[0].Y = -length;
        points[1].X = -12;
        points[1].Y = 0;
        points[2].X = 0;
        points[2].Y = 12;
        points[3].X = 12;
        points[3].Y = 0;

        g.FillPolygon (brush, points);
    }

    void InitializeTransform (Graphics g)
    {
        // Apply transforms that move the origin to the center
        // of the form and scale all output to fit the form's width
        // or height
        g.ResetTransform ();
        g.TranslateTransform (ClientSize.Width / 2,
            ClientSize.Height / 2);
```

```
        float scale = System.Math.Min (ClientSize.Width,
            ClientSize.Height) / 200.0f;
        g.ScaleTransform (scale, scale);
    }


    static void Main ()
    {
        Application.Run (new MyForm ());
    }
}
```

Units of Measure

Just as a *Graphics* object's *Transform* property governs the conversion of world coordinates to page coordinates, the *PageUnit* and *PageScale* properties play important roles in the conversion of page coordinates to device coordinates. *PageUnit* identifies a system of units and can be set to any value defined in the *System.Drawing.GraphicsUnit* enumeration: *Pixel* for pixels, *Inch* for inches, and so on. *PageScale* specifies the scaling factor. It can be used in lieu of or in combination with *ScaleTransform* to scale most output. Some types of output, including fonts, can be scaled only with *PageScale*.

PageUnit's default value is *GraphicsUnit.Display*, which means that one unit in page coordinates equals one pixel on the screen. The following *OnPaint* method sets the unit of measurement to inches and draws the ruler shown in Figure 4-9:

```
protected override void OnPaint (PaintEventArgs e)
{
    Pen pen = new Pen (Color.Black, 0);
    SolidBrush yellow = new SolidBrush (Color.Yellow);
    SolidBrush black = new SolidBrush (Color.Black);

    // Set the unit of measurement to inches
    e.Graphics.PageUnit = GraphicsUnit.Inch;

    // Add 0.5 to all x and y coordinates
    e.Graphics.TranslateTransform (0.5f, 0.5f);

    // Draw the body of the ruler
    e.Graphics.FillRectangle (yellow, 0, 0, 6, 1);
    e.Graphics.DrawRectangle (pen, 0, 0, 6, 1);

    // Draw tick marks
    for (float x=0.25f; x<6.0f; x+=0.25f)
        e.Graphics.DrawLine (pen, x, 0.0f, x, 0.08f);

    for (float x=0.5f; x<6.0f; x+=0.5f)
        e.Graphics.DrawLine (pen, x, 0.0f, x, 0.16f);
```

(continued)

```
for (float x=1.0f; x<6.0f; x+=1.0f)
    e.Graphics.DrawLine (pen, x, 0.0f, x, 0.25f);

// Draw numeric labels
StringFormat format = new StringFormat ();
format.Alignment = StringAlignment.Center;
format.LineAlignment = StringAlignment.Center;

for (float x=1.0f; x<6.0f; x+=1.0f) {
    string label = String.Format ("{0}", Convert.ToInt32 (x));
    RectangleF rect =
        new RectangleF (x - 0.25f, 0.25f, 0.5f, 0.25f);
    e.Graphics.DrawString (label, Font, black, rect, format);
}

// Dispose of GDI+ objects
pen.Dispose ();
yellow.Dispose ();
black.Dispose ();
}
```

The same ruler could be drawn using the default *PageUnit* value by using the *Graphics* object's *DpiX* and *DpiY* properties to manually convert between inches and pixels. But expressing coordinates and distances in inches makes the code more readable. Note the call to *TranslateTransform* offsetting all *x* and *y* coordinates by a half-inch to move the ruler out of the upper left corner of the form. Also note the 0 passed to *Pen*'s constructor. The 0 sets the pen width to 1 pixel, no matter what system of units is selected. Without the 0, a pen defaults to a width of 1 unit. In the *GraphicsUnit.Inch* system of measurement, 1 unit equals 1 inch, so a 1-unit-wide pen would be a very wide pen indeed.

One nuance you should be aware of is that values expressed in inches are *logical* values, meaning the ruler probably won't measure exactly 6 inches long. Logical values differ slightly from physical values because Windows doesn't know precisely how many pixels per inch your screen can display. To compensate, it uses an assumed resolution of 96 dots per inch.

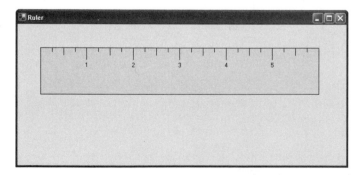

Figure 4-9 Ruler drawn using inches as the unit of measurement.

Menus

Menus are a staple of GUI applications. Nearly everyone who sits down in front of a computer understands that clicking an item in an overhead menu displays a drop-down list of commands. Even novices quickly catch on once they see menus demonstrated a time or two.

Because menus are such an important part of a user interface, the .NET Framework provides a great deal of support to applications that use them. The *System.Windows.Forms* classes listed in the following table play a role in menu creation and operation. The next several sections discuss these and other menu-related classes and offer examples demonstrating their use.

System.Windows.Forms Menu Classes

Class	Description
Menu	Abstract base class for other menu classes
MainMenu	Represents main menus
ContextMenu	Represents context menus
MenuItem	Represents the items in a menu

Main Menus

A main menu, sometimes called a *top-level menu*, is one that appears in a horizontal bar underneath a window's title bar. The following code creates a main menu containing two drop-down menus labeled "File" and "Edit" and attaches it to the form:

```
// Create a MainMenu object
MainMenu menu = new MainMenu ();

// Add a File menu and populate it with items
MenuItem item = menu.MenuItems.Add ("&File");
item.MenuItems.Add ("&New", new EventHandler (OnFileNew));
item.MenuItems.Add ("&Open...", new EventHandler (OnFileOpen));
item.MenuItems.Add ("&Save", new EventHandler (OnFileSave));
item.MenuItems.Add ("Save &As...", new EventHandler (OnFileSaveAs));
item.MenuItems.Add ("-"); // Menu item separator (horizontal bar)
item.MenuItems.Add ("E&xit", new EventHandler (OnFileExit));

// Add an Edit menu and populate it, too
item = menu.MenuItems.Add ("&Edit");
item.MenuItems.Add ("Cu&t", new EventHandler (OnEditCut));
item.MenuItems.Add ("&Copy", new EventHandler (OnEditCopy));
item.MenuItems.Add ("&Paste", new EventHandler (OnEditPaste));

// Attach the menu to the form
Menu = menu;
```

The first statement creates a *MainMenu* object and captures the returned *MainMenu* reference in a variable named *menu*. All menus, including instances of *MainMenu*, inherit a property named *MenuItems* from *Menu* that represents the items in the menu. Calling *Add* on the *MenuItemCollection* represented by *MenuItems* adds an item to the menu and optionally registers an event handler that's called when a user selects the item. The statements

```
MenuItem item = menu.MenuItems.Add ("&File");
item = menu.MenuItems.Add ("&Edit");
```

add top-level items named "File" and "Edit" to the main menu. The remaining calls to *Add* add items to the File and Edit menus. (The ampersand in the menu text identifies a keyboard shortcut. The ampersand in *"&File"* designates Alt+F as the shortcut for File and automatically underlines the F.) The final statement attaches the *MainMenu* to the form by assigning the *MainMenu* to the form's *Menu* property. All forms inherit the *Menu* property from *System.Windows.Forms.Form*.

Processing Menu Commands

Selecting an item from a menu fires a *Click* event and activates the *Click* event handler, if any, registered for that item. The code sample in the previous section registers handlers named *OnFileNew*, *OnFileOpen*, and so on for its menu items. *Click* event handlers are prototyped this way:

```
void HandlerName (Object sender, EventArgs e)
```

Thus, the *OnFileExit* handler registered for the File/Exit command might be implemented like this:

```
void OnFileExit (Object sender, EventArgs e)
{
    Close (); // Close the form
}
```

The first parameter passed to the event handler identifies the menu item that the user selected. The second parameter is a container for additional information about the event that precipitated the call. Menu item event handlers typically ignore this parameter because *EventArgs* contains no information of interest.

An alternative method for connecting menu items to event handlers is to use C#'s += syntax, as shown here:

```
MenuItem exit = item.MenuItems.Add ("E&xit");
exit.Click += new EventHandler (OnFileExit);
```

I prefer to identify event handlers in *Add* simply because doing so makes my code more concise. You should do what works best for you.

Context Menus

Many applications pop up context menus in response to clicks of the right mouse button. Inside a context menu is a context-sensitive list of commands that can be applied to the target of the click. In Windows Forms applications, *ContextMenu* objects represent context menus. *ContextMenus* are populated with items in the same way that *MainMenus* are. One way to display a context menu is to call *ContextMenu.Show*. Here's an example that creates a context menu containing three items and displays it on the screen:

```
ContextMenu menu = new ContextMenu ();
menu.MenuItems.Add ("&Open", new EventHandler (OnOpen));
menu.MenuItems.Add ("&Rename", new EventHandler (OnRename));
menu.MenuItems.Add ("&Delete", new EventHandler (OnDelete));
menu.Show (this, new Point (x, y));
```

The first parameter to *ContextMenu.Show* identifies the form that the menu belongs to. (It's this form's event handlers that are called when items are selected from the context menu.) The second parameter specifies where the menu is to be displayed. The units are pixels, and the coordinates are relative to the upper left corner of the form identified in *Show*'s first parameter.

If an application uses one context menu to serve an entire form—that is, if it displays the same context menu no matter where in the form a right-click occurs—there's an easier way to display a context menu. Simply create a *ContextMenu* object and assign it to the form's *ContextMenu* property, as shown here:

```
ContextMenu menu = new ContextMenu ();
    .
    .
    .
ContextMenu = menu;
```

The .NET Framework responds by displaying the context menu when the form is right-clicked.

As with items in a main menu, context menu items fire *Click* events when clicked. And like main menu items, you can identify event handlers when adding items to the menu or wire them up separately with the += operator.

Menu Item States

Many applications change the states of their menu items on the fly to reflect changing states in the application. For example, if nothing is selected in an application that features an Edit menu, protocol demands that the application disable its Cut and Copy commands.

Windows Forms applications control menu item states by manipulating the properties of *MenuItem* objects. A *MenuItem*'s *Checked* property determines whether the corresponding item is checked or unchecked. *Enabled* determines whether the item is enabled or disabled, and *Text* exposes the text of a menu item. If *item* is a *MenuItem* object, the following statement places a check mark next to it:

```
item.Checked = true;
```

And this statement removes the check mark:

```
item.Checked = false;
```

MFC programmers are familiar with the concept of *update handlers*, which are functions whose sole purpose is to update menu item states. MFC calls update handlers just before a menu appears on the screen, affording the handlers the opportunity to update the items in the menu before the user sees them. Update handlers are useful because they decouple the logic that changes the state of an application from the logic that updates the state of the application's menu items.

You can write update handlers for Windows Forms menu items, too. The secret is to register a handler for the *Popup* event that fires when the menu containing the item you want to update is clicked and to do the updating in the *Popup* handler. The following example registers a *Popup* handler for the Edit menu and updates the items in the menu to reflect the current state of the application:

```
MenuItem item = menu.MenuItems.Add ("&Edit");
item.Popup += new EventHandler (OnPopupEditMenu);
    .
    .
    .
void OnPopupEditMenu (Object sender, EventArgs e)
{
    MenuItem menu = (MenuItem) sender;
    foreach (MenuItem item in menu.MenuItems) {
        switch (item.Text) {
        case "Cu&t":
        case "&Copy":
            item.Enabled = IsSomethingSelected ();
            break;
        case "&Paste":
            item.Enabled = IsSomethingOnClipboard ();
            break;
        }
    }
}
```

IsSomethingSelected and *IsSomethingOnClipboard* are fictitious methods, but hopefully their intent is clear nonetheless. By processing *MenuItem.Popup* events, an application can delay updating its menu items until they need to be updated and eliminate the possibility of forgetting to update them at all.

Accelerators

A final note concerning menus regards accelerators. Accelerators are keys or key combinations that, when pressed, invoke menu commands. Ctrl+O (for Open) is an example of a commonly used accelerator; Ctrl+S (for Save) is another. Windows programmers implement accelerators by loading accelerator resources. Windows Forms programmers have it much easier. They *new* up a *MenuItem* and identify the accelerator in the *MenuItem* constructor's third parameter. Then they add the resulting item to the menu with *MenuItemCollection.Add*:

```
item.MenuItems.Add (new MenuItem ("&Open...",
    new EventHandler (OnFileOpen), Shortcut.CtrlO));
```

CtrlO is a member of the *Shortcut* enumeration defined in *System.Windows.Forms*. *Shortcut* contains a long list of elements representing all the different accelerators you can choose from.

The ImageView Application

The application shown in Figures 4-10 and 4-11 is a Windows Forms image viewer that's capable of displaying a wide variety of image files. The heart of the application is the statement

```
Bitmap bitmap = new Bitmap (FileName);
```

which creates a new *System.Drawing.Bitmap* object encapsulating the image in the file identified by *FileName*. Having the ability to load an image with a single statement is powerful. The *Bitmap* class is capable of reading BMPs, GIFs, JPEGs, and other popular image file formats. To accomplish the same thing in a traditional (unmanaged) Windows application, you'd have to write reams of code or purchase a third-party graphics library.

Equally interesting is the statement

```
g.DrawImage (MyBitmap, ClientRectangle);
```

which draws the bitmap on the form. (*MyBitmap* is a private field that stores a reference to the currently displayed bitmap.) Windows programmers who want to display bitmaps have to grapple with memory device contexts and *BitBlt*s. Windows Forms programmers simply call *Graphics.DrawImage*.

ImageView demonstrates other important principles of Windows Forms programming as well. Here are some of the highlights:

- How to use menus, menu handlers, and menu update handlers

- How to size a form by writing to its *ClientSize* property

- How to use Open File dialog boxes (instances of *System.Windows.Forms.OpenFileDialog*) to solicit file names from users

- How to use *MessageBox.Show* to display message boxes

- How to create a scrollable form by setting a form's *AutoScroll* property to true and its *AutoScrollMinSize* property to the size of the virtual viewing area

- How to properly dispose of *Bitmap* objects

The final item in this list is an important one because without it, Image-View would leak memory like a sieve. Rather than open an image file and assign the *Bitmap* reference to *MyBitmap* in one statement, like this:

```
MyBitmap = new Bitmap (FileName);
```

ImageView does this:

```
Bitmap bitmap = new Bitmap (FileName);
if (MyBitmap != null)
    MyBitmap.Dispose (); // Important!
MyBitmap = bitmap;
```

See what's happening? *Bitmap* objects encapsulate bitmaps, which are unmanaged resources that can consume a lot of memory. By calling *Dispose* on the old *Bitmap* after opening a new one, ImageView disposes of the encapsulated bitmap immediately rather than wait for the garbage collector to call the *Bitmap*'s *Finalize* method. Remember the dictum in Chapter 2 that admonished developers to always call *Close* or *Dispose* on objects that wrap unmanaged resources? This code is the embodiment of that dictum and a fine example of why programmers must constantly be on their guard to avoid the debilitating side effects of nondeterministic destruction.

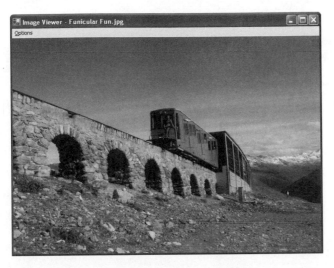

Figure 4-10   ImageView showing a JPEG file.

ImageView.cs

```csharp
using System;
using System.Windows.Forms;
using System.Drawing;

class MyForm : Form
{
    MenuItem NativeSize;
    MenuItem FitToWindow;
    bool ShowNativeSize = true;
    int FilterIndex = -1;
    Bitmap MyBitmap = null;

    MyForm ()
    {
        // Set the form's title
        Text = "Image Viewer";

        // Set the form's size
        ClientSize = new Size (640, 480);

        // Create a menu
        MainMenu menu = new MainMenu ();
        MenuItem item = menu.MenuItems.Add ("&Options");
        item.Popup += new EventHandler (OnPopupOptionsMenu);
        item.MenuItems.Add (new MenuItem ("&Open...",
            new EventHandler (OnOpenImage), Shortcut.Ctrl0));
```

Figure 4-11   ImageView source code.

ImageView.cs *(continued)*

```csharp
        item.MenuItems.Add ("-");
        item.MenuItems.Add (FitToWindow =
            new MenuItem ("Size Image to &Fit Window",
            new EventHandler (OnFitToWindow))
        );
        item.MenuItems.Add (NativeSize =
            new MenuItem ("Show Image in &Native Size",
            new EventHandler (OnNativeSize))
        );
        item.MenuItems.Add ("-");
        item.MenuItems.Add (new MenuItem ("E&xit",
            new EventHandler (OnExit)));

        // Attach the menu to the form
        Menu = menu;
    }

    // Handler for Options menu popups
    void OnPopupOptionsMenu (object sender, EventArgs e)
    {
        NativeSize.Checked = ShowNativeSize;
        FitToWindow.Checked = !ShowNativeSize;
    }

    // Handler for the Open command
    void OnOpenImage (object sender, EventArgs e)
    {
        OpenFileDialog ofd = new OpenFileDialog ();

        ofd.Filter = "Image Files (JPEG, GIF, BMP, etc.)|" +
            "*.jpg;*.jpeg;*.gif;*.bmp;*.tif;*.tiff;*.png|" +
            "JPEG files (*.jpg;*.jpeg)|*.jpg;*.jpeg|"       +
            "GIF Files (*.gif)|*.gif|"                      +
            "BMP Files (*.bmp)|*.bmp|"                      +
            "TIFF Files (*.tif;*.tiff)|*.tif;*.tiff|"       +
            "PNG Files (*.png)|*.png|"                      +
            "All files (*.*)|*.*";

        if (FilterIndex != -1)
            ofd.FilterIndex = FilterIndex;

        if (ofd.ShowDialog () == DialogResult.OK) {
            String FileName = ofd.FileName;
            if (FileName.Length != 0) {
                FilterIndex = ofd.FilterIndex;
                try {
                    Bitmap bitmap = new Bitmap (FileName);
```

```
                    if (MyBitmap != null)
                        MyBitmap.Dispose (); // Important!
                MyBitmap = bitmap;
                string[] parts = FileName.Split ('\\');
                Text = "Image Viewer - " + parts[parts.Length - 1];
                if (ShowNativeSize) {
                    AutoScroll = true;
                    AutoScrollMinSize = MyBitmap.Size;
                    AutoScrollPosition = new Point (0, 0);
                }
                Invalidate ();
            }
            catch (ArgumentException) {
                MessageBox.Show (String.Format ("{0} is not " +
                    "a valid image file", FileName), "Error",
                    MessageBoxButtons.OK, MessageBoxIcon.Error);
            }
        }
    }
    ofd.Dispose ();
}

// Handler for the Size Image to Fit Window command
void OnFitToWindow (object sender, EventArgs e)
{
    ShowNativeSize = false;
    SetStyle (ControlStyles.ResizeRedraw, true);
    if (MyBitmap != null) {
        AutoScroll = false;
        Invalidate ();
    }
}

// Handler for the Show Image in Native Size command
void OnNativeSize (object sender, EventArgs e)
{
    ShowNativeSize = true;
    SetStyle (ControlStyles.ResizeRedraw, false);
    if (MyBitmap != null) {
        AutoScroll = true;
        AutoScrollMinSize = MyBitmap.Size;
        AutoScrollPosition = new Point (0, 0);
        Invalidate ();
    }
}

// Handler for the Exit command
void OnExit (object sender, EventArgs e)
{
```

(continued)

ImageView.cs   *(continued)*

```
        Close ();
    }


    // OnPaint handler
    protected override void OnPaint (PaintEventArgs e)
    {
        if (MyBitmap != null) {
            Graphics g = e.Graphics;
            if (ShowNativeSize)
                g.DrawImage (MyBitmap,
                    AutoScrollPosition.X, AutoScrollPosition.Y,
                    MyBitmap.Width, MyBitmap.Height);
            else
                g.DrawImage (MyBitmap, ClientRectangle);
        }
    }

    static void Main ()
    {
        Application.Run (new MyForm ());
    }
}
```

Mouse and Keyboard Input

ImageView takes all its input from menus, but forms can also process mouse and keyboard input. Windows notifies forms about mouse and keyboard input events using messages. The WM_LBUTTONDOWN message, for example, signifies a press of the left mouse button in a form's client area. Windows forms process mouse and keyboard input by overriding virtual methods inherited from *Form*. The following table lists the virtual methods that correspond to mouse and keyboard events. The rightmost column identifies the type of event argument passed in the method's parameter list.

Form Methods for Processing Mouse and Keyboard Input

Method	Called When	Argument Type
OnKeyDown	A key is pressed	*KeyEventArgs*
OnKeyPress	A character is typed on the keyboard	*KeyPressEventArgs*
OnKeyUp	A key is released	*KeyEventArgs*
OnMouseDown	A mouse button is pressed	*MouseEventArgs*
OnMouseEnter	The mouse cursor enters a form	*EventArgs*

Form **Methods for Processing Mouse and Keyboard Input**   *(continued)*

Method	Called When	Argument Type
OnMouseHover	The mouse cursor pauses over a form	*EventArgs*
OnMouseLeave	The mouse cursor leaves a form	*EventArgs*
OnMouseMove	The mouse cursor moves over a form	*MouseEventArgs*
OnMouseUp	A mouse button is released	*MouseEventArgs*
OnMouseWheel	The mouse wheel is rolled	*MouseEventArgs*

Processing Keyboard Input

The *OnKeyDown* and *OnKeyUp* methods correspond to WM_KEYDOWN and WM_KEYUP messages in Windows. If overridden in a derived class, they're called when keys are pressed and released. The *KeyCode* property of the *KeyEventArgs* passed to *OnKeyDown* and *OnKeyUp* identify the key that generated the event. Here's an example that traps presses of function key F1:

```
protected override void OnKeyDown (KeyEventArgs e)
{
    if (e.KeyCode == Keys.F1) {
        // Function key F1 was pressed
    }
}
```

KeyEventArgs also includes properties named *Alt*, *Control*, *Shift*, and *Modifiers* that you can use to determine whether the Ctrl, Alt, or Shift key (or some combination thereof) was held down when the keyboard event occurred.

A related method named *OnKeyPress* corresponds to WM_CHAR messages in Windows. It's called when a character is input from the keyboard. Not all keys generate character input. Some, such as the A through Z keys, do, but others, such as F1 and F2, do not. To process input from noncharacter keys, you override *OnKeyDown*. To process input from character keys, you generally override *OnKeyPress* instead. Why? Because *OnKeyPress* receives a *KeyPressEventArgs* whose *KeyChar* property tells you what character was entered, taking into account the state of other keys on the keyboard (such as Shift) that affect the outcome. If a user presses the C key, *OnKeyDown* tells you that the C key was pressed. *OnKeyPress* tells you whether the C is uppercase or lowercase. Here's an *OnKeyPress* handler that responds one way to an uppercase C and another way to a lowercase C:

```
protected override void OnKeyPress (KeyPressEventArgs e)
{
    if (e.KeyChar == 'C') {
        // Do something
    }
    else if (e.KeyChar == 'c') {
```

(continued)

```
        // Do something else
    }
}
```

Processing Mouse Input

Pressing and releasing a mouse button with the cursor over a form calls the form's *OnMouseDown* and *OnMouseUp* methods, in that order. Both methods receive a *MouseEventArgs* containing a *Button* property identifying the button that was clicked (*MouseButtons.Left, MouseButtons.Middle,* or *MouseButtons.Right*), a *Clicks* property indicating whether an *OnMouseDown* signifies a single click (*Clicks* == 1) or double-click (*Clicks* == 2), and *X* and *Y* properties identifying the cursor position. Coordinates are always expressed in pixels and are always relative to the upper left corner of the form in which the click occurred. The coordinate pair (100,200), for example, indicates that the event occurred with the cursor 100 pixels to the right of and 200 pixels below the form's upper left corner.

The following *OnMouseDown* method draws a small X at the current cursor position each time the left mouse button is pressed:

```
protected override void OnMouseDown (MouseEventArgs e)
{
    if (e.Button == MouseButtons.Left) {
        Graphics g = Graphics.FromHwnd (Handle);
        Pen pen = new Pen (Color.Black);
        g.DrawLine (pen, e.X - 4, e.Y - 4, e.X + 4, e.Y + 4);
        g.DrawLine (pen, e.X - 4, e.Y + 4, e.X + 4, e.Y - 4);
        pen.Dispose ();
        g.Dispose ();
    }
}
```

This code sample demonstrates another important Windows Forms programming principle: how to draw in a form outside *OnPaint*. The secret? Pass the form's window handle, which is stored in *Form.Handle*, to the static *Graphics.FromHwnd* method. You get back a *Graphics* object. Don't forget to call *Dispose* on the *Graphics* object when you're finished with it because a *Graphics* object acquired this way, unlike a *Graphics* object passed in a *PaintEventArgs*, is not disposed of automatically.

An alternate way to sense mouse clicks is to override *Form* methods named *OnClick* and *OnDoubleClick*. The former is called when a form is clicked with the left mouse button; the latter is called when the form is double-clicked. Neither method receives information about click coordinates. *OnClick* and *OnDoubleClick* are generally more interesting to control developers than to form developers because forms that process mouse clicks typically want to know where the clicks occur.

To track mouse movement over a form, override *OnMouseMove* in the derived class. *OnMouseMove* corresponds to Windows WM_MOUSEMOVE messages. The *X* and *Y* properties of the *MouseEventArgs* passed to *OnMouseMove* identify the latest cursor position. The *Button* property identifies the button or buttons that are held down. If both the left and right buttons are depressed, for example, *Button* will equal *MouseButtons.Left* and *MouseButtons.Right* logically ORed together.

The *OnMouseEnter*, *OnMouseHover*, and *OnMouseLeave* methods enable a form to determine when the cursor enters it, hovers motionlessly over it, and leaves it. One use for these methods is to update a real-time cursor coordinate display. The code for the MouseTracker application shown in Figure 4-13 demonstrates how to go about it. As the mouse moves over the form, *OnMouseMove* updates a coordinate display in the center of the form. (See Figure 4-12.) When the mouse leaves the form, *OnMouseLeave* blanks out the coordinate display. No *OnMouseEnter* handler is needed because an *OnMouseEnter* call is always closely followed by an *OnMouseMove* call identifying the cursor position.

Figure 4-12   MouseTracker displaying real-time cursor coordinates.

MouseTracker.cs
```
using System;
using System.Windows.Forms;
using System.Drawing;

class MyForm : Form
{
    int cx;
    int cy;

    MyForm ()
    {
        Text = "Mouse Tracker";
```

Figure 4-13   MouseTracker source code.

MouseTracker.cs   *(continued)*

```csharp
        Graphics g = Graphics.FromHwnd (Handle);
        SizeF size = g.MeasureString ("MMMM, MMMM", Font);
        cx = (Convert.ToInt32 (size.Width) / 2) + 8;
        cy = (Convert.ToInt32 (size.Height) / 2) + 8;
        g.Dispose ();
    }

    protected override void OnMouseMove (MouseEventArgs e)
    {
        Graphics g = Graphics.FromHwnd (Handle);
        EraseCoordinates (g);
        ShowCoordinates (e.X, e.Y, g);
        g.Dispose ();
    }

    protected override void OnMouseLeave (EventArgs e)
    {
        Graphics g = Graphics.FromHwnd (Handle);
        EraseCoordinates (g);
        g.Dispose ();
    }

    void EraseCoordinates (Graphics g)
    {
        int x = ClientRectangle.Width / 2;
        int y = ClientRectangle.Height / 2;

        SolidBrush brush = new SolidBrush (BackColor);
        g.FillRectangle (brush, x - cx, y - cy, x + cx, y + cy);
        brush.Dispose ();
    }

    void ShowCoordinates (int x, int y, Graphics g)
    {
        StringFormat format = new StringFormat ();
        format.Alignment = StringAlignment.Center;
        format.LineAlignment = StringAlignment.Center;

        string coords = String.Format ("{0}, {1}", x, y);

        SolidBrush brush = new SolidBrush (Color.Black);
        g.DrawString (coords, Font, brush, ClientRectangle, format);
        brush.Dispose ();
    }

    static void Main ()
    {
        Application.Run (new MyForm ());
    }
```

Chapter 4   Windows Forms   **127**

The NetDraw Application

Here's another sample application to chew on, one that processes both mouse and keyboard input. It's called NetDraw, and it's a simple sketching application inspired by the Scribble tutorial that comes with Visual C++. (See Figure 4-14.) To draw, press and hold the left mouse button and begin moving the mouse. To clear the drawing area, press the Del key.

NetDraw's source code appears in Figure 4-15. The *OnMouseDown*, *OnMouseMove*, and *OnMouseUp* methods do most of the heavy lifting. *OnMouseDown* creates a new *Stroke* object representing the stroke the user has just begun drawing and records it in *CurrentStroke*. *OnMouseMove* adds the latest *x-y* coordinate pair to the *Stroke* object that *OnMouseDown* created. *OnMouseUp* adds the *Stroke* to *Strokes*, which is an *ArrayList* that records all the strokes that the user draws. When the form needs repainting, *OnPaint* iterates through the *Strokes* array calling *Stroke.Draw* to reproduce each and every stroke.

Stroke is a class defined in NetDraw.cs. It wraps an *ArrayList* that stores an array of *Points*. Thanks to the *ArrayList*, one *Stroke* object is capable of holding a virtually unlimited number of *x-y* coordinate pairs. *Stroke*'s *Draw* method uses *Graphics.DrawLine* to draw lines connecting the pairs.

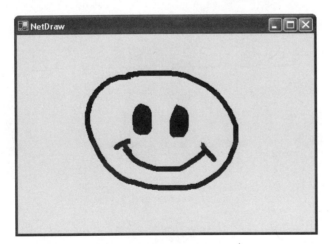

Figure 4-14   NetDraw in action.

NetDraw.cs

```csharp
using System;
using System.Collections;
using System.Windows.Forms;
using System.Drawing;
using System.Drawing.Drawing2D;

class MyForm : Form
{
    Stroke CurrentStroke = null;
    ArrayList Strokes = new ArrayList ();

    MyForm ()
    {
        Text = "NetDraw";
    }

    protected override void OnPaint (PaintEventArgs e)
    {
        // Draw all currently recorded strokes
        foreach (Stroke stroke in Strokes)
            stroke.Draw (e.Graphics);
    }

    protected override void OnMouseDown (MouseEventArgs e)
    {
        if (e.Button == MouseButtons.Left) {
            // Create a new Stroke and assign it to CurrentStroke
            CurrentStroke = new Stroke (e.X, e.Y);
        }
    }

    protected override void OnMouseMove (MouseEventArgs e)
    {
        if ((e.Button & MouseButtons.Left) != 0 && CurrentStroke != null) {
            // Add a new segment to the current stroke
            CurrentStroke.Add (e.X, e.Y);
            Graphics g = Graphics.FromHwnd (Handle);
            CurrentStroke.DrawLastSegment (g);
            g.Dispose ();
        }
    }

    protected override void OnMouseUp (MouseEventArgs e)
    {
```

Figure 4-15   NetDraw source code.

```
        if (e.Button == MouseButtons.Left && CurrentStroke != null) {
            // Complete the current stroke
            if (CurrentStroke.Count > 1)
                Strokes.Add (CurrentStroke);
            CurrentStroke = null;
        }
    }

    protected override void OnKeyDown (KeyEventArgs e)
    {
        if (e.KeyCode == Keys.Delete) {
            // Delete all strokes and repaint
            Strokes.Clear ();
            Invalidate ();
        }
    }

    static void Main ()
    {
        Application.Run (new MyForm ());
    }
}

class Stroke
{
    ArrayList Points = new ArrayList ();

    public int Count
    {
        get { return Points.Count; }
    }

    public Stroke (int x, int y)
    {
        Points.Add (new Point (x, y));
    }

    public void Add (int x, int y)
    {
        Points.Add (new Point (x, y));
    }

    public void Draw (Graphics g)
    {
        Pen pen = new Pen (Color.Black, 8);
        pen.EndCap = LineCap.Round;
        for (int i=0; i<Points.Count - 1; i++)
            g.DrawLine (pen, (Point) Points[i], (Point) Points[i + 1]);
        pen.Dispose ();
    }
```

(continued)

NetDraw.cs *(continued)*

```
public void DrawLastSegment (Graphics g)
{
    Point p1 = (Point) Points[Points.Count - 2];
    Point p2 = (Point) Points[Points.Count - 1];
    Pen pen = new Pen (Color.Black, 8);
    pen.EndCap = LineCap.Round;
    g.DrawLine (pen, p1, p2);
    pen.Dispose ();
}
}
```

Other Form-Level Events

A class that derives from *Form* inherits a long list of virtual methods whose names begin with *On*. *On* methods are called in response to form-level events. They exist to simplify event processing. If there were no *On* methods, every event handler you write would have to be wrapped in a delegate and manually connected to an event.

OnKeyDown, *OnMouseDown*, and *OnPaint* are just a few of the *On* methods that you can override in a derived class to respond to the various events that take place over a form's lifetime. The following table lists some of the others. If you want to know when your form is resized, simply override *OnSizeChanged* in the derived class. *OnSizeChanged* is the Windows Forms equivalent of WM_SIZE messages and is called whenever a form's size changes. Want to know when a form is about to close so you can warn the user if your application contains unsaved data? If so, override *OnClosing*. If you want, you can even prevent the form from closing by setting the *Cancel* property of the *CancelEventArgs* parameter passed to *OnClosing* to true.

Virtual Methods That Correspond to Form-Level Events

Method	Called When
OnActivated	A form is activated
OnClosed	A form is closed
OnClosing	A form is about to close
OnDeactivate	A form is deactivated
OnGotFocus	A form receives the input focus
OnLoad	A form is created
OnLocationChanged	A form is moved
OnLostFocus	A form loses the input focus
OnPaintBackground	A form's background needs repainting
OnSizeChanged	A form is resized

The sample program shown in Figure 4-16 demonstrates one application for *OnClosing*. When the user clicks the Close button in the form's upper right corner, Windows begins closing the form and the framework calls *OnClosing*. This implementation of *OnClosing* displays a message box asking the user to click Yes to close the form or No to cancel the operation. If the answer is yes, *OnClosing* sets *CancelEventArgs.Cancel* to false and the form closes. If, however, the answer is no, *OnClosing* sets *CancelEventArgs.Cancel* to true and the form remains on the screen.

```
CloseDemo.cs
using System;
using System.Windows.Forms;
using System.ComponentModel;

class MyForm : Form
{
    MyForm ()
    {
        Text = "OnClosing Demo";
    }

    protected override void OnClosing (CancelEventArgs e)
    {
        DialogResult result =
            MessageBox.Show ("Close this form?", "Please Verify",
            MessageBoxButtons.YesNo, MessageBoxIcon.Question);
        e.Cancel = (result == DialogResult.No);
    }

    static void Main ()
    {
        Application.Run (new MyForm ());
    }
}
```

Figure 4-16   CloseDemo source code.

Controls

Windows includes more than 20 built-in control types that programmers can use to conserve development time and give applications a look and feel that is consistent with other Windows applications. Push buttons and list boxes are examples of controls; so are tree views, toolbars, and status bars. Controls have been a staple of the Windows operating system since version 1, and the roster has grown over the years to include a rich and varied assortment of control types.

The *System.Windows.Forms* namespace provides managed wrappers around the built-in Windows controls and throws in a few controls of its own that have no direct analogue in the operating system. The following table lists them all. Each class exposes properties that vastly simplify control programming. Want to create a stylized button with a bitmapped background? No problem. Just wrap an image in a *Bitmap* object and assign it to the button's *BackgroundImage* property. Another example involves control colors. Ever tried to customize the background color of an edit control? Other developers have, because I get e-mail asking about doing this all the time. In Windows Forms, it's easy: you just write the color to the control's *BackColor* property and then sit back and let the .NET Framework do the rest.

System.Windows.Forms Control Classes

Class	Description
Button	Push buttons
CheckBox	Check boxes
CheckedListBox	List boxes whose items include check boxes
ComboBox	Combo boxes
DataGrid	Controls that display tabular data
DataGridTextBox	Edit controls hosted by *DataGrid* controls
DateTimePicker	Controls for selecting dates and times
GroupBox	Group boxes
HScrollBar	Horizontal scroll bars
Label	Label controls that display static text
LinkLabel	Label controls that display hyperlinks
ListBox	List boxes
ListView	List views (display flat lists of items in a variety of styles)
MonthCalendar	Month-calendar controls
NumericUpDown	Spinner buttons (up-down controls)
PictureBox	Controls that display images
PrintPreviewControl	Controls that display print previews
ProgressBar	Progress bars
PropertyGrid	Controls that list the properties of other objects
RadioButton	Radio buttons
RichTextBox	Rich-edit controls

System.Windows.Forms Control Classes   *(continued)*

Class	Description
StatusBar	Status bars
TabControl	Tab controls
TextBox	Edit controls
ToolBar	Toolbars
ToolTip	Tooltips
TrackBar	Track bars (slider controls)
TreeView	Tree views (display hierarchical lists of items)
VScrollBar	Vertical scroll bars

Creating a control and making it appear in a form is a three-step process:

1. Instantiate the corresponding control class.

2. Initialize the control by setting its property values.

3. Add the control to the form by calling *Add* on the form's *Controls* collection.

The following code creates a push button control and adds it to a form. The button measures 96 pixels by 24 pixels, and its upper left corner is positioned 16 pixels to the right of and 16 pixels below the form's upper left corner. The text on the face of the button reads "Click Me":

```
Button MyButton; // Field
  .
  .
  .
MyButton = new Button ();
MyButton.Location = new Point (16, 16);
MyButton.Size = new Size (96, 24);
MyButton.Text = "Click Me";
Controls.Add (MyButton);
```

Most controls fire events that apprise their owner of actions taken by the user. For example, button controls fire *Click* events when clicked. A form that wants to respond to clicks of *MyButton* can register an event handler this way:

```
MyButton.Click += new EventHandler (OnButtonClicked);
  .
  .
  .
void OnButtonClicked (Object sender, EventArgs e)
{
    // TODO: Respond to the button click
}
```

EventHandler is a delegate defined in the *System* namespace. Recall that a delegate is a type-safe wrapper around a callback function and that delegates are especially useful for wiring events to event handlers. The event handler's first parameter identifies the control that fired the event. The second parameter provides additional information about the event. As with events involving menu items, *EventArgs* contains no useful information. However, some controls pass other argument types to their event handlers. For example, tree view controls fire *AfterExpand* events after a branch of the tree expands. *AfterExpand* uses *TreeViewEventHandler* as its delegate. The second parameter passed to a *TreeViewEventHandler* is a *TreeViewEventArgs* that identifies the branch of the tree that was expanded.

How do you know what events a given control fires? You read the documentation. Look up *ListBox*, for example, and you'll see that it defines an event named *DoubleClick* that's fired whenever the user double-clicks an item in the list box. *DoubleClick* is prototyped this way:

```
public event EventHandler DoubleClick;
```

From this statement, you know that handlers for *DoubleClick* events must be wrapped in *EventHandler* delegates. And because *EventHandler* is prototyped this way:

```
public delegate void EventHandler (Object sender, EventArgs e);
```

you know the signature for *DoubleClick* event handlers, too.

The ControlDemo Application

The application depicted in Figure 4-17 demonstrates the basics of Windows Forms control usage. Its one and only form contains four controls: a *Label* control, a *TextBox* control, a *ListBox* control, and a *Button* control. To put ControlDemo through its paces, start it up, type a path name (for example, C:\Winnt) into the *TextBox* control, and click the Show File Names button. A list of all the files in that directory will appear in the *ListBox*. Next double-click one of the file names to pop up a message box revealing when the file was created and when it was last modified.

ControlDemo's source code appears in Figure 4-18. The application's main form is an instance of *MyForm*. *MyForm*'s constructor instantiates the controls and stores references to them in private fields. Then it adds the controls to the form's *Controls* collection so that they will physically appear in the form. Event handlers named *OnShowFileNames* and *OnShowFileInfo* respond to the push button's *Click* events and the list box's *DoubleClick* events. These handlers use static methods belonging to the *System.IO* namespace's *Directory* and *File* classes to enumerate files and retrieve file information.

Note the statements that assign numeric values to the *TextBox*, *ListBox*, and *Button* controls' *TabIndex* properties. *TabIndex* specifies the order in which the input focus cycles between the controls when the user presses the Tab key. The logic for moving the focus is provided by the framework; your only responsibility is to provide the order. The *Label* control isn't assigned a tab index because it never receives the input focus.

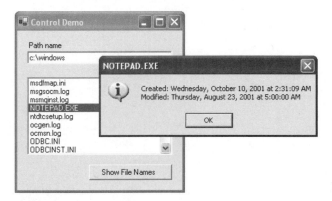

Figure 4-17   ControlDemo showing file details.

ControlDemo.cs
```
using System;
using System.Windows.Forms;
using System.Drawing;
using System.IO;

class MyForm : Form
{
    Label PathNameLabel;
    TextBox PathNameBox;
    ListBox FileNameBox;
    Button ShowFileNamesButton;

    string CurrentPath;

    MyForm ()
    {
        // Set the form's title
        Text = "Control Demo";

        // Set the form's size
        ClientSize = new Size (256, 248);
```

Figure 4-18   ControlDemo source code.

ControlDemo.cs   *(continued)*

```csharp
        // Create the form's controls
        PathNameLabel = new Label ();
        PathNameLabel.Location = new Point (16, 16);
        PathNameLabel.Size = new Size (224, 16);
        PathNameLabel.Text = "Path name";

        PathNameBox = new TextBox ();
        PathNameBox.Location = new Point (16, 32);
        PathNameBox.Size = new Size (224, 24);
        PathNameBox.TabIndex = 1;

        FileNameBox = new ListBox ();
        FileNameBox.Location = new Point (16, 72);
        FileNameBox.Size = new Size (224, 128);
        FileNameBox.TabIndex = 2;
        FileNameBox.DoubleClick += new EventHandler (OnShowFileInfo);

        ShowFileNamesButton = new Button ();
        ShowFileNamesButton.Location = new Point (112, 208);
        ShowFileNamesButton.Size = new Size (128, 24);
        ShowFileNamesButton.Text = "Show File Names";
        ShowFileNamesButton.TabIndex = 3;
        ShowFileNamesButton.Click +=
            new EventHandler (OnShowFileNames);

        // Add the controls to the form
        Controls.Add (PathNameLabel);
        Controls.Add (PathNameBox);
        Controls.Add (ShowFileNamesButton);
        Controls.Add (FileNameBox);
    }

    // Handler for the Show File Names button
    void OnShowFileNames (object sender, EventArgs e)
    {
        // Extract the path name from the TextBox control
        string path = PathNameBox.Text;

        if (path.Length > 0) {
            // Make sure the path name is valid
            if (Directory.Exists (path)) {
                // Empty the list box
                FileNameBox.Items.Clear ();

                // Get a list of all the files in the directory
                string[] files = Directory.GetFiles (path);

                // Put the file names (minus path names) in the
```

```
                    // list box
                    foreach (string file in files) {
                        FileAttributes attr = File.GetAttributes (file);
                        if ((attr & FileAttributes.Hidden) == 0)
                            FileNameBox.Items.Add (Path.GetFileName (file));
                    }

                    // Save the path name in case the user double-
                    // clicks a file name
                    CurrentPath = Path.GetFullPath (PathNameBox.Text);
                }
                // If the path isn't valid, notify the user
                else
                    MessageBox.Show (path + " is not a valid path",
                        "Error", MessageBoxButtons.OK, MessageBoxIcon.Error);
            }
        }

        // Handler for DoubleClick events from the ListBox
        void OnShowFileInfo (object sender, EventArgs e)
        {
            // Create a fully qualified file name from the file name
            // that the user double-clicked
            string file = CurrentPath;
            if (!file.EndsWith (":") && !file.EndsWith ("\\"))
                file += "\\";
            file += FileNameBox.SelectedItem.ToString ();

            // Display the dates and times that the file was created
            // and last modified
            DateTime created = File.GetCreationTime (file);
            DateTime modified = File.GetLastWriteTime (file);

            string msg = "Created: " + created.ToLongDateString () +
                " at " + created.ToLongTimeString () + "\n" +
                "Modified: " + modified.ToLongDateString () +
                " at " + modified.ToLongTimeString ();

            MessageBox.Show (msg, FileNameBox.SelectedItem.ToString (),
                MessageBoxButtons.OK, MessageBoxIcon.Information);
        }

        static void Main ()
        {
            Application.Run (new MyForm ());
        }
    }
}
```

Anchoring

When the Windows Forms team in Redmond drew up the blueprints for their part of the .NET Framework, they decided to include a few bells and whistles, too. One of those bells and whistles is a feature called *anchoring*. Anchoring enables forms designers to create forms whose controls move and resize as the form is resized. Figure 4-19 shows how ControlDemo looks if its form is expanded. Even though the form is larger, the controls retain their original size. Figure 4-20 shows the same form with anchoring enabled. The controls now "flow" with the size of the form.

Anchoring is applied on a control-by-control basis. It's enabled for a given control by initializing the *Anchor* property that the control inherits from *Control*. *Anchor* can be set to any combination of the following values to tell the control what to do when its container is resized:

Anchor Style	Meaning
AnchorStyles.Left	Maintain a constant distance between the left edge of the control and the left edge of the form
AnchorStyles.Right	Maintain a constant distance between the right edge of the control and the right edge of the form
AnchorStyles.Top	Maintain a constant distance between the top edge of the control and the top edge of the form
AnchorStyles.Bottom	Maintain a constant distance between the bottom edge of the control and the bottom edge of the form
AnchorStyles.None	Don't maintain a constant distance between the control and any edge of the form

If you want a control to move to the right when the container is widened, anchor the right edge of the control to the right edge of the form, like this:

```
MyControl.Anchor = AnchorStyles.Right;
```

If you want the control to widen rather than move when the form is widened, anchor both the left and right edges, like this:

```
MyControl.Anchor = AnchorStyles.Left | AnchorStyles.Right;
```

By applying various combinations of anchor styles, you can configure a control to flow how you want it to when its container is resized.

To see anchoring in action first-hand, add the following statements to *MyForm*'s constructor in ControlDemo.cs:

```
PathNameBox.Anchor = AnchorStyles.Left | AnchorStyles.Right |
    AnchorStyles.Top;
FileNameBox.Anchor = AnchorStyles.Left | AnchorStyles.Right |
    AnchorStyles.Bottom | AnchorStyles.Top;
ShowFileNamesButton.Anchor = AnchorStyles.Right | AnchorStyles.Bottom;
```

These statements produce the result that you see in Figure 4-20. Specifically, they configure the *TextBox* control to expand horizontally as the form expands but to remain fixed with respect to the top of the form; they configure the *ListBox* control to stretch horizontally and vertically as the form expands; and they configure the *Button* control to remain fixed in size but move with the lower right corner of the form.

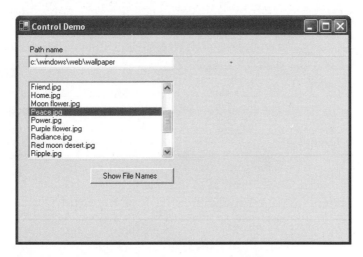

Figure 4-19   ControlDemo without anchoring.

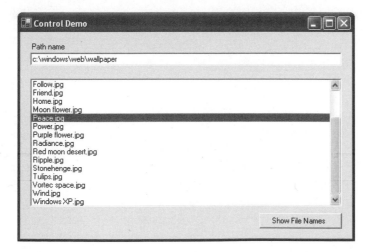

Figure 4-20   ControlDemo with anchoring.

Dialog Boxes

A dialog box is a form used to solicit input from a user. Dialog boxes, or simply "dialogs," as they are often called, come in two styles: modal and modeless. When a modal dialog is displayed, its owner, which is typically the application's main form, is temporarily disabled. The Open File dialog featured in countless Windows applications is an example of a modal dialog. Modeless dialogs don't disable their owners; users are free to "click back" to the main form at any time. The Find and Replace dialog in Microsoft Word is an example of a modeless dialog.

To a developer versed in programming Windows using the Windows API, dialog boxes are special creatures that are just different enough from ordinary windows to be a bit of a nuisance. In Windows Forms, dialog boxes are nothing special; they're just forms. Literally. In fact, just three characteristics differentiate a dialog box from an ordinary form:

- Dialogs have slightly different styles than ordinary forms. For example, dialogs rarely have minimize and maximize buttons, so most dialog constructors set the form's *MinimizeBox* and *MaximizeBox* properties to false.

- Dialogs generally have OK and Cancel buttons. A couple of lines of code in a Windows Forms dialog identifies these buttons to the framework and enables the framework to automatically dismiss the dialog when either button is clicked.

- To show an ordinary form, you call its *Show* method. To display a modal dialog, you call *ShowDialog*.

Experienced Windows developers are often shocked to find that Windows Forms dialogs create their controls programmatically. Traditional Windows applications use dialog resources that enable a dialog to be created, controls and all, with a simple function call. Windows Forms doesn't use dialog resources, so every dialog class contains code to create each and every control that it hosts.

Windows features an assortment of so-called "system dialogs" or "common dialogs" that developers can use to display Open File dialogs, Print dialogs, and other types of dialogs that are commonly found in Windows applications. The FCL wraps the common dialogs with easy-to-use classes. The following table lists the common dialog classes. All are defined in *System.Windows.Forms*. You've seen one of these dialogs—*OpenFileDialog*—already in this chapter's ImageView application. Use these classes whenever appropriate to save on development time and give your Windows Forms applications a look and feel that is consistent with other Windows applications.

Common Dialog Classes Defined in *System.Windows.Forms*

Class	Dialog Type
ColorDialog	Color dialog boxes for choosing colors
FontDialog	Font dialog boxes for choosing fonts
OpenFileDialog	Open File dialog boxes for choosing files
PageSetupDialog	Page Setup dialog boxes for entering page setup parameters
PrintDialog	Print dialog boxes for entering print parameters
SaveFileDialog	Save File dialog boxes for entering file names

The DialogDemo Application

Figure 4-22 contains the source code for a simple Windows Forms application that displays a dialog box in response to a menu command. To display the dialog, select the Edit Ellipse command from the Options menu. In the dialog are controls that you can use to change the width and height of the ellipse in the application's main form. (See Figure 4-21.) You can also select the system of units—inches, centimeters, or pixels—that the width and height are measured in.

DialogDemo's dialog class is named *MyDialog*. Code in the class constructor initializes the dialog's properties. The first statement sizes the dialog:

```
ClientSize = new Size (296, 196);
```

The second statement sets the dialog's *StartPosition* property to *FormStartPosition.CenterParent*, which centers the dialog in the parent form each time it's displayed:

```
StartPosition = FormStartPosition.CenterParent;
```

The next statement gives the dialog a "fixed dialog" border, which prevents the dialog from being resized:

```
FormBorderStyle = FormBorderStyle.FixedDialog;
```

The next two statements remove the minimize and maximize buttons that appear in the dialog's title bar by default, and the statement after that sets the text in the dialog's title bar:

```
MaximizeBox = false;
MinimizeBox = false;
Text = "Edit Ellipse";
```

The final statement prevents the dialog from causing a button to appear in the system's task bar:

```
ShowInTaskbar = false;
```

Top-level forms should appear in the task bar, but dialog boxes should not.

Most of the remaining code in *MyDialog*'s constructor creates the dialog's controls and adds them to the *Controls* collection. But notice these two statements:

```
AcceptButton = OKButton;
CancelButton = NotOKButton;
```

AcceptButton and *CancelButton* are properties that *MyDialog* inherits from *Form*. *AcceptButton* identifies the dialog's OK button; *CancelButton* identifies the Cancel button. OK and Cancel buttons are special because they dismiss the dialog box—that is, cause it to disappear from the screen. The statements above identify the OK and Cancel buttons to the framework so that it can dismiss the dialog when either button is clicked.

The following statements instantiate and display the dialog:

```
MyDialog dlg = new MyDialog ();
    .
    .
    .
if (dlg.ShowDialog (this) == DialogResult.OK) {
```

The dialog appears on the screen when *ShowDialog* is called. *ShowDialog* is a blocking call; it doesn't return until the dialog is dismissed. Its return value tells you *how* the dialog was dismissed. *DialogResult.OK* means the user clicked the OK button. *DialogResult.Cancel* means the user clicked Cancel. Most applications ignore what was entered into the dialog if the Cancel button is clicked. DialogDemo discards the input if *ShowDialog*'s return value is anything other than *DialogResult.OK*, which means the user can cancel out of the dialog without affecting the ellipse in any way.

MyDialog exposes the input that the user enters through public properties named *UserWidth*, *UserHeight*, and *UserUnits*. When read, these properties extract data from the dialog's controls. When written to, they transfer data to the controls. Before calling *ShowDialog* to display the dialog, DialogDemo initializes the dialog's controls by initializing the corresponding properties:

```
dlg.UserWidth = MyWidth;
dlg.UserHeight = MyHeight;
dlg.UserUnits = (int) MyUnits;
```

And when the dialog is dismissed (provided it's dismissed with the OK button), DialogDemo extracts the user input by reading *MyDialog* property values:

```
MyWidth = dlg.UserWidth;
MyHeight = dlg.UserHeight;
MyUnits = (MyForm.Units) dlg.UserUnits;
```

Thus, public properties in the dialog class serve as a mechanism for transferring data to and from the dialog's controls. This mechanism is typically how Windows Forms applications get data in and out of dialogs.

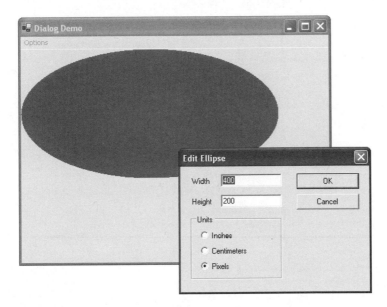

Figure 4-21   DialogDemo in action.

```
DialogDemo.cs
using System;
using System.Windows.Forms;
using System.Drawing;

class MyForm : Form
{
    enum Units {
        Inches,
        Centimeters,
        Pixels
    }

    int MyWidth = 400;
    int MyHeight = 200;
    Units MyUnits = Units.Pixels;
```

Figure 4-22   The DialogDemo source code.

DialogDemo.cs *(continued)*

```csharp
MyForm ()
{
    // Set the form's title
    Text = "Dialog Demo";

    // Set the form's size
    ClientSize = new Size (640, 480);

    // Create a menu
    MainMenu menu = new MainMenu ();
    MenuItem item = menu.MenuItems.Add ("&Options");
    item.MenuItems.Add ("Edit Ellipse...",
        new EventHandler (OnEditEllipse));
    item.MenuItems.Add ("-");
    item.MenuItems.Add ("E&xit", new EventHandler (OnExit));

    // Attach the menu to the form
    Menu = menu;
}

// Handler for the Edit Ellipse command
void OnEditEllipse (object sender, EventArgs e)
{
    // Create the dialog
    MyDialog dlg = new MyDialog ();

    // Initialize the dialog
    dlg.UserWidth = MyWidth;
    dlg.UserHeight = MyHeight;
    dlg.UserUnits = (int) MyUnits;

    // Display the dialog
    if (dlg.ShowDialog (this) == DialogResult.OK) {
        // If the dialog was dismissed with the OK button,
        // extract the user input and repaint the form
        MyWidth = dlg.UserWidth;
        MyHeight = dlg.UserHeight;
        MyUnits = (MyForm.Units) dlg.UserUnits;
        Invalidate ();
    }

    // Dispose of the dialog
    dlg.Dispose ();
}

// Handler for the Exit command
void OnExit (object sender, EventArgs e)
{
```

```
        Close ();
    }

    // OnPaint handler
    protected override void OnPaint (PaintEventArgs e)
    {
        int multiplier = 1;

        switch (MyUnits) {

        case Units.Inches:
            e.Graphics.PageUnit = GraphicsUnit.Inch;
            break;

        case Units.Centimeters:
            e.Graphics.PageUnit = GraphicsUnit.Millimeter;
            multiplier = 10;
            break;

        case Units.Pixels:
            e.Graphics.PageUnit = GraphicsUnit.Pixel;
            break;
        }

        SolidBrush brush = new SolidBrush (Color.Magenta);
        e.Graphics.FillEllipse (brush, 0, 0, MyWidth * multiplier,
            MyHeight * multiplier);
        brush.Dispose ();
    }

    static void Main ()
    {
        Application.Run (new MyForm ());
    }
}

class MyDialog : Form
{
    Label WidthLabel;
    Label HeightLabel;
    TextBox WidthBox;
    TextBox HeightBox;
    GroupBox UnitsGroup;
    RadioButton InchesButton;
    RadioButton CentimetersButton;
    RadioButton PixelsButton;
    Button OKButton;
    Button NotOKButton;
```

(continued)

DialogDemo.cs *(continued)*

```csharp
    public int UserWidth
    {
        get { return Convert.ToInt32 (WidthBox.Text); }
        set { WidthBox.Text = value.ToString (); }
    }

    public int UserHeight
    {
        get { return Convert.ToInt32 (HeightBox.Text); }
        set { HeightBox.Text = value.ToString (); }
    }

    public int UserUnits
    {
        get
        {
            for (int i=0; i<UnitsGroup.Controls.Count; i++) {
                RadioButton button =
                    (RadioButton) UnitsGroup.Controls[i];
                if (button.Checked)
                    return i;
            }
            return -1;
        }
        set
        {
            RadioButton button =
                (RadioButton) UnitsGroup.Controls[value];
            button.Checked = true;
        }
    }

public MyDialog ()
{
    // Initialize the dialog's visual properties
    ClientSize = new Size (296, 196);
    StartPosition = FormStartPosition.CenterParent;
    FormBorderStyle = FormBorderStyle.FixedDialog;
    MaximizeBox = false;
    MinimizeBox = false;
    Text = "Edit Ellipse";
    ShowInTaskbar = false;

    // Create the dialog's controls
    WidthLabel = new Label ();
    WidthLabel.Location = new Point (16, 16);
    WidthLabel.Size = new Size (48, 24);
    WidthLabel.Text = "Width";
```

```
HeightLabel = new Label ();
HeightLabel.Location = new Point (16, 48);
HeightLabel.Size = new Size (48, 24);
HeightLabel.Text = "Height";

WidthBox = new TextBox ();
WidthBox.Location = new Point (64, 12);
WidthBox.Size = new Size (96, 24);
WidthBox.TabIndex = 1;

HeightBox = new TextBox ();
HeightBox.Location = new Point (64, 44);
HeightBox.Size = new Size (96, 24);
HeightBox.TabIndex = 2;

UnitsGroup = new GroupBox ();
UnitsGroup.Location = new Point (16, 76);
UnitsGroup.Size = new Size (144, 100);
UnitsGroup.Text = "Units";

InchesButton = new RadioButton ();
InchesButton.Location = new Point (16, 24);
InchesButton.Size = new Size (112, 16);
InchesButton.Text = "Inches";

CentimetersButton = new RadioButton ();
CentimetersButton.Location = new Point (16, 48);
CentimetersButton.Size = new Size (112, 16);
CentimetersButton.Text = "Centimeters";

PixelsButton = new RadioButton ();
PixelsButton.Location = new Point (16, 72);
PixelsButton.Size = new Size (112, 16);
PixelsButton.Text = "Pixels";

OKButton = new Button ();
OKButton.Location = new Point (184, 12);
OKButton.Size = new Size (96, 24);
OKButton.TabIndex = 3;
OKButton.Text = "OK";
OKButton.DialogResult = DialogResult.OK;

NotOKButton = new Button ();
NotOKButton.Location = new Point (184, 44);
NotOKButton.Size = new Size (96, 24);
NotOKButton.TabIndex = 4;
NotOKButton.Text = "Cancel";
NotOKButton.DialogResult = DialogResult.Cancel;
```

(continued)

DialogDemo.cs *(continued)*

```
        AcceptButton = OKButton;
        CancelButton = NotOKButton;

        // Add the controls to the dialog
        Controls.Add (WidthLabel);
        Controls.Add (HeightLabel);
        Controls.Add (WidthBox);
        Controls.Add (HeightBox);
        Controls.Add (UnitsGroup);
        UnitsGroup.Controls.Add (InchesButton);
        UnitsGroup.Controls.Add (CentimetersButton);
        UnitsGroup.Controls.Add (PixelsButton);
        Controls.Add (OKButton);
        Controls.Add (NotOKButton);
    }
}
```

Windows Forms and Visual Studio .NET

Building applications by hand is a great way to learn the mechanics of Windows Forms, but in practice, most Windows Forms developers use Visual Studio .NET to craft their wares. Visual Studio .NET is the version of Visual Studio for .NET Framework developers. Its many features include an integrated editor, compiler, and debugger, context-sensitive help in the form of IntelliSense, and a built-in forms designer that simplifies the task of laying out and implementing Windows forms.

To acquaint you with Windows Forms development Visual Studio .NET–style, the remaining sections of this chapter provide step-by-step instructions for building a very practical Windows Forms application—a reverse Polish notation (RPN) calculator capable of performing addition, subtraction, multiplication, and division. Figure 4-23 shows the finished product.

Figure 4-23   The NetCalc application.

In case you're not familiar with RPN calculators, here's a brief tutorial. To add 2 and 2 on a conventional calculator, you press the following keys:

```
2
+
2
=
```

To add 2 and 2 on an RPN calculator, you do this instead:

```
2
Enter
2
+
```

The first two key presses—2 and Enter—push a 2 onto the calculator's internal evaluation stack. Pressing 2 again pushes another 2 onto the stack and moves the other one up one slot. Pressing the plus key (+) pops both 2s off the stack, adds them together, and pushes the result onto the stack. A 4 appears in the calculator's output window because the value at the top of the stack is always shown there.

One of the beauties of RPN calculators is that you don't need parentheses, and even complex expressions can be evaluated with a minimum of effort. Suppose, for example, you were given the following expression:

```
((2 + 2) * 6) / 3
```

Evaluating this expression would be a chore on a conventional calculator (especially one that lacks parentheses), but not on an RPN calculator. Here's the sequence of keystrokes:

```
2
Enter
2
+
6
*
3
/
```

RPN was popularized on Hewlett-Packard scientific calculators in the 1970s. Once you get used to crunching numbers the RPN way, you'll never want to use a conventional calculator again. But enough about the virtues of RPN. Let's write some code.

Step 1: Create a Project

The first step in creating a Windows Forms application in Visual Studio .NET is to create a project. To begin, choose the New/Project command from Visual Studio .NET's File menu. When the New Project dialog appears, make sure Visual C# Projects is selected in the Project Types box, as shown in Figure 4-24. Then choose Windows Application to identify the kind of application you intend to create. Type "NetCalc" into the Name box to give the project a name, and then click the OK button.

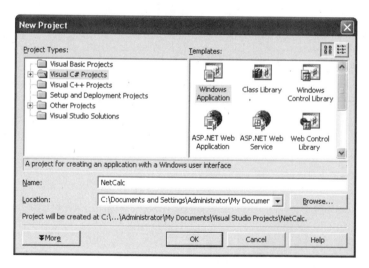

Figure 4-24   Creating a C# Windows Forms project.

Step 2: Design the Form

After creating the project, Visual Studio .NET will drop you into its forms designer, which is a visual tool for adding controls to forms, setting properties on those controls, writing event handlers, and more. The forms designer initially displays a blank form.

The next order of business is to customize the title at the top of the form. The default is "Form1." Change that by locating the form's *Text* property in the Properties window (by default, the Properties window appears in the lower right corner of Visual Studio .NET's main window) and changing "Form1" to "NetCalc." The new title should appear in the form's title bar in the forms designer. While you're at it, make the form nonresizable by setting its *FormBorderStyle* property to FixedDialog, and disable its maximize box by setting *MaximizeBox* to false. The following table summarizes the properties that need to be changed:

Property	Value
Text	"NetCalc"
FormBorderStyle	FixedDialog
MaximizeBox	False

On the left side of the Visual Studio .NET window is a vertical button labeled "Toolbox." Moving the cursor over the button and pausing momentarily causes a palette to appear, listing the various controls that you can add to a Windows form. Create a form that resembles the one shown in Figure 4-25 by selecting *Button* and *TextBox* controls from the palette and positioning them on the form. Then use the Properties window to apply the following properties to the *TextBox*:

Property	Value
TextAlign	Right
TabStop	False
Text	"0.00"
ReadOnly	True
BackColor	Window
Cursor	Default
Name	"Display"
Font	10-point Microsoft Sans Serif

Next use the Properties window to assign the following values to the buttons' *Text* and *Name* properties:

Text	Name	Text	Name
"Enter"	"EnterButton"	"1"	"OneButton"
"Fix"	"FixButton"	"2"	"TwoButton"
"Clear"	"ClearButton"	"3"	"ThreeButton"
"Del"	"DeleteButton"	"4"	"FourButton"
"."	"DecimalButton"	"5"	"FiveButton"
"-"	"SubtractButton"	"6"	"SixButton"
"+"	"AddButton"	"7"	"SevenButton"
"x"	"MultiplyButton"	"8"	"EightButton"
"÷"	"DivideButton"	"9"	"NineButton"
"0"	"ZeroButton"		

Change the font size on the plus, minus, multiply, and divide buttons to 12 points, and then finish up by setting each control's *TabStop* property to false. Setting *TabStop* to false in all the controls (*TextBox* included) prevents the Tab key from moving the input focus around the form. Sometimes it makes sense to support tabbing between controls. But in step 7, you'll endow NetCalc with a separate keyboard interface that's vastly superior to one that merely passes around the input focus.

You just finished designing NetCalc's user interface. Now it's time to add the logic that makes NetCalc behave like a calculator.

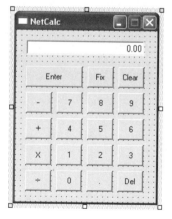

Figure 4-25   The NetCalc form in Visual Studio .NET's forms designer.

Step 3: Add Fields

Add the following private fields to the *Form1* class. *Form1* represents the form you designed in step 2. It was created automatically when the project was created, and it derives from *System.Windows.Forms.Form*:

Type	Name	Initial Value
Stack	*RegStack*	new Stack ()
string	*FormatString*	"f2"
bool	*FixPending*	False
bool	*DecimalInString*	False
bool	*EntryInProgress*	False
const int	*MaxChars*	21

You can add fields to *Form1* by hand, or you can let Visual Studio .NET add them for you. Simply click the Class View tab that appears (by default) near the right edge of the Visual Studio .NET window to display a list of the classes in your project. Then right-click *Form1* and select the Add/Add Field command from the ensuing context menu. When the Add Field wizard appears, fill it in with information about the field you want to add. Here's what the statements that declare and initialize the fields should look like when you've finished:

```
private Stack RegStack = new Stack ();
private string FormatString = "f2";
private bool FixPending = false;
private bool DecimalInString = false;
private bool EntryInProgress = false;
private const int MaxChars = 21;
```

If you use the Add Field wizard to create these statements, you'll have to edit them by hand to add the member initializers—for example, *"= false"*. The Add Field wizard won't add member initializers to fields that aren't *const*.

Incidentally, *RegStack* is an instance of *System.Collections.Stack*. It represents the calculator's internal register stack. We'll use its *Push* and *Pop* methods to move values on and off the stack, just like a real RPN calculator. You don't have to add a

```
using System.Collections;
```

statement to Form1.cs because Visual Studio .NET added it for you.

Step 4: Modify the Form's Class Constructor

Open Form1.cs and scroll down until you find *Form1*'s class constructor. Inside that constructor is the following comment:

```
//
// TODO: Add any constructor code after InitializeComponent call
//
```

Add the following statements after the comment:

```
RegStack.Push (0.0);
DisplayXRegister ();
```

The *Push* statement initializes the calculator's internal stack by pushing a 0 onto it. The second statement initializes the calculator's display by copying the value in the *X* register (the uppermost item on the stack) to the *TextBox* control.

Step 5: Add Helper Methods

Add the following helper methods to the *Form1* class:

Method Name	Return Type	Parameter List
ProcessDigit	void	int *Value*
Reset	void	None
ConditionalResetDisplay	void	None
InitializeXRegisterFromDisplay	void	None
DisplayXRegister	void	None
ReportError	void	string *Message*

You can add these methods by hand (in Form1.cs), or you can add them by right-clicking *Form1* in the Class View window and selecting the Add/Add Method command. Make all of the methods private. Fill in the method bodies with the code shown for the finished methods in Figure 4-26. If you use the Add Method command to add these methods, Visual Studio .NET adds empty method bodies for you. It's still up to you to enter code between the curly braces.

Step 6: Add *Click* Handlers

Go back to the forms designer and, one by one, double-click (with the left mouse button) the form's 19 push buttons. Each double-click adds a *Click* event handler to *Form1* and wires the handler to a button. The handlers are named

OneButton_Click, *TwoButton_Click*, and so on. Fill in the empty method bodies with the code in Figure 4-26.

Step 7: Add Keyboard Handlers

NetCalc is now a functional application, but it lacks a keyboard interface. A usable calculator applet must support keystroke entry. To that end, go back to the forms designer and change the form's *KeyPreview* property from false to true. Turning *KeyPreview* on enables the form to see keystrokes before its controls do, even if one of its controls has the input focus.

Next override the following methods in *Form1* to trap keyboard events:

Method Name	Return Type	Parameter List
OnKeyPress	void	*KeyPressEventArgs* e
OnKeyDown	void	*KeyEventArgs* e

As usual, you can add these methods by hand, or you can add them with the Add Method command. Mark all of these methods *protected*. If you use Add Method, be sure to check the Override box to include the *override* keyword in the method declaration. Finish up by implementing these methods as you did the ones shown in Figure 4-26.

Step 8: Override *ProcessDialogKey*

If you were to build and run NetCalc right now, you'd find that the keyboard interface works only if you use the keyboard exclusively. For example, if you click the 2 button with the mouse and then press Enter on the keyboard, another 2 appears in the calculator window. Why? Because the click sets the input focus to the 2 button, and when a button has the input focus, the system interprets the Enter key to mean that the button should be clicked.

This problem is solved by overriding an obscure method that *Form1* inherits from *Form*. The method is named *ProcessDialogKey*. It's called by the framework when certain keys (such as Enter) are pressed to give the form a chance to process the keystroke. Your job is to override the method like this:

```
protected override bool ProcessDialogKey(Keys keyData)
{
    return keyData == Keys.Enter ?
        false : base.ProcessDialogKey (keyData);
}
```

This implementation of *ProcessDialogKey* performs default processing on keys other than Enter by calling the base class's implementation of *ProcessDialogKey*. When the Enter key is pressed, however, *ProcessDialogKey* refrains from calling the base class to prevent the system from grabbing the keystroke. The Enter key becomes just another key on the keyboard, and pressing it activates your *OnKeyDown* handler even if a control currently has the input focus.

Step 9: Build and Run the Application

Build the application by selecting the Build command from Visual Studio .NET's Build menu. Run it by selecting the Start Without Debugging command from the Debug menu (or invoking its keyboard equivalent, Ctrl+F5). Verify that the code is working properly by adding, subtracting, multiplying, and dividing a few numbers. Also click the Fix button followed by the 4 button to change the calculator's display precision from two places to four. If four numbers appear to the right of the decimal point, you're set.

The NetCalc Source Code

The finished version of Form1.cs is shown in Figure 4-26. The lines that I typed in are shown in boldface type; all others were generated by Visual Studio .NET. I won't take the time to analyze each and every line, but I will point out a few highlights:

- Near the top of the file you'll find the statements that declare instances of *Button* and *TextBox* as private fields. These statements were added when you added the controls to the form in the forms designer.

- The wizard-generated portion of the form's class constructor contains a call to a local method named *InitializeComponent*. *InitializeComponent* instantiates the *Button* and *TextBox* controls and initializes their property values. Much of this code was added when you added the controls to the form. The remainder was added when you used the Properties window to edit the controls' properties.

- *InitializeComponent* also includes statements that wire the *Button* controls to *Click* handlers. Here is one such statement:

```
this.MultiplyButton.Click +=
    new System.EventHandler(this.MultiplyButton_Click);
```

These statements were added when you double-clicked the buttons in the forms designer window.

- Near the end of *InitializeComponent* is a single statement that adds all the controls to the form. Rather than call *Add* repeatedly, the forms designer adds the controls to the form in one fell swoop by calling *AddRange* on the form's *Controls* collection.

■ The *Click* handlers for the calculator's numeric buttons call a helper method named *ProcessDigit*. That method either adds a digit to the number shown in the calculator window or changes the display precision. Clicking the Fix button toggles an internal flag named *Fix-Pending* indicating whether the next number entered represents the desired precision or a numeric input.

■ Clicking the Enter button activates *EnterButton_Click*, which pushes the value currently displayed in the calculator window onto the calculator's internal stack.

■ Clicking any of the arithmetic buttons (plus, minus, multiply, or divide) applies the specified operation to the first two values popped off the stack. If one of these buttons is pressed and the value in the calculator window isn't currently on the stack, it's pushed onto the stack so that it can serve as an operand in the forthcoming calculation.

Visual Studio .NET is a big help in building form-based applications such as NetCalc because it reduces the tedium of sizing and positioning controls and assigning values to control properties. Less tedium means shorter development cycles and faster times to market. That's a winning proposition no matter how you look at it.

Form1.cs

```
using System;
using System.Drawing;
using System.Collections;
using System.ComponentModel;
using System.Windows.Forms;
using System.Data;

namespace NetCalc
{
    /// <summary>
    /// Summary description for Form1.
    /// </summary>
    public class Form1 : System.Windows.Forms.Form
    {
        private System.Windows.Forms.Button FixButton;
        private System.Windows.Forms.Button EnterButton;
        private System.Windows.Forms.TextBox Display;
        private System.Windows.Forms.Button ClearButton;
        private System.Windows.Forms.Button SubtractButton;
```

Form1.cs *(continued)*

Figure 4-26 The NetCalc source code.

```
private System.Windows.Forms.Button SevenButton;
private System.Windows.Forms.Button EightButton;
private System.Windows.Forms.Button NineButton;
private System.Windows.Forms.Button FiveButton;
private System.Windows.Forms.Button FourButton;
private System.Windows.Forms.Button AddButton;
private System.Windows.Forms.Button SixButton;
private System.Windows.Forms.Button ThreeButton;
private System.Windows.Forms.Button MultiplyButton;
private System.Windows.Forms.Button OneButton;
private System.Windows.Forms.Button TwoButton;
private System.Windows.Forms.Button ZeroButton;
private System.Windows.Forms.Button DivideButton;
private System.Windows.Forms.Button DeleteButton;
private System.Windows.Forms.Button DecimalButton;
/// <summary>
/// Required designer variable.
/// </summary>
private System.ComponentModel.Container components = null;

public Form1()
{
    //
    // Required for Windows Form Designer support
    //
    InitializeComponent();

    //
    // TODO: Add any constructor code after InitializeComponent call
    //
    RegStack.Push (0.0);
    DisplayXRegister ();
}

/// <summary>
/// Clean up any resources being used.
/// </summary>
protected override void Dispose( bool disposing )
{
    if( disposing )
    {
        if (components != null)
        {
            components.Dispose();
        }
    }
```

```
            base.Dispose( disposing );
    }


    #region Windows Form Designer generated code
    /// <summary>
    /// Required method for Designer support - do not modify
    /// the contents of this method with the code editor.
    /// </summary>
    private void InitializeComponent()
    {
        this.FixButton = new System.Windows.Forms.Button();
        this.EnterButton = new System.Windows.Forms.Button();
        this.Display = new System.Windows.Forms.TextBox();
        this.ClearButton = new System.Windows.Forms.Button();
        this.SubtractButton = new System.Windows.Forms.Button();
        this.SevenButton = new System.Windows.Forms.Button();
        this.EightButton = new System.Windows.Forms.Button();
        this.NineButton = new System.Windows.Forms.Button();
        this.FiveButton = new System.Windows.Forms.Button();
        this.FourButton = new System.Windows.Forms.Button();
        this.AddButton = new System.Windows.Forms.Button();
        this.SixButton = new System.Windows.Forms.Button();
        this.ThreeButton = new System.Windows.Forms.Button();
        this.MultiplyButton = new System.Windows.Forms.Button();
        this.OneButton = new System.Windows.Forms.Button();
        this.TwoButton = new System.Windows.Forms.Button();
        this.ZeroButton = new System.Windows.Forms.Button();
        this.DivideButton = new System.Windows.Forms.Button();
        this.DeleteButton = new System.Windows.Forms.Button();
        this.DecimalButton = new System.Windows.Forms.Button();
        this.SuspendLayout();
        //
        // FixButton
        //
        this.FixButton.Location = new System.Drawing.Point(112, 57);
        this.FixButton.Name = "FixButton";
        this.FixButton.Size = new System.Drawing.Size(40, 32);
        this.FixButton.TabIndex = 14;
        this.FixButton.TabStop = false;
        this.FixButton.Text = "Fix";
        this.FixButton.Click +=
            new System.EventHandler(this.FixButton_Click);
        //
        // EnterButton
        //
        this.EnterButton.Location = new System.Drawing.Point(16, 57);
        this.EnterButton.Name = "EnterButton";
        this.EnterButton.Size = new System.Drawing.Size(88, 32);
        this.EnterButton.TabIndex = 15;
```

(continued)

Form1.cs *(continued)*

```csharp
            this.EnterButton.TabStop = false;
            this.EnterButton.Text = "Enter";
            this.EnterButton.Click +=
                new System.EventHandler(this.EnterButton_Click);
            //
            // Display
            //
            this.Display.BackColor = System.Drawing.SystemColors.Window;
            this.Display.Cursor = System.Windows.Forms.Cursors.Default;
            this.Display.Font =
                new System.Drawing.Font("Microsoft Sans Serif", 9.75F,
                System.Drawing.FontStyle.Regular,
                System.Drawing.GraphicsUnit.Point, ((System.Byte)(0)));
            this.Display.Location = new System.Drawing.Point(16, 17);
            this.Display.Name = "Display";
            this.Display.ReadOnly = true;
            this.Display.Size = new System.Drawing.Size(184, 22);
            this.Display.TabIndex = 13;
            this.Display.TabStop = false;
            this.Display.Text = "0.00";
            this.Display.TextAlign =
                System.Windows.Forms.HorizontalAlignment.Right;
            //
            // ClearButton
            //
            this.ClearButton.Location = new System.Drawing.Point(160, 57);
            this.ClearButton.Name = "ClearButton";
            this.ClearButton.Size = new System.Drawing.Size(40, 32);
            this.ClearButton.TabIndex = 11;
            this.ClearButton.TabStop = false;
            this.ClearButton.Text = "Clear";
            this.ClearButton.Click +=
                new System.EventHandler(this.ClearButton_Click);
            //
            // SubtractButton
            //
            this.SubtractButton.Font =
                new System.Drawing.Font("Microsoft Sans Serif", 12F,
                System.Drawing.FontStyle.Regular,
                System.Drawing.GraphicsUnit.Point, ((System.Byte)(0)));
            this.SubtractButton.Location = new System.Drawing.Point(16, 97);
            this.SubtractButton.Name = "SubtractButton";
            this.SubtractButton.Size = new System.Drawing.Size(40, 32);
            this.SubtractButton.TabIndex = 12;
            this.SubtractButton.TabStop = false;
            this.SubtractButton.Text = "-";
            this.SubtractButton.Click +=
                new System.EventHandler(this.SubtractButton_Click);
```

```
//
// SevenButton
//
this.SevenButton.Location = new System.Drawing.Point(64, 97);
this.SevenButton.Name = "SevenButton";
this.SevenButton.Size = new System.Drawing.Size(40, 32);
this.SevenButton.TabIndex = 19;
this.SevenButton.TabStop = false;
this.SevenButton.Text = "7";
this.SevenButton.Click +=
    new System.EventHandler(this.SevenButton_Click);
//
// EightButton
//
this.EightButton.Location = new System.Drawing.Point(112, 97);
this.EightButton.Name = "EightButton";
this.EightButton.Size = new System.Drawing.Size(40, 32);
this.EightButton.TabIndex = 20;
this.EightButton.TabStop = false;
this.EightButton.Text = "8";
this.EightButton.Click +=
    new System.EventHandler(this.EightButton_Click);
//
// NineButton
//
this.NineButton.Location = new System.Drawing.Point(160, 97);
this.NineButton.Name = "NineButton";
this.NineButton.Size = new System.Drawing.Size(40, 32);
this.NineButton.TabIndex = 18;
this.NineButton.TabStop = false;
this.NineButton.Text = "9";
this.NineButton.Click +=
    new System.EventHandler(this.NineButton_Click);
//
// FiveButton
//
this.FiveButton.Location = new System.Drawing.Point(112, 137);
this.FiveButton.Name = "FiveButton";
this.FiveButton.Size = new System.Drawing.Size(40, 32);
this.FiveButton.TabIndex = 16;
this.FiveButton.TabStop = false;
this.FiveButton.Text = "5";
this.FiveButton.Click +=
    new System.EventHandler(this.FiveButton_Click);
//
// FourButton
//
this.FourButton.Location = new System.Drawing.Point(64, 137);
this.FourButton.Name = "FourButton";
```

(continued)

Form1.cs   *(continued)*

```
        this.FourButton.Size = new System.Drawing.Size(40, 32);
        this.FourButton.TabIndex = 17;
        this.FourButton.TabStop = false;
        this.FourButton.Text = "4";
        this.FourButton.Click +=
            new System.EventHandler(this.FourButton_Click);
        //
        // AddButton
        //
        this.AddButton.Font =
            new System.Drawing.Font("Microsoft Sans Serif", 12F,
            System.Drawing.FontStyle.Regular,
            System.Drawing.GraphicsUnit.Point, ((System.Byte)(0)));
        this.AddButton.Location = new System.Drawing.Point(16, 137);
        this.AddButton.Name = "AddButton";
        this.AddButton.Size = new System.Drawing.Size(40, 32);
        this.AddButton.TabIndex = 4;
        this.AddButton.TabStop = false;
        this.AddButton.Text = "+";
        this.AddButton.Click +=
            new System.EventHandler(this.AddButton_Click);
        //
        // SixButton
        //
        this.SixButton.Location = new System.Drawing.Point(160, 137);
        this.SixButton.Name = "SixButton";
        this.SixButton.Size = new System.Drawing.Size(40, 32);
        this.SixButton.TabIndex = 5;
        this.SixButton.TabStop = false;
        this.SixButton.Text = "6";
        this.SixButton.Click +=
            new System.EventHandler(this.SixButton_Click);
        //
        // ThreeButton
        //
        this.ThreeButton.Location = new System.Drawing.Point(160, 177);
        this.ThreeButton.Name = "ThreeButton";
        this.ThreeButton.Size = new System.Drawing.Size(40, 32);
        this.ThreeButton.TabIndex = 3;
        this.ThreeButton.TabStop = false;
        this.ThreeButton.Text = "3";
        this.ThreeButton.Click +=
            new System.EventHandler(this.ThreeButton_Click);
        //
        // MultiplyButton
        //
        this.MultiplyButton.Font =
            new System.Drawing.Font("Microsoft Sans Serif", 12F,
```

```
        System.Drawing.FontStyle.Regular,
        System.Drawing.GraphicsUnit.Point, ((System.Byte)(0)));
    this.MultiplyButton.Location = new System.Drawing.Point(16, 177);
    this.MultiplyButton.Name = "MultiplyButton";
    this.MultiplyButton.Size = new System.Drawing.Size(40, 32);
    this.MultiplyButton.TabIndex = 1;
    this.MultiplyButton.TabStop = false;
    this.MultiplyButton.Text = "x";
    this.MultiplyButton.Click +=
        new System.EventHandler(this.MultiplyButton_Click);
    //
    // OneButton
    //
    this.OneButton.Location = new System.Drawing.Point(64, 177);
    this.OneButton.Name = "OneButton";
    this.OneButton.Size = new System.Drawing.Size(40, 32);
    this.OneButton.TabIndex = 2;
    this.OneButton.TabStop = false;
    this.OneButton.Text = "1";
    this.OneButton.Click +=
        new System.EventHandler(this.OneButton_Click);
    //
    // TwoButton
    //
    this.TwoButton.Location = new System.Drawing.Point(112, 177);
    this.TwoButton.Name = "TwoButton";
    this.TwoButton.Size = new System.Drawing.Size(40, 32);
    this.TwoButton.TabIndex = 9;
    this.TwoButton.TabStop = false;
    this.TwoButton.Text = "2";
    this.TwoButton.Click +=
        new System.EventHandler(this.TwoButton_Click);
    //
    // ZeroButton
    //
    this.ZeroButton.Location = new System.Drawing.Point(64, 217);
    this.ZeroButton.Name = "ZeroButton";
    this.ZeroButton.Size = new System.Drawing.Size(40, 32);
    this.ZeroButton.TabIndex = 10;
    this.ZeroButton.TabStop = false;
    this.ZeroButton.Text = "0";
    this.ZeroButton.Click +=
        new System.EventHandler(this.ZeroButton_Click);
    //
    // DivideButton
    //
    this.DivideButton.Font =
        new System.Drawing.Font("Microsoft Sans Serif", 12F,
        System.Drawing.FontStyle.Regular,
```

(continued)

Form1.cs *(continued)*

```
            System.Drawing.GraphicsUnit.Point, ((System.Byte)(0))));
        this.DivideButton.Location = new System.Drawing.Point(16, 217);
        this.DivideButton.Name = "DivideButton";
        this.DivideButton.Size = new System.Drawing.Size(40, 32);
        this.DivideButton.TabIndex = 8;
        this.DivideButton.TabStop = false;
        this.DivideButton.Text = "÷";
        this.DivideButton.Click +=
            new System.EventHandler(this.DivideButton_Click);
        //
        // DeleteButton
        //
        this.DeleteButton.Location = new System.Drawing.Point(160, 217);
        this.DeleteButton.Name = "DeleteButton";
        this.DeleteButton.Size = new System.Drawing.Size(40, 32);
        this.DeleteButton.TabIndex = 6;
        this.DeleteButton.TabStop = false;
        this.DeleteButton.Text = "Del";
        this.DeleteButton.Click +=
            new System.EventHandler(this.DeleteButton_Click);
        //
        // DecimalButton
        //
        this.DecimalButton.Location = new System.Drawing.Point(112, 217);
        this.DecimalButton.Name = "DecimalButton";
        this.DecimalButton.Size = new System.Drawing.Size(40, 32);
        this.DecimalButton.TabIndex = 7;
        this.DecimalButton.TabStop = false;
        this.DecimalButton.Text = ".";
        this.DecimalButton.Click +=
            new System.EventHandler(this.DecimalButton_Click);
        //
        // Form1
        //
        this.AutoScaleBaseSize = new System.Drawing.Size(5, 13);
        this.ClientSize = new System.Drawing.Size(218, 266);
        this.Controls.AddRange(new System.Windows.Forms.Control[] {
            this.FixButton,
            this.EnterButton,
            this.Display,
            this.ClearButton,
            this.SubtractButton,
            this.SevenButton,
            this.EightButton,
            this.NineButton,
            this.FiveButton,
            this.FourButton,
            this.AddButton,
```

```
                this.SixButton,
                this.ThreeButton,
                this.MultiplyButton,
                this.OneButton,
                this.TwoButton,
                this.ZeroButton,
                this.DivideButton,
                this.DeleteButton,
                this.DecimalButton});
        this.FormBorderStyle =
            System.Windows.Forms.FormBorderStyle.FixedDialog;
        this.KeyPreview = true;
        this.MaximizeBox = false;
        this.Name = "Form1";
        this.Text = "NetCalc";
        this.ResumeLayout(false);
    }
    #endregion

    /// <summary>
    /// The main entry point for the application.
    /// </summary>
     [STAThread]
    static void Main()
    {
        Application.Run(new Form1());
    }

    private Stack RegStack = new Stack ();
    private string FormatString = "f2";
    private bool FixPending = false;
    private bool DecimalInString = false;
    private bool EntryInProgress = false;
    private const int MaxChars = 21;


    //
    // Process a press of one of the numeric buttons. If Fix was
    // the last button pressed, change the calculator's output
    // precision by modifying FormatString. Otherwise, reset the
    // display if necessary and append the number to any numbers
    // previously entered.
    //
    private void ProcessDigit(int Value)
    {
        if (FixPending) {
            FormatString = "f" + Value.ToString ();
            if (EntryInProgress)
                InitializeXRegisterFromDisplay ();
            DisplayXRegister ();
```

(continued)

Form1.cs   *(continued)*

```
            FixPending = false;
        }
        else {
            ConditionalResetDisplay ();
            if (Display.Text.Length < MaxChars)
                Display.Text += Value.ToString ();
        }
    }


    //
    // Reset the calculator's internal flags.
    //
    private void Reset()
    {
        DecimalInString = false;
        FixPending = false;
        EntryInProgress = false;
    }


    //
    // Blank out the value displayed in the calculator window
    // if an entry isn't already in progress.
    //
    private void ConditionalResetDisplay()
    {
        if (!EntryInProgress) {
            EntryInProgress = true;
            Display.Text = "";
        }
    }


    //
    // Convert the text in the calculator display to a numeric
    // value and push it onto the stack.
    //
    private void InitializeXRegisterFromDisplay()
    {
        double x = (Display.Text.Length == 0 || Display.Text == ".") ?
            0.0 : Convert.ToDouble (Display.Text);
        RegStack.Push (x);
    }


    //
    // Show the value at the top of the stack in the calculator
    // window. Check for overflow and underflow and display an
    // error message if either has occurred.
    //
    private void DisplayXRegister()
```

```
{
    double x = (double) RegStack.Peek ();
    if (x > Double.MaxValue || x < Double.MinValue)
        ReportError ("Overflow");
    else {
        string display = x.ToString (FormatString);
        if (display.Length > MaxChars ||
            (Math.Abs (x) > 0.0 && Math.Abs (x) < 0.0000000001))
            display = x.ToString ("e");
        Display.Text = display;
    }
}


//
// Report an error to the user by displaying an error
// message in the calculator window. Also reset the
// calculator's internal state so the next button press
// will start things over again.
//
private void ReportError(string Message)
{
    Display.Text = Message;
    RegStack.Clear ();
    RegStack.Push (0.0);
    Reset ();
}


//
// Handlers for the calculator's numeric buttons (0-9).
//
private void ZeroButton_Click(object sender, System.EventArgs e)
{
    ProcessDigit (0);
}


private void OneButton_Click(object sender, System.EventArgs e)
{
    ProcessDigit (1);
}


private void TwoButton_Click(object sender, System.EventArgs e)
{
    ProcessDigit (2);
}


private void ThreeButton_Click(object sender, System.EventArgs e)
{
    ProcessDigit (3);
}
```

(continued)

Form1.cs   *(continued)*

```csharp
        private void FourButton_Click(object sender, System.EventArgs e)
        {
            ProcessDigit (4);
        }

        private void FiveButton_Click(object sender, System.EventArgs e)
        {
            ProcessDigit (5);
        }

        private void SixButton_Click(object sender, System.EventArgs e)
        {
            ProcessDigit (6);
        }

        private void SevenButton_Click(object sender, System.EventArgs e)
        {
            ProcessDigit (7);
        }

        private void EightButton_Click(object sender, System.EventArgs e)
        {
            ProcessDigit (8);
        }

        private void NineButton_Click(object sender, System.EventArgs e)
        {
            ProcessDigit (9);
        }

        //
        // Handlers for the Add, Subtract, Multiply, and
        // Divide buttons.
        //
        // General strategy employed by all four handlers:
        // 1) Push the value in the calculator display onto the
        //    stack if it hasn't been pushed already.
        // 2) Pop two values from the stack to use as operands.
        // 3) Compute the sum, difference, product, or quotient.
        // 4) Push the result onto the stack.
        // 5) Display the result.
        //
        private void SubtractButton_Click(object sender, System.EventArgs e)
        {
            if (EntryInProgress)
                InitializeXRegisterFromDisplay ();
```

```
        if (RegStack.Count >= 2) {
            double op1 = (double) RegStack.Pop ();
            double op2 = (double) RegStack.Pop ();
            RegStack.Push (op2 - op1);
            DisplayXRegister ();
            Reset ();
        }
    }

    private void AddButton_Click(object sender, System.EventArgs e)
    {
        if (EntryInProgress)
            InitializeXRegisterFromDisplay ();

        if (RegStack.Count >= 2) {
            double op1 = (double) RegStack.Pop ();
            double op2 = (double) RegStack.Pop ();
            RegStack.Push (op2 + op1);
            DisplayXRegister ();
            Reset ();
        }
    }

    private void MultiplyButton_Click(object sender, System.EventArgs e)
    {
        if (EntryInProgress)
            InitializeXRegisterFromDisplay ();

        if (RegStack.Count >= 2) {
            double op1 = (double) RegStack.Pop ();
            double op2 = (double) RegStack.Pop ();
            RegStack.Push (op2 * op1);
            DisplayXRegister ();
            Reset ();
        }
    }

    private void DivideButton_Click(object sender, System.EventArgs e)
    {
        if (EntryInProgress)
            InitializeXRegisterFromDisplay ();

        if (RegStack.Count >= 2) {
            if ((double) RegStack.Peek () == 0.0)
                ReportError ("Divide by zero");
            else {
                double op1 = (double) RegStack.Pop ();
                double op2 = (double) RegStack.Pop ();
                RegStack.Push (op2 / op1);
```

(continued)

Form1.cs   *(continued)*

```csharp
                    DisplayXRegister ();
                    Reset ();
                }
            }
        }


        //
        // Handler for the Enter button.
        //
        private void EnterButton_Click(object sender, System.EventArgs e)
        {
            InitializeXRegisterFromDisplay ();
            DisplayXRegister ();
            Reset ();
        }


        //
        // Handler for the Fix button.
        //
        private void FixButton_Click(object sender, System.EventArgs e)
        {
            FixPending = !FixPending;
        }


        //
        // Handler for the Clear button.
        //
        private void ClearButton_Click(object sender, System.EventArgs e)
        {
            RegStack.Clear ();
            RegStack.Push (0.0);
            DisplayXRegister ();
            Reset ();
        }


        //
        // Handler for the Delete button.
        //
        private void DeleteButton_Click(object sender, System.EventArgs e)
        {
            int len = Display.Text.Length;
            if (len > 0 && EntryInProgress) {
                if (Display.Text[len - 1] == '.')
                    DecimalInString = false;
                Display.Text = Display.Text.Substring (0, len - 1);
            }
        }
```

```csharp
//
// Handler for the '.' button.
//
private void DecimalButton_Click(object sender, System.EventArgs e)
{
    ConditionalResetDisplay ();
    if (Display.Text.Length < MaxChars && !DecimalInString) {
        Display.Text += ".";
        DecimalInString = true;
    }
}


//
// Handler for KeyPress events. Comprises half of NetCalc's
// keyboard interface.
//
protected override void OnKeyPress(KeyPressEventArgs e)
{
    switch (e.KeyChar) {

    case '0':
        ZeroButton_Click (ZeroButton, new EventArgs ());
        break;

    case '1':
        OneButton_Click (OneButton, new EventArgs ());
        break;

    case '2':
        TwoButton_Click (TwoButton, new EventArgs ());
        break;

    case '3':
        ThreeButton_Click (ThreeButton, new EventArgs ());
        break;

    case '4':
        FourButton_Click (FourButton, new EventArgs ());
        break;

    case '5':
        FiveButton_Click (FiveButton, new EventArgs ());
        break;

    case '6':
        SixButton_Click (SixButton, new EventArgs ());
        break;

    case '7':
        SevenButton_Click (SevenButton, new EventArgs ());
```

(continued)

Form1.cs *(continued)*

```
            break;

        case '8':
            EightButton_Click (EightButton, new EventArgs ());
            break;

        case '9':
            NineButton_Click (NineButton, new EventArgs ());
            break;

        case '.':
            DecimalButton_Click (DecimalButton, new EventArgs ());
            break;

        case '-':
            SubtractButton_Click (SubtractButton, new EventArgs ());
            break;

        case '+':
            AddButton_Click (AddButton, new EventArgs ());
            break;

        case '*':
            MultiplyButton_Click (MultiplyButton, new EventArgs ());
            break;

        case '/':
            DivideButton_Click (DivideButton, new EventArgs ());
            break;
        }
    }

    //
    // Handler for KeyDown events. The other half of NetCalc's
    // keyboard interface.
    //
    protected override void OnKeyDown(KeyEventArgs e)
    {
        switch (e.KeyCode) {

        case Keys.C:
            ClearButton_Click (ClearButton, new EventArgs ());
            break;

        case Keys.F:
            FixButton_Click (FixButton, new EventArgs ());
            break;

        case Keys.Enter:
            EnterButton_Click (EnterButton, new EventArgs ());
```

```
                break;

        case Keys.Delete:
            DeleteButton_Click (DeleteButton, new EventArgs ());
            break;
        }
    }

    //
    // The following override prevents the form from "stealing"
    // the Enter key and using it to simulate button clicks.
    //
    protected override bool ProcessDialogKey(Keys keyData)
    {
        return keyData == Keys.Enter ?
            false : base.ProcessDialogKey (keyData);
    }
    }
}
```

Windows Forms Retrospective

Windows Forms are an important part of the .NET Framework because they enable developers to build applications that present rich graphical interfaces to their users. To the extent that Microsoft succeeds in convincing developers to embrace the .NET initiative and adopt the .NET Framework, Windows Forms will eventually supplant today's Windows applications. At a not-too-distant date in the future, it's entirely conceivable that the Windows API, MFC, and other tools that have fueled the software industry for years will be historical anachronisms. To programmers who have struggled to overcome the limitations of today's platforms, that day won't come a moment too soon.

Part 2
ASP.NET

5

Web Forms

In recent years, the cutting edge of software development has shifted from traditional "fat client" apps to Web apps. The integration of back-end systems and seamless data sharing, once the holy grail of corporate IT departments, have given way to concerns over lower total cost of ownership (TCO), zero-footprint installs, and the ability to run applications from anywhere an Internet connection is available. The number one challenge that confronts developers today? "Make this software run on the Web." Unfortunately, Web programming isn't easy. Writing applications like Microsoft Word and Microsoft Excel is a well understood art form. Writing applications like eBay and Amazon.com is not. To make matters worse, Web development today is practiced with first-generation tools and technologies that have more in common with 1960s-era Dartmouth BASIC than the modern platforms and development environments that developers have become accustomed to.

Microsoft's answer to the sordid state of Web programming today is a second-generation programming model called *Web Forms*. The Web Forms model is part of ASP.NET, which in turn is part of the Microsoft .NET Framework. Just as Active Server Pages (ASP) revolutionized Web programming in the 1990s with an easy-to-use model for dynamically generating HTML on Web servers, ASP.NET advances the state of the art in Web programming by introducing reusable server controls that render HTML to browser clients and fire events that can be processed by server-side scripts. That's Web Forms in a nutshell: Web pages built around controls and event handlers. If the concept is alluring, the implementation is downright brilliant. Once you learn to build Web apps the Web Forms way, you'll never want to build them any other way again.

This chapter introduces the Web Forms programming model by describing how to build Web forms both with and without Visual Studio .NET. First you'll nail down the basics by building Web forms by hand. Then you'll switch to

Visual Studio .NET and experience rapid application development (RAD), Internet-style. Along the way, you'll be introduced to important Web Forms programming techniques such as code-behind and dynamic control initialization.

Before you begin, it's worth noting what software you need to run this chapter's sample programs. First and foremost, you need the .NET Framework. Second, you need Microsoft Internet Information Services (IIS), which is Microsoft's Web server software. Finally, you need ASP.NET. ASP.NET is automatically installed when you install the .NET Framework SDK on a platform that supports ASP.NET. Currently those platforms include Windows 2000 and Windows XP. Be sure to install IIS before you install the Framework SDK, or you'll have to go back and install ASP.NET separately.

Web Application Primer

The most proficient developers are those who possess an intimate understanding of the platforms they program and the tools they use to program them. Because it's difficult to understand how Web forms work if you lack a more general understanding of Web applications and the protocols that drive them, the next several sections provide a working introduction to the operation of Web apps. They're for developers who have little or no Web programming experience. If you're already familiar with HTTP, HTML forms, and other Web-related technologies, feel free to skip ahead to the section entitled "Your First Web Form." If, however, Web apps are a new frontier for you, you'll find the following discussion helpful in building an in-depth understanding of the Web Forms programming model.

Hypertext Transfer Protocol

The Hypertext Transfer Protocol, better known as HTTP, is the protocol that drives the World Wide Web. Invented by Tim Berners-Lee ("father of the Web") and documented in RFC 2068, which is available online at *www.w3.org/Protocols/rfc2068/rfc2068*, HTTP is arguably the most important network protocol ever invented, with the notable exception of TCP/IP.

HTTP defines how Web browsers and Web servers communicate with each other. It's entirely text based, and it's typically transmitted over TCP connections linking Web browsers to Web servers. Suppose the following HTML file is deployed on a Web server, that its name is Simple.html, and that its URL is *www.wintellect.com/simple.html*:

```
<html>
<body>
Hello, world
</body>
</html>
```

If a user types *http://www.wintellect.com/simple.html* into Internet Explorer's address bar, Internet Explorer (IE) uses the Internet's Domain Name System (DNS) to convert *www.wintellect.com* into an IP address (for example, 66.45.26.25). Then IE opens a socket connection to the server at that address using a well-known port number (port 80) and transmits an HTTP request similar to this one:

```
GET /simple.html HTTP/1.1
Accept: */*
Accept-Language: en-us
Accept-Encoding: gzip, deflate
If-Modified-Since: Wed, 24 Oct 2001 14:12:36 GMT
If-None-Match: "50b0d3ee955cc11:a78"
User-Agent: Mozilla/4.0.(compatible; MSIE.6.0; Windows NT 5.1)
Host: www.wintellect.com
Connection: Keep-Alive
[blank line]
```

The first line of the request is called the *start line*. It consists of a method name (GET), the name of the resource being requested (simple.html), and an HTTP version number (1.1). GET is one of seven methods defined in HTTP 1.1; it requests a resource from a Web server. The next eight lines make up the *message header*. Each line, or *header*, contains additional information about the request, including information about the browser that originated the request (*User-Agent*). A blank line (a simple carriage return/line feed pair) marks the end of the message header and also the end of the request.

How does the Web server respond to the GET command? Assuming /simple.html is a valid resource identifier and security settings don't prevent the file from being returned, the server transmits an HTTP response like this one:

```
HTTP/1.1 200 OK
Server: Microsoft-IIS/5.0
Date: Wed, 24 Oct 2001 14:12:37 GMT
Content-Type: text/html
Accept-Ranges: bytes
Last-Modified: Wed, 24 Oct 2001 14:00:53 GMT
ETag: "d02acf81975cc11:a78"
Content-Length: 46
[blank line]
```

(continued)

```
<html>
<body>
Hello, world
</body>
</html>
```

Upon receiving the response, the browser parses the HTML returned by the Web server and displays the resulting Web page. The *Content-Type* header identifies the returned data as HTML, while *Content-Length* tells the browser how much HTML was returned. The "200" in the first line of the response is an HTTP status code signifying that the server fulfilled the browser's request. The HTTP specification defines about 40 different status codes, including the infamous 401 ("Unauthorized") code indicating that the user isn't authorized to view this resource.

Conversations such as these form the backbone for communications over the Web. As you surf the Web by typing URLs and clicking hyperlinks, your browser issues one GET command after another. Tools such as NetMon—the network packet-sniffing utility that comes with server editions of Windows—let you spy on the HTTP traffic flying back and forth. You don't have to be an HTTP guru to write ASP.NET applications, but a knowledge of basic HTTP semantics and a familiarity with commonly used request and response headers are a big help in understanding the ASP.NET object model.

HTML Forms

Simple.html is a far cry from a full-blown Web application. It's a static HTML file that solicits no user input. Real Web applications like the ones located at *www.amazon.com* and *www.ebay.com* accept input from their users, and they vary the HTML that they return to Web browsers based on the contents of that input.

At the heart of almost every genuine Web application is an HTML form. An HTML form is the portion of an HTML document that appears between <form> and </form> tags. The HTML in Figure 5-1 describes a simple form representing a Web-based adding machine. The form contains two text input fields for the user to type numbers into and an equals button that submits the form back to the server. Figure 5-2 shows how the form appears in Internet Explorer. As you can see, the browser renders an <input type="text"> tag as a text input field and an <input type="submit"> tag as a push button. Similar tags can be used to create check boxes, radio buttons, list boxes, and other basic control types.

Calc.html

```
<html>
  <body>
    <form>
      <input type="text" name="op1" />
      +
      <input type="text" name="op2" />
      <input type="submit" value="  =  " />
    </form>
  </body>
</html>
```

Figure 5-1   A simple HTML form.

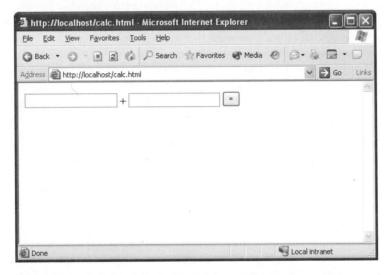

Figure 5-2   Calc.html displayed in Internet Explorer.

A submit button (<input type="submit">) plays a special role in an HTML form. When clicked, it submits the form to a Web server. To be more precise, the *browser* submits the form along with any input in the form's controls. How the form is submitted depends on whether the <form> tag includes a *Method* attribute and the value of that attribute, if present. If the <form> tag lacks a *Method* attribute or includes a *method*="get" attribute, the browser sends an HTTP GET command to the server with the user's input appended to the URL in the form of a query string:

```
GET /calc.html?op1=2&op2=2 HTTP/1.1
  .
  .
  .
Connection: Keep-Alive
[blank line]
```

If, on the other hand, the <form> tag includes a *method*="post" attribute, the form is submitted to the server using an HTTP POST command. Rather than transmit user input in the URL, with a POST command the browser passes it in the body of the HTTP request:

```
POST /calc.html HTTP/1.1
         .
         .
         .

Content-Type: application/x-www-form-urlencoded
Content-Length: 11
[blank line]
op1=2&op2=2
```

Regardless of whether a GET or a POST command is used, when input from an HTML form is submitted back to the server, we say that a "postback" has occurred. Remember that term because you'll encounter it repeatedly in this and the next several chapters.

For a first-hand look at HTML forms in action, copy Calc.html to your PC's \Inetpub\wwwroot directory and call it up in Internet Explorer by typing the following URL:

```
http://localhost/calc.html
```

Now type 2 into each of the form's text boxes and click the = button. As evidence that a postback occurred, observe what appears in the browser's address bar (shown in Figure 5-3). If you change the <form> tag to

```
<form method="post">
```

and repeat the experiment, you won't see any change in the URL. But the postback occurs just the same, and the Web server can access the user's input by examining the body of the request.

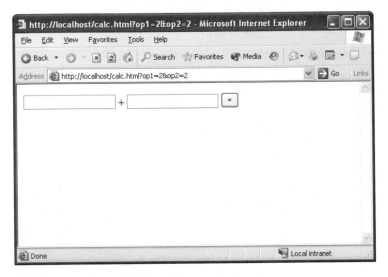

Figure 5-3   Calc.html following a postback.

Server-Side Processing

So far, so good. As Calc.html demonstrates, building the client half of a Web application is easy. After all, it's just HTML. The hard part is building the code that runs on the Web server. *Something* has to be running there to extract the user input from the URL (or from the body of the HTTP request if the postback was performed with POST instead of GET) and generate a new Web page that displays the sum of the inputs next to the = button. In other words, if the user enters 2 and 2 and clicks the = button, we'd like the Web server to respond by returning the following HTML:

```
<html>
  <body>
    <form>
      <input type="text" name="op1" value="2" />
      +
      <input type="text" name="op2" value="2" />
      <input type="submit" value="  =  " />
      4
    </form>
  </body>
</html>
```

Note the *Value* attributes added to the <input type="text"> tags. Including the inputs in the page returned from the Web server following a postback perpetuates the illusion that the user is seeing one Web page when in fact he or she is seeing two in succession.

There are many ways to write applications that process input from HTML forms. One solution is an application that uses the Common Gateway Interface (CGI). CGI defines a low-level programmatic interface between Web servers and applications that run on Web servers. Applications that use it are typically written in a programming language called Perl, but they can be written in other languages as well. CGI applications read the input accompanying postbacks through server environment variables and standard input (stdin), and they write HTTP responses to standard output (stdout). CGI has a reputation for being slow because many implementations of it launch a new process to handle each incoming request. Despite this, CGI enjoys widespread use on UNIX-based Web servers. It's rarely used on the Windows platform.

Another solution—one that's more likely to find favor among Windows developers—is an ISAPI extension DLL. ISAPI stands for Internet Server Application Programming Interface. ISAPI extensions are Windows DLLs that are hosted by Internet Information Services. They're referenced by URL just like HTML files (for example, *http://www.wintellect.com/calc.dll*). IIS forwards HTTP requests to an ISAPI DLL by calling a special function exported from the DLL. The DLL, in turn, generates HTTP responses. ISAPI DLLs are faster than CGI applications because they (typically) run in the same process as IIS. And once loaded, they remain in memory awaiting subsequent requests. The downside to ISAPI DLLs is that they're difficult to write. An ISAPI developer must be comfortable with the architecture of Windows DLLs and also be willing to deal with HTTP messages at a very low level.

Curious to know what an ISAPI DLL looks like? Figure 5-4 shows the C++ source code for an ISAPI DLL that implements a Web calculator identical to the one shown in Figure 5-2. The heart of the DLL is the *HttpExtensionProc* function, which IIS calls on each and every request. The *pECB* parameter points to a structure containing information about the request, including a pointer to the query string (if any) accompanying the request. If the query string is empty, this implementation of *HttpExtensionProc* returns an HTML page depicting an empty calculator. Following a postback, however, it parses the *op1* and *op2* parameters from the query string and returns an HTML page that includes the sum of the inputs. In other words, it returns precisely the HTML we set as our goal a moment ago.

Calc.cpp
```
#include <windows.h>
#include <httpext.h>
#include <string.h>
#include <stdlib.h>
```

Figure 5-4   Source code for an ISAPI DLL.

```
int GetParameter (LPSTR pszQueryString, LPSTR pszParameterName);

BOOL WINAPI DllMain (HINSTANCE hInstance, DWORD fdwReason,
    LPVOID lpvReserved)
{
    return (TRUE);
}

BOOL WINAPI GetExtensionVersion (HSE_VERSION_INFO* pVer)
{
    pVer->dwExtensionVersion =
        MAKELONG (HSE_VERSION_MINOR, HSE_VERSION_MAJOR);
    lstrcpy (pVer->lpszExtensionDesc, "Calc ISAPI Extension");
    return (TRUE);
}

DWORD WINAPI HttpExtensionProc (EXTENSION_CONTROL_BLOCK* pECB)
{
    static char* szPrePostbackMessage =
        "<html>\r\n"                                       \
        "<body>\r\n"                                       \
        "<form>\r\n"                                       \
        "<input type=\"text\" name=\"op1\" />\r\n"         \
        "+\r\n"                                            \
        "<input type=\"text\" name=\"op2\" />\r\n"         \
        "<input type=\"submit\" value=\"  =  \" />\r\n"    \
        "</form>\r\n"                                      \
        "</body>\r\n"                                      \
        "</html>";

    static char* szPostPostbackMessage =
        "<html>\r\n"                                                 \
        "<body>\r\n"                                                 \
        "<form>\r\n"                                                 \
        "<input type=\"text\" name=\"op1\" value=\"%d\" />\r\n"      \
        "+\r\n"                                                      \
        "<input type=\"text\" name=\"op2\" value=\"%d\" />\r\n"      \
        "<input type=\"submit\" value=\"  =  \" />\r\n"             \
        "%d\r\n"                                                     \
        "</form>\r\n"                                                \
        "</body>\r\n"                                                \
        "</html>";

    //
    // Build the response message body.
    //
    char szMessage[512];

    if (lstrlen (pECB->lpszQueryString) == 0) {
        // If the query string is empty, return a page that shows
        // an empty calculator.
        lstrcpy (szMessage, szPrePostbackMessage);
    }
    else {
        // If the query string is not empty, extract the user input,
```

(continued)

Calc.cpp *(continued)*

```cpp
        // process it, and return a page that shows inputs and outputs.
        int a = GetParameter (pECB->lpszQueryString, "op1");
        int b = GetParameter (pECB->lpszQueryString, "op2");
        wsprintf (szMessage, szPostPostbackMessage, a, b, a + b);
    }

    //
    // Build the response message header.
    //
    char szHeader[128];
    DWORD dwCount = lstrlen (szMessage);

    wsprintf (szHeader, "Content-type: text/html\r\n" \
        "Content-Length: %lu\r\n\r\n", dwCount);

    //
    // Output the response message header.
    //
    HSE_SEND_HEADER_EX_INFO shei;
    shei.pszStatus = "200 OK";
    shei.pszHeader = szHeader;
    shei.cchStatus = lstrlen (shei.pszStatus);
    shei.cchHeader = lstrlen (shei.pszHeader);
    shei.fKeepConn = FALSE;

    pECB->ServerSupportFunction (pECB->ConnID,
        HSE_REQ_SEND_RESPONSE_HEADER_EX, &shei, NULL, NULL);

    //
    // Output the response message body.
    //
    pECB->WriteClient (pECB->ConnID, szMessage, &dwCount, 0);

    //
    // Indicate that the request was processed successfully.
    //
    return HSE_STATUS_SUCCESS;
}

int GetParameter (LPSTR pszQueryString, LPSTR pszParameterName)
{
    char* p = strstr (pszQueryString, pszParameterName);

    if (p != NULL) {
        p += strlen (pszParameterName) + 1;
        for (char* tmp = p; *tmp != '&' && *tmp != 0; tmp++)
            ;
        int len = tmp - p;
        char* buffer = new char[len + 1];
        strncpy (buffer, p, len);
        int val = atoi (buffer);
        delete buffer;
        return val;
    }
    return 0;
}
```

The Active Server Pages Solution

A third solution to the problem of processing input from HTML forms on Web servers, and the one that made Windows a popular platform for Web applications in the second half of the 1990s, is Active Server Pages (ASP). Active Server Pages lower the barrier to entry for Web developers by allowing HTML and server-side script to be freely mixed in ASP files. Scripts are typically written in JScript (Microsoft's version of JavaScript) or VBScript, but they can be written in other languages as well. Intrinsic objects available to those scripts abstract the low-level details of HTTP and make it exceedingly easy to write code that generates HTML content dynamically. Just how easy is ASP? Compare the code in Figures 5-4 and 5-5 and judge for yourself.

When an Active Server Page is requested, ASP parses the page and executes any scripts contained inside it. Scripts access the input accompanying the request by using the ASP *Request* object, and they write HTML to the HTTP response using the ASP *Response* object. Figure 5-5 shows the ASP version of Calc.html. The VBScript between <% and %> tags checks the incoming request for inputs named *op1* and *op2*. If the inputs aren't present, an empty calculator is rendered back to the client. If the inputs are present—that is, if *Request ("op1")* and *Request ("op2")* evaluate to non-null strings—the server-side script converts the inputs to integers, adds them together, converts the result to a string, and writes the string to the HTTP response using *Response.Write*.

To prevent the numbers typed into the text boxes from disappearing following a postback, Calc.asp uses ASP's inline output syntax (<%= ... %>) to initialize the *Value* attributes returned in the <input type="text"> tags. When the page is first requested from the server, *Request ("op1")* and *Request ("op2")* return empty strings, so the tags output to the client produce empty text boxes:

```
<input type="text" name="op1" value=""/>
<input type="text" name="op2" value=""/>
```

But when the form is rendered again following a postback, *Request ("op1")* and *Request ("op2")* return the values input by the user and are echoed to the client in the tags' *Value* attributes:

```
<input type="text" name="op1" value="2"/>
<input type="text" name="op2" value="2"/>
```

To verify that this is the case, drop Calc.asp into \Inetpub\wwwroot and bring it up by typing *http://localhost/calc.asp*. Then enter a couple of numbers, click the = button, and use the View/Source command in Internet Explorer to view the HTML returned by ASP.

The appeal of ASP—and the reason it caught on so quickly after its introduction in 1996—is that it provides an easy-to-use model for dynamically generating HTML on Web servers. ASP provides a higher level of abstraction than either CGI or ISAPI, which means a flatter learning curve and faster time to market. And ASP integrates seamlessly with ActiveX Data Objects (ADO), which makes it a great solution for writing Web apps that interact with back-end databases.

```
Calc.asp
<%@ Language="VBScript" %>

<html>
  <body>
    <form>
      <input type="text" name="op1" value="<%= Request ("op1") %>"/>
      +
      <input type="text" name="op2" value="<%= Request ("op2") %>" />
      <input type="submit" value="  =  " />
      <%
        If Request ("op1") <> "" And Request ("op2") <> "" Then
            a = CInt (Request ("op1"))
            b = CInt (Request ("op2"))
            Response.Write (CStr (a + b))
        End If
      %>
    </form>
  </body>
</html>
```

Figure 5-5   ASP calculator applet.

Your First Web Form

ASP is a fine solution for performing server-side processing of HTML form input and dynamically generating HTML, but despite its youth, ASP has already grown long in the tooth. What's wrong with ASP? For starters, it's slow. ASP scripts are interpreted rather than compiled, so you incur the cost of recompiling your scripts on each and every page access. Another problem is that ASP lacks a true encapsulation model. It's not possible, for example, to build reusable ASP controls that encapsulate complex rendering and behavioral logic without resorting to COM.

Enter ASP.NET Web forms. Web forms bring object-oriented programming to the Web. They also combine ASP's ease of use with the speed of compiled code. Figure 5-6 holds the source code for the Web Forms version of Calc.asp. The .aspx file name extension identifies the file as an ASP.NET resource. Figure 5-7 shows how Calc.aspx appears in Internet Explorer. Here's how to run it on your PC:

1.   Copy Calc.aspx to your PC's \Inetpub\wwwroot directory.

2. Start Internet Explorer or the browser of your choice and type *http:/
/localhost/calc.aspx* in the browser's address bar. The Web form will
appear in the browser window.

3. Type 2 and 2 into the input fields and click the = button. The number
4 should appear to the right of the button.

The \Inetpub\wwwroot directory is an IIS virtual directory; it's created
automatically when you install IIS. If you'd prefer not to clutter \Inet-
pub\wwwroot, you can set up virtual directories of your own using the Internet
Services Manager applet found under Administrative Tools. You could, for
example, put Calc.aspx in a directory named Samples and make Samples a virtual directory. If you assign the Samples directory the logical name "Samples"
(virtual directory names don't have to equal physical directory names, although
they often do), you'd run Calc by typing *http://localhost/samples/calc.aspx* in
the browser's address bar. The same goes for other ASPX files presented in this
chapter and throughout the remainder of the book.

Calc.aspx
```
<html>
  <body>
    <form runat="server">
      <asp:TextBox ID="op1" RunAt="server" />
      +
      <asp:TextBox ID="op2" RunAt="server" />
      <asp:Button Text="  =  " OnClick="OnAdd" RunAt="server" />
      <asp:Label ID="Sum" RunAt="server" />
    </form>
  </body>
</html>

<script language="C#" runat="server">
  void OnAdd (Object sender, EventArgs e)
  {
      int a = Convert.ToInt32 (op1.Text);
      int b = Convert.ToInt32 (op2.Text);
      Sum.Text = (a + b).ToString ();
  }
</script>
```

Figure 5-6   ASP.NET Web form calculator.

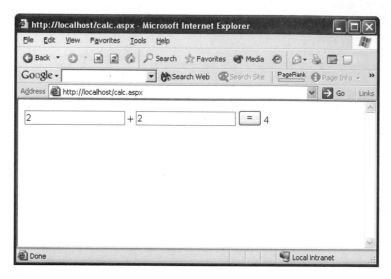

Figure 5-7   Calc.aspx in action.

Web forms are built from a combination of HTML and server controls. Calc.aspx contains four server controls: two *TextBox* controls, a *Button* control, and a *Label* control. *TextBox*, *Button*, and *Label* are classes defined in the *System.Web.UI.WebControls* namespace in the .NET Framework class library (FCL). Each time Calc.aspx is requested, ASP.NET instantiates *TextBox*, *Button*, and *Label* objects and asks each object to render itself into HTML. The HTML returned by the controls is included in the HTTP response. Execute a View/ Source command while Calc.aspx is displayed in Internet Explorer and you'll see the following HTML:

```
<html>
  <body>
    <form name="_ctl0" method="post" action="calc.aspx" id="_ctl0">
      <input type="hidden" name="__VIEWSTATE" value="dDwx0TE0NDY40DE20zs+" />

      <input name="op1" type="text" id="op1" />
      +
      <input name="op2" type="text" id="op2" />
      <input type="submit" name="_ctl1" value="  =  " />
      <span id="Sum"></span>
    </form>
  </body>
</html>
```

The *TextBox* controls turned into <input type="text"> tags, the *Button* control turned into an <input type="submit"> tag, and the *Label* control turned into a

<span> tag. In effect, these controls "project" a user interface to the browser by rendering themselves into HTML.

What about the <input> tag named __VIEWSTATE in the HTML returned by Calc.aspx? That's the mechanism ASP.NET uses to round-trip data from the server to the client and back to the server again. You'll learn all about it in Chapter 8.

Control Properties

Server controls do more than render HTML. They also implement methods, properties, and events that make them highly programmable. For example, *TextBox*, *Button*, and *Label* controls each expose text through a read/write property named *Text*. If you wanted "2" to appear in the *TextBox* controls by default, you could modify the control tags as follows:

```
<asp:TextBox Text="2" ID="op1" RunAt="server" />
<asp:TextBox Text="2" ID="op2" RunAt="server" />
```

Any public property that a control implements and that can be represented as a name/value pair can be initialized by using the property name as an attribute in the tag that declares the control.

Properties can also be accessed from server-side scripts. In Calc.aspx, the server-side script is the code that appears between the <script> and </script> tags. The statements

```
int a = Convert.ToInt32 (op1.Text);
int b = Convert.ToInt32 (op2.Text);
```

extract user input from the *TextBox* controls by reading their *Text* properties, while the statement

```
Sum.Text = (a + b).ToString ();
```

displays the sum of the inputs by writing to the *Label* control's *Text* property. The names *op1*, *op2*, and *Sum* are the controls' programmatic IDs. Control IDs are defined by including *ID* attributes in control tags. In Calc.aspx, the *Label* control serves as a placeholder for the Web form's output. Because the default value of a *Label* control's *Text* property is an empty string, nothing appears in the form where the *Label* control is positioned until the server-side script assigns a string to the control's *Text* property.

Control Events

The ability to encapsulate complex rendering and behavioral logic in reusable control classes is one of the fundamental tenets of the Web Forms programming model. Another is the use of events and event handling. Most server controls fire events in response to user input. *Button* controls, for example, fire *Click* events when they're clicked. Wiring an event to an event handler is accomplished by prefixing the event name with "On" and using the resulting text as an attribute in the tag that declares the control. In Calc.aspx, the statement

```
<asp:Button Text="  =  " OnClick="OnAdd" RunAt="server" />
```

serves the dual purpose of declaring a *Button* control and designating *OnAdd* as the handler for the *Button* control's *Click* events. That's why the code in *OnAdd* executed when you clicked the = button. Knowing this, it's a simple matter to consult the documentation for the list of events a control is capable of firing and connecting handlers to the events that interest you.

What happens under the hood to support the Web Forms event model is a little more complex. Look again at the HTML returned by Calc.aspx. Notice that it contains an HTML form and a submit button. Clicking the button posts the form back to the server using an HTTP POST. Recognizing that the POST command represents a postback that occurred because the user clicked the = button, ASP.NET notifies the *Button* object and the *Button* responds by firing a *Click* event on the server. ASP.NET subsequently calls *OnAdd* and then renders the page again into HTML. Because the *Label* control's *Text* property now has a non-null string assigned to it, this time the HTML output by the *Label* control includes a text string between the <span> and </span> tags.

Implementation Notes

Calc.aspx contains no code to prevent the numbers typed into the *TextBox* controls from disappearing following a postback. The <asp:TextBox> tags in Figure 5-6 lack *Value* attributes such as the ones in Figure 5-5's <input type= "text"> tags. Yet the inputs don't disappear when you click the = button. Why? Because *TextBox* controls automatically persist their contents across postbacks. Check the HTML returned to the browser following the postback and you'll find that <input type="text"> tags rendered by the *TextBox* controls have *Value* attributes that equal the text typed by the user.

To make Calc.aspx as simple as possible, I purposely omitted error checking code. To see what I mean, type something other than a simple integer value (say, "hello") into one of the text boxes and click the = button. The page you see is ASP.NET's way of responding to unhandled exceptions. To prevent this error, rewrite Calc.aspx's *OnAdd* method as follows:

```
void OnAdd (Object sender, EventArgs e)
{
    try {
        int a = Convert.ToInt32 (op1.Text);
        int b = Convert.ToInt32 (op2.Text);
        Sum.Text = (a + b).ToString ();
    }
    catch (FormatException) {
```

```
        Sum.Text = "Error";
    }
}
```

This version of *OnAdd* catches the exception thrown when *Convert.ToInt32* is unable to convert the input to an integer and responds by displaying the word "Error" to the right of the push button.

The Web Forms Programming Model

Calc.aspx demonstrates three important principles of the Web Forms programming model:

- A Web form's user interface is "declared" using a combination of HTML and server controls. Controls can be customized by using control properties as attributes in the tags that declare the controls. Controls are also bona fide objects that are instantiated and executed each time the page that hosts them is requested.

- Server controls fire events that can be handled by server-side scripts. In effect, ASP.NET abstracts the divide between client and server by creating the illusion that events are fired and handled on the same machine. In reality, events fire on the server when an external stimulus (such as the click of a button) causes the form to post back to the server.

- Server-side scripts aren't scripts in the conventional sense of the word. Unlike ASP scripts, which are interpreted rather than compiled and therefore run rather slowly, server-side scripts in ASP.NET are compiled to common intermediate language (CIL) and executed by the common language runtime. Although ASP.NET pages incur more processing overhead than static HTML pages, they tend to execute much faster than ASP pages.

You probably noticed the *RunAt*="server" attributes sprinkled throughout Calc.aspx. *RunAt*="server" is the key that unlocks the door to the magic of Web forms; it signals ASP.NET to "execute" the tag rather than treat it as static HTML. *RunAt*="server" is not optional. It must be used in every tag that ASP.NET is to process, including the <form> tag that marks the beginning of a form containing server controls.

Web Controls

TextBox, *Button*, and *Label* are server controls. They're also examples of *Web controls*—server controls defined in the FCL's *System.Web.UI.WebControls* namespace. The Web controls family includes almost 30 different control types that you can use in ASP.NET Web forms. The following table lists the Web controls provided in version 1 of the .NET Framework class library:

Web Controls

Class Name	Description
AdRotator	Displays rotating banners in Web forms
Button	Generates submit buttons
Calendar	Displays calendars with selectable dates
CheckBox	Displays a check box in a Web form
CheckBoxList	Displays a group of check boxes
CompareValidator	Validates user input by comparing it to another value
CustomValidator	Validates user input using the algorithm of your choice
DataGrid	Displays data in tabular format
DataList	Displays items in single-column or multicolumn lists using HTML templates
DropDownList	Generates HTML drop-down lists
HyperLink	Generates hyperlinks
Image	Displays images in Web forms
ImageButton	Displays graphical push buttons
Label	Generates programmable text fields
LinkButton	Generates hyperlinks that post back to the server
ListBox	Generates HTML list boxes
Literal	Generates literal text in a Web form
Panel	Groups other controls
RadioButton	Displays a radio button in a Web form
RadioButtonList	Displays a group of check boxes
RangeValidator	Verifies that user input falls within a specified range
RegularExpressionValidator	Validates user input using regular expressions
Repeater	Displays items using HTML templates
RequiredFieldValidator	Verifies that an input field isn't empty
Table	Generates HTML tables
TextBox	Generates text input fields

(continued)

Web Controls   *(continued)*

Class Name	Description
ValidationSummary	Displays a summary of validation errors
Xml	Displays XML documents and optionally formats them using XSLT

Some Web controls are simple devices that produce equally simple HTML. Others produce more complex HTML, and some even return client-side script. *Calendar* controls, for example, emit a rich mixture of HTML and JavaScript. It's not easy to add a calendar to a Web page by hand (especially if you want dates in the calendar to be clickable), but calendars are no big deal in Web forms: you simply include an <asp:Calendar> tag in an ASPX file. *DataGrid* is another example of a sophisticated control type. One *DataGrid* control can replace reams of old ASP code that queries a database and returns the results in a richly formatted HTML table. You'll learn all about the *DataGrid* and other Web controls in the next chapter.

HTML Controls

Most Web forms are built from Web controls, but ASP.NET supports a second type of server control called *HTML controls*. HTML controls are instances of classes defined in the FCL's *System.Web.UI.HtmlControls* namespace. They're declared by adding *RunAt*="server" (or, if you'd prefer, *runat*="server"; capitalization doesn't matter in HTML) attributes to ordinary HTML tags. For example, the statement

```
<input type="text" />
```

declares a standard HTML text input field. However, the statement

```
<input type="text" runat="server" />
```

declares an HTML control—specifically, an instance of *System.Web.UI.HtmlControls.HtmlInputText*. At run time, ASP.NET sees the *runat*="server" attribute and creates an *HtmlInputText* object. The *HtmlInputText* object, in turn, emits an <input type="text"> tag that's ultimately returned to the browser.

Without realizing it, you used an HTML control in Calc.aspx. The line

```
<form runat="server">
```

caused an instance of *System.Web.UI.HtmlControls.HtmlForm* to be created on the server. *HtmlForm* returned the <form> tag that you saw when you viewed the page's HTML source code with the View/Source command:

```
<form name="_ctl0" method="post" action="calc.aspx" id="_ctl0">
```

HtmlInputText and *HtmlForm* are but two of many controls defined in the *System.Web.UI.HtmlControls* namespace. The following table lists all the HTML controls that the FCL supports and the tags that produce them.

HTML Controls

Tag	Corresponding HTML Control
<a runat="server">	*HtmlAnchor*
<button runat="server">	*HtmlButton*
<form runat="server">	*HtmlForm*
<img runat="server">	*HtmlImage*
<input type="button" runat="server">	*HtmlInputButton*
<input type="reset" runat="server">	*HtmlInputButton*
<input type="submit" runat="server">	*HtmlInputButton*
<input type="checkbox" runat="server">	*HtmlInputCheckBox*
<input type="file" runat="server">	*HtmlInputFile*
<input type="hidden" runat="server">	*HtmlInputHidden*
<input type="image" runat="server">	*HtmlInputImage*
<input type="radio" runat="server">	*HtmlInputRadioButton*
<input type="password" runat="server">	*HtmlInputText*
<input type="text" runat="server">	*HtmlInputText*
<select runat="server">	*HtmlSelect*
<table runat="server">	*HtmlTable*
<td runat="server">	*HtmlTableCell*
<th runat="server">	*HtmlTableCell*
<tr runat="server">	*HtmlTableRow*
<textarea runat="server">	*HtmlTextArea*
Any other tag with *runat*="server"	*HtmlGenericControl*

It's important to know which *HtmlControls* class corresponds to a given HTML tag because only by knowing the class name can you consult the documentation to determine which properties you can use with that tag and which events the resulting control fires. For example, here's the HTML controls version of Calc.aspx:

```
<html>
  <body>
    <form runat="server">
      <input type="text" id="op1" runat="server" />
```

```
        +
        <input type="text" id="op2" runat="server" />
        <input type="submit" value="  =  " OnServerClick="OnAdd"
          runat="server" />
        <span id="Sum" runat="server" />
     </form>
  </body>
</html>

<script language="C#" runat="server">
  void OnAdd (Object sender, EventArgs e)
  {
      int a = Convert.ToInt32 (op1.Value);
      int b = Convert.ToInt32 (op2.Value);
      Sum.InnerText = (a + b).ToString ();
  }
</script>
```

Besides the different way in which the form's controls are declared, the HTML controls version of this Web form differs from the Web controls version in three important respects:

- The attribute that wires the button control to the event handler is named *OnServerClick* rather than *OnClick*. Why? Because an <input type="button" runat="server" /> tag translates into an instance of *HtmlInputButton*, and *HtmlInputButton* controls, unlike *Button* controls, don't fire *Click* events. They fire *ServerClick* events.

- *OnAdd* reads input from the text boxes using the property name *Value* rather than *Text*. *HtmlInputText* controls don't have *Text* properties as *Label*s and *TextBox*es do; instead, they expose their contents using *Value* properties.

- *OnAdd* writes its output by initializing *Sum*'s *InnerText* property instead of its *Text* property. The <span runat="server"> tag creates an instance of *HtmlGenericControl*. *HtmlGenericControl* doesn't have a *Text* property, but it does have an *InnerText* property.

Once you know which class ASP.NET instantiates as a result of applying a *runat*="server" tag to an otherwise ordinary HTML tag, you can figure out from the documentation what the tag's programmatic interface looks like.

Why does ASP.NET support HTML controls when Web controls do everything HTML controls do and then some? HTML controls simplify the task of turning existing HTML forms into Web forms. It takes a while to convert a couple of hundred <input> tags and <select> tags and other HTML tags into Web controls. It doesn't take long to add *runat*="server" to each of them.

Page-Level Events

Server controls that render HTML and fire events are a cornerstone of the Web Forms programming model, but controls aren't the only entities that fire events. Pages do, too. To understand page-level events, it helps to understand what goes on behind the scenes when ASP.NET processes the first HTTP request for an ASPX file:

1. It creates a temporary file containing a class derived from *System.Web.UI.Page*. The *Page* class is one of the most important classes in ASP.NET; it represents ASP.NET Web pages.

2. ASP.NET copies the code in the ASPX file, as well as some code of its own, to the *Page*-derived class. A method named *OnAdd* in a <script> block in an ASPX file becomes a member method of the derived class.

3. ASP.NET compiles the derived class and places the resulting DLL in a system folder. The DLL is cached so that steps 1 and 2 won't have to be repeated unless the contents of the ASPX file change.

4. ASP.NET instantiates the derived class and "executes" it by calling a series of methods on it. It is during this execution phase that the *Page* object instantiates any controls declared inside it and solicits their output.

As a *Page* object executes, it fires a series of events that can be processed by server-side scripts. The most important are *Init*, which is fired when the page is first instantiated, and *Load*, which is fired after the page's controls are initialized but before the page renders any output. The *Load* event is particularly important to ASP.NET developers because a *Load* handler is the perfect place to initialize any controls that require dynamic (that is, run-time) initialization. The next section offers an example.

If you want to see the DLLs that ASP.NET generates from your ASPX files, you'll find them in subdirectories under the Windows (or Winnt) directory's Microsoft.NET\Framework\v*n.n.nnnn*\Temporary ASP.NET Files subdirectory, where *n.n.nnnn* is the version number of the .NET Framework installed on your PC. Drill down in the directory tree under Temporary ASP.NET Files\root, for example, and you'll find a DLL containing the class that ASP.NET derived from *Page* to serve Calc.aspx (assuming you ran Calc.aspx from \Inetpub\wwwroot). If the subdirectory contains several DLLs, open them with ILDASM, and you'll find one containing a *Page*-derived class named *Calc_aspx*. (See Figure 5-8.) That's the class ASP.NET instantiates each time a request arrives for Calc.aspx. If Calc.aspx changes, ASP.NET recompiles the DLL on the next request. Otherwise, the DLL remains on your hard disk so that ASP.NET can reuse it as needed.

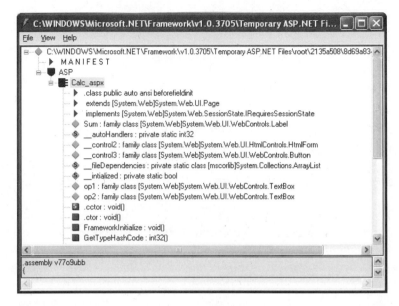

Figure 5-8   DLL generated from Calc.aspx.

The *Page.Load* Event and the *Page.IsPostBack* Property

Suppose you want to build a Web form that displays today's date and the four days following it in a drop-down list. If today is January 1, 2002, one solution is to statically initialize a *DropDownList* control:

```
<asp:DropDownList ID="MyList" RunAt="server">
  <asp:ListItem Text="January 1, 2002" RunAt="server" />
  <asp:ListItem Text="January 2, 2002" RunAt="server" />
  <asp:ListItem Text="January 3, 2002" RunAt="server" />
  <asp:ListItem Text="January 4, 2002" RunAt="server" />
  <asp:ListItem Text="January 5, 2002" RunAt="server" />
</asp:DropDownList>
```

The problem with this approach is obvious: every day you'll have to modify the form to update the dates. A smarter approach is to write a handler for the page's *Load* event that initializes the *DropDownList* at run time:

```
<asp:DropDownList ID="MyList" RunAt="server" />
  .
  .
  .
<script language="C#" runat="server">
  void Page_Load (Object sender, EventArgs e)
  {
```

(continued)

```
    if (!IsPostBack) {
        for (int i=0; i<5; i++) {
            DateTime date =
                DateTime.Today + new TimeSpan (i, 0, 0, 0);
            MyList.Items.Add (date.ToString ("MMMM dd, yyyy"));
        }
    }
}
</script>
```

A *Page_Load* method prototyped this way is automatically called by ASP.NET when the page fires a *Load* event. You don't have to manually wire the event to the handler as you do for controls. The same is true for all page-level events. You can respond to any event fired by *Page* by writing a method named *Page_EventName*, where *EventName* is the name of the event you want to handle.

The *Page_Load* handler in the previous example adds items to the *DropDownList* by calling *Add* on the control's *Items* collection. *Items* represents the items in the *DropDownList*. Significantly, this implementation of *Page_Load* initializes the control only if a value named *IsPostBack* is false. *IsPostBack* is one of several properties defined in the *Page* class. Because all code in an ASPX file executes in the context of a class derived from *Page*, your code enjoys intrinsic access to *Page* properties and methods. *IsPostBack* is a particularly important property because it reveals whether your code is executing because the page was requested from the Web server with an HTTP GET (*IsPostBack*==false) or because the page was posted back to the server (*IsPostBack*==true). In general, you don't want to initialize a Web control during a postback because ASP.NET maintains the control's state for you. If you call *Add* on the control's *Items* collection the first time the page is fetched and then call it again when the page is posted back, the control will have twice as many items in it following the first postback.

The *Page.Init* Event

Page_Load methods are handy for performing run-time control initializations. You can also write *Page_Init* methods that fire in response to *Init* events. One use for *Init* events is to create controls and add them to the page at run time. Another is to programmatically wire events to event handlers. For example, instead of connecting *Click* events to an event handler with an *OnClick* attribute, like this:

```
<asp:Button Text="  =  " OnClick="OnAdd" RunAt="server" />
    .
    .
    .
<script language="C#" runat="server">
```

```
    void OnAdd (Object sender, EventArgs e)
    {
        int a = Convert.ToInt32 (op1.Text);
        int b = Convert.ToInt32 (op2.Text);
        Sum.Text = (a + b).ToString ();
    }
</script>
```

you could connect them programmatically in this manner:

```
<asp:Button Text="  =  " ID="EqualsButton" RunAt="server" />
    .
    .
    .
<script language="C#" runat="server">
  void Page_Init (Object sender, EventArgs e)
  {
      EqualsButton.Click += new EventHandler (OnAdd);
  }

  void OnAdd (Object sender, EventArgs e)
  {
      int a = Convert.ToInt32 (op1.Text);
      int b = Convert.ToInt32 (op2.Text);
      Sum.Text = (a + b).ToString ();
  }
</script>
```

This is the technique that Visual Studio .NET uses to wire events to event handlers. You'll see an example at the end of this chapter when you build a Web Forms application with Visual Studio .NET.

Page-Level Directives

ASP.NET supports a number of commands called *page-level directives* that you can put in ASPX files. They're sometimes called @ *directives* because all directive names begin with an @ sign: @ *Page*, @ *Import*, and so on. Page-level directives appear between <% and %> symbols and must be positioned at the top of an ASPX file. In practice, @ directives appear in all but the simplest of ASPX files. The following table lists the directives that ASP.NET supports. Succeeding sections document the most commonly used directives. Other directives are discussed as circumstances warrant elsewhere in the book.

ASP.NET @ Directives

Directive	Description
@ Page	Defines general attributes and compilation settings for ASPX files
@ Control	Defines general attributes and compilation settings for ASCX files

(continued)

ASP.NET @ Directives *(continued)*

Directive	Description
@ Import	Imports a namespace
@ Assembly	Enables linkage to assemblies not linked to by default
@ Register	Registers user controls and custom controls for use in a Web form
@ OutputCache	Exerts declarative control over page caching and fragment caching
@ Reference	Adds a reference to an external ASPX or ASCX file
@ Implements	Identifies an interface implemented by a Web page

The *@ Page* Directive

Of the various page-level directives that ASP.NET supports, *@ Page* is the one used most often. The following *@ Page* directive changes the default language for all scripts that don't specify otherwise from Visual Basic .NET to C#. It's especially useful when you "inline" code in an ASPX file by placing it between <% and %> tags:

```
<%@ Page Language="C#" %>
```

And here's an ASPX file that uses it:

```
<%@ Page Language="C#" %>

<html>
  <body>
    <%
      Response.Write ("Hello, world");
    %>
  </body>
</html>
```

As this example demonstrates, ASP.NET pages can use *Response* and other intrinsic objects in the same way ASP pages can. Because you can't include *Language*="C#" attributes in <% %> blocks, you either need an *@ Page* directive telling ASP.NET which compiler to pass your code to or a Web.config file that changes the default language on a directory-wide basis. (If you're not familiar with Web.config files just yet, don't worry about it for now. You'll learn all about them in Chapter 9.)

Another common use for *@ Page* directives is to enable debugging support. By default, ASP.NET builds release-build DLLs from your ASPX files. If you encounter a run-time error and need to debug it, you need DLLs with debugging symbols. The statement

```
<%@ Page Debug="true" %>
```

commands ASP.NET to create debug DLLs rather than release DLLs and enriches the information available to you when you debug a malfunctioning Web form.

As you can see, *@ Page* is overloaded to support a variety of uses. In all, it supports some 28 different attributes such as *Language* and *Debug*. A page can have only one *@ Page* directive, but that directive can contain any number of attributes. For example, the statement

```
<%@ Page Language="C#" Debug="true" %>
```

enables debugging and sets the page's default language to C#.

The *@ Import* Directive

Next to *@ Page*, the directive that ASP.NET programmers use the most is *@ Import*. The *@ Import* directive is ASP.NET's equivalent of C#'s *using* directive. Its purpose is to import a namespace so that the types in that namespace are known to the compiler. You need *@ Import* any time you use an FCL data type that's defined in a namespace that ASP.NET doesn't import by default. For example, the statement

```
<%@ Import Namespace="System.Data" %>
```

makes all the data types defined in *System.Data* available to a Web form.

What namespaces does ASP.NET import by default? Here's a complete list:

- *System*
- *System.Collections*
- *System.Collections.Specialized*
- *System.Configuration*
- *System.IO*
- *System.Text*
- *System.Text.RegularExpressions*
- *System.Web*
- *System.Web.Caching*
- *System.Web.Security*
- *System.Web.SessionState*
- *System.Web.UI*
- *System.Web.UI.HtmlControls*
- *System.Web.UI.WebControls*

Because *System.Data* isn't imported automatically, you must import it yourself if you want to use *System.Data* types (for example, *DataSet*) in a Web form. Otherwise, you'll receive an error message the first time ASP.NET attempts to compile the page. *System.Web.Mail* is another example of a commonly used namespace that isn't imported automatically. Look back at Chapter 3's SendMail program (Figure 3-7), and you'll see an *@ Import* statement importing *System.Web.Mail* on the very first line of the ASPX file.

Unlike *@ Page*, *@ Import* can appear multiple times in a Web page. The following statements import three namespaces and are often used together in ASPX files that access SQL Server databases:

```
<%@ Import Namespace="System.Data" %>
<%@ Import Namespace="System.Data.SqlClient" %>
<%@ Import Namespace="System.Data.SqlTypes" %>
```

The *@ Assembly* Directive

The *@ Import* directive identifies namespaces containing an application's data types; *@ Assembly* identifies assemblies. The .NET Framework class library is implemented in a series of single-file assemblies: Mscorlib.dll, System.dll, and others. If ASP.NET is to compile your page, it must know which assemblies the page references so that it can provide that information to the compiler. The following assembly names are provided to the compiler by default and therefore require no *@ Assembly* directive:

- Mscorlib.dll

- System.dll

- System.Data.dll

- System.Drawing.dll

- System.EnterpriseServices.dll

- System.Web.dll

- System.Web.Services.dll

- System.Xml.dll

These assemblies include the data types that Web forms are most likely to use. But suppose you want to use the FCL's *System.DirectoryServices.DirectorySearcher* class in a <script> block to perform a query against Active Directory. Because *DirectorySearcher* lives in an assembly (System.DirectoryServices.dll) that ASP.NET doesn't reference by default, its use requires an *@ Assembly* directive. In the following example, *@ Import* is required also because *DirectorySearcher* is defined in a nondefault namespace:

```
<%@ Import Namespace="System.DirectoryServices" %>
<%@ Assembly Name="System.DirectoryServices" %>
```

It's coincidental that the namespace name and assembly name are one and the same; that's not always the case. Note that an assembly name passed to @ *Assembly* must *not* include the filename extension (.dll). In addition, the list of "default" assemblies can be changed by editing a machine-wide configuration file named Machine.config or augmented by dropping a Web.config file containing an <assemblies> section into an application root. Like @ *Import*, @ *Assembly* can appear multiple times in a Web page.

The @ *OutputCache* Directive

One of the best ways to optimize the performance of ASP.NET applications is to cache Web pages generated from ASPX files so that they can be delivered straight from the cache if they're requested again. ASP.NET supports two forms of caching: *page caching*, which caches entire pages, and *fragment* (or *subpage*) *caching*, which caches portions of pages. The @ *OutputCache* directive enables an application to exert declarative control over page and fragment caching.

Because examples have a way of lending clarity to a subject (funny how that works, isn't it?), here's a simple one that demonstrates @ *OutputCache*:

```
<%@ Page Language="C#" %>
<%@ OutputCache Duration="60" VaryByParam="None" %>

<html>
  <body>
    Today is <%= DateTime.Now.ToLongDateString () %>
  </body>
</html>
```

This ASPX file displays today's date in a Web page. (The <%= ... %> syntax is an alternative to using *Response.Write*. It's an easy way to inject text into the page's output.) Since today's date changes only every 24 hours, it's wasteful to reexecute this page every time it's requested. Therefore, the page includes an @ *OutputCache* directive that caches the output for 60 seconds at a time. Subsequent requests for the page come straight from the cache. When the cache expires and ASP.NET receives another request for the page, ASP.NET reexecutes (and recaches) the page. The *Duration* attribute controls the length of time that the cached page output is valid.

In real life, Web pages are rarely this simple. The output from an ASPX file often varies based on input provided by users. The designers of ASP.NET anticipated this and gave the page cache the ability to hold multiple versions of a page, qualified by the user input that produced each version. Imagine, for example, that you wrote a Web form that takes a city name and state name as input and returns a satellite image of that city from a database. (Sound far-fetched? It's not. Chapter 11 includes an application that does just that.) If the city and state names accompanying each request are transmitted in variables called *city* and *state*, the following directive caches a different version of the page for each city and state requested for up to 1 hour:

```
<%@ OutputCache Duration="3600" VaryByParam="city;state" %>
```

It's that simple. You can even use a shortened form of the *VaryByParam* attribute to cache a separate version of the page for *every* different input:

```
<%@ OutputCache Duration="3600" VaryByParam="*" %>
```

Now if two users request a satellite image of Knoxville, Tennessee, 30 minutes apart, the second of the two requests will be fulfilled very quickly.

A Web Forms Currency Converter

Figure 5-9 shows a Web form that performs currency conversions using exchange rates stored in an XML file. To see it in action, copy Converter.aspx and Rates.xml, which are listed in Figures 5-10 and 5-11, to \Inetpub\wwwroot and type *http://localhost/converter.aspx* in your browser's address bar. Then pick a currency, enter an amount in U.S. dollars, and click the Convert button to convert dollars to the currency of your choice.

Here are some points of interest regarding the source code:

■ Because it uses the *DataSet* class defined in the *System.Data* namespace, Converter.aspx begins with an @ *Import* directive importing *System.Data*.

■ Rather than show a hard-coded list of currency types in the list box, Converter.aspx reads them from Rates.xml. *Page_Load* reads the XML file and initializes the list box. To add new currency types to the application, simply add new *Rate* elements to Rates.xml. They'll automatically appear in the list box the next time the page is fetched.

■ For good measure, Converter.aspx wires the Convert button to the *Click* handler named *OnConvert* programmatically rather than declaratively. The wiring is done in *Page_Init*.

Notice how easily Converter.aspx reads XML from Rates.xml. It doesn't parse any XML; it simply calls *ReadXml* on a *DataSet* and provides an XML file name. *ReadXml* parses the file and initializes the *DataSet* with the file's contents. Each *Rate* element in the XML file becomes a row in the *DataSet*, and each row, in turn, contains fields named "Currency" and "Exchange". Enumerating all the currency types is a simple matter of enumerating the *DataSet*'s rows and reading each row's "Currency" field. Retrieving the exchange rate for a given currency is almost as easy. *OnConvert* uses *DataTable.Select* to query the *DataSet* for all rows matching the currency type. Then it reads the Exchange field from the row returned and converts it to a decimal value with *Convert.ToDecimal*.

One reason I decided to use a *DataSet* to read the XML file is that a simple change would enable the Web form to read currencies and exchange rates from a database. Were Converter.aspx to open the XML file and parse it using the FCL's XML classes, more substantial changes would be required to incorporate database input.

A word of caution regarding this Web form: Don't use it to perform real currency conversions! The exchange rates in Rates.xml were accurate when I wrote them, but they'll be outdated by the time you read this. Unless you devise an external mechanism for updating Rates.xml in real time, consider the output from Converter.aspx to be for educational purposes only.

Figure 5-9 Web form currency converter.

Converter.aspx

```
<%@ Import Namespace=System.Data %>

<html>
  <body>
    <h1>Currency Converter</h1>
    <hr>
    <form runat="server">
      Target Currency<br>
      <asp:ListBox ID="Currencies" Width="256" RunAt="server" /><br>
      <br>
      Amount in U.S. Dollars<br>
      <asp:TextBox ID="USD" Width="256" RunAt="server" /><br>
      <br>
```

Figure 5-10 Currency converter source code.

Converter.aspx *(continued)*

```
        <asp:Button Text="Convert" ID="ConvertButton" Width="256"
          RunAt="server" /><br>
        <br>
        <asp:Label ID="Output" RunAt="server" />
    </form>
  </body>
</html>

<script language="C#" runat="server">
  void Page_Init (Object sender, EventArgs e)
  {
      // Wire the Convert button to OnConvert
      ConvertButton.Click += new EventHandler (OnConvert);
  }

  void Page_Load (Object sender, EventArgs e)
  {
      // If this isn't a postback, initialize the ListBox
      if (!IsPostBack) {
          DataSet ds = new DataSet ();
          ds.ReadXml (Server.MapPath ("Rates.xml"));
          foreach (DataRow row in ds.Tables[0].Rows)
              Currencies.Items.Add (row["Currency"].ToString ());
          Currencies.SelectedIndex = 0;
      }
  }

  void OnConvert (Object sender, EventArgs e)
  {
      // Perform the conversion and display the results
      try {
          decimal dollars = Convert.ToDecimal (USD.Text);
          DataSet ds = new DataSet ();
          ds.ReadXml (Server.MapPath ("Rates.xml"));
          DataRow[] rows = ds.Tables[0].Select ("Currency = '" +
              Currencies.SelectedItem.Text + "'");
          decimal rate = Convert.ToDecimal (rows[0]["Exchange"]);
          decimal amount = dollars * rate;
          Output.Text = amount.ToString ("f2");
      }
      catch (FormatException) {
          Output.Text = "Error";
      }
  }
</script>
```

Rates.xml

```xml
<?xml version="1.0"?>
<Rates>
  <Rate>
    <Currency>British Pound</Currency>
    <Exchange>0.698544</Exchange>
  </Rate>
```

Figure 5-11 XML file used by Converter.aspx.

```
<Rate>
  <Currency>Canadian Dollar</Currency>
  <Exchange>1.57315</Exchange>
</Rate>
<Rate>
  <Currency>French Franc</Currency>
  <Exchange>7.32593</Exchange>
</Rate>
<Rate>
  <Currency>German Mark</Currency>
  <Exchange>2.18433</Exchange>
</Rate>
<Rate>
  <Currency>Italian Lira</Currency>
  <Exchange>2162.67</Exchange>
</Rate>
<Rate>
  <Currency>Japanese Yen</Currency>
  <Exchange>122.742</Exchange>
</Rate>
<Rate>
  <Currency>Mexican Peso</Currency>
  <Exchange>9.22841</Exchange>
</Rate>
<Rate>
  <Currency>Swiss Franc</Currency>
  <Exchange>1.64716</Exchange>
</Rate>
</Rates>
```

Code-Behind Programming

While it's perfectly legal to put HTML and code in the same ASPX file, in the real world you should segregate the two by placing them in separate files. Proper separation of code and data is achieved in ASP.NET by using a technique called *code-behind programming*. A Web form that uses code-behind is divided into two parts: an ASPX file containing HTML, and a source code file containing code. Here are two reasons why all commercial Web forms should employ code-behind:

- Robustness. If a programming error prevents the code in an ASPX file from compiling, the error won't come to light until the first time the page is accessed. Careful testing will take care of this, but how often do unit tests achieve 100 percent code coverage?

- Maintainability. ASP files containing thousands of lines of spaghetti-like mixtures of HTML and script are not uncommon. Clean separation of code and data makes applications easier to write and to maintain.

Code-behind is exceptionally easy to use. Here's a recipe for using code-behind in Web forms coded in C#:

1. Create a CS file containing event handlers, helper methods, and other code—everything that would normally appear between <script> and </script> tags in an ASPX file. Make each of these source code elements members of a class derived from *System.Web.UI.Page*.

2. In your *Page*-derived class, declare protected fields whose names mirror the IDs of the controls declared in the ASPX file. For example, if the Web form includes a pair of *TextBox* controls whose IDs are *UserName* and *Password*, include the following statements in your class declaration:

    ```
    protected TextBox UserName;
    protected TextBox Password;
    ```

    Without these fields, the CS file won't compile because references to *UserName* and *Password* are unresolvable. At run time, ASP.NET maps these fields to the controls of the same name so that reading *UserName.Text*, for example, reads the text typed into the *TextBox* control named *UserName*.

3. Compile the CS file into a DLL and place the DLL in a subdirectory named bin in the virtual directory that holds the ASPX file.

4. Place the HTML portion of the Web form—everything between the <html> and </html> tags—in an ASPX file. Include in the ASPX file an *@ Page* directive containing an *Inherits* attribute that identifies the *Page*-derived class in the DLL.

That's it; that's all there is to it. You get all the benefits of embedding code in an ASPX file but none of the drawbacks. The application in the next section demonstrates code-behind at work.

The Lander Application

In 1969, Neil Armstrong landed the Apollo 11 Lunar Excursion Module (LEM) on the moon with just 12 seconds of fuel to spare. You can duplicate Armstrong's feat with a Web-based lunar lander simulation patterned after the lunar lander game popularized on mainframe computers in the 1970s. This version of the game is built from an ASP.NET Web form, and it uses code-behind to separate code and HTML. It's called Lander, and it's shown in Internet Explorer in Figure 5-12. Its source code appears in Figure 5-13.

To run the program, copy Lander.aspx to your PC's \Inetpub\wwwroot directory. If \Inetpub\wwwroot lacks a subdirectory named bin, create one. Then compile Lander.cs into a DLL and place the DLL in the bin subdirectory. Here's the command to compile the DLL:

```
csc /t:library Lander.cs
```

Next, start your browser and type

```
http://localhost/lander.aspx
```

into the address bar. Begin your descent by entering a throttle value (any percentage from 0 to 100, where 0 means no thrust and 100 means full thrust) and a burn time in seconds. Click the Calculate button to input the values and update the altitude, velocity, acceleration, fuel, and elapsed time read-outs. Repeat until you reach an altitude of 0, meaning you've arrived at the moon's surface. A successful landing is one that occurs with a downward velocity of 4 meters per second or less. Anything greater and you dig your very own crater in the moon.

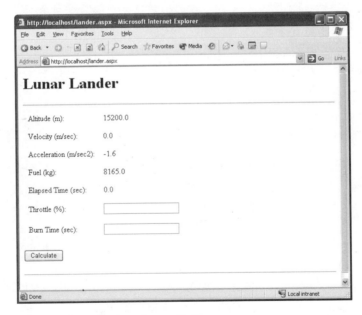

Figure 5-12   The Lander application.

Lander.aspx is a Web form built from a combination of ordinary HTML and ASP.NET server controls. Clicking the Calculate button submits the form to the server and activates the DLL's *OnCalculate* method, which extracts the throttle and burn time values from the input fields and updates the onscreen flight parameters using equations that model the actual flight physics of the Apollo 11

LEM. Like many Web pages, Lander.aspx uses an HTML table with invisible borders to visually align the page's controls.

Lander.aspx differs from the ASPX files presented thus far in this chapter in that it contains no source code. Lander.cs contains the form's C# source code. Inside is a *Page*-derived class named *LanderPage* containing the *OnCalculate* method that handles *Click* events fired by the Calculate button. Protected fields named *Altitude*, *Velocity*, *Acceleration*, *Fuel*, *ElapsedTime*, *Output*, *Throttle*, and *Seconds* serve as proxies for the controls of the same names in Lander.aspx. *LanderPage* and *OnCalculate* are declared public, which is essential if ASP.NET is to use them to serve the Web form defined in Lander.aspx.

Lander.aspx

```
<%@ Page Inherits="LanderPage" %>

<html>
  <body>
    <h1>Lunar Lander</h1>
    <form runat="server">
      <hr>
      <table cellpadding="8">
        <tr>
          <td>Altitude (m):</td>
          <td><asp:Label ID="Altitude" Text="15200.0"
            RunAt="Server" /></td>
        </tr>
        <tr>
          <td>Velocity (m/sec):</td>
          <td><asp:Label ID="Velocity" Text="0.0"
            RunAt="Server" /></td>
        </tr>
        <tr>
          <td>Acceleration (m/sec2):</td>
          <td><asp:Label ID="Acceleration" Text="-1.6"
            RunAt="Server" /></td>
        </tr>
        <tr>
          <td>Fuel (kg):</td>
          <td><asp:Label ID="Fuel" Text="8165.0" RunAt="Server" /></td>
        </tr>
        <tr>
          <td>Elapsed Time (sec):</td>
          <td><asp:Label ID="ElapsedTime" Text="0.0"
            RunAt="Server" /></td>
        </tr>
        <tr>
          <td>Throttle (%):</td>
          <td><asp:TextBox ID="Throttle" RunAt="Server" /></td>
        </tr>
        <tr>
```

Figure 5-13 The Lander source code.

```
            <td>Burn Time (sec):</td>
            <td><asp:TextBox ID="Seconds" RunAt="Server" /></td>
        </tr>
      </table>
      <br>
      <asp:Button Text="Calculate" OnClick="OnCalculate"
        RunAt="Server" />
      <br><br>
      <hr>
      <h3><asp:Label ID="Output" RunAt="Server" /></h3>
    </form>
  </body>
</html>
```

Lander.cs

```csharp
using System;
using System.Web.UI;
using System.Web.UI.WebControls;

public class LanderPage : Page
{
    const double gravity = 1.625;      // Lunar gravity
    const double landermass = 17198.0; // Lander mass

    protected Label Altitude;
    protected Label Velocity;
    protected Label Acceleration;
    protected Label Fuel;
    protected Label ElapsedTime;
    protected Label Output;
    protected TextBox Throttle;
    protected TextBox Seconds;

    public void OnCalculate (Object sender, EventArgs e)
    {
        double alt1 = Convert.ToDouble (Altitude.Text);

        if (alt1 > 0.0) {
            // Check for blank input fields
            if (Throttle.Text.Length == 0) {
                Output.Text = "Error: Required field missing";
                return;
            }

            if (Seconds.Text.Length == 0) {
                Output.Text = "Error: Required field missing";
                return;
            }

            // Extract and validate user input
            double throttle;
            double sec;

            try {
                throttle = Convert.ToDouble (Throttle.Text);
```

(continued)

Lander.cs *(continued)*

```csharp
            sec = Convert.ToDouble (Seconds.Text);
    }
    catch (FormatException) {
        Output.Text = "Error: Invalid input";
        return;
    }

    if (throttle < 0.0 || throttle > 100.0) {
        Output.Text = "Error: Invalid throttle value";
        return;
    }

    if (sec <= 0.0) {
        Output.Text = "Error: Invalid burn time";
        return;
    }

    // Extract flight parameters from the Label controls
    double vel1 = Convert.ToDouble (Velocity.Text);
    double fuel1 = Convert.ToDouble (Fuel.Text);
    double time1 = Convert.ToDouble (ElapsedTime.Text);

    // Compute thrust and remaining fuel
    double thrust = throttle * 1200.0;
    double fuel = (thrust * sec) / 2600.0;
    double fuel2 = fuel1 - fuel;

    // Make sure there's enough fuel
    if (fuel2 < 0.0) {
        Output.Text = "Error: Insufficient fuel";
        return;
    }

    // Compute new flight parameters
    Output.Text = "";
    double avgmass = landermass + ((fuel1 + fuel2) / 2.0);
    double force = thrust - (avgmass * gravity);
    double acc = force / avgmass;

    double vel2 = vel1 + (acc * sec);
    double avgvel = (vel1 + vel2) / 2.0;
    double alt2 = alt1 + (avgvel * sec);
    double time2 = time1 + sec;

    // If altitude <= 0, then we've landed
    if (alt2 <= 0.0) {
        double mul = alt1 / (alt1 - alt2);
        vel2 = vel1 - ((vel1 - vel2) * mul);
        alt2 = 0.0;
        fuel2 = fuel1 - ((fuel1 - fuel2) * mul);
        time2 = time1 - ((time1 - time2) * mul);

        if (vel2 >= -4.0)
            Output.Text = "The Eagle has landed";
        else
            Output.Text = "Kaboom!";
    }
```

```
                // Update the Labels to show latest flight parameters
                Altitude.Text = alt2.ToString ("f1");
                Velocity.Text = vel2.ToString ("f1");
                Acceleration.Text = acc.ToString ("f1");
                Fuel.Text = fuel2.ToString ("f1");
                ElapsedTime.Text = time2.ToString ("f1");
            }
        }
    }
```

How Code-Behind Works

A logical question to ask at this point is, "How does code-behind work?" The answer is deceptively simple. When you put Web forms code in an ASPX file and a request arrives for that page, ASP.NET derives a class from *System.Web.UI.Page* to process the request. The derived class contains the code that ASP.NET extracts from the ASPX file. When you use code-behind, ASP.NET derives a class from *your* class—the one identified with the *Inherits* attribute—and uses it to process the request. In effect, code-behind lets you specify the base class that ASP.NET derives from. And since you write the base class, you control what goes in it.

Figure 5-14 shows (in ILDASM) the class that ASP.NET derived from *LanderPage* the first time Lander.aspx was requested. You can clearly see the name of the ASP.NET-generated class—*Lander_aspx*—as well as the name of its base class: *LanderPage*.

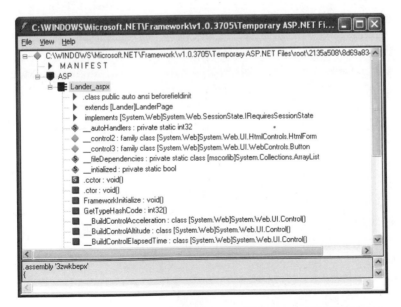

Figure 5-14   DLL generated from a page that uses code-behind.

Using Code-Behind Without Precompiling: The *Src* Attribute

If you like the idea of separating code and data into different files but for some reason would prefer *not* to compile the source code files yourself, you can use code-behind and still allow ASP.NET to compile the code for you. The secret? Place the CS file in the same directory as the ASPX file and add a *Src* attribute to the ASPX file's @ *Page* directive. Here's how Lander.aspx's *Page* directive would look if it were modified to let ASP.NET compile Lander.cs:

```
<%@ Page Inherits="LanderPage" Src="Lander.cs" %>
```

Why anyone would want to exercise code-behind this way is a question looking for an answer. But it works, and the very fact that the *Src* attribute exists means someone will probably find a legitimate use for it.

Using Non-ASP.NET Languages in ASP.NET Web Forms

Code embedded in ASPX files has to be written in one of three languages: C#, Visual Basic .NET, or JScript. Why? Because even though compilers are available for numerous other languages, ASP.NET uses parsers to strip code from ASPX files and generate real source code files that it can pass to language compilers. The parsers are language-aware, and ASP.NET includes parsers only for the aforementioned three languages. To write a Web form in C++, you have to either write a C++ parser for ASP.NET or figure out how to bypass the parsers altogether. Code-behind is a convenient mechanism for doing the latter.

Code-behind makes it possible to code Web forms in C++, COBOL, and any other language that's supported by a .NET compiler. Figure 5-15 contains the C++ version of Lander.cs. Lander.cpp is an example of C++ with Managed Extensions, better known as *managed* C++. That's Microsoft's term for C++ code that targets the .NET Framework. When you see language extensions such as __gc, which declares a managed type, being used, you know you're looking at managed C++.

The following command compiles Lander.cpp into a managed DLL and places it in the current directory's bin subdirectory:

```
cl /clr lander.cpp /link /dll /out:bin\Lander.dll
```

You can replace the DLL created from the CS file with the DLL created from the CPP file and Lander.aspx is none the wiser; it still works the same as it did before. All it sees is a managed DLL containing the *LanderPage* type identified by the *Inherits* attribute in the ASPX file. It neither knows nor cares how the DLL was created or what language it was written in.

Lander.cpp

```cpp
#using <system.dll>
#using <mscorlib.dll>
#using <system.web.dll>

using namespace System;
using namespace System::Web::UI;
using namespace System::Web::UI::WebControls;

public __gc class LanderPage : public Page
{
protected:
    static const double gravity = 1.625;      // Lunar gravity
    static const double landermass = 17198.0; // Lander mass

    Label* Altitude;
    Label* Velocity;
    Label* Acceleration;
    Label* Fuel;
    Label* ElapsedTime;
    Label* Output;
    TextBox* Throttle;
    TextBox* Seconds;

public:
    void OnCalculate (Object* sender, EventArgs* e)
    {
        double alt1 = Convert::ToDouble (Altitude->Text);

        if (alt1 > 0.0) {
            // Check for blank input fields
            if (Throttle->Text->Length == 0) {
                Output->Text = "Error: Required field missing";
                return;
            }

            if (Seconds->Text->Length == 0) {
                Output->Text = "Error: Required field missing";
                return;
            }

            // Extract and validate user input
            double throttle;
            double sec;

            try {
                throttle = Convert::ToDouble (Throttle->Text);
                sec = Convert::ToDouble (Seconds->Text);
            }
            catch (FormatException*) {
                Output->Text = "Error: Invalid input";
                return;
            }
```

Figure 5-15   Managed C++ version of Lander.cs.

Lander.cpp *(continued)*

```cpp
    if (throttle < 0.0 || throttle > 100.0) {
        Output->Text = "Error: Invalid throttle value";
        return;
    }

    if (sec <= 0.0) {
        Output->Text = "Error: Invalid burn time";
        return;
    }

    // Extract flight parameters from the Label controls
    double vel1 = Convert::ToDouble (Velocity->Text);
    double fuel1 = Convert::ToDouble (Fuel->Text);
    double time1 = Convert::ToDouble (ElapsedTime->Text);

    // Compute thrust and remaining fuel
    double thrust = throttle * 1200.0;
    double fuel = (thrust * sec) / 2600.0;
    double fuel2 = fuel1 - fuel;

    // Make sure there's enough fuel
    if (fuel2 < 0.0) {
        Output->Text = "Error: Insufficient fuel";
        return;
    }

    // Compute new flight parameters
    Output->Text = "";
    double avgmass = landermass + ((fuel1 + fuel2) / 2.0);
    double force = thrust - (avgmass * gravity);
    double acc = force / avgmass;

    double vel2 = vel1 + (acc * sec);
    double avgvel = (vel1 + vel2) / 2.0;
    double alt2 = alt1 + (avgvel * sec);
    double time2 = time1 + sec;

    // If altitude <= 0, then we've landed
    if (alt2 <= 0.0) {
        double mul = alt1 / (alt1 - alt2);
        vel2 = vel1 - ((vel1 - vel2) * mul);
        alt2 = 0.0;
        fuel2 = fuel1 - ((fuel1 - fuel2) * mul);
        time2 = time1 - ((time1 - time2) * mul);

        if (vel2 >= -4.0)
            Output->Text = "The Eagle has landed";
        else
            Output->Text = "Kaboom!";
    }
```

```
           // Update the Labels to show latest flight parameters
           Altitude->Text = (new Double (alt2))->ToString ("f1");
           Velocity->Text = (new Double (vel2))->ToString ("f1");
           Acceleration->Text = (new Double (acc))->ToString ("f1");
           Fuel->Text = (new Double (fuel2))->ToString ("f1");
           ElapsedTime->Text = (new Double (time2))->ToString ("f1");
       }
   }
};
```

Web Forms and Visual Studio .NET

Now that you know what makes Web forms tick, it's time to learn to build Web forms the Visual Studio .NET way. Visual Studio .NET brings rapid application development to the Web. You design forms by choosing controls from a palette and dropping them onto forms. You write event handlers by double-clicking controls and filling in empty method bodies. And you compile and run your application by executing simple menu commands. It's no accident that building Web forms with Visual Studio .NET feels a lot like building Windows applications with Visual Basic. That's exactly the feel Microsoft intended to convey.

This chapter closes with a step-by-step tutorial describing how to build a Web-based mortgage payment calculator with Visual Studio .NET. Figure 5-16 shows the finished product. Enter a loan amount, interest rate, and term (length of the loan in months), and click the Compute Payment button. The corresponding monthly payment appears at the bottom of the page.

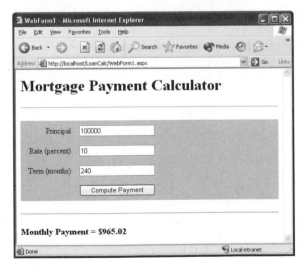

Figure 5-16   Web-based mortgage payment calculator.

Step 1: Create a Virtual Directory

When you create a Web application project with Visual Studio .NET, you don't tell Visual Studio .NET where to the store the files by entering a path name; you enter a URL. Assuming you want to store the files on your PC but don't want to clutter \Inetpub\wwwroot with project subdirectories, your first step is to create a project directory and turn it into a virtual directory so that it's URL-addressable. Here are the steps:

1. Create a folder named Projects somewhere on your hard disk to hold your Web application projects. Then create a Projects subdirectory named LoanCalc.

2. Start the Internet Information Services applet in Windows. You'll find it under Administrative Tools.

3. In the left pane of the Internet Information Services window, expand the Local Computer\Web Sites folder, and select Default Web Site.

4. Select the New/Virtual Directory command from the Action menu to start the Virtual Directory Creation Wizard.

5. When the wizard asks for an alias, type "LoanCalc." When it asks for a path name, enter the path to the LoanCalc directory you created in step 1. Click the Next and Finish buttons until the wizard closes.

You just created a physical directory named LoanCalc and converted it into a virtual directory. Its URL is *http://localhost/loancalc*. Before proceeding, verify that LoanCalc appears with the other virtual directories listed under Default Web Site in the Internet Information Services window, as shown in Figure 5-17.

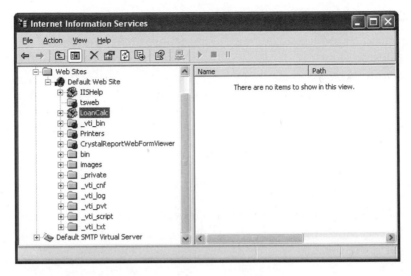

Figure 5-17   Internet Information Services window.

Step 2: Create a Web Application Project

Start Visual Studio .NET, and then select the File/New/Project command. Fill in the New Project dialog *exactly* as shown in Figure 5-18. Verify that the statement "Project will be created at http://localhost/LoanCalc" appears near the bottom of the dialog, that Visual C# Projects is selected in the Project Types box, and that ASP.NET Web Application is selected in the Templates box. Then click OK to create a new project named LoanCalc in the LoanCalc directory you created a moment ago.

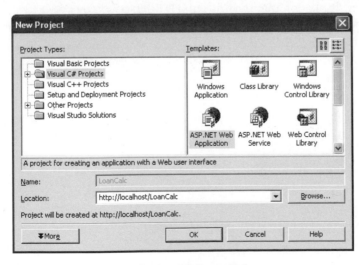

Figure 5-18   Creating the LoanCalc project.

Step 3: Change to Flow Layout Mode

The next screen you see is the Visual Studio .NET Web forms designer. Here you design forms by dragging and dropping controls. Before you begin, however, you have a decision to make.

The forms designer supports two layout modes: grid layout and flow layout. Grid layout mode lets you place controls anywhere in a form. It relies on CSS-P (Cascading Style Sheets-Position) to achieve precise positioning of controls and other HTML elements. Flow layout mode eschews CSS-P and relies on the normal rules of HTML layout. Flow layout mode is more restrictive, but it's compatible with all contemporary browsers.

So that LoanCalc will be compatible with as wide a range of browsers as possible, go to Visual Studio .NET's Properties window and change to flow layout mode by changing the document's *pageLayout* property from GridLayout, which is the default, to FlowLayout. Note that "DOCUMENT" must be selected in the combo box at the top of the Properties window for the *pageLayout* property to appear. If DOCUMENT doesn't appear in the drop-down list, click the empty form in the forms designer.

Before proceeding, click the form and select the Snap To Grid command from Visual Studio .NET's Format menu. This setting will make it easier to size and position the form's controls consistently with respect to one another.

Step 4: Add a Table

Since you're working in flow layout mode, tables are your best friend when it comes to positioning and aligning controls on a page. Click the Web form design window to set the focus to the designer. Then use Visual Studio .NET's Table/Insert/Table command to add an HTML table to the Web form. When the Insert Table dialog appears, fill it in as shown in Figure 5-19. In particular, set Rows to 4, Columns to 2, Width to 100 percent, Border Size to 0, and Cell Padding to 8. When you click OK, the table appears in the forms designer window.

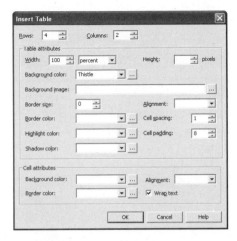

Figure 5-19   Adding a table to a Web form.

Step 5: Insert Text

Click the cell in the table's upper left corner. A caret appears signaling that any text you type will appear inside the table cell. Type "Principal". Then go to the Properties window and change the cell's *align* property to "right" to right align the text. Repeat the process to add "Rate (percent)" to the cell in the next row, and "Term (months)" to the cell below that. Finish up by dragging the vertical divider between table cells until the table's leftmost column is just wide enough to fit the text. Figure 5-20 shows how the table should look when you've finished.

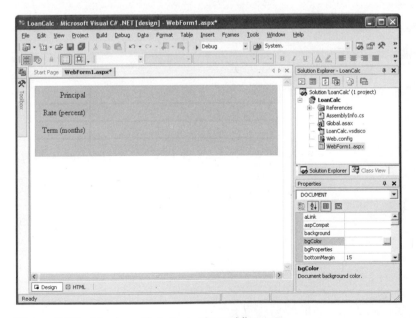

Figure 5-20   The LoanCalc form after adding text.

Step 6: Add *TextBox* Controls

If the Toolbox window isn't displayed somewhere in the Visual Studio .NET window (it appears at the far left by default), choose the Toolbox command from the View menu to display it. Click the Toolbox's Web Forms button to display a list of Web controls, and then use drag-and-drop to add *TextBox* controls to the right-hand cells in the table's first three rows. (See Figure 5-21.) Finish up by using the Properties window to change the *TextBox* controls' IDs to "Principal", "Rate", and "Term", respectively.

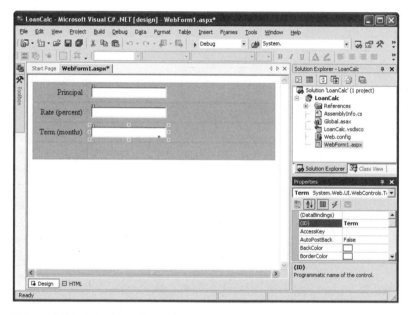

Figure 5-21   The LoanCalc form after adding *TextBox* controls.

Step 7: Add a *Button* Control

Add a *Button* control to the rightmost cell in the table's bottom row, as shown in Figure 5-22. Size the button so that its width equals that of the text box above it. Change the button text to "Compute Payment" and the button ID to "PaymentButton".

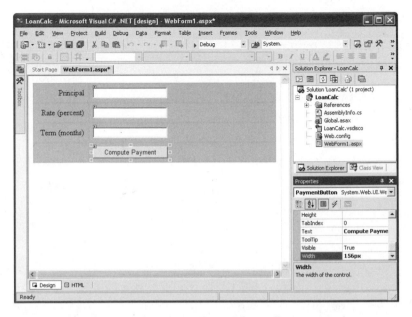

Figure 5-22   The LoanCalc form after adding a *Button* control.

Step 8: Add a *Label* Control

Select a *Label* control from the Toolbox, and add it to the form just below the table, as shown in Figure 5-23. Change the *Label* control's text to an empty string and its ID to "Output".

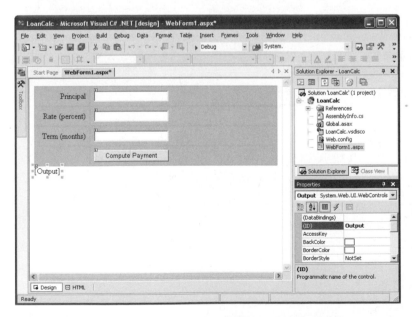

Figure 5-23   The LoanCalc form after adding a *Label* control.

Step 9: Edit the HTML

The next step is to dress up the form by adding a few HTML elements. Start by clicking the HTML button at the bottom of the designer window to view the HTML generated for this Web form. Manually add the following statements between the <body> tag and the <form> tag:

```
<h1>Mortgage Payment Calculator</h1>
<hr>
```

Next scroll to the bottom of the file and add these statements between the </table> tag and the <asp:Label> tag:

```
<br>
<hr>
<br>
<h3>
```

As a last step, move the </h3> tag that Visual Studio .NET inserted so that it comes after the <asp:Label> tag. Now click the Design button at the bottom of the forms designer to switch out of HTML view and back to design view. Figure 5-24 shows how the modified form should look.

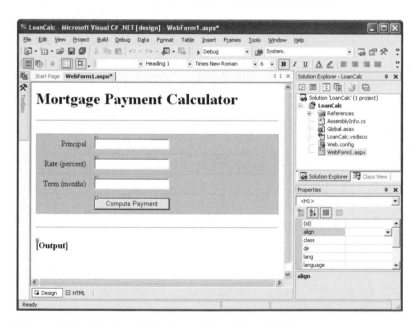

Figure 5-24   The LoanCalc form after adding HTML tags.

Step 10: Add a *Click* Handler

Double-click the form's Compute Payment button. Visual Studio .NET responds by adding a method named *PaymentButton_Click* to WebForm1.aspx.cs and showing the method in the program editor. Add the following code to the empty method body:

```
try {
    double principal = Convert.ToDouble (Principal.Text);
    double rate = Convert.ToDouble (Rate.Text) / 100;
    double term = Convert.ToDouble (Term.Text);
    double tmp = System.Math.Pow (1 + (rate / 12), term);
    double payment = principal * (((rate / 12) * tmp) / (tmp - 1));
    Output.Text = "Monthly Payment = " + payment.ToString ("c");
}
catch (Exception) {
    Output.Text = "Error";
}
```

PaymentButton_Click isn't an ordinary method; it's an event handler. Check out the *InitializeComponent* method that Visual Studio .NET wrote into WebForm1.aspx.cs and you'll find a statement that registers *PaymentButton_Click* to be called in response to the Compute Payment button's *Click* events. *InitializeComponent* is called by *OnInit*, which is called when the page fires an *Init* event. The handler that you just implemented responds to *Click* events by extracting user input from the form's *TextBox* controls, computing the corresponding monthly payment, and displaying the result in the *Label* control.

Step 11: Build and Test

You're now ready to try out your handiwork. Select BuildLoanCalc from the Build menu to compile your code. If it builds without errors, choose Start (or Start Without Debugging) from the Debug menu to run it. When the Web form pops up in Internet Explorer, verify that it works properly by entering the following three inputs:

- Principal: 100000
- Rate: 10
- Term: 240

Now click the Compute Payment button. If "Monthly Payment = $965.02" appears at the bottom of the page, give yourself a pat on the back. You just built your first Web form with Visual Studio .NET.

The LoanCalc Source Code

Of the many files in the LoanCalc directory, WebForm1.aspx and WebForm1.aspx.cs are the two that interest us the most. They contain Loan-Calc's source code. (If you're curious to know what all those other files are for, be patient. You'll learn about many of them—particularly Global.asax and Web.config—in Chapter 9. Most of the extra files are superfluous in this example, but Visual Studio .NET insists on creating them anyway.) WebForm1.aspx contains no code; only HTML. Visual Studio .NET *always* uses code-behind in its Web forms, so all the C# code is located in WebForm1.aspx.cs. Figure 5-25 shows the finished versions of both files. Most of the content that you see was generated by Visual Studio .NET. The statements that you added are shown in boldface type.

Given what you already know about Web forms, there isn't much in Loan-Calc's source code to write home about. The ASPX file defines the user interface using a mixture of HTML and Web controls, and the CS file contains the Compute Payment button's *Click* handler as well as the code that connects the button to the handler. Neither file contains anything you couldn't have written by hand, but it should be apparent that building Web forms visually is faster and less error prone than building them manually.

```
WebForm1.aspx
<%@ Page language="c#" Codebehind="WebForm1.aspx.cs" AutoEventWireup="false"
  Inherits="LoanCalc.WebForm1" %>
<!DOCTYPE HTML PUBLIC "-//W3C//DTD HTML 4.0 Transitional//EN" >
<HTML>
  <HEAD>
    <title>WebForm1</title>
    <meta name="GENERATOR" Content="Microsoft Visual Studio 7.0">
    <meta name="CODE_LANGUAGE" Content="C#">
    <meta name="vs_defaultClientScript" content="JavaScript">
    <meta name="vs_targetSchema"
      content="http://schemas.microsoft.com/intellisense/ie5">
  </HEAD>
  <body>
    <h1>Mortgage Payment Calculator</h1>
    <hr>
    <form id="Form1" method="post" runat="server">
      <TABLE id="Table1" cellSpacing="1" cellPadding="8" width="100%"
        bgColor="thistle" border="0">
        <TR>
          <TD align="right" style="WIDTH: 99px">Principal</TD>
          <TD><asp:TextBox id="Principal" runat="server"></asp:TextBox></TD>
        </TR>
        <TR>
          <TD align="right" style="WIDTH: 99px">Rate (percent)</TD>
```

Figure 5-25   The LoanCalc source code.

```
          <TD><asp:TextBox id="Rate" runat="server"></asp:TextBox></TD>
        </TR>
        <TR>
          <TD align="right" style="WIDTH: 99px">Term (months)</TD>
          <TD><asp:TextBox id="Term" runat="server"></asp:TextBox></TD>
        </TR>
        <TR>
          <TD style="WIDTH: 99px"></TD>
          <TD><asp:Button id="PaymentButton" runat="server"
            Text="Compute Payment" Width="156px"></asp:Button></TD>
        </TR>
      </TABLE>
      <br>
      <hr>
      <br>
      <h3>
        <asp:Label id="Output" runat="server"></asp:Label>
      </h3>
    </form>
  </body>
</HTML>
```

WebForm1.aspx.cs

```
using System;
using System.Collections;
using System.ComponentModel;
using System.Data;
using System.Drawing;
using System.Web;
using System.Web.SessionState;
using System.Web.UI;
using System.Web.UI.WebControls;
using System.Web.UI.HtmlControls;

namespace LoanCalc
{
    /// <summary>
    /// Summary description for WebForm1.
    /// </summary>
    public class WebForm1 : System.Web.UI.Page
    {
        protected System.Web.UI.WebControls.TextBox Rate;
        protected System.Web.UI.WebControls.TextBox Term;
        protected System.Web.UI.WebControls.Button PaymentButton;
        protected System.Web.UI.WebControls.TextBox Principal;
        protected System.Web.UI.WebControls.Label Output;

        private void Page_Load(object sender, System.EventArgs e)
        {
            // Put user code to initialize the page here
        }

        #region Web Form Designer generated code
        override protected void OnInit(EventArgs e)
        {
```

(continued)

WebForm1.aspx.cs *(continued)*

```csharp
        //
        // CODEGEN: This call is required by the ASP.NET
        // Web Form Designer.
        //
        InitializeComponent();
        base.OnInit(e);
    }

    /// <summary>
    /// Required method for Designer support - do not modify
    /// the contents of this method with the code editor.
    /// </summary>
    private void InitializeComponent()
    {
        this.PaymentButton.Click +=
            new System.EventHandler(this.PaymentButton_Click);
        this.Load += new System.EventHandler(this.Page_Load);
    }
    #endregion

    private void PaymentButton_Click(object sender, System.EventArgs e)
    {
        try {
            double principal = Convert.ToDouble (Principal.Text);
            double rate = Convert.ToDouble (Rate.Text) / 100;
            double term = Convert.ToDouble (Term.Text);
            double tmp = System.Math.Pow (1 + (rate / 12), term);
            double payment =
                principal * (((rate / 12) * tmp) / (tmp - 1));
            Output.Text = "Monthly Payment = " + payment.ToString ("c");
        }
        catch (Exception) {
            Output.Text = "Error";
        }
    }
}
```

A Glimpse into the Future

A lot of developers—not all of them Microsoft employees—believe that Web forms are a glimpse into the future of Web programming. The idea of encapsulating complex rendering and behavioral logic in reusable control classes and having those controls fire events that can be processed on Web servers is one whose time has come. Server controls provide the building blocks for sophisticated Web forms while shielding the developer from the nuances of HTML and client-side scripting. That's a win no matter how you look at it (or which computer company—Sun or Microsoft—you swear allegiance to).

You now know more about Web forms than 99.999 percent of the people on the planet. But there's still much to learn. In the next chapter, you'll continue the journey to Web Forms enlightenment by learning about all the different controls in *System.Web.UI.WebControls*. After that, you'll learn how to build Web controls of your own, structure applications around Web forms, create secure Web forms, and much more. Most important, you'll discover that putting your software on the Web isn't such a scary proposition after all.

6

Web Controls

Now that you're acquainted with the Web Forms programming model, the next step on the road to becoming an ASP.NET programmer is getting to know the various types of server controls that the Microsoft .NET Framework places at your disposal. You've seen three of them already: *TextBox*, *Button*, and *Label*. Now it's time to learn about the others.

Recall from Chapter 5 that ASP.NET supports two distinctly different types of server controls: HTML controls and Web controls. HTML controls are instances of classes defined in the *System.Web.UI.HtmlControls* namespace. When you add *runat*="server" to a conventional HTML tag (as in <input type="text" runat="server">), the .NET Framework responds by instantiating an HTML control. Web controls come from classes defined in *System.Web.UI.Web-Controls*. They're declared explicitly by prefixing class names with *asp:*, and, of course, including *runat*="server" attributes (for example, <asp:TextBox RunAt="server">). HTML controls exist primarily to ease the chore of migrating existing HTML forms to ASP.NET. Web controls are richer and more diverse in scope than HTML controls, so the focus of this chapter is Web controls.

To lend order to the otherwise dizzying array of Web controls defined in the *WebControls* namespace, I've divided the Web controls in the .NET Framework class library (FCL) into the following categories:

- "Simple" controls, so called because (in general) they wrap simple HTML control tags

- Button controls, which create various types of buttons in Web forms

- List controls, which display simple lists of items

- Data-bound controls, which use data binding to display information obtained from databases and other data sources

- Calendar controls, whose sole member, *Calendar*, adds interactive calendars to Web forms

- Validation controls, which validate user input before and after forms are submitted to the server

The more you know about Web controls, the better equipped you'll be to build sophisticated Web forms that take advantage of the best features ASP.NET has to offer.

Simple Controls

The simple controls are so named because most emit only a few lines of HTML. Some return client-side script too, but only under special circumstances. They're exceedingly easy to use, and thus are a great starting point for an exploration of Web controls.

TextBox Controls

TextBox controls are the ASP.NET equivalent of <input type="text/password"> and <textarea> tags in HTML. Their purpose? To create text input fields in Web forms. The statement

```
<asp:TextBox ID="UserName" RunAt="server" />
```

creates a text input field in a Web form and assigns it the programmatiç ID "UserName". You can use a *TextBox*'s *Text* property to declaratively insert text into a *TextBox* and also to read and write *TextBox* text from a server-side script. The following statement creates a *TextBox* that initially contains the string "Elmo":

```
<asp:TextBox ID="UserName" Text="Elmo" RunAt="server" />
```

And the following server-side script reads the contents of the *TextBox*:

```
string name = UserName.Text;
```

Text is one of several public properties that the *TextBox* class exposes. Others include *Rows* and *Columns*, which size a *TextBox* by setting the number of rows and columns that it displays; *MaxLength*, which limits the number of characters a *TextBox* will accept; *ReadOnly*, which, when true, prevents the *TextBox* from accepting input; *Wrap*, which determines whether text wraps in a multiline *TextBox*; and *TextMode*, which can be set to SingleLine (the default) to create single-line input fields, MultiLine to create multiline input fields, or Password to create password input fields—fields that display asterisks or other characters in place of the actual characters that the user types. The following statement creates a password input field named "Password":

```
<asp:TextBox ID="Password" TextMode="Password" RunAt="server" />
```

To create a multiline input field, set *TextMode* to MultiLine and *Rows* to the number of rows you want the *TextBox* to display:

```
<asp:TextBox ID="Comments" TextMode="MultiLine" Rows="10"
  RunAt="server" />
```

The *Rows* attribute is ignored unless you explicitly set *TextMode* to MultiLine.

A *TextBox* renders itself as an <input type="text">, <input type="password">, or <textarea> tag, depending on the value assigned to its *TextMode* property. Here are three <asp:TextBox> tags and the HTML that they produce:

```
// Before
<asp:TextBox ID="UserName" RunAt="server" />
<asp:TextBox ID="Password" TextMode="Password" RunAt="server" />
<asp:TextBox ID="Comments" TextMode="MultiLine" Rows="10"
  RunAt="server" />

// After
<input name="UserName" type="text" id="UserName" />
<input name="Password" type="password" id="Password" />
<textarea name="Comments" rows="10" id="Comments"></textarea>
```

Examining the HTML that Web controls return is a great way to get acquainted with Web controls and learn more about how they work.

TextChanged Events and the *AutoPostBack* Property

TextBox controls fire *TextChanged* events following a postback if the text inside them has changed. An *OnTextChanged* attribute in an <asp:TextBox> tag designates a handler for *TextChanged* events:

```
<asp:TextBox ID="UserName" OnTextChanged="OnNameChanged"
  RunAt="server" />
    .
    .
    .
<script language="C#" runat="server">
  void OnNameChanged (Object sender, EventArgs e)
  {
      // Name changed; read it from the TextBox
      string name = UserName.Text;
  }
</script>
```

TextChanged events fire only when the page posts back to the server. By default, *TextBox* controls don't generate postbacks themselves and therefore fire *TextChanged* events only when another control on the page forces a postback. However, you can set a *TextBox* control's *AutoPostBack* property to true to force postbacks to occur (and *TextChanged* events to fire) the moment the text inside the control changes:

```
<asp:TextBox ID="UserName" OnTextChanged="OnNameChanged"
  AutoPostBack="true" RunAt="server" />
```

Unlike Windows edit controls, which fire EN_CHANGE notifications in response to each and every character that the user enters, *TextBox* controls with *AutoPostBack* enabled fire *TextChanged* events only when they lose the input focus (that is, when the user moves to another control in the Web page) following a text change. That's good, because a page that posts back to the server every time a character is entered into a *TextBox* would be a slow page indeed.

How does setting *AutoPostBack* to true cause postbacks to occur when a *TextBox* loses the input focus? With a sprinkle of JavaScript and a dash of Dynamic HTML (DHTML). Enter this statement into a Web form:

```
<asp:TextBox ID="UserName" AutoPostBack="true" RunAt="server" />
```

and the control outputs this:

```
<input name="UserName" type="text" id="UserName"
  onchange="__doPostBack('UserName','')" language="javascript" />
    .
    .
    .
<script language="javascript">
<!--
  function __doPostBack(eventTarget, eventArgument) {
    var theform = document.ctl0;
      .
      .
      .
    theform.submit();
  }
// -->
</script>
```

The <input> tag includes an *onchange* attribute that activates a JavaScript function named *__doPostBack* on the client when the control loses the input focus following a text change. The *__doPostBack* function programmatically posts the page back to the server by calling the *Submit* method of the DHTML object that represents the form.

TextBox isn't the only Web control that features an *AutoPostBack* property; *CheckBox*, *RadioButton*, and several other controls support it as well. Whenever *AutoPostBack* appears in a control's property list, setting it to true causes postbacks to occur (and events to fire) the moment a change occurs in the state of the control. Otherwise, the control's events won't fire until an external stimulus forces a postback.

Label Controls

Label controls are among the simplest—if not *the* simplest—of all Web controls. They add programmable textual labels to Web forms. A *Label* control's *Text* property exposes the control text. The following statement adds "Hello" to a Web page:

```
<asp:Label Text="Hello" RunAt="server" />
```

A *Label* control declared this way renders itself to the Web page as a <span> tag:

```
<span>Hello</span>
```

Spans are benign HTML tags that are used to group other HTML elements.

Label controls frequently serve as placeholders for output written by server-side scripts. The following statement declares an empty *Label* control and assigns it the programmatic ID "Output":

```
<asp:Label ID="Output" RunAt="server" />
```

And this statement in a server-side script writes "Hello" to the Web page where the *Label* control is positioned:

```
Output.Text = "Hello";
```

Use a *Label* control whenever you want to add text to a Web page and change that text from a server-side script. For static labels, use ordinary HTML text instead. Static HTML text improves performance by preventing ASP.NET from having to instantiate and execute a control each time the page is requested from the server.

HyperLink Controls

HyperLink controls add hyperlinks to Web forms. *HyperLink* controls come in two forms: text hyperlinks and image hyperlinks. The following statement creates a hyperlink that renders itself as a text string and points to *www.wintellect.com*:

```
<asp:HyperLink Text="Click here"
  NavigateUrl="http://www.wintellect.com" RunAt="server" />
```

A slight modification transforms the hyperlink into an image that targets the same URL:

```
<asp:HyperLink ImageUrl="logo.jpg"
  NavigateUrl="http://www.wintellect.com" RunAt="server" />
```

Text hyperlinks render as <a href> tags; image hyperlinks render as <img> tags enclosed in <a href> tags. You normally include either a *Text* or an *ImageUrl* attribute in an <asp:HyperLink> tag, but not both. However, if you do specify both, the control uses the text you specify as a tool tip in supportive browsers.

The *HyperLink* class exposes a *Target* property that can be used to control how the targeted Web page is displayed. For example, the statement

```
<asp:HyperLink Text="Click here" Target="_new"
  NavigateUrl="http://www.wintellect.com" RunAt="server" />
```

opens the page in a new browser window. Any value that's valid for a *Target* attribute in an <a> tag is also valid in a *HyperLink*. Another use for *Target* attributes is to open pages in specific windows or frames.

Like *Label* controls, *HyperLink* controls should be used only when you want to change the properties of the control dynamically—that is, when ordinary <a href> tags won't do. The following code initializes the target of a hyperlink when the page loads:

```
<asp:HyperLink ID="MyLink" Text="Web page du jour" RunAt="server" />
  .
  .
  .
<script language="C#" runat="server">
  void Page_Load (Object sender, EventArgs e)
  {
      MyLink.NavigateUrl = "www.wintellect.com";
  }
</script>
```

One motivation for initializing a *HyperLink* control in this way is to retrieve the targeted URL from a database or an XML file.

Image Controls

Image controls add images to Web forms by emitting <img> tags. *Image*'s most important properties are *ImageUrl*, which specifies the URL of the image that the control renders; *ImageAlign*, which controls the alignment of the image; and *AlternateText*, which specifies the image's alternate text. Alternate text is displayed in place of the image in text-only browsers. The following statement declares an *Image* control in a Web form:

```
<asp:Image ImageUrl="logo.jpg" AlternateText="Company Logo"
  RunAt="server" />
```

Image controls are perfect for displaying images whose URLs are assigned at run time, possibly in response to user input. For static images, you can reduce overhead by using conventional <img> tags instead.

CheckBox Controls

CheckBox controls place check boxes in Web forms. (Surprise!) A *CheckBox*'s *Checked* property determines whether the check box is checked (true) or unchecked (false), and its *Text* property controls the text displayed beside the check box. The following code declares a *CheckBox* control in a Web form:

```
<asp:CheckBox ID="Confirm" Text="E-mail my confirmation"
  RunAt="server" />
```

And this server-side script determines whether the check box is checked when the form is submitted to the server:

```
if (Confirm.Checked) {
    // The box is checked
}
else {
    // The box is not checked
}
```

On the off chance that you'd like to reverse the positions of a check box and the text that normally appears to its right, include a *TextAlign*="Left" attribute in the control tag.

 CheckBox controls fire *CheckedChanged* events when they're checked and unchecked. By default, a *CheckedChanged* event doesn't fire the moment the check box is clicked; it waits until the page posts back to the server. To respond immediately to changes in a check box's state, set the control's *Auto-PostBack* property to true to force postbacks:

```
<asp:CheckBox ID="Confirm" Text="E-mail my confirmation"
  AutoPostBack="true" OnCheckedChanged="DoItNow" RunAt="server" />
    .
    .
    .
<script language="C#" runat="server">
  void DoItNow (Object sender, EventArgs e)
  {
      // The check box was just checked or unchecked; do something!
  }
</script>
```

Don't set *AutoPostBack* to true unless you really need *CheckedChanged* events to fire immediately. One justification for setting *AutoPostBack* to true is to dynamically change the contents of the page each time the check box is clicked.

RadioButton Controls

RadioButton controls create radio buttons in Web forms. Radio buttons present users with mutually exclusive lists of choices. Clicking a radio button checks that radio button and unchecks other radio buttons in the group.

RadioButton derives from *CheckBox* and therefore supports the same properties and events that *CheckBox* supports. It also adds a *GroupName* property for designating the group that a radio button belongs to. The following code declares five *RadioButton* controls and divides them into two groups: one group of three and another group of two. It also uses the *RadioButton.Checked* property to check the first radio button in each group:

```
<asp:RadioButton Text="Red" ID="Button1" Checked="true"
  GroupName="Colors" RunAt="server" /><br>
<asp:RadioButton Text="Green" ID="Button2"
  GroupName="Colors" RunAt="server" /><br>
<asp:RadioButton Text="Blue" ID="Button3"
  GroupName="Colors" RunAt="server" /><br>
<br>
<asp:RadioButton Text="Circle" ID="Button4" Checked="true"
  GroupName="Shape" RunAt="server" /><br>
<asp:RadioButton Text="Square" ID="Button5"
  GroupName="Shape" RunAt="server" />
```

Grouping these controls by using the *GroupName* attribute is important because it tells the browser which radio buttons to uncheck when a radio button is checked.

Figuring out which radio button in a group of radio buttons is checked from a server-side script requires checking each button's *Checked* property one by one. A better way to add radio buttons to a Web page is to use a *RadioButtonList*. Its *SelectedIndex* property identifies the button that's checked. *RadioButtonList* also simplifies the task of arranging radio buttons on a page. You'll learn all about *RadioButtonList* later in this chapter.

Table Controls

Table controls add HTML tables to Web forms. They render a combination of <table>, <tr>, and <td> tags to browsers. Here's one way to add a table to a Web form:

```
<table>
  <tr>
    <td>Row 1, Column 1</td>
    <td>Row 1, Column 2</td>
  </tr>
  <tr>
    <td>Row 2, Column 1</td>
    <td>Row 2, Column 2</td>
  </tr>
</table>
```

And here's the equivalent table created with a *Table* control:

```
<asp:Table ID="MyTable" RunAt="server">
  <asp:TableRow>
    <asp:TableCell>Row 1, Column 1</asp:TableCell>
    <asp:TableCell>Row 1, Column 2</asp:TableCell>
  </asp:TableRow>
  <asp:TableRow>
    <asp:TableCell>Row 2, Column 1</asp:TableCell>
    <asp:TableCell>Row 2, Column 2</asp:TableCell>
  </asp:TableRow>
</asp:Table>
```

Table controls add value to a Web form when you want to change a table's contents dynamically. For example, the following server-side script modifies the text in each of the table cells:

```
MyTable.Rows[0].Cells[0].Text = "Cell 1";
MyTable.Rows[0].Cells[1].Text = "Cell 2";
MyTable.Rows[1].Cells[0].Text = "Cell 3";
MyTable.Rows[1].Cells[1].Text = "Cell 4";
```

This script builds the entire table at run time:

```
<asp:Table ID="MyTable" RunAt="server" />
  .
  .
  .
<script language="C#" runat="server">
  void Page_Load (Object sender, EventArgs e)
  {
      for (int i=0; i<2; i++) {
```

(continued)

```
        TableRow row = new TableRow ();
        for (int j=0; j<2; j++) {
            TableCell cell = new TableCell ();
            cell.Text = String.Format ("Row {0}, Column {1}",
                i + 1, j + 1);
            row.Cells.Add (cell);
        }
        MyTable.Rows.Add (row);
    }
}
</script>
```

These scripts work because a *Table* object exposes the rows that it contains through a property named *Rows*. Each row in the *Rows* collection is an instance of *TableRow*. Within a row, each cell is represented as a *TableCell* object that's accessible through the row's *Cells* collection. Calling *Add* on a *Rows* or *Cells* collection programmatically adds a row to a table or a cell to a row.

By default, a *Table* control's borders are invisible. You can change that by setting the control's *GridLines* property to Horizontal, Vertical, or Both. Other useful *Table* properties include *CellPadding* and *CellSpacing*, which, like the HTML attributes of the same name, control the spacing within and between cells, and *BackImageUrl*, which identifies a background image. Tables are often used in Web pages to paint colored backgrounds. To change a *Table* object's background color, use the *BackColor* property that *Table* inherits from *Web-Control*.

Panel Controls

Panel controls serve as containers for other controls. One use for *Panel* controls is to control the visibility of a group of controls. The following Web form toggles four *Label* controls on and off by setting a *Panel* control's *Visible* property to true or false each time a check box is clicked. Note the *AutoPostBack*="true" attribute in the <asp:CheckBox> tag:

```
<html>
  <body>
    <form runat="server"><br>
      <asp:CheckBox ID="Toggle" Text="Show Labels" Checked="true"
        AutoPostBack="true" OnCheckedChanged="OnToggle"
        RunAt="server" />
      <asp:Panel ID="MyPanel" RunAt="server">
        <asp:Label Text="John" RunAt="server" /><br>
        <asp:Label Text="Paul" RunAt="server" /><br>
```

```
            <asp:Label Text="George" RunAt="server" /><br>
            <asp:Label Text="Ringo" RunAt="server" /><br>
        </asp:Panel>
      </form>
   </body>
</html>

<script language="C#" runat="server">
  void OnToggle (Object sender, EventArgs e)
  {
      MyPanel.Visible = Toggle.Checked;
  }
</script>
```

Another use for *Panel* controls is to specify horizontal alignment for a group of controls:

```
<asp:Panel HorizontalAlign="Center" ID="MyPanel" RunAt="server">
  <asp:Label Text="John" RunAt="server" /><br>
  <asp:Label Text="Paul" RunAt="server" /><br>
  <asp:Label Text="George" RunAt="server" /><br>
  <asp:Label Text="Ringo" RunAt="server" /><br>
</asp:Panel>
```

Panel controls render as HTML <div> tags. Therefore, it's appropriate to use them any time you would ordinarily use a <div> tag but want to change the attributes of that tag dynamically.

Button Controls

The Web controls family includes three types of button controls: *Button*, *Link-Button*, and *ImageButton*. Functionally, all three do exactly the same thing: they submit the form that hosts them to the server. The difference lies in their physical appearance. A *Button* control looks like a push button, a *LinkButton* looks like a hyperlink, and an *ImageButton* renders itself using an image you supply. Nearly every Web form uses one or more buttons to enable the user to submit the form to the server.

The following statements declare an instance of each control type in a Web form:

```
<asp:Button Text="Sort" RunAt="server" />
<asp:LinkButton Text="Sort" RunAt="server" />
<asp:ImageButton ImageUrl="sort.jpg" RunAt="server" />
```

The *Text* property specifies the text that appears on the face of a *Button* or *LinkButton*. *ImageUrl* identifies the image displayed by an *ImageButton*.

All three button controls fire two kinds of events when clicked: a *Click* event and a *Command* event. An *OnClick* attribute in the control tag wires a button to a *Click* handler. *Click* handlers for *Button* and *LinkButton* controls are prototyped this way:

```
void OnClick (Object sender, EventArgs e)
{
    // Event handling code goes here
}
```

But *Click* handlers for *ImageButton* controls are prototyped like this:

```
void OnClick (Object sender, ImageClickEventArgs e)
{
    // Extract the click coordinates
    int x = e.X;
    int y = e.Y;
}
```

The *ImageClickEventArgs* passed to an *ImageButton*'s *Click* handler contains public fields named *X* and *Y* that specify where in the image the click occurred. *X* and *Y* are measured in pixels and represent distances from the image's upper left corner.

Using *Command* events rather than *Click* events affords the developer the opportunity to pass additional information via the control's *CommandName* and *CommandArgument* properties. The following example assigns the command name "Sort" and the command argument "Asc" to a *Button* control and toggles the command argument between "Asc" and "Desc" to perform alternating ascending and descending sorts:

```
<asp:Button Text="Sort" ID="SortButton" OnCommand="OnSort"
  CommandName="Sort" CommandArgument="Asc" RunAt="server" />
      .
      .
      .
<script language="C#" runat="server">
  void OnSort (Object sender, CommandEventArgs e)
  {
      if (e.CommandName == "Sort" &&
          e.CommandArgument.ToString () == "Asc") {
          // TODO: Perform ascending sort
          SortButton.CommandArgument = "Desc";
      }
      else if (e.CommandName == "Sort" &&
          e.CommandArgument.ToString () == "Desc") {
          // TODO: Perform descending sort
          SortButton.CommandArgument = "Asc";
      }
  }
</script>
```

Command events are useful for "overloading" button controls and having them perform different actions based on the value of *CommandArgument*. They can also be used to connect multiple buttons to a single handler and have the handler respond differently depending on which button was clicked.

List Controls

The list controls family has four members: *ListBox*, *DropDownList*, *CheckBoxList*, and *RadioButtonList*. All four have two important characteristics in common: they all derive from *System.Web.UI.WebControls.ListControl*, and they're all designed to present lists of items to the user. *ListBox* and *DropDownList* controls display textual items that the user can select. Both render back to the browser as HTML <select> tags. *CheckBoxList* and *RadioButtonList* display arrays of check boxes and radio buttons and render as <input type="checkbox"> and <input type="radio"> tags, respectively. The <input> tags are optionally contained in an HTML table for alignment purposes.

Items in a list control are represented by instances of *ListItem*. Instances of *ListItem* are declared with <asp:ListItem> tags. Inside a *ListItem* are string properties named *Text* and *Value*. *Text* exposes the text that represents the item in a list control; *Value* allows an arbitrary string to be associated with the item. *ListItem* also exposes a Boolean property named *Selected* that determines whether the item is selected. The following statements declare a *ListBox* control containing four items and select the second item:

```
<asp:ListBox ID="MyListBox" RunAt="server">
  <asp:ListItem Text="John" RunAt="server" />
  <asp:ListItem Text="Paul" Selected="true" RunAt="server" />
  <asp:ListItem Text="George" RunAt="server" />
  <asp:ListItem Text="Ringo" RunAt="server" />
</asp:ListBox>
```

A minor change to the code produces a *DropDownList* instead of a *ListBox*:

```
<asp:DropDownList ID="MyDropDownList" RunAt="server">
  <asp:ListItem Text="John" RunAt="server" />
  <asp:ListItem Text="Paul" Selected="true" RunAt="server" />
  <asp:ListItem Text="George" RunAt="server" />
  <asp:ListItem Text="Ringo" RunAt="server" />
</asp:DropDownList>
```

In a *ListBox* or *DropDownList*, a *ListItem*'s *Selected* property determines whether the item is selected (true) or not selected (false). In a *CheckBoxList* or *RadioButtonList*, the same property determines whether the corresponding control is checked or unchecked.

Following a postback, a server-side script doesn't have to examine every item in a list control to determine which one is currently selected. List controls inherit public properties named *SelectedIndex* and *SelectedItem* from the base class *ListControl*. Thus, a script can determine which radio button in a *RadioButtonList* is selected by reading its 0-based index:

```
int index = MyRadioButtonList.SelectedIndex;
```

SelectedIndex and *SelectedItem* aren't that interesting for *CheckBoxList* controls because multiple check boxes in the list might be checked, but they're extremely useful for other types of list controls.

List controls fire *SelectedIndexChanged* events when the selection changes—that is, when a new item is selected in a *ListBox* or *DropDownList* or a button is clicked in a *CheckBoxList* or *RadioButtonList*. By default, the event doesn't fire until something else on the page causes a postback. However, all list controls inherit an *AutoPostBack* property from *ListControl* that you can set to true to fire *SelectedIndexChanged* events immediately.

DropDownList Controls

DropDownList controls display items in a drop-down list that resembles a Windows combo box. A classic use for *DropDownList* controls is to display a list of the 50 U.S. states in a form that solicits an address. The following code sample presents such a list and echoes the user's choice to the Web page:

```
<html>
  <body>
    <form runat="server">
      <asp:DropDownList ID="StateList" RunAt="server">
        <asp:ListItem Text="AL" RunAt="server" />
        <asp:ListItem Text="AK" RunAt="server" />
        <asp:ListItem Text="AR" RunAt="server" />
            .
            .
            .
        <asp:ListItem Text="WI" RunAt="server" />
        <asp:ListItem Text="WV" RunAt="server" />
        <asp:ListItem Text="WY" RunAt="server" />
      </asp:DropDownList>
      <asp:Button Text="Submit" OnClick="OnSubmit" RunAt="server" />
```

```
      <br>
      <asp:Label ID="Output" RunAt="server" />
    </form>
  </body>
</html>

<script language="C#" runat="server">
  void OnSubmit (Object sender, EventArgs e)
  {
      Output.Text = StateList.SelectedItem.Text;
  }
</script>
```

Figure 6-21 later in the chapter contains a complete listing for a *DropDownList* control that displays the abbreviations of all 50 U.S. states plus the District of Columbia.

ListBox Controls

ListBox controls are similar to *DropDownList* controls, but they display their items in a static list rather than in a drop-down list. The following example creates a *ListBox* control that displays the names of the U.S. states and writes the user's selection to the Web page:

```
<html>
  <body>
    <form runat="server">
      <asp:ListBox ID="StateList" Rows="10" RunAt="server">
        <asp:ListItem Text="Alabama" RunAt="server" />
        <asp:ListItem Text="Alaska" RunAt="server" />
        <asp:ListItem Text="Arkansas" RunAt="server" />
           .
           .
           .
        <asp:ListItem Text="Wisconsin" RunAt="server" />
        <asp:ListItem Text="West Virginia" RunAt="server" />
        <asp:ListItem Text="Wyoming" RunAt="server" />
      </asp:ListBox>
      <asp:Button Text="Submit" OnClick="OnSubmit" RunAt="server" />
      <br>
      <asp:Label ID="Output" RunAt="server" />
    </form>
  </body>
</html>
```

(continued)

```
<script language="C#" runat="server">
  void OnSubmit (Object sender, EventArgs e)
  {
      Output.Text = StateList.SelectedItem.Text;
  }
</script>
```

By default, a *ListBox* control is sized to display only four items at a time. The *Rows* attribute in the <asp:ListBox> tag above increases the *ListBox* height to 10 items.

The only functional difference between a *ListBox* control and a *DropDownList* is that the former can be programmed to support multiple selections. A *SelectionMode*="Multiple" attribute in the control tag creates a multiple-selection *ListBox*:

```
<asp:ListBox ID="StateList" SelectionMode="Multiple"
  Rows="10" RunAt="server">
```

Unfortunately, the *ListBox* class lacks a public method or property for retrieving the indices of the items selected in a multiple-selection list box. To figure out which items the user selected, you have to iterate through all the list box's items, checking their *Selected* properties one by one. The following method takes a *ListBox* reference as an input parameter and returns an array of integers containing the 0-based indices of all selected items:

```
int[] GetSelectedIndices (ListBox lb)
{
    ArrayList a = new ArrayList ();
    for (int i=0; i<lb.Items.Count; i++) {
        if (lb.Items[i].Selected)
            a.Add (i);
    }
    int [] indices = new int[a.Count];
    a.CopyTo (indices);
    return indices;
}
```

With *GetSelectedIndices* defined this way, the statement

```
int[] indices = GetSelectedIndices (StateList);
```

identifies all the items selected in the multiple-selection *ListBox* named "StateList."

CheckBoxList Controls

The *CheckBoxList* control creates an array of check boxes. The following statements display four vertically stacked check boxes:

```
<asp:CheckBoxList ID="MyCheckBoxList" RunAt="server">
  <asp:ListItem Text="John" RunAt="server" />
  <asp:ListItem Text="Paul" RunAt="server" />
  <asp:ListItem Text="George" RunAt="server" />
  <asp:ListItem Text="Ringo" RunAt="server" />
</asp:CheckBoxList>
```

To determine whether a given check box is checked, read its *Selected* property from a server-side script:

```
// Is the third check box checked?
if (MyCheckBoxList.Items[2].Selected) {
    // The check box is checked
else {
    // The check box is not checked
}
```

Creating an array of check boxes with *CheckBoxList* is generally preferable to using an array of <asp:CheckBox> tags because *CheckBoxList* makes it easy to align check boxes in rows and columns and to control the spacing between check boxes. Two properties control the check boxes' layout: *RepeatColumns* and *RepeatDirection*. The following statements create an array of check boxes divided into four rows and three columns. The first row contains the check boxes whose indices are 0–2, the second row check boxes 3–5, and so on:

```
<asp:CheckBoxList ID="MyCheckBoxList" RepeatColumns="3"
    RepeatDirection="Horizontal" RunAt="server">
  <asp:ListItem Text="Item 0" RunAt="server" />
  <asp:ListItem Text="Item 1" RunAt="server" />
  <asp:ListItem Text="Item 2" RunAt="server" />
  <asp:ListItem Text="Item 3" RunAt="server" />
  <asp:ListItem Text="Item 4" RunAt="server" />
  <asp:ListItem Text="Item 5" RunAt="server" />
  <asp:ListItem Text="Item 6" RunAt="server" />
  <asp:ListItem Text="Item 7" RunAt="server" />
  <asp:ListItem Text="Item 8" RunAt="server" />
  <asp:ListItem Text="Item 9" RunAt="server" />
  <asp:ListItem Text="Item 10" RunAt="server" />
  <asp:ListItem Text="Item 11" RunAt="server" />
</asp:CheckBoxList>
```

Changing *RepeatDirection* to Vertical modifies the array so that the first column contains check boxes 0–3, the second column contains check boxes 4–7, and the third column contains check boxes 8–11:

```
<asp:CheckBoxList ID="MyCheckBoxList" RepeatColumns="3"
    RepeatDirection="Vertical" RunAt="server">
```

To change the spacing between check boxes, use *CheckBoxList*'s *CellPadding* and *CellSpacing* properties. The values that you specify are attached to the <table> tag that the *CheckBoxList* returns.

RadioButtonList Controls

RadioButtonList simplifies the task of creating groups of radio buttons and finding out which radio button in a group is selected. The statements

```
<asp:RadioButtonList ID="MyRadioButtonList" RunAt="server">
  <asp:ListItem Text="John" Selected="true" RunAt="server" />
  <asp:ListItem Text="Paul" RunAt="server" />
  <asp:ListItem Text="George" RunAt="server" />
  <asp:ListItem Text="Ringo" RunAt="server" />
</asp:RadioButtonList>
```

create a column of radio buttons and check the first one. A server-side script can use *RadioButtonList.SelectedIndex* to determine which button the user selected:

```
int index = MyRadioButtonList.SelectedIndex;
```

Like *CheckBoxList*, *RadioButtonList* features properties named *RepeatColumns* and *RepeatDirection* that can be used to align the radio buttons in rows and columns, and properties named *CellPadding* and *CellSpacing* that control the spacing between radio buttons. Because radio buttons never appear by themselves (that is, without other radio buttons), and because *SelectedIndex* makes it so easy to find out which radio button is selected, *RadioButtonList* all but obviates the need for *RadioButton* to even exist.

Data Binding with List Controls

Think back for a moment to the currency converter Web form named Converter.aspx presented in Chapter 5. Converter.aspx uses a *ListBox* to display a list of international currencies. But rather than statically defining the *ListBox*'s contents with <asp:ListItem> tags, Converter.aspx adds items to the *ListBox* by reading entries from an XML file and calling *Add* on the *ListBox*'s *Items* collection. Here's that code again:

```
DataSet ds = new DataSet ();
ds.ReadXml (Server.MapPath ("Rates.xml"));
foreach (DataRow row in ds.Tables[0].Rows)
    Currencies.Items.Add (row["Currency"].ToString ());
```

Because initializing list controls at run time using the results of database queries or data extracted from XML files is so common, ASP.NET's list controls support a feature called *data binding*. Rather than initialize the *ListBox* control by calling *ListItemCollection.Add* repeatedly, Converter.aspx could have done this:

```
DataSet ds = new DataSet ();
ds.ReadXml (Server.MapPath ("Rates.xml"));
Currencies.DataSource = ds;
Currencies.DataTextField = "Currency";
Currencies.DataBind ();
```

This method is simpler and more intuitive. It also makes the code more generic by eliminating direct interactions with the *DataSet*.

How does data binding work? All list controls inherit from *ListControl* properties named *DataSource*, *DataTextField*, and *DataValueField*. *DataSource* identifies a data source. It can be initialized with a reference to any object that implements the FCL's *IEnumerable* or *IListSource* interface. *IEnumerable* is an enumeration interface that allows a control to interact with a data source using a well-defined protocol. *IListSource* permits objects that don't implement *IEnumerable* themselves but that have subobjects that implement *IList* (which derives from *IEnumerable*) to expose their subobjects' *IList* interfaces. Because *DataSet* implements *IListSource*, a list control can enumerate the rows in the *DataTable* that a *DataSet* contains. *DataTextField* connects the *Text* property of the list control's items to a field in the data source. *DataValueField* specifies which field, if any, provides the items' *Value* properties. List controls also inherit a method named *DataBind* from the *ListControl* base class. *DataBind* commands the control to initialize itself from the data source.

Literally dozens of FCL classes implement *IEnumerable*, meaning a list control can bind to a wide variety of data sources. The following example initializes a *ListBox* named "MyListBox" by binding to an array of strings. The example works because an array is an instance of *System.Array*, and *System.Array* implements *IList*:

```
string[] names = { "John", "Paul", "George", "Ringo" };
MyListBox.DataSource = names;
MyListBox.DataBind ();
```

There's no need to initialize *DataTextField* when binding to an array because an array holds a single column of data. That column is automatically bound to the list items' *Text* property.

You can write custom data types that support binding to list controls by implementing *IEnumerable* in those types. The following example defines a class named *Beatles* that serves up the names of the Fab Four. It implements *IEnumerable*'s one and only method, *GetEnumerator*, by returning an *IEnumerator* interface implemented by a nested class named *Enumerator*.

```
class Beatles : IEnumerable
{
    protected Enumerator enumerator = new Enumerator ();
```

(continued)

```csharp
    public IEnumerator GetEnumerator ()
    {
        return enumerator;
    }

    public class Enumerator : IEnumerator
    {
        protected int index = -1;
        protected string[] names =
            { "John", "Paul", "George", "Ringo" };

        public object Current
        {
            get
            {
                if (index == -1)
                    index = 0; // Just in case
                return names[index];
            }
        }

        public bool MoveNext ()
        {
            if (index < (names.Length - 1)) {
                index++;
                return true;
            }
            return false;
        }

        public void Reset ()
        {
            index = -1;
        }
    }
}
```

Two simple statements initialize a *ListBox* control with the names encapsulated in *Beatles*:

```csharp
MyListBox.DataSource = new Beatles ();
MyListBox.DataBind ();
```

Figure 6-1 contains a modified version of Converter.aspx that populates its list box by binding to a *DataSet* containing the currency and exchange values read from Rates.xml. It also stores exchange rates in the list box items' *Value* properties, eliminating the need to access the XML file again when *OnConvert* is called. Changes are highlighted in bold.

Converter2.aspx

```
<%@ Import Namespace=System.Data %>

<html>
  <body>
    <h1>Currency Converter</h1>
    <hr>
    <form runat="server">
      Target Currency<br>
      <asp:ListBox ID="Currencies" Width="256" RunAt="server" /><br>
      <br>
      Amount in U.S. Dollars<br>
      <asp:TextBox ID="USD" Width="256" RunAt="server" /><br>
      <br>
      <asp:Button Text="Convert" ID="ConvertButton" Width="256"
        RunAt="server" /><br>
      <br>
      <asp:Label ID="Output" RunAt="server" />
    </form>
  </body>
</html>

<script language="C#" runat="server">
  void Page_Init (Object sender, EventArgs e)
  {
      // Wire the Convert button to OnConvert
      ConvertButton.Click += new EventHandler (OnConvert);
  }

  void Page_Load (Object sender, EventArgs e)
  {
      // If this isn't a postback, initialize the ListBox
      if (!IsPostBack) {
          DataSet ds = new DataSet ();
          ds.ReadXml (Server.MapPath ("Rates.xml"));
          Currencies.DataSource = ds;
          Currencies.DataTextField = "Currency";
          Currencies.DataValueField = "Exchange";
          Currencies.DataBind ();
          Currencies.SelectedIndex = 0;
      }
  }

  void OnConvert (Object sender, EventArgs e)
  {
      // Perform the conversion and display the results
```

Figure 6-1   A currency converter that takes advantage of data binding.

Converter2.aspx   *(continued)*

```
        try {
            decimal dollars = Convert.ToDecimal (USD.Text);
            decimal rate =
                Convert.ToDecimal (Currencies.SelectedItem.Value);
            decimal amount = dollars * rate;
            Output.Text = amount.ToString ("f2");
        }
        catch (FormatException) {
            Output.Text = "Error";
        }
    }
</script>
```

Data-Bound Controls

Speaking of data binding: the *WebControls* namespace includes three controls whose primary mission in life is to bind to data sources and display the results as HTML. The controls are *Repeater*, *DataList*, and *DataGrid*. *Repeater* controls use *UI templates*—snippets of HTML that define the appearance of the controls' output—to render items obtained from a data source. *DataList* controls also use UI templates, but they add support for multicolumn formatting, item selection, and item editing. *DataGrid* controls display tabular data in highly customizable HTML tables and support paging, sorting, editing, and other features. *Repeater*, *DataList*, and *DataGrid* are arguably the three most powerful members of the Web control family. Let's see why real-world developers consider them to be an indispensable part of their toolbox.

Repeater Controls

Repeater controls provide a flexible and easy-to-use mechanism for displaying repetitive lists of items. A repeater has no default user interface; you tell a *Repeater* what to display and how to display it. Here's a simple example that uses a *Repeater* to display a list of text strings stored in an array:

```
<html>
  <body>
    <form runat="server">
      <asp:Repeater ID="MyRepeater" RunAt="server">
        <ItemTemplate>
          <%# Container.DataItem %><br>
        </ItemTemplate>
      </asp:Repeater>
```

```
      </form>
   </body>
</html>

<script language="C#" runat="server">
   void Page_Load (Object sender, EventArgs e)
   {
      if (!IsPostBack) {
         string[] beatles = { "John", "Paul", "George", "Ringo" };
         MyRepeater.DataSource = beatles;
         MyRepeater.DataBind ();
      }
   }
</script>
```

ItemTemplate is a *Repeater* property that defines the appearance of individual items. Content bracketed by <ItemTemplate> and </ItemTemplate> tags consti- tutes an *item template* that's invoked repeatedly to render all the items in the data source. Statements between <%# and %> symbols are data-binding expres- sions. Inside a data-binding expression, *Container.DataItem* represents the item that the control is currently binding to—for example, the current row in a *DataTable* or the current string in a string array.

An item template forms the core of a *Repeater* control, but *Repeater* con- trols support other template types as well. For example, you can render alter- nating items differently by using *alternating item templates*. The following example displays alternating lines in different colors:

```
<asp:Repeater ID="MyRepeater" RunAt="server">
   <ItemTemplate>
     <%# Container.DataItem %><br>
   </ItemTemplate>
   <AlternatingItemTemplate>
     <span style="background-color:gainsboro;width:128;">
       <%# Container.DataItem %>
     </span><br>
   </AlternatingItemTemplate>
</asp:Repeater>
```

Header templates and footer templates enable a *Repeater* to render HTML elements that require start and end tags (such as tables and lists):

```
<asp:Repeater ID="MyRepeater" RunAt="server">
   <HeaderTemplate>
     <ul>
   </HeaderTemplate>
   <ItemTemplate>
```

(continued)

```
        <li><%# Container.DataItem %><br>
      </ItemTemplate>
      <AlternatingItemTemplate>
        <li><span style="background-color:gainsboro;width:128;">
          <%# Container.DataItem %>
        </span><br>
      </AlternatingItemTemplate>
      <FooterTemplate>
        </ul>
      </FooterTemplate>
</asp:Repeater>
```

Repeater controls also support separator templates delimited by <SeparatorTemplate> and </SeparatorTemplate> tags. You can use them to place separators (for example, <hr> tags) between individual items.

In practice, *Repeater* controls rarely bind to simple arrays. Typically, they bind to more complex data sources such as *DataReader* and *DataSet* objects. The following example uses a *Repeater* to display the books listed in the Pubs database that comes with Microsoft SQL Server. Each "item" consists of a book title obtained from the "title" field of the current record and a price obtained from the "price" field, as shown in Figure 6-2.

```
<%@ Import Namespace="System.Data" %>
<%@ Import Namespace="System.Data.SqlClient" %>

<html>
  <body>
    <form runat="server">
      <asp:Repeater ID="MyRepeater" RunAt="server">
        <ItemTemplate>
          <%# DataBinder.Eval (Container.DataItem, "title") +
            " (" +
            DataBinder.Eval (Container.DataItem, "price", "{0:c}") +
            ")" %><br>
        </ItemTemplate>
      </asp:Repeater>
    </form>
  </body>
</html>

<script language="C#" runat="server">
  void Page_Load (Object sender, EventArgs e)
  {
    if (!IsPostBack) {
      SqlConnection connection = new SqlConnection
        ("server=localhost;database=pubs;uid=sa;pwd=");
```

```
        try {
            connection.Open ();
            SqlCommand command = new SqlCommand
                ("select * from titles where price != 0",
                connection);
            SqlDataReader reader = command.ExecuteReader ();
            MyRepeater.DataSource = reader;
            MyRepeater.DataBind ();
        }
        finally {
            connection.Close ();
        }
    }
}
</script>
```

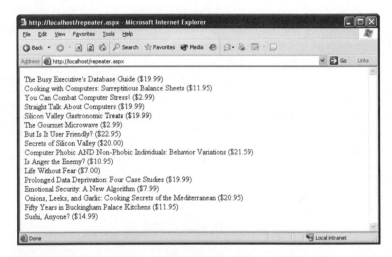

Figure 6-2   A portion of the Pubs database rendered by a *Repeater* control.

Note the use of *DataBinder.Eval*, which is common in data-binding expressions. *DataBinder* is a class defined in the *System.Web.UI* namespace; *Eval* is a static method that uses reflection to evaluate a data-binding expression. The second parameter passed to *DataBinder.Eval* identifies a field in the current record; the optional third parameter is a formatting string specifying how that field is converted into a string. *DataBinder.Eval* vastly simplifies data-binding syntax. Without it, the *Repeater* control in the previous example would have to have been defined this way:

```
<asp:Repeater ID="MyRepeater" RunAt="server">
  <ItemTemplate>
    <%# ((System.Data.Common.DbDataRecord)
      Container.DataItem)["title"] + " (" +
      String.Format ("{0:c}",
      ((System.Data.Common.DbDataRecord)
      Container.DataItem)["price"]) + ")" %><br>
  </ItemTemplate>
</asp:Repeater>
```

Besides simplifying data-binding syntax, *DataBinder.Eval* provides an added level of indirection between data-binding expressions and data sources. Without *DataBinder.Eval*, changing the data source from a *DataReader* to a *DataSet* would also require changing the data-binding expression. With *DataBinder.Eval*, no such change is necessary.

The *Repeater* class defines three events: *ItemCreated*, *ItemDataBound*, and *ItemCommand*. *ItemCreated* and *ItemDataBound* events fire each time an item is created and each time an item binds to a data source, respectively. They let the developer further customize a *Repeater*'s output. *ItemCommand* events fire when a button declared within a *Repeater* control is clicked. The *CommandSource* property of the *RepeaterCommandEventArgs* passed to the event handler identifies the button that prompted the event. The *CommandName* and *CommandArgument* properties identify the values of the same names assigned to the button control. The following example wraps the output from the *Repeater* control in a table and adds an "Add to Cart" button to each row (Figure 6-3). Clicking a button displays the selected title at the bottom of the page:

```
<%@ Import Namespace="System.Data" %>
<%@ Import Namespace="System.Data.SqlClient" %>

<html>
  <body>
    <form runat="server">
      <asp:Repeater ID="MyRepeater" OnItemCommand="OnItemCommand"
        RunAt="server">
        <HeaderTemplate>
          <table border="1">
            <tr>
              <td align="center">Title</td>
              <td align="center">Price</td>
              <td align="center">Action</td>
            </tr>
        </HeaderTemplate>
        <ItemTemplate>
          <tr>
            <td>
              <%# DataBinder.Eval (Container.DataItem, "title") %>
            </td>
```

```
              <td align="center">
                <%# DataBinder.Eval (Container.DataItem, "price",
                  "{0:c}") %>
              </td>
              <td align="center">
                <asp:Button Text="Add to Cart" RunAt="server"
                  CommandArgument='<%# DataBinder.Eval
                  (Container.DataItem, "title") %>' />
              </td>
            </tr>
          </ItemTemplate>
          <FooterTemplate>
            </table>
          </FooterTemplate>
        </asp:Repeater>
        <asp:Label ID="Output" RunAt="server" />
      </form>
    </body>
</html>
<script language="C#" runat="server">
  void Page_Load (Object sender, EventArgs e)
  {
      if (!IsPostBack) {
          SqlConnection connection = new SqlConnection
              ("server=localhost;database=pubs;uid=sa;pwd=");
          try {
              connection.Open ();
              SqlCommand command;
              command = new SqlCommand
                  ("select * from titles where price != 0",
                   connection);
              SqlDataReader reader = command.ExecuteReader ();
              MyRepeater.DataSource = reader;
              MyRepeater.DataBind ();
          }
          finally {
              connection.Close ();
          }
      }
  }

  void OnItemCommand (Object sender, RepeaterCommandEventArgs e)
  {
      Output.Text = e.CommandArgument.ToString ();
  }
</script>
```

To simplify the process of figuring out which item in the control corresponds to the button that was clicked, this example initializes the *CommandArgument* property of each *Button* control with the book title stored in the current record's "title" field using a data-binding expression in the <asp:Button> tag.

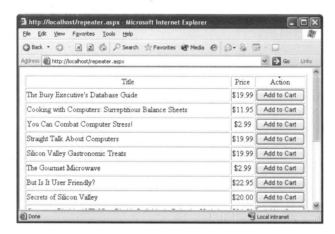

Figure 6-3 *Repeater* control with buttons.

The MyComicsRepeater Page

For a first-hand look at a *Repeater* control in action, check out the Web form in Figure 6-4. Named MyComicsRepeater.aspx, it uses a *Repeater* control to display the contents of a SQL Server database named MyComics that stores information about a collection of fictitious comic books. Each item in the control includes a thumbnail-size cover scan, a title and issue number, and other relevant information about the corresponding comic. (In case you wondered, the "CGC" column specifies whether the numerical grade in the column to the left is an official CGC grade or an estimated CGC grade. CGC stands for Comics Guaranty Corporation, one of the world's most respected authorities on comic books.) Clicking a thumbnail image displays a full-size scan of the cover.

Before you can run MyComicsRepeater.aspx, you must do the following:

1. Create the MyComics database. The CD that comes with this book contains a SQL script file named MyComics.sql that creates and initializes the database. To execute the script, open a command prompt window and type

   ```
   osql -U sa -P -i mycomics.sql
   ```

   in the directory where MyComics.sql is stored. This assumes, of course, that Microsoft SQL Server is installed on your PC.

2.   Either copy the MyComics folder that was created when you installed the CD to \Inetpub\wwwroot, or use the IIS configuration manager to make MyComics a virtual directory.

If you copy MyComics to wwwroot, you can open the Web form by typing

```
http://localhost/mycomicsrepeater.aspx
```

into your browser's address bar. If you make MyComics a virtual directory and name it "MyComics," type the following instead:

```
http://localhost/mycomics/mycomicsrepeater.aspx
```

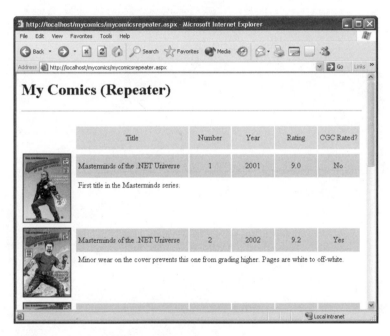

Figure 6-4   The MyComicsRepeater page.

MyComicsRepeater.aspx is listed in Figure 6-5. At its heart is a *Repeater* control that binds to the records returned by a query executed in *Page_Load*. Each item rendered by the *Repeater* includes a table for visual formatting purposes. Most of the data-binding expressions do little more than embed text in table cells. These, however, do more:

```
<a href='Images/Large/<%# DataBinder.Eval
  (Container.DataItem, "LargeCover") %>'>
  <img src='Images/Small/<%# DataBinder.Eval
  (Container.DataItem, "SmallCover") %>'
</a>
```

This code embeds an <img> tag in each item output by the *Repeater* control. The *Src* attribute references one of the thumbnails in the Images\Small subdirectory. Furthermore, the <img> tag is enclosed in an <a> tag whose *Href* attribute references one of the larger and more detailed cover images in the Images\Large subdirectory. That's why clicking a thumbnail displays a close-up image of the comic book cover. The names of the files containing the cover scans come from the database's "SmallCover" and "LargeCover" fields and are appended to the path names to form URLs.

MyComicsRepeater.aspx

```
<%@ Import Namespace="System.Data" %>
<%@ Import Namespace="System.Data.SqlClient" %>

<html>
  <body>
    <h1>My Comics (Repeater)</h1>
    <hr>
    <form runat="server">
      <table width="100%">
        <tr>
          <td width="104" />
          <td>
            <table cellpadding="4" width="100%">
              <tr height="48" bgcolor="yellow">
                <td width="40%" align="center">
                  Title
                </td>
                <td width="15%" align="center">
                  Number
                </td>
                <td width="15%" align="center">
                  Year
                </td>
                <td width="15%" align="center">
                  Rating
                </td>
                <td width="15%" align="center">
                  CGC Rated?
                </td>
              </tr>
            </table>
          </td>
        </tr>
      </table>
      <asp:Repeater ID="MyRepeater" RunAt="server">
        <ItemTemplate>
```

Figure 6-5   MyComicsRepeater source code.

```
      <table width="100%">
        <tr>
          <td width="104">
            <a href='Images/Large/<%# DataBinder.Eval
              (Container.DataItem, "LargeCover") %>'>
              <img src='Images/Small/<%# DataBinder.Eval
                (Container.DataItem, "SmallCover") %>'
            </a>
          </td>
          <td>
            <table cellpadding="4" height="100%" width="100%">
              <tr height="48" bgcolor="gainsboro">
                <td width="40%">
                  <%# DataBinder.Eval
                    (Container.DataItem, "Title") %>
                </td>
                <td width="15%" align="center">
                  <%# DataBinder.Eval
                    (Container.DataItem, "Number") %>
                </td>
                <td width="15%" align="center">
                  <%# DataBinder.Eval
                    (Container.DataItem, "Year") %>
                </td>
                <td width="15%" align="center">
                  <%# DataBinder.Eval
                    (Container.DataItem, "Rating", "{0:f1}") %>
                </td>
                <td width="15%" align="center">
                  <%# ((bool) DataBinder.Eval
                    (Container.DataItem, "CGC")) ?
                      "Yes" : "No" %>
                </td>
              </tr>
              <tr>
                <td colspan="5">
                  <%# DataBinder.Eval
                    (Container.DataItem, "Comment") %>
                </td>
              </tr>
            </table>
          </td>
        </tr>
      </table>
    </ItemTemplate>
</asp:Repeater>
```

(continued)

MyComicsRepeater.aspx *(continued)*

```
      </form>
    </body>
</html>

<script language="C#" runat="server">
    void Page_Load (Object sender, EventArgs e)
    {
        if (!IsPostBack) {
            SqlConnection connection = new SqlConnection
                ("server=localhost;database=mycomics;uid=sa;pwd=");

            try {
                connection.Open ();
                SqlCommand command;
                command = new SqlCommand
                    ("select * from books order by title, number",
                    connection);
                SqlDataReader reader = command.ExecuteReader ();
                MyRepeater.DataSource = reader;
                MyRepeater.DataBind ();
            }
            finally {
                connection.Close ();
            }
        }
    }
</script>
```

DataList Controls

DataList controls are similar to *Repeater* controls, but they include features that *Repeater*s don't. Specifically, they add support for multicolumn formatting, item selection, and item editing. Multicolumn layouts are controlled with the *Repeat-Columns* and *RepeatDirection* properties. Item selection is controlled with the *SelectedIndex* property, which holds the 0-based index of the item that's currently selected, and the *SelectedItemStyle* and *SelectedItemTemplate* properties, which govern the appearance of items that are in the selected state. To enable users to edit the items in a *DataList*, use the control's *EditItemStyle* and *EditItemTemplate* properties to define the appearance of the item that's being edited. The related *EditItemIndex* property specifies which item is currently being edited.

Developers accustomed to working with Windows controls are often surprised to learn that the selection in a *DataList* is controlled manually. A *DataList* doesn't automatically highlight an item when the item is clicked. Rather, it's up to a server-side event handler to do the highlighting by setting the control's *SelectedIndex* property equal to the index of the item. Each item rendered by a *DataList* that supports selection must include a control that activates a server-side event handler. In the following example, the *DataList*'s item template includes a *LinkButton* control. When the *LinkButton* is clicked, the *DataList* fires an *ItemCommand* event, and the *OnItemCommand* handler selects the item that was clicked. For good measure, this *DataList* also takes advantage of multicolumn formatting by arranging its items in two columns:

```html
<html>
  <body>
    <form runat="server">
      <asp:DataList ID="MyDataList" RunAt="server"
        RepeatColumns="2" RepeatDirection="Horizontal"
        OnItemCommand="OnItemCommand">
        <ItemTemplate>
          <asp:LinkButton Text="<%# Container.DataItem %>"
            RunAt="server" /><br>
        </ItemTemplate>
        <SelectedItemStyle BackColor="gainsboro" />
      </asp:DataList>
    </form>
  </body>
</html>

<script language="C#" runat="server">
  void Page_Load (Object sender, EventArgs e)
  {
      if (!IsPostBack) {
          string[] beatles = { "John", "Paul", "George", "Ringo" };
          MyDataList.DataSource = beatles;
          MyDataList.DataBind ();
      }
  }

  void OnItemCommand (Object sender, DataListCommandEventArgs e)
  {
      MyDataList.SelectedIndex = e.Item.ItemIndex;
  }
</script>
```

The <SelectedItemStyle> tag in this example highlights the currently selected item by setting its background color to gainsboro (light gray). Other aspects of the item's appearance, however, are defined by the item template. If you want to, you can use a <SelectedItemTemplate> tag to specify the look of selected items independent of the item template.

Incidentally, the statement

```
<SelectedItemStyle BackColor="gainsboro" />
```

initializes the subproperty named *BackColor* of the property named *SelectedItemStyle*. If you'd prefer, you can initialize subproperties in the tag that declares a control by separating property and subproperty names with hyphens, as in

```
<asp:DataList ID="MyDataList" RunAt="server"
  RepeatColumns="2" RepeatDirection="Horizontal"
  OnItemCommand="OnItemCommand"
  SelectedItemStyle-BackColor="gainsboro">
```

This syntax isn't limited to *DataList* controls. It's applicable to all controls that implement properties and subproperties, including *Repeater*, *DataGrid*, and *Calendar* controls.

The MyComicsDataList Page

The Web form in Figure 6-6 uses a *DataList* rather than a *Repeater* to put a face on the MyComics database. The underlying ASPX file, MyComicsDataList.aspx, appears in Figure 6-7. The *DataList*'s item template renders a one-row, two-column table whose left cell contains a thumbnail cover image and whose right cell contains the comic book title, issue number, and other information. The top row of text is rendered as a *LinkButton*. Clicking the *LinkButton* invokes *OnItemCommand*, which selects the item that was clicked and displays descriptive text in the yellow bar at the top of the page. That text comes from the database's "Comment" field, which is passed to the event handler using the *LinkButton*'s *CommandArgument* property. As with the *Repeater* control version of this page, clicking one of the cover thumbnails displays a close-up scan of the cover, thanks to an <a> tag surrounding the <img> tag emitted by the *DataList* control.

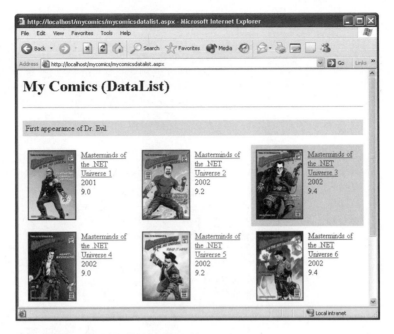

Figure 6-6   The MyComicsDataList page.

MyComicsDataList.aspx

```
<%@ Import Namespace="System.Data" %>
<%@ Import Namespace="System.Data.SqlClient" %>

<html>
  <body>
    <h1>My Comics (DataList)</h1>
    <hr>
    <form runat="server">
      <asp:Table Width="100%" Height="32" CellPadding="4"
        BackColor="yellow" RunAt="server">
        <asp:TableRow>
          <asp:TableCell ID="Output" />
        </asp:TableRow>
      </asp:Table>
      <br>
      <asp:DataList ID="MyDataList" RepeatColumns="3"
        RepeatDirection="Horizontal" CellPadding="4"
        OnItemCommand="OnItemCommand" RunAt="server">
        <ItemTemplate>
          <table width="100%" cellpadding="4">
```

Figure 6-7   MyComicsDataList source code.

MyComicsDataList.aspx   *(continued)*

```html
            <tr>
              <td width="100">
                <a href='Images/Large/<%# DataBinder.Eval
                  (Container.DataItem, "LargeCover") %>'>
                  <img src='Images/Small/<%# DataBinder.Eval
                    (Container.DataItem, "SmallCover") %>'>
                </a>
              </td>
              <td valign="top">
                <asp:LinkButton CommandName="Select" RunAt="server"
                  CommandArgument='<%# DataBinder.Eval
                  (Container.DataItem, "Comment") %>'
                  Text='<%# DataBinder.Eval (Container.DataItem,
                  "Title") + " " +
                  DataBinder.Eval (Container.DataItem,
                  "Number") %>' /><br>
                <%# DataBinder.Eval (Container.DataItem,
                  "Year") %><br>
                <%# DataBinder.Eval (Container.DataItem, "Rating",
                  "{0:f1}") %><br>
              </td>
            </tr>
          </table>
        </ItemTemplate>
        <SelectedItemStyle BackColor="gainsboro" />
      </asp:DataList>
    </form>
  </body>
</html>

<script language="C#" runat="server">
  void Page_Load (Object sender, EventArgs e)
  {
      if (!IsPostBack) {
          SqlConnection connection = new SqlConnection
              ("server=localhost;database=mycomics;uid=sa;pwd=");

          try {
              connection.Open ();
              SqlCommand command;
              command = new SqlCommand
                  ("select * from Books order by title, number",
                   connection);
              SqlDataReader reader = command.ExecuteReader ();
              MyDataList.DataSource = reader;
```

```
              MyDataList.DataBind ();
        }
        finally {
            connection.Close ();
        }
    }
}

void OnItemCommand (Object sender, DataListCommandEventArgs e)
{
    if (e.CommandName == "Select") {
        MyDataList.SelectedIndex = e.Item.ItemIndex;
        Output.Text = e.CommandArgument.ToString ();
    }
}
}
</script>
```

DataGrid Controls

DataGrid controls are the most complex of the data-bound Web controls for the simple reason that they offer the richest variety of options. The *DataGrid*'s purpose is to display tabular data. A single *DataGrid* control can replace reams of old ASP code that queries a database and manually outputs a table using repeated calls to *Response.Write*. Here's an example that uses a *DataGrid* to display the contents of the SQL Server Pubs database's "Titles" table. The output is shown in Figure 6-8.

```
<%@ Import Namespace="System.Data" %>
<%@ Import Namespace="System.Data.SqlClient" %>

<html>
  <body>
    <form runat="server">
      <asp:DataGrid ID="MyDataGrid" RunAt="server" />
    </form>
  </body>
</html>

<script language="C#" runat="server">
  void Page_Load (Object sender, EventArgs e)
  {
      if (!IsPostBack) {
          SqlConnection connection = new SqlConnection
              ("server=localhost;database=pubs;uid=sa;pwd=");

          try {
```

(continued)

```
        connection.Open ();
        SqlCommand command = new SqlCommand
            ("select * from titles where price != 0",
            connection);
        SqlDataReader reader = command.ExecuteReader ();
        MyDataGrid.DataSource = reader;
        MyDataGrid.DataBind ();
    }
    finally {
        connection.Close ();
    }
    }
}
</script>
```

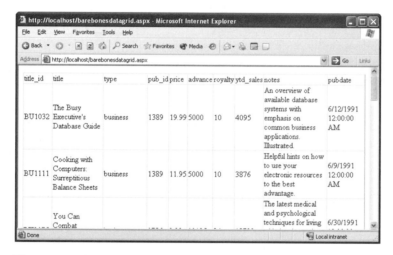

Figure 6-8 Bare-bones *DataGrid* control.

That's a lot of output for a relatively small amount of code, but aesthetically, the output leaves something to be desired. Fortunately, *DataGrid* controls support a wide range of formatting options. Some of those options are controlled by using properties such as *BorderColor* and *BackColor* as attributes in control tags. Others are exercised by using the *Columns* property to specify what columns should appear in the table and how those columns should be rendered. A *DataGrid* supports the following column types:

Column Type	Description
BoundColumn	Creates a column whose content comes from a field in the data source.
ButtonColumn	Creates a column of buttons (push buttons or link buttons).
EditColumn	Creates a column of buttons enabling *DataGrid* items to be edited and changes to be accepted or rejected.
HyperLinkColumn	Creates a column of hyperlinks. Hyperlink text can be static or drawn from a field in the data source.
TemplateColumn	Creates a column of items whose appearance is defined by a UI template.

By default, a *DataGrid* control contains one *BoundColumn* for every field in the data source. You can change that by setting the *DataGrid*'s *AutoGenerateColumns* property to false and manually creating columns. The following example uses a *DataGrid* to display the contents of the Pubs database's "Titles" table—the same table depicted in Figure 6-8. But this time, the results are more pleasing to the eye, as you can see in Figure 6-9.

```
<%@ Import Namespace="System.Data" %>
<%@ Import Namespace="System.Data.SqlClient" %>

<html>
  <body>
    <form runat="server">
      <asp:DataGrid ID="MyDataGrid"
        AutoGenerateColumns="false" CellPadding="2"
        BorderWidth="1" BorderColor="lightgray"
        Font-Name="Verdana" Font-Size="8pt"
        GridLines="vertical" Width="90%"
        OnItemCommand="OnItemCommand" RunAt="server">
        <Columns>
          <asp:BoundColumn HeaderText="Item ID"
            DataField="title_id" />
          <asp:BoundColumn HeaderText="Title"
            DataField="title" />
          <asp:BoundColumn HeaderText="Price"
            DataField="price" DataFormatString="{0:c}"
            HeaderStyle-HorizontalAlign="center"
            ItemStyle-HorizontalAlign="right" />
          <asp:ButtonColumn HeaderText="Action" Text="Add to Cart"
            HeaderStyle-HorizontalAlign="center"
            ItemStyle-HorizontalAlign="center"
            CommandName="AddToCart" />
        </Columns>
        <HeaderStyle BackColor="teal" ForeColor="white"
```

(continued)

```
                    Font-Bold="true" />
                <ItemStyle BackColor="white" ForeColor="darkblue" />
                <AlternatingItemStyle BackColor="beige"
                    ForeColor="darkblue" />
            </asp:DataGrid>
            <br>
            <asp:Label ID="Output" RunAt="server" />
        </form>
    </body>
</html>

<script language="C#" runat="server">
    void Page_Load (Object sender, EventArgs e)
    {
        if (!IsPostBack) {
            SqlConnection connection = new SqlConnection
                ("server=localhost;database=pubs;uid=sa;pwd=");

            try {
                connection.Open ();
                SqlCommand command = new SqlCommand
                    ("select * from titles where price != 0",
                    connection);
                SqlDataReader reader = command.ExecuteReader ();
                MyDataGrid.DataSource = reader;
                MyDataGrid.DataBind ();
            }
            finally {
                connection.Close ();
            }
        }
    }

    void OnItemCommand (Object sender, DataGridCommandEventArgs e)
    {
        if (e.CommandName == "AddToCart")
            Output.Text = e.Item.Cells[1].Text;
    }
</script>
```

This *DataGrid* contains three *BoundColumn*s and one *ButtonColumn*. The *BoundColumn*s bind to the "title_id," "title," and "price" fields of the data source, as indicated by the *DataField* attributes. The *ButtonColumn* renders a column of *LinkButton*s labeled "Add to Cart." Clicking a *LinkButton* activates *OnItemCommand*, which uses the *Label* control at the bottom of the page to display the title of the book whose "Add to Cart" button was clicked. Just like

Repeater controls and *DataList* controls, a *DataGrid* control that renders buttons fires an *ItemCommand* event whenever one of those buttons is clicked.

When an *ItemCommand* event fires, the handler receives a *DataGridCommandEventArgs* whose *Item* property represents the row whose button was clicked. As the example in the previous paragraph demonstrates, the handler can read the contents of the row by reading the *TableCell*s in *Item*'s *Cells* collection. Each *TableCell*'s *Text* property exposes the text contained in one of the row's cells.

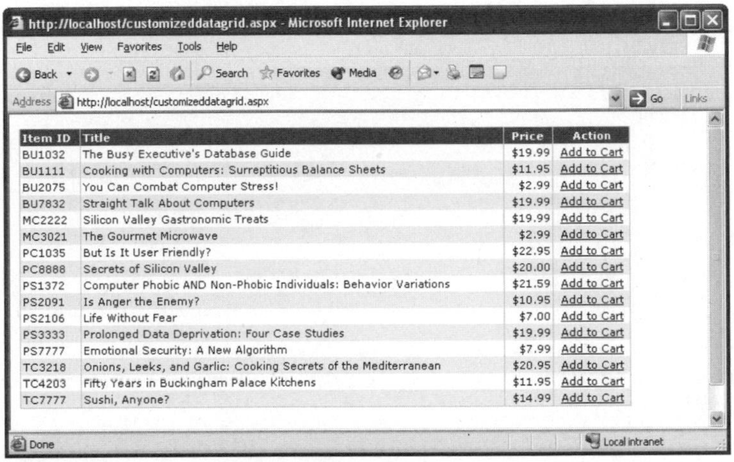

Figure 6-9   Customized *DataGrid* control.

Sortable *DataGrid* Controls

By default, items appear in a *DataGrid* in the same order in which they're enumerated from the data source. You can sort the contents of a *DataGrid* by binding to a *DataView* instead of a *DataReader* or *DataSet*. *DataView* is an ADO.NET class used to create logical views of the records in a data source. A *DataView* can be sorted by assigning a sort expression to its *Sort* property. For example, the sort expression "Title ASC" sorts the *DataView* in ascending order based on the contents of its "Title" column. The sort expression "Price DESC" sorts the *DataView* in descending order based on the contents of its "Price" column. The following code fragment demonstrates how you'd modify the

Page_Load method in the previous example to sort the *DataGrid* output by book title:

```
void Page_Load (Object sender, EventArgs e)
{
    SqlDataAdapter adapter = new SqlDataAdapter
        ("select * from titles where price != 0",
        "server=localhost;database=pubs;uid=sa;pwd=");
    DataSet ds = new DataSet ();
    adapter.Fill (ds);
    DataView view = new DataView (ds.Tables[0]);
    view.Sort = "Title ASC";
    MyDataGrid.DataSource = view;
    MyDataGrid.DataBind ();
}
```

In this example, the *DataView* wraps a *DataTable*. The *DataTable* comes from a *DataSet* initialized with a *DataAdapter*. Setting the *DataView*'s *Sort* property to "Title ASC" sorts items enumerated from the *DataView* by title.

*DataGrid*s also support interactive sorting. Here's a recipe for creating a sortable *DataGrid*—one whose contents can be sorted by clicking a column header:

1. Set the *DataGrid*'s *AllowSorting* property to true.

2. Include a *SortExpression* attribute in each *BoundColumn* that supports sorting. The sort expression "Title ASC" performs an ascending sort on the "Title" field.

3. Write a handler for the *SortCommand* event that a *DataGrid* fires when the header atop a sortable column is clicked. In the event handler, bind the *DataGrid* to a *DataView*. Initialize the *DataView*'s *Sort* property with the sort expression in the *SortExpression* property of the *DataGridSortCommandEventArgs* passed to the event handler.

4. Use an *OnSortCommand* attribute in the <asp:DataGrid> tag to connect the *DataGrid* to the *SortCommand* event handler.

To demonstrate, the following example shows how to modify the *Data-Grid* control shown in the previous section to support interactive sorting by title and price. Changes are highlighted in bold:

```
<asp:DataGrid ID="MyDataGrid"
  AutoGenerateColumns="false" CellPadding="2"
  BorderWidth="1" BorderColor="lightgray"
  Font-Name="Verdana" Font-Size="8pt"
  GridLines="vertical" Width="90%"
```

```
    OnItemCommand="OnItemCommand" RunAt="server"
    AllowSorting="true" OnSortCommand="OnSort">
    <Columns>
      <asp:BoundColumn HeaderText="Item ID"
        DataField="title_id" />
      <asp:BoundColumn HeaderText="Title"
        DataField="title" SortExpression="title ASC" />
      <asp:BoundColumn HeaderText="Price"
        DataField="price" DataFormatString="{0:c}"
        HeaderStyle-HorizontalAlign="center"
        ItemStyle-HorizontalAlign="right"
        SortExpression="price DESC" />
        .
        .
        .
</asp:DataGrid>
    .
    .
    .
// In the <script> block
void OnSort (Object sender, DataGridSortCommandEventArgs e)
{
    SqlDataAdapter adapter = new SqlDataAdapter
        ("select * from titles where price != 0",
        "server=localhost;database=pubs;uid=sa;pwd=");
    DataSet ds = new DataSet ();
    adapter.Fill (ds);
    DataView view = new DataView (ds.Tables[0]);
    view.Sort = e.SortExpression.ToString (); // e.g., "Title ASC"
    MyDataGrid.DataSource = view;
    MyDataGrid.DataBind ();
}
```

The value passed in the *SortExpression* property of the *DataGridSortCommandEventArgs* is the same *SortExpression* value assigned to the *BoundColumn* whose header was clicked. Figure 6-10 shows how the *DataGrid* appears after it's sorted by title. Note the underlining that appears in the headers atop the "Title" and "Price" columns indicating that these columns support sorting.

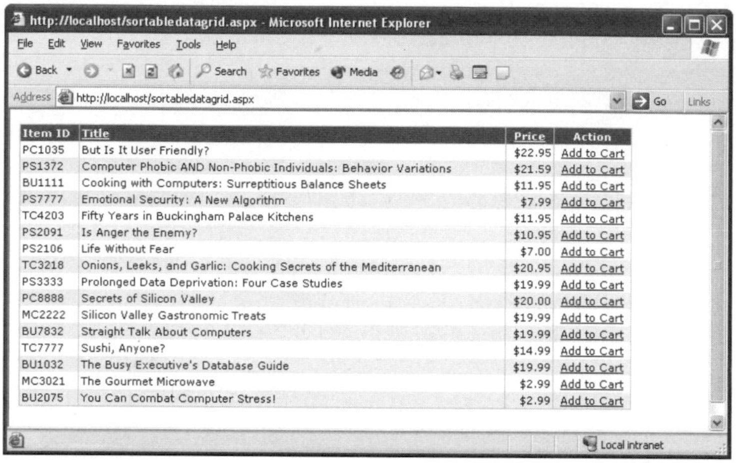

Figure 6-10   Sortable *DataGrid* control.

Pageable *DataGrid* Controls

DataGrid controls also support paging. Paging enables you to paginate the output when you bind to a data source containing a long list of items. The following example displays records from the Microsoft SQL Server Northwind database's "Products" table in a pageable *DataGrid*:

```
<%@ Import Namespace="System.Data" %>
<%@ Import Namespace="System.Data.SqlClient" %>

<html>
  <body>
    <form runat="server">
      <asp:DataGrid ID="MyDataGrid"
        AutoGenerateColumns="false" CellPadding="2"
        BorderWidth="1" BorderColor="lightgray"
        Font-Name="Verdana" Font-Size="8pt"
        GridLines="vertical" Width="90%" RunAt="server"
        AllowPaging="true" PageSize="10"
        OnPageIndexChanged="OnNewPage">
        <Columns>
          <asp:BoundColumn HeaderText="Product ID"
            DataField="ProductID"
            HeaderStyle-HorizontalAlign="center"
            ItemStyle-HorizontalAlign="center" />
          <asp:BoundColumn HeaderText="Product Name"
            DataField="ProductName"
            HeaderStyle-HorizontalAlign="center" />
          <asp:BoundColumn HeaderText="Unit Price"
```

```
                    DataField="UnitPrice"
                    HeaderStyle-HorizontalAlign="center"
                    ItemStyle-HorizontalAlign="right"
                    DataFormatString="{0:c}" />
                  <asp:BoundColumn HeaderText="Unit"
                    DataField="QuantityPerUnit"
                    HeaderStyle-HorizontalAlign="center" />
              </Columns>
              <HeaderStyle BackColor="teal" ForeColor="white"
                Font-Bold="true" />
              <ItemStyle BackColor="white" ForeColor="darkblue" />
              <AlternatingItemStyle BackColor="beige"
                ForeColor="darkblue" />
          </asp:DataGrid>
       </form>
    </body>
</html>

<script language="C#" runat="server">
  void Page_Load (Object sender, EventArgs e)
  {
      if (!IsPostBack) {
          SqlDataAdapter adapter =
              new SqlDataAdapter ("select * from products",
              "server=localhost;database=northwind;uid=sa;pwd=");
          DataSet ds = new DataSet ();
          adapter.Fill (ds);
          MyDataGrid.DataSource = ds;
          MyDataGrid.DataBind ();
      }
  }

  void OnNewPage (Object sender, DataGridPageChangedEventArgs e)
  {
      MyDataGrid.CurrentPageIndex = e.NewPageIndex;
      SqlDataAdapter adapter =
          new SqlDataAdapter ("select * from products",
          "server=localhost;database=northwind;uid=sa;pwd=");
      DataSet ds = new DataSet ();
      adapter.Fill (ds);
      MyDataGrid.DataSource = ds;
      MyDataGrid.DataBind ();
  }
</script>
```

The output from this code is shown in Figure 6-11. Clicking one of the arrows at the bottom of the page displays the next or previous page. The *Allow-Paging* attribute in the <asp:DataGrid> tag enables paging. The *PageSize* attribute sizes each page to display 10 items, and the *OnPageIndexChanged* attribute identifies the event handler—*OnNewPage*—that's called when an arrow is clicked. *OnNewPage* displays the next or previous page by reinitializing the *DataSet* and setting the *DataGrid*'s *CurrentPageIndex* property equal to the page number passed in the *DataGridPageChangedEventArgs*. The *DataGrid* does the hard part by extracting the data for the current page from the *DataSet*.

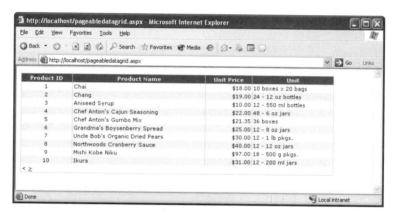

Figure 6-11   Pageable *DataGrid* control.

You can further customize a pageable *DataGrid* by using its *PagerStyle* property. Adding the following attributes to the <asp:DataGrid> tag changes the arrows displayed at the bottom of the control to the strings "Previous Page" and "Next Page:"

```
PagerStyle-PrevPageText="Previous Page"
PagerStyle-NextPageText="Next Page"
```

The attribute shown in the next statement replaces the arrows with page numbers, providing random access to the *DataGrid*'s pages:

```
PagerStyle-Mode="NumericPages"
```

For a list of other changes you can effect with *PagerStyle*, consult the list of *DataGridPagerStyle* members in the .NET Framework SDK documentation.

One drawback to paging a *DataGrid* using the technique shown in the previous example is that it's inefficient. *OnNewPage* retrieves the entire "Products" table each time it's called, even though it needs only 10 records. That's why *DataGrid* controls support an alternative form of paging called *custom paging.* Setting a *DataGrid*'s *AllowCustomPaging* property to true enables custom paging and frees the *PageIndexChanged* handler to fetch just the records shown on the current page. Custom paging can deliver dramatic performance benefits when the data source contains hundreds or thousands of records rather than just a few.

The MyComicsDataGrid Page

The Web page shown in Figure 6-12 rounds out this chapter's treatment of data-bound Web controls by using a *DataGrid* to expose the contents of the MyComics database used in earlier examples. In addition to showing how to use *BoundColumn*s to expose selected fields in a data source, MyComicsData-Grid.aspx, shown in Figure 6-13, demonstrates how to use *TemplateColumn*s to create user-defined columns. The statements

```
<asp:TemplateColumn HeaderText="CGC"
  HeaderStyle-HorizontalAlign="center">
  <ItemTemplate>
    <center>
      <%# ((bool) DataBinder.Eval (Container.DataItem,
        "CGC")) == false ? "N" : "Y" %>
    </center>
  </ItemTemplate>
</asp:TemplateColumn>
```

create a column that programmatically binds to the database's "CGC" field and displays either "Y" if the field contains a 1 or "N" if it contains a 0. *DataGrid* controls don't support UI templates per se, but *TemplateColumn*s do. One common use for *TemplateColumn*s is to create columns containing *TextBox* controls that the user can type information into.

The *DataGrid* in this example also uses a *ButtonColumn* to put "View Cover" buttons in the grid's leftmost column. Clicking a button fires an *Item-Command* event that activates the page's *OnItemCommand* method, which displays a close-up of the comic book cover by calling *Response.Redirect* with the URL of the corresponding image in the Images/Large directory. *Response.Redirect* is one of the most important methods in all of ASP.NET; it transfers control to another Web page. You'll learn more about it later in this chapter.

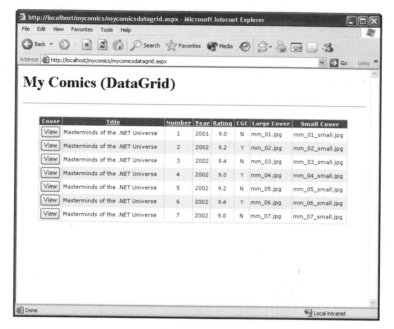

Figure 6-12   The MyComicsDataGrid page.

MyComicsDataGrid.aspx

```
<%@ Import Namespace="System.Data" %>
<%@ Import Namespace="System.Data.SqlClient" %>

<html>
  <body>
    <h1>My Comics (DataGrid)</h1>
    <hr>
    <form runat="server">
      <center>
        <asp:DataGrid ID="MyDataGrid" AutoGenerateColumns="false"
          BorderWidth="1" BorderColor="lightgray" CellPadding="2"
          Font-Name="Verdana" Font-Size="8pt" GridLines="vertical"
          OnItemCommand="OnItemCommand" OnSortCommand="OnSort"
          Width="90%" AllowSorting="true" RunAt="server">
          <Columns>
            <asp:ButtonColumn ButtonType="PushButton"
              HeaderText="Cover" Text="View"
              HeaderStyle-HorizontalAlign="center"
              ItemStyle-HorizontalAlign="center"
              CommandName="ViewComic" />
            <asp:BoundColumn HeaderText="Title" DataField="Title"
              SortExpression="Title ASC"
```

Figure 6-13   MyComicsDataGrid source code.

```
                    HeaderStyle-HorizontalAlign="center" />
                <asp:BoundColumn HeaderText="Number" DataField="Number"
                    SortExpression="Number ASC"
                    HeaderStyle-HorizontalAlign="center"
                    ItemStyle-HorizontalAlign="center" />
                <asp:BoundColumn HeaderText="Year" DataField="Year"
                    SortExpression="Year ASC"
                    HeaderStyle-HorizontalAlign="center"
                    ItemStyle-HorizontalAlign="center" />
                <asp:BoundColumn HeaderText="Rating" DataField="Rating"
                    DataFormatString="{0:f1}" SortExpression="Rating ASC"
                    HeaderStyle-HorizontalAlign="center"
                    ItemStyle-HorizontalAlign="center" />
                <asp:TemplateColumn HeaderText="CGC"
                    HeaderStyle-HorizontalAlign="center">
                    <ItemTemplate>
                      <center>
                        <%# ((bool) DataBinder.Eval (Container.DataItem,
                            "CGC")) == false ? "N" : "Y" %>
                      </center>
                    </ItemTemplate>
                </asp:TemplateColumn>
                <asp:BoundColumn HeaderText="Large Cover"
                    DataField="LargeCover"
                    HeaderStyle-HorizontalAlign="center" />
                <asp:BoundColumn HeaderText="Small Cover"
                    DataField="SmallCover"
                    HeaderStyle-HorizontalAlign="center" />
            </Columns>
            <HeaderStyle BackColor="teal" ForeColor="white"
                Font-Bold="true" />
            <ItemStyle BackColor="white" ForeColor="darkblue" />
            <AlternatingItemStyle BackColor="beige"
                ForeColor="darkblue" />
          </asp:DataGrid>
        </center>
      </form>
    </body>
</html>

<script language="C#" runat="server">
  void Page_Load (Object sender, EventArgs e)
  {
      if (!IsPostBack) {
          SqlDataAdapter adapter = new SqlDataAdapter
```

(continued)

MyComicsDataGrid.aspx   *(continued)*

```
                ("select * from books order by title, number",
                "server=localhost;database=mycomics;uid=sa;pwd=");
            DataSet ds = new DataSet ();
            adapter.Fill (ds);
            MyDataGrid.DataSource = ds;
            MyDataGrid.DataBind ();
        }
    }

    void OnSort (Object sender, DataGridSortCommandEventArgs e)
    {
        SqlDataAdapter adapter = new SqlDataAdapter
            ("select * from books order by title, number",
            "server=localhost;database=mycomics;uid=sa;pwd=");
        DataSet ds = new DataSet ();
        adapter.Fill (ds);
        DataView view = new DataView (ds.Tables[0]);
        view.Sort = e.SortExpression.ToString ();
        MyDataGrid.DataSource = view;
        MyDataGrid.DataBind ();
    }

    void OnItemCommand (Object sender, DataGridCommandEventArgs e)
    {
        if (e.CommandName == "ViewComic")
            Response.Redirect ("Images/Large" + e.Item.Cells[6].Text);
    }
</script>
```

Calendar Controls

One of the most thankless tasks in Web programming is building calendars into Web pages. Creating an HTML table that resembles a calendar is easy enough. Writing code that customizes that table to display an arbitrary month and year and to allow the user to select dates from the calendar is not.

Creating calendars is a piece of cake in Web forms thanks to the FCL's *Calendar* class. The following statement displays the calendar seen in Figure 6-14. The calendar automatically shows the current month unless told to do otherwise, automatically fires an event when a date is selected, and automatically shows the next or previous month when either of its navigation buttons (the arrows in the control's title bar) is clicked:

```
<asp:Calendar RunAt="server" />
```

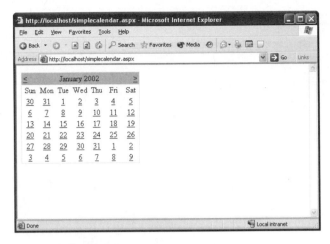

Figure 6-14   Simple calendar control.

Of course, self-respecting developers want controls to be attractive as well as functional. *Calendar* controls expose a rich assortment of properties and subproperties that allow them to be customized in a variety of ways. Here's an excerpt from a Web form that uses some of those properties to customize a calendar's UI:

```
<asp:Calendar
  DayNameFormat="FirstLetter"
  ShowGridLines="true"
  BackColor="beige" ForeColor="darkblue"
  SelectedDayStyle-BackColor="red"
  SelectedDayStyle-ForeColor="white"
  SelectedDayStyle-Font-Bold="true"
  TitleStyle-BackColor="darkblue"
  TitleStyle-ForeColor="white"
  TitleStyle-Font-Bold="true"
  NextPrevStyle-BackColor="darkblue"
  NextPrevStyle-ForeColor="white"
  DayHeaderStyle-BackColor="red"
  DayHeaderStyle-ForeColor="white"
  DayHeaderStyle-Font-Bold="true"
  OtherMonthDayStyle-BackColor="white"
  OtherMonthDayStyle-ForeColor="lightblue"
  Width="256px" RunAt="Server">
</asp:Calendar>
```

Among other things, the attributes added to the control tag display one-letter (rather than three-letter) abbreviations for the days of the week, add grid lines, and customize the control's colors. They even highlight the days in the current month using a different color. Figure 6-15 shows the result.

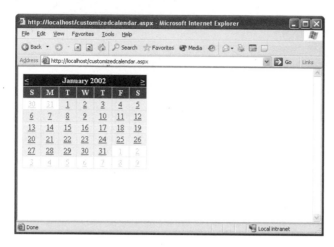

Figure 6-15   Customized calendar control.

Calendar controls fire three kinds of events:

■ *SelectionChanged* events, which indicate that the user has selected a new date.

■ *VisibleMonthChanged* events, which indicate that the user has navigated to another month.

■ *DayRender* events, which fire as the calendar renders individual cells, giving the developer the opportunity to customize each cell's appearance.

A server-side script can select a date in a *Calendar* control by writing to the calendar's *SelectedDate* property. If "MyCalendar" is a *Calendar* control, the following statement selects today's date:

```
MyCalendar.SelectedDate = DateTime.Now;
```

Similarly, a script can retrieve the currently selected date by reading *SelectedDate*. The next example responds to *SelectionChanged* events by writing the date that's currently selected to a *Label* control whose ID is "Output":

```
<asp:Calendar ID="MyCalendar" OnSelectionChanged="OnDateSelected"
  RunAt="server" />
  .
  .
  .
<script language="C#" runat="server">
```

```
void OnDateSelected (Object sender, EventArgs e)
{
    Output.Text = MyCalendar.SelectedDate.ToLongDateString ();
}
</script>
```

By default, a *Calendar* control allows only one day to be selected at a time. You can change that by setting the control's *SelectionMode* property, which defaults to Day, to DayWeek, DayWeekMonth, or None. DayWeek allows days or weeks to be selected; DayWeekMonth permits days, weeks, or entire months to be selected; and None prevents anything—even individual days—from being selected. DayWeek adds arrows to the left margin of the calendar for selecting entire weeks. DayWeekMonth adds arrows for selecting weeks and a double arrow for selecting the entire month. Regardless of what the user selects—a day, a week, or a month—the control fires a *SelectionChanged* event. A server-side script determines which dates are selected by reading the *Calendar*'s *SelectedDates* property. *SelectedDates* is a *SelectedDatesCollection* containing a list of all the dates that are currently selected. The following example sets the calendar's *SelectionMode* to DayWeekMonth and writes the entire array of selected dates to a *Label* control:

```
<html>
  <body>
    <form runat="server"><br>
      <asp:Calendar ID="MyCalendar" SelectionMode="DayWeekMonth"
        OnSelectionChanged="OnDateSelected" RunAt="server" />
      <br>
      <asp:Label ID="Output" RunAt="server" />
    </form>
  </body>
</html>

<script language="C#" runat="server">
  void OnDateSelected (Object sender, EventArgs e)
  {
      StringBuilder builder = new StringBuilder ();
      foreach (DateTime date in MyCalendar.SelectedDates) {
          builder.Append (date.ToLongDateString ());
          builder.Append ("<br>");
      }
      Output.Text = builder.ToString ();
  }
</script>
```

If you run this sample and select the week of January 6, 2002, you'll see the following output:

```
Sunday, January 06, 2002
Monday, January 07, 2002
Tuesday, January 08, 2002
Wednesday, January 09, 2002
Thursday, January 10, 2002
Friday, January 11, 2002
Saturday, January 12, 2002
```

A server-side script can select a range of dates by calling the *SelectRange* method on the control's *SelectedDates* collection. The following code selects January 1, 2002, through January 3, 2002, and changes the month displayed by the calendar to January 2002 so that the selection can be seen:

```
DateTime start = new DateTime (2002, 1, 1);
DateTime end = new DateTime (2002, 1, 3);
MyCalendar.SelectedDates.SelectRange (start, end);
MyCalendar.VisibleDate = start;
```

Calendar controls render a lengthy mix of HTML and JavaScript to browsers. Do a View/Source on a page containing a *Calendar* control and you'll see what I mean. The JavaScript is necessary to force a postback when the visible month or selection changes. Fortunately, the JavaScript is benign enough to permit *Calendar* controls to work with virtually any browser that supports client-side scripting.

Advanced Customization: The *DayRender* Event

Whenever I speak about *Calendar* controls in classes and at conferences, I'm inundated with questions about customization. A typical question is, "Is it possible to restrict the dates the user can select from?" or, "Can I add text or images to individual cells in a *Calendar* control?" The answer is almost always yes, thanks to *DayRender* events.

DayRender events are fired for each and every cell that a *Calendar* control renders. By processing *DayRender* events, you can customize individual cells ("days") by inserting your own HTML. The following example displays the word "Christmas" in tiny red letters on December 25 (shown in Figure 6-16):

```
<asp:Calendar ID="MyCalendar" ShowGridLines="true"
  OnDayRender="OnDayRender" RunAt="server" />
    .
    .
    .
<script language="C#" runat="server">
  void OnDayRender (Object sender, DayRenderEventArgs e)
```

```
    {
        e.Cell.Width = 80;
        e.Cell.Height = 64;

        string html =
            "<br><font color=\"red\" face=\"verdana\" size=\"1\">" +
            "Christmas</font>";

        if (e.Day.Date.Month == 12 && e.Day.Date.Day == 25) {
            e.Cell.Controls.AddAt (0, new LiteralControl ("<br>"));
            e.Cell.Controls.Add (new LiteralControl (html));
        }
    }
}
</script>
```

DayRender event handlers receive *DayRenderEventArgs* parameters whose *Day* and *Cell* properties contain everything a handler needs to customize a calendar cell. *Day* contains a *Date* property that identifies the date being rendered. *Cell* is a *TableCell* object that provides programmatic access to the corresponding table cell. *Cell*'s *Controls* collection exposes the controls defined in the table cell. By default, the *Controls* collection contains a *LiteralControl* that renders a number into the cell. The *OnDayRender* method in the previous example calls *AddAt* on the *Controls* collection to insert a line break (<br>) before the number and *Add* to insert additional HTML after. You could modify this sample to inject images into a *Calendar* control by emitting <img> tags instead of text.

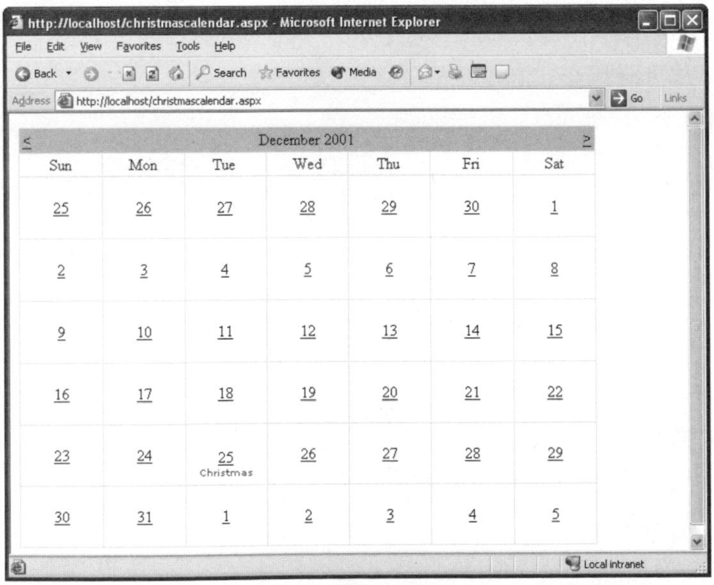

Figure 6-16   *Calendar* control with December 25 customized.

That's one example of what you can accomplish with *DayRender* events. Here's another. Suppose you want to place a calendar in a Web form but prevent the user from selecting anything other than weekdays. The following *DayRender* handler demonstrates the solution:

```
void OnDayRender (Object sender, DayRenderEventArgs e)
{
    e.Day.IsSelectable =
        !(e.Day.Date.DayOfWeek == DayOfWeek.Saturday ||
        e.Day.Date.DayOfWeek == DayOfWeek.Sunday);
}
```

How does it work? *Day* is an instance of *CalendarDay*, which features a get/set property named *IsSelectable* that can be set to false to prevent the control from placing a hyperlink in the corresponding cell. This example sets *IsSelectable* to false for Saturdays and Sundays and true for other days, producing the calendar shown in Figure 6-17. A similar technique can be used to prevent dates prior to today's date from being selected:

```
void OnDayRender (Object sender, DayRenderEventArgs e)
{
    e.Day.IsSelectable = e.Day.Date >= DateTime.Today;
}
```

A little knowledge of *DayRender* events goes a long way when it comes to making *Calendar* controls work the way you want them to.

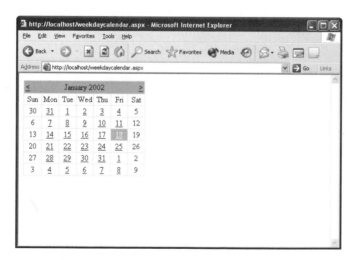

Figure 6-17 *Calendar* control that limits selections to weekdays.

Showtime

The Web form shown in Figure 6-18 is the front end for an online ordering service that allows patrons to order Broadway show tickets. It uses a *DropDownList*, a *Calendar*, and, for good measure, a graphical *ImageButton*. Pick a show and a date and your selections appear at the bottom of the Web page.

The program's source code appears in Figure 6-19. The *Calendar* control uses a *DayRender* handler to limit the user to Fridays and Saturdays that occur on or after today's date and also to highlight selectable dates by painting their background color beige. The code that changes the cell's background color refrains from acting if the day being rendered is the day selected in the *Calendar* control. This simple precaution prevents *OnDayRender* from overriding the colors specified in the control tag with *SelectedDayStyle*.

Figure 6-18   The Showtime Web form.

Showtime.aspx

```
<html>
  <body>
    <h1>Showtime</h1>
    <hr>
    <form runat="server">
      Pick a show:<br>
      <asp:DropDownList ID="ShowName" RunAt="Server">
        <asp:ListItem Text="Cats" Selected="true" RunAt="server" />
        <asp:ListItem Text="Phantom of the Opera" RunAt="server" />
        <asp:ListItem Text="Les Miserables" RunAt="server" />
        <asp:ListItem Text="Cabaret" RunAt="server" />
      </asp:DropDownList>
      <br><br>
      Pick a date:<br>
      <asp:Calendar
        ID="ShowDate"
        ShowGridLines="true"
        ForeColor="darkblue"
        SelectedDayStyle-BackColor="darkblue"
        SelectedDayStyle-ForeColor="white"
        SelectedDayStyle-Font-Bold="true"
        TitleStyle-BackColor="darkblue"
        TitleStyle-ForeColor="white"
        TitleStyle-Font-Bold="true"
        NextPrevStyle-BackColor="darkblue"
        NextPrevStyle-ForeColor="white"
        DayHeaderStyle-BackColor="beige"
        DayHeaderStyle-ForeColor="darkblue"
        DayHeaderStyle-Font-Bold="true"
        OtherMonthDayStyle-ForeColor="lightgray"
        OnSelectionChanged="OnDateSelected"
        OnDayRender="OnDayRender"
        RunAt="Server" />
      <br>
      <asp:ImageButton ImageUrl="OrderBtn.gif" OnClick="OnOrder"
        RunAt="server" />
      <br><br><hr>
      <h3><asp:Label ID="Output" RunAt="server" /></h3>
    </form>
  </body>
</html>

<script language="C#" runat="server">
  void OnOrder (Object sender, ImageClickEventArgs e)
  {
```

Figure 6-19   Showtime source code.

```
        if (ShowDate.SelectedDate.Year > 1900)
            Output.Text = "You selected " +
                ShowName.SelectedItem.Text + " on " +
                ShowDate.SelectedDate.ToLongDateString ();
        else
            Output.Text = "Please select a date";
    }

    void OnDateSelected (Object sender, EventArgs e)
    {
        Output.Text = "";
    }

    void OnDayRender (Object sender, DayRenderEventArgs e)
    {
        e.Day.IsSelectable =
            (e.Day.Date.DayOfWeek == DayOfWeek.Friday ||
            e.Day.Date.DayOfWeek == DayOfWeek.Saturday) &&
            e.Day.Date >= DateTime.Today &&
            !e.Day.IsOtherMonth;

        if (e.Day.IsSelectable && e.Day.Date != ShowDate.SelectedDate)
            e.Cell.BackColor = System.Drawing.Color.Beige;
    }
</script>
```

Validation Controls

Six of the controls found in *System.Web.UI.WebControls* are provided to help you validate user input in Web forms. Known as *validation controls,* or simply *validators*, these controls are some of the most interesting—and potentially useful—of all the controls in ASP.NET. Here are two reasons why:

■ Validation checking—for example, verifying that a required field isn't blank or a date selected by the user falls within a specified range— is a common requirement in Web applications.

■ ASP.NET's validation controls are smart. They do their checking on both the client and the server. Validation controls emit JavaScript that executes in the browser and prevents postbacks from occurring if a page contains invalid input. And after a postback occurs, validators check the input again on the server.

Why do validation controls recheck the input on the server? One, rechecking prevents spoofing. Two, it enables the input to undergo a validation check even if it originated from a browser that doesn't support client-side scripting.

Validating user input on the client side is a Good Thing because it prevents postbacks from occurring that would ultimately be rejected by the server anyway. Checking on the client side is nothing new; Web programmers have been doing it for years. Unfortunately, writing client-side validation scripts requires a non-trivial knowledge of Dynamic HTML and client-side scripting. Validation controls lower the barrier to entry by encapsulating the required logic in easy-to-use classes. You simply attach validators to the controls you want to validate, and the validators do the rest.

What kinds of checks are validation controls capable of performing? For starters, they can verify that

■   An input field isn't blank (*RequiredFieldValidator*)

■   An input value falls within a specified range (*RangeValidator*)

■   An input string conforms to a pattern matching a regular expression (*RegularExpressionValidator*)

■   An input value is equal to, not equal to, less than, equal to or less than, greater than, or greater than or equal to either a specified value or another input value (*CompareValidator*)

If none of these validation types fit the bill, you can use a *CustomValidator* control to enact validation routines of your own. And the *ValidationSummary* control enables error messages provided by other validators to be displayed as a group.

One nuance you should be aware of regarding validator controls is that the client-side validation code they emit doesn't work with all browsers. The JavaScript that they return makes extensive use of the browser's DHTML document object model (DOM). Before the W3C standardized the DOM, Internet Explorer and Netscape Navigator implemented incompatible DOMs. Client-side validation works fine in Internet Explorer 4 and later. ASP.NET sniffs out the browser type and doesn't even attempt to return client-side validation code to Navigator.

The good news is that the incompatibilities affect only *client-side* validation. Server-side validation works regardless of the browser type, so someone using a down-level browser won't be able to submit invalid data without you knowing about it. They will, however, incur a round trip to the server and back each time they try.

Using the Validation Controls

All validator control classes with the exception of *ValidationSummary* derive from a common base class—*BaseValidator*—and therefore share many traits, including the following:

- All feature a property named *ControlToValidate* that identifies the control whose input the validator validates.

- All have a property named *ErrorMessage* that defines the error message the control displays if it deems an input invalid. Where on the Web page the error message appears depends on where on the page the validator is located. Position the validator to the right of a *TextBox* control, for example, and the validator's error message appears to the right of the *TextBox*, too.

- All have a property named *ForeColor* that specifies the color in which error messages are rendered. The default is red.

- All have a property named *Display* that determines how a validator's error message is displayed. *Display* can be set to Static, which statically reserves space in the Web page for the error message; Dynamic, which doesn't reserve space for the error message (and therefore might alter the page layout if the validator fires); and None, which prevents the error message from displaying at all. Use the None option when you intend to display the validators' error messages in a *ValidationSummary* control.

- All have a property named *EnableClientScript* that allows client-side validation to be selectively enabled or disabled. *EnableClientScript* defaults to true. Setting it to false prevents the control from emitting client-side JavaScript and therefore disables client-side error checking. Checks are still performed on the server, however.

Here's an example demonstrating how some of these properties are used. The following code declares a *TextBox* and attaches a *RequiredFieldValidator* to it. It also specifies the error message displayed if the validator fires, ensures that space is reserved for the error message even if it isn't displayed (possibly preventing the page layout from changing if the error message does appear), and sets the error message's color to blue:

```
<asp:TextBox ID="Password" TextMode="Password" RunAt="server" />

<asp:RequiredFieldValidator
  ControlToValidate="Password"
  ErrorMessage="Required field"
  Display="static"
  ForeColor="blue"
  RunAt="server"
/>
```

If you'd prefer, you can omit the *ErrorMessage* attribute and place the error message between the validator's start and end tags:

```
<asp:RequiredFieldValidator
  ControlToValidate="Password"
  Display="static"
  ForeColor="blue"
  RunAt="server"
>
Required Field
</asp:RequiredFieldValidator>
```

The downside to defining an error message this way is that it prevents the error message from working in conjunction with *ValidationSummary* controls. The upside is that it lets you create "rich" error messages that include HTML tags.

A validator can be attached to only one control, but any number of validator controls can be declared on a page. In addition, a given control can have several validators attached to it. The following example combines a *RequiredFieldValidator* and a *RegularExpressionValidator* to verify that a password field isn't blank *and* that it contains at least eight characters:

```
<asp:TextBox ID="Password" TextMode="Password" RunAt="server" />

<asp:RequiredFieldValidator
  ControlToValidate="Password"
  ErrorMessage="Required field"
  Display="dynamic"
  ForeColor="blue"
  RunAt="server"
/>

<asp:RegularExpressionValidator
  ControlToValidate="Password"
  ValidationExpression=".{8,}"
  ErrorMessage="You must enter at least 8 characters"
  Display="dynamic"
  ForeColor="blue"
  RunAt="server"
/>
```

At first glance, it might seem as if the *RequiredFieldValidator* is superfluous because the *RegularExpressionValidator* verifies that the *TextBox* contains at least eight characters. However, *RegularExpressionValidator* performs validation checks only on nonblank fields. The same is true of other validators as well. Therefore, if you want to verify that an input field isn't blank and that it meets other validation criteria too, you must combine *RequiredFieldValidator* with other validation controls.

In the preceding example, note that the validators' *Display* properties are set to Dynamic rather than Static. The reason? If you write *Display*="static," the *RegularExpressionValidator*'s error message, if displayed, appears far to the right of the *TextBox* because of the space reserved for the *RequiredFieldValidator*'s error message. *Display*="dynamic" prevents either control from claiming space that might be used by the other and therefore enables either error message to appear in the same place.

RequiredFieldValidator

As I mentioned, the *RequiredFieldValidator* control validates input by verifying that the corresponding field isn't blank. It's perfect for *TextBox* controls representing required fields in a form because if any of those *TextBox*es is blank, the *RequiredFieldValidator* won't allow the form to be submitted to the server.

Here's an example that verifies that a *TextBox* named "EMail" isn't blank:

```
<asp:TextBox ID="EMail" RunAt="server" />

<asp:RequiredFieldValidator
  ControlToValidate="EMail"
  ErrorMessage="Required field"
  Display="static"
  RunAt="server"
/>
```

Because required fields are so common in Web forms, *RequiredFieldValidator* has the potential to see more use than all the other validation controls combined. It's often used in conjunction with other validation controls because none of the others run their validation checks on blank fields.

RangeValidator

The *RangeValidator* control is the answer to the question, "How do I ensure that an input value falls within a specified range?" Suppose you ask the user to type in a percentage and that valid values range from 0 to 100, inclusive. Here's how to reject any numbers that fall outside that range:

```
<asp:TextBox ID="Percent" RunAt="server" />

<asp:RangeValidator
  ControlToValidate="Percent"
  MinimumValue="0"
  MaximumValue="100"
  Type="Integer"
  ErrorMessage="Value out of range"
  Display="static"
  RunAt="server"
/>
```

The *Type* attribute tells a *RangeValidator* what type of data to use in the comparison. If you don't specify a type, *Type* defaults to String. *Type*="Integer" performs a numeric comparison involving integers. Other valid *Type* attributes include Currency, Date, and Double. The following example displays an error message if the date typed into a *TextBox* doesn't fall in the fourth quarter of 2002:

```
<asp:TextBox ID="MyDate" RunAt="server" />

<asp:RangeValidator
  ControlToValidate="MyDate"
  MinimumValue="10/01/2002"
  MaximumValue="12/31/2002"
  Type="Date"
  ErrorMessage="Date out of range"
  Display="static"
  RunAt="server"
/>
```

In practice, checking a range of dates with *RangeValidator* is of limited usefulness because well-designed sites permit users to pick dates from a calendar. Manually entered dates are problematic because they're culture-sensitive (many parts of the world put days before months, for example) and because *RangeValidator* understands a limited set of date formats.

CompareValidator

The *CompareValidator* control validates input by comparing it to a constant value specified with a *ValueToCompare* attribute or to a value in another control identified with a *ControlToCompare* attribute. *ControlToCompare* makes *CompareValidator* a valuable control for validating input based on other input.

Suppose you invite the user to enter minimum and maximum values denoting the ends of a range. It doesn't make sense to accept a maximum that's less than the minimum, so you could use a *CompareValidator* to ensure the integrity of the input. In the following example, the validator signals an error if the maximum is less than the minimum. The *Operator* attribute specifies that the value entered in the *TextBox* named "Maximum" must be equal to or greater than the value entered in the *TextBox* named "Minimum." The *Type* attribute identifies the type of data involved in the comparison:

```
<asp:TextBox ID="Minimum" RunAt="server" />
<asp:TextBox ID="Maximum" RunAt="server" />

<asp:CompareValidator
  ControlToValidate="Maximum"
  ControlToCompare="Minimum"
  Type="Integer"
  Operator="GreaterThanEqual"
  ErrorMessage="Invalid maximum"
  Display="static"
  RunAt="server"
/>
```

Other supported values for *Operator* are Equal, NotEqual, GreaterThan, Less-Than, LessThanEqual, and DataTypeCheck. The last of these values validates the type of data entered by verifying that it matches the type specified in the *Type* attribute. If you simply wanted to verify that the user input an integer, for example, you could set *Type* to Integer and *Operator* to DataTypeCheck.

Another use for *CompareValidator* is to compare two passwords on pages that ask the user to enter a password and then enter it again to validate the first. Here's the code to compare two passwords:

```
<asp:TextBox ID="Password1" TextMode="Password" RunAt="server" />
<asp:TextBox ID="Password2" TextMode="Password" RunAt="server" />

<asp:CompareValidator
  ControlToValidate="Password2"
  ControlToCompare="Password1"
  Type="String"
  Operator="Equal"
  ErrorMessage="Mismatch"
  Display="static"
  RunAt="server"
/>
```

In scenarios like this one, it's important to validate the second of the two inputs rather than the first to prevent the *CompareValidator* from firing when the focus moves from the first *TextBox* to the second.

Be aware that string comparisons performed by *CompareValidator* are case-sensitive. With passwords that's typically what you want, but for some forms of text input, you might not want the comparison to be case-sensitive.

RegularExpressionValidator

The most versatile validation control by far is the *RegularExpressionValidator*, which validates input by verifying that it conforms to a format specified in a regular expression. You can use a *RegularExpressionValidator* to perform a variety of common validation chores, from verifying that an input value contains only numbers to ensuring that e-mail addresses, zip codes, and credit card numbers are well formed.

Here's a very simple example—one that uses a *RegularExpressionValidator* to reject input containing nonnumeric characters:

```
<asp:TextBox ID="Quantity" RunAt="server" />

<asp:RegularExpressionValidator
  ControlToValidate="Quantity"
  ValidationExpression="^\d+$"
  ErrorMessage="Digits only"
  Display="static"
  RunAt="server"
/>
```

In a regular expression, \d represents the digits 0–9 and + means "one or more of." The expression \d+ means "one or more characters that are digits." If the user tries to slip in a string with a letter in it, the validator will reject it.

The next example validates an e-mail address. It can't actually verify that the address is valid, but it can (and does) verify that the address is well formed:

```
<asp:TextBox ID="EMail" RunAt="server" />

<asp:RegularExpressionValidator
  ControlToValidate="EMail"
  ValidationExpression="^[\w\.-]+@[\w-]+\.[\w\.-]+$"
  ErrorMessage="Invalid e-mail address"
  Display="static"
  RunAt="server"
/>
```

Let's dissect the regular expression. ^ means "start at the beginning of the string." That's important because otherwise a string with a substring matching the regular expression (for example, "!@#$%^&* name@domain.com") would fool the validator into validating the input. The same goes for the $ at the end: it prevents "name@domain.com !@#$%^&*" from resulting in a false match. [\w\.-]+ means "one or more of the following characters: letters, numbers, underscores, periods, and hyphens." @ means the characters must be followed by an @ sign. [\w-]+ indicates that the @ sign must be followed by one or more letters, numbers, underscores, or hyphens, and \. means all that must be followed by a period. Finally, [\w\.-]+ stipulates that the string must end with one or more letters, numbers, underscores, or hyphens. Strings such as "jeff-pro@wintellect.com" and "jeff.pro@win-tellect.com" pass the test just fine, but "jeffpro," "jeffpro@wintellect," and "jeffpro@**&&^^%%.com" do not.

CustomValidator

When none of the other validators fits the bill, *CustomValidator* will do the job that no others can. As its name implies, *CustomValidator* validates input using an algorithm that you supply. If you want *CustomValidator* to check input on the client side, you provide a JavaScript function to do the checking and identify the function with a *ClientValidationFunction* attribute. (You can use VBScript if you'd like, but realize that doing so sacrifices compatibility with browsers other than Internet Explorer. Future versions of ASP.NET will probably support client-side validation in selected third-party browsers.) If you want the input checked on the server as well, you provide the validation method and identify it with an *OnServerValidate* attribute. The following example uses *CustomValidator* to verify that an input value is an even multiple of 10:

```
<asp:TextBox ID="Amount" RunAt="server" />

<asp:CustomValidator
  ControlToValidate="Amount"
  ClientValidationFunction="__validateAmount"
  OnServerValidate="ValidateAmount"
  ErrorMessage="Amount must be a multiple of 10"
  Display="static"
  RunAt="server"
/>
       .
       .
       .
<script language="JavaScript">
<!--
  function __validateAmount (source, args)
  {
      args.IsValid = (args.Value % 10 == 0);
  }
-->
</script>

<script language="C#" runat="server">
  void ValidateAmount (Object sender, ServerValidateEventArgs e)
  {
```

```
        try {
            e.IsValid = (Convert.ToInt32 (e.Value) % 10 == 0);
        }
        catch (FormatException) {
            // In case a non-numeric value is entered
            e.IsValid = false;
        }
    }
</script>
```

The key is to set *args.IsValid* to true or false on the client side and *e.IsValid* to true or false on the server side to indicate whether the input is valid. *CustomValidator* can be used to apply any validation algorithm you want as long as you're willing to write the code to back it up.

ValidationSummary

ValidationSummary is a different sort of validation control. It doesn't perform any validation of its own. It does, however, offer an alternative method for displaying other validators' error messages by "batching them up" and displaying them as a group. The following example uses a *ValidationSummary* control to summarize all the validation errors encountered on the page. Note that the other validator controls' *Display* attributes are set to None, which prevents them from displaying error messages on their own. Before the page is submitted to the server, the *ValidationSummary* control checks the other validators. If any of the validation checks failed, the *ValidationSummary* control displays the corresponding error messages in a bulleted list:

```
<asp:TextBox ID="UserName" RunAt="server" />

<asp:RequiredFieldValidator
  ControlToValidate="UserName"
  ErrorMessage="The user name can't be blank"
  Display="none"
  RunAt="server"
/>

<asp:TextBox ID="Password" TextMode="Password" RunAt="server" />

<asp:RequiredFieldValidator
  ControlToValidate="Password"
  ErrorMessage="The password can't be blank"
  Display="none"
  RunAt="server"
/>
```

```
<asp:RegularExpressionValidator
  ControlToValidate="Password"
  ValidationExpression=".{8,}"
  Display="none"
  ErrorMessage="The password must contain at least 8 characters"
  RunAt="server"
/>

<asp:ValidationSummary
  DisplayMode="BulletList"
  HeaderText="This page contains the following errors"
  RunAt="server"
/>
```

The *ValidationSummary* control's *DisplayMode* attribute can be set to BulletList, which displays error messages in a bulleted list; List, which displays error messages in a list without bullets; or SingleParagraph, which displays error messages without bullets or line breaks. *HeaderText* specifies the text, if any, that appears above the error messages.

A *ValidationSummary* control's *ShowMessageBox* and *ShowSummary* properties can be used to further customize the control's output. By default, *ShowMessageBox* is false and *ShowSummary* is true, meaning that error messages are displayed in the Web page. However, setting *ShowMessageBox* to true and *ShowSummary* to false displays the error messages in a pop-up message box (what JavaScript programmers refer to as an *alert box* because of the JavaScript command used to display it: *alert*):

```
<asp:ValidationSummary
  DisplayMode="BulletList"
  HeaderText="This page contains the following errors"
  ShowMessageBox="true"
  ShowSummary="false"
  RunAt="server"
/>
```

Setting both *ShowMessageBox* and *ShowSummary* to true causes the validation summary to appear in a message box *and* in the Web page. (Talk about getting someone's attention!)

Spammers, Incorporated

Ever been spammed? Just in case you don't get enough spam already, the application in Figure 6-21 displays a form from a fictitious company named Spammers, Inc., that invites users to enter a name, e-mail address, and other personal information and receive spam in return. It collects most of its input from *Text-*

Box controls and validates the input using an assortment of *RequiredFieldValidator*s and *RegularExpressionValidator*s. Specifically, it uses the following validators:

- *RequiredFieldValidator*s to verify that a name and e-mail address are provided

- A *RegularExpressionValidator* to verify that the e-mail address is well formed

- A *RegularExpressionValidator* to verify that the zip code, if entered, consists of five numeric characters, optionally followed by a hyphen and four more numeric characters

- A *RegularExpressionValidator* to verify that the credit card number, if entered, is well formed—specifically, that it contains from 15 to 20 characters and that all characters are either digits or hyphens

Figure 6-20 shows the Spammers, Inc., home page after several validators have fired.

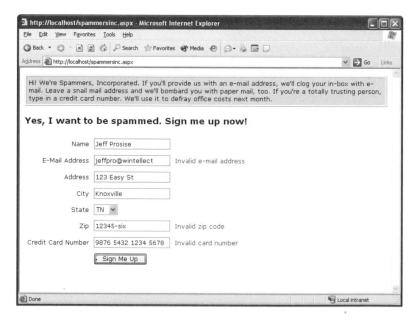

Figure 6-20 The Spammers, Inc., home page.

An item of interest concerning SpammersInc.aspx's implementation is that the *OnSignMeUp* method, which executes on the server when the Sign Me Up button is clicked, does nothing if *IsValid* is false:

```
void OnSignMeUp (Object sender, EventArgs e)
{
    if (IsValid) {
        ...
    }
}
```

IsValid is a *System.Web.UI.Page* property. When the client is Internet Explorer 4 or later, checking *IsValid* is redundant unless you're concerned about someone intentionally circumventing the client-side script in order to submit invalid data. When the client is any other browser (particularly Netscape Navigator), checking *IsValid* is essential if you want input to be validated. Validation controls don't do any input checking on the client side in those browsers, so if you fail to check *IsValid* on the server side, bad input can slip by undetected. *IsValid* is set to false on the server if any of the page's validation controls flags an error. An *IsValid* value equal to true means all of the page's input conforms to the criteria specified by the validators. If you want validation controls to work regardless of browser type, *always* check the page's *IsValid* property on the server side just in case the input wasn't validated on the client side.

```
SpammersInc.aspx
<html>
  <head>
    <style>
    <!--
      body { font: 10pt verdana };
      table { font: 10pt verdana };
      input { font: 10pt verdana };
    -->
    </style>
  </head>
  <body>
    <table cellpadding="4" border="1">
      <tr bgcolor="yellow">
        <td>
        Hi! We're Spammers, Incorporated. If you'll provide us with an
        e-mail address, we'll clog your inbox with email.
        Leave a snail mail address and we'll bombard you with paper
        mail, too. If you're a totally trusting person, type in a
        credit card number. We'll use it to defray office costs
        next month.
```

Figure 6-21   Source code for Spammers, Inc.

SpammersInc.aspx   *(continued)*

```
          </td>
       </tr>
    </table>
    <h3>Yes, I want to be spammed. Sign me up now!</h3>
    <form runat="server">
      <table cellpadding="4">
        <tr>
          <td align="right">
            Name
          </td>
          <td>
            <asp:TextBox ID="Name" RunAt="server" />
          </td>
          <td>
            <asp:RequiredFieldValidator
              ControlToValidate="Name"
              ErrorMessage="Please enter your name"
              Display="dynamic"
              RunAt="server"
            />
          </td>
        </tr>
        <tr>
          <td align="right">
            E-Mail Address
          </td>
          <td>
            <asp:TextBox ID="EMail" RunAt="server" />
          </td>
          <td>
            <asp:RequiredFieldValidator
              ControlToValidate="EMail"
              ErrorMessage="Please enter your e-mail address"
              Display="dynamic"
              RunAt="server"
            />
            <asp:RegularExpressionValidator
              ControlToValidate="EMail"
              ValidationExpression="^[\w\.-]+@[\w-]+\.[\w\.-]+$"
              ErrorMessage="Invalid e-mail address"
              Display="dynamic"
              RunAt="server"
            />
          </td>
        </tr>
        <tr>
          <td align="right">
            Address
          </td>
```

```
      <td>
        <asp:TextBox ID="Address" RunAt="server" />
      </td>
      <td>
      </td>
    </tr>
    <tr>
      <td align="right">
        City
      </td>
      <td>
        <asp:TextBox ID="City" RunAt="server" />
      </td>
      <td>
      </td>
    </tr>
    <tr>
      <td align="right">
        State
      </td>
      <td>
        <asp:DropDownList ID="StateList" RunAt="server">
          <asp:ListItem Text="AL" RunAt="server" />
          <asp:ListItem Text="AK" RunAt="server" />
          <asp:ListItem Text="AR" RunAt="server" />
          <asp:ListItem Text="AZ" RunAt="server" />
          <asp:ListItem Text="CA" RunAt="server" />
          <asp:ListItem Text="CO" RunAt="server" />
          <asp:ListItem Text="CT" RunAt="server" />
          <asp:ListItem Text="DC" RunAt="server" />
          <asp:ListItem Text="DE" RunAt="server" />
          <asp:ListItem Text="FL" RunAt="server" />
          <asp:ListItem Text="GA" RunAt="server" />
          <asp:ListItem Text="HI" RunAt="server" />
          <asp:ListItem Text="IA" RunAt="server" />
          <asp:ListItem Text="ID" RunAt="server" />
          <asp:ListItem Text="IL" RunAt="server" />
          <asp:ListItem Text="IN" RunAt="server" />
          <asp:ListItem Text="KS" RunAt="server" />
          <asp:ListItem Text="KY" RunAt="server" />
          <asp:ListItem Text="LA" RunAt="server" />
          <asp:ListItem Text="MA" RunAt="server" />
          <asp:ListItem Text="MD" RunAt="server" />
          <asp:ListItem Text="ME" RunAt="server" />
          <asp:ListItem Text="MI" RunAt="server" />
          <asp:ListItem Text="MN" RunAt="server" />
          <asp:ListItem Text="MO" RunAt="server" />
```

(continued)

SpammersInc.aspx *(continued)*

```
                        <asp:ListItem Text="MS" RunAt="server" />
                        <asp:ListItem Text="MT" RunAt="server" />
                        <asp:ListItem Text="NC" RunAt="server" />
                        <asp:ListItem Text="ND" RunAt="server" />
                        <asp:ListItem Text="NE" RunAt="server" />
                        <asp:ListItem Text="NH" RunAt="server" />
                        <asp:ListItem Text="NJ" RunAt="server" />
                        <asp:ListItem Text="NM" RunAt="server" />
                        <asp:ListItem Text="NV" RunAt="server" />
                        <asp:ListItem Text="NY" RunAt="server" />
                        <asp:ListItem Text="OH" RunAt="server" />
                        <asp:ListItem Text="OK" RunAt="server" />
                        <asp:ListItem Text="OR" RunAt="server" />
                        <asp:ListItem Text="PA" RunAt="server" />
                        <asp:ListItem Text="RI" RunAt="server" />
                        <asp:ListItem Text="SC" RunAt="server" />
                        <asp:ListItem Text="SD" RunAt="server" />
                        <asp:ListItem Text="TN" RunAt="server" />
                        <asp:ListItem Text="TX" RunAt="server" />
                        <asp:ListItem Text="UT" RunAt="server" />
                        <asp:ListItem Text="VA" RunAt="server" />
                        <asp:ListItem Text="VT" RunAt="server" />
                        <asp:ListItem Text="WA" RunAt="server" />
                        <asp:ListItem Text="WI" RunAt="server" />
                        <asp:ListItem Text="WV" RunAt="server" />
                        <asp:ListItem Text="WY" RunAt="server" />
                    </asp:DropDownList>
                </td>
                <td>
                </td>
            </tr>
            <tr>
                <td align="right">
                    Zip
                </td>
                <td>
                    <asp:TextBox ID="ZipCode" RunAt="server" />
                </td>
                <td>
                    <asp:RegularExpressionValidator
                        ControlToValidate="ZipCode"
                        ValidationExpression="^(\d{5}|\d{5}\-\d{4})$"
                        ErrorMessage="Invalid zip code"
                        Display="dynamic"
                        RunAt="server"
                    />
```

```
              </td>
          </tr>
          <tr>
            <td align="right">
              Credit Card Number
            </td>
            <td>
              <asp:TextBox ID="CreditCardNumber" RunAt="server" />
            </td>
            <td>
              <asp:RegularExpressionValidator
                ControlToValidate="CreditCardNumber"
                ValidationExpression="^[\d\-]{15,20}$"
                ErrorMessage="Invalid card number"
                Display="dynamic"
                RunAt="server"
              />
            </td>
          </tr>
          <tr>
            <td>
            </td>
            <td>
              <asp:Button Text="Sign Me Up" OnClick="OnSignMeUp"
                RunAt="server" />
            </td>
            <td>
            </td>
          </tr>
        </table>
      </form>
    </body>
</html>

<script language="C#" runat="server">
  void OnSignMeUp (Object sender, EventArgs e)
  {
      if (IsValid) {
          StringBuilder sb =
              new StringBuilder ("Thanks.aspx?Name=", 256);
          sb.Append (Name.Text);
          sb.Append ("&EMail=");
          sb.Append (EMail.Text);

          string address = Address.Text;
          string city = City.Text;
          string state = StateList.SelectedItem.Text;
          string zip = ZipCode.Text;
```

(continued)

SpammersInc.aspx *(continued)*

```
            if (address.Length > 0 && city.Length > 0 &&
                zip.Length > 0) {
                sb.Append ("&Address=");
                sb.Append (address);
                sb.Append ("&City=");
                sb.Append (city);
                sb.Append ("&State=");
                sb.Append (state);
                sb.Append ("&ZipCode=");
                sb.Append (zip);
            }

            string number = CreditCardNumber.Text;

            if (number.Length > 0) {
                sb.Append ("&CreditCardNumber=");
                sb.Append (number);
            }

            Response.Redirect (sb.ToString ());
        }
    }
</script>
```

Thanks.aspx

```
<%@ Page Language="C#" %>

<html>
  <body>
    Here's the information you entered:<br><br>
    <ul>
      <%
        Response.Write ("<li>Name: " + Request["Name"]);
        Response.Write ("<li>E-mail address: " + Request["EMail"]);

        if (Request["Address"] != null) {
            StringBuilder sb =
                new StringBuilder ("<li>Address: ", 64);
            sb.Append (Request["Address"]);
            sb.Append (", ");
            sb.Append (Request["City"]);
            sb.Append (", ");
            sb.Append (Request["State"]);
            sb.Append (" ");
            sb.Append (Request["ZipCode"]);
            Response.Write (sb.ToString ());
        }
```

```
        if (Request["CreditCardNumber"] != null)
            Response.Write ("<li>Credit card number: " +
                Request["CreditCardNumber"]);
    %>
    </ul>
    Thanks for signing up with Spammers, Inc.!
  </body>
</html>
```

Connecting Web Forms with *Response.Redirect*

In addition to showing validators at work, Spammers, Inc., demonstrates another important technique for programming Web forms: how to transfer control from one page to another and transmit data in the process. The application contains not one, but two Web forms: SpammersInc.aspx and Thanks.aspx. When the user clicks the Sign Me Up button, SpammersInc.aspx uses *Response.Redirect* to transfer control to Thanks.aspx, which displays a summary of the user input along with a thank you (Figure 6-22).

How is the input transmitted to Thanks.aspx? SpammersInc.aspx appends it to the URL in the form of a query string. For example, if the user types "Jeff" in the name field and "jeffpro@wintellect.com" in the e-mail address field, *Response.Redirect* is passed the following URL:

```
Thanks.aspx?Name=Jeff&EMail=jeffpro@wintellect.com
```

Thanks.aspx extracts the data from the query string using the ASP.NET *Request* object and writes it to the HTTP response using *Response.Write*:

```
Response.Write ("<li>Name: " + Request["Name"]);
Response.Write ("<li>E-mail address: " + Request["EMail"]);
```

The names used to retrieve data from the *Response* object must match the parameter names used in the query string. Code that relies on *Request* and *Response* objects looks more like ASP code than ASP.NET code, but this is nonetheless an efficient and extremely common technique for moving between pages in ASP.NET.

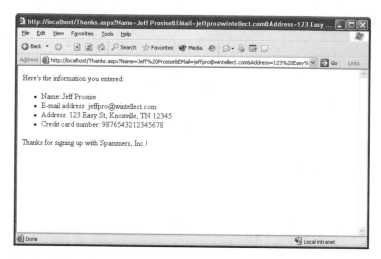

Figure 6-22 The Spammers, Inc., "thank you" page.

The *StringBuilder* Class

To formulate the URL passed to *Response.Redirect*, SpammersInc.aspx uses a *StringBuilder* object. *StringBuilder* is defined in the FCL's *System.Text* namespace; it provides an efficient and easy-to-use mechanism for building strings on the fly.

Strings in managed applications are instances of *System.String*, but *System.Strings* are immutable, meaning once defined, they can't be changed. The following code works but is inefficient because each concatenation operation results in a memory allocation and a memory copy:

```
string s = "";
for (int i=1; i<=99; i++) {
    s += i.ToString ();
    s += ", ";
}
```

The following code produces the same string, but it does so in a fraction of the time. Why? Because it builds the string in a buffer large enough to hold 512 characters:

```
StringBuilder sb = new StringBuilder (512);
for (int i=1; i<=99; i++) {
    sb.Append (i.ToString ());
    sb.Append (", ");
}
string s = sb.ToString ();
```

StringBuilder.Append will enlarge the buffer if necessary, but if you know approximately how long the string will be before you start, you can size the buffer accordingly and keep new memory allocations to a minimum.

Building URLs with *StringBuilder.Append* is a performance optimization. Thanks.aspx also uses *StringBuilder* to build strings dynamically—not to build URLs, but to build the address that it outputs to the page. A few milliseconds per request might not seem like much, but if your application receives thousands of requests per second, a little can add up to a lot.

Conditional Validation

The vast majority of the time, input validation is unconditional. An e-mail address that needs validating one time needs it every time. But occasionally the need arises to validate conditionally—usually based on the state of something else on the page, such as a check box. For example, you might want to validate an e-mail address only if a check box labeled "E-mail my confirmation" is checked.

The Web page in Figures 6-23 and 6-24 demonstrates how to enact conditional validation. In this example, the user is invited to enter his or her name for the purpose of registering a product. The user can optionally enter an e-mail address and check a box to have a confirmation e-mailed. If the box is checked, the e-mail address is validated using a *RequiredFieldValidator* and a *RegularExpressionValidator*. If the box isn't checked, validation is skipped—even if the user enters something into the e-mail field.

Notice the *Enabled*="false" attributes in the tags that declare the validators. *Enabled* is a property that validators inherit from *System.Web.UI.WebControls.WebControl*. It defaults to true, meaning the validator will work as normal. Setting *Enabled* to false disables the validator and prevents it from performing its validation checks.

Now look at the <asp:CheckBox> tag. It sets *AutoPostBack* to true, forcing a postback to occur any time the check box is clicked. It also registers a handler—*OnCheckBoxClicked*—for the *CheckedChanged* event that fires each time the check box is clicked. *OnCheckBoxClicked* enables or disables the validators based on the state of the check box. It enables them if the box is checked and disables them if it's not. Here's the relevant code:

```
EMailRequiredValidator.Enabled = Confirm.Checked;
EMailExpressionValidator.Enabled = Confirm.Checked;
```

"EMailRequiredValidator" and "EMailExpressionValidator" are the validators' programmatic IDs; "Confirm" is the *CheckBox* ID. By enabling the validators only when the check box is checked, ConditionalValidate.aspx prevents the validators from firing if the input from the control they're attached to is meaningless.

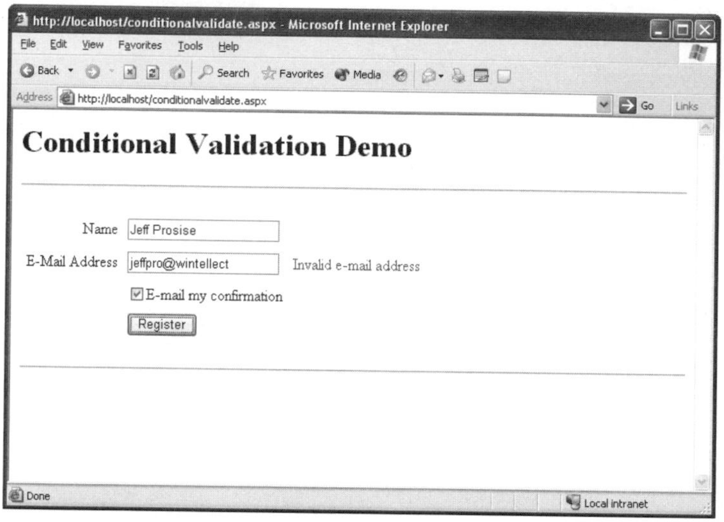

Figure 6-23   The ConditionalValidate application.

ConditionalValidate.aspx

```
<html>
  <body>
    <h1>Conditional Validation Demo</h1>
    <hr>
    <form runat="server">
      <table cellpadding="4">
        <tr>
          <td align="right">
            Name
          </td>
          <td>
            <asp:TextBox ID="Name" RunAt="server" />
          </td>
          <td>
            <asp:RequiredFieldValidator
              ControlToValidate="Name"
              ErrorMessage="Please enter your name"
              Display="dynamic"
              Color="red"
              RunAt="server"
            />
          </td>
        </tr>
        <tr>
```

Figure 6-24   Conditional input validation.

```
      <td align="right">
        E-Mail Address
      </td>
      <td>
        <asp:TextBox ID="EMail" RunAt="server" />
      </td>
      <td>
        <asp:RequiredFieldValidator
          ControlToValidate="EMail"
          ErrorMessage="Please enter your e-mail address"
          Display="dynamic"
          Color="red"
          Enabled="false"
          ID="EMailRequiredValidator"
          RunAt="server"
        />
        <asp:RegularExpressionValidator
          ControlToValidate="EMail"
          ValidationExpression="^[\w\.-]+@[\w-]+\.[\w\.-]+$"
          ErrorMessage="Invalid e-mail address"
          Display="dynamic"
          Color="red"
          Enabled="false"
          ID="EMailExpressionValidator"
          RunAt="server"
        />
      </td>
    </tr>
    <tr>
      <td>
      </td>
      <td>
        <asp:CheckBox ID="Confirm"
          Text="E-mail my confirmation"
          OnCheckedChanged="OnCheckBoxClicked"
          AutoPostBack="true" RunAt="server" />
      </td>
      <td>
      </td>
    </tr>
    <tr>
      <td>
      </td>
      <td>
```

(continued)

ConditionalValidate.aspx   *(continued)*

```
                <asp:Button Text="Register" OnClick="OnRegister"
                    RunAt="server" />
            </td>
            <td>
            </td>
        </tr>
    </table>
    <br><hr><br>
    <asp:Label ID="Output" RunAt="server" />
    </form>
  </body>
</html>

<script language="C#" runat="server">
  void OnCheckBoxClicked (Object sender, EventArgs e)
  {
      EMailRequiredValidator.Enabled = Confirm.Checked;
      EMailExpressionValidator.Enabled = Confirm.Checked;
  }
  void OnRegister (Object sender, EventArgs e)
  {
      if (IsValid) {
          if (Confirm.Checked) {
              Output.Text =
                  "Confirmation will be e-mailed to " +
                  EMail.Text + ".";
          }
          else {
              Output.Text =
                  "At your request, no confirmation will " +
                  "be sent.";
          }
      }
  }
</script>
```

Odds, Ends, and the *WebControl* Base Class

All Web controls implement a long list of properties that enable them to be customized in a variety of ways. Some of those properties are defined in the control classes themselves; others are inherited from the *WebControl* base class. For
example, all Web controls have properties named *Width* and *Height* because
both of these properties are members of *WebControl*.

Not all *WebControl* properties are as ordinary as *Width* and *Height*. Take,
for example, *WebControl*'s *CssClass* property. I'm frequently asked whether

Web controls support cascading style sheets (CSS). The answer? Yes they do, thanks to the *CssClass* property that they inherit from *WebControl*. The following example defines a CSS class named *Input* and uses it to modify a *TextBox* control to display text in red 10-point Verdana type:

```
<html>
  <head>
    <style>
      .Input { font: 10pt verdana; color: red; }
    </style>
  </head>
  <body>
    <form runat="server">
      <asp:TextBox CssClass="Input" RunAt="server" />
    </form>
  </body>
</html>
```

ToolTip is another property that Web controls inherit from *WebControl*. Want to display a tooltip window when the cursor hovers over a control? Then include a *ToolTip* attribute in the control tag, like this:

```
<asp:TextBox ToolTip="Type your name here" RunAt="server" />
```

There's virtually no end to the customizations you can perform when you have a firm grasp of all the properties and events that ASP.NET's Web controls expose. And when the built-in Web controls don't do what you want, you can always build controls of your own—which is precisely what the next two chapters are all about.

7

User Controls

Web forms bring component-based programming to the Internet by enabling complex rendering and behavioral logic to be encoded in reusable server control classes. Classes such as *Calendar* and *DataGrid* form the backbone of Web forms and enable developers who have only a rudimentary knowledge of HTML and client-side scripting to build sophisticated Web pages.

But the story of componentization in ASP.NET doesn't end with server controls. ASP.NET supports a second type of component called the *user control*. A user control is a custom control built from HTML and server-side script. It's an intuitive and easily understood means for capturing and sharing functionality without resorting to the server-side includes (SSIs) so prevalent in ASP programming. And it's a mechanism for building reusable ASP.NET components that's simpler than writing full-blown server controls. A developer familiar with the Web Forms programming model can have a basic user control up and running in no time flat. Then he or she can instantiate that control in Web forms by using declarative tags much like those used to declare *DataGrid*s and other server controls.

User controls enjoy three primary uses:

■ To factor out complex UI elements and convert them into reusable components

■ To create dynamic pages that are personalized for individual users

■ To facilitate output caching at the subpage level—that is, to cache a page's static content while allowing other parts of the page to be rendered dynamically

This chapter is all about user controls—what they are, how to write them, how to use them, and why you'd want to use them in the first place. You'll see some real working examples of user controls, including one that implements Web navigation bars, and learn how to combine user controls with HTTP cookies to create personalized content. Finally, you'll learn how user controls can improve the performance of applications built around Web forms.

User controls are one of the most important facets of the Web Forms programming model—so important, in fact, that time delayed in learning about them is time wasted. In the words of a famous American, let's roll.

User Control Fundamentals

User controls live in ASCX files, just as Web forms live in ASPX files. ASPX files contain <form> tags defining HTML forms. ASCX files never have <form> tags because they're designed to be inserted into existing forms. Here's a very simple user control:

```
<h1>Hello, world</h>
```

Assume that this HTML is stored in a file named Hello.ascx. Furthermore, assume that someone wants to insert this user control into a Web form. Here's an ASPX file that does just that:

```
<%@ Register TagPrefix="user" TagName="Hello" src="Hello.ascx" %>

<html>
  <body>
    <form runat="server">
      <user:Hello RunAt="server" />
    </form>
  </body>
</html>
```

When executed, this Web form displays "Hello, world" in big bold letters, thanks to the HTML embedded in the user control. The <user:Hello> tag declares an instance of the control. The @ *Register* directive at the top of the file tells ASP.NET what to do when it encounters a <user:Hello> tag. The *Src* attribute identifies the control's ASCX file. *TagName* assigns a name to the control ("Hello"), and *TagPrefix* defines the prefix that precedes the name ("user") in a tag that declares a control instance. You don't have to use "user" as your tag prefix; you can use "foo" or your company name or whatever you like. However, every ASPX file that incorporates a user control must have an @ *Register* directive defining the tag name and tag prefix and linking both to an ASCX file.

Hello.ascx is so simple that it barely qualifies as a user control, but it nonetheless demonstrates three important principles:

- User controls are stored in ASCX files

- *@ Register* directives declare tag names and tag prefixes and map them to ASCX files

- Tags registered with *@ Register* add user controls to Web forms

What this example doesn't show is that user controls can have methods, properties, and events, just like server controls. Moreover, they can include server-side scripts, just like ASPX files. In a moment, we'll build a more sophisticated user control that demonstrates these principles and others. But first, there's another directive you should know about: *@ Control*.

The *@ Control* Directive

ASPX files often include *@ Page* directives that provide directions to the ASP.NET compilation engine, enable and disable certain features of ASP.NET, and more. ASCX files never contain *@ Page* directives. They contain *@ Control* directives instead.

The *@ Control* and *@ Page* directives share many common attributes and in fact are nearly identical save for the directive name. For example, suppose you wanted to enable debugging support in an ASCX file. Instead of putting this statement at the top of the file:

```
<%@ Page Debug="true" %>
```

you'd put this one:

```
<%@ Control Debug="true" %>
```

To enable debugging support and specify the default language for inline code blocks, you'd write this:

```
<%@ Control Debug="true" Language="C#" %>
```

Like *@ Page* directives, *@ Control* directives can appear only once in a file. But you can include as many attributes in an *@ Control* directive as you want.

ASCX files can contain *@ Import* and *@ Assembly* directives just like ASPX files. If, in an ASCX file, you use types belonging to namespaces that aren't imported by default or types in assemblies that ASP.NET doesn't link to auto-matically, you can use *@ Import* and *@ Assembly* to resolve the differences. The syntax for these directives is exactly the same in ASCX files as it is in ASPX files. For a review of *@ Import* and *@ Assembly*, see Chapter 5.

Your First User Control

With these fundamentals in mind, let's build a more ambitious user control—a login control that accepts user names and passwords typed by the user. We'll build the control in steps. The end result will be the control shown in Figure 7-1, which not only accepts user names and passwords, but also performs some simple validation on them.

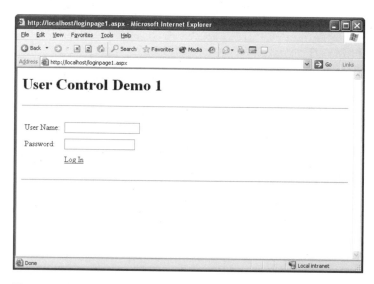

Figure 7-1   Login user control.

Step 1 in building the login control is to create a text file named LoginControl1.ascx. Step 2 is to type in the code in Figure 7-2. That code declares three Web controls—two *TextBox* controls and one *LinkButton* con-trol—and uses an HTML table to align them on the page. The *TextBox* controls provide input fields for user names and passwords. The *LinkButton* control submits the form containing the login control to the server.

LoginControl1.ascx

```
<table cellpadding="4">
  <tr>
    <td>User Name:</td>
    <td><asp:TextBox ID="MyUserName" RunAt="server" /></td>
  </tr>
  <tr>
    <td>Password:</td>
    <td><asp:TextBox ID="MyPassword" TextMode="password"
      RunAt="server" /></td>
  </tr>
  <tr>
    <td></td>
    <td><asp:LinkButton Text="Log In" RunAt="server" /></td>
  </tr>
</table>
```

Figure 7-2   Login control, version 1.

To test the login control, you need a Web form. Figure 7-3 contains the source code for a Web form named LoginPage1.aspx that declares an instance of the login control with the statement

```
<user:LoginControl RunAt="server" />
```

The *@ Register* directive at the top of the file defines the tag prefix *user* and the tag name *LoginControl* and associates them with LoginControl1.ascx. When this page is executed, ASP.NET derives a class from *System.Web.UI.UserControl* and adds the content found in LoginControl1.ascx to the derived class. Then it instantiates the derived class, adds the resulting object to the page's control tree (a hierarchical list of the controls defined on the page), and executes the control along with any other controls declared on the page.

LoginPage1.aspx

```
<%@ Register TagPrefix="user" TagName="LoginControl"
  src="LoginControl1.ascx" %>

<html>
  <body>
    <h1>User Control Demo 1</h1>
    <hr>
    <form runat="server">
      <user:LoginControl RunAt="server" />
    </form>
    <hr>
  </body>
</html>
```

Figure 7-3   Test page for LoginControl1.

If you open LoginControl1.aspx in your browser right now, you'll see the page in Figure 7-1. The login control is present, but it's not functional yet. One reason it's not functional is that a server-side script can't read user input from the *TextBox*es. Even if you assign the login control an ID (for example, "MyLogin"), the following statement won't compile because *MyUserName* is a protected member of the class that ASP.NET generates to represent the login control:

```
string name = MyLogin.MyUserName.Text;
```

The solution is to add public properties enabling scripts to access the data encapsulated in the login control. The next section describes how.

Adding Properties

User controls can have properties just like server controls. When you design a user control, you should try to anticipate all the different ways that other developers will want to customize it and then make it easy for them by exposing properties that they can use to customize the control's appearance and behavior.

Adding a property to a user control is simple. You define the property in a <script> block in the control's ASCX file. At run time, ASP.NET adds the code in the script block to the class that it derives to represent the user control. Any properties declared in the <script> block become members of that class.

The ASCX file in Figure 7-4 adds three public properties to the login control:

- A *BackColor* property that exposes the control's background color

- A *UserName* property that exposes the text in the "MyUserName" *TextBox*

- A *Password* property that exposes the text in the "MyPassword" *Text-Box*

Changes are highlighted in bold so that you can more easily distinguish the differences between LoginControl1.ascx and LoginControl2.ascx. The *BackColor* property does nothing more than read and write the *BgColor* property of the underlying table, which, thanks to the *runat*="server" attribute in the <table> tag, is an instance of *System.Web.UI.HtmlControls.HtmlTable*.

LoginControl2.ascx

```
<table id="MyTable" cellpadding="4" runat="server">
  <tr>
    <td>User Name:</td>
    <td><asp:TextBox ID="MyUserName" RunAt="server" /></td>
  </tr>
  <tr>
    <td>Password:</td>
    <td><asp:TextBox ID="MyPassword" TextMode="password"
      RunAt="server" /></td>
  </tr>
  <tr>
    <td></td>
    <td><asp:LinkButton Text="Log In" RunAt="server" /></td>
  </tr>
</table>

<script language="C#" runat="server">
  public string BackColor
  {
      get { return MyTable.BgColor; }
      set { MyTable.BgColor = value; }
  }

  public string UserName
  {
      get { return MyUserName.Text; }
      set { MyUserName.Text = value; }
  }

  public string Password
  {
      get { return MyPassword.Text; }
      set { MyPassword.Text = value; }
  }
</script>
```

Figure 7-4   Login control with *BackColor*, *UserName*, and *Password* properties.

The ASPX file in Figure 7-5 displays the modified login control. Once more, changes are highlighted in bold. Note the *BackColor* attribute in the control tag. It changes the control's background color by initializing the control's *BackColor* property. In addition, a server-side script now displays a personalized greeting on the Web page using the name typed into the user name *Text-Box*. (See Figure 7-6.) The script retrieves the contents of the *TextBox* by reading the control's *UserName* property. If you want, *UserName* and *Password* can also be used as attributes in the control tag to preload the *TextBox*es with text.

```
LoginPage2.aspx
<%@ Register TagPrefix="user" TagName="LoginControl"
  src="LoginControl2.ascx" %>

<html>
  <body>
    <h1>User Control Demo 2</h1>
    <hr>
    <form runat="server">
      <user:LoginControl ID="MyLogin" BackColor="#ccccff"
        RunAt="server" />
    </form>
    <hr>
    <h3><asp:Label ID="Output" RunAt="server" /></h3>
  </body>
</html>

<script language="C#" runat="server">
  void Page_Load (Object sender, EventArgs e)
  {
      if (IsPostBack)
          Output.Text = "Hello, " + MyLogin.UserName;
  }
</script>
```

Figure 7-5   Test page for LoginControl2.

So far, so good. At least the login control is usable. But observe how the server-side script traps the postback generated when the user clicks the Log In button: it processes the *Page.Load* event that fires when the postback occurs. A better solution—and one more in keeping with the Web Forms programming model—is to have the login control fire an event of its own when the user clicks the Log In button. That's precisely what you'll do in the next section.

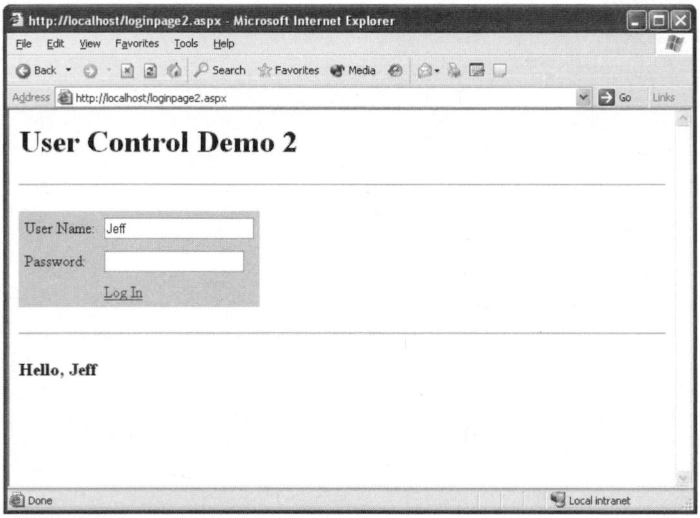

Figure 7-6   LoginControl2 in a Web form.

Adding Events

You add events to a user control by declaring them in a <script> block. Like properties declared in a <script> block, events declared there become members of the class that ASP.NET derives from *UserControl* to represent the control.

Figure 7-7 contains version 3 of the login control. This version declares an event named *Login*. It also wires the Log In button to a *Click* handler named *OnLoginButtonClicked* that fires a *Login* event if neither *TextBox* is empty. The revised test page in Figure 7-8 adds an *OnLogin* attribute to the <user:Login-Control> tag that responds to *Login* events by activating *OnLoginUser*. You can try it out by typing a user name and password and clicking the Log In button. The user name that you typed should appear at the bottom of the page. This design is better than the one in the previous section because the greeting is displayed *only* when the Log In button is clicked—even if the page includes other controls that cause postbacks.

LoginControl3.ascx
```
<table id="MyTable" cellpadding="4" runat="server">
  <tr>
    <td>User Name:</td>
    <td><asp:TextBox ID="MyUserName" RunAt="server" /></td>
  </tr>
  <tr>
    <td>Password:</td>
    <td><asp:TextBox ID="MyPassword" TextMode="password"
      RunAt="server" /></td>
```

Figure 7-7   Login control with a *Login* event added.

LoginControl3.ascx *(continued)*

```
</tr>
  <tr>
    <td></td>
    <td><asp:LinkButton Text="Log In" OnClick="OnLoginButtonClicked"
      RunAt="server" /></td>
  </tr>
</table>

<script language="C#" runat="server">
  public string BackColor
  {
      get { return MyTable.BgColor; }
      set { MyTable.BgColor = value; }
  }

  public string UserName
  {
      get { return MyUserName.Text; }
      set { MyUserName.Text = value; }
  }

  public string Password
  {
      get { return MyPassword.Text; }
      set { MyPassword.Text = value; }
  }

  public event EventHandler Login;

  void OnLoginButtonClicked (Object sender, EventArgs e)
  {
      if (Login != null && UserName.Length > 0 && Password.Length > 0)
          Login (this, new EventArgs ()); // Fire Login event
  }
</script>
```

LoginPage3.aspx

```
<%@ Register TagPrefix="user" TagName="LoginControl"
  src="LoginControl3.ascx" %>

<html>
  <body>
    <h1>User Control Demo 3</h1>
    <hr>
    <form runat="server">
      <user:LoginControl ID="MyLogin" BackColor="#ccccff"
```

Figure 7-8 Test page for LoginControl3.

```
     OnLogin="OnLoginUser" RunAt="server" />
   </form>
   <hr>
   <h3><asp:Label ID="Output" RunAt="server" /></h3>
  </body>
</html>

<script language="C#" runat="server">
  void OnLoginUser (Object sender, EventArgs e)
  {
     Output.Text = "Hello, " + MyLogin.UserName;
  }
</script>
```

Using Code-Behind with User Controls

With the addition of properties and events, the login control is now a self-contained component. For the final step in its evolution, we'll use code-behind to get the C# code out of the ASCX file and into a compiled DLL. While we're at it, we'll make the login control a little smarter by having it run some simple validation code on the user name and password that the user enters. Furthermore, rather than type handlers for *Login* events as generic *EventHandler*s, we'll define a custom delegate named *LoginEventHandler* that receives a *LoginEventArgs* revealing whether the login is valid. *LoginEventArgs* is a custom data type that we'll include in the same DLL that holds the code-behind class.

The revised source code for the login control appears in Figure 7-9. The ASCX file contains the HTML that defines the control and an @ *Control* directive whose *Inherits* attribute identifies the login control's base class. Normally ASP.NET would derive the control class from *UserControl*. Now, however, it will derive from *LoginBase*, which itself derives from *UserControl*.

LoginBase.cs contains the source code for the *LoginBase* class. *LoginBase* declares fields named *MyTable*, *MyUserName*, and *MyPassword* that map to the controls of the same names in the ASCX file. It declares a custom delegate named *LoginEventHandler*, and it declares an event named *Login*, whose type is *LoginEventHandler*. When the Log In button is clicked, *LoginBase* fires a *Login* event accompanied by a *LoginEventArgs* object whose *IsValid* property is true if the login is valid or false if it's not. To judge whether the user's credentials are valid, *OnLoginButtonClicked* checks for the user name "jeffpro" and the password "imbatman." In real life, it would validate against a back-end database (or at least an XML file), but the principle is valid nonetheless.

LoginControl4.ascx

```
<%@ Control Inherits="LoginBase" %>

<table id="MyTable" cellpadding="4" runat="server">
  <tr>
    <td>User Name:</td>
    <td><asp:TextBox ID="MyUserName" RunAt="server" /></td>
  </tr>
  <tr>
    <td>Password:</td>
    <td><asp:TextBox ID="MyPassword" TextMode="password"
      RunAt="server" /></td>
  </tr>
  <tr>
    <td></td>
    <td><asp:LinkButton Text="Log In" OnClick="OnLoginButtonClicked"
      RunAt="server" /></td>
  </tr>
</table>
```

LoginBase.cs

```
using System;
using System.Web.UI;
using System.Web.UI.HtmlControls;
using System.Web.UI.WebControls;

public class LoginEventArgs
{
    private bool LoginValid;

    public LoginEventArgs (bool IsValid)
    {
        LoginValid = IsValid;
    }

    public bool IsValid
    {
        get { return LoginValid; }
    }
}

public class LoginBase : UserControl
{
    protected HtmlTable MyTable;
    protected TextBox MyUserName;
    protected TextBox MyPassword;
```

Figure 7-9   Login control with code-behind.

```
     public string BackColor
     {
         get { return MyTable.BgColor; }
         set { MyTable.BgColor = value; }
     }

     public string UserName
     {
         get { return MyUserName.Text; }
         set { MyUserName.Text = value; }
     }

     public string Password
     {
         get { return MyPassword.Text; }
         set { MyPassword.Text = value; }
     }

     public delegate void LoginEventHandler (Object sender,
         LoginEventArgs e);

     public event LoginEventHandler Login;

     public void OnLoginButtonClicked (Object sender, EventArgs e)
     {
         if (Login != null) {
             bool IsValid = (UserName.ToLower () == "jeffpro" &&
                 Password == "imbatman");
             Login (this, new LoginEventArgs (IsValid));
         }
     }
}
```

The test page in Figure 7-10 responds to *Login* events by displaying a greeting if the login is valid or an error message if it's not. Before you run LoginPage4.aspx, you must compile LoginBase.cs and place the resulting DLL in the application root's bin directory so that ASP.NET can find it. Here's the command to create the DLL:

```
csc /t:library LoginBase.cs
```

If you run LoginPage4.aspx from wwwroot, place the DLL in wwwroot\bin.

```
LoginPage4.aspx
<%@ Register TagPrefix="user" TagName="LoginControl"
  src="LoginControl4.ascx" %>

<html>
  <body>
    <h1>User Control Demo 4</h1>
    <hr>
    <form runat="server">
      <user:LoginControl ID="MyLogin" BackColor="#ccccff"
        OnLogin="OnLoginUser" RunAt="server" />
    </form>
    <hr>
    <h3><asp:Label ID="Output" RunAt="server" /></h3>
  </body>
</html>

<script language="C#" runat="server">
  void OnLoginUser (Object sender, LoginEventArgs e)
  {
      if (e.IsValid)
          Output.Text = "Hello, " + MyLogin.UserName;
      else {
          Output.Text = "Invalid login";
          MyLogin.UserName = "";
          MyLogin.Password = "";
      }
  }
</script>
```

Figure 7-10   Test page for LoginControl4.

The XmlNavBar Control

Surf the Web, and you'll find numerous pages with lists of links to other pages running down the left-hand side. Known as *navigation bars* or simply *navbars*, these ubiquitous UI elements are nearly as common in Web pages as menus are in Windows applications. They also make ideal user controls. Why? Because they typically appear not once but many times throughout a site. A navbar implemented as a user control doesn't have to be physically replicated on each and every page. A simple tag creates the control wherever it's needed. And updating every navbar on the site requires changing just one source code file.

The Web page in Figure 7-11 features a navbar user control I call the Xml-NavBar. XmlNavBar retrieves the items that it displays and the URLs that they point to from an XML file. It also has properties for controlling its width and height, its foreground and background colors, and the font that it uses to render its items. XmlNavBar even supports mouseovers. If you include a *MouseOver-Color* attribute in the control tag, the navbar highlights items using the specified color when the cursor passes over them.

The navbar in Figure 7-11 contains four items. Clicking an item takes you to the corresponding Web page: News.aspx, Sports.aspx, Stocks.aspx, or Weather.aspx. All four are provided on the CD that accompanies this book, but because they're virtually identical, only one is shown in this section (Figure 7-12). You can see the *@ Register* directive that registers the control and the <user:XmlNavBar> tag that creates it. You can also see the *XmlSrc* attribute identifying the XML file from which the control derives its content. Individual items are represented by *Item* elements in the XML file. For a given item, *Name* and *Link* elements define the item text and the URL that the item refers to. Because XmlNavBar configures itself from an external file, you could customize it on every page by pointing it to different XML files. The XML file used in this example—Links.xml—appears in Figure 7-13.

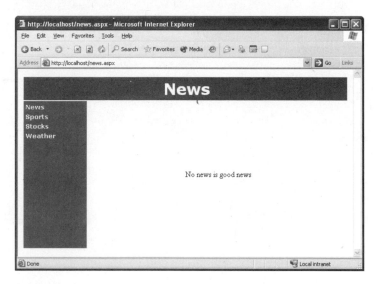

Figure 7-11   Web page featuring an XmlNavBar user control.

News.aspx

```
<%@ Register TagPrefix="user" TagName="XmlNavBar"
  Src="XmlNavBar.ascx" %>

<html>
  <body>
    <form runat="server">
      <table width="100%" height="100%">
        <tr height="48">
          <td bgcolor="teal" align="center" colspan="2">
            <span style="color: white; font-family: verdana;
              font-size: 24pt; font-weight: bold">
              News
            </span>
          </td>
        </tr>
        <tr>
          <td width="128" valign="top" bgcolor="royalblue">
            <user:XmlNavBar XmlSrc="Links.xml" ForeColor="white"
              Font-Name="verdana" Font-Size="10pt" Font-Bold="true"
              MouseOverColor="black" RunAt="server" />
          </td>
          <td align="center" valign="center">
            No news is good news
          </td>
        </tr>
      </table>
    </form>
  </body>
</html>
```

Figure 7-12   Web form that uses XmlNavBar.

Links.xml

```
<?xml version="1.0">
<Items>
  <Item>
    <Text>News</Text>
    <Link>News.aspx</Link>
  </Item>
  <Item>
    <Text>Sports</Text>
    <Link>Sports.aspx</Link>
  </Item>
  <Item>
    <Text>Stocks</Text>
    <Link>Stocks.aspx</Link>
```

Figure 7-13   XML source file for configuring an XmlNavBar.

```
    </Item>
      <Item>
        <Text>Weather</Text>
        <Link>Weather.aspx</Link>
      </Item>
    </Items>
```

XmlNavBar is defined in the source code file XmlNavBar.ascx (Figure 7-14). That file contains just one line of HTML:

```
<asp:Table ID="MyTable" RunAt="server" />
```

Everything else is server-side script. *Page_Load* builds the XmlNavBar at run time by adding rows to "MyTable." (Even though a user control isn't a "page" in the classical sense, *Page_Load* is still the handler name for the event that fires when the control loads.) Each row contains one cell. Inside the cell is a single item consisting of item text surrounded by an HTML <a> element referencing the item's URL. Here's a typical item:

```
<a href="News.aspx" onmouseover="defcolor=this.style.color;
this.style.color='Black'" onmouseout="this.style.color=defcolor"
style="text-decoration: none; font-family: verdana; font-size: 10pt;
font-weight: bold; color: White">News</a>
```

The *Href* attribute comes from one of the *Link* elements in the XML file. The *MouseOverColor* attribute in the <user:XmlNavBar> tag translates into *OnMouseOver* and *OnMouseOut* attributes that change the color of the item underneath the cursor. *Font* and *ForeColor* attributes, if used, translate into *Style* attributes in the <a> tags.

XmlNavBar reads XML files the same way Chapter 5's Converter.aspx reads XML files: by reading them into a *DataSet* and iterating over the *DataSet*'s rows. *DataSet.ReadXml* reduces the complex task of parsing an XML file to one simple method call. Once the file is read, XmlNavBar retrieves the names and URLs of the items it generates by using the element names in the XML file as indexes into the *DataSet*'s *DataRows*.

XmlNavBar.ascx adapts portions of its output to the browser that originated the request. Rather than blindly emit *OnMouseOver* and *OnMouseOut* attributes when a *MouseOverColor* attribute is present in the control tag, Xml-NavBar outputs them only if the requestor is Internet Explorer 4 or later. Mouse-overs are a royal pain to implement in Navigator, and they don't work in early versions of Internet Explorer, either. How does XmlNavBar know the type and version of the browser that transmitted the request? Like this:

```
if (Request.Browser.Type.ToUpper ().IndexOf ("IE") > -1
    && Request.Browser.MajorVersion >= 4) {
    .
    .
    .
}
```

Web servers receive information about browser types and version numbers in the *User-Agent* headers accompanying HTTP requests. ASP.NET examines *User-Agent* headers and makes the information gleaned from them available to server-side scripts through the *Request* object's *Browser* property. *Type*, *Major-Version*, *MinorVersion*, *JavaScript*, *Cookies*, and other *Browser* properties provide information about the browser that originated the request and the features that it supports. For a complete list of *Browser* properties, see the documentation for *System.Web.HttpBrowserCapabilities* in the .NET Framework SDK.

A final item of interest regarding XmlNavBar.ascx is how it implements the *Font* property. *Font* is nothing more than a container for subproperties named *Name*, *Size*, and *Weight*. When ASP.NET encounters an attribute such as this one:

```
Font-Name="verdana"
```

it generates code that looks something like this:

```
ctrl.Font.Name="verdana";
```

For this to work, *Font* must be an instance of a type that implements a string property named *Name*. In XmlNavBar.ascx, *Font* is implemented this way:

```
MyFontInfo MyFont = new MyFontInfo ();
    .
    .
    .
public MyFontInfo Font
{
    get { return MyFont; }
    set { MyFont = value; }
}
```

MyFontInfo, which is also defined in XmlNavBar.ascx, implements *Name* this way:

```
string FontName;
    .
    .
    .
```

```
public string Name
{
    get { return FontName; }
    set { FontName = value; }
}
```

The *Font* property that Web controls inherit from *WebControl* is implemented in much the same way. Now that you've seen how it works, you can write properties that have subproperties any time the situation calls for it.

Incidentally, when I designed XmlNavBar, I didn't intend to write a *MyFontInfo* class. I planned to use the FCL's *FontInfo* (*System.Web.UI.WebControls.FontInfo*) class instead. However, *FontInfo* can't be instantiated directly because it lacks a public constructor. So I wrote a version of my own and included it in XmlNavBar.ascx.

XmlNavBar.ascx

```
<%@ Import Namespace="System.Data" %>
<%@ Import Namespace="System.Drawing" %>

<asp:Table ID="MyTable" RunAt="server" />

<script language="C#" runat="server">
  string MyXmlSrc;
  Color MyBackColor;
  Color MyForeColor;
  Color MyMouseOverColor;
  MyFontInfo MyFont = new MyFontInfo ();

  public string XmlSrc
  {
      get { return MyXmlSrc; }
      set { MyXmlSrc = value; }
  }

  public Color BackColor
  {
      get { return MyBackColor; }
      set { MyBackColor = value; }
  }

  public Color ForeColor
  {
      get { return MyForeColor; }
      set { MyForeColor = value; }
  }
```

Figure 7-14   XmlNavBar user control.

XmlNavBar.ascx   *(continued)*

```csharp
public Color MouseOverColor
  {
      get { return MyMouseOverColor; }
      set { MyMouseOverColor = value; }
  }

  public MyFontInfo Font
  {
      get { return MyFont; }
      set { MyFont = value; }
  }

  void Page_Load (Object sender, EventArgs e)
  {
      if (MyXmlSrc != null) {
          DataSet ds = new DataSet ();
          ds.ReadXml (Server.MapPath (MyXmlSrc));

          foreach (DataRow item in ds.Tables[0].Rows) {
              TableRow row = new TableRow ();
              TableCell cell = new TableCell ();

              StringBuilder builder = new StringBuilder ();
              builder.Append ("<a href=\"");
              builder.Append (item["Link"]);
              builder.Append ("\" ");

              if (MyMouseOverColor != Color.Empty &&
                  Request.Browser.Type.ToUpper ().IndexOf ("IE") > -1
                  && Request.Browser.MajorVersion >= 4) {
                  builder.Append ("onmouseover=\"" +
                      "defcolor=this.style.color; " +
                      "this.style.color=\'");
                  builder.Append (MyMouseOverColor.Name);
                  builder.Append ("\'\" onmouseout=\"" +
                      "this.style.color=defcolor\" ");
              }

              builder.Append ("style=\"text-decoration: none; ");

              if (MyFont.Name != null) {
                  builder.Append ("font-family: ");
                  builder.Append (MyFont.Name);
                  builder.Append ("; ");
              }

              if (MyFont.Size != FontUnit.Empty) {
                  builder.Append ("font-size: ");
                  builder.Append (MyFont.Size.ToString ());
```

```
                              builder.Append ("; ");
                    }

                    if (MyFont.Bold)
                        builder.Append ("font-weight: bold; ");

                    if (MyForeColor != Color.Empty) {
                        builder.Append ("color: ");
                        builder.Append (MyForeColor.Name);
                    }

                    builder.Append ("\">");
                    builder.Append (item["Text"]);
                    builder.Append ("</a>");

                    cell.Text = builder.ToString ();
                    row.Cells.Add (cell);
                    MyTable.Rows.Add (row);
                }

                if (MyBackColor != Color.Empty)
                    MyTable.BackColor = MyBackColor;
            }
        }

        public class MyFontInfo
        {
            string FontName;
            FontUnit FontSize;
            bool FontBold = false;

            public string Name
            {
                get { return FontName; }
                set { FontName = value; }
            }

            public FontUnit Size
            {
                get { return FontSize; }
                set { FontSize = value; }
            }

            public bool Bold
            {
                get { return FontBold; }
                set { FontBold = value; }
            }
        }
</script>
```

Dynamic Loading (and Cookies, Too!)

It's easy enough to create user controls declaratively by including tags in your ASPX files. But user controls can also be created programmatically, a procedure referred to as *dynamic loading*. The *Page* class's *LoadControl* method loads a user control at run time. It takes an ASCX file name as input and returns a generic *Control* reference representing the control that it loaded. The following example does away with the need for a <user:XmlNavBar> tag by loading Xml-NavBar dynamically:

```
Control navbar = LoadControl ("XmlNavBar.ascx");
Controls.Add (navbar);
```

The first statement loads the control. The second adds it to the page by calling *Add* on the page's *Controls* collection. In practice, adding a dynamically loaded control to the page is rarely this simple. Typically, you call *Add* on the *Controls* collection of a table cell or a <span> element to control where on the page the control appears. If the container hosts other controls as well, you can use *AddAt* instead of *Add* to specify where in the container's *Controls* collection the new control should be added.

LoadControl makes dynamic loading a breeze. The only catch is that the *Control* reference that it returns doesn't enable you to access any of the methods, properties, or events defined in the ASCX file. The following code, for example, won't compile because *XmlSrc* isn't a member of *Control*:

```
Control navbar = LoadControl ("XmlNavBar.ascx");
// Attempt to point the control to an XML source file
navbar.XmlSrc = "Links.xml"; // Won't compile!
```

The solution is to cast the *Control* reference to an *XmlNavBar_ascx* reference:

```
XmlNavBar_ascx navbar = (XmlNavBar_ascx) LoadControl ("XmlNavBar.ascx");
// Attempt to point the control to an XML source file
navbar.XmlSrc = "Links.xml"; // It works!
```

Where did *XmlNavBar_ascx* come from? That's the name of the class that ASP.NET generated to represent the XmlNavBar control. It simply strips the file name extension from the ASCX file's file name and appends _ascx. If you'd prefer to name the class yourself, you can do so by including an @ *Control* directive in the ASCX file:

```
<%@ Control ClassName="XmlNavBarControl" %>
```

The code to load and initialize the control would then look like this:

```
XmlNavBarControl navbar = (XmlNavBarControl) LoadControl ("XmlNavBar.ascx");
navbar.XmlSrc = "Links.xml";
```

Regardless of whether you specify a class name or settle for the default, you *must* register the control with an *@ Register* directive if you cast *LoadControl*'s return value. Otherwise, the compiler will complain that the type you cast to is an undefined type.

The question you're probably asking yourself is, "Why would I want to load a user control dynamically?" The answer is that it's a great way to customize a Web form on the basis of user preferences. Suppose you offer your users the option of displaying a stock ticker on your company's home page. You could implement the stock ticker as a user control and load it at run time only for those users who indicate that they want the stock ticker to appear. Users who don't want a stock ticker won't be bothered by it, and those who want one will get their wish.

Cookies

One problem with writing a Web page that supports user preferences is figuring out where to store those preferences. HTTP is a stateless protocol. As a user browses your site, all the Web server sees is a succession of HTTP requests coming from an arbitrary IP address. Chances are those requests are mixed with requests coming from other IP addresses, too. To store preferences, you either have to store them on the server and somehow correlate each incoming HTTP request to a set of stored preferences, or come up with a way to encode the user preferences in the individual requests. Cookies are a convenient mechanism for doing the latter.

A cookie is nothing more than a chunk of data that's transmitted from a browser to a Web server in each and every request. Cookies are transmitted in HTTP headers—specifically, in *Cookie* headers. Here's an HTTP request containing a cookie:

```
GET /mypage.html HTTP/1.1
Accept: */*
    .

    .

    .
User-Agent: Mozilla/4.0.(compatible; MSIE.6.0; Windows NT 5.1)
Host: www.wintellect.com
Cookie: FavoriteColor=Blue
```

Cookies have names and values. In this example, the cookie's name is "Favor-iteColor," and its value is "Blue." A browser can transmit several cookies at once by encoding them in a semicolon-separated list, as in

```
Cookie: FavoriteColor=Blue; FavoriteNumber=3
```

Lots of Web sites use cookies to identify returning users. Sometimes cookies contain user preferences; other times they carry authentication information to prevent you from having to log in again and again to sites that require logins. ASP.NET uses cookies to correlate returning visitors to sessions stored on the Web server—something you'll learn all about in the next chapter. ASP.NET also uses cookies to identify users who've been validated using forms authentication. (I'll cover forms authentication in more detail in Chapter 10.) Here's a cookie that could be used to signify that the requestor wants to see the latest prices of Amazon, Intel, and Microsoft stock on a personalized home page:

```
Cookie: Stocks=AMZN&INTC&MSFT
```

When a request containing a cookie arrives, it's up to the server to parse and interpret the cookie. Cookies are highly application-specific. Their purpose and contents vary widely among applications that use them.

Most browsers permit cookies to be disabled. Some sites warn you that they won't work properly if cookies aren't enabled. That's usually because they use cookies to round-trip user preferences, login information, or something similar. Cookies have gotten a bad rap in the press, but by and large they're harmless and in fact are quite useful to have around because we're stateful beings who use a stateless protocol as our primary means of transmitting digital information around the world.

How are cookies created? How does a browser know when to send a cookie and what to send? A Web server creates a cookie by returning it in the *Set-Cookie* header of an HTTP response. The following response returns a cookie to the requestor:

```
HTTP/1.1 200 OK
Server: Microsoft-IIS/5.0
Date: Wed, 24 Oct 2001 14:12:37 GMT
Content-Type: text/html
Content-Length: 46
    .
    .
    .

Set-Cookie: FavoriteColor=Blue; path=/
```

The *Path* component of the *Set-Cookie* header tells the requestor which subset of URLs at this domain the cookie applies to. The "path=/" attribute says that the cookie should be transmitted in every request to this domain. By default, "this domain" is the domain that the original request was directed to. However, cookies can optionally include *Domain* attributes that identify other domains. For example, if the Web server returns this *Set-Cookie* header:

```
Set-Cookie: FavoriteColor=Blue; domain=www.wintellect.com/; path=/
```

the "FavoriteColor" cookie will be transmitted in subsequent requests sent to www.wintellect.com, regardless of what domain the cookie was created in. Browsers don't have to honor *Set-Cookie* headers, but most do if cookies aren't disabled. A browser that accepts a cookie caches it so that it can transmit it back to the server in future requests.

How the browser caches a cookie depends on the cookie type. *Session cookies* are valid only until the browser closes and are typically cached in memory. *Persistent cookies* have deterministic lifetimes that are independent of the browser's lifetime. They're stored on the client's hard disk. (If you're an Internet Explorer user, look in Documents and Settings*UserName*\\Cookies to peek at the cookies stored on your hard disk.) What differentiates a session cookie from a persistent cookie, and how does the browser know when a persistent cookie expires? The *Expires* attribute. The following response header creates a persistent cookie that expires at noon on December 31, 2009:

```
Set-Cookie: FavoriteColor=Blue; expires=Thu, 31-Dec-2009 12:00:00 GMT; path=/
```

A cookie that lacks an *Expires* attribute is a session cookie; a cookie with an *Expires* attribute is a persistent cookie. Cookies can also include *Secure* attributes that prevent browsers from transmitting them over unencrypted (non-HTTPS) channels. The *Secure* attribute is handy if you use cookies to transmit sensitive information that mustn't fall into the wrong hands.

Cookies and ASP.NET

The .NET Framework class library simplifies cookie usage by providing a wrapper class named *HttpCookie* (a member of the *System.Web* namespace). One simple statement creates a cookie and assigns it a name and a value:

```
HttpCookie cookie = new HttpCookie ("FavoriteColor", "Blue");
```

Public *HttpCookie* properties named *Domain*, *Path*, *Expires*, and *Secure* wrap the cookie attributes of the same names. The following statement sets a cookie to expire one week from today:

```
cookie.Expires = DateTime.Now + new TimeSpan (7, 0, 0, 0);
```

These statements assign the cookie an absolute (rather than relative) expiration date and tag it with a *Secure* attribute, too:

```
cookie.Expires = new DateTime (2009, 12, 31); // December 31, 2009
cookie.Secure = true;
```

If you want to change a cookie's name or value after creating it, you can do so by using the cookie's *Name* and *Value* properties.

HttpCookie makes cookie creation simple. But how do you return a cookie that you create with *HttpCookie* to the browser in a *Set-Cookie* header? Easy: you add the cookie to the *Response* object's *Cookies* collection. The following statements create a session cookie named "FavoriteColor" (note the lack of statements assigning the cookie an expiration date, which makes the cookie a session cookie) and add it to the HTTP response:

```
HttpCookie cookie = new HttpCookie ("FavoriteColor", "Blue");
Response.Cookies.Add (cookie);
```

It's that simple. Adding the cookie to the *Response* object's *Cookies* collection ensures that the cookie will be returned in the HTTP response. You can add as many cookies as you like. They'll all be returned in the response.

Of course, cookies are of no use at all unless you can read them from incoming requests. To that end, the ASP.NET *Request* object contains a *Cookies* collection of its own that exposes the cookies (if any) accompanying an HTTP request. The following code reads a single cookie (by name) from the request, verifies that the cookie is indeed present in the request, and extracts the cookie's value:

```
HttpCookie cookie = Request.Cookies["FavoriteColor"];
if (cookie != null) {
    string FavoriteColor = cookie.Value;
    .
    .
    .
}
```

The *Request* object's *Cookies* property is of type *HttpCookieCollection*. If you'd like, you can use *HttpCookieCollection* properties such as *Keys*, *AllKeys*, and *Count* to enumerate the cookies accompanying an HTTP request.

Cookies can be deleted by the user or by the Web server. A user destroys a session cookie by simply closing his or her browser. Persistent cookies are destroyed by deleting the files they're stored in. That's typically done using a browser command (such as Internet Explorer's Delete Cookies command), but the operation can be performed manually or with the help of third-party utilities, too. Web servers delete cookies by doing the following:

- Returning *Set-Cookie* headers containing the names of the cookies to be deleted, accompanied by null values

- Including in those *Set-Cookie* headers expiration dates identifying dates in the past

This *Set-Cookie* header commands the browser to delete the cookie named "FavoriteColor," and works regardless of whether "FavoriteColor" is a session cookie or a persistent cookie:

```
Set-Cookie: FavoriteColor=; expires=Wed, 30-Sep-1959 07:15:00 GMT
```

In an ASP.NET application, you delete the "FavoriteColor" cookie this way:

```
HttpCookie cookie = new HttpCookie ("FavoriteColor");
cookie.Expires = new DateTime (1959, 9, 30);
Response.Cookies.Add (cookie);
```

Passing a single value to *HttpCookie*'s constructor assigns the cookie a name but no value, producing a *Set-Cookie* header very much like the one just shown.

Multivalue Cookies

It's not uncommon for cookie values to include multiple name/value pairs. For example, the following *Cookie* header transmits a cookie containing a user name and password:

```
Cookie: AuthInfo=UserName=Jeffpro&Password=imbatman
```

This is perfectly legal because the cookie technically still has just one value: "UserName=Jeffpro&Password=imbatman." The application running on the server can read that value and parse it to extract its subitems.

To make dealing with multivalue cookies easier (and to prevent you from having to manually parse out the subitems), *HttpCookie* exposes properties named *HasKeys* and *Values*. *HasKeys* is a Boolean; it reveals whether the cookie value contains subitems. *Values* is a collection that exposes the subitems. The following statements create and return a cookie that contains two subitems:

```
HttpCookie cookie = new HttpCookie ("AuthInfo");
cookie.Values["UserName"] = "Jeffpro";
cookie.Values["Password"] = "imbatman";
Response.Cookies.Add (cookie);
```

And this code retrieves the user name and password encapsulated in the cookie from the HTTP request:

```
HttpCookie cookie = Request.Cookies["AuthInfo"];
if (cookie != null) {
    string UserName = cookie.Values["UserName"];
    string Password = cookie.Values["Password"];
}
```

You can also enumerate the subitems contained in the *Values* property by using members of the *NameValueCollection* class. (*Values* is of type *NameValueCollection*.) Enumeration is useful when you don't know the names of the subitems up front.

The MyQuotes Page

The application in Figures 7-15 and 7-16 demonstrates how dynamically loaded user controls and cookies can be combined to create personalized Web pages. When initially displayed, MyQuotes.aspx contains nothing but a check box labeled "Show quotes." Checking the box dynamically loads the user control defined in MyQuotes.ascx and adds it to the page. MyQuotes.ascx goes out on the Web, fetches the most recent quotes for Amazon, Intel, and Microsoft stock, and displays them in a *DataGrid*. Refreshing the page refreshes the stock prices as well.

Checking the Show Quotes box does more than just load MyQuotes.ascx; it also creates a cookie named "MyQuotes" and returns it to the requestor. The cookie is a persistent one that's good for one year. Each time the page loads, the *Page_Load* handler checks for the "MyQuotes" cookie and loads the user control if the cookie is found. Consequently, you can check the box, close and reopen your browser, and go back to MyQuotes.aspx, and the user control comes back automatically. Unchecking the box deletes the cookie and prevents the control from being loaded again.

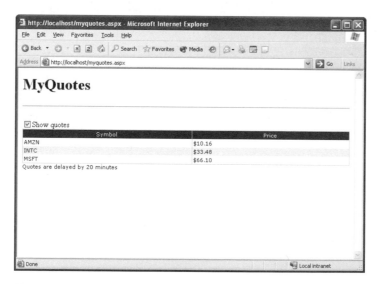

Figure 7-15   The MyQuotes page.

The stock quotes displayed by the user control are real, although they're delayed by 20 minutes. How does MyQuotes fetch real-time (or near-real-time) stock prices? It uses a Web service. Specifically, it uses the Delayed Stock Quote Web service written and supported by XMethods (*www.xmethods.com*). I haven't formally introduced Web services just yet, but you'll learn all about them in Chapter 11. I decided to use one here to make the sample more tantalizing. The downside to using a Web service is that there's no guarantee that it will be there tomorrow. MyQuotes worked fine when I wrote it, but if by some chance the Delayed Stock Quote service is no longer available when you read this, or if its URL or programmatic interface has changed, MyQuotes will be a dull sample indeed.

In order to run MyQuotes, you must copy the supplied DLL (MyQuotes.dll) to the bin directory of the application root. If MyQuotes.aspx and MyQuotes.ascx are in wwwroot, the DLL must be in wwwroot\bin. MyQuotes.dll contains a Web service proxy class named *netxmethodsservicesstockquoteStockQuoteService* that enables the user control to talk to the Delayed Stock Quote service using SOAP (Simple Object Access Protocol) messages transmitted over HTTP. Thanks to the proxy class, retrieving stock prices is as simple as this (with exception-handling code omitted for clarity):

```
netxmethodsservicesstockquoteStockQuoteService qs =
    new netxmethodsservicesstockquoteStockQuoteService ();

decimal amzn;
decimal intc;
decimal msft;

amzn = (decimal) qs.getQuote ("AMZN");
intc = (decimal) qs.getQuote ("INTC");
msft = (decimal) qs.getQuote ("MSFT");
```

MyQuotes.dll was generated from the source code file MyQuotes.cs, which in turn was generated by Wsdl.exe. Don't worry if this makes no sense right now; it'll become crystal clear in Chapter 11. A lot of people feel that Web services are the future of the Internet. If this sample doesn't make you hungry to know more, I don't know what will.

MyQuotes.aspx

```
<%@ Register TagPrefix="user" TagName="MyQuotes" Src="MyQuotes.ascx" %>

<html>
  <body>
    <h1>MyQuotes</h1>
    <hr>
    <form runat="server">
      <asp:CheckBox ID="ShowQuotes" Text="Show quotes" RunAt="server"
        AutoPostBack="true" OnCheckedChanged="OnCheckBoxClicked" />
      <span ID="PlaceHolder" runat="server" />
    </form>
  </body>
</html>

<script language="C#" runat="server">
  const string CookieName = "MyQuotes";
  const string CookieVal = "ShowQuotes";

  void Page_Load (Object sender, EventArgs e)
  {
      if (!IsPostBack) {
          // If a "MyQuotes" cookie is present, load the
          // user control and check the "Show quotes" box
          HttpCookie cookie = Request.Cookies["MyQuotes"];
          if (cookie != null) {
              MyQuotes_ascx ctrl =
                  (MyQuotes_ascx) LoadControl ("MyQuotes.ascx");
              ctrl.Width = Unit.Percentage (100);
              PlaceHolder.Controls.Add (ctrl);
              ShowQuotes.Checked = true;
          }
      }
  }

  void OnCheckBoxClicked (Object sender, EventArgs e)
  {
      if (ShowQuotes.Checked) {
          // Load the user control
          MyQuotes_ascx ctrl =
              (MyQuotes_ascx) LoadControl ("MyQuotes.ascx");
          ctrl.Width = Unit.Percentage (100);
          PlaceHolder.Controls.Add (ctrl);

          // Return a "MyQuotes" cookie that's good for one year
          HttpCookie cookie = new HttpCookie (CookieName, CookieVal);
          cookie.Expires = DateTime.Now + new TimeSpan (365, 0, 0, 0);
          Response.Cookies.Add (cookie);
      }
```

Figure 7-16   MyQuotes source code.

```
        else {
            // Delete the "MyQuotes" cookie
            HttpCookie cookie = new HttpCookie (CookieName);
            cookie.Expires = new DateTime (1959, 9, 30);
            Response.Cookies.Add (cookie);
        }
    }
}
</script>
```

MyQuotes.ascx

```
<%@ Import Namespace="System.Data" %>
<%@ Import Namespace="System.Drawing" %>

<asp:DataGrid ID="MyGrid" RunAt="server"
  BorderWidth="1" BorderColor="lightgray" CellPadding="2"
  Font-Name="Verdana" Font-Size="8pt" GridLines="vertical">
  <HeaderStyle BackColor="maroon" ForeColor="white"
    HorizontalAlign="center" />
  <ItemStyle BackColor="white" ForeColor="black" />
  <AlternatingItemStyle BackColor="beige" ForeColor="black" />
</asp:DataGrid>
<span style="font-family: verdana; font-size: 8pt">
  Quotes are delayed by 20 minutes
</span>

<script language="C#" runat="server">
  Unit MyWidth;

  public Unit Width
  {
      get { return MyWidth; }
      set { MyWidth = value; }
  }

  void Page_Load (Object sender, EventArgs e)
  {
      if (MyWidth != Unit.Empty)
          MyGrid.Width = MyWidth;

      // Get quotes for AMZN, INTC, and MSFT
      netxmethodsservicesstockquoteStockQuoteService qs =
          new netxmethodsservicesstockquoteStockQuoteService ();

      decimal amzn;
      decimal intc;
```

(continued)

MyQuotes.ascx   *(continued)*

```
    decimal msft;

    try {
        amzn = (decimal) qs.getQuote ("AMZN");
    }
    catch {
        amzn = -1.0m;
    }

    try {
        intc = (decimal) qs.getQuote ("INTC");
    }
    catch {
        intc = -1.0m;
    }

    try {
        msft = (decimal) qs.getQuote ("MSFT");
    }
    catch {
        msft = -1.0m;
    }

    // Add the quotes to a DataSet
    DataSet ds = new DataSet ();
    DataTable dt = new DataTable ("Quotes");
    ds.Tables.Add (dt);

    DataColumn col1 = new DataColumn ("Symbol", typeof (string));
    DataColumn col2 = new DataColumn ("Price", typeof (string));
    dt.Columns.Add (col1);
    dt.Columns.Add (col2);

    DataRow row = dt.NewRow ();
    row["Symbol"] = "AMZN";
    row["Price"] = (amzn == -1.0m) ? "Unavailable" :
        String.Format ("{0:c}", amzn);
    dt.Rows.Add (row);

    row = dt.NewRow ();
    row["Symbol"] = "INTC";
    row["Price"] = (intc == -1.0m) ? "Unavailable" :
        String.Format ("{0:c}", intc);
    dt.Rows.Add (row);

    row = dt.NewRow ();
    row["Symbol"] = "MSFT";
    row["Price"] = (msft == -1.0m) ? "Unavailable" :
```

```
        String.Format ("{0:c}", msft);
    dt.Rows.Add (row);

    // Bind the DataGrid to the DataSet
    MyGrid.DataSource = ds;
    MyGrid.DataBind ();
}
</script>
```

Fragment Caching

In Chapter 5, I briefly touched on the subject of output caching and described how to improve the performance of Web forms by including @ *OutputCache* directives in your ASPX files. For example, adding the statement

```
<%@ OutputCache Duration="60" VaryByParam="None" %>
```

to an ASPX file instructs ASP.NET to generate the page once and to hold a copy of it in the output cache for 60 seconds. Until one minute elapses and the cached page becomes invalid, ASP.NET satisfies subsequent requests for the page by returning cached HTML. Caching improves performance by preventing a page from having to be executed over and over again to obtain its output.

One of the limitations of using @ *OutputCache* directives in ASPX files is lack of granularity. You either cache the entire page or nothing at all: there's no in-between. User controls offer a middle ground by allowing portions of a page to be cached while the rest continues to be generated dynamically. Called *sub-page caching* or *fragment caching*, this form of caching is a boon to performance because it enables ASP.NET output caching to be used with pages that mix static and dynamic content.

Here's how fragment caching works. You begin by apportioning your pages into areas that contain static content (content that doesn't change from request to request and is therefore amenable to caching) and areas that contain dynamic content (content that changes—or could change—from request to request and should therefore not be cached). Then you implement the static portions of the page as user controls. In the controls' ASCX files, you include @ *OutputCache* directives that enable output caching. Significantly, caching is performed *just for the content generated from the ASCX files* and not for other content on the page. You can even include *VaryByControl* attributes in @ *OutputCache* directives to cache different instances of the same control based on the property values assigned to those instances.

Perhaps an example or two will help clarify matters. You might have noticed that the MyQuotes application presented earlier in this chapter is slow. Every time you check the Show Quotes box, the control retrieves stock prices from a Web service. You could alleviate the performance problem somewhat by adding an @ *OutputCache* directive to MyQuotes.aspx, but if the page contained other controls (and in real life it would), their output would be cached, too. A better solution is to add the following directive to MyQuotes.ascx:

```
<%@ OutputCache Duration="60" VaryByParam="None" %>
```

Now only the stock quotes grid will be cached and you're free to generate content dynamically elsewhere on the page. Sure, stock quotes can now be up to 60 seconds out-of-date, but when they're delayed for 20 minutes anyway, who cares? You just freed up your Web server to process potentially thousands more requests per second.

Admittedly, this example is overly simplistic because MyQuotes is such a simple control: it looks the same on every Web page. This chapter's XmlNavBar control offers a more realistic example. Once initialized, an XmlNavBar never varies its HTML output unless its properties are changed dynamically. That means it lends itself extraordinarily well to output caching. However, you might use several XmlNavBars on your site and configure each of them differently, in which case different versions of the control need to be cached.

That's what the *VaryByControl* attribute is for. With it, you can instruct ASP.NET to cache different versions of a user control based on the property values assigned to it. For example, if you use two different XmlNavBar controls and initialize each with a different XML file, you could cache a version for each XML file by listing the *XmlSrc* property in a *VaryByControl* attribute:

```
<%@ OutputCache Duration="3600" VaryByParam="None"  VaryByControl="XmlSrc" %>
```

If you customize XmlNavBar controls by varying multiple properties, you can separate the property names with semicolons in the @ *OutputCache* directive:

```
<%@ OutputCache Duration="3600" VaryByParam="None"
  VaryByControl="XmlSrc;ForeColor;MouseOverColor" %>
```

Now the control won't be physically executed more than once an hour, and no matter how many pages contain XmlNavBars and how often those pages are requested, you've reduced the load on your server commensurately. That's a bargain by any measure.

Incidentally, ASP.NET performs output caching on a per-application basis. That means if you use two different navbars in two different applications, you don't have to bother with *VaryByControl* attributes. ASP.NET will automatically cache two versions.

Next Up: Custom Controls

User controls are powerful devices for capturing complex rendering and behavioral logic in reusable components that can be shared among developers and shared among Web pages. Because the ASP.NET output cache is ASCX-aware, user controls play an important role in performance tuning, too.

The first time I read about user controls, I flatly failed to understand their potential. "Nice," I thought to myself. "Maybe I'll find a use for them someday." Since then, I've found more uses for user controls than I ever could have imagined. In fact, I've come to believe that user controls are among the top three or four most important features of ASP.NET, if only for making Web applications perform better by permitting selected regions of a page to be served from a cache while other regions are generated anew in each request.

Web controls are also high on my favorite features list. Not just because the FCL includes a set of prepackaged controls, but because developers can write controls of their own, better known as "custom controls," to supplement and extend what the FCL has to offer. Custom controls enjoy powers that user controls never dreamed of and are the key to extending ASP.NET. But don't take my word for it. Turn the page and see for yourself.

8

Custom Controls

As you learned in Chapter 6, the .NET Framework class library (FCL) features a rich collection of server controls that provide ready-made building blocks for Web forms. FCL control types range from the simple (*Label*) to the sublime (*Calendar*, *DataGrid*, *Repeater*, and others), and they enable developers to build sophisticated Web applications without getting lost in a maze of HTML and client-side scripting.

Diverse as they are, the FCL's built-in server controls can't possibly accommodate the needs of every developer. The time will come when you need a control that's not part of the FCL. Then you'll have two choices: purchase the control from a third party or write it yourself. This chapter is about the latter: how to write custom controls that look and feel like FCL controls but encapsulate functionality that FCL controls don't. Among other things, you'll learn how controls render themselves to Web pages, how controls process postback data and generate postbacks of their own, how controls use view state to persist data across requests, how to write controls that do some of their processing on the client side by emitting JavaScript, and how to build controls that escape the bonds of HTML by deriving their appearance from dynamically generated images. You'll see many working examples, including one that paints a realistic-looking odometer onto a Web page and another that creates numbers-only text input fields.

ASP.NET's server control architecture is such that writing a simple control is relatively easy and writing a complex control is—well—complex. Still, the ability to write custom controls is an essential skill that every ASP.NET developer should possess. Even if you never intend to write a custom control, you'll find the knowledge in this chapter edifying because it speaks volumes about how ASP.NET works.

Custom Control Basics

The starting point for a custom control is *System.Web.UI.Control*, which defines the fundamental characteristics of a server control. You build a custom control by deriving from *Control*, overriding a few virtual methods here and there, and adding the methods, properties, and events that make your control unique. It's also possible to write custom controls by deriving from FCL control classes such as *DataGrid*, but I'm assuming here and throughout the remainder of this chapter that your intent is to build controls from scratch rather than modify existing ones.

Control's most important virtual method, and the method that's overridden in almost every custom control, is *Render*. *Render* is called each time a control is executed—that is, when the page that hosts the control is requested. It affords a control the opportunity to render itself by emitting HTML to the client. *Render* receives through its parameter list an *HtmlTextWriter* reference whose *Write* method writes HTML to the output stream.

Your First Custom Control

Figure 8-1 contains the source code for a simple control that writes "Hello, world" to a Web page. The *using* statements at the top of the file identify the namespaces containing the types that the control uses. The *namespace* statement encloses the class definition in a custom namespace named *Wintellect*. Namespaces aren't optional when you write custom controls; control classes *must* be scoped to a namespace. The *Hello* class represents the control itself. It derives from *System.Web.UI.Control*, and it overrides the *Render* method that it inherits from its base class. *Render* does nothing more than write "Hello, world" to the output stream by calling *HtmlTextWriter.Write*.

Despite its simplicity, this example demonstrates three important principles of custom control programming:

- Classes representing custom controls derive from *System.Web.UI.Control*

- Custom controls render themselves to the client by overriding *Control.Render*

- Custom control classes must be enclosed in namespaces

There's more (of course!), but these principles permeate the fabric of custom control programming and are embodied in each and every sample presented in this chapter.

Before you can test the *Hello* control, you need to compile it. Here's the command:

```
csc /t:library /out:HelloControl.dll hello1.cs
```

The output is a DLL named HelloControl.dll that contains the control's implementation. HelloControl.dll should be placed in the bin subdirectory of the application that uses the control. As you're well aware by now, the application root's bin subdirectory is a magic place that ASP.NET looks to resolve references to types not found in the assemblies ASP.NET links to by default. "Application root" is any directory that is an IIS virtual directory.

Hello1.cs
```
using System;
using System.Web.UI;

namespace Wintellect
{
    public class Hello : Control
    {
        protected override void Render (HtmlTextWriter writer)
        {
            writer.Write ("Hello, world");
        }
    }
}
```

Figure 8-1   A simple custom control.

Testing the *Hello* Control

The Web form in Figure 8-2 uses the *Hello* control to write "Hello, world" to a Web page. The statement

```
<win:Hello RunAt="server" />
```

declares a control instance. The statement

```
<%@ Register TagPrefix="win" Namespace="Wintellect"
  Assembly="HelloControl" %>
```

enables ASP.NET to make sense of the declaration. *TagPrefix* defines the prefix used in tags that declare instances of the control. *Namespace* identifies the namespace that the control belongs to. *Assembly* identifies the assembly in which the control is implemented. Note the absence of a *TagName* attribute. *TagName* isn't needed for custom controls, as it is for user controls, because the control's class name doubles as its tag name.

Hello1.aspx

```
<%@ Register TagPrefix="win" Namespace="Wintellect"
  Assembly="HelloControl" %>

<html>
  <body>
    <form runat="server">
      <win:Hello RunAt="server" />
    </form>
  </body>
</html>
```

Figure 8-2   Using the *Hello* control.

Here's a three-step procedure for testing the *Hello* control:

1.   Copy Hello1.aspx to your PC's wwwroot directory.

2.   Copy HelloControl.dll to wwwroot\bin.

3.   Start your browser and type http://localhost/hello1.aspx into the address bar.

In response, a bare-bones Web page containing the text "Hello, world" should appear, as shown in Figure 8-3.

Figure 8-3   Output from the *Hello* control.

Improving the *Hello* Control: Adding Properties

Hello demonstrates the basics of custom control authoring, but it's merely a
start. When you design a custom control, you should strive to make it as programmable as possible by including public properties that developers can use
to tweak its appearance and behavior. Public properties double as attributes in
tags that declare control instances and can also be utilized by server-side
scripts. Adding a property is easy: you simply declare the property in the control class and implement its *get* and *set* methods as you would for any other
managed type.

Figure 8-4 lists an improved version of the *Hello* control that implements
a public property named *Name*. Rather than write "Hello, world" to the host
page, the revised control writes "Hello" followed by the value encapsulated in
the *Name* property.

Hello2.cs

```
using System;
using System.Web.UI;

namespace Wintellect
{
    public class Hello : Control
    {
        string MyName = "";

        public string Name
        {
            get { return MyName; }
            set { MyName = value; }
        }

        protected override void Render (HtmlTextWriter writer)
        {
            writer.Write ("<h1>Hello, " + Name + "</h1>");
        }
    }
}
```

Figure 8-4   Improved *Hello* control.

The Web form in Figure 8-5 uses the new and improved *Hello* control. The
Name attribute in the control tag initializes the control's *Name* property with the
string "Jeff", changing the text that appears in the Web page to "Hello, Jeff".
Because the output is enclosed in an <h1> element, the text appears in a head-
line font (Figure 8-6).

Hello2.aspx
```
<%@ Register TagPrefix="win" Namespace="Wintellect"
  Assembly="HelloControl" %>

<html>
  <body>
    <form runat="server">
      <win:Hello Name="Jeff" RunAt="server" />
    </form>
  </body>
</html>
```

Figure 8-5   Using the improved *Hello* control.

Figure 8-6   Output from the improved *Hello* control.

More About *HtmlTextWriter*

Write is one of many *HtmlTextWriter* methods that you can use in a control's *Render* method to output HTML. *WriteFullBeginTag*, *WriteEndTag*, and other *HtmlTextWriter* methods simplify rendering code by letting the developer think in terms of HTML tags and attributes rather than raw text. For example, rather than write this:

```
writer.Write ("<h1>Hello, " + Name + "</h1>");
```

You can write this:

```
writer.WriteFullBeginTag ("h1");
writer.Write ("Hello, " + Name);
writer.WriteEndTag ("h1");
```

WriteFullBeginTag writes out the specified tag in angle brackets, while *WriteEnd-Tag* outputs the specified tag surrounded by angle brackets and prefixed with a / symbol, as in </h1>.

This simple example belies the dramatic improvements that *WriteEndTag* and other *HtmlTextWriter* methods can lend to your code. Here's a code snippet that uses *Write* to output an HTML <input> tag containing a number of attributes:

```
writer.Write ("<input type=\"text\"");

writer.Write (" name=\"");
writer.Write (UniqueID);
writer.Write ("\"");

writer.Write (" id=\"");
writer.Write (ClientID);
writer.Write ("\"");

writer.Write (" value=\"");
writer.Write (Text);
writer.Write ("\"");

writer.Write (">");
```

Here's the equivalent code recast to use *WriteBeginTag*, *WriteEndTag*, and *WriteAttribute*. The *WriteBeginTag* method emits an HTML tag without a closing angle bracket so that attributes can be added. The *WriteAttribute* method adds an attribute to a tag started with *WriteBeginTag*:

```
writer.WriteBeginTag ("input");
writer.WriteAttribute ("type", "text");
writer.WriteAttribute ("name", UniqueID);
writer.WriteAttribute ("id", ClientID);
writer.WriteAttribute ("value", Text);
writer.Write (HtmlTextWriter.TagRightChar);
```

The rewritten code not only reads better, it executes faster, too. You'll see numerous examples like this one in the chapter's remaining sample controls.

Postbacks and Postback Data

Suppose you wanted to build a custom control similar to the FCL's *TextBox* control. On the surface, this sounds easy enough. You'd start by deriving from *Control* and overriding its *Render* method with one that outputs an <input

type="text"> tag. Most likely, you'd also implement a *Text* property to expose the control's text. Here's what the derived class might look like:

```
using System;
using System.Web.UI;

namespace Wintellect
{
    public class MyTextBox : Control
    {
        string MyText = "";

        public string Text
        {
            get { return MyText; }
            set { MyText = value; }
        }

        protected override void Render (HtmlTextWriter writer)
        {
            writer.WriteBeginTag ("input");
            writer.WriteAttribute ("type", "text");
            writer.WriteAttribute ("name", UniqueID);

            if (ID != null)
                writer.WriteAttribute ("id", ClientID);

            if (Text.Length > 0)
                writer.WriteAttribute ("value", Text);

            writer.Write (HtmlTextWriter.TagRightChar);
        }
    }
}
```

This code sample illustrates a pair of subtle but important points that control developers should take to heart:

■ If a tag output by a control includes a *Name* attribute, the value of that attribute should be taken from the *UniqueID* property that the control inherits from *Control*.

■ If a tag output by a control includes an *Id* attribute, the value of that attribute should be taken from the *ClientID* property that the control inherits from *Control*.

UniqueID and *ClientID* are important because, unlike the *ID* property, they're never null. Even if the tag that declares a custom control instance lacks an *Id* attribute, *UniqueID* and *ClientID* assume values defined by the system that give the control a unique identity. And unlike *ID*, *UniqueID* and *ClientID* give each control instance a unique identity even when a replicator-type control (such as a *Repeater*) is used to create multiple control instances.

Here's a tag that declares a *MyTextBox* instance in a Web form:

```
<win:MyTextBox ID="UserName" Text="Bill" RunAt="server" />
```

And here's the output:

```
<input type="text" name="UserName" id="UserName" value="Bill">
```

So far, there's nothing here that you haven't seen already. But now comes the hard part. When a postback occurs, *MyTextBox* should update its *Text* property from the postback data so that a server-side script can read the text typed into the control. In other words, let's say the user types "Gates" into the text box and submits the form back to the server, generating an HTTP POST with the following message body:

```
UserName=Gates
```

The *MyTextBox* control created on the server must read the message body and update its *Text* property accordingly. Which brings up a question: how?

The *IPostBackDataHandler* Interface

The answer is an interface named *IPostBackDataHandler*, which belongs to the FCL's *System.Web.UI* namespace. Implementing *IPostBackDataHandler* enables a control to access data accompanying a postback and update its properties accordingly. The interface defines two methods, both of which must be implemented in a class that derives from it:

- *LoadPostData*, which the .NET Framework calls to pass postback data to the control

- *RaisePostDataChangedEvent*, which is called after *LoadPostData* to give the control the opportunity to fire events stemming from changes in its internal state following a postback

Forget about *RaisePostDataChangedEvent* for a moment; we'll talk about it later. *LoadPostData* is the method that interests us for now because it's the one we can use to grab the text typed into a text box created by *MyTextBox*. *LoadPostData* is prototyped this way:

```
bool LoadPostData (string postDataKey, NameValueCollection postCollection)
```

When *LoadPostData* is called, *postCollection* holds all the data that accompanied the postback—not just for the control whose *LoadPostData* method was called, but for all controls. The individual data items in *postCollection* are indexed, and *postDataKey* holds the index of the data item that corresponds to the control whose *LoadPostData* method was called. (The index is actually the control ID, but that's an implementation detail that has no bearing on the code you write.) If the control emits an <input type="text"> tag and the user types "Gates" into it, *postCollection*[*postDataKey*] equals "Gates" when *LoadPostData* is called.

Figure 8-7 contains the source code for a *MyTextBox* control whose *Text* property is updated on each and every postback. *MyTextBox* derives not only from *Control* but from *IPostBackDataHandler*. Yes, it's true that a managed type can have only one base class, but it's perfectly legal to derive from one base class and one or more interfaces. All an interface does is define abstract methods that must be overridden in a derived class. The fact that *MyTextBox* derives from *IPostBackDataHandler* indicates that it implements the *IPostBack-DataHandler* interface. And because it derives from *IPostBackDataHandler*, it's obliged to override the *LoadPostData* and *RaisePostDataChangedEvent* methods. *MyTextBox*'s *LoadPostData* method retrieves the postback data generated from the text that the user typed into the input field. Then it writes the value to its own *Text* property.

MyTextBox1.cs
```csharp
using System;
using System.Web.UI;
using System.Collections.Specialized;

namespace Wintellect
{
    public class MyTextBox : Control, IPostBackDataHandler
    {
        string MyText = "";

        public string Text
        {
            get { return MyText; }
            set { MyText = value; }
        }
```

Figure 8-7   *MyTextBox* control.

```
        public bool LoadPostData (string postDataKey,
            NameValueCollection postCollection)
        {
            Text = postCollection[postDataKey];
            return false;
        }

        public void RaisePostDataChangedEvent ()
        {
        }

        protected override void Render (HtmlTextWriter writer)
        {
            writer.WriteBeginTag ("input");
            writer.WriteAttribute ("type", "text");
            writer.WriteAttribute ("name", UniqueID);

            if (ID != null)
                writer.WriteAttribute ("id", ClientID);

            if (Text.Length > 0)
                writer.WriteAttribute ("value", Text);

            writer.Write (HtmlTextWriter.TagRightChar);
        }
    }
}
```

You can try out *MyTextBox* with the Web form in Figure 8-8. First compile MyTextBox1.cs into an assembly named MyTextBoxControl.dll and place it in the application root's bin directory. Then bring up the page in your browser, type something into the text box, and click the Test button. The text that you typed should appear below the text box, proof that the control updated its *Text* property from the postback data.

MyTextBoxPage1.aspx

```
<%@ Register TagPrefix="win" Namespace="Wintellect"
  Assembly="MyTextBoxControl" %>

<html>
  <body>
    <form runat="server">
      <win:MyTextBox ID="Input" Text="Type something here"
        RunAt="server" />
      <asp:Button Text="Test" OnClick="OnTest" RunAt="server" /><br>
      <asp:Label ID="Output" RunAt="server" />
```

Figure 8-8   *MyTextBox* test page.

MyTextBoxPage1.aspx *(continued)*

```
      </form>
  </body>
</html>

<script language="C#" runat="server">
  void OnTest (Object sender, EventArgs e)
  {
      Output.Text = Input.Text;
  }
</script>
```

Are you surprised by the complexity of *MyTextBox*? Who would have thought that a control as simple as *TextBox*—the FCL class that *MyTextBox* is patterned after—would have to do so much just to do so little? *TextBox* is an exemplary class because despite its outward simplicity, its implementation is moderately complex. It also demonstrates some of the key facets of the server control programming model. In the next several sections, we'll enhance *MyTextBox* until it's practically a plug-in replacement for *TextBox*. The goal isn't to build a better *TextBox*: it's to understand the intricacies of control programming using a familiar control type as a baseline.

View State

Most controls fire events of one type or another. For example, *Button* controls fire *Click* events, and *ListBoxes* fire *SelectedIndexChanged* events. *TextBox*es fire *TextChanged* events when the text submitted via a postback doesn't match the text that the *TextBox* returned to the browser.

Sounds simple, right? But there's a huge gotcha waiting to ensnare the unwary developer. A server control's lifetime matches that of a single HTTP request. If MyTextBoxPage.aspx is requested 100 times, ASP.NET creates 100 different *MyTextBox* objects to fulfill those requests. Because *MyTextBox* is reinstantiated each and every time a request arrives, it can't very well use data members to store state from one request to the next. In other words, *MyTextBox* can't possibly determine whether its text has changed by doing this:

```
public bool LoadPostData (string postDataKey,
    NameValueCollection postCollection)
{
    string NewText = postCollection[postDataKey];
    if (NewText != MyText) {
        // The control's text has changed
    }
    return false;
}
```

Why? Because *MyText* won't necessarily equal what you set it to in the last request. Instead, it will hold the value it was initialized with when the control was instantiated.

One of the most difficult aspects of building stateful programs on top of stateless protocols is figuring out how to hold state between requests. That's why ASP.NET offers a mechanism called *view state*. View state is a place where controls can store state in such a way that it remains valid from one request to the next. It's particularly useful for controls that fire change events and that therefore require a mechanism for retaining state across requests. ASP.NET does the hard part by storing the state. Your job is to tell it what to store.

ASP.NET exposes its view state mechanism through a *Control* property named *ViewState*. The property's type is *StateBag*, which is a dictionary-like class that stores key/value pairs. The following statement adds an integer to view state and keys it with the string "Count":

```
ViewState["Count"] = 1;
```

The next statement reads the integer back from view state. The cast is necessary because view state is typed to store generic *Objects*:

```
int count = (int) ViewState["Count"];
```

The magic here is that "Count" can be written to view state in one request and read back in the next one. Therefore, view state is an exceedingly easy-to-use means for persisting a control's internal state from one page invocation to the next.

Change Events

Now that you know about view state, you're prepared for the next logical step in *MyTextBox*'s evolution: adding *TextChanged* events. Declaring an event is no big deal; events were discussed briefly in Chapter 2 and again in Chapter 7. The following statement declares an event named *TextChanged* whose type is *EventHandler*. Recall that *EventHandler* is one of the standard delegates defined in the *System* namespace:

```
public event EventHandler TextChanged;
```

With the event thusly declared, firing a *TextChanged* event is as simple as this:

```
if (TextChanged != null)
    TextChanged (this, new EventArgs ());
```

The question that remains is when to fire the event. That's where *IPostBackDataHandler*'s other method, *RaisePostDataChangedEvent*, comes in.

RaisePostDataChangedEvent exists for the sole purpose of enabling controls that update their properties from postback data to fire change events. *RaisePostDataChangedEvent* is called right after *LoadPostData*, but it's called only if *LoadPostData* returns true. In Figure 8-7, *RaisePostDataChangedEvent* contains no code because it's never called (note *LoadPostData*'s return value). Here's the proper way to implement *LoadPostData* and *RaisePostDataChangedEvent* in controls that support change events:

■ Persist property values that serve as the basis for change events in view state.

■ In *LoadPostData*, extract the new property values from the postback data and the old property values from view state and then compare the two. If a property changed, return true so that *RaisePostDataChangedEvent* will be called. Otherwise, return false.

■ In *RaisePostDataChangedEvent*, fire your change events.

Figure 8-9 contains a modified version of *MyTextBox* that fires *TextChanged* events. The data member *MyText* is gone; it's no longer needed now that *Text* is stored in view state. *LoadPostData* has been modified to compare the old text to the new and return true if they're unequal. And *RaisePostDataChangedEvent* fires a *TextChanged* event to let interested parties know that a change occurred.

```
MyTextBox2.cs
using System;
using System.Web.UI;
using System.Collections.Specialized;

namespace Wintellect
{
    public class MyTextBox : Control, IPostBackDataHandler
    {
        public event EventHandler TextChanged;

        public string Text
        {
            get
            {
                string text = (string) ViewState["MyText"];
                return (text == null) ? "" : text;
            }
```

Figure 8-9 *MyTextBox* control with *TextChanged* events.

```
        set { ViewState["MyText"] = value; }
    }

    public bool LoadPostData (string postDataKey,
        NameValueCollection postCollection)
    {
        string temp = Text;
        Text = postCollection[postDataKey];
        return (temp != Text);
    }

    public void RaisePostDataChangedEvent ()
    {
        if (TextChanged != null)
            TextChanged (this, new EventArgs ()); // Fire event
    }

    protected override void Render (HtmlTextWriter writer)
    {
        writer.WriteBeginTag ("input");
        writer.WriteAttribute ("type", "text");
        writer.WriteAttribute ("name", UniqueID);

        if (ID != null)
            writer.WriteAttribute ("id", ClientID);

        if (Text.Length > 0)
            writer.WriteAttribute ("value", Text);

        writer.Write (HtmlTextWriter.TagRightChar);
    }
  }
}
```

The Web form in Figure 8-10 responds to *TextChanged* events by displaying a message underneath the control. To see for yourself, open MyTextBoxPage2.aspx in your browser (don't forget to regenerate MyTextBox-Control.dll by compiling MyTextBox2.cs first) and click the Test button to force a postback. Nothing visible should happen because the input text didn't change. Now edit "Type something here" and click Test again. This time, "Text changed" should appear under the control, demonstrating that it fired a *TextChanged* event.

MyTextBoxPage2.aspx
```
<%@ Register TagPrefix="win" Namespace="Wintellect"
  Assembly="MyTextBoxControl" %>

<html>
  <body>
    <form runat="server">
      <win:MyTextBox ID="Input" Text="Type something here"
        OnTextChanged="OnTextChanged" RunAt="server" />
      <asp:Button Text="Test" RunAt="server" /><br>
      <asp:Label ID="Output" RunAt="server" />
    </form>
  </body>
</html>

<script language="C#" runat="server">
  void Page_Load (Object sender, EventArgs e)
  {
      Output.Text = ""; // Reset the Label control
  }

  void OnTextChanged (Object sender, EventArgs e)
  {
      Output.Text = "Text changed";
  }
</script>
```

Figure 8-10   Revised test page for *MyTextBox*.

How View State Works

Are you curious to know how ASP.NET saves the data that you write to view state? Bring up MyTextBoxPage2.aspx in your browser, click the Test button, and check out the HTML that comes back. Here's what you'll see:

```
<html>
  <body>
    <form name="_ctl0" method="post" action="mytextboxpage2.aspx" id="_ctl0">
      <input type="hidden" name="__VIEWSTATE"
        value="dDwtNzIwNTMyODUzO3Q8O8O2w8aTwxPjs+O2w8dDw7bDxpPDE+O2k8NT47PjtsPH
        Q8cDxsPE15VGV4dDs+O2w8VHlwZSBzb211dGhpbmcgaGVyZTs+Pjs7Pjt0PHA8cDxsPFR
        leHQ7PjtsPFFx1Oz4+Oz47Oz47Pj47Pj47Pg==" />
```

```
        <input type="text" name="Input" value="Type something here">
        <input type="submit" name="_ctl1" value="Test" /><br>
        <span id="Output"></span>
    </form>
  </body>
</html>
```

The key is the hidden input control named __VIEWSTATE. It doesn't show up in the Web page because it's marked *type*="hidden." It has no UI because it doesn't need one; it's there for the sole purpose of round-tripping view state to the client and back. View state isn't stored on the Web server. It's transmitted to the client in a hidden control and then transmitted back to the server as part of the form's postback data. The value of __VIEWSTATE is a base-64 encoded version of all the data written to view state by all the page's controls, plus any view state saved by the page itself, plus a hash value generated from the page's contents that enables ASP.NET to detect changes to the page.

This answers one of the most common questions that newcomers ask about ASP.NET: "What's all that __VIEWSTATE stuff I see when I do a View/Source?" Now you know. That's how ASP.NET components persist state across round trips. View state is typically used to detect changes in control state, but it has other uses, too. I once used it to help a sortable *DataGrid* remember which column it was last sorted on. I didn't have to modify *DataGrid*. In the page that hosted the *DataGrid*, I simply wrote a sort expression to view state when the *DataGrid* was sorted and retrieved it from view state whenever I needed it. Because *Page* derives indirectly from *Control*, and because pages are instances of classes derived from *Page*, pages can access view state using the same *ViewState* property that controls use.

View State Security

If you submit a Web form over an unencrypted channel, it's entirely conceivable that someone could intercept the view state accompanying the request and modify it, possibly for malicious purposes. To guard against such occurrences without resorting to HTTPS, include the following statement at the top of your ASPX files:

```
<%@ Page EnableViewStateMac="true" %>
```

The "Mac" in *EnableViewStateMac* stands for *message authentication code*. Setting *EnableViewStateMac* to true appends a hash of view state combined with a validation key to every __VIEWSTATE value returned from this page. Following a postback, ASP.NET verifies that view state wasn't tampered with by rehashing it and comparing the new hash value to the one round-tripped to the client. A snooper can't alter __VIEWSTATE and escape detection without updating the hash too. But updating the hash is next to impossible because the validation key is known only to the server.

EnableViewStateMac ensures that alterations don't go unnoticed, but it doesn't protect view state from prying eyes or physically prevent it from being altered. For an extra measure of security over unencrypted connections, add the following entry to your Web server's Machine.config file:

```
<machineKey validation="3DES" />
```

Henceforth, ASP.NET will encrypt view state using symmetric Triple DES encryption. Encrypted view state can't be read by mere mortals unless they manage to compromise your Web server and steal the encryption key. That key is randomly generated by ASP.NET (unless you specify otherwise using additional entries in Machine.config) and stored by the Web server's Local Security Authority (LSA).

Generating Postbacks

MyTextBox is now a reasonable facsimile of *TextBox*, but it still lacks an important ingredient: an *AutoPostBack* property. Setting *AutoPostBack* to true programs a *TextBox* to fire a *TextChanged* event the moment it loses the input focus following a text change. Without *AutoPostBack*, *TextChanged* events don't fire until the page posts back to the server for some other reason, such as a button click. *AutoPostBack* forces the postback to occur immediately. How it forces postbacks isn't obvious to the casual observer. Rather than explain how *AutoPostBack* works and follow up with a code sample, I'll show you the code first and then explain how it works.

Figure 8-11 contains the third and final version of *MyTextBox*. Unlike the previous versions, this one implements a public property named *AutoPostBack* whose value is stored in a private field (*MyAutoPostBack*). The latest version also implements *Render* differently: it adds an *OnChange* attribute to the <input type="text"> tag. Here's the relevant code:

```
if (AutoPostBack)
    writer.WriteAttribute ("onchange", "javascript:" +
        Page.GetPostBackEventReference (this));
```

Execute a View/Source command after fetching MyTextBoxPage3.aspx (Figure 8-12) and you'll see this:

```
<input type="text" name="Input" id="Input" value="Type something here"
  onchange="javascript:__doPostBack('Input','')">
  .
  .
  .
<input type="hidden" name="__EVENTTARGET" value="" />
```

```
<input type="hidden" name="__EVENTARGUMENT" value="" />
<script language="javascript">
<!--
    function __doPostBack(eventTarget, eventArgument) {
        var theform = document._ctl0;
        theform.__EVENTTARGET.value = eventTarget;
        theform.__EVENTARGUMENT.value = eventArgument;
        theform.submit();
    }
// -->
</script>
```

See how it works? The *OnChange* attribute designates a handler for DHTML *OnChange* events. A text input field fires an *OnChange* event when it loses the input focus following a text change. *Page.GetPostBackEventReference* returns code that calls a JavaScript function named *__doPostBack*. It also writes *__doPostBack* to a script block returned to the client. When the *__doPostBack* function is called in response to an *OnChange* event, it programmatically submits the form to the server by calling *submit* on the DHTML object representing the form (*theform*). In other words, *AutoPostBack* works its magic with some clever client-side script. And the script is simple enough that it works with just about any browser that supports JavaScript.

MyTextBox3.cs

```
using System;
using System.Web.UI;
using System.Collections.Specialized;

namespace Wintellect
{
    public class MyTextBox : Control, IPostBackDataHandler
    {
        bool MyAutoPostBack = false;
        public event EventHandler TextChanged;

        public string Text
        {
            get
            {
                string text = (string) ViewState["MyText"];
                return (text == null) ? "" : text;
            }
            set { ViewState["MyText"] = value; }
        }
```

Figure 8-11   *MyTextBox* control with *AutoPostBack*.

MyTextBox3.cs *(continued)*

```csharp
    public bool AutoPostBack
    {
        get { return MyAutoPostBack; }
        set { MyAutoPostBack = value; }
    }

    public bool LoadPostData (string postDataKey,
        NameValueCollection postCollection)
    {
        string temp = Text;
        Text = postCollection[postDataKey];
        return (temp != Text);
    }

    public void RaisePostDataChangedEvent ()
    {
        if (TextChanged != null)
            TextChanged (this, new EventArgs ()); // Fire event
    }

    protected override void Render (HtmlTextWriter writer)
    {
        writer.WriteBeginTag ("input");
        writer.WriteAttribute ("type", "text");
        writer.WriteAttribute ("name", UniqueID);

        if (ID != null)
            writer.WriteAttribute ("id", ClientID);

        if (Text.Length > 0)
            writer.WriteAttribute ("value", Text);

        if (AutoPostBack)
            writer.WriteAttribute ("onchange", "javascript:" +
                Page.GetPostBackEventReference (this));

        writer.Write (HtmlTextWriter.TagRightChar);
    }
  }
}
```

You can try out the *AutoPostBack* property with the Web page in Figure 8-12. MyTextBoxPage3.aspx is identical to MyTextBoxPage2.aspx save for the *AutoPostBack* attribute in the <win:MyTextBox> tag. Press the Tab key a few times to move the input focus around on the page. Then tab to the *MyTextBox* control, edit its text, and press Tab again. This time, "Text changed" should appear underneath the control indicating that a *TextChanged* event fired—this despite the fact that you didn't click the Test button to submit the form to the server.

MyTextBoxPage3.aspx

```
<%@ Register TagPrefix="win" Namespace="Wintellect"
  Assembly="MyTextBoxControl" %>

<html>
  <body>
    <form runat="server">
      <win:MyTextBox ID="Input" Text="Type something here"
        OnTextChanged="OnTextChanged" AutoPostBack="true"
        RunAt="server" />
      <asp:Button Text="Test" RunAt="server" /><br>
      <asp:Label ID="Output" RunAt="server" />
    </form>
  </body>
</html>

<script language="C#" runat="server">
  void Page_Load (Object sender, EventArgs e)
  {
      Output.Text = "";  // Reset the Label control
  }

  void OnTextChanged (Object sender, EventArgs e)
  {
      Output.Text = "Text changed";
  }
</script>
```

Figure 8-12   Final test page for *MyTextBox*.

The *IPostBackEventHandler* Interface

IPostBackDataHandler is for controls that update their properties from postback data. Because FCL controls such as *TextBox*, *CheckBox*, *RadioButton*, and *ListBox* all wrap HTML elements that transmit postback data, all implement the *IPostBackDataHandler* interface, too.

The .NET Framework defines a second postback-related interface named *IPostBackEventHandler*. Not to be confused with *IPostBackDataHandler*, *IPostBackEventHandler* enables controls that generate postbacks to be notified when they cause postbacks to occur. *LinkButton* is one example of an FCL control that implements *IPostBackEventHandler*. Its server-side processing regimen includes firing *Click* and *Command* events, but only if it was the *LinkButton* that caused the postback to occur in the first place.

IPostBackEventHandler's sole method, *RaisePostBackEvent*, is called by ASP.NET when a control that implements *IPostBackEventHandler* posts a page back to the server. *RaisePostBackEvent* is prototyped this way:

```
void RaisePostBackEvent (string eventArgument)
```

The one and only parameter passed to *RaisePostBackEvent* is the second parameter passed to *__doPostBack* to generate the postback. Here's the line again in *MyTextBox* that adds an *OnChange* attribute to the <input> tag when *AutoPostBack* is true:

```
writer.WriteAttribute ("onchange", "javascript:" +
    Page.GetPostBackEventReference (this));
```

And here's the resulting output:

```
onchange="javascript:__doPostBack('Input','')"
```

In this example, *RaisePostBackEvent*'s *eventArgument* parameter is an empty string because *__doPostBack*'s second parameter is an empty string. But suppose you called *GetPostBackEventReference* this way:

```
writer.WriteAttribute ("onchange", "javascript:" +
    Page.GetPostBackEventReference (this, "Hello"));
```

Now the *OnChange* attribute looks like this:

```
onchange="javascript:__doPostBack('Input','Hello')"
```

And *RaisePostBackEvent* can read the string from its parameter list:

```
void RaisePostBackEvent (string eventArgument)
{
    string arg = eventArgument; // "Hello"
}
```

The ability to pass application-specific data to controls that generate postbacks comes in handy when the action taken by the control in *RaisePostBackEvent* depends on the action that generated the postback on the client side. You'll see what I mean in the next section. But first let's see a real-world example of *IPostBackEventHandler* in action.

The source code in Figure 8-13 is that of a control named *MyLinkButton*. Like its FCL namesake, *LinkButton*, it creates a hyperlink that posts back to the server. When the postback occurs, the control fires a *Click* event. Here are two important elements of its design:

- *MyLinkButton*'s *Render* method emits a text string surrounded by an HTML <a> element. The element's *Href* attribute points to __doPostBack, which submits the form to the server.

- *MyLinkButton* implements *IPostBackEventHandler*. When the postback occurs, ASP.NET calls the control's *RaisePostBackEvent* method, which in turn fires a *Click* event. If the page contains 100 *MyLinkButtons*, only one fires a *Click* event because only one has its *RaisePostBackEvent* method called.

Figure 8-14 contains a very simple Web form that you can use to test *MyLinkButton*. Because the *@ Register* directive refers to an assembly named MyLinkButtonControl, you need to compile MyLinkButton.cs into a DLL named MyLinkButtonControl.dll before executing the page.

MyLinkButton.cs
```
using System;
using System.Web.UI;

namespace Wintellect
{
    public class MyLinkButton : Control, IPostBackEventHandler
    {
        string MyText = "";
        public event EventHandler Click;

        public string Text
        {
            get { return MyText; }
            set { MyText = value; }
        }

        public void RaisePostBackEvent (string eventArgument)
        {
            if (Click != null)
                Click (this, new EventArgs ());
        }

        protected override void Render (HtmlTextWriter writer)
        {
```

Figure 8-13   *MyLinkButton* control.

MyLinkButton.cs *(continued)*

```
                            // Output an <a> tag
                            writer.WriteBeginTag ("a");
                            if (ID != null)
                                writer.WriteAttribute ("id", ClientID);
                            writer.WriteAttribute ("href", "javascript:" +
                                Page.GetPostBackEventReference (this));
                            writer.Write (HtmlTextWriter.TagRightChar);

                            // Output the text bracketed by <a> and </a> tags
                            if (Text.Length > 0)
                                writer.Write (Text);

                            // Output a </a> tag
                            writer.WriteEndTag ("a");
                        }
                    }
                }
```

MyLinkButtonPage.aspx

```
<%@ Register TagPrefix="win" Namespace="Wintellect"
  Assembly="MyLinkButtonControl" %>

<html>
  <body>
    <form runat="server">
      <win:MyLinkButton Text="Click Me" OnClick="OnClick"
        RunAt="server" /><br>
      <asp:Label ID="Output" RunAt="server" />
    </form>
  </body>
</html>

<script language="C#" runat="server">
  void OnClick (Object sender, EventArgs e)
  {
      Output.Text = "Click!";
  }
</script>
```

Figure 8-14 *MyLinkButton* test page.

The *AutoCounter* Control

Let's sum up what you've learned thus far with a custom control that handles postback data and postback events. The control is named *AutoCounter*. *Auto-Counter* renders a text box sandwiched between < and > buttons (Figure 8-15). When clicked, < and > increment or decrement the value in the text box and fire an *Increment* or a *Decrement* event. Manually typing a number into the text box and submitting the form to the server fires a *CountChanged* event. *Auto-Counter* exposes one property—*Count*—that you can use to read and write the value displayed. Typing a non-numeric value into the control resets the count to 0.

AutoCounter's source code, shown in Figure 8-16, reveals the innermost secrets of its design and operation. There's nothing here you haven't seen before; the difference is that this time, it's all under one roof. *AutoCounter* implements *IPostBackDataHandler* in order to update its *Count* property (and fire a *CountChanged* event) when the user types a value into the text box and posts back to the server. It also implements *IPostBackEventHandler* so that it can fire *Increment* and *Decrement* events when the < and > buttons are clicked. To generate postbacks, *AutoCounter*'s *Render* method encloses the < and > in HTML anchor elements (<a>) whose *Href* attributes point to the *__doPostBack* function returned by *GetPostBackEventReference*.

Pay particular attention to how *GetPostBackEventReference* is called. For the < button, it's called this way:

```
writer.WriteAttribute ("href", "javascript:" +
    Page.GetPostBackEventReference (this, "dec"));
```

And for the > button, it's called like this:

```
writer.WriteAttribute ("href", "javascript:" +
    Page.GetPostBackEventReference (this, "inc"));
```

RaisePostBackEvent uses the second parameter passed to *GetPostBackEventReference* to determine whether to fire an *Increment* event or a *Decrement* event:

```
if (eventArgument == "dec") {
    . . .
    if (Decrement != null)
        Decrement (this, new EventArgs ());
}
else if (eventArgument == "inc") {
    . . .
    if (Increment != null)
        Increment (this, new EventArgs ());
}
```

This is a great example of how *GetPostBackEventReference*'s optional second parameter can be used on the server to determine what generated the postback when a control emits multiple postback elements.

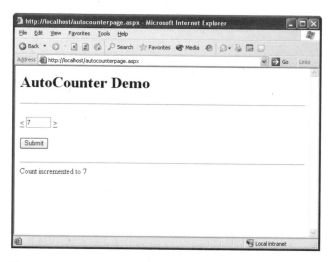

Figure 8-15 *AutoCounter* control in action.

AutoCounter.cs
```csharp
using System;
using System.Web.UI;
using System.Collections.Specialized;

namespace Wintellect
{
    public class AutoCounter : Control, IPostBackDataHandler,
        IPostBackEventHandler
    {
        public event EventHandler Decrement;
        public event EventHandler Increment;
        public event EventHandler CountChanged;

        public int Count
        {
            get
            {
                int count = 0;
                if (ViewState["Count"] != null)
                    count = (int) ViewState["Count"];
                return count;
            }
            set { ViewState["Count"] = value; }
        }

        public bool LoadPostData (string postDataKey,
            NameValueCollection postCollection)
```

Figure 8-16 *AutoCounter* control.

```
    {
        int temp = Count;
        try {
            Count = Convert.ToInt32 (postCollection[postDataKey]);
        }
        catch (FormatException) {
            Count = 0;
        }
        return (temp != Count);
    }

    public void RaisePostDataChangedEvent ()
    {
        if (CountChanged != null)
            CountChanged (this, new EventArgs ());
    }

    public void RaisePostBackEvent (string eventArgument)
    {
        if (eventArgument == "dec") {
            Count--;
            if (Decrement != null)
                Decrement (this, new EventArgs ());
        }
        else if (eventArgument == "inc") {
            Count++;
            if (Increment != null)
                Increment (this, new EventArgs ());
        }
    }

    protected override void Render (HtmlTextWriter writer)
    {
        // Output an <a> tag
        writer.WriteBeginTag ("a");
        writer.WriteAttribute ("href", "javascript:" +
            Page.GetPostBackEventReference (this, "dec"));
        writer.Write (HtmlTextWriter.TagRightChar);

        // Output a less-than sign
        writer.Write ("&lt;");

        // Output a </a> tag
        writer.WriteEndTag ("a");

        // Output an <input> tag
        writer.Write (" ");
        writer.WriteBeginTag ("input");
        writer.WriteAttribute ("type", "text");
```

(continued)

AutoCounter.cs   *(continued)*

```
            writer.WriteAttribute ("name", UniqueID);
            if (ID != null)
                writer.WriteAttribute ("id", ClientID);
            writer.WriteAttribute ("value", Count.ToString ());
            writer.WriteAttribute ("size", "3");
            writer.Write (HtmlTextWriter.TagRightChar);
            writer.Write (" ");

            // Output another <a> tag
            writer.WriteBeginTag ("a");
            writer.WriteAttribute ("href", "javascript:" +
                Page.GetPostBackEventReference (this, "inc"));
            writer.Write (HtmlTextWriter.TagRightChar);

            // Output a greater-than sign
            writer.Write ("&gt;");

            // Output a </a> tag
            writer.WriteEndTag ("a");
        }
    }
}
```

As usual, you need to compile AutoCounter.cs and place the resulting DLL in the bin directory before you run it. Then use AutoCounterPage.aspx (Figure 8-17) to take it for a test drive. AutoCounterPage.aspx responds to *Increment*, *Decrement*, and *CountChanged* events by displaying descriptive text at the bottom of the page. Click the < and > buttons a time or two to see what I mean. Then type a number into the control's text box and click Submit. The value that you entered should be echoed to the page.

AutoCounterPage.aspx

```
<%@ Register TagPrefix="win" Namespace="Wintellect"
  Assembly="AutoCounterControl" %>

<html>
  <body>
    <h1>AutoCounter Demo</h1>
    <hr>
    <form runat="server">
      <win:AutoCounter ID="MyCounter" Count="5"
        OnDecrement="OnDecrement" OnIncrement="OnIncrement"
        OnCountChanged="OnCountChanged" RunAt="server" />
        <br><br>
      <asp:Button Text="Submit" RunAt="server" />
    </form>
```

Figure 8-17   *AutoCounter test page.*

```
    <hr>
    <asp:Label ID="Output" RunAt="server" />
  </body>
</html>

<script language="c#" runat="server">
  void Page_Load (Object sender, EventArgs e)
  {
      Output.Text = "";
  }

  void OnDecrement (Object sender, EventArgs e)
  {
      Output.Text = "Count decremented to " + MyCounter.Count;
  }

  void OnIncrement (Object sender, EventArgs e)
  {
      Output.Text = "Count incremented to " + MyCounter.Count;
  }

  void OnCountChanged (Object sender, EventArgs e)
  {
      Output.Text = "Count changed to " + MyCounter.Count;
  }
</script>
```

Composite Controls

Occasionally, building custom controls by combining other controls is useful. A control that serves as a container for other controls is called a *composite control*, and it, too, is an important element of ASP.NET's server control architecture.

All *Control*-derived classes have the innate ability to act as containers for other controls. Contained controls, or *child controls*, are exposed through the parent control's *Controls* property, which is inherited from *Control*. *Controls'* type is *ControlCollection*, which provides methods and properties for adding controls, removing controls, enumerating controls, and more. *System.Web.UI.Page* counts *Control* among its base types. Its *Controls* collection defines all the controls on the page.

Composite controls come in two basic varieties: declarative and programmatic. A declarative custom control contains other controls declared in a Web form. The FCL's *Panel* control is one example of a declarative composite. It acts as a container for other controls and allows them to be manipulated programmatically, but it doesn't create the controls that it contains: you create these controls by declaring them between <asp:Panel> and </asp:Panel> tags. By contrast, a programmatic composite creates the controls that it hosts programmatically. Both types of composites are discussed in the sections that follow.

Declarative Composites

Here's the simplest composite control you can build:

```
using System.Web.UI;

namespace Wintellect
{
    public class CompositeControl : Control
    {
    }
}
```

On the surface, it doesn't seem as if this control could do anything useful. But check this out:

```
<%@ Register TagPrefix="win" Namespace="Wintellect"
    Assembly="CompositeControl" %>

<html>
  <body>
    <form runat="server">
      <win:CompositeControl ID="MyComposite" RunAt="server">
        <asp:Label Text="Hello!" RunAt="server" /><br>
        <asp:Label Text="Goodbye!" Runat="server" />
      </win:CompositeControl>
    </form>
  </body>
</html>
```

In this example, *CompositeControl* serves as a container for a pair of *Label* controls. ASP.NET automatically adds the *Label* controls to the *CompositeControl's Controls* collection. Furthermore, *CompositeControl's* inherited *Render* method calls the child controls' *Render* methods. If a server-side script prevents *CompositeControl's Render* method from being called by setting the control's *Visible* property (which it inherits from *Control*) to false, like this:

```
MyComposite.Visible = false;
```

the children's *Render* methods won't be called either. Consequently, the children will disappear from the Web page—all because you turned off the control that contains them.

The *GroupBox* Control

Windows developers are familiar with the group box control, which draws a stylish border around other controls and visually groups them together. HTML 4 and later versions support a <fieldset> element that looks very much like a group box. The following HTML displays three radio buttons surrounded by a group box:

```
<html>
  <body>
    <form>
      <fieldset>
        <legend>Colors</legend>
        <input type="radio" name="Color" value="red">Red<br>
        <input type="radio" name="Color" value="green">Green<br>
        <input type="radio" name="Color" value="blue">Blue
      </fieldset>
    </form>
  </body>
</html>
```

The <fieldset> element is an ideal candidate to be encapsulated in a custom control, and a composite control fits the bill perfectly. Figure 8-19 contains the source code for an ASP.NET *GroupBox* control. It renders its children by calling the base class's *Render* method, but it surrounds the child controls' output with <fieldset> and </fieldset> tags. Figure 8-20 contains a *GroupBox* test page, and Figure 8-18 shows the output. Clicking the check box at the top of the page toggles the *GroupBox* control (and by extension, its children) on and off by alternately setting the *GroupBox*'s *Visible* property to true and false.

RadioButtonList is a composite control, too, so this example nests one composite control inside another. The *ListItems* are children of the *RadioButtonList*, and the *RadioButtonList* is a child of the *GroupBox*. That means—you guessed it—the *GroupBox* has grandchildren!

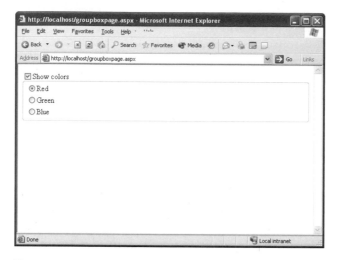

Figure 8-18 Controls grouped with a *GroupBox* control.

GroupBox.cs
```csharp
using System;
using System.Web.UI;

namespace Wintellect
{
    public class GroupBox : Control
    {
        string MyText = "";

        public string Text
        {
            get { return MyText; }
            set { MyText = value; }
        }

        protected override void Render (HtmlTextWriter writer)
        {
            // Output a <fieldset> tag
            writer.WriteBeginTag ("fieldset");
            if (ID != null)
                writer.WriteAttribute ("id", ClientID);
            writer.Write (HtmlTextWriter.TagRightChar);

            // Output a <legend> element
            if (Text.Length > 0) {
                writer.WriteBeginTag ("legend");
                writer.Write (Text);
                writer.WriteEndTag ("legend");
```

Figure 8-19 *GroupBox* control.

```
        }

            // Output the content between <fieldset> and </fieldset> tags
            base.Render (writer);

            // Output a </fieldset> tag
            writer.WriteEndTag ("fieldset");
        }
    }
}
```

GroupBoxPage.aspx
```
<%@ Register TagPrefix="win" Namespace="Wintellect"
    Assembly="GroupBoxControl" %>

<html>
  <body>
    <form runat="server">
      <asp:CheckBox ID="Toggle" Text="Show colors"
        OnCheckedChanged="OnToggle" AutoPostBack="true"
        Checked="true" RunAt="server" /><br>
      <win:GroupBox ID="MyGroupBox" Text="Colors" RunAt="server">
        <asp:RadioButtonList RunAt="server">
          <asp:ListItem Text="Red" Selected="true" RunAt="server" />
          <asp:ListItem Text="Green" RunAt="server" />
          <asp:ListItem Text="Blue" RunAt="server" />
        </asp:RadioButtonList>
      </win:GroupBox>
    </form>
  </body>
</html>

<script language="C#" runat="server">
  void OnToggle (Object sender, EventArgs e)
  {
      MyGroupBox.Visible = Toggle.Checked;
  }
</script>
```

Figure 8-20   *GroupBox* test page.

Programmatic Composites

Programmatic composite controls create child controls programmatically. All controls inherit a virtual *CreateChildControls* method from *Control* that can be overridden in a derived class. The .NET Framework calls *CreateChildControls* very early in the control's lifetime, so it's the perfect place to instantiate child controls. The following control is the programmatic equivalent of the declarative control presented a few moments ago—the one containing *Label* controls with the greetings "Hello!" and "Goodbye!"

```
using System.Web.UI;
using System.Web.UI.WebControls;

namespace Wintellect
{
    public class CompositeControl : Control
    {
        protected override void CreateChildControls ()
        {
            Label label1 = new Label ();
            label1.Text = "Hello!";
            Controls.Add (label1);
            Controls.Add (new LiteralControl ("<br>"));
            Label label2 = new Label ();
            label2.Text = "Goodbye!";
            Controls.Add (label2);
        }
    }
}
```

In its override of *CreateChildControls*, *CompositeControl* instantiates the *Label* controls with *new* and adds them to its *Controls* collection with *ControlCollection.Add*. It also uses a *Literal* control to insert a <br> element between the *Labels*.

The *LoginControl*

The Web page in Figure 8-21 is built around a composite control named *LoginControl*. *LoginControl* is functionally similar to the login control presented in Chapter 7. When instantiated, it creates two *TextBox* controls and a *Button* control and adopts them as child controls. If the user enters a user name and password and clicks the button, the control fires a *Login* event. A server-side script can process the event and retrieve the user name and password by reading the control's *UserName* and *Password* properties. *LoginControl*'s source code appears in Figure 8-22. You'll find a page to test it with in Figure 8-23.

One nuance of composite controls that you should be aware of regards the *INamingContainer* interface. All but the most trivial composite controls should derive from *INamingContainer*. If they don't, they're liable to suffer strange maladies, including events that don't fire properly. *INamingContainer*'s purpose is to allow ASP.NET to assign child controls names that are unique with respect to other controls on the page. Fortunately, *INamingContainer* requires no implementation. It's a signal interface, meaning it has no methods. Simply including *INamingContainer* in a control's list of base types is sufficient to "implement" the interface.

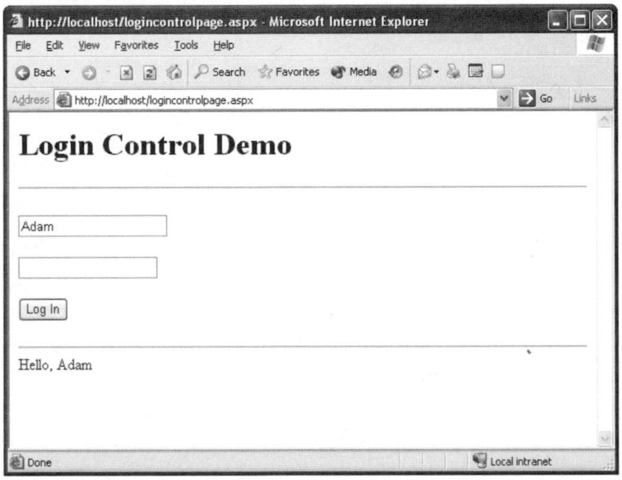

Figure 8-21   Custom login control.

LoginControl.cs
```
using System;
using System.Web.UI;
using System.Web.UI.WebControls;

namespace Wintellect
{
    public class LoginControl : Control, INamingContainer
    {
        TextBox MyUserName = new TextBox ();
        TextBox MyPassword = new TextBox ();
        public event EventHandler Login;

        public string UserName
        {
            get { return MyUserName.Text; }
            set { MyUserName.Text = value ; }
        }

        public string Password
        {
```

Figure 8-22   *LoginControl* source code.

LoginControl.cs   *(continued)*

```csharp
            get { return MyPassword.Text; }
            set { MyPassword.Text = value ; }
        }

        protected override void CreateChildControls ()
        {
            Controls.Add (MyUserName);
            Controls.Add (new LiteralControl ("<br>"));
            Controls.Add (new LiteralControl ("<br>"));

            MyPassword.TextMode = TextBoxMode.Password;
            Controls.Add (MyPassword);
            Controls.Add (new LiteralControl ("<br>"));
            Controls.Add (new LiteralControl ("<br>"));

            Button button = new Button ();
            button.Text = "Log In";
            Controls.Add (button);

            button.Click += new EventHandler (OnLogin);
        }

        protected void OnLogin (Object sender, EventArgs e)
        {
            if (Login != null && UserName.Length > 0 &&
                Password.Length > 0)
                Login (this, new EventArgs ());
        }
    }
}
```

LoginControlPage.aspx

```
<%@ Register TagPrefix="win" Namespace="Wintellect"
  Assembly="LoginControl" %>

<html>
  <body>
    <h1>Login Control Demo</h1>
    <hr>
    <form runat="server">
      <win:LoginControl ID="Login" OnLogin="OnLogin" RunAt="server" />
    </form>
    <hr>
    <asp:Label ID="Output" RunAt="server" />
</html>
```

Figure 8-23   *LoginControl* test page.

```
<script language="C#" runat="server">
  void OnLogin (Object sender, EventArgs e)
  {
      Output.Text = "Hello, " + Login.UserName;
  }
</script>
```

Server Controls and Client-Side Scripting

You can do a lot with custom server controls by returning ordinary HTML to the client. But some of the most exotic (and potentially useful) server controls in the world return client-side script as well. The ASP.NET validation controls are a great example. They couldn't validate user input on the client side without some help from the browser, and one way to get the browser involved in the execution of a control is to return script that the browser understands.

The chief benefit of writing controls that return client-side script is performance. The more you can do on the client, the better a page will perform. Why? Because executing code in a browser is far faster than sending HTTP requests to a server. Years ago I took part in an online discussion forum that diagrammed message threads with a browser-based tree control. Using the forum was a nightmare because each time you clicked a plus sign to expand a branch of the tree, a request went back to the server, which generated a new GIF depicting the tree with the branch expanded and streamed the GIF back to the client. With a dial-up connection, a branch took a minute or more to expand! That was a classic example of how *not* to design Web pages. Now that most browsers support client-side scripting, the same tree control can be implemented in script and branches can be expanded and collapsed locally, without incurring round trips to the server.

High-performance tree controls are just one example of the wonders you can accomplish with client-side script. Server controls and scripting are a match made in heaven because a control can hide the script that it relies on under the hood where it belongs. Few veteran Windows developers are experts in client-side scripting too, but they don't have to be to use controls that generate script. That, after all, is what encapsulation is all about: hiding difficult implementation details behind the veil of reusable components so that anyone can write sophisticated applications, regardless of their background or experience level.

Most controls that emit client-side script return JavaScript, also known as *JScript* and *ECMAScript*, rather than VBScript. VBScript works fine in Internet Explorer, but it's unsupported in other browsers. Returning JavaScript provides a measure of browser independence. In reality, that independence is more measured than we would like because it's difficult to write scripts that work equally well in Internet Explorer, Netscape Navigator, and other browsers. Still, I'll use JavaScript for all the sample controls in this chapter that return client-side script and, when necessary, customize the script on the fly to match the browser type, enabling it to work in Internet Explorer and Navigator.

Returning JavaScript to the Client

The simplest way to return JavaScript from a custom control is to output it from the control's *Render* method. The control in Figure 8-24 does just that. It's a simple control called *MessageButton* that renders out an <input type="submit"> tag. Inside the tag is an *OnClick* attribute that calls JavaScript's *alert* function when the button is clicked. If you declare a control instance like this:

```
<win:MessageButton Text="Click Me" Message="Hello, world" RunAt="server" />
```

the control renders itself this way:

```
<input type="submit" name="_ctl1" value="Click Me"
  onclick="javascript:alert ('Hello, world')">
```

As a result, clicking the button pops up "Hello, world!" in a message box.

```
MessageButton1.cs
using System;
using System.Web.UI;

namespace Wintellect
{
    public class MessageButton : Control
    {
        string MyText = "";
        string MyMessage = "";

        public string Text
        {
            get { return MyText; }
            set { MyText = value; }
        }

        public string Message
        {
            get { return MyMessage; }
            set { MyMessage = value; }
        }
```

Figure 8-24   *MessageButton* control, version 1.

```
        protected override void Render (HtmlTextWriter writer)
        {
            writer.WriteBeginTag ("input");
            writer.WriteAttribute ("type", "submit");
            writer.WriteAttribute ("name", UniqueID);

            if (ID != null)
                writer.WriteAttribute ("id", ClientID);

            if (Text.Length > 0)
                writer.WriteAttribute ("value", Text);

            if (Message.Length > 0)
                writer.WriteAttribute ("onclick",
                    "javascript:alert (\'" + Message + "\')");

            writer.Write (HtmlTextWriter.TagRightChar);
        }
    }
}
```

The *RegisterClientScriptBlock* Method

Returning client-side script from a control's *Render* method is fine when the script is simple enough to be embedded in control tags, but what about more complex scripts? Many controls return client-side script blocks containing functions that are called from control tags. Here's how the *OnClick* attribute in the previous section would look if instead of calling *alert* directly, it called a local function named *doAlert*:

```
<script language="javascript">
<!--
function doAlert (message)
{
    alert (message);
}
-->
</script>
    .
    .
    .
<input type="submit" name="_ctl1" value="Click Me"
  onclick="javascript:doAlert ('Hello, world')">
```

Rather than return blocks of client-side script by manually writing them out with *HtmlTextWriter*, controls should return them with *Page.RegisterClientScriptBlock*. *RegisterClientScriptBlock* returns a block of client-side script and ensures that it's returned only once, no matter how many controls on the page use it. *RegisterClientScriptBlock* accepts two string parameters: one that assigns the script a name, and another that contains the script itself. If a control outputs a block of script using *HtmlTextWriter*, a page containing 10 instances of the control will see the same script block replicated 10 times. If the control uses *RegisterClientScriptBlock*, however, the block is returned only one time because each control instance registers the script block using the same name.

The version of *MessageButton* in Figure 8-25 displays message boxes by calling a local function in a client-side script block. The block is returned by *RegisterClientScriptBlock*. Note where *RegisterClientScriptBlock* is called: in the *OnPreRender* override. ASP.NET calls *OnPreRender* on every control on a page before calling any of the controls' *Render* methods. Calling *RegisterClientScript-Block* from *OnPreRender* ensures that the script block is registered early enough in the page rendering process to allow ASP.NET to control the position of the script block in the output. As you've probably already surmised, *OnPre-Render* is another of the virtual methods that a control inherits from *Control*.

```
MessageButton2.cs
using System;
using System.Web.UI;

namespace Wintellect
{
    public class MessageButton : Control
    {
        string MyText = "";
        string MyMessage = "";

        public string Text
        {
            get { return MyText; }
            set { MyText = value; }
        }

        public string Message
        {
            get { return MyMessage; }
            set { MyMessage = value; }
        }

        protected override void OnPreRender (EventArgs e)
        {
```

Figure 8-25 *MessageButton* control, version 2.

```
        Page.RegisterClientScriptBlock (
            "MessageButtonScript",
            "<script language=\"javascript\">\n" +
            "<!--\n"                           +
            "function doAlert (message)\n"     +
            "{\n"                              +
            "    alert (message);\n"           +
            "}\n"                              +
            "-->\n"                            +
            "</script>"
        );
    }

    protected override void Render (HtmlTextWriter writer)
    {
        writer.WriteBeginTag ("input");
        writer.WriteAttribute ("type", "submit");
        writer.WriteAttribute ("name", UniqueID);

        if (ID != null)
            writer.WriteAttribute ("id", ClientID);

        if (Text.Length > 0)
            writer.WriteAttribute ("value", Text);

        if (Message.Length > 0)
            writer.WriteAttribute ("onclick",
                "javascript:doAlert (\'" + Message + "\')");

        writer.Write (HtmlTextWriter.TagRightChar);
    }
  }
}
```

RegisterClientScriptBlock prevents a function from being downloaded to a page multiple times. ASP.NET supports a similar method named *RegisterStartupScript* whose purpose isn't to return client-side JavaScript functions but to return ordinary script—code that's not contained in functions—that executes when the page loads. The difference between *RegisterClientScriptBlock* and *RegisterStartupScript* is the location at which they position the scripts registered with them. *RegisterClientScriptBlock* puts the scripts near the top of the document, shortly after the <form> tag. *RegisterStartupScript* puts them just before the </form> tag. The placement of the startup script is important because if the script interacts with other elements on the page, those elements must be loaded before the script executes. Placing startup script near the end of the document ensures that other elements on the page are present and accounted for when the script runs.

Keeping Your Code Off the Client

The <script> tag supports a *Src* attribute that permits scripts to be referenced remotely. The following code creates a message button that calls a function named *doAlert* from a JS file on the server:

```
<script language="javascript" src="/jscript/messagebutton.js">
</script>
    .
    .
    .
<input type="submit" value="Click Me"
  onclick="javascript:doAlert ('Hello, world')">
```

Messagebutton.js contains *doAlert*'s implementation. Keeping the code on the server serves two purposes:

■   It hides your client-side script so that it can't be seen with a View/ Source command. (It does not, however, prevent technically savvy users from retrieving scripts from the browser cache.)

■   If multiple pages on your site use a common set of JavaScript functions, packaging the functions in a JS file and referencing them on the server means you can update every page that uses them by modifying one source-code file.

This is precisely how ASP.NET's validation controls work. They emit a modest amount of client-side script to the browser, but most of their work is done by functions in a script file named WebUIValidation.js that's stored on the server.

Figure 8-26 contains the final version of *MessageButton*—one that emits a <script> tag with a *Src* attribute pointing to a JavaScript file on the server. Functionally, this version is identical to the previous two. But view the source code returned to the browser, and you'll see that the *doAlert* function is no longer visible.

```
MessageButton3.cs
using System;
using System.Web.UI;

namespace Wintellect
{
    public class MessageButton : Control
    {
        string MyText = "";
        string MyMessage = "";

        public string Text
```

Figure 8-26   *MessageButton* control, version 3, and the associated JavaScript file.

```csharp
    {
        get { return MyText; }
        set { MyText = value; }
    }

    public string Message
    {
        get { return MyMessage; }
        set { MyMessage = value; }
    }

    protected override void OnPreRender (EventArgs e)
    {
        Page.RegisterClientScriptBlock (
            "MessageButtonRemoteScript",
            "<script language=\"javascript\" " +
                "src=\"/JScript/MessageButton.js\"></script>");
    }

    protected override void Render (HtmlTextWriter writer)
    {
        writer.WriteBeginTag ("input");
        writer.WriteAttribute ("type", "submit");
        writer.WriteAttribute ("name", UniqueID);

        if (ID != null)
            writer.WriteAttribute ("id", ClientID);

        if (Text.Length > 0)
            writer.WriteAttribute ("value", Text);

        if (Message.Length > 0)
            writer.WriteAttribute ("onclick",
                "javascript:doAlert (\'" + Message + "\')");

        writer.Write (HtmlTextWriter.TagRightChar);
    }
}
}
```

MessageButton.js
```javascript
function doAlert (message)
{
    alert (message);
}
```

Now that you've seen the mechanics of how controls return client-side script, let's put this newfound knowledge to work building some intelligent controls that do their work without incurring round trips to the server.

The *RolloverImageLink* Control

One of the most common scripted elements found on Web sites is the "rollover image." When the cursor goes over the top of it, the image changes; when the cursor moves away, the image reverts to its original form. Usually, the image is combined with a hyperlink so that clicking it jumps to another URL. The rollover effect adds visual flair that draws the user's attention and says "click here."

Rollover images are relatively simple to implement with JavaScript and DHTML. The following HTML file demonstrates how image rollovers work. An <img> tag is enclosed in an *anchor* element. The *anchor* element includes *OnMouseOver* and *OnMouseOut* attributes that dynamically change the image's *Src* attribute when the mouse enters and leaves the image:

```
<html>
  <body>
    <a href="next.html"
      onmouseover="javascript:document.myimage.src='logo2.jpg'"
      onmouseout="javascript:document.myimage.src='logo1.jpg'">
      <img name="myimage" src="logo1.jpg">
    </a>
  </body>
</html>
```

The *RolloverImageLink* control in Figure 8-27 encapsulates this behavior in a custom control. Assuming *RolloverImageLink* is compiled into a DLL named RolloverImageLinkControl.dll, creating a rollover image hyperlink is as simple as this:

```
<%@ Register TagPrefix="win" Namespace="Wintellect"
  Assembly="RolloverImageLinkControl" %>
  .
  .
  .
<win:RolloverImageLink NavigateUrl="next.html" RunAt="server"
  OnImageUrl="image1.jpg" OffImageUrl="image2.jpg" />
```

The control has three public properties: *NavigateUrl*, *OnImageUrl*, and *OffImageUrl*. *NavigateUrl* identifies the target of the hyperlink. *OnImageUrl* and

OffImageUrl identify the images shown when the cursor is over the image and when it's not. The source code should be easy to understand given that the control's output looks very much like the HTML shown previously.

```csharp
RolloverImageLink.cs
using System;
using System.Web.UI;

namespace Wintellect
{
    public class RolloverImageLink : Control
    {
        string MyNavigateUrl = "";
        string MyOnImageUrl = "";
        string MyOffImageUrl = "";

        public string NavigateUrl
        {
            get { return MyNavigateUrl; }
            set { MyNavigateUrl = value; }
        }

        public string OnImageUrl
        {
            get { return MyOnImageUrl; }
            set { MyOnImageUrl = value; }
        }

        public string OffImageUrl
        {
            get { return MyOffImageUrl; }
            set { MyOffImageUrl = value; }
        }

        protected override void Render (HtmlTextWriter writer)
        {
            // Output an <a> tag
            writer.WriteBeginTag ("a");

            if (NavigateUrl.Length > 0)
                writer.WriteAttribute ("href", NavigateUrl);

            if (OnImageUrl.Length > 0 && OffImageUrl.Length > 0) {
                writer.WriteAttribute ("onmouseover",
                    "javascript:document." + ClientID + ".src=\'" +
                    OnImageUrl + "\'");
```

Figure 8-27 *RolloverImageLink* control.

RolloverImageLink.cs   *(continued)*

```
            writer.WriteAttribute ("onmouseout",
                "javascript:document." + ClientID + ".src=\'" +
                OffImageUrl + "\'");
        }
        writer.Write (HtmlTextWriter.TagRightChar);

        // Output an <img> tag
        writer.WriteBeginTag ("img");
        writer.WriteAttribute ("name", ClientID);
        if (OffImageUrl.Length > 0)
            writer.WriteAttribute ("src", OffImageUrl);
        writer.Write (HtmlTextWriter.TagRightChar);

        // Output a </a> tag
        writer.WriteEndTag ("a");
    }
  }
}
```

The *NumTextBox* Control

For years, Windows developers have customized edit controls by processing the EN_CHANGE notifications that fire as individual characters are typed and filtering out unwanted characters. A common application for this technique is to build numeric edit controls that accept numbers but reject letters and other symbols.

You can achieve the same effect in Web applications with JavaScript and DHTML. Modern browsers fire *OnKeyDown* events as characters are typed into a text box. A Web page can register a handler for *OnKeyDown* events and filter out unwanted characters by returning false from the event handler. The following Web page demonstrates how it works. The *OnKeyDown* attribute in the <input type ="text"> tag activates the JavaScript *isKeyValid* function on each keystroke. The *isKeyValid* function examines the key code and returns true if the key represents a numeric character or any of a number of auxiliary keys, such as Tab, Backspace, and Delete. Try it out and you'll find that the input field won't accept any characters other than the numbers 0 through 9:

```
<html>
  <head>
    <script language="javascript">
    <!--
      var keys = new Array (8, 9, 13, 33, 34, 35, 36, 37, 39, 45, 46);

      function isKeyValid (keyCode)
      {
```

```
         return ((keyCode >= 48 && keyCode <= 57) ||
             isAuxKey (keyCode));
     }

     function isAuxKey (keyCode)
     {
         for (i=0; i<keys.length; i++)
             if (keyCode == keys[i])
                 return true;
         return false;
     }
   -->
   </script>
 </head>
 <body>
   <form>
     <input type="text" name="quantity"
     onkeydown="javascript:return isKeyValid (window.event.keyCode)">
   </form>
 </body>
</html>
```

This example works in Internet Explorer 4 and later. To work in Netscape Navigator 4 and later, the script must be modified:

```
<html>
  <head>
    <script language="javascript">
    <!--
      function isKeyValid (keyCode)
      {
          return ((keyCode >= 48 && keyCode <= 57) ||
              keyCode == 8 || keyCode== 13);
      }
    -->
    </script>
  </head>
  <body>
    <form>
      <input type="text" name="quantity"
        onkeydown="javascript:return isKeyValid (event.which)">
    </form>
  </body>
</html>
```

Once more, this behavior is begging to be encapsulated in a custom control to shield the developer from the nuances of DHTML and client-side script. It also presents the perfect opportunity to demonstrate *adaptive rendering*—varying the script that a control outputs based on the browser it renders to.

Figure 8-28 contains the source code for a *NumTextBox* control that trivializes the task of creating numbers-only text boxes:

```
<%@ Register TagPrefix="win" Namespace="Wintellect"
   Assembly="NumTextBoxControl" %>
     .
     .
     .

<win:NumTextBox ID="Quantity" RunAt="server" />
```

NumTextBox exposes its content through a *Text* property that throws an exception if a noninteger value is assigned. It uses *RegisterClientScriptBlock* to register the <script> block containing *isKeyValid* and its helpers. And it works with both Internet Explorer and Netscape Navigator, thanks to adaptive rendering logic that returns one set of client-side script to Internet Explorer and another to Navigator. If the requestor is neither Internet Explorer nor Navigator (or is a down-level version of either), the control returns no client-side script because chances are it won't work anyway.

How does *NumTextBox* adapt its output to the browser type? By using the *Request* object's *Browser* property, which contains a variety of information about the browser that made the request, including its make and version number. As described in Chapter 7, ASP.NET reads the *User-Agent* headers accompanying HTTP requests and populates the *Browser* property with information inferred from those headers. *NumTextBox* checks the browser's type and version number by reading *Browser's Type* and *MajorVersion* properties:

```
string browser = Context.Request.Browser.Type.ToUpper ();
int version = Context.Request.Browser.MajorVersion;
     .
     .
     .

if (browser.IndexOf ("IE") > -1 && version >= 4) {
    // Internet Explorer 4 or later
}
else if (browser.IndexOf ("NETSCAPE") > -1 && version >= 4) {
    // Netscape Navigator 4 or later
}
```

For Internet Explorer, *Browser.Type* returns a string of the form "IE4," while for Navigator it returns a string such as "Netscape4." Using *String.IndexOf* to check for the substrings "IE" and "Netscape" detects requests emanating from these browsers.

NumTextBox.cs

```
using System;
using System.Web.UI;

namespace Wintellect
{
    public class NumTextBox : Control
    {
        string MyText = "";

        string IEClientScriptBlock =
            "<script language=\"javascript\">\n"                      +
            "<!--\n"                                                  +
            "var keys = new Array (8, 9, 13, 33, 34, 35, "           +
                "36, 37, 39, 45, 46);\n"                             +
            "function isKeyValid (keyCode)\n"                        +
            "{\n"                                                    +
            "    return ((keyCode >= 48 && keyCode <= 57) || "      +
                "isAuxKey (keyCode));\n"                             +
            "}\n"                                                    +
            "function isAuxKey (keyCode)\n"                          +
            "{\n"                                                    +
            "    for (i=0; i<keys.length; i++)\n"                    +
            "        if (keyCode == keys[i])\n"                      +
            "            return true;\n"                             +
            "    return false;\n"                                   +
            "}\n"                                                    +
            "-->\n"                                                  +
            "</script>";

        string NetscapeClientScriptBlock =
            "<script language=\"javascript\">\n"                     +
            "<!--\n"                                                 +
            "function isKeyValid (keyCode)\n"                        +
            "{\n"                                                    +
            "    return ((keyCode >= 48 && keyCode <= 57) || "      +
                "keyCode == 8 || keyCode == 13);\n"                 +
            "}\n"                                                    +
            "-->\n"                                                  +
            "</script>";
```

Figure 8-28   *NumTextBox* control.

NumTextBox.cs *(continued)*

```csharp
    public string Text
    {
        get { return MyText; }
        set
        {
            // Make sure value is numeric before storing it
            Convert.ToInt64 (value);
            MyText = value;
        }
    }

    protected override void OnPreRender (EventArgs e)
    {
        string browser = Context.Request.Browser.Type.ToUpper ();
        int version = Context.Request.Browser.MajorVersion;

        if (browser.IndexOf ("IE") > -1 && version >= 4)
            Page.RegisterClientScriptBlock ("NumTextBoxScript",
                IEClientScriptBlock);
        else if (browser.IndexOf ("NETSCAPE") > -1 && version >= 4)
            Page.RegisterClientScriptBlock ("NumTextBoxScript",
                NetscapeClientScriptBlock);
    }

    protected override void Render (HtmlTextWriter writer)
    {
        string browser = Context.Request.Browser.Type.ToUpper ();
        int version = Context.Request.Browser.MajorVersion;

        writer.WriteBeginTag ("input");
        writer.WriteAttribute ("type", "text");
        writer.WriteAttribute ("name", UniqueID);

        if (ID != null)
            writer.WriteAttribute ("id", ClientID);

        if (Text.Length > 0)
            writer.WriteAttribute ("value", Text);

        if (browser.IndexOf ("IE") > -1 && version >= 4)
            writer.WriteAttribute ("onkeydown",
                "javascript:return isKeyValid (window.event.keyCode)");
        else if (browser.IndexOf ("NETSCAPE") > -1 && version >= 4)
            writer.WriteAttribute ("onkeydown",
                "javascript:return isKeyValid (event.which)");

        writer.Write (HtmlTextWriter.TagRightChar);
    }
}
```

Graphical Controls

By writing to the output stream with *HtmlTextWriter*, a custom control can render anything that can be expressed in HTML. Controls that require more latitude than HTML provides can return graphical images. The images can be stored statically (for example, in JPEG files) on the server, or they can be generated at run time and even customized for each request. Returning dynamically generated images frees controls from the limitations of HTML and opens the door to a world of possibilities, from controls that render graphs and pie charts to controls that render maps, formatted reports, and virtually anything else you can dream up.

The secret to authoring a graphical control is to code its *Render* method to return an <img> tag. If the image is static—that is, if it's stored in a file on the server—the tag's *Src* attribute identifies the image file:

```
<img src="staticimage.jpg">
```

If the image is dynamically generated, however, the *Src* attribute must point to a URL that creates the image on the fly. The following <img> tag references a URL that dynamically generates an image based on input passed in the query string:

```
<img src="imagegen.ashx?shape=circle&color=red">
```

What is ImageGen.ashx? It's not a file; it's an HTTP handler. Specifically, it's an HTTP handler you write that parses a query string and returns a dynamically generated image. We haven't talked about HTTP handlers yet. Let's remedy that shortcoming right now.

HTTP Handlers

HTTP handlers are one of the fundamental building blocks of ASP.NET. An HTTP handler is a class that handles HTTP requests for a specific endpoint (URL) or set of endpoints on a Web server. HTTP handlers built into ASP.NET handle requests for ASPX files, ASCX files, and other ASP.NET file types. In addition, you can extend ASP.NET with HTTP handlers of your own. Entries in Web.config map URLs to HTTP handlers. (We haven't talked about Web.config and the role that it plays in configuring ASP.NET applications yet, but don't worry: you'll learn all about it in the next chapter.) The following statements in a Web.config file map requests for ImageGen.ashx targeted at this directory (the directory that hosts Web.config) and its subdirectories to a class named *Image-Gen* in an assembly named DynaImageLib.dll:

```
<httpHandlers>
  <add verb="*" path="ImageGen.ashx" type="ImageGen, DynaImageLib" />
</httpHandlers>
```

When an HTTP request arrives for ImageGen.ashx, ASP.NET instantiates *ImageGen* and passes it the request. Assuming *ImageGen* is an image generator, it responds by creating an image and returning it in the HTTP response. Here's a generic template for an HTTP handler that creates an image in memory and returns it to the requestor as a JPEG. The hard part—building the image and writing it out to the HTTP response as a JPEG-formatted bit stream—is vastly simplified by the FCL's *Bitmap* and *Graphics* classes:

```
public class ImageGen : IHttpHandler
{
    public void ProcessRequest (HttpContext context)
    {
        // Create a bitmap that measures 128 pixels square
        Bitmap bitmap = new Bitmap (128, 128,
            PixelFormat.Format32bppArgb);

        // Create a Graphics object for drawing to the bitmap
        Graphics g = Graphics.FromImage (bitmap);

        // TODO: Use Graphics methods to draw the image

            .
            .
            .

        // Set the response's content type to image/jpeg
        context.Response.ContentType = "image/jpeg";

        // Write the image to the HTTP response
        bitmap.Save (context.Response.OutputStream, ImageFormat.Jpeg);

        // Clean up before returning
        bitmap.Dispose ();
        g.Dispose ();
    }

    public bool IsReusable
    {
        // Returning true enables instances of this class to be
        // pooled and reused. Return false if ImageGen instances
        // should NOT be reused.
        get { return true; }
    }
}
```

ImageGen can be deployed in its own assembly or in the same assembly as a control. Once deployed, it's invoked by ASP.NET whenever an HTTP request arrives for ImageGen.ashx. "Invoke" means ASP.NET instantiates *ImageGen* and calls its *ProcessRequest* method. *ProcessRequest* receives an *Http-Context* object whose *Request* property provides access to input parameters encoded in the query string. *ProcessRequest* writes to the HTTP response using the *HttpContext* object's *Response* property. To return an image, *ProcessRequest* saves the bits making up the image to the stream represented by *HttpContext.Response.OutputStream*.

Incidentally, it doesn't matter that there is no file named ImageGen.ashx; what's important is that ImageGen.ashx is mapped to *ImageGen* via Web.config. You don't have to use the file name extension ASHX for HTTP handlers, but ASHX is a widely used convention. Using ASHX as the handler's file name extension also prevents you from having to register a special file name extension in the IIS metabase. (If you picked an arbitrary file name extension—say, IGEN—for your HTTP handler, you'd also have to map *.igen to Aspnet_isapi.dll in the IIS metabase. Otherwise, IIS wouldn't forward requests for IGEN files to ASP.NET.) ASHX files are already mapped to ASP.NET in the IIS metabase, so requests for files with ASHX file name extensions are automatically handed off to ASP.NET. You can also write ASPX files that generate and return images, but using a dedicated HTTP handler is cleaner because it requires no additional files on the server.

With this background in mind, let's close the chapter with a control that returns a dynamically generated image depicting an odometer. One application for such a control is to implement the ubiquitous hit counters found on sites all over the Web.

The *Odometer* Control

The *Odometer* control shown in Figure 8-29 renders itself using dynamically generated images. The control's programmatic interface consists of the following public properties:

Property	Description
Count	Gets and sets the value displayed by the control
Digits	Gets and sets the number of digits displayed
Width	Gets and sets the control's width
Height	Gets and sets the control's height
ForeColor	Gets and sets the color of the control's numbers
BackColor1	Gets and sets the first of two background colors behind the numbers
BackColor2	Gets and sets the second of two background colors behind the numbers
BorderColor	Gets and sets the color of the control's border

The two *BackColor* properties merit further explanation. The *Odometer* control uses a pair of *LinearGradientBrush*es (discussed in Chapter 4) to paint the background behind the numbers. It exposes the colors of these brushes through *BackColor1* and *BackColor2*. By default, *BackColor1* is black and *BackColor2* is light gray, which produces a background that fades from black to light gray and then back to black again, yielding the realistic look depicted in Figure 8-29. If you prefer a flat background, set *BackColor1* and *BackColor2* to the same color. Setting both to red produces red cells behind the numbers.

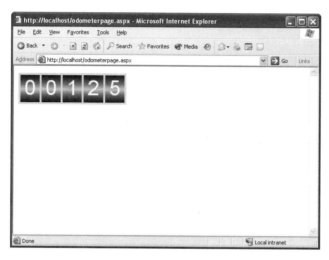

Figure 8-29   The *Odometer* control in action.

It's simple to add an *Odometer* control to a Web page and configure it to display the number 1,000:

```
<%@ Register TagPrefix="win" Namespace="Wintellect"
  Assembly="OdometerControl" %>
    .
    .
    .
<win:Odometer Count="1000" RunAt="server" />
```

The following statement configures the control to display five digits ("01000") instead of the four that would normally be displayed for 1,000:

```
<win:Odometer Count="1000" Digits="5" RunAt="server" />
```

The next statement does the same thing, but it also configures the control to display numbers against a flat black background:

```
<win:Odometer Count="1000" Digits="5" RunAt="server"
  BackColor1="black" BackColor2="black" />
```

If you'd like, you can set *Count*'s value at run time by initializing it from a *Page_Load* handler:

```
<win:Odometer ID="MyOdometer" RunAt="server" />
    .
    .
    .
<script language="C#" runat="server">
  void Page_Load (Object sender, EventArgs e)
  {
      MyOdometer.Count = 1000;
  }
</script>
```

In all likelihood, you'd retrieve the count from a database or other data source rather than hardcode into the ASPX file.

Before using the control in a Web page, you must do the following:

■ Compile Odometer.cs into a DLL and place the DLL in the application root's bin directory. The @ *Register* directive in the preceding example assumes the DLL's name is OdometerControl.dll.

■ Copy the Web.config file in Figure 8-30 to the application root (or to any subdirectory containing an ASPX file that uses an *Odometer* control). If the directory already contains a Web.config file, simply add the <httpHandlers> section to the existing file.

Odometer outputs <img> tags whose *Src* attributes reference Odometer-ImageGen.ashx. Web.config maps requests for OdometerImageGen.ashx to the HTTP handler *OdometerImageGen*, which lives in the same DLL as the control.

```
Web.config
<configuration>
  <system.web>
    <httpHandlers>
      <add verb="*" path="OdometerImageGen.ashx"
        type="Wintellect.OdometerImageGen, OdometerControl" />
    </httpHandlers>
  </system.web>
</configuration>
```

Figure 8-30   Web.config file for the *Odometer* control.

How the *Odometer* Control Works

Odometer.cs (Figure 8-31) is a fine example of how to write custom controls that output dynamically generated images. The *Odometer* class represents the control itself. Its *Render* method outputs an <img> tag that points to Odometer-ImageGen.ashx as the image source. The URL includes a query string that provides the handler with all the information it needs regarding the odometer's appearance:

```
<img src="OdometerImageGen.ashx?Count=1000&Digits=5...">
```

When the browser fetches OdometerImageGen.ashx from the server, ASP.NET activates *OdometerImageGen* thanks to the following statement in Web.config:

```
<add verb="*" path="OdometerImageGen.ashx"
  type="Wintellect.OdometerImageGen, OdometerControl" />
```

OdometerImageGen is implemented in Odometer.cs alongside *Odometer*. Its *ProcessRequest* method generates an image based on the inputs contained in the query string. *ProcessRequest* offloads the actual work of creating the image to a local method named *GenerateImage*. It then transmits the image back in the HTTP response by calling *Bitmap.Save* on the *Bitmap* returned by *GenerateImage* and directing the output to the *Response* object's *OutputStream*.

```
Odometer.cs
using System;
using System.Web;
using System.Web.UI;
using System.Drawing;
using System.Drawing.Drawing2D;
using System.Drawing.Imaging;
using System.Text;

namespace Wintellect
{
    public class Odometer : Control
    {
        int MyCount = 0;
        int MyDigits = 0;
        int MyWidth = 128;
        int MyHeight = 48;
        Color MyForeColor = Color.White;
        Color MyBackColor1 = Color.Black;
        Color MyBackColor2 = Color.LightGray;
        Color MyBorderColor = Color.Gray;

        public int Count
```

Figure 8-31 *Odometer* control.

```
{
    get { return MyCount; }
    set
    {
        if (value >= 0)
            MyCount = value;
        else
            throw new ArgumentOutOfRangeException ();
    }
}

public int Digits
{
    get { return MyDigits; }
    set
    {
        if (value >= 0)
            MyDigits = value;
        else
            throw new ArgumentOutOfRangeException ();
    }
}

public int Width
{
    get { return MyWidth; }
    set
    {
        if (value >= 0)
            MyWidth = value;
        else
            throw new ArgumentOutOfRangeException ();
    }
}

public int Height
{
    get { return MyHeight; }
    set
    {
        if (value >= 0)
            MyHeight = value;
        else
            throw new ArgumentOutOfRangeException ();
    }
}

public Color ForeColor
{
```

(continued)

Odometer.cs   *(continued)*

```
        get { return MyForeColor; }
        set { MyForeColor = value; }
    }

    public Color BackColor1
    {
        get { return MyBackColor1; }
        set { MyBackColor1 = value; }
    }

    public Color BackColor2
    {
        get { return MyBackColor2; }
        set { MyBackColor2 = value; }
    }

    public Color BorderColor
    {
        get { return MyBorderColor; }
        set { MyBorderColor = value; }
    }

    protected override void Render (HtmlTextWriter writer)
    {
        StringBuilder builder = new StringBuilder ();

        builder.Append ("OdometerImageGen.ashx?");
        builder.Append ("Count=");
        builder.Append (Count);
        builder.Append ("&Digits=");
        builder.Append (Digits);
        builder.Append ("&Width=");
        builder.Append (Width);
        builder.Append ("&Height=");
        builder.Append (Height);
        builder.Append ("&ForeColor=");
        builder.Append (ForeColor.ToArgb ().ToString ());
        builder.Append ("&BackColor1=");
        builder.Append (BackColor1.ToArgb ().ToString ());
        builder.Append ("&BackColor2=");
        builder.Append (BackColor2.ToArgb ().ToString ());
        builder.Append ("&BorderColor=");
        builder.Append (BorderColor.ToArgb ().ToString ());

        writer.WriteBeginTag ("img");
        writer.WriteAttribute ("src", builder.ToString ());
        if (ID != null)
            writer.WriteAttribute ("id", ClientID);
```

```
                writer.Write (HtmlTextWriter.TagRightChar);
        }
}

public class OdometerImageGen : IHttpHandler
{
    public void ProcessRequest (HttpContext context)
    {
        // Extract input values from the query string
        int Count = Convert.ToInt32 (context.Request["Count"]);
        int Digits = Convert.ToInt32 (context.Request["Digits"]);
        int Width = Convert.ToInt32 (context.Request["Width"]);
        int Height = Convert.ToInt32 (context.Request["Height"]);

        Color ForeColor = Color.FromArgb
            (Convert.ToInt32 (context.Request["ForeColor"]));
        Color BackColor1 = Color.FromArgb
            (Convert.ToInt32 (context.Request["BackColor1"]));
        Color BackColor2 = Color.FromArgb
            (Convert.ToInt32 (context.Request["BackColor2"]));
        Color BorderColor = Color.FromArgb
            (Convert.ToInt32 (context.Request["BorderColor"]));

        // Generate an image to return to the client
        Bitmap bitmap = GenerateImage (Count, Digits,
            Width, Height, ForeColor, BackColor1, BackColor2,
            BorderColor);

        // Set the content type to image/jpeg
        context.Response.ContentType = "image/jpeg";

        // Write the image to the HTTP response
        bitmap.Save (context.Response.OutputStream,
            ImageFormat.Jpeg);

        // Clean up
        bitmap.Dispose ();
    }

    public bool IsReusable
    {
        get { return true; }
    }

    Bitmap GenerateImage (int Count, int Digits,
        int Width, int Height, Color ForeColor, Color BackColor1,
        Color BackColor2, Color BorderColor)
    {
        const int BorderWidth = 4;
```

(continued)

Odometer.cs   *(continued)*

```
const int MinCellWidth = 16;
const int MinCellHeight = 24;

// Make sure Digits is sufficient for Count to be displayed
int digits = Digits;
int places = Places (Count);
if (digits < places)
    digits = places;

// Compute the width of a single character cell and
// the width and height of the entire image
int CellWidth = System.Math.Max (Width / digits,
    MinCellWidth);
Width = (CellWidth * digits) + BorderWidth;
Height = System.Math.Max (Height, MinCellHeight);

// Create an in-memory bitmap
Bitmap bitmap = new Bitmap (Width, Height,
    PixelFormat.Format32bppArgb);

// Create the fonts and brushes that will be used to
// generate the image
Font font = new Font ("Arial", Height / 2);
Brush brushForeColor = new SolidBrush (ForeColor);
Brush brushBorderColor = new SolidBrush (BorderColor);

// Create a Graphics object that can be used to draw to
// the bitmap
Graphics g = Graphics.FromImage (bitmap);

// Fill the bitmap with the border color
g.FillRectangle (brushBorderColor, 0, 0, Width, Height);

// Create a StringFormat object for displaying text
// that is centered horizontally and vertically
StringFormat format = new StringFormat ();
format.Alignment = StringAlignment.Center;
format.LineAlignment = StringAlignment.Center;

// Initialize the values used to extract individual
// digits from Count
int div1 = (int) System.Math.Pow (10, digits);
int div2 = div1 / 10;

// Draw the digits and their backgrounds
for (int i=0; i<digits; i++) {
    Rectangle rect =
        new Rectangle (i * CellWidth + BorderWidth,
```

```
                    BorderWidth, CellWidth - BorderWidth,
                    Height - (2 * BorderWidth));

            Rectangle top = rect;
            top.Height = (rect.Height / 2) + 1;
            Rectangle bottom = rect;
            bottom.Y += rect.Height / 2;
            bottom.Height = rect.Height / 2;

            Brush brushBackColor1 =
                new LinearGradientBrush (top, BackColor1,
                BackColor2, LinearGradientMode.Vertical);

            Brush brushBackColor2 =
                new LinearGradientBrush (bottom, BackColor2,
                BackColor1, LinearGradientMode.Vertical);

            g.FillRectangle (brushBackColor2, bottom);
            g.FillRectangle (brushBackColor1, top);

            string num = ((Count % div1) / div2).ToString ();
            g.DrawString (num, font, brushForeColor, rect, format);

            div1 /= 10;
            div2 /= 10;

            brushBackColor1.Dispose ();
            brushBackColor2.Dispose ();
        }

        // Clean up and return
        font.Dispose ();
        brushForeColor.Dispose ();
        brushBorderColor.Dispose ();
        g.Dispose ();

        return bitmap;
    }

    // Compute the number of places (digits) in an input value
    int Places (int val)
    {
        int count = 1;
        while (val / 10 > 0) {
            val /= 10;
            count++;
        }
        return count;
    }
  }
}
```

Summary

Here's a summary of the important concepts presented in this chapter:

- Custom controls are authored by deriving from *System.Web.UI.Control*.

- A custom control overrides the *Render* method it inherits from *Control* to render itself to a Web page.

- Implementing *IPostBackDataHandler* enables a control to update property values using data transmitted in postbacks and also to fire change events.

- Controls that fire change events persist property values in view state in order to detect changes in property values.

- Controls can force postbacks by rendering HTML elements that use client-side scripts to submit forms to the server. *Page.GetPostBack-EventReference* outputs the postback script and returns code that calls the postback function.

- Implementing *IPostBackEventHandler* enables a control to fire events when an element it rendered to a page causes a postback.

- Composite controls serve as containers for other controls. A composite can be populated with child controls declaratively or programmatically.

- Controls have the option of returning client-side script when they render themselves to a Web page. *Page.RegisterClientScriptBlock* ensures that functions returned in a script block are returned just once per request.

- Controls can use the *Browser* property of the *Request* object to determine which type of browser submitted the request and adapt their output accordingly.

- Graphical controls can be authored by returning <img> tags whose *Src* attributes reference image files stored on the server or HTTP handlers that generate images and return them to the client.

- The @ *Register* directive enables custom controls to be used in Web forms.

Controls are the atoms from which Web forms are composed. Encapsulating complex rendering and behavioral logic in custom controls is a great way to share your knowledge with other developers and shield them from implementation details at the same time. As you design and implement controls of your own, keep in mind the principles discussed in this chapter. And feel free to use the samples contained herein as the basis for controls of your own.

9

Web Applications

Knowing Web forms inside and out is an important first step on the road to becoming an ASP.NET programmer. But Web forms alone do not an application make. Building full-fledged Web applications like the ones at Amazon, eBay, and other popular Web sites requires infrastructure above and beyond what Web forms provide, including per-user data stores to hold shopping carts and other information that's unique to individual users, caching services to boost performance, and security services to identify users and prevent unauthorized accesses. ASP.NET provides all these services and more. Once you know the ropes, ASP.NET lets you build commercial-quality sites in a fraction of the time required by older Web programming technologies such as ASP and CGI.

This chapter is about the facilities that ASP.NET provides for turning Web forms into Web applications. Among other things, you'll learn about Web.config and Global.asax files and the roles that they play in ASP.NET applications; how to use application state and the ASP.NET application cache to improve performance by caching frequently used data in memory; how to use session state to store per-user data for visitors to your site; and about the various session state configuration options that ASP.NET places at your disposal. You'll also learn how to build applications that are compatible with Web farms. To top it off, the chapter concludes with a full-blown Web application that brings many of these concepts together under one roof and demonstrates some of the most important principles of ASP.NET-style Web programming.

There's a lot to cover, so let's get started.

Structure of an ASP.NET Application

A logical way to begin a chapter on ASP.NET applications is to define the term "ASP.NET application." An ASP.NET application consists of all the files in a virtual directory and its subdirectories. If your Web server has a subdirectory named MyApp and MyApp is a virtual directory, all the files in MyApp and any subdirectories that stem from it make up an ASP.NET application. Typically, an application includes one or more of the following file types:

- ASPX files containing Web forms

- ASCX files containing user controls

- Web.config files containing configuration settings

- A Global.asax file containing global application elements

- DLLs containing custom types employed by the application

An application can contain an unlimited number of ASPX and ASCX files, each representing a different Web page or portion of a page. Only one Global.asax file is permitted. The number of Web.config files isn't restricted, but each must reside in a different directory. ASP.NET places no limit on the number of DLLs an application uses. DLLs are normally found in the application root's bin directory.

Figure 9-1 diagrams the physical structure of a very simple ASP.NET application that consists of a lone Web form in an ASPX file. The directory containing the ASPX file has been transformed into a virtual directory with the IIS configuration manager and is therefore URL-addressable on the server.

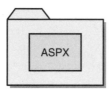

Figure 9-1   A simple ASP.NET application.

Figure 9-2 depicts an ASP.NET application that's more representative of those found in the real world. The virtual directory at the top of the directory hierarchy (the "application root") houses several ASPX files, each representing a single page in the application, as well as ASCX files containing user controls. It also holds a Global.asax file containing event handlers and other elements that are global to the application. Underneath the virtual root is a pair of subdirectories containing ASPX files of their own. Each directory contains a Web.config file containing configuration information for the file or files in that directory.

Inside the virtual root's bin subdirectory are DLLs containing code-behind classes, custom controls, and other custom types used by the application.

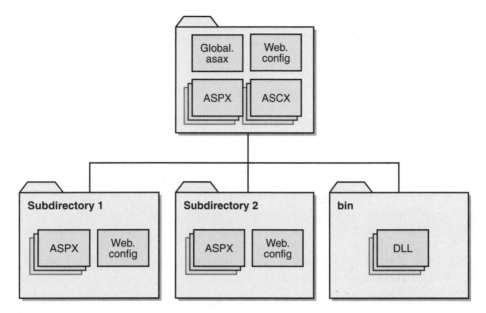

Figure 9-2 A more complex ASP.NET application.

The Web.config File

One of the goals of the Microsoft .NET Framework from the outset was to support XCOPY installs—that is, the ability to install applications by copying them to a directory on your hard disk and uninstall them by deleting files and directories. Having this ability means, among other things, that managed applications don't store configuration settings in the registry as traditional Windows applications do. Instead, they store them in text-based XML files. Web.config is the XML file in which ASP.NET applications store configuration data.

Here's the general structure of a typical Web.config file:

```
<configuration>
  <appSettings>
    <!-- appSettings values go here -->
  </appSettings>
  <system.web>
    <!-- ASP.NET configuration settings go here -->
  </system.web>
</configuration>
```

This file is partitioned into two sections: an *appSettings* section that holds application-specific data items such as database connection strings, and a *system.web* section that holds ASP.NET configuration settings. These sections aren't the only ones that can appear in a Web.config file, but they are the most common. Web.config's architecture is extensible, enabling developers to define custom sections when circumstances warrant.

<appSettings>

The *appSettings* section of Web.config holds application-specific values (strings) that are keyed by other strings. Its purpose is to parameterize an application's behavior, and to allow that behavior to be modified without changing any source code.

Suppose, for example, that you coded the following statements into a *Page_Load* handler:

```
SqlDataAdapter adapter = new SqlDataAdapter
    ("select * from titles where price != 0",
     "server=hawkeye;database=pubs;uid=sa;pwd=");
DataSet ds = new DataSet ();
adapter.Fill (ds);
```

The only problem with this code is that if the database connection string changes—if the database moves to another machine, for example, or if the user name or password changes—you have to modify the code to update the database connection string. If you work in a big company, code modifications probably trigger a mountain of paperwork and require all or part of the application to be retested and reapproved.

A better solution to encoding connection strings and other data that's subject to change over the lifetime of an application is to put it in the *appSettings* section of Web.config. The following Web.config file declares a connection string and assigns it the name "MyConnectionString":

```
<configuration>
  <appSettings>
    <add key="MyConnectionString"
      value="server=hawkeye;database=pubs;uid=sa;pwd=" />
  </appSettings>
</configuration>
```

Page_Load can be rewritten to extract the connection string from Web.config:

```
string conn = ConfigurationSettings.AppSettings["MyConnectionString"];
SqlDataAdapter adapter = new SqlDataAdapter
    ("select * from titles where price != 0", conn);
DataSet ds = new DataSet ();
adapter.Fill (ds);
```

AppSettings is a static method belonging to the *ConfigurationSettings* class in the FCL's *System.Configuration* namespace. It retrieves values by name from the *appSettings* section of Web.config. The benefit to doing it this way? Storing the database connection string in Web.config enables you to change it without touching any actual program code. It's analogous to storing program settings in the registry in a Windows application, and it comes with all the perks but none of the drawbacks.

<system.web>

The *system.web* section of Web.config holds configuration settings used by ASP.NET. Its content is categorized by subsections. Although the type and number of subsections that can appear is technically unlimited—as developers are free to define custom subsections—the ones listed in the following table are supported by default and can be used without writing custom configuration handlers.

<system.web> Subsections

Section Name	Description
authentication	Sets the authentication mode and specifies settings for the mode selected
authorization	Specifies who is allowed to access resources in this directory and its subdirectories
browserCaps	Maps user-agent data to browser capabilities
clientTarget	Maps user-agent data to browser types
compilation	Specifies run-time compilation settings such as whether executables should be compiled with debug symbols, maps file name extensions and *Language* attributes to compilers, and identifies the assemblies that ASP.NET links to
customErrors	Enables the use of custom error pages and specifies how errors should be reported on clients and servers
httpRuntime	Specifies request time-outs and other settings used by the ASP.NET runtime
globalization	Specifies character encodings for requests and responses
httpHandlers	Maps URLs to HTTP handlers (for example, maps requests for ASPX files to *System.Web.UI.PageHandlerFactory*)
httpModules	Identifies HTTP modules called in response to HTTP requests

\<system.web\> Subsections   *(continued)*

Section Name	Description
identity	Controls the identity that ASP.NET assigns to individual requests
machineKey	Specifies encryption and validation settings (for example, the key and algorithm used to encrypt authentication cookies)
pages	Specifies page-level configuration settings such as whether output buffering, session state, and view state are enabled
processModel	Specifies configuration settings for ASP.NET worker processes
securityPolicy	Maps trust levels to CONFIG files containing security policies
sessionState	Specifies session state settings (for example, where session state is stored)
trace	Enables and disables tracing and specifies trace settings
trust	Specifies the code access security trust level
webControls	Identifies the location on the server of client scripts used by ASP.NET Web controls
webServices	Contains Web service settings

Here's a sample Web.config file that enables tracing. Drop it in the application root, and ASP.NET appends useful trace information (including strings written to trace output with *Trace.Write* and *Trace.Warn*) to the application's pages:

```
<configuration>
  <system.web>
    <trace enabled="true" />
  </system.web>
</configuration>
```

Here's another Web.config file that enables tracing, instructs ASP.NET to compile debug executables, moves session state to a back-end SQL Server database (a topic you'll learn about later in this chapter), tells ASP.NET to assume code found in the application's files is written in C# unless otherwise noted, and enables view state validation by appending hashes to view state values round-tripped to the client:

```
<configuration>
  <system.web>
    <trace enabled="true" />
    <sessionState
      mode="SQLServer"
      sqlConnectionString="server=localhost;uid=sa;pwd="
    />
```

```
      <compilation debug="true" defaultLanguage="c#" />
      <pages enableViewStateMac="true" />
   </system.web>
</configuration>
```

Because element and attribute names in XML are case-sensitive, statements in Web.config are case-sensitive, too. For example, the statement

```
<Pages enableviewstatemac="true" />
```

isn't valid and will generate an error message. Even attribute values are case-sensitive. The statement

```
<pages enableViewStateMac="True" />
```

is invalid because the T in "true" must be lowercase.

If you're going to use Web.config files to affect configuration changes, knowing what the default settings are so that you know what needs changing and what doesn't is helpful. Default configuration settings are defined in Machine.config, which is located in the Windows (or Winnt) directory's Microsoft.NET\Framework*vn.n.nnnn*\Config directory. For example, tracing is disabled by default as the result of the following statement in Machine.config:

```
<trace enabled="false" ... />
```

Because Machine.config holds configuration settings for all managed applications on the host machine, modifying Machine.config changes the defaults machine-wide. If you want tracing to be enabled by default, simply edit the statement above to read

```
<trace enabled="true" ... />
```

Settings in Web.config, by contrast, apply only to local applications.

The Microsoft .NET SDK documents most of the elements and attributes that Web.config supports out of the box. But the ultimate source of reference is Machine.config. It's sprinkled with comments placed there by Microsoft developers documenting the options available and the syntax of individual elements. If you have a question about Web.config and can't find an answer in the documentation, turn to Machine.config; chances are it'll have the answer you're looking for.

Configuration Inheritance

One of the hallmarks of Web.config files is configuration inheritance. Simply put, configuration inheritance means that settings specified in a Web.config file pertain to all files in the host directory (the one that holds Web.config) and its subdirectories. In other words, if you put the following Web.config file in wwwroot:

```
<configuration>
  <system.web>
    <compilation defaultLanguage="c#" />
  </system.web>
</configuration>
```

the default language for subdirectories stemming from wwwroot is also C#. Why? Because subdirectories inherit configuration settings from parent directories.

Subdirectories inherit their parents' configuration settings, but they can override those settings with Web.config files of their own. As an example, consider the directory structure in Figure 9-3. The top-level directory contains a Web.config file that sets the default language to C#. One of its subdirectories holds a Web.config file that sets the default language to Visual Basic .NET; the other subdirectory has no Web.config file. In this case, C# is the default language in wwwroot and wwwroot\CSharpFiles, but Visual Basic .NET is the default language in wwwroot\VBFiles. If the subdirectories contained subdirectories of their own, those subdirectories too would inherit settings from their parents. Specifically, subdirectories underneath wwwroot\CSharpFiles would default to C# and subdirectories beneath wwwroot\VBFiles would default to Visual Basic .NET. Those settings, of course, could be overridden by placing Web.config files in the subdirectory's subdirectories.

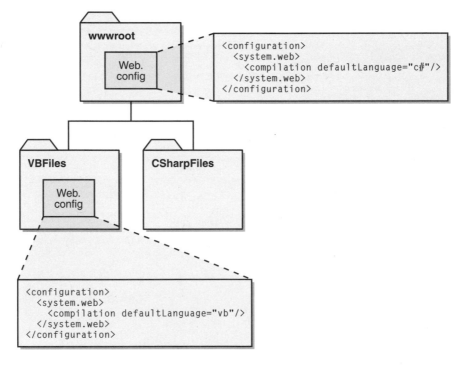

Figure 9-3 Configuration inheritance.

Machine.config sits at the top of the inheritance hierarchy. Default settings for the .NET Framework, ASP.NET included, are defined in Machine.config and are inherited by all framework applications. That's why settings in Machine.config apply to every managed application on the machine, and why you can look to Machine.config to determine what a server's default settings are. When you drop a Web.config file into a local directory, all you're really doing is overriding settings inherited from Machine.config.

The Global.asax File

Global.asax is a text file that houses application-level event handlers, declarations that pertain to all parts of the application, and other global application elements. ASP.NET applications don't have to include Global.asax files, but most do. An application can have only one Global.asax file. That file must be located in the application's virtual root directory.

What's inside a Global.asax file? Global.asax supports three element types:

■   Global directives

■   Global event handlers

■   Global object tags

Of the three, the first two are used more often. Global event handlers are particularly important and are the number one reason why developers include Global.asax files in their applications. We'll discuss global directives first and global event handlers second. Then, for completeness, we'll talk about global object tags, too.

Global Directives

Global directives, also known as *application directives*, provide application-wide instructions to the ASP.NET compilation engine. A Global.asax file supports three types of global directives:

■   *@ Application* directives

■   *@ Import* directives

■   *@ Assembly* directives

Global.asax can contain just one *@ Application* directive, but it places no limit on the number of *@ Import* and *@ Assembly* directives.

The *@ Application* Directive

@ Application directives serve two purposes: they enable developers to add descriptive text to applications, and they facilitate code-behind programming in Global.asax files. An *@ Application* directive accompanied by a *Description* attribute adds descriptive text, as in

```
<%@ Application Description="My First ASP.NET Application" %>
```

ASP.NET ignores *Description* attributes, so descriptions declared with it are visible only to those persons with access to your Global.asax files.

The *@ Application* directive also supports an *Inherits* attribute that enables code to be removed from Global.asax and packaged in a separate DLL. Suppose, for example, that you included the following Global.asax file in an application:

```
<%@ Import Namespace="System.Data" %>

<script language="C#" runat="server">
  void Application_Start ()
  {
      DataSet ds = new DataSet ();
      ds.ReadXml (Server.MapPath ("GlobalData.xml"));
      Application["GlobalData"] = ds;
  }
</script>
```

Coded this way, *Application_Start*, which is an event handler that fires each time the application starts up, is compiled the first time Global.asax is accessed by ASP.NET. To avoid run-time compilation, you can remove *Application_Start* from Global.asax and code it into a class that derives from *System.Web.HttpApplication*:

```
using System.Web;
using System.Data;

public class MyApp : HttpApplication
{
    public void Application_Start ()
    {
        DataSet ds = new DataSet ();
        ds.ReadXml ("GlobalData.xml");
        Application["GlobalData"] = ds;
    }
}
```

Then you compile the CS file into a DLL, place the DLL in the application root's bin directory, and reduce Global.asax to one simple statement:

```
<%@ Application Inherits="MyApp" %>
```

Code-behind offers the same benefits to Global.asax that it offers to ASPX files: it catches compilation errors before the application is deployed, and it enables developers to code handlers in C++ and other languages that ASP.NET doesn't explicitly support.

A look behind the scenes reveals why code-behind classes used by Global.asax files derive from *HttpApplication*. ASP.NET starts an application running when the very first request for that application arrives. Starting an application involves launching a process named Aspnet_wp.exe (commonly referred to as the *ASP.NET worker process*) if it isn't already running and creating a new application domain in that process to host the application and segregate it from other running ASP.NET applications. In the absence of code-behind, startup also involves parsing Global.asax and placing any content found there into a temporary file containing a class derived from *HttpApplication*, compiling the temporary file into a DLL, and instantiating the derived class. The resulting *HttpApplication* object handles the request that prompted the application to start up. As a performance optimization, ASP.NET maintains a pool of such objects and uses them to service incoming requests.

One implication of this design is that any code you include in Global.asax executes in the context of an *HttpApplication* object. That means you can call *HttpApplication* instance methods and access *HttpApplication* instance properties from anywhere in Global.asax. It also explains why using code-behind in Global.asax means deriving from *System.Web.HttpApplication* rather than *System.Web.UI.Page*. Because the system places Global.asax code in an *HttpApplication*-derived class, you must do the same if you want to get your code out of Global.asax and into a DLL.

The @ *Import* Directive

The @ *Import* directive serves the same purpose in Global.asax that it serves in ASPX files: it imports namespaces that ASP.NET doesn't import by default. For example, let's say you include the following <script> block in Global.asax:

```
<script language="C#" runat="server">
  void Application_Start ()
  {
      DataSet ds = new DataSet ();
      ds.ReadXml (Server.MapPath ("GlobalData.xml"));
      Application["GlobalData"] = ds;
  }
</script>
```

Because *DataSet* is defined in the *System.Data* namespace and *System.Data* isn't imported by default, you must either fully qualify all references to *DataSet* by including the namespace name or place the following directive at the top of Global.asax:

```
<%@ Import Namespace="System.Data" %>
```

@ Import directives in Global.asax pertain *only* to code in Global.asax. They do not import namespaces into other of the application's files.

The *@ Assembly* Directive

The *@ Assembly* directive does for Global.asax what *@ Assembly* does for ASPX files: it identifies assemblies Global.asax uses that ASP.NET doesn't link to by default. (For a list of default assemblies, see Chapter 5.)

As an example, suppose your Global.asax file uses classes in the *System.DirectoryServices* namespace. Because that namespace isn't imported by default and because the types that belong to that namespace live in System.DirectoryServices.dll, which ASP.NET doesn't link to by default, you need to include the following statements in Global.asax:

```
<%@ Import Namespace="System.DirectoryServices" %>
<%@ Assembly Name="System.DirectoryServices" %>
```

If you don't, ASP.NET will greet you with an error message the moment the application starts up.

Global Event Handlers

The most common reason for including Global.asax files in ASP.NET applications is to handle global events—events that aren't specific to a particular page but that apply to the application as a whole. Some global events are fired by the *HttpApplication* instances that process individual requests. Others are fired by HTTP modules—plug-in components that provide services such as authentication and output caching to ASP.NET. Some events fire on every request. Others fire at predictable junctures in an application's lifetime, such as when the application starts or stops. Still others fire conditionally—for example, when an unhandled exception occurs. Regardless of when a global event fires or who fires it, you can process it by including a handler in Global.asax.

Start and End Events

ASP.NET fires global events named *Start* and *End* when an application starts and stops. To process these events, include handlers named *Application_Start* and *Application_End* in Global.asax:

```
<script language="C#" runat="server">
  void Application_Start ()
  {
    ...
  }

  void Application_End ()
  {
    ...
  }
</script>
```

Application_Start is called when the application receives its first request. This handler is frequently used to initialize application state or the ASP.NET application cache (both of which are introduced later in this chapter) with data that is global to the application—that is, shared by all of its users. *Application_End* is called when the application shuts down. Typically, that happens when the application has run for 20 minutes without receiving an HTTP request. *Application_End* isn't used all that often because ASP.NET applications don't have to clean up after themselves by deleting objects created in *Application_Start*, but it's sometimes used to write data to a persistent storage medium prior to shutdown so that the data can be reloaded the next time the application starts and to dispose of objects that encapsulate unmanaged resources such as database connections.

Later in this chapter, you'll learn about ASP.NET session state. Session state is a mechanism for storing per-user information (such as shopping carts) in Web applications and preserving it across requests. Session state services are provided by an HTTP module named *SessionStateModule*, which fires a *Start* event each time it creates a session and an *End* event each time a session ends. You can process these events by including handlers named *Session_Start* and *Session_End* in Global.asax:

```csharp
<script language="C#" runat="server">
  void Session_Start ()
  {
    ...
  }

  void Session_End ()
  {
    ...
  }
</script>
```

Session_Start is called when a user visits your site who hasn't been there recently (usually in the last 20 minutes). *Session_End* is typically called when a session times out, which by default happens 20 minutes after the last request is received from the user for whom the session was created. The most common use for *Session_Start* is to initialize session state with data that is unique to each user. You'll see examples later in this chapter.

Per-Request Events

Global.asax can also include handlers for events fired by *HttpApplication* instances. If present in Global.asax, the following methods are called in every request in response to *HttpApplication* events. They're listed in the order in which they're called.

Per-Request Global Event Handlers

Method	Description
Application_BeginRequest	Called at the beginning of each request
Application_AuthenticateRequest	Called to authenticate the caller
Application_AuthorizeRequest	Called to determine whether the caller is authorized to access the requested resource
Application_ResolveRequestCache	Called to resolve the current request by providing content from a cache
Application_AcquireRequestState	Called to associate the current request with a session and populate session state
Application_PreRequestHandlerExecute	Called to prepend content to the HTTP response
Application_PostRequestHandlerExecute	Called to append content to the HTTP response
Application_ReleaseRequestState	Called to release (store) any state associated with this session
Application_UpdateRequestCache	Called to update a cache with content returned in the response
Application_EndRequest	Called at the end of each request

These handlers let you customize ASP.NET by plugging into the request processing pipeline. For example, *Application_ResolveRequestCache* and *Application_UpdateRequestCache* could be used to implement a custom output cache. *Application_AuthenticateRequest* and *Application_AuthorizeRequest* provide hooks for modifying ASP.NET's security apparatus. The event handlers *Application_PreRequestHandlerExecute* and *Application_PostRequestHandlerExecute* enable HTTP responses to be modified before they're returned to clients. The following Global.asax file uses the latter of these two methods to place a copyright notice at the bottom of each and every page (assuming, of course, that your pages use HTML flow layout rather than absolute positioning):

```
<script language="C#" runat="server">
  void Application_PostRequestHandlerExecute (Object sender, EventArgs e)
  {
      HttpApplication app = (HttpApplication) sender;
      app.Context.Response.Write ("<hr><center><i>" +
          "Copyright © 2002 by Me, Myself, and I</i></center>");
  }
</script>
```

Outputting a copyright notice this way rather than duplicating it in every ASPX file lets you change it in one place to modify it everywhere it shows up.

Error Events

The events listed above fire in each and every request. *HttpApplication* also defines an *Error* event that fires if ASP.NET throws an unhandled exception. You can process *Error* events by including an *Application_Error* handler in Global.asax. Here's a Global.asax file that logs unhandled exceptions in the NT event log. It uses the FCL's *System.Diagnostics.EventLog* class to write to the event log:

```
<%@ Import Namespace="System.Diagnostics" %>

<script language="C#" runat="server">
  void Application_Error (Object sender, EventArgs e)
  {
      // Formulate a message to write to the event log
      string msg = "Error accessing " + Request.Path + "\n" +
          Server.GetLastError ().ToString ();

      // Write an entry to the event log
      EventLog log = new EventLog ();
      log.Source = "My ASP.NET Application";
      log.WriteEntry (msg, EventLogEntryType.Error);
  }
</script>
```

It's not unwise to include a handler like this one in *every* ASP.NET application so that you can detect unhandled exceptions by periodically checking the NT event log. You could even modify the handler to send an e-mail message to a system administrator to apprise him or her of unhandled exceptions (a sure sign of a sick or buggy application) the moment they occur.

Don't be surprised if you encounter a Global.asax file containing an event handler that's not mentioned here. *HttpApplication* fires a few other events that I haven't listed because they're rarely used or used internally by ASP.NET. Plus, ASP.NET can be extended with HTTP modules that fire global events of their own. HTTP modules can also sink global events, which is precisely how the HTTP modules built into ASP.NET work much of their magic. A full discussion is beyond the scope of this chapter, but further information regarding HTTP modules and events is available in the Microsoft .NET Framework SDK.

Global Object Tags

Global object tags create object instances declaratively. Suppose you want a new instance of *ShoppingCart* created for each user that visits your site. Rather than do this:

```
<script>
  void Session_Start ()
  {
      Session["MyShoppingCart"] = new ShoppingCart ();
  }
</script>
```

you can do this:

```
<object id="MyShoppingCart" class="ShoppingCart" scope="session"
  runat="server" />
```

Assuming *ShoppingCart* has an *Add* method, a Web form could add an item to a user's shopping cart by doing this:

```
MyShoppingCart.Add (...);
```

This code might not make a lot of sense right now, but it'll make plenty of sense by the end of the chapter.

An <object> tag's *Scope* attribute assigns a scope to the object instances it creates. *Scope*="Application" creates one object instance, which is shared by all users of the application. *Scope*="Session" creates one object instance per session (that is, per user). *Scope*="Pipeline" creates a unique instance of the object for each and every request.

ASP.NET doesn't create objects declared with <object> tags unless it has to—that is, until they're requested for the first time. "Lazy instantiation" prevents objects from being created unnecessarily if the application doesn't use them.

Application State

ASP.NET offers two mechanisms for improving application performance by caching frequently used data: application state and the application cache. The former is a holdover from ASP. The latter is new to ASP.NET and largely obviates the need for application state. It also offers compelling features that application state does not. Application state might be useful for quickly porting old ASP code to ASP.NET, but new ASP.NET applications should use the application cache instead.

Application state and the application cache have three important characteristics in common:

■ Both make the data that they store available to all parts of an application. Store a product list in application state or the application cache, for example, and items in the list are available to every page in (and every user of) the application.

■ Both store data in memory and offer no options for storing it anywhere else. This means that application state and the application cache are fine places for caching data to avoid performance-inhibiting accesses to external data stores, but also that neither should store important data that can't be regenerated if the server goes down.

■ Both store dictionaries of key/value pairs and are generically typed to store anything that derives from *System.Object*. Since all managed types derive from *System.Object*, you can store instances of any managed type in application state and the application cache and key those instances with strings.

When is it appropriate to use application state or the application cache? Imagine you're writing a Web application that serves up real-time stock prices and that the application is backed by a massive database of stock prices that's updated periodically. Rather than query the database every time someone asks for a stock price, you could query it every few minutes, cache the results in application state or the application cache, and retrieve prices directly from memory. Prices fetched from your site might be a few minutes old, but the decreased number of database accesses will enable the application to respond to individual requests much more quickly.

Using Application State

Application state is physically represented by instances of *System.Web.HttpApplicationState*. Pages access instances of *HttpApplicationState* through the *Application* property that they inherit from *Page*; Global.asax files access them through the *Application* property that they inherit from *HttpApplication*.

HttpApplicationState properties and methods expose the contents of application state. The following statements add three stock prices keyed by stock symbols to application state and work equally in an ASPX file, in Global.asax, or in a code-behind file:

```
Application["AMZN"] = 10.00m;
Application["INTC"] = 20.00m;
Application["MSFT"] = 30.00m;
```

You can also add items to application state using *HttpApplicationState.Add*:

```
Application.Add ("AMZN", 10.00m);
Application.Add ("INTC", 20.00m);
Application.Add ("MSFT", 30.00m);
```

However, *Add* and *[]* behave slightly differently when adding items to application state. *Add* adds an item even if an item with the specified key already exists; *[]* does not. These statements add two separate items to application state:

```
Application.Add ("AMZN", 10.00m);
Application.Add ("AMZN", 11.00m);
```

You can retrieve both items by iterating over the contents of application state, but if you simply ask for the item keyed by "AMZN," you'll get back 10. The following example, by contrast, adds just one item to application state. The first statement creates the item and assigns it the value 10. The second statement changes the item's value to 11:

```
Application["AMZN"] = 10.00m;
Application["AMZN"] = 11.00m;
```

How do you read values from application state? The following statements retrieve the stock prices inserted earlier:

```
decimal amzn = (decimal) Application["AMZN"];
decimal intc = (decimal) Application["INTC"];
decimal msft = (decimal) Application["MSFT"];
```

The casts are necessary to convert the generic *System.Object* references retrieved from application state to strong types. To remove items from application state, call *Remove, RemoveAt, RemoveAll,* or *Clear* through the *Application* property. *Clear* and *RemoveAll* are semantically equivalent; they empty application state by removing all items.

Locking and Unlocking

Internally, ASP.NET uses a reader/writer lock to synchronize access to application state so that two threads representing two concurrent requests can't read it and write it at the same time. However, if you perform multistep operations on application state and need them to be treated as one atomic operation—that is, to ensure thread A can't read from application state while thread B performs a multistep update—you should surround the updates with calls to *Lock* and *UnLock,* as shown here:

```
Application.Lock ();
Application["ItemsSold"] = (int) Application["ItemsSold"] + 1;
Application["ItemsLeft"] = (int) Application["ItemsLeft"] - 1;
Application.UnLock ();
```

In between calls to *Lock* and *UnLock*, other threads that call *Lock* and *UnLock* can neither read nor write application state. Locking and unlocking is necessary only when multiple operations performed on application state must be treated as one.

The AppCounter Application

The application in Figure 9-4 uses application state to keep a running count of the number of times its pages are requested. Its one and only page is App-Counter.aspx, which reads the count from application state, increments it, writes the incremented count back to application state, and displays it. The *Application_Start* handler in Global.asax writes the count to application state each time the application starts up. The count is persistent—that is, it doesn't reset to 0 when the application shuts down—because Global.asax includes an *Application_End* handler that saves the count in a text file named Count.txt when the application ends. Next time the application starts up, *Application_Start* reads the count from the file. Only if the file doesn't exist or contains invalid data does *Application_Start* initialize the count to 0.

Application_Start calls *Server.MapPath* to convert Count.txt's URL into a physical path name. Rather than do the same, *Application_End* reads the path from a static field (*_path*) initialized by *Application_Start*. The reason? *Server.MapPath* throws an exception if called from *Application_End*. By the time *Application_End* is called, the application has almost shut down and some *HttpApplication* facilities normally available to handlers in Global.asax are no longer usable. *Server.MapPath* happens to be one of those facilities.

Take the application for a spin by copying the two source code files to wwwroot (or the virtual directory of your choice) and calling up App-Counter.aspx in your browser. The resulting page should show a count of 1. Refresh the page a few times and observe that each refresh increments the count. Now close your browser, open a command prompt window, and type *iisreset* to restart IIS. This command shuts down the application, which causes *Application_End* to be called, which writes the count to Count.txt. Call up App-Counter.aspx again and the count should pick up right where it left off.

Global.asax

```
<%@ Import NameSpace="System.IO" %>

<script language="C#" runat="server">
  static string _path;

  void Application_Start ()
  {
      StreamReader reader = null;

      try {
          // If Count.txt exists, read the count from it and
          // store the count in application state
          _path = Server.MapPath ("/Count.txt");
          reader = new StreamReader (_path);
          string line = reader.ReadLine ();
          int count = Convert.ToInt32 (line);
          Application["Count"] = count;
      }
      catch (Exception) {
          // If Count.txt does not exist or contains an invalid
          // count, store a 0 in application state
          Application["Count"] = 0;
      }
      finally {
          // Close the StreamReader
          if (reader != null)
              reader.Close ();
      }
  }

  void Application_End ()
  {
      StreamWriter writer = null;

      try {
          // Save the current count in Count.txt
          writer = new StreamWriter (_path, false);
          writer.Write (Application["Count"]);
      }
```

Figure 9-4   AppCounter source code.

```
        finally {
            // Close the StreamWriter
            if (writer != null)
                writer.Close ();
        }
    }
</script>
```

AppCounter.aspx

```
<%@ Page Language="C#" %>

<html>
  <body>
    <%
        // Fetch the count and increment it by 1. Lock application state
        // to prevent the count from changing as it's being updated.
        Application.Lock ();
        int count = (int) Application["Count"] + 1;
        Application["Count"] = count;
        Application.UnLock ();

        // Write the count to the page
        Response.Write ("Pages in this application " +
            "have been requested " + count + " time");
        if (count > 1)
            Response.Write ("s");
        Response.Write (".");
    %>
  </body>
</html>
```

The Application Cache

Now that you know about application state, forget that it even exists. The ASP.NET application cache does everything application state does and more, and it's loaded with features that make it bigger and better than application state in every way.

What is the ASP.NET application cache? It's a per-application, in-memory data store that, like application state, can store instances of any managed type, including complex types such as *DataSet* and *Hashtable*, and key them with strings. Unlike items placed in application state, items placed in the application cache can be assigned expiration policies. If you want an item to expire 15 minutes after it's placed in the cache or when the file it was initialized from changes, for example, you simply say so and ASP.NET automatically removes the item at the prescribed time. If that's still not enough to convince you to forget about application state, consider this: ASP.NET will optionally call the callback method of your choice when it removes an item from the cache. You can refresh the cache by writing callback methods that replace deleted items. Finally, when memory grows short, ASP.NET discards items in the application cache based on usage patterns (such as which items have been accessed the least recently) or on priorities that you assign.

Adding and Removing Items

The application cache is represented by instances of *System.Web.Caching.Cache*. Like application state, the application cache is exposed to program code through properties in ASP.NET base classes. Pages access the application cache through *Page.Cache*; Global.asax files access it through *HttpApplication.Context.Cache*. The following statements add three items—once more, decimal stock prices keyed by stock symbols—to the application cache from Global.asax:

```
Context.Cache["AMZN"] = 10.00m;
Context.Cache["INTC"] = 20.00m;
Context.Cache["MSFT"] = 30.00m;
```

ASPX files add items to the application cache without using *Context* as an intermediary:

```
Cache["AMZN"] = 10.00m;
Cache["INTC"] = 20.00m;
Cache["MSFT"] = 30.00m;
```

Items can also be added to the application cache with *Cache.Insert*:

```
Cache.Insert ("AMZN", 10.00m);
Cache.Insert ("INTC", 20.00m);
Cache.Insert ("MSFT", 30.00m);
```

Both *Insert* and *[]* replace an existing item if an existing key is specified. In other words, the following statements add just one item to the cache but modify its value three times:

```
Cache["AMZN"] = 10.00m;
Cache["AMZN"] = 11.00m;
Cache.Insert ("AMZN", 12.00m);
Cache.Insert ("AMZN", 13.00m);
```

Here's how a Web form retrieves items from the application cache:

```
decimal amzn = (decimal) Cache["AMZN"];
decimal intc = (decimal) Cache["INTC"];
decimal msft = (decimal) Cache["MSFT"];
```

As with application state, the cast is necessary to let the compiler know what kind of items were retrieved from the cache. To remove an item from the application cache, call *Cache.Remove*.

Locking and Unlocking

The application cache doesn't have *Lock* and *UnLock* methods as application state does. But that doesn't mean locking isn't necessary; it means you have to come up with your own mechanism for doing it. *System.Threading.ReaderWriterLock* is the perfect tool for the job. Assuming *rwlock* is an instance of *ReaderWriterLock*, here's how you'd lock the application cache during an update:

```
rwlock.AcquireWriterLock (Timeout.Infinite);
try {
    Cache["ItemsSold"] = (int) Cache["ItemsSold"] + 1;
    Cache["ItemsLeft"] = (int) Cache["ItemsLeft"] - 1;
}
finally {
    rwlock.ReleaseWriterLock ();
}
```

And here's how you'd read "ItemsSold" and "ItemsLeft" values from the cache:

```
rwlock.AcquireReaderLock (Timeout.Infinite);
try {
    int sold = (int) Cache["ItemsSold"];
    int left = (int) Cache["ItemsLeft"];
}
finally {
    rwlock.ReleaseReaderLock ();
}
```

As with application state, locking the application cache is necessary only when performing multistep updates that are to be treated as atomic operations.

Expiration Policies

If you use the application cache as shown above—that is, if you do nothing more than add static items and later retrieve them—then the application cache is little better than application state. The real power of the cache comes into play when you assign items expiration policies and process the callbacks that fire when the items expire. The following example, which is taken from a Global.asax file, initializes the application cache with a *Hashtable* containing three stock prices when the application starts up. It also sets the item to expire 5 minutes after it's added to the cache:

```
<script language="C#" runat="server">
  void Application_Start ()
  {
      Hashtable stocks = new Hashtable ();
      stocks.Add ("AMZN", 10.00m);
      stocks.Add ("INTC", 20.00m);
      stocks.Add ("MSFT", 30.00m);

      Context.Cache.Insert ("Stocks", stocks, null,
          DateTime.Now.AddMinutes (5), Cache.NoSlidingExpiration);
  }
</script>
```

Insert's fourth parameter—a *DateTime* value specifying a time 5 minutes hence—tells ASP.NET to remove the item from the cache in 5 minutes. That's called an *absolute expiration*. As an alternative, you can assign the item a *sliding expiration* by passing a *TimeSpan* value in the fifth parameter and *Cache.NoAbsoluteExpiration* in the fourth. A sliding expiration configures the item to expire when it has not been accessed (retrieved from the cache) for a specified length of time.

Absolute expirations and sliding expirations are one way to define expiration policies. Another option is to use *Insert*'s third parameter to establish a dependency between an item added to the cache and one or more files or directories. When the file or directory changes—when the file is modified, for example—ASP.NET removes the item from the cache. The following code sample initializes a *DataSet* from an XML file, adds the *DataSet* to the application cache, and creates a dependency between the *DataSet* and the XML file so that the *DataSet* is automatically removed from the cache if someone modifies the XML file:

```
DataSet ds = new DataSet ();
ds.ReadXml (Server.MapPath ("Stocks.xml"));
Context.Cache.Insert ("Stocks", ds,
    new CacheDependency (Server.MapPath ("Stocks.xml")));
```

Used this way, a *CacheDependency* object defines a dependency between a cached item and a file or directory. You can also use *CacheDependency* to set an item to expire when another item in the cache expires. Simply pass an array of key names identifying the item or items on which your item depends in the second parameter to *CacheDependency*'s constructor. If you don't want to establish a file or directory dependency also, pass null in the constructor's first parameter.

Cache.Insert also lets you assign priorities to items added to the application cache. When memory grows short, ASP.NET uses these priorities to determine which items to remove first. If you don't specify otherwise, an item's priority is *CacheItemPriority.Normal*. Other valid *CacheItemPriority* values, in order of lowest to highest priorities, are *Low*, *BelowNormal*, *AboveNormal*, *High*, and *NotRemovable*. Priority values are specified in *Insert*'s sixth parameter. The following statement inserts a *DataSet* named *ds* into the application cache, sets it to expire 1 hour after the last access, and assigns it a relatively high priority so that items with default or lower priority will be purged first in low-memory situations:

```
Context.Cache.Insert ("Stocks", ds, null,
    Cache.NoAbsoluteExpiration, TimeSpan.FromHours (1),
    CacheItemPriority.AboveNormal, null);
```

Specifying a *CacheItemPriority* value equal to *NotRemovable* is the *only* way to ensure that an item added to the cache will still be there when you retrieve it. That's important, because it means code that retrieves an item from the application cache should always verify that the reference to the item returned by the cache isn't null—unless, of course, the item was marked *NotRemovable*.

Cache Removal Callbacks

All items except those marked *NotRemovable* are subject to removal from the cache at any time if ASP.NET needs the memory for other purposes. If you'd like to be notified when an item is removed, you can pass a *CacheItemRemovedCallback* delegate to *Insert* identifying the method you want ASP.NET to call if and when it removes the item from the cache. The following example extends one of the examples in the previous section by adding a *DataSet* to the application cache, configuring it to expire when the XML file it's initialized from changes, and automatically replacing the old *DataSet* with a new one using a callback method:

```
<%@ Import Namespace="System.Data" %>

<script language="C#" runat="server">
  static Cache _cache;
  static string _path;

  void Application_Start ()
  {
      _cache = Context.Cache;
      _path = Context.Server.MapPath ("Stocks.xml");

      DataSet ds = new DataSet ();
      ds.ReadXml (_path);
```

(continued)

```
        _cache.Insert ("Stocks", ds, new CacheDependency (_path),
            Cache.NoAbsoluteExpiration, Cache.NoSlidingExpiration,
            CacheItemPriority.Default,
            new CacheItemRemovedCallback (RefreshDataSet));
    }

    static void RefreshDataSet (String key, Object item,
        CacheItemRemovedReason reason)
    {
        DataSet ds = new DataSet ();
        ds.ReadXml (_path);

        _cache.Insert ("Stocks", ds, new CacheDependency (_path),
            Cache.NoAbsoluteExpiration, Cache.NoSlidingExpiration,
            CacheItemPriority.Default,
            new CacheItemRemovedCallback (RefreshDataSet));
    }
</script>
```

When *RefreshDataSet* (or any other *CacheItemRemovedCallback* method) is called, the first parameter identifies the string that the item was keyed with, the second identifies the item itself, and the third specifies why the item was removed. This example is simple enough that no callback parameters need to be examined. In a more complex application that stores multiple items in the application cache, however, you'd probably use at least the first of the three parameters to determine which item needs refreshing.

The *Cache.Add* Method

Earlier, I showed you how to add items to the application cache using *Insert* and *[]*. You can also add items with *Cache.Add*. Unlike *Insert*, however, *Add* isn't overloaded to support simplified usage; when you call it, you have to provide seven different parameters, as shown here:

```
Context.Cache.Add ("Stocks", ds, null,
    Cache.NoAbsoluteExpiration, Cache.NoSlidingExpiration,
    CacheItemPriority.Default, null);
```

Add doesn't behave exactly like *Insert*. *Add* adds an item to the cache, but only if the key you specify in *Add*'s first parameter doesn't already exist. By contrast, *Insert* always adds an item to the cache. If the key specified in *Insert*'s first parameter already exists, *Insert* simply replaces the old item with the new one.

The SmartQuotes Application

For an example of how the ASP.NET application cache might be used to improve performance, consider the following ASPX file:

```
<%@ Import Namespace="System.IO" %>

<html>
  <body>
    <asp:Label ID="Output" RunAt="server" />
  </body>
</html>

<script language="C#" runat="server">
  void Page_Load (Object sender, EventArgs e)
  {
      ArrayList quotes = new ArrayList ();
      StreamReader reader = new StreamReader (Server.MapPath ("Quotes.txt"));

      for (string line = reader.ReadLine (); line != null;
          line = reader.ReadLine ())
          quotes.Add (line);

      reader.Close ();

      Random rand = new Random ();
      int index = rand.Next (0, quotes.Count - 1);
      Output.Text = (string) quotes[index];
  }
</script>
```

Each time this ASPX file is requested, it opens a text file named Quotes.txt, reads its contents, and displays a randomly selected line. If Quotes.txt contains a collection of famous quotations, a randomly selected quotation appears each time the page is refreshed.

So what's wrong with this picture? Nothing—unless, that is, you value performance. Each time the page is requested, it opens and reads the text file. Consequently, each and every request results in a physical file access. File accesses impede performance because file I/O is a relatively time-consuming undertaking.

This ASPX file, simple as it is, can benefit greatly from the ASP.NET application cache. Suppose that instead of reading Quotes.txt every time the page is requested, you read it once—when the application starts up—and store it in the application cache. Rather than physically access the file, the ASPX file could then retrieve a line directly from the application cache. Furthermore, the cached data could be configured so that it's deleted from the cache if the file that it comes from changes. You could write a callback method that refreshes the cache when the data is removed. That way, the application would incur just one physical file access at startup and would never access the file again unless the contents of the file change.

Figure 9-5 shows what the output looks like for a Web application that fits the description in the previous paragraph. Figure 9-6 contains the source code. Global.asax's *Application_Start* method reads the contents of Quotes.txt into an *ArrayList* and inserts the *ArrayList* into the application cache. It also establishes a dependency between the *ArrayList* and Quotes.txt so that if the latter changes, the *ArrayList* is removed from the cache and Global.asax's *Refresh-Quotes* method is called. *RefreshQuotes* refreshes the cache by rereading the file and placing the resulting *ArrayList* in the cache. The ASPX file—Smart-Quotes.aspx—retrieves the *ArrayList* and displays a randomly selected line. And just in case it hits the cache after the *ArrayList* is deleted and before the new one is added, SmartQuotes.aspx displays a "Server busy" message if the cache read returns a null reference. Refreshing the page again should replace "Server busy" with a famous quotation. To try the application for yourself, copy the source code files to wwwroot or the virtual directory of your choice, open SmartQuotes.aspx in your browser, and refresh the page a few times.

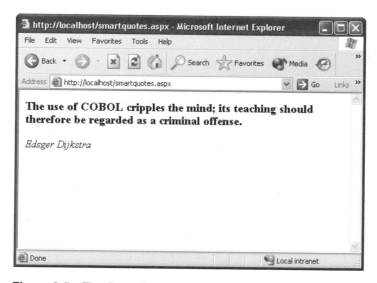

Figure 9-5 The SmartQuotes Web page in action.

Global.asax

```
<%@ Import NameSpace="System.IO" %>

<script language="C#" runat="server">

  static Cache _cache = null;
  static string _path = null;

  void Application_Start ()
  {
      _cache = Context.Cache;
      _path = Server.MapPath ("Quotes.txt");

      ArrayList quotes = ReadQuotes ();

      if (quotes != null) {
          _cache.Insert ("Quotes", quotes, new CacheDependency (_path),
              Cache.NoAbsoluteExpiration, Cache.NoSlidingExpiration,
              CacheItemPriority.Default,
              new CacheItemRemovedCallback (RefreshQuotes));
      }
  }

  static void RefreshQuotes (String key, Object item,
      CacheItemRemovedReason reason)
  {
      ArrayList quotes = ReadQuotes ();

      if (quotes != null) {
          _cache.Insert ("Quotes", quotes, new CacheDependency (_path),
              Cache.NoAbsoluteExpiration, Cache.NoSlidingExpiration,
              CacheItemPriority.Default,
              new CacheItemRemovedCallback (RefreshQuotes));
      }
  }

  static ArrayList ReadQuotes ()
  {
      ArrayList quotes = new ArrayList ();
      StreamReader reader = null;

      try {
          reader = new StreamReader (_path);
          for (string line = reader.ReadLine (); line != null;
              line = reader.ReadLine ())
              quotes.Add (line);
      }
```

Figure 9-6   The SmartQuotes source code.

Global.asax *(continued)*

```
        catch (IOException) {
            return null;
        }
        finally {
            if (reader != null)
                reader.Close ();
        }
        return quotes;
    }
</script>
```

SmartQuotes.aspx

```
<%@ Import Namespace="System.IO" %>

<html>
  <body>
    <asp:Label ID="Output" RunAt="server" />
  </body>
</html>

<script language="C#" runat="server">
  void Page_Load (Object sender, EventArgs e)
  {
      ArrayList quotes = (ArrayList) Cache["Quotes"];

      if (quotes != null) {
          Random rand = new Random ();
          int index = rand.Next (0, quotes.Count - 1);
          Output.Text = (string) quotes[index];
      }
      else {
          Output.Text = "Server busy";
      }
  }
</script>
```

Quotes.txt

```
<h3>Give me chastity and continence, but not yet.</h3>
<i>Saint Augustine</i>
<h3>The use of COBOL cripples the mind; its teaching should
  therefore be regarded as a criminal offense.</h3><i>Edsger
  Dijkstra</i>
<h3>C makes it easy to shoot yourself in the foot; C++ makes it
  harder, but when you do, it blows away your whole leg.</h3>
  <i>Bjarne Stroustrup</i>
<h3>A programmer is a device for turning coffee into code.</h3>
```

```
<i>Jeff Prosise (with an assist from Paul Erdos)</i>
<h3>I have not failed. I've just found 10,000 ways that won't
  work.</h3><i>Thomas Edison</i>
<h3>Blessed is the man who, having nothing to say, abstains from
  giving wordy evidence of the fact.</h3><i>George Eliot</i>
<h3>I think there is a world market for maybe five computers.</h3>
  <i>Thomas Watson</i>
<h3>Computers in the future may weigh no more than 1.5 tons.</h3>
  <i>Popular Mechanics</i>
<h3>I have traveled the length and breadth of this country and talked
  with the best people, and I can assure you that data processing is a
  fad that won't last out the year.</h3><i>Prentice-Hall business books
  editor</i>
<h3>640K ought to be enough for anybody.</h3><i>Bill Gates</i>
```

Session State

One of the more difficult problems in Web programming is storing per-user state. Suppose you intend to write a site that lets visitors drop items into virtual shopping carts by clicking Add to Cart buttons. It sounds simple enough, but remember: the Web server sees the button clicks as a series of unrelated HTTP requests, and the requests generated by one user are mixed in with similar requests from other users. Finding a place to store the contents of your shopping carts—in memory on the server, for example, or in hidden <input> fields round-tripped to the client and back—is only half the battle; the other half involves examining each incoming request, determining whether that request came from a user for whom a shopping cart has been created, and either correlating the request to an existing shopping cart or creating a brand new shopping cart. The challenge is far less trivial than most people realize.

ASP offers a convenient and easy-to-use solution to the per-user-state problem in the form of *sessions*. When a user who hasn't visited an ASP-driven site recently (typically in the last 20 minutes) submits a request to that site, ASP creates a session for that user and returns a cookie that uniquely identifies the session. In subsequent requests from the same user, ASP uses the cookie to correlate the request to the session it created earlier. If hundreds of users browse a site simultaneously, each is assigned his or her own session, and each session implements a data store that's exposed to ASP scripts through a *session object*. Information written to that data store is called *session state*. One simple statement in an ASP script writes a value to session state or reads it back. And because each session corresponds to exactly one user, data written to session state is stored strictly on a per-user basis.

Despite its elegance, ASP's session state implementation suffers from two fatal flaws:

- ASP session state is stored in memory, which means it's incompatible with Web farms—clusters of Web servers that act as one—and also that it's destroyed if IIS is restarted or the server is rebooted.

- ASP session state relies on cookies to correlate users to sessions. If a user disables cookies in his or her browser, an ASP Web server is powerless to map incoming requests to sessions.

For these reasons, many large sites that rely on ASP either don't use session state or use a custom implementation that replaces ASP's default session state provider with one of their own.

ASP.NET also uses sessions to enable Web applications to store per-user state. ASP.NET's session state implementation is better thought out and more robust, however, and it suffers from none of the shortcomings of ASP session state. It supports a variety of storage models, enabling session state to be physically stored in-process to ASP.NET, in another process, on another machine, or even in a database, and it supports cookieless operation for the benefit of browsers that don't support cookies (or that have cookies turned off). All in all, it's a huge improvement over ASP and one of ASP.NET's greatest strengths. And it's the perfect place to store shopping carts or anything else that requires unique storage for each visitor to your site.

Using Session State

Using ASP.NET session state is simplicity itself. Pages access it through the *Session* property that they inherit from *System.Web.UI.Page*. Global.asax files access it through the *Session* property inherited from *System.Web.HttpApplication*. In both cases, the *Session* property maps to an instance of *System.Web.SessionState.HttpSessionState* specially created by ASP.NET to store data for the user who originated the request.

HttpSessionState.Add adds an item to session state. As are items stored in application state or the application cache, an "item" is an instance of any managed type keyed by a string. The following statement adds an item named "10012552" to session state and assigns it the value "Quantity=1":

```
Session.Add ("10012552", "Quantity=1");
```

Or, if you'd prefer, you can add it this way:

```
Session["10012552"] = "Quantity=1";
```

The *Add* method and *[]* operator are semantically equivalent. In other words, both add items to session state, and both replace an existing item if an existing key is specified.

Retrieving an item from session state is equally painless:

```
string value = Session["10012552"];
```

The same can be said about enumerating items and the strings that they're keyed with:

```
NameObjectCollectionBase.KeysCollection keys = Session.Keys;
foreach (string key in keys) {
    // key is the item's key
    // Session[key] returns the item's value
    .
    .
    .
}
```

To remove items from session state, use *HttpSessionState*'s *Remove*, *RemoveAt*, and *RemoveAll* methods. You can also use *Clear*, which is equivalent to *RemoveAll*.

ASP.NET uses randomly generated session IDs, which aren't unlike COM GUIDs (globally unique identifiers), to identify sessions. If you'd like to know what the ID of a given session is, you can retrieve it from the *SessionID* property of the corresponding *HttpSessionState* object. Another interesting *HttpSessionState* property is *IsNewSession*, which reveals whether the session ID was generated for the current request (true) or a previous request (false).

Incidentally, if you perform a multistep update on session state and are concerned that a read from another thread at just the wrong time might catch the data in an indeterminate state, don't fret. ASP.NET locks session state when an *HttpApplication* instance fires an *AcquireRequestState* event and unlocks it following the next *ReleaseRequestState* event. The practical effect is that it's impossible for two requests to read and write session state at the same time, even in the unlikely event that two requests that correspond to the same session overlap each other.

The SessionSpy Page

For a firsthand look at session state in action, check out the Web page in Figure 9-7. Called SessionSpy.aspx, it uses session state to store a count of the number of times a user visits the site. The first time you request the page, you'll be greeted as a first-time visitor and shown the ID of the session that was created for you. Each time thereafter, you'll be told how many times you've visited the site (that is, requested the page).

The count is a simple integer stored in session state and keyed with the string "Count". SessionSpy.aspx reads the *HttpSessionState* object's *IsNewSession* property to determine whether this access is the first one to the page and its *SessionID* property to get the session ID.

```
SessionSpy.aspx
<%@ Page Language="C#" %>

<html>
  <body>
    <%
      if (Session.IsNewSession || Session["Count"] == null) {
          Session["Count"] = 1;
          Response.Write ("Welcome! Because this is your first " +
              "visit to this site, a new session has been created " +
              "for you. Your session ID is " + Session.SessionID +
              ".");
      }
      else {
          Session["Count"] = (int) Session["Count"] + 1;
          Response.Write ("You have visited this site " +
              Session["Count"] + " times. Your session ID is still " +
              Session.SessionID + ".");
      }
    %>
  </body>
</html>
```

Figure 9-7   The SessionSpy page.

After you've played with the page for a few moments, start a second instance of your browser and open SessionSpy.aspx. Because the new browser instance represents a new "session" and doesn't share cookies with the first, you're greeted as a first-time user. But use your browser's New Window command (Ctrl+N in most browsers) to start a third instance, and you'll be greeted as a returning user. Why? A browser started with the New Window command doesn't represent a new session. It shares cookies and other resources with the first instance and thus shares its session state on the server, too.

Cookieless Session State

By default, ASP.NET, like ASP, uses cookies to correlate returning users to sessions on the server. Unlike ASP, ASP.NET supports cookieless session state as well. Cookieless sessions are enabled by adding *cookieless*="true" to the *sessionState* element in Web.config or Machine.config:

```
<sessionState cookieless="true" />
```

How does ASP.NET correlate users and sessions when cookies are disabled? By using *URL munging*. Check out the screen in Figure 9-8, which was taken after a client retrieved a page from an ASP.NET application running in cookieless mode. The strange-looking value in parentheses in the browser's address bar is the session ID. Before returning the page to the client, ASP.NET inserts the session ID into the URL. When the page posts back to the server, ASP.NET strips the session ID from the URL and uses it to associate the request with a session. URL munging isn't perfect because there's nothing preventing the user from editing the URL and invalidating the session ID. But it's better than nothing, and it prevents ASP.NET session state from being unusable with browsers that don't honor cookies.

You're probably wondering, "Is there a way I can ask ASP.NET whether cookies are enabled in a browser, and if so, can I enable cookieless operation on the fly if I detect that a request came from a browser that doesn't support cookies?" The short answer is no and no. ASP.NET doesn't attempt to determine whether a browser supports cookies, so if you want to know, you have to find out yourself. The usual technique is to return a cookie to a browser and use *Response.Redirect* to redirect to a page that checks for the cookie. If the cookie's not there, you know the browser ignored it. Another approach is to return a cookie along with some client-side script that checks for it. Even if you determine at run time that cookies aren't supported, however, there's not much you can do about it as far as session state is concerned because cookieless operation can't be enabled and disabled programmatically. If you want to know whether cookieless session state is in effect, however, you can read the *IsCookieless* property of any *HttpSessionState* object.

Bottom line? If you want session state to work with as many browsers as possible, configure your application to use cookieless session state up front. If you don't like URL munging and don't care that your application might not work properly with browsers that have cookies disabled (many applications test for cookie support and display a warning indicating that they might not work properly if cookies are disabled), then stick with the default: *cookieless*="false."

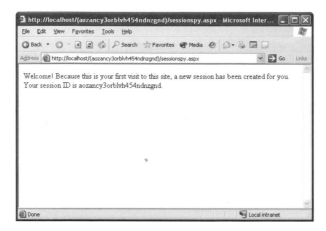

Figure 9-8   URL containing a session ID.

Session State Process Models

Cookieless sessions are an important enhancement to ASP.NET, but even more important are ASP.NET's new session state process models. ASP session state is always stored in memory, which makes it incompatible with Web farms (a session—and session ID—created on server A are undefined on server B). It also means that you lose everything in session state if the Web server goes down. That's a big deal to a site like Amazon.com, which at any given time might have millions of dollars worth of potential sales sitting in virtual shopping carts. Web farms are a big deal, too, because setting up clusters of Web servers is a classic and relatively inexpensive way to scale an application to meet the demands of a growing customer base.

That's why ASP.NET doesn't limit session to memory on the Web server as ASP does. ASP.NET supports three session state process models:

Model	Description
In-proc	Stores session state in-process to ASP.NET (that is, in Aspnet_wp.exe)
State server	Stores session state in an external "state server" process on the Web server or on a remote machine
SQL Server	Stores session state in a Microsoft SQL Server database on the Web server or on a remote machine

The default is in-proc, which is very ASP-like, but simple configuration changes applied via Web.config or Machine.config switch to the state server or SQL Server model and get session state out of the ASP.NET worker process Aspnet_wp.exe and into the location of your choosing. The sections that follow describe the necessary configuration changes and also shed light on the pros and cons of the individual process models.

In-Proc Session State

In-proc session state is the fastest, but it's also the least robust; restart IIS or reboot your Web server and in-proc session state goes away for good. In-proc is the default because of the following statement in Machine.config:

```
<sessionState ... mode="InProc" />
```

To be absolutely certain that in-proc session state is in effect regardless of what might be in Machine.config, add a Web.config file to your application's virtual root directory and include this statement in it:

```
<sessionState mode="InProc" />
```

In-proc session state is appropriate when you prefer speed to robustness and your application runs on a single server rather than a Web farm.

State Server Session State

The state server session state model is new in ASP.NET. It moves session state out of Aspnet_wp.exe and into a dedicated "state server" process managed by the system. The state server is actually a running instance of a service named Aspnet_state.exe. If you want to use the state server model, you must do the following:

- Start Aspnet_state.exe. You can start it manually (from the command line) by executing the following command:

  ```
  net start aspnet_state
  ```

  Or you can configure it to start automatically each time the system is started by using Windows' Services control panel applet (Figure 9-9).

- Add a *mode*="StateServer" attribute and a *stateConnectionString* attribute to the *sessionState* element in Machine.config or a local Web.config file. The latter of these two attributes identifies the machine that hosts the state server process.

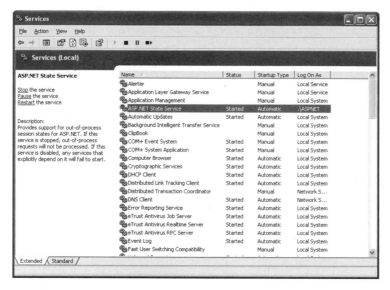

Figure 9-9 The ASP.NET State service.

Here's a Web.config file that configures an application to store session state in a state server process on the same Web server that hosts the application:

```
<configuration>
  <system.web>
    <sessionState
      mode="StateServer"
      stateConnectionString="tcpip=localhost:42424"
    />
  </system.web>
</configuration>
```

And here's one that places session state in a state server process on another machine identified by IP address:

```
<configuration>
  <system.web>
    <sessionState
      mode="StateServer"
      stateConnectionString="tcpip=192.168.1.2:42424"
    />
  </system.web>
</configuration>
```

By default, ASP.NET uses port 42424 to communicate with the state server process. That's why "42424" appears in the state connection string. In the unlikely event that 42424 conflicts with another application on your Web server, you can change the port number by doing the following:

■   Add the desired port number to the registry at HKEY_LOCAL_
MACHINE\System\CurrentControlSet\Services\aspnet_state\
Parameters\Port.

■   Replace 42424 with the new port number in *stateConnectionString*.

As an example, here's a Web.config file that changes the session state mode to
"StateServer" and directs ASP.NET to use port 31313 to connect Aspnet_wp.exe
to Aspnet_state.exe:

```
<configuration>
  <system.web>
    <sessionState
      mode="StateServer"
      stateConnectionString="tcpip=192.168.1.2:31313"
    />
  </system.web>
</configuration>
```

The state server model is slower than in-proc session state because data
read from and written to session state must travel across process or machine
boundaries. However, the state server model prevents session state from being
lost if IIS is restarted, and should the state server process be on another
machine, it even allows session state to survive if the entire Web server is
rebooted. Switching to the state server model is also one way to build ASP.NET
applications that work with Web farms.

Figure 9-10 illustrates how the state server model solves the Web farm
compatibility problem. In this example, the Web farm contains three servers.
The application runs in worker processes on all three servers, but each server
is configured to store session state in a state server process on a fourth machine.
It's perfectly acceptable now for data to be written to session state on server A
and read back on server B because both servers refer to machine D for their
session state. If you don't want to dedicate a machine to host the state server
process, no problem: simply designate one of the Web servers as the state
server and point the other servers to it with *stateConnectionString*.

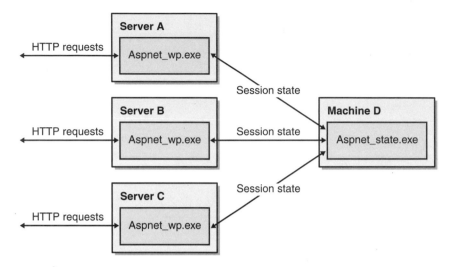

Figure 9-10 Web farm with session state in a remote state server process.

SQL Server Session State

The SQL Server process model offers the ultimate in scalability and reliability. Like the state server model, it moves session state out of Aspnet_wp.exe. But rather than store session state in an external process, the SQL Server model stores it in a Microsoft SQL Server database. You gain Web farm compatibility because you can point all your servers to a common back-end machine (the one that hosts the database). You also achieve robustness because session state is preserved no matter what—even if IIS is restarted or the Web server is rebooted. If SQL Server is clustered or otherwise configured to survive hard failures, you can reboot the database server itself and still preserve the contents of session state.

Configuring ASP.NET to use the SQL Server process model is a breeze. Here are the steps required:

■ Create the database that holds the session state. The .NET Framework SDK provides a script that creates the database for you; it's called InstallSqlState.sql. To run it, open a command prompt window and type the following command:

```
osql -S localhost -U sa -P -i installsqlstate.sql
```

This command creates a SQL Server database named ASPState on the host machine and adds to it all the tables, stored procedures, and other infrastructure that ASP.NET uses to access the database, as shown in Figure 9-11.

■ Add a *mode*="SQLServer" attribute and a *sqlConnectionString* attribute to the *sessionState* element in Machine.config or a local

Web.config file. The latter of these two attributes provides the information ASP.NET needs to connect to the database.

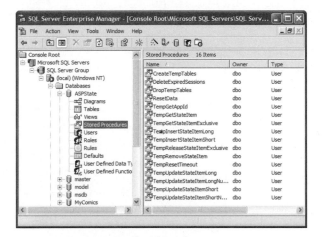

Figure 9-11   The ASPState database.

The following Web.config file configures an ASP.NET application to store session state in a SQL Server database on the Web server:

```
<configuration>
  <system.web>
    <sessionState
      mode="SQLServer"
      sqlConnectionString="server=localhost;uid=sa;pwd="
    />
  </system.web>
</configuration>
```

The next one does the same, but it points ASP.NET to a SQL Server database on a remote machine named "Hawkeye":

```
<configuration>
  <system.web>
    <sessionState
      mode="SQLServer"
      sqlConnectionString="server=hawkeye;uid=sa;pwd="
    />
  </system.web>
</configuration>
```

Performance-wise, the SQL Server model is the slowest of them all, but in return for speed it virtually guarantees that session state won't be lost. Figure 9-12 shows how the SQL Server option factors into Web farms. A dedicated server holds the state database, and all the Web servers point ASP.NET to that database. If you intend to use ASP.NET to build large, industrial-strength e-commerce sites, this is the architecture you want.

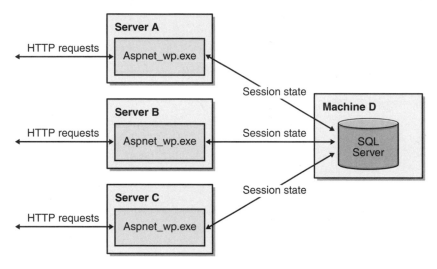

Figure 9-12   Web farm with session state in a remote SQL Server database.

State Servers, SQL Servers, and Serializable Objects

One gotcha to be aware of if you plan to use the state server or SQL Server session state model is that both require types stored in session state to be serializable. Serialization is the process of writing out the data that defines an object instance to a designated storage medium for the purpose of re-creating, or *rehydrating*, it at a later time or in another place. ASP.NET must be able to serialize objects stored in session state if it's to transfer them to a state server process or a SQL Server database. And it must be able to deserialize them if they're to be read back. Nonserializable types work just fine with the in-proc session state model, but try to write a nonserializable type to session state using either of the other process models and ASP.NET will throw an exception.

Here's an example to help clarify. Suppose you write a class named *ShoppingCart* to serve as a virtual container for items that users select from your site:

```
public class ShoppingCart
{
    . . .
}
```

Defined this way, a *ShoppingCart* instance can be written to session state without any problem as long as session state is stored in-proc:

```
ShoppingCart cart = new ShoppingCart ();
Session["MyShoppingCart"] = cart;
```

But the same code throws an exception if you switch to the state server or SQL Server model. To remedy that, make the class serializable by adding a *Serializable* attribute:

```
[Serializable]
public class ShoppingCart
{
  ...
}
```

This quick-and-easy change enables ASP.NET to serialize and deserialize *ShoppingCart* objects using *System.Runtime.Serialization.Formatters.Binary.BinaryFormatter*, better known as the .NET Framework's binary formatter. When you create custom data types with the intention of storing them in session state, *always* include a *Serializable* attribute unless you're certain you'll only use the types in-proc. It's never harmful, and it will pay off in spades if you or anyone else attempts to write an instance of the class to session state in an application that uses the state server or SQL Server model.

Session Lifetimes

ASP.NET creates sessions for you. It also deletes them (in reality, hands them over to the garbage collector) when it's done. Knowing when to delete them requires a bit of guesswork. ASP.NET can't know definitively when a session is no longer needed because it has no way of knowing whether a given request is that user's last. So it does the next best thing: if a prescribed time period elapses and ASP.NET receives no requests from a user for whom a session was created, it discards the corresponding session. The default time-out period is 20 minutes, as specified in Machine.config:

```
<sessionState ... timeout="20" />
```

You can change the session time-out period in three ways. Option number one is to edit Machine.config. Option number two is to place a statement like this one, which sets the session time-out to 60 minutes, in a local Web.config file:

```
<sessionState timeout="60" />
```

And option number three is to write a time-out value (in minutes) to the *Time-out* property of an *HttpSessionState* object:

```
Session.Timeout = 60;
```

Which route you should choose depends on the desired scope of the change. Setting the time-out interval in Machine.config changes the default for all ASP.NET applications on the Web server. Setting it in a local Web.config file changes it for a single application, and setting it with *Session.Timeout* changes it for an individual session. The proper time-out interval is both subjective and application-specific. Twenty minutes is fine for most applications, but if you'd like a user to be able to go out to lunch and come back to find his or her shopping cart still full (assuming you're storing shopping carts in session state), then you might want to up the time-out interval to an hour or more.

You can see session time-outs in action by calling up Figure 9-7's Session-Spy.aspx in your browser, refreshing it a time or two, waiting for 20 minutes, and then refreshing the page again. Because your session timed out while you were away, you'll be greeted as a first-time visitor. Increase the session time-out, and you'll be able to stay away for longer periods of time.

An application can explicitly close a session by calling the session's *Abandon* method:

```
Session.Abandon ();
```

This option is sometimes used by sites that permit users to log out (or that forcibly log them out) after completing a transaction.

Disabling Session State

Session state can also be disabled altogether. Session state exacts a modest price in both memory and performance, so if you don't use it, you should disable it. You can disable session state for an individual page (ASPX file) with the following @ *Page* directive:

```
<%@ Page EnableSessionState="false" %>
```

You can disable it for an entire application by including this statement in Web.config:

```
<sessionState mode="Off" />
```

Or you can disable it for all applications by adding a *mode*="Off" attribute to the *sessionState* element in Machine.config.

A Word on Web Farms

Moving session state to a remote machine and pointing all your Web servers to that machine is essential to building Web applications that are compatible with server farms. But there's something else you have to do to deploy an ASP.NET application on a Web farm. First, a bit of background.

Each server's Machine.config file contains a *machineKey* element that assigns values to a pair of cryptographic keys:

```
<machineKey ... validationKey="AutoGenerate" decryptionKey="AutoGenerate" />
```

When configured to prevent tampering by appending hashes to view state values and forms authentication cookies (a topic I'll cover in Chapter 10), ASP.NET uses *validationKey* to generate the hashes. If the protection level is sufficiently high, ASP.NET goes even further and uses *decryptionKey* to encrypt view state and authentication cookies. "AutoGenerate" tells ASP.NET to generate a random key and store it in the host machine's Local Security Authority (LSA). Randomly generated keys are fine for single-server installations, but in a Web farm, each server must use identical keys; otherwise, a value encrypted on one machine can't be unencrypted on another.

Before deploying an ASP.NET application on a Web farm, you should make the following configuration change on *every server in the Web farm*. The change can be made in Machine.config or in a local Web.config file:

- Set *machineKey*'s *validationKey* attribute to *validation-Key="mmmm,"* where *mmmm* is a random value from 40 to 128 characters in length. Longer values provide stronger encryption.

- Set *machineKey*'s *decryptionKey* attribute to *decryptionKey="nnnn,"* where *nnnn* is a random value either 16 or 48 characters in length. The latter provides stronger encryption but works only on servers that support 128-bit encryption.

Here's a sample Web.config file that, if used on every server on which your application is installed, configures each server to use identical validation and encryption keys:

```
<configuration>
  <system.web>
    <machineKey
      validationKey="DD2B3BB0B07F4FE6917B60DAFEB0D01532C1C3BB07F533A1"
      decryptionKey="C89EFEF650CA4D9C9BC986061211329A9717DC2260BC6199"
    />
  </system.web>
</configuration>
```

Values for *validationKey* and *decryptionKey* should by cryptographically strong to make values encrypted with them difficult to break. Various tools are available for producing cryptographically strong keys. You can even write your own key generator using the FCL's *System.Security.Cryptography.RNGCryptoServiceProvider* class. (RNG stands for Random Number Generator.) However you derive your keys, be sure to apply them in a CONFIG file or your Web farm–compatible application might not be so Web farm–compatible after all.

The Congo.com Application

The application pictured in Figure 9-13 breathes life into many of the concepts presented in this chapter. Called Congo.com, it's a virtual storefront for a fictitious online bookseller. Congo.com's catalog consists of titles obtained from the SQL Server Pubs database. The main page, Congo.aspx, fetches the titles from the database and displays them in a *DataGrid*. Each row in the *DataGrid* contains an Add to Cart button that, when clicked, adds the corresponding book to a virtual shopping cart. Clicking the View Cart button at the top of the page shows the shopping cart's contents, again using a *DataGrid*. This *DataGrid* has Remove buttons that delete items from the shopping cart.

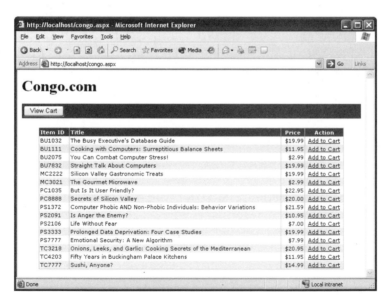

Figure 9-13   Congo.com.

Here's how to install Congo.com on your Web server:

- Copy Web.config, Global.asax, Congo.aspx, and ViewCart.aspx to wwwroot or the virtual directory of your choice.

- Compile Congo.cs and place the resulting DLL in the virtual directory's bin subdirectory. The following command performs the compilation:

```
csc /t:library congo.cs
```

Once deployment is complete, call up Congo.aspx in your browser and click a few Add to Cart buttons. Then click View Cart to view your shopping cart's contents. Now do the same using a second instance of your browser. You'll find that the two browser instances track items added to the shopping cart independently. Why? Because each represents a separate session and is therefore assigned its own session (and own session state) on the server.

Inside Congo.com

Congo.com's source code, shown in Figure 9-14, is remarkably compact considering the amount of functionality it provides. If you don't believe me, try coding the application as an ISAPI DLL. You'll see what I mean.

The action begins in Global.asax. Each time a new user requests a page from the site, ASP.NET creates a session for that user and calls Global.asax's *Session_Start* handler. *Session_Start* creates a new *ShoppingCart* object to serve as a container for the user's selections and stores a reference to it in session state, keying it with the name "MyShoppingCart":

```
Session["MyShoppingCart"] = new ShoppingCart ();
```

When the user calls up Congo.aspx and clicks an Add to Cart button, Congo.aspx's *OnItemCommand* method is called on the server. *OnItemCommand* retrieves the product ID, title, and price of the corresponding book from the *DataGrid* and encapsulates them in a *BookOrder* object:

```
BookOrder order = new BookOrder (e.Item.Cells[0].Text,
    e.Item.Cells[1].Text, Convert.ToDecimal
    (e.Item.Cells[2].Text.Substring (1)), 1);
```

OnItemCommand then retrieves the reference to the user's *ShoppingCart* from session state and adds the *BookOrder* to the *ShoppingCart*:

```
ShoppingCart cart = (ShoppingCart) Session["MyShoppingCart"];
if (cart != null)
    cart.AddOrder (order);
```

Congo.aspx's *Page_Load* handler populates the *DataGrid* by binding it to a *DataSet* holding the results of a database query.

When the user clicks the View Cart button at the top of the page, Congo.com redirects the user to ViewCart.aspx with *Response.Redirect*:

```
Response.Redirect ("ViewCart.aspx");
```

ViewCart.aspx declares a *DataGrid* that's similar to the one declared in Congo.aspx. But ViewCart.aspx's *DataGrid* control doesn't bind to a *DataSet* encapsulating the results of a database query; it binds to the *ShoppingCart* object in session state. Here's the code that does the binding:

```
ShoppingCart cart = (ShoppingCart) Session["MyShoppingCart"];
      .
      .
      .
MyDataGrid.DataSource = cart.Orders;
MyDataGrid.DataBind ();
```

Clearly, *ShoppingCart* plays a huge role in Congo.com's operation. Not only does it keep a record of the items the user selected, but it implements an *Orders* property that supports data binding. Where does *ShoppingCart* come from, and what's the magic that enables it to work with data-binding controls?

ShoppingCart is a custom data type defined in Congo.cs. It's accompanied by *BookOrder*, which is also defined in Congo.cs. The *ShoppingCart* class is basically a wrapper around a *Hashtable*. It implements a private field named *_Orders* that holds a *Hashtable* reference, and public methods that enable *BookOrder* objects to be added to the *Hashtable* and removed. It also implements a public property named *Orders* that exposes the *Hashtable*'s *ICollection* interface:

```
public ICollection Orders
{
    get { return _Orders.Values; }
}
```

That's why a *DataGrid* can bind to a *ShoppingCart*: because its *Orders* property exposes the underlying *Hashtable*'s *ICollection* interface. The statement

```
MyDataGrid.DataSource = cart.Orders;
```

does nothing more than put the *Hashtable*'s *ICollection* interface into the hands of the *DataGrid*.

Both *ShoppingCart* and *BookOrder* are tagged with *Serializable* attributes. That's so they can be stored in session state regardless of the session state process model selected. As I said earlier, it's wise to mark types that you intend to store in session state as serializable so that your source code doesn't have to change if the process model changes.

What role does Web.config play in Congo.com's operation? It stores the connection string that Congo.aspx uses to connect to the Pubs database. Storing the connection string in Web.config rather than hardcoding it into Congo.aspx enables it to be changed without modifying any C# code.

Web.config
```
<configuration>
  <appSettings>
    <add key="connectString"
      value="server=localhost;database=pubs;uid=sa;pwd=" />
  </appSettings>
</configuration>
```

Figure 9-14   Congo.com source code.

Global.asax
```
<script language="C#" runat="server">
  void Session_Start ()
  {
      Session["MyShoppingCart"] = new ShoppingCart ();
  }
</script>
```

Congo.aspx
```
<%@ Import Namespace="System.Data" %>
<%@ Import Namespace="System.Data.SqlClient" %>

<html>
  <body>
    <h1>Congo.com</h1>
    <form runat="server">
      <table width="100%" bgcolor="teal">
        <tr>
          <td>
            <asp:Button Text="View Cart" OnClick="OnViewCart"
              RunAt="server" />
          </td>
        </tr>
      </table>
      <br>
```

Congo.aspx   *(continued)*

```
      <center>
        <asp:DataGrid ID="MyDataGrid"
          AutoGenerateColumns="false" CellPadding="2"
          BorderWidth="1" BorderColor="lightgray"
          Font-Name="Verdana" Font-Size="8pt"
          GridLines="vertical" Width="90%"
          OnItemCommand="OnItemCommand" RunAt="server">
          <Columns>
            <asp:BoundColumn HeaderText="Item ID"
              DataField="title_id" />
            <asp:BoundColumn HeaderText="Title"
              DataField="title" />
            <asp:BoundColumn HeaderText="Price"
              DataField="price" DataFormatString="{0:c}"
              HeaderStyle-HorizontalAlign="center"
              ItemStyle-HorizontalAlign="right" />
            <asp:ButtonColumn HeaderText="Action" Text="Add to Cart"
              HeaderStyle-HorizontalAlign="center"
              ItemStyle-HorizontalAlign="center"
              CommandName="AddToCart" />
          </Columns>
          <HeaderStyle BackColor="teal" ForeColor="white"
            Font-Bold="true" />
          <ItemStyle BackColor="white" ForeColor="darkblue" />
          <AlternatingItemStyle BackColor="beige"
            ForeColor="darkblue" />
        </asp:DataGrid>
    </center>
    </form>
  </body>
</html>

<script language="C#" runat="server">
  void Page_Load (Object sender, EventArgs e)
  {
      if (!IsPostBack) {
          string ConnectString =
              ConfigurationSettings.AppSettings["connectString"];
          SqlDataAdapter adapter = new SqlDataAdapter
              ("select * from titles where price != 0", ConnectString);
          DataSet ds = new DataSet ();
          adapter.Fill (ds);
          MyDataGrid.DataSource = ds;
          MyDataGrid.DataBind ();
      }
  }

  void OnItemCommand (Object sender, DataGridCommandEventArgs e)
  {
```

```
        if (e.CommandName == "AddToCart") {
            BookOrder order = new BookOrder (e.Item.Cells[0].Text,
                e.Item.Cells[1].Text, Convert.ToDecimal
                (e.Item.Cells[2].Text.Substring (1)), 1);
            ShoppingCart cart = (ShoppingCart) Session["MyShoppingCart"];
            if (cart != null)
                cart.AddOrder (order);
        }
    }

    void OnViewCart (Object sender, EventArgs e)
    {
        Response.Redirect ("ViewCart.aspx");
    }
</script>
```

ViewCart.aspx

```
<html>
  <body>
    <h1>Shopping Cart</h1>
    <form runat="server">
      <table width="100%" bgcolor="teal">
        <tr>
          <td>
            <asp:Button Text="Return to Shopping" OnClick="OnShop"
              RunAt="server" />
          </td>
        </tr>
      </table>
      <br>
      <center>
        <asp:DataGrid ID="MyDataGrid"
          AutoGenerateColumns="false" CellPadding="2"
          BorderWidth="1" BorderColor="lightgray"
          Font-Name="Verdana" Font-Size="8pt"
          GridLines="vertical" Width="90%"
          OnItemCommand="OnItemCommand" RunAt="server">
          <Columns>
            <asp:BoundColumn HeaderText="Item ID"
              DataField="ItemID" />
            <asp:BoundColumn HeaderText="Title"
              DataField="Title" />
            <asp:BoundColumn HeaderText="Price"
              DataField="Price" DataFormatString="{0:c}"
              HeaderStyle-HorizontalAlign="center"
              ItemStyle-HorizontalAlign="right" />
            <asp:BoundColumn HeaderText="Quantity"
              DataField="Quantity"
```

(continued)

ViewCart.aspx *(continued)*

```
                    HeaderStyle-HorizontalAlign="center"
                    ItemStyle-HorizontalAlign="center" />
                <asp:ButtonColumn HeaderText="Action" Text="Remove"
                    HeaderStyle-HorizontalAlign="center"
                    ItemStyle-HorizontalAlign="center"
                    CommandName="RemoveFromCart" />
            </Columns>
            <HeaderStyle BackColor="teal" ForeColor="white"
                Font-Bold="true" />
            <ItemStyle BackColor="white" ForeColor="darkblue" />
            <AlternatingItemStyle BackColor="beige"
                ForeColor="darkblue" />
        </asp:DataGrid>
      </center>
      <h3><asp:Label ID= "Total" RunAt="server" /></h3>
    </form>
  </body>
</html>

<script language="C#" runat="server">
  void Page_Load (Object sender, EventArgs e)
  {
      ShoppingCart cart = (ShoppingCart) Session["MyShoppingCart"];
      if (cart != null) {
          MyDataGrid.DataSource = cart.Orders;
          MyDataGrid.DataBind ();
          Total.Text = String.Format ("Total Cost: {0:c}",
              cart.TotalCost);
      }
  }

  void OnItemCommand (Object sender, DataGridCommandEventArgs e)
  {
      if (e.CommandName == "RemoveFromCart") {
          ShoppingCart cart = (ShoppingCart) Session["MyShoppingCart"];
          if (cart != null) {
              cart.RemoveOrder (e.Item.Cells[0].Text);
              MyDataGrid.DataBind ();
              Total.Text = String.Format ("Total Cost: {0:c}",
                  cart.TotalCost);
          }
      }
  }

  public void OnShop (Object sender, EventArgs e)
  {
      Response.Redirect ("Congo.aspx");
  }
</script>
```

Congo.cs

```csharp
using System;
using System.Collections;

[Serializable]
public class BookOrder
{
    string _ItemID;
    string _Title;
    decimal _Price;
    int _Quantity;

    public string ItemID
    {
        get { return _ItemID; }
        set { _ItemID = value; }
    }

    public string Title
    {
        get { return _Title; }
        set { _Title = value; }
    }

    public decimal Price
    {
        get { return _Price; }
        set { _Price = value; }
    }

    public int Quantity
    {
        get { return _Quantity; }
        set { _Quantity = value; }
    }

    public BookOrder (string ItemID, string Title, decimal Price,
        int Quantity)
    {
        _ItemID = ItemID;
        _Title = Title;
        _Price = Price;
        _Quantity = Quantity;
    }
}

[Serializable]
public class ShoppingCart
```

(continued)

Congo.cs *(continued)*

```csharp
{
    Hashtable _Orders = new Hashtable ();

    public ICollection Orders
    {
        get { return _Orders.Values; }
    }

    public decimal TotalCost
    {
        get
        {
            decimal total = 0;
            foreach (DictionaryEntry entry in _Orders) {
                BookOrder order = (BookOrder) entry.Value;
                total += (order.Price * order.Quantity);
            }
            return total;
        }
    }

    public void AddOrder (BookOrder Order)
    {
        BookOrder order = (BookOrder) _Orders[Order.ItemID];
        if (order != null)
            order.Quantity += Order.Quantity;
        else
            _Orders.Add (Order.ItemID, Order);
    }

    public void RemoveOrder (string ItemID)
    {
        if (_Orders[ItemID] != null)
            _Orders.Remove (ItemID);
    }
}
```

On Your Own

Congo.com uses the default session time-out, which normally equals 20 minutes. To experience the impact of shortened time-out intervals firsthand, add the following statement to Web.config:

```
<sessionState timeout="1" />
```

Call up Congo.aspx, click a few Add to Cart buttons, verify that the items were added to the shopping cart, and return to Congo.aspx. Now wait a couple of minutes and check the shopping cart again. Because the session time-out is a mere 1 minute, the cart should be empty. Finish up by deleting the *sessionState* element from Web.config in order to reset the time-out interval to 20 minutes.

Because it lacks a Web.config file specifying otherwise, Congo.com settles for the default session state process model. To demonstrate the effect of moving session state out of Aspnet_wp.exe, try this simple experiment:

1. Open Congo.aspx in your browser.

2. Add a few items to the shopping cart.

3. Open a command prompt window and restart IIS by typing *iisreset*.

4. View the shopping cart. How many items does it contain?

The answer should be zero because restarting IIS restarts ASP.NET, and restarting ASP.NET shuts down Aspnet_wp.exe. Since that's where session is stored in the in-proc model, restarting IIS destroys all active session state, too. Now do the following:

1. In a command prompt window, type

    ```
    net start aspnet_state
    ```

    to start the ASP.NET state server process running.

2. Add the following statement to the *system.web* section of Web.config:

    ```
    <sessionState
      mode="StateServer"
      stateConnectionString="tcpip=localhost:42424"
    />
    ```

3. Bring up Congo.aspx in your browser and add a few items to your shopping cart.

4. Type *iisreset* again to restart IIS.

5. Check your shopping cart.

This time, the shopping cart's contents should still be there because session state is no longer stored in Aspnet_wp.exe. It's in Aspnet_state.exe, which isn't restarted when ASP.NET is restarted. If you go the extra mile and move the state server process to another machine (or use a SQL Server database on another machine to store session state), you can reboot your entire server without losing session state.

As a final learning exercise, try modifying Congo.aspx to store the *DataSet* that it binds to the *DataGrid* in the application cache. As it stands now, a physical database access is performed every time Congo.aspx is requested. Assuming the contents of the database don't change very often, it would be far more efficient to query the database periodically, store the results in the application cache, and populate the *DataGrid* from the cache. Here's a blueprint for making the change:

1. Add an *Application_Start* method to Global.asax.

2. In *Application_Start*, populate a *DataSet* with a database query and add the *DataSet* to the application cache. Specify that the *DataSet* expires 5 minutes after it's added to the cache, and provide a reference to a callback method that's called when the *DataSet* expires.

3. Code the callback method to reexecute the database query and place a new *DataSet* in the application cache.

4. Modify Congo.aspx's *Page_Load* handler to bind to the *DataSet* stored in the application cache rather than populate a new *DataSet* with the results of a database query.

Once these changes are made, a physical database access will occur only every 5 minutes, no matter how often the page is requested. The performance difference will be negligible if you have only a few users, but as the load on the server increases, the improvement will be more and more noticeable. Caching frequently used data in memory is a tried-and-true means of increasing performance, and ASP.NET's application cache is the perfect tool for the job.

10

ASP.NET Security

An old adage among developers is that building security into software is like paying taxes. You know it's important and you know you must do it sooner or later, but you put it off as long as you can and when you finally do it, you do so only because you have to. You might not go to jail for building insecure applications, but security is no less important because of it. In many applications—Web applications in particular—security isn't a luxury; it's a necessity.

Security is a Big Deal in network applications because by nature those applications are available to (and vulnerable to misuse by and outright attacks from) a larger population of users. When the network an application is deployed on is the Internet, security becomes even more important because the list of potential users grows to about 4 billion. Web security is a broad and complicated subject. Much of the ongoing research in the field has to do with hardening Web servers against attacks. Administrators who work on networks where IIS is deployed are all too aware of the security holes in IIS and of the constant stream of patches and security updates from Redmond. But this chapter isn't about protecting servers from buffer overruns and other hack attacks; it's about using ASP.NET to build secure sites that serve up pages only to authorized users.

Most sites built with ASP.NET fall into one of three categories:

■ Sites whose content is freely available to everyone.

■ Internet sites that serve the general population but require a login before displaying certain pages. eBay is a great example of such a site. Anyone can browse eBay and view the ongoing auctions, but when you place a bid, eBay requires a user name and password. eBay also has a feature named "My eBay" that lets you review the auctions you've bid on. Because My eBay pages are personalized for individual users and because they contain private information such as maximum bid prices, you must log in before viewing them.

■ Intranet sites that expose content to a controlled population of users—a company's employees, for example—who have accounts in a Windows domain (or set of domains). Sometimes these sites support a limited degree of Internet access too, so authorized users can access them from anywhere an Internet connection is available.

Sites that fall into the first category require no special protection beyond what the Web server provides. Sites in the second and third categories require some form of application-level security to identify authorized users and prevent illicit accesses. ASP.NET provides that application-level security. It works in conjunction with IIS and the Windows security subsystem to provide a solid foundation for building secure sites. And ASP.NET builds on what IIS has to offer to make deploying secure sites as easy as possible.

Understanding Web Security

At the application level, Web security is first and foremost about securing pages so that they can't be retrieved by unauthorized users—for example, preventing nonmanagers from viewing pages containing salary data and performance evaluations on the company intranet or preventing other people from viewing your My eBay pages. At a slightly deeper level, you might want to know who requested a page so that you can personalize it for that individual. Either form of protection requires two overt actions on the part of the application:

■ Identify the originator of each request

■ Define rules that govern who can access which pages

A Web server identifies callers using a mechanism known as *authentication*. Once a caller is identified, *authorization* determines which pages that caller is allowed to view. ASP.NET supports a variety of authentication and authorization models. Understanding the options that are available and how they interrelate is an important first step in designing a site that restricts access to some or all of its resources or that personalizes content for individual users.

Authentication

Authentication enables the recipient of a request to ascertain the caller's identity. The caller might claim to be Bob, but you don't know he's Bob unless you authenticate him. ASP.NET supports three types of authentication:

■   Windows authentication

■   Passport authentication

■   Forms authentication

When Windows authentication is selected, ASP.NET looks to IIS for help. IIS does the hard part by authenticating the caller. Then it makes the caller's identity available to ASP.NET. Let's say Windows authentication is enabled and Bob requests an ASPX file. IIS authenticates Bob and forwards the request to ASP.NET along with an access token identifying Bob. ASP.NET uses the token to make sure Bob has permission to retrieve the page he requested. ASP.NET also makes the token available to the application that handles the request so that at its discretion, the application can impersonate Bob—that is, temporarily assume Bob's identity—to prevent code executed within the request from accessing resources that Bob lacks permission to access.

For Web applications, Windows authentication is typically used in the following scenarios:

■   Your application is deployed on a company's intranet and everyone who uses it has an account that they can use to log in and access network resources.

■   Your application is primarily intended for use on a company intranet, but you'd also like employees to be able to log in and use the application remotely—that is, from outside the firewall.

The overarching goal of Windows authentication is to map incoming requests to user accounts on your Web server (or in the Web server's domain). In addition to preventing users who lack the proper login credentials from accessing parts of your site that require authenticated access, Windows authentication lets you use the operating system's built-in security mechanisms to protect files and other resources from unauthorized access by authenticated users.

Passport authentication relies on Microsoft Passport to authenticate users. Passport is a Web service that serves as a front end to a massive database of user names and passwords maintained by Microsoft. Users who register with Passport can be authenticated anywhere on the Internet by applications that present login credentials to Passport. If Passport determines that the credentials are valid, it returns an authentication ticket that the application can encode in a cookie to prevent the user from having to log in time and time again. Further information about Passport can be found in the Passport SDK, which you can download for no charge from Microsoft's Web site.

Forms authentication relies on login forms in Web pages to authenticate users. Figure 10-1 shows an example of forms authentication in action on eBay. You can surf most of eBay's site without logging in, but to bid on an item or go to My eBay, you have to enter a user name and password to let eBay know who you are. Windows authentication isn't very practical in this scenario because eBay doesn't want to assign each of its millions of users a Windows account on its servers. Forms authentication fits the bill nicely because it doesn't require users to have Windows accounts. It's perfect for Internet sites designed to serve the general population but that have to know who a user is before allowing him or her access to certain pages. Forms authentication is as old as the Web, but ASP.NET makes it incredibly easy. You'll see what I mean later in this chapter.

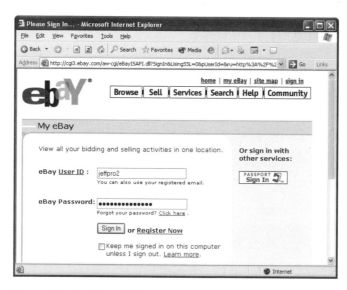

Figure 10-1　eBay login form.

You tell ASP.NET what type of authentication, if any, to use through Web.config files. The following Web.config file enables forms authentication for the corresponding application:

```
<configuration>
  <system.web>
    <authentication mode="Forms" />
  </system.web>
</configuration>
```

Other valid *mode* values include None, Windows, and Passport. The default, defined in Machine.config, is Windows. The authentication mode is an application-wide setting that can be set only in the application root and can't be overridden in subordinate Web.config files. You can't use Windows authentication in one part of an application and forms authentication in another.

Authorization

Authentication is an important element of Web security—indeed, of network security in general—because it establishes trust. You can't trust a user if you don't know who he or she is.

Authorization is the other half of the security equation. Once you know who a user is, authorization determines what resources that person can access. On a company intranet, for example, you might want to prevent rank-and-file employees from accessing files and directories containing payroll data. That's what authorization is for. ASP.NET supports two forms of authorization:

■   ACL (access control list) authorization, also known as *file authorization*

■   URL authorization

ACL authorization is based on file system permissions. Most Web servers that run IIS and ASP.NET use the NTFS file system. NTFS uses ACLs to protect file system resources—that is, files and directories. It's trivial, for example, to tag a file with an ACL that permits only system administrators to read it. You simply pop up the file's property sheet, go to the Security page, remove the security principals (users and groups) that are currently listed, and add administrators. If you don't want Bob to view a particular ASPX file, you can deny Bob read access to the file in an ACL and Bob will be greeted with an access denied error when he tries to view the page. Because ACL checks are performed against access tokens representing Windows security principals, ACL authorization is typically used in scenarios in which Windows authentication is used too.

URL authorization works differently. Rather than rely on NTFS permissions to protect resources, it relies on configuration directives in Web.config files. URL authorization is wholly a function of ASP.NET and does not require the complicity of IIS. It's most often used with forms authentication, but it can be used with other authentication types as well.

IIS Security

IIS is a Web server. Its primary job is to accept connections from remote clients and respond to HTTP requests arriving through those connections. Most of the requests are HTTP GET and POST commands requesting HTML files, JPEG files, ASPX files, and other file system resources. Obviously, you don't want someone who connects to your Web server to be able to retrieve just any file that resides there. IIS protects a server's content in four ways:

- Web applications are deployed in virtual directories that are URL-addressable on the server. Remote clients can't arbitrarily grab files outside virtual directories and their subdirectories.

- IIS assigns every request an access token representing a Windows security principal. The access token enables the operating system to perform ACL checks on resources targeted by the request. If the request runs as Bob and Bob isn't allowed to read Hello.html, the request will fail when it attempts to read Hello.html. In addition, IIS makes Bob's access token available to ASP.NET so that ASP.NET can perform access checks of its own.

- IIS supports IP address and domain name restrictions, enabling requests to be granted and denied based on the IP address or domain of the requestor.

- IIS supports encrypted HTTP connections using the Secure Sockets Layer (SSL) family of protocols. SSL doesn't protect resources on the server per se, but it does prevent eavesdropping on conversations between Web servers and remote clients.

All of these protection mechanisms are important to ASP.NET programmers, but item number 2 merits special consideration because ACL checks are entirely dependent upon the identity assigned to a request, and when Windows authentication is the chosen form of authentication, ASP.NET works closely with IIS to resolve issues involving identity.

IIS runs in a process named Inetinfo.exe. Inetinfo.exe typically runs using the identity of the built-in SYSTEM account, which is highly privileged on the host machine. Requests forwarded to ASP.NET by IIS don't run as SYSTEM, however. They're assigned the identity of a specific user. Which user depends on the configuration of the requested resource.

Through the IIS configuration manager found under Administrative Tools, IIS permits authentication control to be applied to individual files and directories. A given file or directory can be configured to allow anonymous access (access by unauthenticated users), authenticated access, or both. Let's say a request comes in for a file that allows anonymous access. By default, the request executes as IUSR_*machinename*, where *machinename* is the Web server's machine name. IUSR_*machinename* is a special account that's created when IIS is installed. You can use the IIS configuration manager to map anonymous requests to other accounts, but assuming you don't change the defaults, requests from anonymous users are tagged with IUSR_*machinename*'s access token. It follows that Web pages intended for anonymous users should not be tagged with ACLs that deny access to IUSR_*machinename*.

If, on the other hand, the requested file requires authenticated access, IIS assigns the request the identity of the account whose credentials the requestor supplies. If the user is Bob and can prove as much to IIS, then the request is tagged with Bob's access token.

How does IIS ascertain a requestor's identity for authenticated accesses? How, for example, does it know that Bob is Bob? It depends on the type of authentication used. IIS supports four different forms of authentication. As far as ASP.NET is concerned, all four fall under the category of Windows authentication:

- Basic authentication

- Digest authentication

- Integrated Windows authentication

- SSL client certificates

Basic and digest authentication rely on user names and passwords to authenticate users. When the client is a browser, the browser prompts the user for a user name and password and transmits them to the Web server. Basic and digest authentication work well over the Internet because they piggyback on HTTP. Integrated Windows authentication uses Windows login credentials to authenticate users. It's ill-suited to general Internet use, in part because both client and server must support Windows security protocols, and also because the client must validate against a domain controller that it can't get to through a firewall. SSL client certificates are also limited primarily to intranet use because they require clients to be outfitted with digital certificates.

ASP.NET Security

Figure 10-2 diagrams the relationship between IIS and ASP.NET. When IIS receives a request for a file registered to ASP.NET (for example, an ASPX file), it hands off the request to an ISAPI DLL named Aspnet_isapi.dll. Aspnet_isapi.dll runs in the same process as IIS—that is, inside Inetinfo.exe. ASP.NET applications run in a separate process named Aspnet_wp.exe. Aspnet_isapi.dll forwards requests to Aspnet_wp.exe using a named pipe. When the request reaches the worker process, it is assigned to a specific application executing in a specific application domain. Once inside an application domain, the request travels through ASP.NET's *HTTP pipeline*, where it is examined by various HTTP modules and ultimately processed by the HTTP handler that corresponds to the resource type requested. Machine.config contains the master list that maps file types to HTTP handlers.

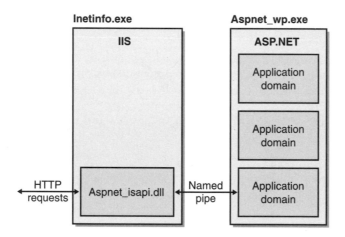

Figure 10-2 The relationship between IIS and ASP.NET.

The architecture shown in Figure 10-2 changes somewhat when ASP.NET is paired with IIS 6.0. Slated for release in 2002, IIS 6.0 features a more robust security model that gives IIS administrators the ability to segregate applications into surrogate processes that are very much like Aspnet_wp.exe. In IIS 6.0, there is no Aspnet_wp.exe; instead, IIS provides the worker process. At the time of this writing, Microsoft planned to connect Inetinfo.exe to worker processes using local procedures calls (LPCs) rather than named pipes.

What does all this have to do with security? When Aspnet_isapi.dll forwards an HTTP request to Aspnet_wp.exe, it also forwards the access token that it obtained from IIS. That access token is typically one of the following:

■ An IUSR_*machinename* token representing an unauthenticated user

■ A token representing an authenticated security principal (for example, Bob)

Before processing the request by sending it through the targeted application's HTTP pipeline, Aspnet_wp.exe does the following:

- It performs an ACL check on the requested resource using the access token presented to it. If, for example, the request is a GET command asking for Foo.aspx, the access token represents Bob, and Foo.aspx has an ACL that denies read permission to Bob, then ASP.NET fails the request with an access denied error. Significantly, ASP.NET performs this ACL check *regardless of whether impersonation is enabled* in ASP.NET.

- It makes the access token available to the application that handles the request so that, *if desired*, the application can impersonate the caller and protect resources guarded by ACLs from code executed during the request.

The importance of these actions cannot be overstated. The ACL check that ASP.NET performs before processing the request means that you can deny Bob access to an ASPX file simply by tagging that file with an ACL that denies Bob read access. The fact that ASP.NET makes the caller's access token available for impersonation purposes means you, the developer, have some latitude in deciding which identity to use when processing the request. The right choice depends on what the application is designed to do and how it's designed to do it. Here's some background to enrich your understanding.

By default, Aspnet_wp.exe runs as ASPNET, a special account that's set up when ASP.NET is installed. ASPNET is a member of the Users group, so it's privileged enough to perform most of the actions a legitimate application might want to perform, but it is restricted enough to prevent certain kinds of attacks. Unless you specify otherwise, requests executed by ASP.NET use Aspnet_wp.exe's identity. Therefore, by default, requests run as ASPNET. Among other things, this means that, barring configuration changes, an ASP.NET application can't perform certain actions, such as modifying entries in the HKEY_LOCAL_MACHINE section of the registry.

The other option is to execute the request using the access token provided by IIS, a technique known as *impersonation*. Impersonation is enabled by including the following statement in the *system.web* section of a top-level Web.config file or modifying the *identity* element already present in Machine.config:

```
<identity impersonate="true" />
```

If IIS assigns a request the identity IUSR_machinename, impersonation won't buy you much because IUSR_machinename is a weak account that enjoys few privileges on the host machine. But if Windows authentication is enabled and IIS presents ASP.NET with a token representing the actual requestor, impersonation ensures that the application can't do anything on the Web server that the requestor isn't allowed to do.

To further complicate matters, Aspnet_wp.exe can be configured to run as a principal other than ASPNET. Suppose you write an ASP.NET application that must have wider-ranging permissions than those afforded ASPNET—for example, the freedom to write to any part of the registry. You can configure Aspnet_wp.exe to run as SYSTEM by changing the statement

```
<processModel userName="machine" ... />
```

in Machine.config to read

```
<processModel userName="SYSTEM" ... />
```

This change enables your application to do almost anything it wants on the host machine, but it also makes ASP.NET less resistant to attacks. SYSTEM was the default when ASP.NET was in beta, but that was changed shortly before the product shipped.

Another possible complication arises from the fact that in IIS 6.0, ASP.NET requests will default to Network Service rather than ASPNET. If you use ACLs to allow access to the ASPNET account while denying access to other security principals and find that requests mysteriously fail with access denied errors after you install IIS 6.0, modify your ACLs to allow access to Network Service rather than ASPNET.

Clearly, the identities assigned to the ASP.NET worker process and to the requests that it executes play crucial roles in determining how successful an application is in carrying out its appointed mission. If your head is spinning right now trying to make sense of it all, don't fret; ASP.NET security will be far easier to grasp once you've experienced it first-hand. In the meantime, here are some guidelines to help you sort through the options and figure out which of them really matter for a given deployment scenario:

- If your application requires no special protection—that is, if all of its pages can be freely browsed by anyone and none are personalized for individual users—you needn't bother with application-level security. Just grant Everyone access to the application's files and be done with it.

- If you're building an intranet application or any application for which permissions are based on mapping incoming requests to Windows accounts on your server, you'll probably use Windows authentication and ACL authorization. In that case, you'll use operating system ACLs to restrict access to pages that aren't intended for everyone. You may or may not enable impersonation, depending on the needs of the application.

■   If you're building an Internet application that serves the general public but want to secure access to certain pages, you'll most likely use forms authentication and URL authorization. In that case, you'll leave impersonation disabled and rely on credentials entered in login forms as the basis for authorizations. Many of the aforementioned issues regarding IIS and access tokens fall by the wayside in this scenario because you grant Everyone access to the application's files and rely on URL authorizations in Web.config to protect them.

A final thought to keep in mind is that if you use ACLs to limit access to directories in an ASP.NET application, *always* grant the ASPNET account—or whatever account Aspnet_wp.exe runs as—read access to them. Otherwise, ASP.NET itself will be unable to retrieve files from the directories and you'll experience all kinds of access denied errors that you probably didn't expect.

Windows Authentication

Windows authentication is one of the options that ASP.NET gives you for identifying callers. Because Windows authentication maps incoming requests to accounts on the Web server or in the Web server's domain, you don't use it to generically expose content to all comers over the Internet. Instead, you use it to serve content to a well-defined populace—a populace that you control through Windows user accounts. Windows authentication on the front end is typically paired with ACL authorization on the back end to control access to the resources that your application exposes. But it works with URL authorization, too.

Recall that Windows authentication comes in four forms: basic, digest, integrated, and certificate. All four forms map incoming requests to accounts on your network, but each does so in a different way. The next several sections describe the inner workings of basic, digest, and integrated Windows authentication and the user experiences that they convey. After that, you'll put Windows authentication to work in a real ASP.NET application.

Basic Authentication

Basic authentication is an HTTP standard. It's documented in RFC 2617, which you can read online at *ftp://ftp.isi.edu/in-notes/rfc2617.txt*. Basic authentication transmits a user name and password in each request. IIS maps the user name and password to an account on the Web server, producing an access token that can be used to perform ACL-based security checks.

It sounds simple, and it is. To demonstrate how basic authentication works, suppose that your company deploys a series of Web pages containing information that only employees should be able to see. The IT staff places the files in a virtual directory on your Web server and configures IIS to disallow anonymous access to that directory and to require basic authentication. The first time you attempt to retrieve a page from that directory, the Web server returns a 401 status code indicating that authentication is required. It also includes in the response a *WWW-Authenticate* header identifying the type (or types) of authentication that it accepts. (The details differ slightly when a proxy server is involved, but the principle is valid nonetheless.) Here's a portion of a response returned by IIS 5.0 indicating that access to the requested resource requires basic authentication:

```
HTTP/1.1 401 Access Denied
Server: Microsoft IIS-5.0
        .
        .
        .
WWW-Authenticate: Basic realm="jupiter"
```

Your browser responds by popping up a dialog box asking for a user name and password (Figure 10-3). It then concatenates the user name and password to a string that identifies the authentication type, base-64-encodes the result, and transmits it to the browser in the *Authorization* header of an HTTP request. Here's the *Authorization* header transmitted by Internet Explorer 6.0 following a login with the user name "Jeff" and the password "imbatman":

```
Authorization: Basic SmVmZjppbWJhdG1hbg==
```

And here are the contents of the base-64-encoded portion of the header after decoding:

```
Jeff:imbatman
```

To prevent you from having to log in again and again, the browser includes the same *Authorization* header in future requests to the same realm. A *realm* is simply a logical security space that encompasses all or part of a Web site.

Figure 10-3   User name and password dialog displayed by Internet Explorer 6.0.

All authentication mechanisms have pros and cons. Here's what's good about basic authentication:

■ It works with virtually all browsers.

■ It provides an easily used and understood means to solicit user names and passwords.

■ It works well with firewalls.

And here's what's bad:

■ Basic authentication transmits user names and passwords in clear text. If used over an unencrypted channel, nothing prevents requests from being intercepted and used to gain access to your server (or other servers on which the caller's credentials are valid).

■ Some users consider pop-up user name and password dialogs intrusive.

If you use basic authentication and the lines to your Web server aren't physically secured, be sure you use it over HTTPS, not HTTP. Otherwise, you'll secure access to honest (or technically unsophisticated) users but leave yourself vulnerable to attacks by others.

Digest Authentication

Digest authentication is similar to basic authentication. When you attempt to access a resource guarded by digest authentication, the browser solicits a user name and password by popping up a dialog box. The Web server uses the credentials that you enter to assign an identity to the request. The big difference between basic and digest authentication is that digest doesn't transmit clear-text passwords. Instead, it passes an authentication token that is cryptographically secure. As a result, you can use it over unencrypted channels without fear of compromising your Web server.

The inner workings of digest authentication are documented in RFC 2617 (*ftp://ftp.isi.edu/in-notes/rfc2617.txt*). When the client first requests a resource guarded by digest authentication, the server returns a 401 error and includes a "nonce"—a string of 1s and 0s—in a *WWW-Authenticate* header. The browser responds by prompting for a user name and password. It then transmits the user name back to the server, along with a hash or "digest" computed from the combined user name, password, and nonce. The server authenticates the request by performing its own hash on the user name, password, and nonce. The password the server uses doesn't come from the client; it comes from the server itself (or from a connected server). If the hashes match, the user is authenticated. Significantly, digest authentication never requires a plain-text password to be transmitted over an HTTP connection. It's also compatible with proxy servers.

Digest authentication offers the following advantages:

■   Like basic authentication, it provides an easily understood means for identifying callers, and it works with firewalls.

■   It's far more secure over ordinary HTTP than basic authentication.

But it has disadvantages, too:

■   Digest authentication requires a modern browser that supports digest authentication. For Internet Explorer users, Internet Explorer 5.0 or later is required.

■   Digest authentication requires passwords to be stored in plain text (or in a reversible encrypted form that can be converted to plain text). This is contrary to the normal Windows security model, which stores one-way password hashes in lieu of plain-text or encrypted passwords to protect the passwords if the server is compromised.

■   Like basic authentication, digest authentication uses pop-up dialog boxes to prompt for user names and passwords.

Because of these restrictions, and because digest authentication doesn't support delegation (the ability to make a call from one machine to another and have the call execute as the caller on the remote machine) on Windows 2000 servers, digest authentication is not widely used.

Integrated Windows Authentication

Integrated Windows authentication uses Windows login credentials to authenticate users. Rather than prompt a user for a user name and password and transmit them over HTTP, a browser asked to identify the user through integrated Windows authentication carries on a conversation with the Web server and identifies the user by using that person's login identity on the client. In other words, if Bob logs in to his Windows PC, starts Internet Explorer, and requests a resource protected by integrated Windows authentication, a handshake ensues between Internet Explorer and the Web server, and Bob's request executes as Bob on the server. Obviously, Bob has to be a valid account on the server (or in a domain that the server can authenticate against) or else access will be denied. Unless configured to do otherwise, the browser asks for a user name and password only if Bob is not a valid account on the server.

Integrated Windows authentication isn't an Internet standard; rather, it is a proprietary authentication protocol that permits Windows login credentials to travel over HTTP. Its inner workings haven't been fully documented by Microsoft, although some details have been published by third parties. The details vary somewhat depending on the security provider being used, which can be either NTLM or Kerberos. In essence, however, the client and server negotiate a trust in a series of exchanges that involve user names, domain names, nonces, and hashes.

Here are the positives regarding integrated Windows authentication:

- It provides a better user experience because it doesn't force users who have already logged in to Windows to provide a user name and password again.

- Integrated Windows authentication is secure, even over unencrypted channels, because plain-text passwords are never transmitted.

And here are the negatives:

- It works in Internet Explorer 2.0 and later but is unsupported by other browsers.

- It's stopped dead in its tracks by firewalls because it relies on ports orthogonal to those that carry HTTP traffic.

Integrated Windows authentication is a great solution for in-house networks that sit behind firewalls and whose browser clients can be carefully controlled—that is, restricted to Internet Explorer. It is poorly suited for general Internet use.

Getting Information About Authenticated Users

ASP.NET exposes information about callers via an *HttpContext* property named *User*. *HttpContext* objects accompany each and every request and are exposed to application code through the *Context* properties of various ASP.NET classes such as *Page*, *WebService*, and *HttpApplication*. Pages (ASPX files) access *User* through *Page.Context.User* or simply *Page.User*.

User's type is *IPrincipal*. *IPrincipal* is an interface defined in the *System.Security.Principal* namespace. It's implemented by the *WindowsPrincipal* and *GenericPrincipal* classes. When a user is authenticated using Windows authentication, *Page.User* refers to a *WindowsPrincipal* object. When a user is authenticated using another form of authentication (for example, forms authentication), *Page.User* refers to a *GenericPrincipal* object. *IPrincipal* has a method named *IsInRole* that you can use to test role memberships. (For users authenticated using Windows authentication, roles correspond to groups. For users authenticated using forms authentication, roles do not exist unless they're programmatically assigned. You'll learn how to use role-based security with forms authentication near the end of this chapter.) *IPrincipal* also has a property named *Identity* that exposes information regarding an authenticated user's identity. *Identity* is actually a reference to an *IIdentity* interface. *IIdentity* has the following members:

Property	Description
AuthenticationType	Reveals which form of authentication was used
IsAuthenticated	Reveals whether the user is authenticated
Name	Reveals an authenticated user's name

All this sounds confusing, but in practice, *User* makes getting information about callers trivially easy. If you want to find out whether a caller is authenticated from code in an ASPX file, do this:

```
if (User.Identity.IsAuthenticated) {
    // The caller is authenticated
}
```

You can also find out whether a caller is authenticated by checking the *Request* object's *IsAuthenticated* property, which under the hood consults *User.Identity.IsAuthenticated*. If you want to know the caller's name (assuming the caller is authenticated), do this:

```
string name = User.Identity.Name;
```

For a user authenticated using Windows authentication, the name is of the form *domainname\username*, where *domainname* is the name of the domain in which the user is registered (or the machine name if the account is a local account instead of a domain account), and *username* is the user's name. For forms authentication, the name is normally the one that the user typed into a login form. One use for the user name is to personalize pages for individual users. The application in the next section demonstrates how.

Windows Authentication in Action

The application shown in Figure 10-6, which I'll refer to as "CorpNet" since it models a simple intranet-type application, uses Windows authentication and ACL authorization to restrict access to some of its pages and to personalize content for individual users. It contains three pages:

- General.aspx, which provides general information about the company

- Salaries.aspx, which lists the salary of the employee who views the page

- Bonuses.aspx, which lists this year's employee bonuses

You'll deploy CorpNet such that anyone in the company can view General.aspx but only selected individuals can view Salaries.aspx and Bonuses.aspx.

Before testing can begin, you need to deploy the application on your Web server and configure it to provide the desired level of security. Here are the steps:

1. Create a directory named Basic somewhere—anywhere—on your Web server.

2. Use the IIS configuration manager to transform Basic into a virtual directory named "Basic."

3. While in the IIS configuration manager, configure Basic to require basic authentication and to disallow anonymous access. How? Right-click Basic in the IIS configuration manager and select Properties from the ensuing context menu. Go to the Directory Security page of the property sheet that pops up and click the Edit button under "Anonymous access and authentication control." In the ensuing dialog box, uncheck "Anonymous access" and check "Basic authentication," as shown in Figure 10-4. OK the changes, and then close the configuration manager.

4. Create two user accounts on your Web server for testing purposes. Name the accounts "Bob" and "Alice." It doesn't matter what passwords you assign, only that Bob and Alice are valid accounts on the server.

5. Copy General.aspx, Salaries.aspx, Bonuses.aspx, Bonuses.xml, and Web.config to the Basic directory.

6. Change the permissions on Salaries.aspx so that only Bob and the ASPNET account are allowed access. At the very least, grant them read permission. Other permissions are optional.

7. Change the permissions on Bonuses.xml (not Bonuses.aspx) to grant access to Everyone but specifically deny access to Alice.

Figure 10-4   Configuring a directory to require basic authentication.

Now give the application a try by performing the following exercises:

1. Type *http://localhost/basic/general.aspx* into your browser's address bar to call up General.aspx. Because the Basic directory requires callers to be authenticated using basic authentication, a dialog box will pop up. Enter Bob's user name and password. When General.aspx appears, observe that it knows your login name. (See Figure 10-5.)

2. Restart your browser and repeat the previous exercise, but this time enter Alice's user name and password rather than Bob's. General.aspx still displays just fine because both Bob and Alice have permission to access it.

Figure 10-5   General.aspx showing the caller's identity.

3. Without restarting your browser, call up Salaries.aspx. Because you're logged in as Alice and Alice isn't allowed to read Salaries.aspx, the server reports that access is denied. (If you're using Internet Explorer, you may have to type Alice's user name and password a few times before being told access is denied.)

4. Restart your browser and try again to call up Salaries.aspx. This time, log in as Bob when prompted for a user name and password. Because Bob is permitted to read Salaries.aspx, the page comes up and Bob's salary appears. Salaries.aspx is capable of displaying salaries for other employees, too, but it uses the caller's login name to personalize the information that it displays.

5. Without restarting your browser, call up Bonuses.aspx. A list of employee bonuses appears.

6. Restart your browser and call up Bonuses.aspx again. This time, log in as Alice. What do you think will happen? Anyone can access Bonuses.aspx, but Bonuses.aspx calls *DataSet.ReadXml* to read Bonuses.xml, and Alice isn't permitted to read Bonuses.xml. You're logged in as Alice. Will Bonuses.aspx report an error?

As you can see, Bonuses.aspx comes up just fine and even shows a list of bonuses. Clearly Bonuses.aspx succeeded in reading Bonuses.xml. How can that happen if Alice lacks permission to read Bonuses.xml? The answer is simple, but also subtle.

IIS tagged the request with Alice's access token, and it passed that access token to ASP.NET. ASP.NET knows that the caller is Alice and won't allow Alice to retrieve an ASPX file (or any other ASP.NET file type) for which Alice lacks access permission. But because Web.config lacks a statement enabling impersonation, any code executed inside the request executes as ASPNET, not as Alice. ASPNET has permission to read Bonuses.xml, so Alice wasn't prevented from viewing employee bonuses.

I purposely laid this trap for you to drive home an important point. ASP.NET performs ACL checks on ASPX files and other ASP.NET file types using the caller's identity, regardless of whether impersonation is enabled. That means you can prevent any caller from retrieving an ASPX file simply by denying that caller permission to read the file. However, if a caller pulls up an ASPX file and the ASPX file programmatically reads another file, you must tell ASP.NET to impersonate the caller if you want the read to be subject to an ACL check using the caller's identity.

You can prevent Alice from seeing the data in Bonuses.xml by modifying Web.config to read as follows. The new line is highlighted in bold:

```
<configuration>
  <system.web>
    <authentication mode="Windows" />
    <identity impersonate="true" />
  </system.web>
</configuration>
```

After making the change to Web.config, restart your browser, log in as Alice, and try to view Bonuses.aspx again. This time, you're greeted with an error message reporting that an error occurred while processing the page. That message is displayed by the exception handler in Bonuses.aspx's *Page_Load* method, which catches the *XmlException* thrown when *ReadXml* can't read Bonuses.xml. Restart your browser and log in as Bob, however, and you can once again view Bonuses.aspx.

CorpNet demonstrates several important principles that you should keep in mind when writing ASP.NET applications that use Windows authentication:

■ Windows authentication is enabled in ASP.NET by including an <authentication mode="Windows" /> statement in Web.config.

■ ASP.NET applications that use Windows authentication can prevent users from viewing files by using ACLs to deny access to selected security principals.

■ ASP.NET applications that use Windows authentication must enable impersonation if they want resources protected by ACLs to be protected from programmatic accesses by code executed within a request.

■   ASP.NET applications that use Windows authentication can personalize content for individual users by reading user names from
Page.User.Identity.Name.

Remember, too, that directories containing ASPX files and other ASP.NET files
must grant read permission to the account that Aspnet_wp.exe runs as (ASPNET
by default) or else ASP.NET itself can't access resources in those directories. To
prove it, temporarily deny ASPNET permission to read from the Basic directory.
Now even Bob can't view Salaries.aspx.

General.aspx

```
<%@ Page Language="C#" %>

<html>
  <body>
    <h1>Welcome to CorpNet!</h1>
    <hr>
Welcome to the corporate intranet! We don't have a lot to offer
right now, but check back in a few days and we'll have information
regarding the massive layoff that has been the subject of so many
rumors. Do remember, though, that we're watching you all the time.
We even know who you are because you had to provide a user name
and password to see this page. To prove it, your user name is
shown below.<br>
    <h3>
      <%
        if (User.Identity.IsAuthenticated)
          Response.Write (User.Identity.Name);
      %>
    </h3>
  </body>
</html>
```

Figure 10-6   CorpNet source code.

Salaries.aspx

```
<%@ Page Language="C#" %>

<html>
  <body>
    <h1>Salaries</h1>
    <hr>
    <%
```

(continued)

Salaries.aspx *(continued)*

```
        if (!User.Identity.IsAuthenticated)
            Response.Write ("Sorry, but no salary information " +
                "is available for unauthenticated users.");
        else {
            if (User.Identity.Name.IndexOf ("Jeff") != -1)
                Response.Write ("Jeff's salary is $10,000.");
            else if (User.Identity.Name.IndexOf ("John") != -1)
                Response.Write ("John's salary is $20,000.");
            else if (User.Identity.Name.IndexOf ("Bob") != -1)
                Response.Write ("Bob's salary is $30,000.");
            else if (User.Identity.Name.IndexOf ("Alice") != -1)
                Response.Write ("Alice's salary is $40,000.");
            else if (User.Identity.Name.IndexOf ("Mary") != -1)
                Response.Write ("Mary's salary is $50,000.");
            else
                Response.Write ("No salary information is " +
                    "available for " + User.Identity.Name);
        }
    %>
  </body>
</html>
```

Bonuses.aspx

```
<%@ Import Namespace="System.Data" %>

<html>
  <body>
    <asp:DataGrid ID="MyDataGrid" Width="40%" RunAt="server" />
    <asp:Label ID="Output" RunAt="server" />
  </body>
</html>

<script language="C#" runat="server">
  void Page_Load (Object sender, EventArgs e)
  {
      try {
          DataSet ds = new DataSet ();
          ds.ReadXml (Server.MapPath ("Bonuses.xml"));
          MyDataGrid.DataSource = ds;
          MyDataGrid.DataBind ();
      }
      catch (Exception) {
          Output.Text = "An error occurred processing this page.";
      }
  }
</script>
```

Bonuses.xml

```xml
<?xml version="1.0" encoding="UTF-8"?>
<Bonuses>
  <Bonus>
    <Name>Jeff</Name>
    <Amount>1000</Amount>
  </Bonus>
  <Bonus>
    <Name>John</Name>
    <Amount>2000</Amount>
  </Bonus>
  <Bonus>
    <Name>Bob</Name>
    <Amount>3000</Amount>
  </Bonus>
  <Bonus>
    <Name>Alice</Name>
    <Amount>4000</Amount>
  </Bonus>
  <Bonus>
    <Name>Mary</Name>
    <Amount>5000</Amount>
  </Bonus>
</Bonuses>
```

Web.config

```xml
<configuration>
  <system.web>
    <authentication mode="Windows" />
  </system.web>
</configuration>
```

Windows Authentication and URL Authorizations

CorpNet currently uses ACL authorizations to restrict access to its pages. But ASP.NET also supports URL authorizations. To demonstrate, create a subdirectory named Secret in the Basic directory and move Salaries.aspx, Bonuses.aspx, and Bonuses.xml into it. Then place the following Web.config file in the Secret directory (and be sure to replace *domainname* with the appropriate machine name or domain name for the Bob account):

```
<configuration>
  <system.web>
    <authorization>
      <allow users="domainname\Bob" />
      <deny users="*" />
    </authorization>
  </system.web>
</configuration>
```

Log in as Bob and you'll be able to access Salaries.aspx and Bonuses.aspx just fine. But log in as anyone else, and it'll be as if the files don't exist.

The chief drawback to URL authorizations is that they only protect files registered to ASP.NET. You can't use them to protect ordinary HTML files, for example. Another limitation is that URL authorizations are based on stringified names rather than Windows security IDs (SIDs). For these reasons, ACL authorizations are typically used in lieu of URL authorizations when Windows authentication is used too.

Windows Authentication and Role-Based Security

Role-based security is a powerful concept in Web applications. Rather than restrict access to callers based on user names, role-based security restricts access based on "roles"—CEO, manager, developer, clerk, or whatever—that those users belong to. If you modify the permissions on the Secret directory to allow access only to members of a group named Managers, for example, you're exercising role-based security. Only users that belong to that group can call up Salaries.aspx and Bonuses.aspx.

Role-based security can also be applied using URL authorizations. The following Web.config file restricts access to the host directory to members of the Managers group. Behind the scenes, ASP.NET handles the chore of mapping the groups to which the caller belongs to roles named in *allow* and *deny* elements:

```
<configuration>
  <system.web>
    <authorization>
      <allow roles="domainname\Managers" />
      <deny users="*" />
    </authorization>
  </system.web>
</configuration>
```

Role-based security applied through URL authorizations suffers from the same limitations as user-based security applied through URL authorizations and is therefore rarely used outside forms authentication.

Forms Authentication

Forms authentication is one of ASP.NET's coolest new features. Simply put, forms authentication is a security mechanism that authenticates a user by asking him or her to type credentials (typically a user name and a password) into a Web form. Through entries in Web.config, you identify the login page and tell ASP.NET which resources the login page protects. The first time a user attempts to access a protected resource, ASP.NET transparently redirects him or her to your login page. If the login is successful, ASP.NET then issues the user an authentication ticket in the form of a cookie and redirects the user to the page originally requested. The ticket allows that user to revisit protected portions of your site without having to log in again and again. You control the ticket's lifetime, so you decide how long the login is good for.

Forms authentication replaces reams of code in ASP applications that checks (often at the top of every page) to see whether a user has logged in, manually redirects the user to a login page if the answer is negative, and then redirects the user to the page originally requested following a successful login. It's perfect for enacting the kind of authentication featured on sites like eBay, where you have to type in a user name and password before viewing personalized pages or placing bids on auction items. It also plays well on the Internet, where Windows authentication is seldom practical.

A First Look at Forms Authentication

Just how easy is forms authentication? Check out the application in Figure 10-9 and you be the judge. The application's user interface consists of two pages: PublicPage.aspx, which can be viewed by anyone, and ProtectedPage.aspx, which is available only to authenticated users. "Authenticated users" means anyone who has logged in through a third page, LoginPage.aspx, which asks for a user name and a password. Valid user names and passwords are stored in Web.config.

Before you dive into the source code, take the application for a test drive. Here's how:

1.   Copy PublicPage.aspx, LoginPage.aspx, and Web.config (application root) to wwwroot or the virtual directory of your choice.

2.   Create a subdirectory named Secret in the virtual root, and then copy ProtectedPage.aspx and Web.config (Secret subdirectory) to the Secret subdirectory.

3. Call up PublicPage.aspx in your browser. If you copied it to wwwroot, the proper URL is *http://localhost/publicpage.aspx*.

4. Click the View Secret Message button.

5. View Secret Message uses *Response.Redirect* to go to Secret/ProtectedPage.aspx. But because ProtectedPage.aspx is viewable only by authenticated users, ASP.NET displays the login form in LoginPage.aspx (Figure 10-7).

6. Type "Jeff" into the user name field and "imbatman" into the password field.

7. ProtectedPage.aspx appears. Because you're now an authenticated user, you've been issued an authentication ticket that accompanies subsequent requests as a cookie.

8. Go back to PublicPage.aspx.

9. Click the View Secret Message button again.

10. ProtectedPage.aspx appears again, this time without asking you for a user name and password. Why? Because the authentication cookie transmitted with the request identified you to ASP.NET's forms authentication module (which listens in on every request) as an authenticated user and even identified you as "Jeff." Note the personalized greeting on the page (Figure 10-8).

11. Close your browser. Start it again, and then call up PublicPage.aspx.

12. Click View Secret Message once more. You're asked to log in again because the cookie containing your authentication ticket is a session cookie, which means it's destroyed when you close your browser.

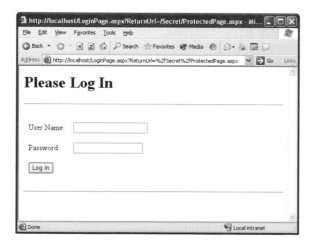

Figure 10-7   Forms authentication login form.

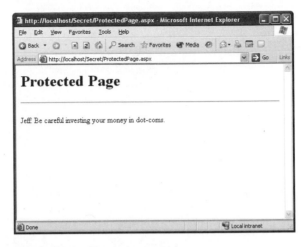

Figure 10-8   The secret message.

What did it take to prevent unauthenticated users from seeing Protect-edPage.aspx and to direct them to our login form when they attempt to call it up? Not a lot, really. The secret lies in Web.config—to be specific, in the two Web.config files that accompany this application. The Web.config file in the application root enables forms authentication and identifies the login page:

```
<authentication mode="Forms">
  <forms loginUrl="LoginPage.aspx">
    .
    .
    .
  </forms>
</authentication>
```

It also contains a *credentials* section listing valid user names and passwords:

```
<credentials passwordFormat="Clear">
  <user name="Jeff" password="imbatman" />
  <user name="John" password="redrover" />
  <user name="Bob" password="mxyzptlk" />
  <user name="Alice" password="nomalice" />
  <user name="Mary" password="contrary" />
</credentials>
```

The Web.config file in the Secret subdirectory plays an equally important role in securing the application. In it, the statements

```
<authorization>
  <deny users="?" />
</authorization>
```

denote a URL authorization. They instruct ASP.NET's URL authorization module (*System.Web.Security.UrlAuthorizationModule*) to deny unauthenticated users access to any ASP.NET files in the host directory. The "?" stands for anonymous users, which is another way of saying unauthenticated users. When someone attempts to view a file in this directory, ASP.NET checks to see whether a valid authentication cookie is attached to the request. If the cookie exists, ASP.NET unencrypts it, validates it to ensure that it hasn't been tampered with, and extracts identity information that it assigns to the current request. (Encryption and validation can be turned off but are enabled by default.) If the cookie doesn't exist, ASP.NET redirects the request to the login page.

The actual authentication—soliciting a user name and password and checking their validity—is performed by LoginPage.aspx. The following statement passes the user name and password that the user entered to the static *System.Web.Security.FormsAuthentication* method named *Authenticate*, which returns true if the user name and password are valid (that is, if they appear in the *credentials* section of Web.config) and false if they're not:

```
if (FormsAuthentication.Authenticate (UserName.Text, Password.Text))
```

If *Authenticate* returns true, the next statement creates an authentication cookie, attaches it to the outgoing response, and redirects the user to the page that he or she originally requested:

```
FormsAuthentication.RedirectFromLoginPage (UserName.Text, false);
```

The second parameter passed to *RedirectFromLoginPage* specifies whether the authentication should be a session cookie (false) or a persistent cookie (true). Many sites that use forms authentication present the user with a check box that lets him or her decide which type of cookie to issue. If you see a check box labeled "Keep me logged in on this site" or something to that effect, checking the box generally issues an authentication cookie whose lifetime is independent of the browser session.

ProtectedPage.aspx is the only ASPX file in the Secret subdirectory, but if there were others, they too would be protected by the login form. Protection is applied on a directory-by-directory basis. Applying two different protection levels to two sets of files requires hosting those files in separate directories. Web.config files in each directory specify exactly how the files are to be protected.

PublicPage.aspx

```
<html>
  <body>
    <h1>Public Page</h1>
    <hr>
    <form runat="server">
      <asp:Button Text="View Secret Message" OnClick="OnViewSecret"
        RunAt="server" />
    </form>
  </body>
</html>

<script language="C#" runat="server">
  void OnViewSecret (Object sender, EventArgs e)
  {
      Response.Redirect ("Secret/ProtectedPage.aspx");
  }
</script>
```

Figure 10-9   Simple forms authentication.

ProtectedPage.aspx

```
<%@ Page Language="C#" %>

<html>
  <body>
    <h1>Protected Page</h1>
    <hr><br>
    <% Response.Write (Context.User.Identity.Name + ": "); %>
    Be careful investing your money in dot-coms.
  </body>
</html>
```

LoginPage.aspx

```
<html>
  <body>
    <h1>Please Log In</h1>
    <hr>
    <form runat="server">
      <table cellpadding="8">
        <tr>
          <td>
            User Name:
          </td>
          <td>
            <asp:TextBox ID="UserName" RunAt="server" />
```

(continued)

LoginPage.aspx *(continued)*

```
            </td>
        </tr>
        <tr>
          <td>
            Password:
          </td>
          <td>
            <asp:TextBox ID="Password" TextMode="password"
              RunAt="server" />
          </td>
        </tr>
        <tr>
          <td>
            <asp:Button Text="Log In" OnClick="OnLogIn"
              RunAt="server" />
          </td>
          <td>
          </td>
        </tr>
      </table>
    </form>
    <hr>
    <h3><asp:Label ID="Output" RunAt="server" /></h3>
  </body>
</html>

<script language="C#" runat="server">
  void OnLogIn (Object sender, EventArgs e)
  {
      if (FormsAuthentication.Authenticate (UserName.Text,
          Password.Text))
          FormsAuthentication.RedirectFromLoginPage (UserName.Text,
              false);
      else
          Output.Text = "Invalid login";
  }
</script>
```

Web.config (Application Root)

```
<configuration>
  <system.web>
    <authentication mode="Forms">
      <forms loginUrl="LoginPage.aspx">
        <credentials passwordFormat="Clear">
          <user name="Jeff" password="imbatman" />
          <user name="John" password="redrover" />
          <user name="Bob" password="mxyzptlk" />
```

```
            <user name="Alice" password="nomalice" />
            <user name="Mary" password="contrary" />
        </credentials>
      </forms>
    </authentication>
  </system.web>
</configuration>
```

Web.config (Secret Subdirectory)
```
<configuration>
  <system.web>
    <authorization>
      <deny users="?" />
    </authorization>
  </system.web>
</configuration>
```

Real-World Forms Authentication

The application in the previous section isn't very realistic for a couple of reasons. First, it's unreasonable to store passwords in clear text. ASP.NET has a fix for that, but I won't even mention it here because it becomes a moot point in light of problem number two—namely, that storing thousands (or hundreds of thousands) of names and passwords in Web.config is completely unrealistic. In the real world, you'd store that information in a database. Storing user names and passwords in a database and still leveraging forms authentication is precisely what this section is about.

Figure 10-11 lists a modified version of the application that stores user names and passwords in a Microsoft SQL Server database named WebLogin. The database's "Users" table contains a list of user names and passwords (Figure 10-10). Only two source code files—LoginPage.aspx and Web.config (the one in the application root)—changed; the others are exactly the same, so they don't appear in the listing. Web.config no longer has a *credentials* section containing user names and passwords. LoginPage.aspx no longer uses *FormsAuthentication.Authenticate* to validate user credentials. Instead, it calls a local method named *CustomAuthenticate*, which uses an SQL query to determine whether the credentials are valid. If the user types "Jeff" into the user name field and "imbatman" into the password field, the query looks like this:

```
select count (*) from users where username = 'Jeff' and
cast (rtrim (password) as varbinary) = cast ('imbatman' as varbinary)
```

This query returns a count of the number of records containing "Jeff" in the "UserName" field and "imbatman" in the "Password" field. A return value of 1 means the credentials are valid. A 0 return means they're invalid because no such record exists in the database.

The purpose of the CAST operators in the query is to make the password comparison case-sensitive. By default, most SQL databases ignore case when performing string comparisons. Casting strings to varbinaries has SQL treat them as binary values rather than strings and is a commonly used trick for making string comparisons case-sensitive. The RTRIM operator applied to the Password field strips trailing spaces from the string. SQL ignores trailing spaces when comparing strings but not when performing binary comparisons. Casting the password to varbinary also prevents spoofing with passwords that are actually SQL commands. (At least I *think* it prevents spoofing; you never know what clever work-arounds evildoers might devise. To be certain, slap *RegularExpressionValidator*s on the *TextBox* controls to reject input containing anything besides letters and numbers. For good form, throw in a couple of *RequireFieldValidator*s too.)

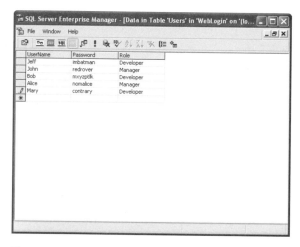

Figure 10-10   The WebLogin database.

This version of LoginPage.aspx has one other feature that the previous version did not: a check box that lets the user decide whether the authentication cookie issued to him or her is temporary or persistent. LoginPage.aspx passes the value of the check box's *Checked* property to *RedirectFromLoginPage*:

```
FormsAuthentication.RedirectFromLoginPage (UserName.Text,
    Persistent.Checked);
```

Checking the box produces a persistent authentication cookie by passing true to *RedirectFromLoginPage*, and leaving the box unchecked produces a temporary (session) authentication cookie by passing false. Check the box before logging in and you'll be able to get back to ProtectedPage.aspx without logging in again, even if you shut down your machine and don't come back until days later.

Before testing the new version of the application, you must create the WebLogin database. The CD included with this book contains a script named WebLogin.sql that creates it for you. Simply open a command prompt window, go to the directory where WebLogin.sql is stored, and type

```
osql -U sa -P -i weblogin.sql
```

The installation script will work, of course, only if Microsoft SQL Server is installed on your PC.

LoginPage.aspx
```
<%@ Import NameSpace="System.Data.SqlClient" %>

<html>
  <body>
    <h1>Please Log In</h1>
    <hr>
    <form runat="server">
      <table cellpadding="8">
        <tr>
          <td>
            User Name:
          </td>
          <td>
            <asp:TextBox ID="UserName" RunAt="server" />
          </td>
        </tr>
        <tr>
          <td>
            Password:
          </td>
          <td>
```

Figure 10-11   Forms authentication utilizing user names and passwords stored in a database.

LoginPage.aspx   *(continued)*

```
            <asp:TextBox ID="Password" TextMode="password"
              RunAt="server" />
          </td>
        </tr>
        <tr>
          <td>
            <asp:Button Text="Log In" OnClick="OnLogIn"
              RunAt="server" />
          </td>
          <td>
            <asp:CheckBox Text="Keep me signed in" ID="Persistent"
              RunAt="server" />
          </td>
        </tr>
      </table>
    </form>
    <hr>
    <h3><asp:Label ID="Output" RunAt="server" /></h3>
  </body>
</html>

<script language="C#" runat="server">
  void OnLogIn (Object sender, EventArgs e)
  {
      if (CustomAuthenticate (UserName.Text, Password.Text))
          FormsAuthentication.RedirectFromLoginPage (UserName.Text,
              Persistent.Checked);
      else
          Output.Text = "Invalid login";
  }

  bool CustomAuthenticate (string username, string password)
  {
      SqlConnection connection = new SqlConnection
          ("server=localhost;database=weblogin;uid=sa;pwd=");

      try {
          connection.Open ();

          StringBuilder builder = new StringBuilder ();
          builder.Append ("select count (*) from users " +
              "where username = \'");
          builder.Append (username);
          builder.Append ("\' and cast (rtrim (password) as " +
              "varbinary) = cast (\'");
          builder.Append (password);
          builder.Append ("\' as varbinary)");
```

```
        SqlCommand command = new SqlCommand (builder.ToString (),
            connection);

        int count = (int) command.ExecuteScalar ();
        return (count > 0);
    }
    catch (SqlException) {
        return false;
    }
    finally {
        connection.Close ();
    }
  }
</script>
```

Web.config (Application Root)
```
<configuration>
  <system.web>
    <authentication mode="Forms">
      <forms loginUrl="LoginPage.aspx" />
    </authentication>
  </system.web>
</configuration>
```

Authentication Cookie Lifetime

When you call *RedirectFromLoginPage* and pass false in the second parameter, ASP.NET issues a session authentication cookie containing a time stamp that limits the cookie's validity to 30 minutes, even if the browser session extends longer than that. The time-out value of 30 minutes is controlled by the *timeout* attribute attached to the <forms> element in Machine.config:

```
<forms ... timeout="30">
```

You can change the time-out by editing Machine.config or including a *timeout* attribute in a local Web.config file. The following Web.config file enables forms authentication and extends the validity of the authentication cookie to 7 days (10,080 minutes):

```
<configuration>
  <system.web>
    <authentication mode="Forms">
      <forms loginUrl="/LoginPage.aspx" timeout="10080" />
    </authentication>
  </system.web>
</configuration>
```

When a session time-out cookie is returned to ASP.NET in a subsequent request, ASP.NET automatically renews it (updates the time stamp) if the cookie's lifetime is more than half over. Thus, even the default time-out of 30 minutes enables you to access a protected page indefinitely as long as the browser remains open and you submit the cookie to ASP.NET at least once every 15 minutes.

If the user checks the "Keep me signed in" box in the login page of the application in the previous section, LoginPage.aspx issues a persistent authentication cookie by passing true to *RedirectFromLoginPage*. Here's that statement again:

```
FormsAuthentication.RedirectFromLoginPage (UserName.Text,
    Persistent.Checked);
```

One drawback to issuing a persistent authentication cookie this way is that the cookie remains valid for 50 years. Furthermore, there is no configuration setting that lets you change this. The *timeout* attribute has no effect on a persistent authentication cookie. Suppose you'd like to issue a persistent authentication cookie but you'd also like to limit its lifetime to, say, 7 days. How do you go about it?

The solution is to programmatically modify the authentication cookie before returning it in the response. Here's a modified version of *OnLogIn* (the handler that's called when the user clicks LoginPage.aspx's Log In button) that sets the authentication cookie's lifetime to 7 days—provided, of course, the cookie is a persistent cookie:

```
void OnLogIn (Object sender, EventArgs e)
{
    if (CustomAuthenticate (UserName.Text, Password.Text)) {
        string url = FormsAuthentication.GetRedirectUrl
            (UserName.Text, Persistent.Checked);

        FormsAuthentication.SetAuthCookie (UserName.Text,
            Persistent.Checked);

        if (Persistent.Checked) {
            HttpCookie cookie =
                Response.Cookies[FormsAuthentication.FormsCookieName];
            cookie.Expires = DateTime.Now + new TimeSpan (7, 0, 0, 0);
        }

        Response.Redirect (url);
    }
    else
        Output.Text = "Invalid login";
}
```

If *CustomAuthenticate* returns true, indicating that the user entered valid credentials, this version of *OnLogIn* uses *FormsAuthentication.GetRedirectUrl* to grab the URL of the page that the user originally requested. Then it calls *FormsAuthentication.SetAuthCookie* to create an authentication cookie and add it to the cookies going out in the response. Before calling *Response.Redirect* to go to the requested page, however, *OnLogIn* modifies the cookie by retrieving it from the response's *Cookies* collection and setting its *Expires* property to a date 7 days hence. This simple modification ensures that the user will have to go through your login page again after 7 days. Of course, you can set the lifetime to any length you want by modifying the *TimeSpan* value. You'll see this technique used in the chapter's final sample program. But first, there's one more topic we need to cover: role-based security.

Forms Authentication and Role-Based Security

The last sample program demonstrated how to combine forms authentication with user names and passwords stored in a SQL Server database. The next one demonstrates how to use role membership to allow some users to view ProtectedPage.aspx while hiding it from others.

The following statement in the Secret directory's Web.config file prevents unauthenticated users from accessing ASPX files in that directory:

```
<deny users="?" />
```

The only problem with this statement is that it allows any authenticated user to view ProtectedPage.aspx. It's not unrealistic to imagine that in some scenarios, you might want to allow *some* authenticated users to view ProtectedPage.aspx without permitting *all* authenticated users to view it. Suppose John and Alice are managers who should be able to call up ProtectedPage.aspx, but Jeff, Bob, and Mary are mere developers who should not. One way to keep Jeff, Bob, and Mary out is to deny access to all users (users="*") but specifically allow access to John and Alice. Here's a Web.config file that does just that:

```
<configuration>
  <system.web>
    <authorization>
      <allow users="John, Alice" />
      <deny users="*" />
    </authorization>
  </system.web>
</configuration>
```

Another way to do it is to specifically deny access to Jeff, Bob, and Mary:

```
<configuration>
  <system.web>
    <authorization>
      <deny users="Jeff, Bob, Mary" />
      <allow users="*" />
    </authorization>
  </system.web>
</configuration>
```

Be aware that when you use <allow> and <deny> in this manner, the entries are order-sensitive. The statements

```
<deny users="*" />
<allow users="John, Alice" />
```

are not equivalent to

```
<allow users="John, Alice" />
<deny users="*" />
```

because ASP.NET will stop at <deny users="*"> and ignore any statements that appear after it.

These Web.config files work just fine, but they're not very practical for sites that serve large volumes of users. Just imagine what a nightmare it would be to edit multimegabyte Web.config files every time someone enters or leaves your company or gets a promotion. For large sites, roles provide a practical solution to the problem of granting access to some authenticated users without granting access to all of them. And roles work well with forms authentication provided you're willing to write a little code to help out.

Look again at the WebLogin database that serves our site. In addition to storing user names and passwords, the "Users" table has a field named "Role" that stores each user's role membership, if any. John and Alice are assigned manager roles, while Jeff, Bob, and Mary are assigned the role of developer. Is it possible to use these role memberships to grant John and Alice—and anyone else assigned the role of manager—access to ProtectedPage.aspx while keeping others away? You bet. All it requires is two simple modifications to the code you've already written.

The first step is the easy one. It involves editing the Secret directory's Web.config file to grant access to managers or deny access to developers. Here's a Web.config file that does the former:

```
<configuration>
  <system.web>
    <authorization>
      <allow roles="Manager" />
      <deny users="*" />
    </authorization>
  </system.web>
</configuration>
```

The *roles* attribute takes the place of the *users* attribute and grants or denies access not to individual users, but to groups of users based on the role or roles that they've been assigned.

The second step is more involved. Somehow we have to map the roles stored in the database to user accounts in each and every request so that ASP.NET can determine whether the requestor is a manager or a developer. The best place to do the mapping is in the *AuthenticateRequest* events that fire at the beginning of every request. You can process *AuthenticateRequest* events in a custom HTTP module or in Global.asax. Here's a Global.asax file that layers roles onto forms authentication:

```
<%@ Import Namespace="System.Security.Principal" %>

<script language="C#" runat="server">
  void Application_AuthenticateRequest (Object sender, EventArgs e)
  {
      HttpApplication app = (HttpApplication) sender;
      if (app.Request.IsAuthenticated &&
          app.User.Identity is FormsIdentity) {
          FormsIdentity identity = (FormsIdentity) app.User.Identity;
          if (identity.Name == "Jeff")
              app.Context.User = new GenericPrincipal (identity,
                  new string[] { "Developer" });
      }
  }
</script>
```

How does it work? After verifying that the user has indeed been authenticated (for forms authentication, "is authenticated" means a valid authentication cookie is attached to the request) and that the authentication was performed using forms authentication, *Application_AuthenticateRequest* extracts the user name from the cookie. It doesn't touch the cookie directly; instead, it casts *User.Identity* to *FormsIdentity*, which works fine as long as the user was authenticated using forms authentication, and reads the user name from the *FormsIdentity* object's *Name* property.

If the user name is "Jeff," *Application_AuthenticateRequest* creates a new *GenericPrincipal* object containing the role name "Developer" and assigns it to the current request by writing it to the *User* property of the request's *HttpContext*. *GenericPrincipal* is a device for representing user identities independent of the authentication protocol being used. When code executed in this request attempts to redirect to ProtectedPage.aspx, ASP.NET compares the role name in the *GenericPrincipal* to the roles granted access through Web.config. Since Jeff is a developer but the Secret directory's Web.config file allows access only to managers, Jeff is denied access to ProtectedPage.aspx. But change the statement

```
app.Context.User = new GenericPrincipal (identity,
    new string[] { "Developer" });
```

to

```
app.Context.User = new GenericPrincipal (identity,
    new string[] { "Manager" });
```

and Jeff is able to view ProtectedPage.aspx just fine.

Figure 10-12 contains the third and final version of our PublicPage/ProtectedPage application. It includes three features that the previous version did not:

■ It retrieves roles from the WebLogin database and assigns them to incoming requests (assuming the requests are authenticated and that they were authenticated using forms authentication).

■ Its Web.config file (the one in the Secrets directory) allows access to managers but not to anyone else.

■ It returns an authentication cookie whose lifetime is 7 days rather than 50 years if the login page's "Keep me signed in" box is checked.

To experience role-based security in action, click PublicPage.aspx's View Secret Message button and type "Jeff" and "imbatman" into the login form. Because Jeff is identified as a developer in the database, you won't be able to view ProtectedPage.aspx. But log in as John (password "redrover"), and you'll pull up ProtectedPage.aspx just fine. Why? Because John's role is manager, and managers are specifically allowed to access resources in the Secrets directory.

By the way, if clicking the View Secret Message button bypasses the login form and goes straight to ProtectedPage.aspx, that's because the cookie you were issued when you tested the previous version of the application still identifies you as an authenticated user. If it's a session cookie, simply restarting your browser will destroy the cookie and let you see the login page again. If it's a persistent cookie, you'll have to delete it. The easiest way to do that is to use your browser's delete cookies command. In Internet Explorer 6.0, you'll find it under Tools/Internet Options.

LoginPage.aspx

```
<%@ Import NameSpace="System.Data.SqlClient" %>

<html>
  <body>
    <h1>Please Log In</h1>
    <hr>
    <form runat="server">
      <table cellpadding="8">
        <tr>
          <td>
            User Name:
          </td>
          <td>
            <asp:TextBox ID="UserName" RunAt="server" />
          </td>
        </tr>
        <tr>
          <td>
            Password:
          </td>
          <td>
            <asp:TextBox ID="Password" TextMode="password"
              RunAt="server" />
          </td>
        </tr>
        <tr>
          <td>
            <asp:Button Text="Log In" OnClick="OnLogIn"
              RunAt="server" />
          </td>
          <td>
            <asp:CheckBox Text="Keep me signed in" ID="Persistent"
              RunAt="server" />
          </td>
        </tr>
      </table>
    </form>
```

Figure 10-12 Forms authentication with role-based security.

LoginPage.aspx *(continued)*

```
    <hr>
    <h3><asp:Label ID="Output" RunAt="server" /></h3>
  </body>
</html>

<script language="C#" runat="server">
  void OnLogIn (Object sender, EventArgs e)
  {
      if (CustomAuthenticate (UserName.Text, Password.Text)) {
          string url = FormsAuthentication.GetRedirectUrl
              (UserName.Text, Persistent.Checked);

          FormsAuthentication.SetAuthCookie (UserName.Text,
              Persistent.Checked);

          if (Persistent.Checked) {
              HttpCookie cookie =
                Response.Cookies[FormsAuthentication.FormsCookieName];
              cookie.Expires = DateTime.Now +
                  new TimeSpan (7, 0, 0, 0);
          }

          Response.Redirect (url);
      }
      else
          Output.Text = "Invalid login";
  }

  bool CustomAuthenticate (string username, string password)
  {
      SqlConnection connection = new SqlConnection
          ("server=localhost;database=weblogin;uid=sa;pwd=");

      try {
          connection.Open ();

          StringBuilder builder = new StringBuilder ();
          builder.Append ("select count (*) from users " +
              "where username = \'");
          builder.Append (username);
          builder.Append ("\' and cast (rtrim (password) as " +
              "varbinary) = cast (\'");
          builder.Append (password);
          builder.Append ("\' as varbinary)");

          SqlCommand command = new SqlCommand (builder.ToString (),
              connection);
```

```
            int count = (int) command.ExecuteScalar ();
            return (count > 0);
        }
        catch (SqlException) {
            return false;
        }
        finally {
            connection.Close ();
        }
    }
}
</script>
```

Global.asax

```
<%@ Import Namespace="System.Data.SqlClient" %>
<%@ Import Namespace="System.Security.Principal" %>

<script language="C#" runat="server">
  void Application_AuthenticateRequest (Object sender, EventArgs e)
  {
      HttpApplication app = (HttpApplication) sender;

      if (app.Request.IsAuthenticated &&
          app.User.Identity is FormsIdentity) {
          FormsIdentity identity = (FormsIdentity) app.User.Identity;

          // Find out what role (if any) the user belongs to
          string role = GetUserRole (identity.Name);

          // Create a GenericPrincipal containing the role name
          // and assign it to the current request
          if (role != null)
              app.Context.User = new GenericPrincipal (identity,
                  new string[] { role });
      }
  }

  string GetUserRole (string name)
  {
      SqlConnection connection = new SqlConnection
          ("server=localhost;database=weblogin;uid=sa;pwd=");

      try {
          connection.Open ();

          StringBuilder builder = new StringBuilder ();
          builder.Append ("select role from users " +
              "where username = \'");
```

(continued)

Global.asax *(continued)*

```
            builder.Append (name);
            builder.Append ("\'");

            SqlCommand command = new SqlCommand (builder.ToString (),
                connection);

            object role = command.ExecuteScalar ();

            if (role is DBNull)
                return null;

            return (string) role;
        }
        catch (SqlException) {
            return null;
        }
        finally {
            connection.Close ();
        }
    }
}
</script>
```

Web.config (Secret Subdirectory)

```
<configuration>
  <system.web>
    <authorization>
      <allow roles="Manager" />
      <deny users="*" />
    </authorization>
  </system.web>
</configuration>
```

As a practical matter, you might prefer to consolidate all your URL authorizations in the top-level Web.config file rather than divide them among Web.config files in individual directories. ASP.NET supports that, too. The following Web.config file, which goes in the application root, enables forms authentication and specifies that only managers are allowed access to resources in the subdirectory named Secret:

```
<configuration>
  <!-- Configuration information for this directory -->
  <system.web>
    <authentication mode="Forms">
      <forms loginUrl="/LoginPage.aspx" />
    </authentication>
  </system.web>
  <!-- Configuration information for the Secret directory -->
```

```
    <location path="Secret">
      <system.web>
        <authorization>
          <allow roles="Manager" />
          <deny users="*" />
        </authorization>
      </system.web>
    </location>
</configuration>
```

The ability to specify configuration settings for multiple directories in one Web.config file isn't limited to URL authorizations; it works for other configuration settings, too.

Multiple Roles

It's not uncommon to encounter organizations in which employees are (or can be) assigned multiple roles. The requestor might be a manager, but he or she could be a developer also or at least want access to material that developers have access to. Does ASP.NET's brand of role-based security support multiple role memberships? Yes it does. The second parameter passed to *GenericPrincipal*'s constructor isn't a string; it's an *array* of strings. To indicate that a given security principal (user) belongs to two or more roles, simply submit an array of role names, as shown here:

```
app.Context.User = new GenericPrincipal (identity,
    new string[] { "Developer", "Manager" });
```

Now the requestor can access any resources that managers or developers enjoy access to.

You can also use *allow* and *deny* elements to allow or deny access to multiple roles. For example, the statements

```
<allow roles="Manager, Developer" />
<deny users="*" />
```

in a Web.config file grant access to developers and managers while denying access to everyone else.

Signing Out

Many sites that rely on forms-style authentication allow users to sign out as well as sign in. Calling any *FormsAuthentication* method that attaches an authentication cookie to the response effectively signs in the user. The *FormsAuthentication.SignOut* method does the opposite: it signs out an authenticated user. It works by returning a *Set-Cookie* header that sets the cookie's value to a null string and sets the cookie's expiration date to a date in the past, effectively destroying the authentication cookie. Here's a snippet of code from a Web form that logs out the current user when the Log Out button is clicked:

```
<asp:Button Text="Log Out" OnClick="OnLogOut" RunAt="server" />
    .
    .
    .
<script language="C#" runat="server">
  void OnLogOut (Object sender, EventArgs e)
  {
      FormsAuthentication.SignOut ();
  }
</script>
```

The practical effect is that the next time this user visits a protected portion of your site, he or she will have to log in again.

Authentication Cookie Security

The *forms* element in Web.config supports the following five attributes:

Attribute	Description	Default
name	Name assigned to authentication cookies	.ASPXAUTH
loginUrl	URL of the login page	login.aspx
protection	Level of protection (validation and encryption) applied to authentication cookies	All
timeout	Lifetime of session authentication tickets in minutes	30
path	Scope of authentication cookies	/

Most of these attributes are self-explanatory, but *protection* deserves special mention. It specifies the desired level of protection for the authentication cookies that ASP.NET uses to identify authenticated users. The default is "All," which instructs ASP.NET to both encrypt and validate authentication cookies. Validation works exactly the same for authentication cookies as it does for view state: the *machineKey* element's *validationKey* is appended to the cookie, the resulting value is hashed, and the hash is appended to the cookie. When the cookie is returned in a request, ASP.NET verifies that it wasn't tampered with by rehashing the cookie and comparing the new hash to the one accompanying the cookie. Encryption works by encrypting the cookie—hash value and all—with *machineKey*'s *decryptionKey* attribute.

Validation consumes less CPU time than encryption and prevents tampering. It does not, however, prevent someone from intercepting an authentication cookie and reading its contents. Nonetheless, if you want ASP.NET to validate but not encrypt authentication cookies, set the *forms* element's *protection* attribute as follows:

```
<forms ... protection="Validation" />
```

Encryption provides a double dose of insurance against tampering and prevents the cookie's contents from being read, too. If you'd like ASP.NET to encrypt authentication cookies but skip the validation procedure, do this:

```
<forms ... protection="Encryption" />
```

Finally, if you want neither validation nor encryption performed, do this:

```
<forms ... protection="None" />
```

The "None" option is useful when authentication cookies travel over HTTPS. After all, there's no need to encrypt them twice.

Speaking of HTTPS: encrypted cookies can't be read or altered, but they can be stolen and used illicitly. Time-outs are the only protection a cookie offers against replay attacks, and they apply to session cookies only. The most reliable way to prevent someone from spoofing your site with a stolen authentication cookie is to use an encrypted communications link. If you'd prefer not to encrypt communications to all parts of your site, consider at least submitting user names and passwords over HTTPS. (When you see buttons on commercial sites that say "Sign in using a secure link," that's exactly what they're doing.) The following *forms* element protects plain-text user names and passwords from prying eyes by connecting to the login form over a secure link:

```
<forms ... loginUrl="https://www.wintellect.com/secure/login.aspx" />
```

This assumes, of course, that your server supports HTTPS and that Login.aspx is stored in a directory configured to use HTTPS.

The *path* attribute can also play a role in securing authentication cookies. Say you place public files in the virtual root and protected files in a subdirectory configured for HTTPS. If you accept the default path of /, the authentication cookie you acquire is transmitted in all requests to the Web site, not just the ones directed to the Secret directory. An intruder can intercept the cookie on its way to a public page and use it to gain access to protected pages. Here's the solution:

```
<forms path="/Secret" />
```

Now the cookie will be transmitted only in requests for resources in the Secret subdirectory and its subdirectories, meaning it's transmitted only over secure channels.

Caveat Emptor

I'll close this chapter with a word of warning regarding forms authentication—something that's vitally important to understand but easily overlooked.

Forms authentication protects only ASP.NET files. I'll say it again: *forms authentication protects only ASP.NET files*. It guards ASPX files, ASMX files, and other file types registered to ASP.NET, but it doesn't protect files that don't belong to ASP.NET—for example, files with .htm or .html extensions. Try it: put a ProtectedPage.html file in the Secret directory used in this chapter's forms authentication samples. You have to go through the login page to get to ProtectedPage.aspx, but ProtectedPage.html requires no login. That's because ASP.NET never sees (and therefore can't intercept and redirect) requests for file types that aren't registered to it.

One solution is to assign HTML files and other non-ASP.NET files that you want to protect with forms authentication the file name extension .aspx. You'll incur additional overhead when accessing the files, but at least you won't leave them alone and unprotected.

11

Web Services

Read any book, paper, or magazine article about Microsoft .NET and you'll encounter one term over and over: "XML Web services." XML Web services, or simply "Web services" as they are more often called, are the cornerstone of the Microsoft .NET initiative. They're the key to Microsoft's vision of a world in which computers talk to each other over the Web using HTTP and other universally supported protocols. And they're the number one reason that the Microsoft .NET Framework exists in the first place—to make it as easy as humanly possible to build Web services and Web service clients.

A Web service is a different kind of Web application. It doesn't have a user interface as does a traditional Web application. Instead, it exposes callable API functions, better known as *Web methods*, over the Internet. It's not designed to serve end users as traditional Web applications are. It's designed to provide *services* to other applications, be they Web applications, GUI applications, or even command-line applications. What kinds of services do Web services provide? That's up to the implementer. A Web service could provide real-time stock quotes to interested parties. It could validate credit cards or provide current information about the weather. Like traditional applications, Web services are as diverse as their creators' imaginations. Microsoft, Sun, IBM, and others foresee a world in which all sorts of interesting information is made available via Web services. To the extent that developers embrace that vision, Web services will one day be the backbone of a highly programmable Internet—an Internet that doesn't just serve end users, but one that allows servers to communicate with each other and applications to be freed from the bonds of the platforms on which they run.

An application that speaks the language of Web services has access to a universe of services that is just now emerging. Already, companies all over the world are exposing content and business logic through Web services. As one of this chapter's sample programs demonstrates, it's easy to build a Web service client that takes city and state names as input and fetches satellite images of said cities, thanks to Microsoft TerraService, which is a front end to a massive database of satellite images, aerial photographs, and topo maps of much of Earth's surface and is freely available to anyone who wants to use it. In the future, you'll see applications that use Web services to check the status of overnight packages or display the soup of the day at your favorite restaurant. Web services have the potential to change the world as few technologies ever have. And Microsoft .NET will play a huge role in that change, primarily because the .NET Framework makes writing Web services and Web service clients so incredibly easy.

Web services are not the property of Microsoft. They're an industry standard built on open protocols such as HTTP and the Simple Object Access Protocol (SOAP). Many of the Web services in operation today run on UNIX servers. You don't need the .NET Framework to write Web services or Web service clients, but you *want* the framework because it makes writing Web services and Web service clients easy. A few button clicks in Visual Studio .NET creates a Web service and exposes Web methods to anyone that you provide a URL to. Creating a Web service client requires equally little effort. You don't even have to use Visual Studio .NET. You can write powerful Web services with Notepad, which is precisely what we'll do in this chapter to introduce the brave new world of Web services and applications that use them.

Web Services

A great place to begin an exploration of Web services is to define precisely what a Web service is. A Web service is an application that:

- Runs on a Web server

- Exposes Web methods to interested callers

- Listens for HTTP requests representing commands to invoke Web methods

- Executes Web methods and returns the results

Most Web services expect their Web methods to be invoked using HTTP requests containing SOAP messages. SOAP is an XML-based vocabulary for performing remote procedure calls using HTTP and other protocols. You can read all about it at *http://www.w3.org/TR/SOAP*. Suppose you write a Web service that publishes Web methods named *Add* and *Subtract* that callers can use to add and subtract simple integers. If the service's URL is www.wintellect.com/ calc.asmx, here's how a client would invoke the *Add* method by transmitting a SOAP envelope in an HTTP request. This example adds 2 and 2:

```
POST /calc.asmx HTTP/1.1
Host: www.wintellect.com
Content-Type: text/xml; charset=utf-8
Content-Length: 338
SOAPAction: "http://tempuri.org/Add"

<?xml version="1.0" encoding="utf-8"?>
<soap:Envelope xmlns:xsi="http://www.w3.org/2001/XMLSchema-instance"
  xmlns:xsd=http://www.w3.org/2001/XMLSchema
  xmlns:soap="http://schemas.xmlsoap.org/soap/envelope/">
  <soap:Body>
    <Add xmlns="http://tempuri.org/">
      <a>2</a>
      <b>2</b>
    </Add>
  </soap:Body>
</soap:Envelope>
```

And here's how the Web service would respond:

```
HTTP/1.1 200 OK
Content-Type: text/xml; charset=utf-8
Content-Length: 353

<?xml version="1.0" encoding="utf-8"?>
<soap:Envelope xmlns:xsi=http://www.w3.org/2001/XMLSchema-instance
  xmlns:xsd=http://www.w3.org/2001/XMLSchema
  xmlns:soap="http://schemas.xmlsoap.org/soap/envelope/">
  <soap:Body>
    <AddResponse xmlns="http://tempuri.org/">
      <AddResult>4</AddResult>
    </AddResponse>
  </soap:Body>
</soap:Envelope>
```

The Web service's job is to parse the SOAP envelope containing the inputs, add 2 and 2, formulate a SOAP envelope containing the sum of 2 and 2, and return it to the client in the body of the HTTP response. This, at the most elemental level, is what Web services are all about.

Web services written with the .NET Framework also allow their Web methods to be invoked using ordinary HTTP GET and POST commands. The following GET command adds 2 and 2 by invoking the Web service's *Add* method:

```
GET /calc.asmx/Add?a=2&b=2 HTTP/1.1
Host: www.wintellect.com
```

The Web service responds as follows:

```
HTTP/1.1 200 OK
Content-Type: text/xml; charset=utf-8
Content-Length: 80


<?xml version="1.0" encoding="utf-8"?>
<int xmlns="http://tempuri.org/">4</int>
```

Here's a POST command that adds 2 and 2:

```
POST /calc.asmx/Add HTTP/1.1
Host: www.wintellect.com
Content-Type: application/x-www-form-urlencoded
Content-Length: 7


a=2&b=2
```

And here's the Web service's response:

```
HTTP/1.1 200 OK
Content-Type: text/xml; charset=utf-8
Content-Length: 80


<?xml version="1.0" encoding="utf-8"?>
<int xmlns="http://tempuri.org/">4</int>
```

As you can imagine, the hard part of writing a Web service is parsing HTTP requests and generating HTTP responses. But as you'll see in the next section and throughout the remainder of this chapter, the .NET Framework insulates developers from the low-level details of HTTP, SOAP, and XML and provides a high-level framework for writing Web services and Web service clients alike.

There are many ways to write Web services. You can write Web services by hand. You can use SOAP toolkits from Microsoft, IBM, and other companies. And you can use the .NET Framework. Because this book is about Microsoft .NET, this chapter is about the latter. Writing Web services with the .NET Framework offers two advantages over all the other methods:

■   The .NET Framework makes writing Web services extremely easy.

■   Web services written with the .NET Framework are managed applications, meaning you shouldn't have to worry about memory leaks, stray pointers, and other maladies that bedevil programmers and cost more than their fair share of development time.

What does it take to write a Web service using the .NET Framework? I'm glad you asked, because that's what the next section is about.

Your First Web Service

The ASMX file shown in Figure 11-1 is a complete Web service. It implements two Web methods: *Add* and *Subtract*. Both take two integers as input and return an integer as well. Deploying the Web service is as simple as copying it to a directory on your Web server that is URL-addressable. If you put Calc.asmx in wwwroot, the Web service's local URL is http://localhost/calc.asmx.

Calc.asmx demonstrates several important principles of Web service programming using the .NET Framework:

■   Web services are implemented in ASMX files. ASMX is a special file name extension registered to ASP.NET (specifically, to an ASP.NET HTTP handler) in Machine.config.

■   ASMX files begin with @ *WebService* directives. At a minimum, the directive must contain a *Class* attribute identifying the class that makes up the Web service.

■   Web service classes can be attributed with optional *WebService* attributes. The one in this example assigns the Web service a name and a description that show up in the HTML page generated when a user calls up Calc.asmx in his or her browser. The *WebService* attribute also supports a *Namespace* parameter that can be used to change the name of the XML namespace that scopes the Web service's members.

■   Web methods are declared by tagging public methods in the Web service class with *WebMethod* attributes. You can build helper methods into a Web service—methods that are used internally by Web methods but that are not exposed as Web methods themselves—by omitting the attribute. The *WebMethod* attributes in Figure 11-1 also assign descriptive text to their Web methods. You'll learn more about *Description* and other *WebMethod* parameters in the section entitled "The *WebMethod* Attribute."

- HTTP, XML, and SOAP are hidden under the hood. You don't have to deal with raw XML data or SOAP messages because the .NET Framework deals with them for you.

Calc.asmx

```
<%@ WebService Language="C#" Class="CalcService" %>

using System;
using System.Web.Services;

[WebService (Name="Calculator Web Service",
    Description="Performs simple math over the Web")]
class CalcService
{
    [WebMethod (Description="Computes the sum of two integers")]
    public int Add (int a, int b)
    {
        return a + b;
    }

    [WebMethod
        (Description="Computes the difference between two integers")]
    public int Subtract (int a, int b)
    {
        return a - b;
    }
}
```

Figure 11-1   Calc Web service.

Despite its brevity, Calc.asmx is a full-blown Web service when installed on a Web server outfitted with ASP.NET. Its Web methods can be invoked with SOAP, HTTP GET, and HTTP POST, and it's capable of returning output in SOAP responses or simple XML wrappers. All we need now is a way to test it out. The .NET Framework lends a hand there too.

Testing a Web Service

How do you test an ASMX Web service? Simple: just call it up in your browser. To demonstrate, copy Calc.asmx to wwwroot and type

```
http://localhost/calc.asmx
```

in your browser's address bar. You'll be greeted with the screen shown in Figure 11-2. What happened? ASP.NET responded to the HTTP request for Calc.asmx by generating an HTML page that describes the Web service. The name and description in the ASMX file's *WebService* attribute appear at the top of the page. Underneath is a list of Web methods that the service exposes, complete with the descriptions spelled out in the *WebMethod* attributes.

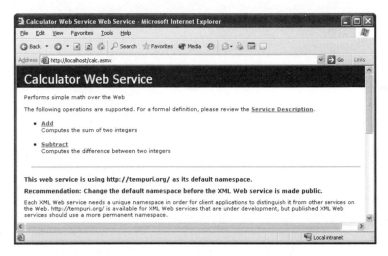

Figure 11-2   Calc.asmx as seen in Internet Explorer.

Like what you've seen so far? It gets better. Click "Add" near the top of the page, and ASP.NET displays a page that you can use to test the *Add* method (Figure 11-3). ASP.NET knows the method name and signature because it reads them from the metadata in the DLL it compiled from Calc.asmx. It even generates an HTML form that you can use to call the *Add* method with your choice of inputs. Type 2 and 2 into the "a" and "b" boxes and click Invoke. The XML returned by the Web method appears in a separate browser window (Figure 11-4).

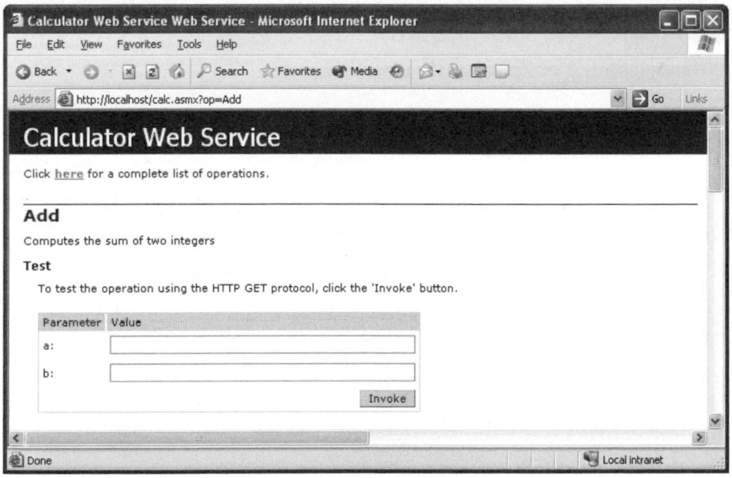

Figure 11-3   Test page for the *Add* method.

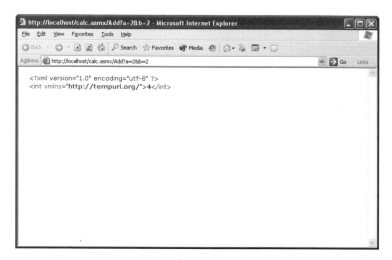

Figure 11-4   XML returned by the *Add* method.

The forms that ASP.NET generates on the fly from ASMX files enable you to test the Web services that you write without writing special clients to test them with. They also let you explore a Web service built with the .NET Framework simply by pointing your browser to it. For kicks, type the following URL into your browser's address bar:

```
http://terraservice.net/terraservice.asmx
```

That's the URL of the Microsoft TerraService, an ultra-cool Web service that provides a programmatic interface to a massive database of geographic data known as the Microsoft TerraServer. Don't worry about the details just yet; you'll be using TerraService to build a Web service client later in this chapter. But do notice how much you can learn about TerraService simply by viewing the page that ASP.NET generated for it.

Web Services and Code-Behind

You can use code-behind to move Web service classes out of ASMX files and into separately compiled DLLs. Figure 11-5 shows how Calc.asmx looks after it's modified to take advantage of code-behind. The ASMX file now contains just one statement. The class referenced in that statement is implemented in Calc.cs. The following command compiles Calc.cs into a DLL named Calc.dll:

```
csc /t:library calc.cs
```

Once compiled, the DLL must be placed in the application root's bin subdirectory (for example, wwwroot\bin).

Calc.asmx

```
<%@ WebService Class="CalcService" %>
```

Calc.cs

```
using System;
using System.Web.Services;

[WebService (Name="Calculator Web Service",
    Description="Performs simple math over the Web")]
class CalcService
{
    [WebMethod (Description="Computes the sum of two integers")]
    public int Add (int a, int b)
    {
        return a + b;
    }

    [WebMethod
        (Description="Computes the difference between two integers")]
    public int Subtract (int a, int b)
    {
        return a - b;
    }
}
```

Figure 11-5   Calc Web service with code-behind.

Code-behind offers the same benefits to Web services that it offers to Web pages: it catches compilation errors before the service is deployed, and it enables you to write Web services in languages that ASP.NET doesn't natively support. For an example of ASP.NET code written in managed C++ and for a refresher on code-behind in general, turn back to Chapter 5.

The *WebService* Base Class

Very often when you see ASMX code samples, the Web service classes inside them derive from a class named *WebService*, as in

```
class CalcService : WebService
{
  ...
}
```

WebService belongs to the *System.Web.Services* namespace. It contributes properties named *Application, Session, Context, Server,* and *User* to derived classes, enabling a Web service to access the ASP.NET objects with the same names. If you don't use these objects in your Web service—for example, if you don't use application state or session state—you don't need to derive from *WebService* either.

The *WebMethod* Attribute

The *WebMethod* attribute tags a method as a Web method. The .NET Framework automatically exposes such methods as Web methods when they're implemented inside a Web service. *WebMethod* is capable of doing much more, however, than simply letting the framework know which methods are Web methods and which are not; it also supports the following parameters:

Parameter Name	Description
BufferResponse	Enables and disables response buffering
CacheDuration	Caches responses generated by this method for the specified number of seconds
Description	Adds a textual description to a Web method
EnableSession	Enables and disables session state for this Web method
MessageName	Specifies the Web method's name
TransactionOption	Specifies the transactional behavior of a Web method

CacheDuration is the ASMX equivalent of an *@ OutputCache* directive in an ASPX or ASCX file: it caches a method's output so that subsequent requests will execute more quickly. Suppose, for example, that you write a Web method that returns the current time:

```
[WebMethod]
public string GetCurrentTime ()
{
    return DateTime.Now.ToShortTimeString ();
}
```

Since *ToShortTimeString* returns a string that includes minutes but not seconds, it's wasteful to execute it too often. The following method declaration uses *CacheDuration* to cache the output for 10 seconds at a time:

```
[WebMethod (CacheDuration="10")]
public string GetCurrentTime ()
{
    return DateTime.Now.ToShortTimeString ();
}
```

Now the data that the method returns could be stale by a few seconds, but if the Web service is getting pounded with calls to *GetCurrentTime,* the load on it will be reduced commensurately.

Web services enjoy access to the same session state facilities that conventional ASP.NET applications do. By default, however, session state is disabled for Web methods. You can enable it with *WebMethod's EnableSession* parameter. If you want to use session state in a Web service, derive from *WebService* (to inherit its *Session* property) and tag each Web method that uses session state with *EnableSession*="true":

```
class CalcService : WebService
{
    [WebMethod (EnableSession="true",
        Description="Adds an item to a shopping cart")]
    public void AddToCart (Item item)
    {
        ShoppingCart cart = (ShoppingCart) Session["MyShoppingCart"];
        cart.Add (item);
    }
}
```

Session state utilization is less common in Web services than in conventional Web applications, but it is an option nonetheless.

The *MessageName* parameter lets you assign a Web method a name other than that of the method that implements it. For example, suppose that you build two *Add* methods into a Web service—one that adds integers and another that adds floating point values—and you tag both of them as Web methods:

```
[WebMethod]
public int Add (int a, int b)
{
    return a + b;
}

[WebMethod]
public float Add (float a, float b)
{
    return a + b;
}
```

The only problem with this code is that it doesn't compile. C# methods can be overloaded, but Web methods cannot. The solution? Either change the method names or add *MessageName* parameters to the *WebMethod* attributes, as demonstrated here:

```
[WebMethod (MessageName="AddInts")]
public int Add (int a, int b)
{
    return a + b;
}


[WebMethod (MessageName="AddFloats")]
public float Add (float a, float b)
{
    return a + b;
}
```

Now the C# methods remain overloaded, but the corresponding Web methods are named *AddInts* and *AddFloats*.

The Web Services Description Language

If other developers are to consume (that is, write clients for) a Web service that you author, they need to know what Web methods your service publishes, what protocols it supports, the signatures of its methods, and the Web service's location (URL), among other things. All this information and more can be expressed in a language called the *Web Services Description Language*, or WSDL for short.

WSDL is a relatively new standard. It's an XML vocabulary devised by IBM, Microsoft, and others. Its syntax is documented at *http://www.w3.org/TR/wsdl*. I won't describe the details of the language here for several reasons. First, the details are already documented in the spec. Second, WSDL is a language for machines, not humans. Third, it's trivial to generate a WSDL contract for a Web service built with the .NET Framework: simply point your browser to the Web service's URL and append a WSDL query string, as in

```
http://www.wintellect.com/calc.asmx?wsdl
```

Figure 11-6 shows the result. Scan through it and you'll find a *service* element that describes the Web service; *operation* elements that document the "operations," or Web methods, that the service supports; *binding* elements that document the protocols that the Web methods support; and other descriptive information.

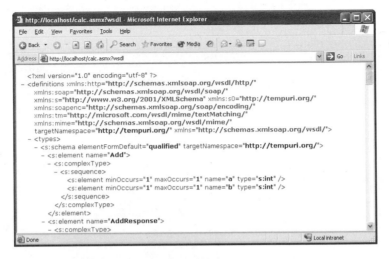

Figure 11-6   WSDL contract for Calc.asmx.

When you publish a Web service, you should also publish a WSDL contract describing it. For a Web service built with the .NET Framework, the contract is usually nothing more than a URL with ?wsdl on the end. Other developers can use the contract to write clients for your Web service. Typically, they don't read the contract themselves. Instead, they run it through a tool that generates a wrapper class containing all the elements needed to talk to a Web service. The .NET Framework SDK includes one such tool: it's called Wsdl.exe. You'll learn all about it later in this chapter when we turn our attention from Web services to Web service clients.

Web Services and Complex Data Types

It's not hard to understand how simple data types can be passed to and from Web methods. After all, integers and other primitive types are defined in one form or another on virtually every platform. But what about more complex types? What if, for example, you define a custom class or struct and want to use it as an input parameter or return value for a Web method? Are complex types supported, and if so, how do you declare them so that they become an intrinsic part of the Web service?

Complex types *are* supported, and they work very well because virtually any type can be represented in XML. As an example, consider the Web service in Figure 11-7. It exposes a Web method named *FindStores* that accepts a state abbreviation (for example, "CA") as input. *FindStores* calls a local method named *FindByState*, which queries the Pubs database that comes with Microsoft SQL Server for all the bookstores in the specified state and returns the results in an array of *Bookstore* objects. (Observe that *FindByState* is not a Web method because it lacks a *WebMethod* attribute.) *FindStores* returns the array to the client. *Bookstore* is a custom type defined in the ASMX file.

Figure 11-8 shows the XML returned when *FindStores* is called with the input string "CA". The array of *Bookstore* objects has been serialized into XML. The serialization is performed by the .NET Framework's *System.Xml.Serialization.XmlSerializer* class, otherwise known as the "XML serializer." A client application that receives the XML and that has a schema describing the structure and content of the data can rehydrate the information into *Bookstore* objects. Or it can take the raw XML and do with it as it pleases.

Locator.asmx

```csharp
<%@ WebService Language="C#" Class="LocatorService" %>

using System;
using System.Web.Services;
using System.Data;
using System.Data.SqlClient;

[WebService (Name="Bookstore Locator Service",
    Description="Retrieves bookstore information from the Pubs database")]
class LocatorService
{
    [WebMethod (Description="Finds bookstores in a specified state")]
    public Bookstore[] FindStores (string state)
    {
        return FindByState (state);
    }

    Bookstore[] FindByState (string state)
    {
        SqlDataAdapter adapter = new SqlDataAdapter
            ("select * from stores where state = \'" + state + "\'",
            "server=localhost;database=pubs;uid=sa;pwd=");
        DataSet ds = new DataSet ();
        adapter.Fill (ds);

        DataTable table = ds.Tables[0];
        Bookstore[] stores = new Bookstore[table.Rows.Count];

        for (int i=0; i<table.Rows.Count; i++) {
            stores[i] = new Bookstore (
                table.Rows[i]["stor_name"].ToString ().TrimEnd
                    (new char[] { ' ' }),
                table.Rows[i]["stor_address"].ToString ().TrimEnd
                    (new char[] { ' ' }),
```

Figure 11-7 Bookstore locator Web service.

```
                            table.Rows[i]["city"].ToString ().TrimEnd
                                (new char[] { ' ' }),
                            table.Rows[i]["state"].ToString ().TrimEnd
                                (new char[] { ' ' })
                    );
            }
            return stores;
        }
    }

public class Bookstore
{
    public string Name;
    public string Address;
    public string City;
    public string State;

    public Bookstore () {}

    public Bookstore (string name, string address, string city,
        string state)
    {
        Name = name;
        Address = address;
        City = city;
        State = state;
    }
}
```

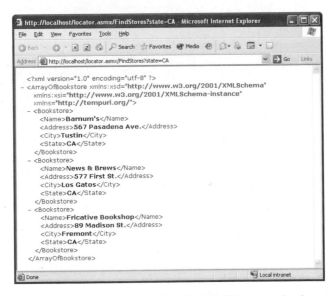

Figure 11-8   XML returned by the *FindStores* method.

Where might a client obtain an XML schema describing the *Bookstore* data type? From the service's WSDL contract, of course. Sneak a peek at Locator.asmx's WSDL contract and you'll see the *Bookstore* data type (and arrays of *Bookstore*s) defined this way in the contract's *types* element:

```
<s:complexType name="ArrayOfBookstore">
  <s:sequence>
    <s:element minOccurs="0" maxOccurs="unbounded"
      name="Bookstore" nillable="true" type="s0:Bookstore" />
  </s:sequence>
</s:complexType>
<s:complexType name="Bookstore">
  <s:sequence>
    <s:element minOccurs="1" maxOccurs="1" name="Name"
      nillable="true" type="s:string" />
    <s:element minOccurs="1" maxOccurs="1" name="Address"
      nillable="true" type="s:string" />
    <s:element minOccurs="1" maxOccurs="1" name="City"
      nillable="true" type="s:string" />
    <s:element minOccurs="1" maxOccurs="1" name="State"
      nillable="true" type="s:string" />
  </s:sequence>
</s:complexType>
```

Given these definitions, a client can define a *Bookstore* class of its own and initialize arrays of *Bookstore* objects by deserializing *Bookstore* elements. It's not as hard as it sounds. If the client is written with the .NET Framework, tools generate the class definitions for you and the framework handles the deserialization.

As Locator.asmx demonstrates, it's not difficult to write Web methods that use custom types. There are, however, two gotchas to be aware of:

■ Because query strings are limited to passing simple name/value pairs, you can't pass complex types to a Web method using HTTP GET and POST. That's not a limitation if you use SOAP to invoke Web methods, but it does prevent ASP.NET from generating test pages for methods that accept complex types. If you go to a test page and see the warning "No test form is available because this method does not support HTTP GET" or something to that effect, you've found a method that accepts an input parameter that can't be represented in a query string. ASP.NET test forms invoke methods using HTTP GET commands.

- Any fields or properties declared in a class or struct that's passed to or from a Web method must be public if they're to be serialized when instances of the class or struct are serialized. That's because the .NET Framework's XML serializer will not serialize nonpublic members.

Keep these caveats in mind and you'll have few problems combining Web methods and custom data types.

Web Service Discovery—DISCO

Once a client has a WSDL contract describing a Web service, it has all the information it needs to make calls to that Web service. But when you publish a Web service by making it available on a Web server, how do clients find out where to get a WSDL contract? For that matter, how do clients know that your Web service exists in the first place?

The answer comes in two parts: DISCO and Universal Description, Discovery, and Integration, better known as UDDI. The former is a file-based mechanism for local Web service discovery—that is, for getting a list of available Web services from DISCO files deployed on Web servers. The latter is a global Web service directory that is itself implemented as a Web service. UDDI is discussed in the next section.

The DISCO (short for "discovery") protocol is a simple one that revolves around XML-based DISCO files. The basic idea is that you publish a DISCO file on your Web server that describes the Web services available on it and perhaps on other servers as well. Clients can interrogate the DISCO file to find out what Web services are available and where the services' WSDL contracts can be found. As an example, suppose you publish two Web services and their URLs are as follows:

- http://www.wintellect.com/calc.asmx

- http://www.wintellect.com/locator.asmx

To advertise these Web services, you can deploy the following DISCO file at a well-known URL on your server. The *contractRef* elements identify the URLs of the Web services' WSDL contracts. URLs can be absolute or relative (relative to the directory in which the DISCO file resides). The optional *docRef* attributes identify the locations of documents describing the Web services, which, because of the self-documenting nature of Web services built with the .NET Framework, are typically the ASMX files themselves:

```
<?xml version="1.0" ?>
<discovery xmlns="http://schemas.xmlsoap.org/disco/"
  xmlns:scl="http://schemas.xmlsoap.org/disco/scl/">
  <scl:contractRef ref="http://www.wintellect.com/calc.asmx?wsdl"
    docRef="http://www.wintellect.com/Calc.asmx" />
  <scl:contractRef ref="http://www.wintellect.com/locator.asmx?wsdl"
    docRef="http://www.wintellect.com/Locator.asmx" />
</discovery>
```

If you'd prefer, you can write DISCO files for individual Web services and reference them in a master DISCO file using *discoveryRef* elements. Here's a DISCO file that points to other DISCO files. Once more, URLs can be absolute or relative:

```
<?xml version="1.0" ?>
<discovery xmlns="http://schemas.xmlsoap.org/disco/">
  <discoveryRef ref="http://www.wintellect.com/calc.disco" />
  <discoveryRef ref="http://www.wintellect.com/locator.disco" />
</discovery>
```

A third option is to deploy a VSDISCO file to enable *dynamic discovery*. The following VSDISCO file automatically exposes all ASMX and DISCO files in a host directory and its subdirectories, with the exception of those subdirectories noted with *exclude* elements:

```
<?xml version="1.0" ?>
<dynamicDiscovery
  xmlns="urn:schemas-dynamicdiscovery:disco.2000-03-17">
  <exclude path="_vti_cnf" />
  <exclude path="_vti_pvt" />
  <exclude path="_vti_log" />
  <exclude path="_vti_script" />
  <exclude path="_vti_txt" />
</dynamicDiscovery>
```

How does dynamic discovery work? ASP.NET maps the file name extension .vsdisco to an HTTP handler that scans the host directory and subdirectories for ASMX and DISCO files and returns a dynamically generated DISCO document. A client that requests a VSDISCO file gets back what appears to be a static DISCO document.

For security reasons, Microsoft disabled dynamic discovery just before version 1.0 of the .NET Framework shipped. You can reenable it by uncommenting the line in the *httpHandlers* section of Machine.config that maps *.vsdisco to *System.Web.Services.Discovery.DiscoveryRequestHandler* and granting the ASP-NET account permission to access the IIS metabase. Microsoft highly discourages dynamic discovery for fear of compromising your Web server, and a bug in version 1.0 of the .NET Framework SDK prevents most DISCO-aware tools from working with VSDISCO anyway. My advice is to forget that VSDISCO files even exist and use static DISCO files instead.

To further simplify Web service discovery, you can link to a master DISCO file from your site's default HTML document. For example, suppose the default HTML document at www.wintellect.com is Default.html and that the same directory also holds a discovery document named Default.disco. Including the following HTML in Default.html enables most tools that read DISCO files to accept the URL www.wintellect.com (as opposed to www.wintellect.com/default.disco):

```
<html>
  <head>
    <link type="text/html" rel="alternate" href="Default.disco">
  </head>
</html>
```

Visual Studio .NET (specifically, its Add Web Reference command) reads DISCO files; so does the Disco.exe utility that comes with the .NET Framework SDK.

DISCO's chief disadvantage is that you can't read a DISCO file if you don't have its URL. So how do you find a Web service if you don't even have a URL to start with? Can you spell U-D-D-I?

Web Service Discovery—UDDI

UDDI is an abbreviation for Universal Description, Discovery, and Integration. Jointly developed by IBM, Microsoft, and Ariba and supported by hundreds of other companies, UDDI is a specification for building distributed databases that enable interested parties to "discover" each other's Web services. No one company owns the databases; anyone is free to publish a UDDI-based business registry. Operator sites have already been established by IBM and Microsoft and are likely to be the first of many such sites that will come on line in the future.

UDDI sites are themselves Web services. They publish a pair of SOAP-based APIs: an *inquiry API* for inquiring about companies and their Web services and a *publisher API* for advertising a company's Web services. Anyone can call the inquiry API, but operator sites typically limit the publisher API to registered members. Documentation regarding these APIs and other information about UDDI can be found at *http://www.uddi.org*. At the time of this writing, Microsoft was beta testing a UDDI .NET SDK featuring managed wrapper classes that simplify interactions with UDDI business registries. For the latest information on this and other UDDI development tools proffered by Microsoft, visit *http://uddi.microsoft.com/default.aspx*.

Most developers will never deal with UDDI APIs directly. Instead, they'll use high-level tools such as Visual Studio .NET to query UDDI business registries and generate wrapper classes that allow them to place calls to the Web services that they find there. The actual placing of UDDI calls will be limited primarily to tools vendors and to clients that wish to locate and bind to Web services dynamically.

Web Service Clients

Now that you've seen Web services up close and personal, it's time to learn about Web service clients—that is, applications that use, or *consume*, Web methods. It's easy to write Web services. Writing Web service clients is even easier, thanks to some high-level support lent by the .NET Framework class library (FCL) and a code-generator named Wsdl.exe. If you have a WSDL contract describing a Web service (or the URL of a DISCO file that points to a WSDL contract), you can be making calls to that Web service in no time.

Web Service Proxies

The key concept to grasp when writing Web service clients is that of the *Web service proxy*. A Web service proxy is an object that provides a local representation of a remote Web service. A proxy is instantiated in the client's own application domain, but calls to the proxy flow through the proxy and out to the Web service that the proxy represents. The Wsdl.exe utility that comes with the .NET Framework SDK (and that is integrated into Visual Studio .NET) generates Web service proxy classes from WSDL contracts. Once a proxy is created, calling the corresponding Web service is a simple matter of calling methods on the proxy, as shown here:

```
CalculatorWebService calc = new CalculatorWebService ();
int sum = calc.Add (2, 2);
```

The methods in the proxy class mirror the Web methods in the Web service. If the Web service exposes Web methods named *Add* and *Subtract*, the Web service proxy also contains methods named *Add* and *Subtract*. When you call one of these methods, the proxy packages up the input parameters and invokes the Web method using the protocol encapsulated in the proxy (typically SOAP). The proxy insulates you from the low-level details of the Web service and of the protocols that it uses. It even parses the XML that comes back and makes the result available as managed types.

Using Wsdl.exe to generate a Web service proxy is simplicity itself. Suppose you want to call a Web service whose URL is http://www.wintellect.com/calc.asmx. If the Web service was written with the .NET Framework, which means you can retrieve a WSDL contract by appending a ?wsdl query string to the service URL, you can generate a proxy for the Web service like this:

```
wsdl http://www.wintellect.com/calc.asmx?wsdl
```

Or you can leave off the query string and let Wsdl.exe supply it for you:

```
wsdl http://www.wintellect.com/calc.asmx
```

If Calc.asmx wasn't written with the .NET Framework, it might not support WSDL query strings. In that case, you find the WSDL contract and pass its URL (or local path name) to Wsdl.exe. The following example assumes that the contract is stored in a local file named Calc.wsdl:

```
wsdl calc.wsdl
```

However you point it to the WSDL contract, Wsdl.exe generates a CS file containing a class that represents the Web service proxy. That's the class you instantiate to invoke the Web service's methods.

The proxy class's name comes from the service name (that is, the *name* attribute accompanying the *service* element) in the WSDL contract. For example, suppose you attribute a Web service as follows in its ASMX file:

```
[WebService (Name="Calculator Web Service")]
```

The resulting <service> tag in the WSDL contract looks like this:

```
<service name="Calculator Web Service">
```

and the resulting proxy class is named *CalculatorWebService*. By default, the name of the CS file that Wsdl.exe generates also derives from the service name (for example, Calculator Web Service.cs). You can override that name by passing Wsdl.exe a */out* switch. The command

```
wsdl /out:Calc.cs http://www.wintellect.com/calc.asmx
```

names the output file Calc.cs regardless of the service name.

Wsdl.exe supports a number of command line switches that you can use to customize its output. For example, if you'd prefer the proxy class to be written in Visual Basic .NET rather than C#, use the */language* switch:

```
wsdl /language:vb http://www.wintellect.com/calc.asmx
```

If you'd like Wsdl.exe to enclose the code that it generates in a namespace (which is extremely useful for preventing collisions between types defined in the generated code and types defined in your application and in the FCL), use the */namespace* switch:

```
wsdl /namespace:Calc http://www.wintellect.com/calc.asmx
```

Classes generated by Wsdl.exe derive from base classes in the FCL's *System.Web.Services.Protocols* namespace. By default, a proxy class derives from *SoapHttpClientProtocol*, which enables it to invoke Web methods using SOAP over HTTP. You can change the invocation protocol with Wsdl.exe's */protocol* switch. The command

```
wsdl /protocol:httpget http://www.wintellect.com/calc.asmx
```

creates a Web service proxy that derives from *HttpGetClientProtocol* and calls Web methods using HTTP GET commands, while the command

```
wsdl /protocol:httppost http://www.wintellect.com/calc.asmx
```

creates a proxy that derives from *HttpPostClientProtocol* and uses HTTP POST. Why would you want to change the protocol that a proxy uses to invoke Web methods? In the vast majority of cases, SOAP is fine. However, if the methods that you're calling are simple methods that use equally simple data types, switching to HTTP GET or POST makes calls slightly more efficient by reducing the amount of data transmitted over the wire.

Incidentally, if you use Visual Studio .NET to write Web service clients, you don't have to run Wsdl.exe manually. When you use the Add Web Reference command found in the Project menu, Visual Studio .NET runs Wsdl.exe for you and adds the proxy class to your project. Add Web Reference also speaks the language of UDDI, making it easy to search Microsoft's UDDI registry for interesting Web services.

A Simple Web Service Client

Want to write a client for Calc.asmx? Here are the steps:

1. Use Wsdl.exe to create a proxy class for Calc.asmx. If you installed Calc.asmx in wwwroot, the proper command is

    ```
    wsdl http://localhost/calc.asmx
    ```

    Wsdl.exe responds by creating a file named Calculator Web Service.cs.

2. Create a new text file named CalcClient.cs and enter the code in Figure 11-9.

3. Compile the CS files into a console application with the following command:

    ```
    csc CalcClient.cs "Calculator Web Service.cs"
    ```

4. Run CalcClient.exe.

    CalcClient.exe instantiates a Web service proxy and calls the service's *Add* method. The resulting output proves beyond the shadow of a doubt that Calc.asmx is smart enough to add 2 and 2 (Figure 11-10).

CalcClient.cs
```
using System;

class MyApp
{
    public static void Main ()
    {
        CalculatorWebService calc = new CalculatorWebService ();
        int sum = calc.Add (2, 2);
        Console.WriteLine ("2 + 2 = " + sum);
    }
}
```

Figure 11-9   Console client for Calc.asmx.

Figure 11-10   Output from CalcClient.exe.

Avoiding Hard-Coded Service URLs

Look through a CS file generated by Wsdl.exe, and you'll see the Web service proxy class as well as the methods that wrap the Web service's Web methods. You'll also see that the Web service's URL is hardcoded into the CS file in the proxy's class constructor. Here's an example:

```
public CalculatorWebService() {
    this.Url = "http://www.wintellect.com/calc.asmx";
}
```

If the Web service moves, you'll have to modify the CS file and regenerate the proxy.

To avoid having to update code when a Web service's URL changes, you can use Wsdl.exe's */appsettingurlkey* (abbreviated */urlkey*) switch. The command

```
wsdl /urlkey:CalcUrl http://www.wintellect.com/calc.asmx
```

produces the following class constructor:

```
public CalculatorWebService() {
    string urlSetting =
System.Configuration.ConfigurationSettings.AppSettings["CalcUrl"];
    if ((urlSetting != null)) {
        this.Url = urlSetting;
    }
    else {
        this.Url = "http://www.wintellect.com/calc.asmx";
    }
}
```

Now you can assign a value to "CalcUrl" in the *appSettings* section of a local Web.config file, like so:

```
<configuration>
  <appSettings>
    <add key="CalcUrl" value="http://www.wintellect.com/calc.asmx" />
  </appSettings>
</configuration>
```

If the URL changes, you can update the proxy simply by editing Web.config. No code changes are required.

Asynchronous Method Calls

Something else you'll notice if you open a CS file generated by Wsdl.exe is that the proxy class contains asynchronous as well as synchronous wrappers around the Web service's methods. The former can be used to invoke Web methods asynchronously. An asynchronous call returns immediately, no matter how long the Web service requires to process the call. To retrieve the results from an asynchronous call, you make a separate call later on.

Here's an example using Calc.asmx's *Add* method that demonstrates how to invoke a Web method asynchronously. The client calls the proxy's *BeginAdd* method to initiate an asynchronous call arfd then goes off to attend to other business. Later it returns to finish the call by calling *EndAdd*:

```
CalculatorWebService calc = new CalculatorWebService ();
IAsyncResult res = calc.BeginAdd (2, 2, null, null);
    .
    .
    .
int sum = calc.EndAdd (res);
```

If the call hasn't completed when *EndAdd* is called, *EndAdd* blocks until it does. If desired, a client can use the *IsCompleted* property of the *IAsyncResult* interface returned by *BeginAdd* to determine whether the call has completed and avoid calling *EndAdd* prematurely:

```
IAsyncResult res = calc.BeginAdd (2, 2, null, null);
    .
    .
    .
if (res.IsCompleted) {
    int sum = calc.EndAdd (res);
}
else {
    // Try again later
}
```

Another option is to ask to be notified when an asynchronous call returns by providing a reference to an *AsyncCallback* delegate wrapping a callback method. In the next example, *EndAdd* won't block because it isn't called until the client is certain the method call has returned:

```
AsyncCallback cb = new AsyncCallback (AddCompleted);
IAsyncResult res = calc.BeginAdd (2, 2, cb, null);
    .
    .
    .
public void AddCompleted (IAsyncResult res)
{
    int sum = calc.EndAdd (res);
}
```

Whatever approach you decide on, the proxy's asynchronous method–call support is extraordinarily useful for calling methods that take a long time to complete. *Add* isn't a very realistic example because it's such a simple method, but the principle is valid nonetheless.

Web Service Clients and Proxy Servers

If a client invokes methods on a Web service from behind a proxy server, the Web service proxy needs to know the address of the proxy server. You can provide that address in two ways. The first option is to pass Wsdl.exe a */proxy* switch specifying the proxy server's URL:

```
wsdl /proxy:http://myproxy http://www.wintellect.com/calc.asmx
```

Option number two is to programmatically initialize the Web service proxy's *Proxy* property (which it inherits from *HttpWebClientProtocol*) with a reference to a *WebProxy* object (*System.Net.WebProxy*) identifying the proxy server:

```
CalculatorWebService calc = new CalculatorWebService ();
calc.Proxy = new WebProxy (http://myproxy, true);
int sum = calc.Add (2, 2);
```

The true passed to *WebProxy*'s constructor bypasses the proxy server for local addresses. Pass false instead to route *all* requests through the proxy server.

The CityView Application

The Web application pictured in Figure 11-11—CityView—is a novel and graphic example of a Web service client. The Web service that it connects to is the Microsoft TerraService (*http://terraservice.net/terraservice.asmx*), which is a Web service front end to the Microsoft TerraServer database. You can read all about TerraServer and TerraService at *http://terraservice.net*. TerraServer is one of the world's largest online databases. Inside it are photographs and maps of much of Earth's surface, made available to the public through a partnership between Microsoft and the U.S. Geological Survey. TerraService exposes TerraServer's content via Web methods. There are 16 Web methods in all, with names such as *ConvertPlaceToLonLatPt* and *GetTile*. As you might expect, TerraService was written with the Microsoft .NET Framework. Its WSDL contract is available at *http://terraservice.net/terraservice.asmx?wsdl*.

Before you can run CityView, you need to install it on your Web server. Here's how:

1. Copy CityView.aspx and CityView.ashx from the CD that came with this book to the virtual directory of your choice.

2. Create a subdirectory named bin in the directory that you copied CityView.aspx and CityView.ashx to. Then copy TerraService.dll to the bin directory. TerraService.dll is a DLL containing a TerraService proxy class named *TerraService*.

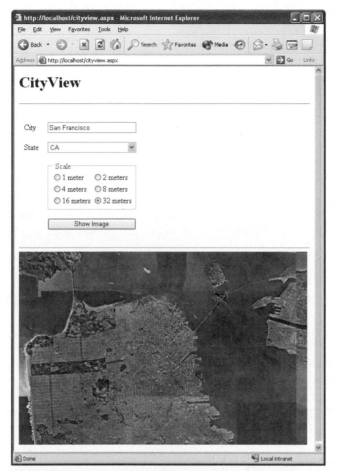

Figure 11-11   CityView showing an aerial view of San Francisco.

Now that CityView is installed, try it out by calling up CityView.aspx in your browser. Enter a city name (for example, "New York") and pick a state. Then click Show Image. After a brief pause, the specified city appears at the bottom of the page. If CityView is unable to fetch the image you requested, it responds by displaying "Image not available" in place of the image. That could mean you entered a city that doesn't exist. Or it could mean that TerraService is temporarily down or your Internet connection is taking a nap.

You can zoom in and out by selecting different scales. The default scale is 8 meters. Choose a smaller number to zoom in or a larger number to zoom out. For a great aerial view of the San Francisco peninsula that includes an overhead shot of the Golden Gate Bridge, enter San Francisco, CA and choose a scale of 32 meters.

How CityView Works

CityView consists of three files:

- CityView.aspx

- CityView.ashx

- TerraService.dll

CityView.aspx is a Web form that defines CityView's user interface. Its source code appears in Figure 11-12. The user interface consists of a *TextBox* for typing city names, a *DropDownList* for selecting states, a *RadioButtonList* for choosing scales, and a *Button* for posting back to the server and fetching images. It also includes an *Image* control whose *ImageUrl* property is programmatically initialized following each postback. Here's the code that assigns a URL to the *Image* control:

```
MyImage.ImageUrl = builder.ToString ();
```

If you enter Redmond, WA, and accept the default scale of 8 meters, the string assigned to *ImageURL* looks like this:

```
CityView.ashx?city=Redmond&state=WA&scale=8
```

which sets the stage perfectly for a discussion of the second component of CityView: namely, CityView.ashx.

CityView.ashx is an HTTP handler. Specifically, it's an HTTP handler that generates and returns a bitmap image of the location named in a query string. When we deployed an HTTP handler in Chapter 8, we coded the handler in a CS file, compiled it into a DLL, and dropped the DLL into the application root's bin directory. We also registered the handler using a Web.config file. City-View.ashx demonstrates the *other* way to deploy HTTP handlers. You simply code an *IHttpHandler*-derived class into an ASHX file and include an @ *Web-Handler* directive that identifies the class name and the language in which the class is written:

```
<%@ WebHandler Language="C#" Class="CityViewImageGen" %>
```

When a client requests an ASHX file containing a *WebHandler* class, ASP.NET compiles the class for you. The beauty of deploying an HTTP handler in an ASHX file is that you don't have to register the handler in a CONFIG file or in the IIS metabase; you just copy the ASHX file to your Web server. The downside, of course, is that you must test the handler carefully to make sure ASP.NET can compile it.

The *CityViewImageGen* class inside CityView.ashx (Figure 11-12) generates the images that CityView.aspx displays. Its heart is the *ProcessRequest* method, which is called on each and every request. *ProcessRequest* calls a local method named *GetTiledImage* to generate the image. Then it returns the image in the HTTP response by calling *Save* on the *Bitmap* object encapsulating the image:

```
bitmap.Save (context.Response.OutputStream, format);
```

Should *GetTiledImage* fail, *ProcessRequest* returns a simple bitmap containing the words "Image not available" instead of an aerial photograph. It also adjusts the format of the bitmap to best fit the type of content returned: JPEG for photographs, and GIF for bitmaps containing text.

GetTiledImage uses three TerraService Web methods:

- *ConvertPlaceToLonLatPt*, which converts a "place" (city, state, country) into a latitude and longitude

- *GetAreaFromPt*, which takes a latitude and longitude and an image size (in pixels) and returns an *AreaBoundingBox* representing the image boundaries

- *GetTile*, which takes a tile ID (obtained from the *AreaBoundingBox*) and returns the corresponding tile

A "tile" is a 200-pixel-square image of a particular geographic location. To build larger images, a TerraService client must fetch multiple tiles and stitch them together to form a composite. That's how *GetTiledImage* generates the 600 x 400 images that it returns. It starts by creating a *Bitmap* object to represent the image. Then it uses *Graphics.DrawImage* to draw each tile onto the image. The logic is wholly independent of the image size, so if you'd like to modify CityView to show larger (or smaller) images, find the statement

```
Bitmap bitmap = GetTiledImage (city, state, res, 600, 400);
```

in CityView.ashx and change the 600 and 400 to the desired width and height.

The third and final component of CityView is TerraService.dll, which contains the TerraService proxy class named *TerraService*. CityView.ashx's *GetTiledImage* method instantiates the proxy class and uses the resulting object to call TerraService's Web methods:

```
TS.TerraService ts = new TS.TerraService ();
```

TerraService.dll was compiled from TerraService.cs, which I generated with the following command:

```
wsdl /namespace:TS http://terraservice.net/terraservice.asmx
```

The namespace was necessary to prevent certain data types defined in TerraService's WSDL contract from conflicting with data types defined in the .NET Framework Class Library. Once TerraService.cs was created, the command

```
csc /t:library terraservice.cs
```

compiled it into a DLL.

CityView.aspx
```
<html>
  <body>
    <h1>CityView</h1>
    <hr>
    <form runat="server">
      <table cellpadding="8">
        <tr>
          <td>
            City
          </td>
          <td>
            <asp:TextBox ID="City" Width="100%" RunAt="server" />
          </td>
          <td>
            <asp:RequiredFieldValidator
              ControlToValidate="City"
              ErrorMessage="*"
              Display="static"
              Color="red"
              RunAt="server"
            />
          </td>
        </tr>
        <tr>
          <td>
            State
          </td>
          <td>
            <asp:DropDownList ID="State" Width="100%" RunAt="server">
              <asp:ListItem Text="AL" RunAt="server" />
              <asp:ListItem Text="AK" RunAt="server" />
              <asp:ListItem Text="AR" RunAt="server" />
              <asp:ListItem Text="AZ" RunAt="server" />
              <asp:ListItem Text="CA" RunAt="server" />
```

Figure 11-12 CityView source code.

```
                    <asp:ListItem Text="CO" RunAt="server" />
                    <asp:ListItem Text="CT" RunAt="server" />
                    <asp:ListItem Text="DC" RunAt="server" />
                    <asp:ListItem Text="DE" RunAt="server" />
                    <asp:ListItem Text="FL" RunAt="server" />
                    <asp:ListItem Text="GA" RunAt="server" />
                    <asp:ListItem Text="HI" RunAt="server" />
                    <asp:ListItem Text="IA" RunAt="server" />
                    <asp:ListItem Text="ID" RunAt="server" />
                    <asp:ListItem Text="IL" RunAt="server" />
                    <asp:ListItem Text="IN" RunAt="server" />
                    <asp:ListItem Text="KS" RunAt="server" />
                    <asp:ListItem Text="KY" RunAt="server" />
                    <asp:ListItem Text="LA" RunAt="server" />
                    <asp:ListItem Text="MA" RunAt="server" />
                    <asp:ListItem Text="MD" RunAt="server" />
                    <asp:ListItem Text="ME" RunAt="server" />
                    <asp:ListItem Text="MI" RunAt="server" />
                    <asp:ListItem Text="MN" RunAt="server" />
                    <asp:ListItem Text="MO" RunAt="server" />
                    <asp:ListItem Text="MS" RunAt="server" />
                    <asp:ListItem Text="MT" RunAt="server" />
                    <asp:ListItem Text="NC" RunAt="server" />
                    <asp:ListItem Text="ND" RunAt="server" />
                    <asp:ListItem Text="NE" RunAt="server" />
                    <asp:ListItem Text="NH" RunAt="server" />
                    <asp:ListItem Text="NJ" RunAt="server" />
                    <asp:ListItem Text="NM" RunAt="server" />
                    <asp:ListItem Text="NV" RunAt="server" />
                    <asp:ListItem Text="NY" RunAt="server" />
                    <asp:ListItem Text="OH" RunAt="server" />
                    <asp:ListItem Text="OK" RunAt="server" />
                    <asp:ListItem Text="OR" RunAt="server" />
                    <asp:ListItem Text="PA" RunAt="server" />
                    <asp:ListItem Text="RI" RunAt="server" />
                    <asp:ListItem Text="SC" RunAt="server" />
                    <asp:ListItem Text="SD" RunAt="server" />
                    <asp:ListItem Text="TN" RunAt="server" />
                    <asp:ListItem Text="TX" RunAt="server" />
                    <asp:ListItem Text="UT" RunAt="server" />
                    <asp:ListItem Text="VA" RunAt="server" />
                    <asp:ListItem Text="VT" RunAt="server" />
                    <asp:ListItem Text="WA" RunAt="server" />
                    <asp:ListItem Text="WI" RunAt="server" />
                    <asp:ListItem Text="WV" RunAt="server" />
                    <asp:ListItem Text="WY" RunAt="server" />
                  </asp:DropDownList>
                </td>
                <td>
```

(continued)

CityView.aspx   *(continued)*

```
            </td>
          </tr>
          <tr>
            <td>
            </td>
            <td>
              <fieldset>
                <legend>Scale</legend>
                <asp:RadioButtonList ID="Scale" RunAt="server"
                  RepeatColumns="2" RepeatDirection="Horizontal">
                  <asp:ListItem Text="1 meter" RunAt="server" />
                  <asp:ListItem Text="2 meters" RunAt="server" />
                  <asp:ListItem Text="4 meters" RunAt="server" />
                  <asp:ListItem Text="8 meters" Selected="true"
                    RunAt="server" />
                  <asp:ListItem Text="16 meters" RunAt="server" />
                  <asp:ListItem Text="32 meters" RunAt="server" />
                </asp:RadioButtonList>
              </fieldset>
            </td>
            <td>
            </td>
          </tr>
          <tr>
            <td>
            </td>
            <td>
              <asp:Button Text="Show Image" OnClick="OnShowImage"
                Width="100%" RunAt="server" />
            </td>
            <td>
            </td>
          </tr>
        </table>
      </form>
      <hr>
      <asp:Image ID="MyImage" RunAt="server" />
  </body>
</html>

<script language="C#" runat="server">
  void OnShowImage (Object sender, EventArgs e)
  {
      StringBuilder builder = new StringBuilder ();
      builder.Append ("CityView.ashx?city=");
      builder.Append (City.Text);
      builder.Append ("&state=");
      builder.Append (State.SelectedItem.Text);
```

```
        builder.Append ("&scale=");

        switch (Scale.SelectedIndex) {
        case 0:
            builder.Append ("1");
            break;

        case 1:
            builder.Append ("2");
            break;

        case 2:
            builder.Append ("4");
            break;

        case 3:
            builder.Append ("8");
            break;

        case 4:
            builder.Append ("16");
            break;

        case 5:
            builder.Append ("32");
            break;
        }

        MyImage.ImageUrl = builder.ToString ();
    }
</script>
```

CityView.ashx

```
<%@ WebHandler Language="C#" Class="CityViewImageGen" %>

using System;
using System.Web;
using System.Drawing;
using System.Drawing.Imaging;
using System.IO;

public class CityViewImageGen : IHttpHandler
{
    public void ProcessRequest (HttpContext context)
    {
        // Extract user input from the query string
        string city = context.Request["City"];
        string state = context.Request["State"];
```

(continued)

CityView.ashx *(continued)*

```
            string scale = context.Request["Scale"];

        if (city != null && state != null) {
            // Determine the scale
            TS.Scale res = TS.Scale.Scale8m;

            if (scale!= null) {
                switch (scale) {
                case "1":
                    res = TS.Scale.Scale1m;
                    break;

                case "2":
                    res = TS.Scale.Scale2m;
                    break;

                case "4":
                    res = TS.Scale.Scale4m;
                    break;

                case "8":
                    res = TS.Scale.Scale8m;
                    break;

                case "16":
                    res = TS.Scale.Scale16m;
                    break;

                case "32":
                    res = TS.Scale.Scale32m;
                    break;
                }
            }

            // Generate the requested image
            string type = "image/jpeg";
            ImageFormat format = ImageFormat.Jpeg;
            Bitmap bitmap = GetTiledImage (city, state, res, 600, 400);

            // If GetTiledImage failed, generate an error bitmap
            if (bitmap == null) {
                bitmap = GetErrorImage ("Image not available");
                type = "image/gif";
                format = ImageFormat.Gif;
            }

            // Set the response's content type
            context.Response.ContentType = type;
```

```
            // Write the image to the HTTP response
            bitmap.Save (context.Response.OutputStream, format);

            // Clean up and return
            bitmap.Dispose ();
        }
    }

    public bool IsReusable
    {
        get { return true; }
    }

    Bitmap GetTiledImage (string City, string State, TS.Scale Scale,
        int cx, int cy)
    {
        Bitmap bitmap = null;
        Graphics g = null;

        try {
            // Instantiate the TerraService proxy
            TS.TerraService ts = new TS.TerraService ();

            // Get the latitude and longitude of the requested city
            TS.Place place = new TS.Place ();
            place.City = City;
            place.State = State;
            place.Country = "USA";
            TS.LonLatPt point = ts.ConvertPlaceToLonLatPt (place);

            // Compute the parameters for a bounding box
            TS.AreaBoundingBox abb = ts.GetAreaFromPt (point,
                TS.Theme.Photo, Scale, cx, cy);

            // Create an image to fit the bounding box
            bitmap = new Bitmap (cx, cy,
                PixelFormat.Format32bppRgb);
            g = Graphics.FromImage (bitmap);

            int x1 = abb.NorthWest.TileMeta.Id.X;
            int y1 = abb.NorthWest.TileMeta.Id.Y;
            int x2 = abb.NorthEast.TileMeta.Id.X;
            int y2 = abb.SouthWest.TileMeta.Id.Y;

            for (int x=x1; x<=x2; x++) {
                for (int y=y1; y>=y2; y--) {
                    TS.TileId tid = abb.NorthWest.TileMeta.Id;
                    tid.X = x;
```

(continued)

CityView.ashx *(continued)*

```
                tid.Y = y;
                Image tile = Image.FromStream
                    (new MemoryStream (ts.GetTile (tid)));
                g.DrawImage (tile,
                    (x - x1) * tile.Width  -
                    (int) abb.NorthWest.Offset.XOffset,
                    (y1 - y) * tile.Height -
                    (int)abb.NorthWest.Offset.YOffset,
                    tile.Width, tile.Height);
                tile.Dispose();
            }
        }

        // Return the image
        return bitmap;
    }
    catch (Exception) {
        if (bitmap != null)
            bitmap.Dispose ();
        return null;
    }
    finally {
        if (g != null)
            g.Dispose ();
    }
}

Bitmap GetErrorImage (string message)
{
    // Determine the width and height of the error message
    Bitmap bitmap =
        new Bitmap (1, 1, PixelFormat.Format32bppRgb);
    Graphics g = Graphics.FromImage (bitmap);
    Font font = new Font ("Verdana", 10);
    SizeF size = g.MeasureString (message, font);
    int cx = (int) size.Width;
    int cy = (int) size.Height;
    bitmap.Dispose ();
    g.Dispose ();

    // Generate a bitmap containing the error message
    bitmap = new Bitmap (cx, cy, PixelFormat.Format32bppRgb);
    g = Graphics.FromImage (bitmap);
    SolidBrush redBrush = new SolidBrush (Color.Red);
    SolidBrush whiteBrush = new SolidBrush (Color.White);

    g.FillRectangle (whiteBrush, 0, 0, 256, 64);
    g.DrawString (message, font, redBrush, 0, 0);
```

```
        whiteBrush.Dispose ();
        redBrush.Dispose ();
        font.Dispose ();
        g.Dispose ();

        // Return the image
        return bitmap;
    }
}
```

For-Fee Web Services

One of the most commonly asked questions regarding Web services has to do with economics rather than programming conundrums. The question can be summarized as follows. I'm thinking about writing a particular Web service. For it to be commercially viable, I have to charge a fee for using it. If I charge for it, I have to know who's calling it. How do I know who's calling my Web service? In other words, how do I identify the originator of a Web method call?

The question is actually one of security. Identifying callers means authenticating callers. There are several ways to authenticate Web service callers. Here are three possibilities:

- Assign authorized callers an authentication key (for example, a password or a random sequence of digits) and require them to pass the key in each method call.

- Transmit user names and passwords in HTTP *Authorization* headers.

- Transmit user names and passwords or some other form of credentials in SOAP headers.

The third of these three options is arguably the most compelling because it transmits authentication data out-of-band and enables developers to leverage the high-level support for SOAP headers built into the .NET Framework. To demonstrate, here's a Web service whose *Add* method can be called successfully only if the SOAP request contains a header named *AuthHeader* that in turn contains a *UserName* element equal to "jeffpro" and a *Password* element equal to "imbatman":

```
<%@ WebService Language="C#" Class="SafeService" %>

using System;
using System.Web;
using System.Web.Services;
using System.Web.Services.Protocols;
```

(continued)

```
public class AuthHeader : SoapHeader
{
    public string UserName;
    public string Password;
}

class SafeService
{
    public AuthHeader header;

    [WebMethod]
    [SoapHeader ("header", Required="true")]
    public int Add (int a, int b)
    {
        if (header.UserName == "jeffpro" &&
            header.Password == "imbatman")
            return a + b;
        else
            throw new HttpException (401, "Not authorized");
    }
}
```

AuthHeader is a custom type derived from *System.Web.Services.Protocols.Soap-Header* that represents a SOAP header. The *SoapHeader* attribute affixed to the *Add* method tells ASP.NET to reject calls (that is, throw *SoapHeaderExceptions*) to *Add* that lack *AuthHeader*s and to map incoming *AuthHeader*s to the *SafeService* field named *header*. The *Add* method extracts the user name and password from the SOAP header and throws an exception if the credentials are invalid.

How does a client attach *AuthHeader*s to outgoing calls? Here's an excerpt from a .NET Framework client that calls *SafeService*'s *Add* method with the proper authorization header:

```
SafeService calc = new SafeService ();
AuthHeader header = new AuthHeader ();
header.UserName = "jeffpro";
header.Password = "imbatman";
calc.AuthHeaderValue = header;
int sum = calc.Add (2, 2);
```

The *AuthHeader* data type is defined in the service's WSDL contract. When Wsdl.exe generated the Web service proxy (*SafeService*), it also generated an *AuthHeader* class definition and added an *AuthHeader* field named *AuthHeaderValue* to *SafeService*. Initializing that field with an *AuthHeader* object transmits the data contained therein in a SOAP header. Here, in fact, is what the outgoing SOAP envelope might look like, with the SOAP header highlighted in boldface text:

```
<?xml version="1.0" encoding="utf-8"?>
<soap:Envelope xmlns:xsi="http://www.w3.org/2001/XMLSchema-instance"
  xmlns:xsd=http://www.w3.org/2001/XMLSchema
  xmlns:soap="http://schemas.xmlsoap.org/soap/envelope/">
  <soap:Header>
    <AuthHeader xmlns="http://tempuri.org/">
      <UserName>jeffpro</UserName>
      <Password>imbatman</Password>
    </AuthHeader>
  </soap:Header>
  <soap:Body>
    <Add xmlns="http://tempuri.org/">
      <a>2</a>
      <b>2</b>
    </Add>
  </soap:Body>
</soap:Envelope>
```

As you can see, the .NET Framework goes to great lengths to insulate you from the nuts and bolts of SOAP and XML. It even provides high-level abstractions for SOAP headers.

A variation on this technique is to include an *Application_AuthenticateRequest* handler in a Global.asax file and examine SOAP headers there. The advantage to this approach is that you don't have to authenticate the caller in each and every Web method. *Application_AuthenticateRequest* centralizes the authentication code and allows you to prevent the Web method from even being called if the caller lacks the proper credentials.

Yet another way to identify callers is to configure IIS to require authenticated access to the directory that hosts the Web service and enable Windows authentication in ASP.NET via a Web.config file. Then derive your Web service class from *System.Web.Services.WebService* and use the inherited *User* property to obtain callers' user names. This form of authentication, unlike methods that perform custom authentication using SOAP headers, is appropriate only if callers have accounts in the Web server's domain. In other words, it's a fine solution for Web services that serve clients on the company's intranet but not for ones that serve the population at large.

Dawn of a New Era

Web services have the potential to change the way we compute. Imagine an Internet featuring millions of TerraServices, each exposing different content and business logic to interested callers. The applications that you write would enjoy access to a rich assortment of data and services unparalleled in the industry today. And writing those applications would require little or no knowledge of the underlying communications protocols, thanks to the .NET Framework, which hides HTTP, XML, and SOAP under the hood and allows you to focus on the logic that makes your application unique rather than on the plumbing that enables it to communicate with remote servers.

True cross-platform distributed computing has been the Holy Grail of computer scientists for years, but only now, with the advent of Web services and tools that simplify them, is the dream finally realizable. Anyone who has spent the last several years wrestling with RPC, DCOM, CORBA, and other remote invocation protocols will agree: Web services are an idea whose time has come. For developers, the time to learn about them is now.

Part 3

The Cutting Edge

12

ADO.NET

Behind every great application lies a database manager. At least it seems that way, especially if your gig is writing Web applications that expose content over the Internet. Amazon.com and eBay are little more than front ends to massive databases designed to serve end users like you and me. The older I get and the wiser I become, the more I realize that programming is about managing and manipulating data, and UI code is just the goo that lets it happen.

Like their counterparts in the unmanaged world, managed applications can and often do utilize industrial-strength databases such as Microsoft SQL Server and Oracle 8i. That's why Microsoft created ADO.NET, an elegant, easy-to-use database API for managed applications. ADO.NET is exposed as a set of classes in the .NET Framework class library's *System.Data* namespace and its descendants. Unlike ADO and OLE DB, its immediate predecessors, ADO.NET was designed from the outset to work in the connectionless world of the Web. It also integrates effortlessly with XML, bridging the gap between relational data and XML and simplifying the task of moving back and forth between them.

If you're like most developers, you believe that the last thing the world needs is another database access API. Why, when we already have ODBC, DAO, ADO, RDO, OLE DB, and others, do we need yet another API? The short answer is that the world has changed, and none of the existing data access technologies maps very well to a world that revolves around that stateless, text-based protocol called HTTP. In addition, managed applications need an efficient and intuitive way to talk to databases. That's ADO.NET in a nutshell—the database language spoken by managed applications. ADO.NET is an essential component of the .NET Framework. Let's see how it works.

A Tale of Two Providers

The very first thing that every developer should know about ADO.NET is that it has a split personality. ADO.NET database accesses go through software modules known as *data providers*. Version 1.0 of the .NET Framework ships with two data providers:

■ The SQL Server .NET provider, which interfaces to Microsoft SQL Server databases without any help from unmanaged providers

■ The OLE DB .NET provider, which interfaces to databases through unmanaged OLE DB providers

OLE DB is a data access technology that originated in the heyday of COM. OLE DB providers layer a uniform object-oriented API over disparate databases, just as Open Database Connectivity (ODBC) drivers provide a procedural front end to different kinds of databases. OLE DB providers are available for a variety of non–SQL Server databases. The .NET Framework's OLE DB .NET provider lets you leverage existing OLE DB providers by calling out to them from managed code. Microsoft has tested the following OLE DB providers and deemed them compatible with the framework's OLE DB .NET provider:

■ The SQLOLEDB provider, which interfaces with SQL Server databases

■ The MSDAORA provider, which interfaces with Oracle databases

■ The Microsoft.Jet.OLEDB.4.0 provider, which interfaces with databases driven by the Microsoft Jet database engine

In the past, some developers used the MSDASQL OLE DB provider to access databases using ODBC. MSDASQL was a generic solution that permitted databases without an OLE DB provider of their own but that had ODBC drivers available to be accessed using the OLE DB API. MSDASQL is not compatible with the .NET Framework, but you can download an ODBC .NET provider that is compatible with the framework from Microsoft's Web site.

So what does all this mean for the developer? For starters, you should decide on a provider before you write the first line of code in a project that relies on a database. Here are your choices:

■ If your application will employ Microsoft SQL Server version 7.0 or later, use the SQL Server .NET provider. It's faster than the OLE DB .NET provider because it doesn't use OLE DB. It goes all the way to the database without leaving the realm of managed code. The OLE DB .NET provider, by contrast, uses the .NET Framework's Platform Invoke (P/Invoke) mechanism to call out to unmanaged OLE DB providers.

■ If your application will use Microsoft SQL Server 6.5 or earlier, use the OLE DB .NET provider paired with the SQLOLEDB OLE DB provider. The SQL Server .NET provider requires SQL Server 7.0 or later.

■ If your application will use a database other than SQL Server—say, an Oracle 8i database—use the OLE DB .NET provider.

If the database is neither Oracle nor Jet but an OLE DB provider is available for it, the provider *might* work. Then again, it might not. It depends on whether the database's unmanaged OLE DB provider is compatible with the .NET Framework's managed OLE DB .NET provider. Not all are. If the OLE DB driver isn't compatible with the .NET Framework (or if it doesn't exist), but an ODBC driver is available for the database in question, download Microsoft's ODBC .NET driver and use it to talk to the database.

The *System.Data.SqlClient* and *System.Data.OleDb* Namespaces

Your choice of provider directly impacts the code that you write. Some ADO.NET classes work with all providers. *DataSet* is a good example. Defined in the *System.Data* namespace, *DataSet* works equally well with SQL Server .NET and OLE DB .NET. But many ADO.NET classes target a specific provider. For example, *DataAdapter* comes in two flavors: *SqlDataAdapter* for the SQL Server .NET provider and *OleDbDataAdapter* for the OLE DB .NET provider. *SqlDataAdapter* and other SQL Server .NET classes belong to the *System.Data.SqlClient* namespace. *OleDbDataAdapter* is defined in *System.Data.OleDb*.

How does this affect the code that you write? Here's a short sample that uses the SQL Server .NET provider to list all the book titles contained in the "Titles" table of the Pubs database that comes with SQL Server:

```
using System.Data.SqlClient;
    .
    .
    .
SqlConnection conn = new SqlConnection
    ("server=localhost;database=pubs;uid=sa;pwd=");
```

(continued)

```
try {
    conn.Open ();
    SqlCommand cmd = new SqlCommand ("select * from titles", conn);
    SqlDataReader reader = cmd.ExecuteReader ();
    while (reader.Read ())
        Console.WriteLine (reader["title"]);
}
catch (SqlException ex) {
    Console.WriteLine (ex.Message);
}
finally {
    conn.Close ();
}
```

And here's the equivalent code rewritten to use the OLE DB .NET provider (via the unmanaged OLE DB provider for SQL Server). Changes are highlighted in bold:

```
using System.Data.OleDb;
    .
    .
    .

OleDbConnection conn = new OleDbConnection
    ("provider=sqloledb;server=localhost;database=pubs;uid=sa;pwd=");

try {
    conn.Open ();
    OleDbCommand cmd =
        new OleDbCommand ("select * from titles", conn);
    OleDbDataReader reader = cmd.ExecuteReader ();
    while (reader.Read ())
        Console.WriteLine (reader["title"]);
}
catch (OleDbException ex) {
    Console.WriteLine (ex.Message);
}
finally {
    conn.Close ();
}
```

Notice that *SqlConnection*, *SqlCommand*, *SqlDataReader*, and *SqlException* became *OleDbConnection*, *OleDbCommand*, *OleDbDataReader*, and *OleDbException*, and that the database connection string changed too. ADO.NET provides a common API for various types of databases, but the details of that API differ slightly depending on the managed provider that you choose.

The good news is that other than class names and connection strings, few differences distinguish the SQL Server .NET and OLE DB .NET providers. The *SqlDataAdapter* and *OleDbDataAdapter* classes, for example, implement the same set of methods, properties, and events. Converting *SqlDataAdapter* code to use *OleDbDataAdapter* instead is mostly a matter of using find-and-replace to change the class names. That's good to know if you originally design your software around a SQL Server database and later decide to switch to Oracle (or vice versa).

In general, I'll use the *Sql* classes for the code samples in this chapter. Unless I say otherwise, you can assume that changing *Sql* to *OleDb* in the class names is sufficient to switch providers. Provider-specific class names without *Sql* or *OleDb* prefixes refer generically to classes of both types. For example, when I use the term *DataReader*, I'm referring to both *SqlDataReader* and *OleDbDataReader*.

Connections, Commands, and *DataReaders*

All interactions with a database using ADO.NET involve, either implicitly or explicitly, connection and command objects. Connection objects represent physical connections to a database. They come in two flavors: *SqlConnection* for Microsoft SQL Server databases and *OleDbConnection* for others. Command objects represent the commands performed on a database. They too come in provider-specific versions: *SqlCommand* and *OleDbCommand*.

The canonical usage pattern for executing database commands in ADO.NET is as follows:

1. Create a connection object encapsulating a connection string.

2. Open the connection by calling *Open* on the connection object.

3. Create a command object encapsulating both an SQL command and the connection that the command will use.

4. Call a method on the command object to execute the command.

5. Close the connection by calling *Close* on the connection object.

SqlCommand and *OleDbCommand* implement several methods that you can call to execute a command. Which method you call and what you get in return depends on the command being executed. If the command is a query, you get back a *DataReader* object (*SqlDataReader* or *OleDbDataReader*) encapsulating the results. *Connection*, *Command*, and *DataReader* are three of the most important types defined in ADO.NET. The next several sections describe them in detail.

The *SqlConnection* Class

Before you can perform an operation on a database, you must open a connection to it. ADO.NET's *System.Data.SqlClient.SqlConnection* class represents connections to SQL Server databases. Inside a *SqlConnection* object is a connection string. The following statements create a *SqlConnection* object and initialize it with a connection string that opens the Pubs database that comes with SQL Server, using the user name "sa" and a blank password:

```
SqlConnection conn = new SqlConnection ();
conn.ConnectionString = "server=localhost;database=pubs;uid=sa;pwd=";
```

ConnectionString is the *SqlConnection* property that stores the connection string. *SqlConnection* features an alternative constructor that creates a *SqlConnection* object and initializes the *ConnectionString* property in one step:

```
SqlConnection conn = new SqlConnection
    ("server=localhost;database=pubs;uid=sa;pwd=");
```

SqlConnection verifies that the connection string is well formed when the string is assigned. The following statement throws a *System.ArgumentException* exception because *Srvr* is not a valid parameter:

```
SqlConnection conn = new SqlConnection
    ("srvr=localhost;database=pubs;uid=sa;pwd=");
```

Parameter values in the connection string aren't tested until you open the connection, so a connection string assignment operation will not throw an exception if the server name, database name, user ID, or password is invalid.

The connection string's *Server* parameter identifies the instance of SQL Server that contains the database and the machine on which it resides. *Server*=localhost, which can also be written *Server*=(local) or *Data Source*=(local), identifies the host machine (the machine that's executing the ADO.NET code) as the one that hosts the database and implicitly identifies the default instance of SQL Server. SQL Server 2000 permits up to 16 different instances to be installed on a given machine. One instance is typically designated as the default instance; others are referenced by name. The following statements create a *SqlCommand* object referencing the Pubs database in an instance of SQL Server named Wintellect on a remote machine named Hawkeye:

```
SqlConnection conn = new SqlConnection
    ("server=hawkeye\wintellect;database=pubs;uid=sa;pwd=");
```

The *Database* parameter, which can also be written *Initial Catalog*, identifies the database. *Uid*, whose alternate form is *User ID*, specifies the user name, and *Pwd*, which can optionally be written *Password*, specifies the password. The abbreviated parameter names are a holdover from ODBC and are officially considered deprecated. Nonetheless, I use them in most of my examples to keep the connection strings as compact as possible.

Server, *Database*, *Uid*, and *Pwd* aren't the only parameters you can include in a SQL Server connection string. A complete list is available in the documentation for the *SqlConnection.ConnectionString* property. Other commonly used connection string parameters include *Min Pool Size* and *Max Pool Size*, which set limits on the size of the connection pool (the defaults are 0 and 100, respectively); *Pooling*, which enables and disables connection pooling (default=true); *Integrated Security*, which enables and disables integrated security (the default is false, which authenticates the user on the basis of the user name and password in the connection string; if *Integrated Security* is true, SQL Server uses Windows access tokens for authentication); and *Connect Timeout*, which specifies the maximum length of time, in seconds, you're willing to wait when opening a connection (default=15). The following statements use some of these parameters to more carefully control the connection attributes:

```
SqlConnection conn = new SqlConnection
    ("server=hawkeye\wintellect;database=pubs;uid=sa;pwd=;" +
    "min pool size=10;max pool size=50;connect timeout=10");
```

Setting the minimum pool size to some value greater than 0 preloads the connection pool with the specified number of connections and helps a data-driven application that expects heavy demand get off to a fast start.

The *OleDbConnection* Class

System.Data.OleDb.OleDbConnection represents connections to databases accessed through the .NET Framework's OLE DB .NET provider. The format of connection strings used with *OleDbConnection* is patterned after OLE DB connection strings and differs slightly from that of *SqlConnection*. The following statement creates an *OleDbConnection* object encapsulating a connection to SQL Server's Pubs database on the local machine:

```
OleDbConnection conn = new OleDbConnection
    ("provider=sqloledb;server=localhost;database=pubs;uid=sa;pwd=");
```

The *Provider* parameter identifies the OLE DB provider used to interact with the database—in this case, SQLOLEDB, which is Microsoft's OLE DB provider for SQL Server. Changing the provider to MSDAORA would target Oracle databases instead.

As with *SqlConnection* connection strings, *OleDbConnection* connection strings are not case-sensitive and can utilize a more verbose syntax in which *Server* equals *Data Source*, *DataBase* equals *Initial Catalog*, *Uid* equals *User ID*, and *Pwd* equals *Password*. The following statement is functionally equivalent to the previous one:

```
OleDbConnection conn = new OleDbConnection
    ("provider=sqloledb;data source=localhost;" +
    "initial catalog=pubs;user id=sa;password=");
```

OleDbConnection connection strings can also include *File Name* parameters targeting Microsoft Data Link (UDL) files and *OLE DB Services* parameters enabling and disabling certain features of the underlying unmanaged provider. For example, the following connection string disables connection pooling:

```
OleDbConnection conn = new OleDbConnection
    ("provider=sqloledb;data source=localhost;OLE DB Services=-2" +
    "initial catalog=pubs;user id=sa;password=");
```

Other *OleDbConnection* connection string parameters are supported, but these tend to vary among providers. Refer to the documentation for individual OLE DB providers for more information on valid connection string parameters.

Opening and Closing Connections

The mere act of creating a *Connection* object and supplying a connection string doesn't physically open a connection to the database. Calling the object's *Open* method does. A connection opened with *Open* should be closed with *Close*. Both *SqlConnection* and *OleDbConnection* feature *Open* and *Close* methods. The following code opens and closes a SQL Server connection:

```
SqlConnection conn = new SqlConnection
    ("server=localhost;database=pubs;uid=sa;pwd=");
conn.Open ();
// TODO: Use the connection
conn.Close ();
```

SqlConnection.Open throws a *SqlException* if it can't establish a connection to the database. Operations performed on the database through an open connection also throw *SqlExceptions* if they fail. Because exceptions should never go uncaught, and because closing an open connection is vitally important, you should enclose statements that close database connections in *finally* blocks, as shown here:

```
SqlConnection conn = new SqlConnection
    ("server=localhost;database=pubs;uid=sa;pwd=");
try {
    conn.Open ();
    // TODO: Use the connection
}
catch (SqlException ex) {
```

```
        // TODO: Handle the exception
    }
    finally {
        conn.Close ();
    }
```

The equivalent code for the OLE DB .NET provider looks like this. Note that the exception type is *OleDbException* rather than *SqlException*:

```
OleDbConnection conn = new OleDbConnection
    ("provider=sqloledb;server=localhost;database=pubs;uid=sa;pwd=");
try {
    conn.Open ();
    // TODO: Use the connection
}
catch (OleDbException ex) {
    // TODO: Handle the exception
}
finally {
    conn.Close ();
}
```

Calling *Close* on a connection that's not open isn't harmful. Structuring your database access code this way ensures that the connection is closed even in the event of untimely errors. Failing to close open connections is debilitating to performance and to the very operation of the application. *Always* close database connections in *finally* blocks in production code.

Command Classes

An open connection to a database is of little value unless you use it to execute commands. To that end, ADO.NET provides a pair of command classes named *SqlCommand* and *OleDbCommand*. Both encapsulate SQL commands performed on a database, both rely on connections established with *SqlConnection* and *OleDbConnection*, and both include methods that you can call to execute the commands encapsulated inside them.

The following example uses a *SqlCommand* object to delete a record from the Pubs database's "Titles" table using an SQL DELETE command:

```
SqlConnection conn = new SqlConnection
    ("server=localhost;database=pubs;uid=sa;pwd=");
try {
    conn.Open ();
    SqlCommand cmd = new SqlCommand ();
    cmd.CommandText = "delete from titles where title_id = 'BU1032'";
    cmd.Connection = conn;
    cmd.ExecuteNonQuery (); // Execute the command
}
```

```
catch (SqlException ex) {
    // TODO: Handle the exception
}
finally {
    conn.Close ();
}
```

You can make your code more concise by creating a *SqlCommand* object and initializing its *Connection* and *CommandText* properties in one step:

```
SqlConnection conn = new SqlConnection
    ("server=localhost;database=pubs;uid=sa;pwd=");
try {
    conn.Open ();
    SqlCommand cmd = new SqlCommand
        ("delete from titles where title_id = 'BU1032'", conn);
    cmd.ExecuteNonQuery (); // Execute the command
}
catch (SqlException ex) {
    // TODO: Handle the exception
}
finally {
    conn.Close ();
}
```

You can also use the command object's *CommandTimeout* property to specify the number of seconds you're willing to give the command for it to complete:

```
SqlCommand cmd = new SqlCommand
    ("delete from titles where title_id = 'BU1032'", conn);
cmd.CommandTimeout = 10; // Allow 10 seconds
cmd.ExecuteNonQuery ();
```

The default command time-out is 30 seconds. A command that times out throws a *SqlException*. To prevent a command from timing out (probably not a good idea), set *CommandTimeout* to 0.

The preceding examples use *ExecuteNonQuery* to execute an SQL command. *Command* objects also have methods named *ExecuteScalar* and *ExecuteReader*. Which of the three you should use depends on the nature of the command that you're executing.

The *ExecuteNonQuery* Method

The *ExecuteNonQuery* method is a vehicle for executing INSERT, UPDATE, DELETE, and other SQL commands that don't return values—for example, CREATE DATABASE and CREATE TABLE commands. When used with INSERT,

UPDATE, or DELETE, *ExecuteNonQuery* returns the number of rows affected by the command. For all other commands, it returns –1.

Here's an example that uses *ExecuteNonQuery* to add a record to the Pubs database's "Titles" table using an INSERT command:

```
SqlConnection conn = new SqlConnection
    ("server=localhost;database=pubs;uid=sa;pwd=");

try {
    conn.Open ();
    SqlCommand cmd = new SqlCommand
        ("insert into titles (title_id, title, type, pubdate) " +
        "values ('JP1001', 'Programming Microsoft .NET', " +
        "'business', 'May 2002')", conn);
    cmd.ExecuteNonQuery ();
}
catch (SqlException ex) {
    // TODO: Handle the exception
}
finally {
    conn.Close ();
}
```

The next example updates the record just added:

```
SqlConnection conn = new SqlConnection
    ("server=localhost;database=pubs;uid=sa;pwd=");

try {
    conn.Open ();
    SqlCommand cmd = new SqlCommand
        ("update titles set title_id = 'JP2002' " +
        "where title_id = 'JP1001'", conn);
    cmd.ExecuteNonQuery ();
}
catch (SqlException ex) {
    // TODO: Handle the exception
}
finally {
    conn.Close ();
}
```

And this one removes the record from the database:

```
SqlConnection conn = new SqlConnection
    ("server=localhost;database=pubs;uid=sa;pwd=");

try {
    conn.Open ();
    SqlCommand cmd = new SqlCommand
```

(continued)

```
        ("delete from titles where title_id = 'JP2002'", conn);
    cmd.ExecuteNonQuery ();
}
catch (SqlException ex) {
    // TODO: Handle the exception
}
finally {
    conn.Close ();
}
```

To create a new database named "MyDatabase" with *ExecuteNonQuery*, simply change the command text to "create database MyDatabase." Follow up with CREATE TABLE and INSERT commands, and you can build a whole new database on the fly.

If *ExecuteNonQuery* fails, it throws an exception accompanied by a *SqlException* object. *SqlException* properties such as *Message*, *Class*, and *Source* contain detailed information about the error. A simple way to respond to a *SqlException* in a console application is to write the error message in the *SqlException* object to the console window:

```
catch (SqlException ex) {
    Console.WriteLine (ex.Message);
}
```

Examples of statements that throw exceptions are UPDATEs with invalid field names and INSERTs that violate primary key constraints. Note that UPDATE and DELETE commands targeting nonexistent records do not constitute errors; *ExecuteNonQuery* simply returns 0.

The *ExecuteScalar* Method

The *ExecuteScalar* method executes an SQL command and returns the first row of the first column in the result set. One of its most common uses is to execute SQL functions such as COUNT, AVG, MIN, MAX, and SUM, which return single-row, single-column result sets. The following example writes the largest advance payment recorded in the Pubs database to a console window:

```
SqlConnection conn = new SqlConnection
    ("server=localhost;database=pubs;uid=sa;pwd=");

try {
    conn.Open ();
    SqlCommand cmd = new SqlCommand
        ("select max (advance) from titles", conn);
    decimal amount = (decimal) cmd.ExecuteScalar ();
    Console.WriteLine ("ExecuteScalar returned {0:c}", amount);
}
```

```
catch (SqlException ex) {
    Console.WriteLine (ex.Message);
}
finally {
    conn.Close ();
}
```

Note the cast that converts *ExecuteScalar*'s return value into a decimal value. *ExecuteScalar* is generically typed to return an *Object*, so a cast is required to convert it into a strong type. If you cast incorrectly, the .NET Framework throws an *InvalidCastException*. In this example, the cast works fine because the "Advance" field in the Pubs database is of type money, and the SQL money data type translates naturally into the .NET Framework's decimal (*System.Decimal*) data type.

Another common use for *ExecuteScalar* is to retrieve BLOBs (binary large objects) from databases. The following example retrieves an image from the "Logo" field of the Pubs database's "Pub_info" table and encapsulates it in a bitmap:

```
MemoryStream stream = new MemoryStream ();
SqlConnection conn = new SqlConnection
    ("server=localhost;database=pubs;uid=sa;pwd=");

try {
    conn.Open ();
    SqlCommand cmd = new SqlCommand
        ("select logo from pub_info where pub_id='0736'", conn);
    byte[] blob = (byte[]) cmd.ExecuteScalar ();
    stream.Write (blob, 0, blob.Length);
    Bitmap bitmap = new Bitmap (stream);
    // TODO: Use the bitmap
    bitmap.Dispose ();
}
catch (SqlException ex) {
    // TODO: Handle the exception
}
finally {
    stream.Close ();
    conn.Close ();
}
```

Once the bitmap is created, you can do whatever you want with it: display it in a Windows form, stream it back in an HTTP response, or whatever. Note that in order for this sample to compile, you must include *using* statements that import the *System.IO* and *System.Drawing* namespaces as well as *System* and *System.Data.SqlClient*.

Incidentally, the previous code sample answers a frequently asked ADO.NET question: "How do I retrieve BLOBs from databases with ADO.NET?" You might be interested in knowing how to write BLOBs to databases, too. The secret is to call *ExecuteNonQuery* on a command object that wraps an INSERT command containing an input parameter whose type is byte[]. To demonstrate, the following example inserts a record into the Pubs database's "Pub_info" table and includes a BLOB in the record's "Logo" field:

```
SqlConnection conn = new SqlConnection
    ("server=localhost;database=pubs;uid=sa;pwd=");

try {
    conn.Open ();
    SqlCommand cmd = new SqlCommand
        ("insert into pub_info (pub_id, logo) values ('9937', @logo)",
         conn);
    cmd.Parameters.Add ("@logo", blob);
    cmd.ExecuteNonQuery ();
}
catch (SqlException ex) {
    // TODO: Handle the exception
}
finally {
    conn.Close ();
}
```

Where does the variable named *blob* come from? It's defined and initialized separately. Here's an example that initializes *blob* with an image read from a file named Logo.jpg:

```
FileStream stream = new FileStream ("Logo.jpg", FileMode.Open);
byte[] blob = new byte[stream.Length];
stream.Read (blob, 0, (int) stream.Length);
stream.Close ();
```

Using the techniques demonstrated here, it's easy to write images or other BLOBs to databases and read them back. Do note that for the preceding INSERT command to work on the Pubs database, you must first add a record to the "Publishers" table containing the "Pub_id" 9937. If you don't, the INSERT will fail because of a foreign key constraint that stipulates that publisher IDs in the "Pub_info" table also appear in the "Publishers" table.

Chapter 10 contains another excellent example of ExecuteScalar usage. That chapter's LoginPage.aspx file uses ExecuteScalar to validate a user name and password by using an SQL COUNT command to see whether the user name and password exist in the database. Here's that code again:

```
SqlConnection connection = new SqlConnection
    ("server=localhost;database=weblogin;uid=sa;pwd=");

try {
    connection.Open ();

    StringBuilder builder = new StringBuilder ();
    builder.Append ("select count (*) from users " +
        "where username = \'");
    builder.Append (username);
    builder.Append ("\' and cast (rtrim (password) as " +
        "varbinary) = cast (\'");
    builder.Append (password);
    builder.Append ("\' as varbinary)");

    SqlCommand command = new SqlCommand (builder.ToString (),
        connection);

    int count = (int) command.ExecuteScalar ();
    return (count > 0);
}
catch (SqlException) {
    return false;
}
finally {
    connection.Close ();
}
```

As described in Chapter 10, casting the password to SQL's *varbinary* data type
is a sneaky way to perform a case-sensitive string comparison.

The *ExecuteReader* Method

The *ExecuteReader* method exists for one purpose and one purpose only: to
perform database queries and obtain the results as quickly and efficiently as
possible. *ExecuteReader* returns a *DataReader* object: *SqlDataReader* if called
on a *SqlCommand* object and *OleDbDataReader* if called on an *OleDbCommand* object. *DataReader* has methods and properties that you can call to iterate over the result set. It is a fast, forward-only, read-only mechanism for
enumerating the results of database queries. It's extremely efficient for retrieving result sets from remote machines because it pulls back only the data that
you ask for. A query might produce a million records, but if you only read 10
of them with a *DataReader*, only a fraction of the total result set is actually
returned.

The following example uses *ExecuteReader* and the resultant *SqlDataReader*
to write the titles of all the books listed in the Pubs database to a console window:

```
SqlConnection conn = new SqlConnection
    ("server=localhost;database=pubs;uid=sa;pwd=");

try {
    conn.Open ();
    SqlCommand cmd = new SqlCommand ("select * from titles", conn);
    SqlDataReader reader = cmd.ExecuteReader ();
    while (reader.Read ())
        Console.WriteLine (reader["title"]);
}
catch (SqlException ex) {
    Console.WriteLine (ex.Message);
}
finally {
    conn.Close ();
}
```

Each call to *SqlDataReader.Read* returns one row from the result set. This example uses a property indexer to extract the value of the record's "Title" field. Fields can be referenced by name or by numeric index (0-based, of course).

You don't have to know a database's schema in advance to query it with a *DataReader*. You can get schema information from the *DataReader* itself. The next example queries for all the records in the "Titles" table and displays the names of the fields:

```
SqlConnection conn = new SqlConnection
    ("server=localhost;database=pubs;uid=sa;pwd=");

try {
    conn.Open ();
    SqlCommand cmd = new SqlCommand ("select * from titles", conn);
    SqlDataReader reader = cmd.ExecuteReader ();
    for (int i=0; i<reader.FieldCount; i++)
        Console.WriteLine (reader.GetName (i));
}
catch (SqlException ex) {
    Console.WriteLine (ex.Message);
}
finally {
    conn.Close ();
}
```

You can also get schema information by calling a *DataReader*'s *GetSchema-Table* method. *GetSchemaTable* returns a *DataTable* object (described later in this chapter) from which you can enumerate fields.

The previous example used *DataReader.GetName* to retrieve field names. *DataReader* also has a *GetValue* method that you can use to retrieve a field's value. *GetValue* returns a generic *Object*, but it's complemented by numerous *Get* methods, such as *GetInt32* and *GetDecimal*, that return strong data types. The following code uses *GetDecimal* to read decimal values from the "Titles" table's "Advance" field. The WHERE clause in the SELECT command skips records whose "Advance" field is null. The call to *GetOrdinal* is required because *GetDecimal* accepts only integer indexes. *GetOrdinal* does exactly the opposite of *GetName*—it converts a field name into a numeric index:

```
SqlConnection conn = new SqlConnection
    ("server=localhost;database=pubs;uid=sa;pwd=");

try {
    conn.Open ();
    SqlCommand cmd = new SqlCommand
        ("select * from titles where advance != 0", conn);
    SqlDataReader reader = cmd.ExecuteReader ();
    int index = reader.GetOrdinal ("advance");
    while (reader.Read ())
    Console.WriteLine ("{0:c}", reader.GetDecimal (index));
}
catch (SqlException ex) {
    Console.WriteLine (ex.Message);
}
finally {
    conn.Close ();
}
```

In the further interest of type safety, *DataReader* also offers methods named *GetFieldType* and *GetDataTypeName* for determining a field's type at run time. The former identifies the .NET Framework data type (for example, *System.Decimal*), while the latter identifies the SQL data type (for example, money).

Closing a *DataReader*

A potential gotcha regarding *DataReader*s has to do with their *Close* methods. By default, *DataReader.Close* does not close the connection encapsulated in the command object that created the *DataReader*. In other words, this is buggy code:

```
SqlDataReader reader = cmd.ExecuteReader ();
```

.
.
.

```
// Close the connection
reader.Close (); // Does NOT close the connection!
```

DataReader.Close closes the *DataReader*, which frees the connection associated with the *DataReader* so that it can be used again. For example, suppose you use a command object to create a *DataReader* and then try to use that command object (or the connection that it encapsulates) for something else, as shown here:

```
SqlCommand cmd = new SqlCommand ("select * from titles", conn);
SqlDataReader reader = cmd.ExecuteReader ();
while (reader.Read ())
    Console.WriteLine (reader["title"]);

cmd.CommandText = "select * from authors";
reader = cmd.ExecuteReader ();
while (reader.Read ())
    Console.WriteLine (reader["au_lname"]);
```

The second call to *ExecuteReader* throws an *InvalidOperationException*. Why? Because the underlying connection is still associated with the first *DataReader*, which hasn't been closed. To correct this error, close the first *DataReader* before reusing the connection:

```
SqlCommand cmd = new SqlCommand ("select * from titles", conn);
SqlDataReader reader = cmd.ExecuteReader ();
while (reader.Read ())
    Console.WriteLine (reader["title"]);

reader.Close ();
cmd.CommandText = "select * from authors";
reader = cmd.ExecuteReader ();
while (reader.Read ())
    Console.WriteLine (reader["au_lname"]);
```

Now the code will work as intended. You don't need to call *Close* on a *Data-Reader* if you don't intend to reuse the connection, but there's no harm in calling *Close* anyway if it makes you feel more comfortable. (Can you spell D-E-F-E-N-S-I-V-E P-R-O-G-R-A-M-M-I-N-G?)

As an aside, you can configure a *DataReader* so that its *Close* method does close the underlying connection. The secret is to pass *ExecuteReader* a "command behavior":

```
reader = cmd.ExecuteReader (CommandBehavior.CloseConnection);
```

If you elect to close a connection this way, be sure to position the statement that closes the *DataReader* in a *finally* block to prevent exceptions from leaking connections.

Transacted Commands

Transacted database operations are an important element of many data-driven applications. A transaction is simply two or more otherwise independent units of work grouped together into one logical unit. A classic example is an application that transfers funds from one bank account to another by debiting money from one account (that is, one database record) and crediting it to another. The updates should be performed within the scope of a transaction. Why? So that if one of the operations fails, the other will fail (or be rolled back), too.

Much has been written in recent years about distributed transactions—transactions that span two or more databases. The .NET Framework supports distributed transactions by leveraging the underlying distributed services in the operating system. In reality, however, the vast majority of database transactions are local rather than distributed—that is, they're performed on a single database. ADO.NET simplifies local transaction management by exposing a *Begin-Transaction* method from its *Connection* classes and offering provider-specific *Transaction* classes to represent the resulting transactions.

To demonstrate, suppose you've created a SQL Server database named MyBank that contains a table named "Accounts." Each record in the table identifies the current balance in the account as well as the account number. Suppose this data is stored in fields named "Balance" and "Account_ID." Here's some simple database access code that transfers funds from account 1111 to account 2222:

```
SqlConnection conn = new SqlConnection
    ("server=localhost;database=mybank;uid=sa;pwd=");

try {
    conn.Open ();

    // Debit $1,000 from account 1111
    SqlCommand cmd = new SqlCommand
        ("update accounts set balance = balance - 1000 " +
        "where account_id = '1111'", conn);
    cmd.ExecuteNonQuery ();

    // Credit $1,000 to account 2222
    cmd.CommandText = "update accounts set balance = " +
        "balance + 1000 where account_id = '2222'";
    cmd.ExecuteNonQuery ();
```

(continued)

```
}
catch (SqlException ex) {
    // TODO: Handle the exception
}
finally {
    conn.Close ();
}
```

This code suffers from two potentially fatal flaws. The first is that if the debit succeeds but the credit fails, money disappears into thin air. Chances are neither account owner will be too happy with the results. The second problem is that if another application were to query for the account balances at exactly the wrong time (that is, after the debit but before the credit), it might get inconsistent results.

Performing these updates inside a transaction solves both problems. If one of the operations succeeds but the other fails, we can effectively fail the one that succeeded by failing the transaction. Also, databases that support transactions use locking to prevent other parties from seeing the results of incomplete transactions. (Locking behavior is dependent on the transaction's isolation level and sometimes does permit a client to read data from an unfinished transaction, but the preceding statement is conceptually accurate nonetheless.) Here's a revised code sample that uses ADO.NET's transaction support to encapsulate the updates in a transaction:

```
SqlTransaction trans = null;
SqlConnection conn = new SqlConnection
    ("server=localhost;database=mybank;uid=sa;pwd=");

try {
    conn.Open ();

    // Start a local transaction
    trans = conn.BeginTransaction (IsolationLevel.Serializable);

    // Create and initialize a SqlCommand object
    SqlCommand cmd = new SqlCommand ();
    cmd.Connection = conn;
    cmd.Transaction = trans;

    // Debit $1,000 from account 1111
    cmd.CommandText = "update accounts set balance = " +
        "balance - 1000 where account_id = '1111'";
    cmd.ExecuteNonQuery ();

    // Credit $1,000 to account 2222
    cmd.CommandText = "update accounts set balance = " +
        "balance + 1000 where account_id = '2222'";
```

```
    cmd.ExecuteNonQuery ();

    // Commit the transaction (commit changes)
    trans.Commit ();
}
catch (SqlException) {
    // Abort the transaction (roll back changes)
    if (trans != null)
        trans.Rollback ();
}
finally {
    conn.Close ();
}
```

The revised code calls *BeginTransaction* on the open *SqlConnection* object to start a local transaction. *IsolationLevel.Serializable* assigns the transaction the highest isolation level possible, which locks down the records involved in the transaction while they're updated so that they can't be read or written. *Serializable* is admittedly too high an isolation level for this simple example, but in the real world, the transaction wouldn't be nearly so simple. At the very least, you'd build in checks for negative balances and write a separate record to another table in the database documenting the transfer of funds. (A full discussion of isolation levels is beyond the scope of this chapter, but copious documentation regarding isolation levels and the various ramifications thereof is available in published literature.) *BeginTransaction* returns a *SqlTransaction* object representing the new transaction. A reference to that object is assigned to the *SqlCommand* object's *Transaction* property. If both updates perform without error, this sample commits the transaction by calling *Commit* on the *SqlTransaction* object. Committing the transaction commits, or writes, the changes to the database. If, however, either update throws an exception, the exception handler aborts the transaction by calling *Rollback* on the *SqlTransaction* object. Aborting a transaction prevents the changes made within it from being committed to the database. On a practical level, it is now impossible to update one of these records without updating the other.

That, in a nutshell, is how ADO.NET handles transacted database operations. Note that because passing an invalid account number in a WHERE clause to an UPDATE command is not considered an error (*ExecuteNonQuery* returns 0 rather than throwing an exception), you must add logic to the sample in the previous paragraph if you want a bad account number to fail the transaction. In real life, that kind of protection is important.

Parameterized Commands

It's not unusual for an application to execute the same command on a database repeatedly, varying only the value or values used in the command. The SQL INSERT command in the previous section is a perfect example. The same basic command was used to debit and credit accounts. The only difference from one invocation to the next was the amount of money involved and the account number.

SQL programmers often use parameterized commands (frequently referred to as "parameterized queries") to code redundant commands, especially commands whose input values come from user input. Here's a parameterized version of the previous section's INSERT command:

```
UPDATE Accounts SET Balance = Balance + ? WHERE Account_ID = ?
```

ADO.NET supports parameterized commands as well. The syntax, however, varies slightly depending on the provider that you use.

The following example demonstrates how to use parameterized commands with the SQL Server .NET provider. Transaction management code is omitted for clarity:

```
SqlConnection conn = new SqlConnection
    ("server=localhost;database=mybank;uid=sa;pwd=");

try {
    conn.Open ();

    // Create and initialize a SqlCommand object
    SqlCommand cmd = new SqlCommand
        ("update accounts set balance = balance + @amount " +
        "where account_id = @id", conn);
    cmd.Parameters.Add ("@amount", SqlDbType.Money);
    cmd.Parameters.Add ("@id", SqlDbType.Char);

    // Debit $1,000 from account 1111
    cmd.Parameters["@amount"].Value = -1000;
    cmd.Parameters["@id"].Value = "1111";
    cmd.ExecuteNonQuery ();

    // Credit $1,000 to account 2222
    cmd.Parameters["@amount"].Value = 1000;
    cmd.Parameters["@id"].Value = "2222";
    cmd.ExecuteNonQuery ();
}
catch (SqlException ex) {
    // TODO: Handle the exception
}
finally {
```

```
    conn.Close ();
}
```

And here's the same example modified to work with the OLE DB .NET provider, with changes highlighted in bold:

```
OleDbConnection conn = new OleDbConnection
    ("provider=sqloledb;server=localhost;database=mybank;uid=sa;pwd=");

try {
    conn.Open ();

    // Create and initialize an OleDbCommand object
    OleDbCommand cmd = new OleDbCommand
        ("update accounts set balance = balance + ? " +
        "where account_id = ?", conn);
    cmd.Parameters.Add ("@amount", OleDbType.Decimal);
    cmd.Parameters.Add ("@id", OleDbType.Char);

    // Debit $1,000 from account 1111
    cmd.Parameters["@amount"].Value = -1000;
    cmd.Parameters["@id"].Value = "1111";
    cmd.ExecuteNonQuery ();

    // Credit $1,000 to account 2222
    cmd.Parameters["@amount"].Value = 1000;
    cmd.Parameters["@id"].Value = "2222";
    cmd.ExecuteNonQuery ();
}
catch (OleDbException ex) {
    // TODO: Handle the exception
}
finally {
    conn.Close ();
}
```

These samples are cleaner than the ones in the previous section and are also easier to maintain. Parameterized commands are to database programming as subroutines are to application programming.

As these examples demonstrate, the general approach to using parameterized commands in ADO.NET is to add *Parameter* (*SqlParameter* or *OleDbParameter*) objects containing the values of the command's replaceable parameters to the *Command* object by calling *Add* on the *Command* object's *Parameters* collection. Besides the obvious differences in class names, here's how parameterized command usage differs between the two providers:

- The SQL Server .NET provider requires replaceable parameters to be named; it does not accept ? characters. The OLE DB .NET provider, by contrast, doesn't accept named parameters; it only accepts question marks.

- The SQL Server .NET provider lets you add parameters in any order. The OLE DB .NET provider requires parameters to appear in the *Parameters* collection in the same order in which they appear in the command.

With regard to that last point, switching the following two statements doesn't affect the SQL Server .NET provider in the least:

```
cmd.Parameters.Add ("@amount", SqlDbType.Money);
cmd.Parameters.Add ("@id", SqlDbType.Char);
```

But reversing the order of the equivalent statements in the OLE DB .NET sample generates a run-time exception. What's scary is that if the two parameters were type-compatible, no exception would occur and the command would happily execute with bogus input parameters. Don't forget about parameter order when using the OLE DB .NET provider! Also be aware that if a parameterized *OleDbCommand* uses one input value multiple times, that value must be added to the *Parameters* collection an equal number of times. The same is not true of parameterized *SqlCommand*s, which use parameter names to resolve multiple references.

Stored Procedures

Both *SqlCommand* and *OleDbCommand* feature *Prepare* methods that you can call to "prepare" a method—that is, compile it so that it can be used again and again without having to be recompiled ad infinitum. However, you shouldn't use *Prepare*. Why? Because commands that are executed repeatedly on a database should be implemented as stored procedures. A stored procedure is nothing more than a user-defined command added to a database. Stored procedures execute faster than the equivalent dynamic SQL statements because they're already compiled; the performance difference is akin to that of compiled code vs. interpreted code. Coding frequently used commands as stored procedures is a common technique for improving the performance of data-driven applications. Back-end databases are often where performance bottlenecks lie, so anything you can do to speed database operations will have a direct impact on overall performance.

ADO.NET supports stored procedures. The syntax is very much like that of parameterized commands. Here's a stored procedure named *proc_TransferFunds* that transfers funds between accounts in the MyBank database used in previous examples. Observe that transaction management logic is built into the stored procedure, ensuring that the UPDATEs succeed or fail as a whole without any overt action on the part of the calling application:

```
CREATE PROCEDURE proc_TransferFunds
    @Amount money,
    @From char (10),
    @To char (10)
AS
    BEGIN TRANSACTION
    UPDATE Accounts SET Balance = Balance - @Amount
        WHERE Account_ID = @From
    IF @@ROWCOUNT = 0
    BEGIN
        ROLLBACK TRANSACTION
        RETURN
    END
    UPDATE Accounts SET Balance = Balance + @Amount
        WHERE Account_ID = @To
    IF @@ROWCOUNT = 0
    BEGIN
        ROLLBACK TRANSACTION
        RETURN
    END
    COMMIT TRANSACTION
GO
```

Here's how an application would call this stored procedure using the SQL Server .NET provider:

```
SqlConnection conn = new SqlConnection
    ("server=localhost;database=mybank;uid=sa;pwd=");

try {
    conn.Open ();
    SqlCommand cmd = new SqlCommand ("proc_TransferFunds", conn);
    cmd.CommandType = CommandType.StoredProcedure;
    cmd.Parameters.Add ("@amount", 1000);
    cmd.Parameters.Add ("@from", 1111);
    cmd.Parameters.Add ("@to", 2222);
    cmd.ExecuteNonQuery ();
}
catch (SqlException ex) {
    // TODO: Handle the exception
}
finally {
    conn.Close ();
}
```

Notice how much simpler the code is. All the application has to do is create a *SqlCommand* object containing the stored procedure's name, set the *CommandType* property to *CommandType.StoredProcedure*, and initialize the *Parameters* collection with values representing the stored procedure's input parameters. It's that easy.

The code would change only slightly if it targeted the OLE DB .NET provider. The connection string would change, and *SqlConnection* and *SqlCommand* would become *OleDbConnection* and *OleDbCommand*. Nothing else would change. However, a gotcha is lurking just beneath the surface. As it does for parameterized commands, the OLE DB .NET provider requires that the order of the parameters in the *Parameters* collection be consistent with the order in which the parameters are defined in the stored procedure. Changing the order of the *Add* method calls would render the stored procedure useless with the OLE DB .NET provider (or worse yet, might do the opposite of what you intended by reversing the account numbers). The SQL Server .NET provider, on the other hand, couldn't care less about parameter order.

What about stored procedures that return data in output parameters? ADO.NET supports them too. Here's a simple stored procedure that takes an account ID as input and returns the account's current balance in an output parameter named *@Balance*. It also returns an integer value indicating whether the call succeeded. A return value of 0 means the call succeeded, while -1 means it did not:

```
CREATE PROCEDURE proc_GetBalance
    @ID char (10),
    @Balance money OUTPUT
AS
    SELECT @Balance = Balance FROM Accounts WHERE Account_ID = @ID
    IF @@ROWCOUNT = 1
        RETURN 0
    ELSE
    BEGIN
        SET @Balance = 0
        RETURN -1
    END
GO
```

The following code sample uses the SQL Server .NET provider to call *proc_GetBalance* and retrieve both the return value and the output parameter:

```
SqlConnection conn = new SqlConnection
    ("server=localhost;database=mybank;uid=sa;pwd=");

try {
    SqlCommand cmd = new SqlCommand ("proc_GetBalance", conn);
    cmd.CommandType = CommandType.StoredProcedure;
```

```
    cmd.Parameters.Add ("@id", 1111);

    SqlParameter bal =
        cmd.Parameters.Add ("@balance", SqlDbType.Money);
    bal.Direction = ParameterDirection.Output;

    SqlParameter ret = cmd.Parameters.Add ("@return", SqlDbType.Int);
    ret.Direction = ParameterDirection.ReturnValue;

    cmd.ExecuteNonQuery ();

    int retval = (int) ret.Value;
    decimal balance = (decimal) bal.Value;
}
catch (SqlException ex) {
    // TODO: Catch the exception
}
finally {
    conn.Close ();
}
```

The key here is setting the *Direction* property of the *SqlParameter* that represents the output parameter to *ParameterDirection.Output* and the *Direction*
property of the *SqlParameter* that represents the return value to *ParameterDi-
rection.ReturnValue*. Only one parameter can be designated as a return value,
but several can be marked as output parameters. (By the way, you can name
the parameter that represents the return value anything you want; it doesn't have
to be named *@Return*.) On return, the application that called the stored procedure retrieves the output by reading it from the parameters' *Value* properties.

DataSets and *DataAdapters*

ADO.NET's *SqlDataReader* and *OleDbDataReader* classes provide stream-based
access to the results of database queries. Streaming access is fast and efficient,
but it's also read-only and forward-only. You can't, for example, back up and
reread the previous record with a *DataReader* or change the results and write
them back to the database. That's why ADO.NET supports set-based data
access as well as stream-based data access. Set-based accesses capture an entire
query in memory and support backward and forward traversal through the
result set. They also let you edit the data obtained through database queries,
propagate the changes back to the data source, and much, much more.

Set-based data accesses revolve around two classes: *DataSet*, which is the
equivalent of an in-memory database and is defined in the *System.Data*

namespace, and *DataAdapter*, which serves as a bridge between *DataSet*s and physical data sources. *DataAdapter* is actually two classes in one because it comes in provider-specific versions: *SqlDataAdapter* and *OleDbDataAdapter*. Learning about *DataSet* and *DataAdapter* unlocks the door to a whole new style of data access that further abstracts the SQL data model and lends itself extraordinarily well to data binding and caching.

The *DataSet* Class

If *DataSet* isn't the most important class in ADO.NET, it's certainly the one that gets the most attention. Think of a *DataSet* as an in-memory database. (See Figure 12-1.) The actual data is stored in *DataTable* objects, which are analogous to tables in a database. The *DataSet.Tables* property exposes a list of the *DataTable*s in a *DataSet*. Records in a *DataTable* are represented by *DataRow* objects, and fields are represented by instances of *DataColumn*. *DataTable* properties named *Rows* and *Columns* expose the collections of *DataRow*s and *DataColumn*s that make up the table. *DataTable* also features a property named *Constraints* that permits constraints to be applied to individual columns. Ensuring that all the values in a column are unique, for example, is as simple as creating a *UniqueConstraint* object identifying the *DataColumn* and adding it to the table's *Constraints* collection. *DataSet*s also support data relations. The *DataSet* class's *Relations* property holds a collection of *DataRelation* objects, each of which defines a relationship between two tables. *DataTable*, *DataRow*, *DataColumn*, *UniqueConstraint*, and *DataRelation* are all members of the *System.Data* namespace and are not provider-specific.

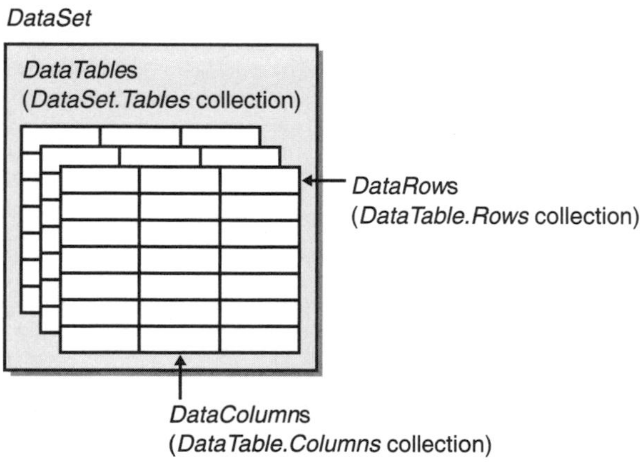

Figure 12-1   The *DataSet* object.

*DataSet*s are ideal for capturing the results of database queries and storing them in memory for the purpose of examining and perhaps modifying the data. Unlike a *DataReader*, which supports forward-only access to the data that it encapsulates, a *DataSet* supports random access. You can also modify the contents of a *DataSet* and propagate the changes back to the database that provided the data in the first place. In addition, *DataSet*s are great for caching, especially in Web applications. Rather than physically query a database every time a page is hit, for example, you can query the database once, capture the results in a *DataSet*, stuff the *DataSet* into ASP.NET's application cache, and satisfy subsequent requests without touching the database. Of course, you would also implement a refresh policy to prevent the data in the cache from becoming stale.

*DataSet*s vs. *DataReader*s

One of the most common questions that developers ask about ADO.NET is which is best, *DataSet*s or *DataReader*s? The answer is: it depends. If your intention is simply to query a database and read through the records one at a time until you find the one you're looking for, then *DataReader* is the right tool for the job. *DataReader*s, unlike *DataSet*s, retrieve only the data that you actually use, and they don't consume memory by storing every record that you read. If, however, you intend to use all the query results (perhaps because you're displaying them in a table), you need the ability to iterate backward and forward through a result set, or you want to cache the result set in memory, use a *DataSet*.

As a corollary to the *DataSet* vs. *DataReader* debate, realize that many controls that support data binding to *DataSet*s are perfectly capable of binding to *DataReader*s as well. Many examples in the .NET Framework SDK and elsewhere that demonstrate data binding to ASP.NET server controls show controls binding to *DataSet*s:

```
DataSet ds = new DataSet ();
// TODO: Initialize the DataSet
MyDataGrid.DataSource = ds;
MyDataGrid.DataBind ();
```

Oftentimes, the same code can be implemented more efficiently with a *DataReader*:

```
SqlDataReader reader = cmd.ExecuteReader ();
MyDataGrid.DataSource = reader;
MyDataGrid.DataBind ();
```

Binding to *DataReader*s is more efficient for the simple reason that it doesn't leave the result set lying around in memory for the garbage collector to clean up.

DataAdapter Classes

While it's perfectly possible to build *DataSet*s in memory, from scratch, without relying on external data sources, in practice *DataSet*s are almost always initialized from database queries or XML documents. *DataSet*s don't interact with databases directly; instead, they let *DataAdapter*s do the dirty work. *DataAdapter*'s purpose is to perform database queries and create *DataTable*s containing the query results. It's also capable of writing changes made to the *DataTable*s back to the database. Figure 12-2 diagrams the relationship between *DataSet*s, *DataAdapter*s, and databases. The *DataAdapter* acts as a go-between, providing a layer of abstraction between the *DataSet* and the physical data source.

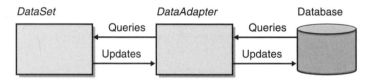

Figure 12-2   The role of *DataAdapter*.

As mentioned earlier, *DataAdapter* is a provider-specific class that comes in two varieties: *SqlDataAdapter*, which interacts with databases using the SQL Server .NET provider, and *OleDbDataAdapter*, which uses the Framework's OLE DB .NET provider. Both derive from a common base class—*System.Data.Common.DbDataAdapter*—and both feature a common set of methods and properties that control their behavior. Chief among a *DataAdapter*'s methods are *Fill* and *Update*. The former queries a database and initializes a *DataSet* (actually, a *DataTable*) with the results. The latter propagates changes back to the database. *Fill* is introduced in the next section. You'll learn all about the *Update* method a few sections hence.

Initializing a *DataSet* from a Database: *DataAdapter.Fill*

The following code sample is representative of the numerous *DataSet* examples found in the .NET Framework SDK and on Web sites that cater to .NET developers:

```
SqlDataAdapter adapter = new SqlDataAdapter ("select * from titles",
    "server=localhost;database=pubs;uid=sa;pwd=");
DataSet ds = new DataSet ();
adapter.Fill (ds, "Titles");
```

What does this code do? A lot. Here's a blow-by-blow of what happens inside the call to *Fill*:

1. *Fill* opens a connection to the Pubs database using the connection string passed to *SqlDataAdapter*'s constructor.

2. It performs a query on the Pubs database using the query string passed to *SqlDataAdapter*'s constructor.

3. It creates a *DataTable* named "Titles" in the *DataSet*.

4. It initializes the *DataTable* with a schema that matches that of the "Titles" table in the database.

5. It retrieves all the records produced by the query and writes them to the *DataTable*.

6. It closes the connection to the database.

Under the hood, the *DataAdapter* uses a *DataReader* to fetch the query results, but that's merely an implementation detail. What matters is that one simple call fills a *DataSet* with data from a database. Furthermore, you control what goes into the *DataSet* because you provide the command that makes up the query. That query can be as complex as you like—whatever it takes to initialize the *DataSet* the way you want it initialized. If you want, you can call *Fill* multiple times with the same *DataSet* but with different table names to populate the *DataSet* with several *DataTables*. And you can use *DataSet.Clear* to clear out old *DataTables* if you've finished with them but want to reuse the *DataSet*.

The preceding code would change only slightly if reconfigured to use the OLE DB .NET provider:

```
OleDbDataAdapter adapter =
    new OleDbDataAdapter ("select * from titles",
    "provider=sqloledb;server=localhost;database=pubs;uid=sa;pwd=");
DataSet ds = new DataSet ();
adapter.Fill (ds);
```

Once the *DataSet* is initialized, it doesn't matter which provider you used to initialize it because *DataSet*s are provider agnostic.

DataTable and Friends

The *DataSet* class gets all the press, but *DataTable* and friends are the unsung heroes of set-based data access. A *DataSet* is first and foremost a collection of *DataTables*, which are often created by *DataAdapters*. To examine the data returned by a *DataAdapter*, you browse the *DataTable* that the *DataAdapter* created. If you want to edit the data, once more the *DataTable* will be the focus of your actions.

The following code iterates through the *Tables* collection of a *DataSet* named *ds* and outputs the name of each table that it encounters:

```
foreach (DataTable table in ds.Tables)
    Console.WriteLine (table.TableName);
```

Individual *DataTable*s in a *DataSet* can be referenced by name or 0-based index. The next example retrieves the first *DataTable* from a *DataSet* and writes the value of the first column in every row to a console window:

```
DataTable table = ds.Tables[0];
foreach (DataRow row in table.Rows)
    Console.WriteLine (row[0]);
```

Columns, too, can be referenced by name as well as numeric index. Thus, if the name assigned to the first column in the *DataTable* is "Account_ID," the preceding example could be rewritten this way:

```
DataTable table = ds.Tables[0];
foreach (DataRow row in table.Rows)
    Console.WriteLine (row["account_id"]);
```

Enumerating a *DataTable*'s columns is equally simple:

```
DataTable table = ds.Tables[0];
foreach (DataColumn col in table.Columns)
    Console.WriteLine ("Name={0}, Type={1}",
        col.ColumnName, col.DataType);
```

A quick and easy way to display a *DataTable* in a Web form is to bind it to a *DataGrid* control, as demonstrated in Chapter 9.

Inserting Records into a *DataTable*

One way to insert records into a database is to call *ExecuteNonQuery* on a *Command* object wrapping an INSERT command, as demonstrated in the first half of this chapter. You can also insert records into databases using *DataSet*s. The general approach is to perform a query with *DataAdapter.Fill*, add records to the resulting *DataTable*, and write the changes to the database. You already know how to call *Fill*. Let's talk about adding records to a *DataTable*.

The following example adds a record to a *DataTable* created from the Pubs database's "Titles" table:

```
SqlDataAdapter adapter = new SqlDataAdapter ("select * from titles",
    "server=localhost;database=pubs;uid=sa;pwd=");

DataSet ds = new DataSet ();
adapter.Fill (ds, "Titles");

// Create a new DataRow
DataTable table = ds.Tables["Titles"];
DataRow row = table.NewRow ();

// Initialize the DataRow
row["title_id"] = "JP1001";
row["title"] = "Programming Microsoft .NET";
row["price"] = "59.99";
row["ytd_sales"] = "1000000";
row["type"] = "business";
row["pubdate"] = "May 2002";

// Add the DataRow to the DataTable
table.Rows.Add (row);
```

You begin by creating a new *DataRow* representing the record to be added. Rather than simply *new* up a *DataRow*, you call the *DataTable*'s *NewRow* method so that the *DataTable* can initialize the *DataRow* with a schema that matches its own. You then assign values to the *DataRow*'s columns. This example takes advantage of the facts that the columns are addressable by the names of the fields retrieved from the database and that nullable columns don't have to be initialized at all. (The Pubs database's "Titles" table contains 10 columns. This example initializes just six of them; the others are set to null.) Once the *DataRow* is initialized, you add it to the *DataTable* by calling *Add* on the table's *Rows* collection. Repeat this process to add as many records as you like.

Incidentally, *DataRow* is happy to convert string values into the actual data types associated with each column, but you can make your code slightly more efficient by using strong types yourself, as shown here:

```
row["title_id"] = "JP1001";
row["title"] = "Programming Microsoft .NET";
row["price"] = 59.99m;
row["ytd_sales"] = 1000000;
row["type"] = "business";
row["pubdate"] = new DateTime (2002, 5, 1);
```

In the revised code, the values assigned to the "Price," "Ytd_sales," and "Pubdate" fields are a decimal, an integer, and a *DateTime*, respectively.

Selecting Records in a *DataTable*

Inserting records into a *DataTable* is easy enough. So are updating and deleting. But before you go updating or deleting, you have to find the records targeted for update or deletion. One way to do this is to iterate through the *DataRows* searching for the record or records you want. A smarter way to find the records is to use the *DataTable.Select* method.

As its name implies, *Select* selects one or more records in a *DataSet*. It returns an array of *DataRow* objects representing the *DataRows* selected. Applied to the *DataTable* in the previous section, the following statement returns an array containing a single *DataRow*—the one added to the table with *Add*:

```
DataRow[] rows = table.Select ("title_id = 'JP1001'");
```

This statement selects (returns) all *DataRows* whose "Price" field contains a value less than 10:

```
DataRow[] rows = table.Select ("price < 10.00");
```

And this one selects records whose "Pubdate" fields hold dates on or after January 1, 2000:

```
DataRow[] rows = table.Select ("pubdate >= '#1/1/2000#'");
```

If you want to know how many rows *Select* returned, read the array's *Length* property.

How complex can the filter expressions passed to *DataTable.Select* be? The syntax is documented in the .NET Framework SDK, but here are some of the highlights. The following comparison operators are supported: <, <=, =, >=, >, and <>. You can also use IN and LIKE, as in the following:

```
// Return all rows where "State" equals CA, TN, or WA
DataRow[] rows = table.Select ("state in ('ca', 'tn', 'wa')");
```

```
// Return all rows where "State" begins with CA
DataRow[] rows = table.Select ("state like 'ca*'");
```

There's also a handful of functions you can use in *Select* clauses. The next example uses the ISNULL function to select all the records in the *DataTable* with null "State" values:

```
DataRow[] rows = table.Select ("isnull (state, 0) = 0");
```

AND, OR, and NOT work, too:

```
DataRow[] rows = table.Select ("state = 'tn' and zip like '37*'");
```

You can create complex Boolean expressions by grouping clauses with parentheses.

Updating Records in a *DataTable*

Once you've identified a record that you want to update in a *DataTable*, performing the update is easy: just replace the values of one or more of the record's fields with values of your own. The following example selects all the records in the Pubs database's "Title" table with year-to-date sales of 10,000 and adds $10.00 to their price:

```
SqlDataAdapter adapter = new SqlDataAdapter ("select * from titles",
    "server=localhost;database=pubs;uid=sa;pwd=");

DataSet ds = new DataSet ();
adapter.Fill (ds, "Titles");

DataRow[] rows = table.Select ("ytd_sales > 10000");
foreach (DataRow row in rows)
    row["price"] = (decimal) row["price"] + 10.00m;
```

Deleting Records from a *DataTable*

Deleting records from a *DataTable* is a simple matter of calling *Delete* on each *DataRow* that you want to remove. The next example deletes all rows whose year-to-date sales are less than 10,000 or equal to null:

```
SqlDataAdapter adapter = new SqlDataAdapter ("select * from titles",
    "server=localhost;database=pubs;uid=sa;pwd=");

DataSet ds = new DataSet ();
adapter.Fill (ds, "Titles");

DataRow[] rows =
    table.Select ("ytd_sales < 10000 OR isnull (ytd_sales, 0) = 0");
foreach (DataRow row in rows)
    row.Delete ();
```

Propagating Changes Back to a Database: *DataAdapter.Update*

Inserts, updates, and deletes performed on a *DataTable* do not automatically propagate back to the database. If you want changes written back to the database, you have to take matters into your own hands. Fortunately, the *DataAdapter.Fill* method makes your job incredibly simple.

Here's a code sample demonstrating how to make changes to a database using a *DataSet* and a *DataAdapter*:

```
SqlDataAdapter adapter =
    new SqlDataAdapter ("select * from titles",
    "server=localhost;database=pubs;uid=sa;pwd=");

SqlCommandBuilder builder = new SqlCommandBuilder (adapter);
DataSet ds = new DataSet ();
adapter.Fill (ds, "Titles");

// Insert a record
DataTable table = ds.Tables["Titles"];
DataRow row = table.NewRow ();
row["title_id"] = "JP1001";
row["title"] = "Programming Microsoft .NET";
row["price"] = 59.99m;
row["ytd_sales"] = 1000000;
row["type"] = "business";
row["pubdate"] = new DateTime (2002, 5, 1);
table.Rows.Add (row);

// Update the database
adapter.Update (table);
```

The *DataAdapter*'s *Update* method examines each row in the table passed to it and writes rows that were inserted, updated, or deleted since the last update (or since the last time the table's *AcceptChanges* method was called) to the database. If a *DataSet* contains multiple *DataTables* that underwent modification, pass the entire *DataSet* to *Update* and all the changes will be propagated at once.

Many samples demonstrating how to use *DataAdapter.Update* call a method named *GetChanges* to create a *DataSet* or *DataTable* containing only rows that were inserted, modified, or deleted. They then pass the "delta" *DataSet* or *DataTable* to *Update*, as shown here:

```
// Update the database
DataTable delta = table.GetChanges ();
adapter.Update (delta);
```

This approach works, but it isn't necessary. *Update* is smart enough to ignore rows that weren't changed in a *DataTable* containing a mixture of modified and unmodified rows. Where *GetChanges* becomes interesting is when you want to control the order in which changes are propagated back to the database. If you want to make sure DELETEs are performed before INSERTs to avoid duplicate key errors, for example, you can do this:

```
// Update the database
DataTable deletes = table.GetChanges (DataRowState.Deleted);
adapter.Update (deletes);
DataTable inserts = table.GetChanges (DataRowState.Added);
adapter.Update (inserts);
```

Another use for *GetChanges* is to minimize the amount of data passed between machines when the update won't be performed locally. Passing a *DataSet* or *DataTable* containing just the rows that changed is more efficient than passing a *DataSet* or *DataTable* containing both modified and unmodified rows.

CommandBuilder Classes

Now ask yourself a question. How does *Update* physically update the database? The short answer is that it executes SQL INSERT commands for rows added to a *DataTable*, UPDATE commands for rows that were modified, and DELETE commands for rows that were deleted. But where do the INSERT, UPDATE, and DELETE commands come from? Are they manufactured out of thin air?

Close. They're manufactured by a *SqlCommandBuilder* object. Note the following statement from the previous code sample:

```
SqlCommandBuilder builder = new SqlCommandBuilder (adapter);
```

If you omit this statement, *Update* throws an exception. The reason? A *Data-Adapter* has four very important properties that control how it communicates with a database:

- *SelectCommand*, which encapsulates the command the *DataAdapter* uses to perform queries

- *InsertCommand*, which encapsulates the command the *DataAdapter* uses to insert rows

- *UpdateCommand*, which encapsulates the command the *Data-Adapter* uses to update rows

- *DeleteCommand*, which encapsulates the command the *Data-Adapter* uses to delete rows

When you create a *DataAdapter* this way:

```
SqlDataAdapter adapter =
    new SqlDataAdapter ("select * from titles",
    "server=localhost;database=pubs;uid=sa;pwd=");
```

the constructor initializes *SelectCommand* with a *SqlCommand* object wrapping the query string, but it leaves *InsertCommand*, *UpdateCommand*, and *Delete-Command* set to null. When *Update* is called and it finds these properties still equal to null, it asks the *SqlCommandBuilder* to provide it with the commands it needs. If there is no *SqlCommandBuilder*, *Update* is powerless to update the database and indicates as much by throwing an exception.

SqlCommandBuilder and its OLE DB counterpart, *OleDbCommand-Builder*, generate INSERT, UPDATE, and DELETE commands on the fly based on information inferred from the *DataAdapter*'s *SelectCommand*. The commands that they generate are simple dynamic SQL commands. You can see these commands for yourself by calling the command builder's *GetInsertCommand*, *GetUpdateCommand*, and *GetDeleteCommand* methods and inspecting the command text found inside the returned command objects:

```
string insert = builder.GetInsertCommand ().CommandText;
string update = builder.GetUpdateCommand ().CommandText;
string delete = builder.GetDeleteCommand ().CommandText;
```

In the vast majority of cases, a builder's auto-generated commands work just fine. However, if you do a lot of database updating with *DataAdapter*s, you might achieve a performance boost by coding your own INSERT, UPDATE, and DELETE commands in stored procedures, wrapping the stored procedures in *SqlCommand* or *OleDbCommand* objects, and assigning those objects to the adapter's *InsertCommand*, *UpdateCommand*, and *DeleteCommand* properties. The *DataAdapter* will respond by using your stored procedures to do its updating.

The *DataView* Class

Database programmers are familiar with the concept of views. A view is a logical table containing rows from one or more physical tables. Views can be used to sort and filter data and also to create fictitious tables that combine data from other tables.

ADO.NET also supports the concept of views. ADO.NET views are represented by instances of *System.Data.DataView*. They support sorting and filtering and are often used to customize the content displayed in controls through data binding. The following ASPX file displays the contents of the Pubs database's "Titles" table in a *DataGrid* and sorts the output on the "Title" column:

```
<%@ Import Namespace="System.Data" %>
<%@ Import Namespace="System.Data.SqlClient" %>

<html>
  <body>
    <form runat="server">
      <asp:DataGrid ID="MyDataGrid" RunAt="server" />
    </form>
  </body>
</html>

<script language="C#" runat="server">
  void Page_Load (object sender, EventArgs e)
  {
      SqlDataAdapter adapter =
          new SqlDataAdapter ("select * from titles",
          "server=localhost;database=pubs;uid=sa;pwd=");
```

```
    DataSet ds = new DataSet ();
    adapter.Fill (ds, "Titles");

    DataView view = new DataView (ds.Tables["Titles"]);
    view.Sort = "title ASC";
    MyDataGrid.DataSource = view;
    MyDataGrid.DataBind ();
}
</script>
```

The view's *Sort* property contains the expression that defines the sort. You can also use a view's *RowFilter* property to filter data from the view. For example, adding the following statement displays only those records whose "Price" field contains a value greater than or equal to 10:

```
view.RowFilter = "price >= 10";
```

DataView also contains a property named *RowStateFilter* that you can use to filter content based on row state—that is, based on which rows have been added, modified, and deleted from the *DataTable*.

It might seem odd that a chapter on ADO.NET doesn't have a large section describing data binding. However, data binding to ASP.NET server controls is discussed at length in Chapter 6. Data binding can be used with Windows Forms controls too. Combined with views, data binding is a powerful concept that vastly simplifies the task of querying databases and displaying the results in GUI applications.

A Word About XML

One of ADO.NET's most touted features is its seamless support for XML. But what does "seamless XML support" really mean? In answer to that question, check out the following code, which calls *ReadXml* on a *DataSet* to read an XML file from disk:

```
DataSet ds = new DataSet ();
ds.ReadXml ("Rates.xml");
```

Chapter 5's Converter program used code remarkably similar to this to read an XML file and populate a ListBox control by iterating over the rows in the resulting DataTable and calling Add on the control's Items collection:

```
foreach (DataRow row in ds.Tables[0].Rows)
    Currencies.Items.Add (row["Currency"].ToString ());
```

The *Currency* elements in the XML file metamorphosed into a "Currency" column in the *DataTable*, and *Exchange* elements representing currency exchange rates became an "Exchange" column.

DataSet.ReadXml is a powerful method that renders a *DataSet* equally capable of handling relational data and XML data. Reading an XML file into a *DataSet* transforms XML data into relational data and vastly simplifies the handling of XML. Once the data is in the *DataSet*, you can perform queries on it using *DataTable.Select* and even write it to a database using a *DataAdapter*. How might that come in handy? Suppose someone sends your company an invoice as an XML file and you want to process the invoice. Reading the XML into a *DataSet* simplifies the process of parsing the data and of storing it permanently in a database along with other records that your company keeps. That's worlds easier than using MSXML or other XML parsers to manually iterate over the data and write it to a database with SQL commands. Nor is *ReadXml* limited to working exclusively with files. It's equally capable of reading from streams and readers.

ReadXml is complemented by a *DataSet* method named *WriteXml*. When I need to create XML documents, I often do so by building a *DataSet* and calling *WriteXml* on it. *WriteXml* is especially convenient for converting relational data into XML. Using a *DataAdapter* to initialize a *DataSet* with a database query and writing the results to an XML file with *WriteXml* makes relational-to-XML data conversions an absolute breeze.

That's seamless integration. XML is a language for machines, not humans, but developers have expended untold hours in recent years using XML parsers to read XML data and XML writers to write XML. With the advent of the .NET Framework, XML becomes light-years easier to deal with in part because of the high level of support for it in *DataSet* and in part thanks to the XML classes in the FCL.

Speaking of XML classes in the FCL: what about them? Shouldn't a book on the .NET Framework describe those classes somewhere? Turn the page and you'll find out.

13

XML

In a few short years, XML has grown from an obscure specification into the world's de facto data language. XML stands for Extensible Markup Language. Whereas HTML is designed to express appearance, XML is designed to express raw information absent any implied notion about how the data should be rendered. It's a simple language that is entirely text based, making it particularly well suited to travel over text-based protocols such as HTTP, and that has no predefined tags as HTML does. XML provides the rules. You provide the rest.

XML finds several applications in business and, increasingly, in everyday life. It provides a common data format for companies that want to exchange documents. It's used by Web services to encode messages and data in a platform-independent manner. It's even used to build Web sites, where it serves as a tool for cleanly separating content from appearance.

There's little remarkable about XML in and of itself. What makes XML important is the fact that the computer industry has accepted it as a standard, and as such numerous tools are available for reading and writing XML. If someone hands you a large free-formatted text file containing thousands of records and your job is to get the records into a database, you'll probably end up writing a parser to extract the records from the file and write them to the database. If the text file is an XML file, your job is much simpler. You can use one of the many XML parsers already available to read the records. XML doesn't make your life easier because it's a great language. It makes your life easier because tools for reading, writing, and manipulating XML data are almost as common as word processors.

When it comes to handling XML, nothing rivals the .NET Framework class library (FCL) for ease of use. A few simple statements will read an entire XML file and write its contents to a database, or query a database and write out the results as XML. It's equally easy to perform XPath queries on XML documents or convert XML into HTML on the fly using XSL transformations.

This chapter is about the XML support in the FCL. A comprehensive treatment of the subject could easily fill 200 pages or more, so I'll attempt to strike a reasonable balance between detail and succinctness. In the pages that follow, you'll learn about the classes and namespaces that form the cornerstone for the FCL's XML support. Before we start slinging code, however, let's take a brief look at XML itself.

XML Primer

XML is a language for describing data and the structure of data. XML data is contained in a document, which can be a file, a stream, or any other storage medium, real or virtual, that's capable of holding text. A proper XML document begins with the following XML declaration, which identifies the document as an XML document and specifies the version of XML that the document's contents conform to:

```
<?xml version="1.0"?>
```

The XML declaration can also include an *encoding* attribute that identifies the type of characters contained in the document. For example, the following declaration specifies that the document contains characters from the Latin-1 character set used by Windows 95, 98, and ME:

```
<?xml version="1.0" encoding="ISO-8859-1"?>
```

The next example identifies the character set as UTF-16, which consists of 16-bit Unicode characters:

```
<?xml version="1.0" encoding="UTF-16"?>
```

The *encoding* attribute is optional if the document consists of UTF-8 or UTF-16 characters because an XML parser can infer the encoding from the document's first five characters: "<?xml". Documents that use other encodings should identify the encodings that they use to ensure that an XML parser can read them.

XML declarations are actually specialized forms of XML *processing instructions*, which contain commands for XML processors. Processing instructions are always enclosed in <? and ?> symbols. Some browsers interpret the following processing instruction to mean that the XML document should be formatted using a style sheet named Guitars.xsl before it's displayed:

```
<?xml-stylesheet type="text/xsl" href="Guitars.xsl"?>
```

You'll see this processing instruction used in an XML Web page near the end of this chapter.

The XML declaration is followed by the document's root element, which is usually referred to as the *document element*. In the following example, the document element is named *Guitars*:

```
<?xml version="1.0"?>
<Guitars>
 ...
</Guitars>
```

The document element is not optional; every document must have one. The following XML is legal because *Guitar* elements are nested within the document element *Guitars*:

```
<?xml version="1.0"?>
<Guitars>
  <Guitar>
    ...
  </Guitar>
  <Guitar>
    ...
  </Guitar>
</Guitars>
```

The document in the next example, however, is not legal because it lacks a document element:

```
<?xml version="1.0"?>
<Guitar>
  ...
</Guitar>
<Guitar>
  ...
</Guitar>
```

Element names conform to a set of rules prescribed in the XML 1.0 specification, which you can read at *http://www.w3.org/TR/REC-xml*. The spec essentially says that element names can consist of letters or underscores followed by letters, digits, periods, hyphens, and underscores. Spaces are not permitted in element names.

Elements

Elements are the building blocks of XML documents. Elements can contain data, other elements, or both, and are always delimited by start and end tags. XML has no predefined elements; you define elements as needed to adequately describe the data contained in an XML document. The following document describes a collection of guitars:

```
<?xml version="1.0"?>
<Guitars>
  <Guitar>
    <Make>Gibson</Make>
    <Model>SG</Model>
    <Year>1977</Year>
    <Color>Tobacco Sunburst</Color>
    <Neck>Rosewood</Neck>
  </Guitar>
  <Guitar>
    <Make>Fender</Make>
    <Model>Stratocaster</Model>
    <Year></Year>
    <Color>Black</Color>
    <Neck>Maple</Neck>
  </Guitar>
</Guitars>
```

In this example, *Guitars* is the document element, *Guitar* elements are children of *Guitars*, and *Make*, *Model*, *Year*, *Color*, and *Neck* are children of *Guitar*. The *Guitar* elements contain no data (just other elements), but *Make*, *Model*, *Year*, *Color*, and *Neck* contain data. The line

```
<Year></Year>
```

signifies an *empty element*—one that contains neither data nor other elements. Empty elements are perfectly legal in XML. An empty *Year* element can optionally be written this way for conciseness:

```
<Year/>
```

Unlike HTML, XML requires that start tags be accompanied by end tags. Therefore, the following XML is never legal:

```
<Year>1977
```

Also unlike HTML, XML is case-sensitive. A <Year> tag closed by a </year> tag is not legal because the cases of the Y's do not match.

Because XML permits elements to be nested within elements, the content of an XML document can be viewed as a tree. Figure 13-1 shows the tree that corresponds to the XML document above. The tree clearly diagrams the parent-child relationships among the document's elements and is helpful in visualizing the document's structure.

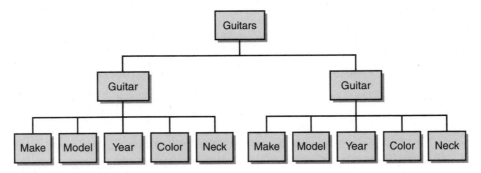

Figure 13-1   An XML tree.

Attributes

XML allows you to attach additional information to elements by including attributes in the elements' start tags. Attributes are name/value pairs. The following *Guitar* element expresses *Year* as an attribute rather than as a child element:

```
<Guitar Year="1977">
  <Make>Gibson</Make>
  <Model>SG</Model>
  <Color>Tobacco Sunburst</Color>
  <Neck>Rosewood</Neck>
</Guitar>
```

Attribute values must be enclosed in single or double quotation marks and may include spaces and embedded quotation marks. (An attribute value delimited by single quotation marks can contain double quotation marks and vice versa.) Attribute names are subject to the same restrictions as element names and therefore can't include spaces. The number of attributes an element can be decorated with is not limited.

When defining a document's structure, it's sometimes unclear—especially to XML newcomers—whether a given item should be defined as an attribute or an element. In general, attributes should be used to define out-of-band data and elements to define data that is integral to the document. In the example above, it probably makes sense to define *Year* as an element rather than an attribute because *Year* provides important information about the instrument in question. But consider the following element definition:

```
<Guitar Image="MySG.jpeg">
  <Make>Gibson</Make>
  <Model>SG</Model>
  <Year>1977</Year>
  <Color>Tobacco Sunburst</Color>
  <Neck>Rosewood</Neck>
</Guitar>
```

The *Image* attribute contains additional information that an application might use to decorate a table containing information about the guitar with a picture. Because no one other than the software processing this document is likely to care about the image, and since the image is an adjunct to (rather than a part of) the guitar's definition, *Image* is properly cast as an attribute instead of an element.

CDATA, PCDATA, and Entity References

Textual data contained in an XML element can be expressed as character data (CDATA), parsed character data (PCDATA), or a combination of the two. Data that appears between <![CDATA[and]]> tags is CDATA; any other data is PCDATA. The following element contains PCDATA:

```
<Color>Tobacco Sunburst</Color>
```

The next element contains CDATA:

```
<Color><![CDATA[Tobacco Sunburst]]></Color>
```

And this one contains both:

```
<Color>Tobacco <![CDATA[Sunburst]]></Color>
```

XML parsers ignore CDATA but parse PCDATA—that is, interpret it as markup language. The practical implication is that you can put anything between <![CDATA[and]]> tags and an XML parser won't care. Data not enclosed in <![CDATA[and]]> tags, however, must conform to the rules of XML.

Why does XML distinguish between CDATA and PCDATA? Certain characters—notably <, >, and &—have special meaning in XML and must be enclosed in CDATA sections if they're to be used verbatim. For example, suppose you wanted to define an element named *Range* whose value is "0 < x < 100". Because < is a reserved character, you can't define the element this way:

```
<Range>0 < x < 100</Range>
```

You can, however, define it this way:

```
<Range><[CDATA[0 < x < 100]]></Range>
```

CDATA sections are useful for including mathematical equations, code listings, and even other XML documents in XML documents.

Another way to include <, >, and & characters in an XML document is to replace them with *entity references*. An entity reference is a string enclosed in & and ; symbols. XML predefines the following entities:

Symbol	Corresponding Entity
<	lt
>	gt
&	amp
'	apos
"	quot

Here's an alternative method for defining a *Range* element with the value "0 < x < 100":

```
<Range>0 &lt; x &lt; 100</Range>
```

You can also represent characters in PCDATA with *character references*, which are nothing more than numeric character codes enclosed in &# and ; symbols, as in

```
<Range>0 &#60; x &#60; 100</Range>
```

Character references are useful for representing characters that can't be typed from the keyboard. Entity references are useful for escaping the occasional special character, but for large amounts of text containing arbitrary content, CDATA sections are far more convenient.

Namespaces

Namespaces, which are documented in the XML namespaces specification at *http://www.w3.org/TR/REC-xml-names*, are a crucial component of XML. Namespaces are a mechanism for qualifying element and attribute names to avoid naming collisions. The following example defines three namespaces and three namespace prefixes. It uses the namespace prefixes to qualify its elements so that the elements won't clash if used in the same document with other elements having the same names but different definitions:

```
<?xml version="1.0"?>
<win:Guitars
  xmlns:win="http://www.wintellect.com/classic-guitars"
  xmlns:gibson="http://www.gibson.com/finishes"
  xmlns:fender="http://www.fender.com/finishes">
  <win:Guitar>
```

```
      <win:Make>Gibson</win:Make>
      <win:Model>SG</win:Model>
      <win:Year>1977</win:Year>
      <gibson:Color>Tobacco Sunburst</gibson:Color>
      <win:Neck>Rosewood</win:Neck>
   </win:Guitar>
   <win:Guitar>
      <win:Make>Fender</win:Make>
      <win:Model>Stratocaster</win:Model>
      <win:Year>1990</win:Year>
      <fender:Color>Black</fender:Color>
      <win:Neck>Maple</win:Neck>
   </win:Guitar>
</win:Guitars>
```

In this example, the namespace names are URLs. You can name a namespace anything you want, but in accordance with the namespaces specification, developers typically use Uniform Resource Identifiers (URIs). The URI doesn't have to point to anything; it just has to be unique. It's not far-fetched to think that two different people somewhere in the world might define an XML element named "Guitar," but it's unlikely that both will assign it to a namespace named *http://www.wintellect.com/classic-guitars*.

A namespace prefix is valid for the element in which the prefix is declared and for the element's children. In the preceding example, the *win* prefix is both declared and used in the same element:

```
<win:Guitars
  xmlns:win="http://www.wintellect.com/classic-guitars"
  ...>
```

It's also used to qualify child elements:

```
<win:Guitar>
  ...
</win:Guitar>
```

Interestingly enough, an element's attributes are not automatically scoped to a namespace, even if the element is. In the following example, the *Image* attribute doesn't belong to a namespace:

```
<win:Guitar Image="MySG.jpeg">
  ...
</win:Guitar>
```

However, you can use namespace prefixes to join attributes to namespaces:

```
<win:Guitar win:Image="MySG.jpeg">
  ...
</win:Guitar>
```

Because attributes are scoped by the elements they're associated with, they're typically used without namespace prefixes unless needs dictate otherwise.

XML also supports the concept of *default namespaces*. A default namespace is declared with an *xmlns* attribute but without a prefix. The element in which a default namespace is declared and all of its children automatically belong to that namespace unless otherwise specified. The following example is equivalent to the first example in this section, but it uses a default namespace—*http://www.wintellect.com/classic-guitars*—to eliminate the repeated *win* prefixes:

```
<?xml version="1.0"?>
<Guitars
  xmlns="http://www.wintellect.com/classic-guitars"
  xmlns:gibson="http://www.gibson.com/finishes"
  xmlns:fender="http://www.fender.com/finishes">
  <Guitar>
    <Make>Gibson</Make>
    <Model>SG</Model>
    <Year>1977</Year>
    <gibson:Color>Tobacco Sunburst</gibson:Color>
    <Neck>Rosewood</Neck>
  </Guitar>
  <Guitar>
    <Make>Fender</Make>
    <Model>Stratocaster</Model>
    <Year></Year>
    <fender:Color>Black</fender:Color>
    <Neck>Maple</Neck>
  </Guitar>
<Guitars>
```

The *Color* elements in this example belong to the *http://www.gibson.com/finishes* and *http://www.fender.com/finishes* namespaces, but all other elements belong to *http://www.wintellect.com/classic-guitars*.

Why do document authors use XML namespaces, and when is it appropriate to omit them? XML elements intended for use by one person or application typically have no need for namespaces because their owner can prevent naming collisions. XML elements intended for public consumption, however, should be qualified with namespaces because their owner can't control how they're used or what other elements they're used with.

Document Validity and Schemas

An XML document that conforms to the rules of XML is said to be a *well-formed document*. The following document is well-formed:

```xml
<?xml version="1.0"?>
<Guitars>
  <Guitar>
    <Make>Gibson</Make>
    <Model>SG</Model>
    <Year>1977</Year>
    <Color>Tobacco Sunburst</Color>
    <Neck>Rosewood</Neck>
  </Guitar>
  <Guitar>
    <Make>Fender</Make>
    <Model>Stratocaster</Model>
    <Year>1990</Year>
    <Color>Black</Color>
    <Neck>Maple</Neck>
  </Guitar>
</Guitars>
```

The document below is not well-formed. In fact, it contains three flaws. Can you spot them?

```xml
<?xml version="1.0"?>
<Guitar>
  <Make>Gibson</Make>
  <Model>SG</Model>
  <Year>1977</Year>
  <Color>Tobacco Sunburst</Color>
  <Neck>Rosewood</Neck>
</guitar>
<Guitar>
  <Make>Fender</Make>
  <Model>Stratocaster</Model>
  <Year>1990
  <Color>Black</Color>
  <Neck>Maple</Neck>
</Guitar>
```

The first flaw is the lack of a document element. The second is the mismatched case in the first *Guitar* element's start and end tags. The third is the complete lack of an end tag for the second *Year* element. Any of these flaws is sufficient to make an XML parser quit and report an error. An easy way to determine whether a document is well-formed is to load it into Internet Explorer. IE will apprise you of any well-formedness errors.

A more stringent test of a document's veracity is whether or not the document is valid. A *valid document* is one that is well-formed *and* that conforms to a schema. Schemas define acceptable document structure and content. If you allow other companies to invoice your company by transmitting XML invoices, you can provide them with a schema specifying what format you expect their

XML documents to be in. When an invoice arrives, you can validate it against the schema to verify that the sender acceded to your wishes.

In the early days of XML, developers used document type definitions (DTDs) to validate XML document content. Today they use XML Schema Definitions (XSDs), which are described at *http://www.w3.org/TR/xmlschema-1* and *http://www.w3.org/TR/xmlschema-2*. XSD is an XML-based language for describing XML documents and the types that they contain. A full treatment of the language could easily fill a book, but just to give you a feel for what XML schemas are all about, here's one that defines the valid format of an XML document describing guitars:

```
<?xml version="1.0"?>
<xsd:schema id="Guitars" xmlns=""
  xmlns:xsd="http://www.w3.org/2001/XMLSchema">
  <xsd:element name="Guitars">
    <xsd:complexType>
      <xsd:choice maxOccurs="unbounded">
        <xsd:element name="Guitar">
          <xsd:complexType>
            <xsd:sequence>
              <xsd:element name="Make" type="xsd:string" />
              <xsd:element name="Model" type="xsd:string" />
              <xsd:element name="Year" type="xsd:gYear"
                minOccurs="0" />
              <xsd:element name="Color" type="xsd:string"
                minOccurs="0" />
              <xsd:element name="Neck" type="xsd:string"
                minOccurs="0" />
            </xsd:sequence>
          </xsd:complexType>
        </xsd:element>
      </xsd:choice>
    </xsd:complexType>
  </xsd:element>
</xsd:schema>
```

This schema, which might be stored in an XSD file, can be used to validate the XML document that leads off this section. It says that a valid document must contain a *Guitars* element, that the *Guitars* element must contain one or more *Guitar* elements, and that a *Guitar* element must contain exactly one *Make* element and one *Model* element and may contain one *Year* element, one *Color* element, and one *Neck* element, in that order. It also says that *Make, Model, Color*, and *Neck* elements contain string data, while *Year* contains a Gregorian calendar year. The following XML document is not valid with respect to this schema because its one and only *Guitar* element lacks a *Make* element and contains two *Color* elements:

```
<?xml version="1.0"?>
<Guitars>
  <Guitar>
    <Model>SG</Model>
    <Year>1977</Year>
    <Color>Tobacco Sunburst</Color>
    <Color>Gun-Metal Gray</Color>
    <Neck>Rosewood</Neck>
  </Guitar>
</Guitars>
```

Schemas are meant to be consumed by computers, not humans. Numerous software tools are available for validating XML documents against schemas and for generating schemas from XML documents. One such tool is the Xsd.exe utility that comes with the .NET Framework SDK. Among other things, Xsd.exe is capable of inferring a schema from an XML document and writing the schema to an XSD file. You may have to tweak the XSD file to make sure the schema reflects your true intent, but changing a few statements here and there in an existing schema is far easier than generating a schema from scratch.

XML Parsers

There's nothing inherently magic about XML itself. What's magic is that software tools called XML parsers are readily available to help you read XML documents and extract data from them while shielding you from the syntax of the language.

Most XML parsers implement one of two popular APIs: DOM or SAX. DOM stands for *Document Object Model* and is described at *http://www.w3.org/TR/DOM-Level-2-Core*. SAX stands for *Simple API for XML* and is an unofficial (that is, non-W3C) standard that grew out of a grass roots effort in the Java community. It's currently documented at *http://www.saxproject.org*. Both APIs define a programmatic interface that abstracts the physical nature of XML documents, but they differ in how they go about it.

SAX is an event-based API. You provide a SAX parser with one or more interfaces containing known sets of callback methods, and as the parser parses the document, it calls you back to let you know what it found. Consider the following XML document:

```
<Greeting>Hello, world</Greeting>
```

An application that wants to read this document using a SAX parser implements a well-known interface containing methods named *startDocument, endDocument, startElement, endElement*, and *characters*, among others. As the parser moves through the document, it invokes these methods on the client in the following order:

```
startDocument    // Signals start of document
startElement     // Signals start of Greeting element
characters       // Transmits "Hello, world"
   ...
endElement       // Signals end of Greeting element
endDocument      // Signals end of document
```

Calls to *startElement* and *endElement* are accompanied by the element names. The ellipsis following *characters* indicates that *characters* is called an indeterminate number of times. Some SAX parsers might call it once and pass "Hello, world" in one chunk, but others might call it several times and transmit "Hello, world" in bite-sized pieces. SAX is extremely useful for parsing large documents because it doesn't require entire documents to be read into memory at once. SAX's chief downside is that it's a forward-only, stream-based API; you can't arbitrarily move backward and forward within a document. Nor can you easily identify relationships between items in the document, since a callback from a SAX parser provides precious little information about the context in which the callback occurred.

DOM is an alternative API that reads a document into memory and supports random access to the document's content items. Microsoft provides a free DOM-style parser in a DLL named MSXML.dll, better known as the "MSXML parser" or simply "MSXML." (Newer versions of MSXML support SAX too.) MSXML layers a DOM Level 2–compliant object model onto XML documents. Individual items within a document—elements, attributes, comments, text, and so on—are represented as *nodes*. Figure 13-2 shows the in-memory node tree that MSXML builds from the following XML document:

```
<?xml version="1.0"?>
<Guitars>
  <Guitar Image="MySG.jpeg">
    <Make>Gibson</Make>
    <Model>SG</Model>
    <Year>1977</Year>
    <Color>Tobacco Sunburst</Color>
    <Neck>Rosewood</Neck>
  </Guitar>
</Guitars>
```

Each block in the diagram represents a node. Rectangles represent element nodes (elements in the XML document), ellipses represent text nodes (textual content within those elements), and the parallelogram represents an attribute. Had the document included processing instructions and other XML items, they too would have been represented as nodes in the tree. Each node is an object that provides methods and properties for navigating the tree and extracting content. For example, each node has a *hasChildNodes* property that reveals whether the node has child nodes, and *firstChild* and *lastChild* properties that return references to child nodes.

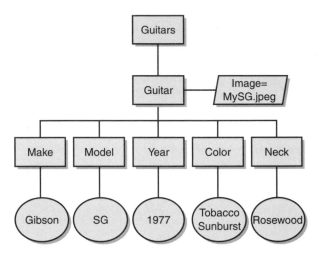

Figure 13-2   DOM representation of a simple XML document.

What's it like to use the DOM API to parse an XML document? Check out the example in Figure 13-4. It's an unmanaged console application written in C++ that uses MSXML to load an XML document and parse it for *Guitar* elements. For each *Guitar* element that it finds, the application reads the values of the *Make* and *Model* subelements and writes them to the console window. If you run it against the XML file in Figure 13-3, the application responds with the following output:

```
Gibson SG
Fender Stratocaster
```

Guitars.xml
```xml
<?xml version="1.0"?>
<Guitars>
  <Guitar Image="MySG.jpeg">
    <Make>Gibson</Make>
    <Model>SG</Model>
    <Year>1977</Year>
    <Color>Tobacco Sunburst</Color>
    <Neck>Rosewood</Neck>
  </Guitar>
  <Guitar Image="MyStrat.jpeg" PreviousOwner="Eric Clapton">
    <Make>Fender</Make>
    <Model>Stratocaster</Model>
    <Year>1990</Year>
    <Color>Black</Color>
    <Neck>Maple</Neck>
  </Guitar>
</Guitars>
```

Figure 13-3   Sample XML document.

How does the ReadXml application work? Briefly, the statement

```
hr = CoCreateInstance (CLSID_DOMDocument, NULL,
    CLSCTX_INPROC_SERVER, IID_IXMLDOMDocument, (void**) &pDoc);
```

instantiates a *DOMDocument* object from a COM class implemented in MSXML.dll and returns an *IXMLDOMDocument* interface pointer. The statement

```
hr = pDoc->load (var, &success);
```

loads an XML document from disk, and the statement

```
hr = pDoc->getElementsByTagName (tag, &pNodeList);
```

asks the *DOMDocument* object for a list of *Guitar* nodes. The list is returned as an *IXMLDOMNodeList* interface. The application enumerates the *Guitar* nodes by calling *get_item* repeatedly on the node list. Each call to *get_item* returns an *IXMLDOMNode* interface pointer representing a node that is in reality a *Guitar* element. The sample program passes the interface pointer to a local function named *ShowGuitarType*, which performs various acrobatics involving a node list of its own to find the *Make* and *Model* subelements and extract their text. Implemented this way, the application can find *Guitar* elements anywhere in any XML file and extract their *Make* and *Model* elements, no matter what order those elements appear in.

```
ReadXml.cpp
#include <stdio.h>
#include <windows.h>

void ShowGuitarType (IXMLDOMNode* pNode);
BOOL GetChildElementByTagName (LPOLESTR pName, IXMLDOMNode* pParent,
    IXMLDOMNode** ppNode);
BOOL IsElementNamed (LPOLESTR pName, IXMLDOMNode* pNode);

int main (int argc, char* argv[])
{
    HRESULT hr = CoInitialize (NULL);

    // Instantiate the MS XML parser
    IXMLDOMDocument* pDoc;
    hr = CoCreateInstance (CLSID_DOMDocument, NULL,
        CLSCTX_INPROC_SERVER, IID_IXMLDOMDocument, (void**) &pDoc);

    if (SUCCEEDED (hr)) {
        // Load Guitars.xml
        VARIANT_BOOL success;
```

Figure 13-4   XML client written in C++.

ReadXml.cpp *(continued)*

```cpp
        BSTR file = SysAllocString (OLESTR ("Guitars.xml"));
        VARIANT var;
        var.vt = VT_BSTR;
        var.bstrVal = file;

        pDoc->put_async (VARIANT_FALSE);
        hr = pDoc->load (var, &success);
        SysFreeString (file);

        if (SUCCEEDED (hr) && hr != S_FALSE) {
            // Get a list of elements named "Guitar"
            IXMLDOMNodeList* pNodeList;
            BSTR tag = SysAllocString (OLESTR ("Guitar"));
            hr = pDoc->getElementsByTagName (tag, &pNodeList);
            SysFreeString (tag);

            if (SUCCEEDED (hr)) {
                // Get a count of the elements returned
                long count;
                hr = pNodeList->get_length (&count);

                if (SUCCEEDED (hr)) {
                    pNodeList->reset ();

                    // Walk the list element by element
                    for (int i=0; i<count; i++) {
                        IXMLDOMNode* pNode;
                        hr = pNodeList->get_item (i, &pNode);

                        if (SUCCEEDED (hr)) {
                            // Show the Make and Model subelements
                            ShowGuitarType (pNode);
                            pNode->Release ();
                        }
                    }
                }
                pNodeList->Release ();
            }
        }
        pDoc->Release ();
    }

    CoUninitialize ();
    return 0;
}

void ShowGuitarType (IXMLDOMNode* pNode)
{
```

```
        IXMLDOMNode* pMakeNode;
        IXMLDOMNode* pModelNode;

        // Get an IXMLDOMNode pointer to the Make subelement
        if (GetChildElementByTagName (OLESTR ("Make"), pNode,
            &pMakeNode)) {
            // Get the Make subelement's text
            BSTR make;
            HRESULT hr = pMakeNode->get_text (&make);

            if (SUCCEEDED (hr) && hr != S_FALSE) {
                // Get an IXMLDOMNode pointer to the Model subelement
                if (GetChildElementByTagName (OLESTR ("Model"), pNode,
                    &pModelNode)) {
                    // Get the Model subelement's text
                    BSTR model;
                    hr = pModelNode->get_text (&model);

                    if (SUCCEEDED (hr) && hr != S_FALSE) {
                        // Output the guitar's make and model
                        wprintf (OLESTR ("%s %s\n"), make, model);
                        SysFreeString (model);
                    }
                    pModelNode->Release ();
                }
                SysFreeString (make);
            }
            pMakeNode->Release ();
        }
    }
}

BOOL GetChildElementByTagName (LPOLESTR pName, IXMLDOMNode* pParent,
    IXMLDOMNode** ppNode)
{
    // Get a list of nodes that are children of pParent
    IXMLDOMNodeList* pNodeList;
    HRESULT hr = pParent->get_childNodes (&pNodeList);

    if (SUCCEEDED (hr)) {
        // Get a count of the nodes returned
        long count;
        hr = pNodeList->get_length (&count);

        if (SUCCEEDED (hr)) {
            pNodeList->reset ();

            // Walk the list node by node
            for (int i=0; i<count; i++) {
                IXMLDOMNode* pNode;
```

(continued)

ReadXml.cpp   *(continued)*

```
                hr = pNodeList->get_item (i, &pNode);

                if (SUCCEEDED (hr)) {
                    // If the node is an element whose name matches
                    // the input name, return an IXMLDOMNode pointer
                    if (IsElementNamed (pName, pNode)) {
                        *ppNode = pNode;
                        pNodeList->Release ();
                        return TRUE;
                    }
                    pNode->Release ();
                }
            }
        }
        pNodeList->Release ();
    }

    return FALSE;
}

BOOL IsElementNamed (LPOLESTR pName, IXMLDOMNode* pNode)
{
    BOOL retval;

    // Get the node type
    DOMNodeType type;
    HRESULT hr = pNode->get_nodeType (&type);

    if (SUCCEEDED (hr) && type == NODE_ELEMENT) {
        // If the node is an element, get its name
        BSTR name;
        hr = pNode->get_nodeName (&name);

        if (SUCCEEDED (hr)) {
            // If the element name matches the input name, return
            // TRUE to indicate a match
            retval = (wcscmp (name, pName) == 0) ? TRUE : FALSE;
            SysFreeString (name);
        }
    }

    return retval;
}
```

Dear reader: the code in Figure 13-4 is hard to write and even harder to maintain. It involves so many COM interface pointers and BSTRs (COM's language-neutral string data type) that the tiniest slip could result in memory leaks.

There's too much code like this in the real world, which is one reason why so many applications leak memory and have to be restarted periodically. Admittedly, the code would have been much simpler had it been written in Visual Basic rather than C++, but the fact remains that this is no way to write production code.

Enter the .NET Framework class library. The FCL features a handy little class named *XmlDocument* that provides a managed DOM implementation and makes parsing truly simple. To demonstrate, Figure 13-5 contains the C# equivalent of the application in Figure 13-4. Which of the two would you rather write and maintain?

```
ReadXml.cs
using System;
using System.Xml;

class MyApp
{
    static void Main ()
    {
        XmlDocument doc = new XmlDocument ();
        doc.Load ("Guitars.xml");
        XmlNodeList nodes = doc.GetElementsByTagName ("Guitar");
        foreach (XmlNode node in nodes) {
            Console.WriteLine ("{0} {1}", node["Make"].InnerText,
                node["Model"].InnerText);
        }
    }
}
```

Figure 13-5   XML client written in C#.

Reading and Writing XML

The FCL's *System.Xml* namespace offers a variety of classes for reading and writing XML documents. For DOM lovers, there's the *XmlDocument* class, which looks and feels like MSXML but is simpler to use. If you prefer a stream-based approach to reading XML documents, you can use *XmlTextReader* or the schema-aware *XmlValidatingReader* instead. A complementary class named *XmlTextWriter* simplifies the process of creating XML documents. These classes are the first line of defense when battle plans call for manipulating XML.

The *XmlDocument* Class

XmlDocument provides a programmatic interface to XML documents that complies with the DOM Level 2 Core specification. It represents a document as an upside-down tree of nodes, with the root element, or document element, at the top. Each node is an instance of *XmlNode*, which exposes methods and properties for navigating DOM trees, reading and writing node content, adding and removing nodes, and more. *XmlDocument* derives from *XmlNode* and adds methods and properties of its own supporting the loading and saving of documents, the creation of new nodes, and other operations.

The following statements create an *XmlDocument* object and initialize it with the contents of Guitars.xml:

```
XmlDocument doc = new XmlDocument ();
doc.Load ("Guitars.xml");
```

Load parses the specified XML document and builds an in-memory representation of it. It throws an *XmlException* if the document isn't well-formed.

A successful call to *Load* is often followed by reading the *XmlDocument*'s *DocumentElement* property. *DocumentElement* returns an *XmlNode* reference to the document element, which is the starting point for a top-to-bottom navigation of the DOM tree. You can find out whether a given node (including the document node) has children by reading the node's *HasChildNodes* property. You can enumerate a node's children by reading its *ChildNodes* property, which returns an *XmlNodeList* representing a collection of nodes. The combination of *HasChildNodes* and *ChildNodes* makes possible a recursive approach to iterating over all the nodes in the tree. The following code loads an XML document and writes a list of its nodes to a console window:

```
XmlDocument doc = new XmlDocument ();
doc.Load ("Guitars.xml");
OutputNode (doc.DocumentElement);
    .
    .
    .
void OutputNode (XmlNode node)
{
    Console.WriteLine ("Type={0}\tName={1}\tValue={2}",
        node.NodeType, node.Name, node.Value);

    if (node.HasChildNodes) {
        XmlNodeList children = node.ChildNodes;
        foreach (XmlNode child in children)
            OutputNode (child);
    }
}
```

Run against Guitars.xml in Figure 13-3, it produces the following output:

```
Type=Element    Name=Guitars    Value=
Type=Element    Name=Guitar     Value=
Type=Element    Name=Make       Value=
Type=Text       Name=#text      Value=Gibson
Type=Element    Name=Model      Value=
Type=Text       Name=#text      Value=SG
Type=Element    Name=Year       Value=
Type=Text       Name=#text      Value=1977
Type=Element    Name=Color      Value=
Type=Text       Name=#text      Value=Tobacco Sunburst
Type=Element    Name=Neck       Value=
Type=Text       Name=#text      Value=Rosewood
Type=Element    Name=Guitar     Value=
Type=Element    Name=Make       Value=
Type=Text       Name=#text      Value=Fender
Type=Element    Name=Model      Value=
Type=Text       Name=#text      Value=Stratocaster
Type=Element    Name=Year       Value=
Type=Text       Name=#text      Value=1990
Type=Element    Name=Color      Value=
Type=Text       Name=#text      Value=Black
Type=Element    Name=Neck       Value=
Type=Text       Name=#text      Value=Maple
```

Notice the varying node types in the listing's first column. Element nodes represent elements in an XML document, and text nodes represent the text associated with those elements. The following table lists the full range of possible node types, which are represented by members of the *XmlNodeType* enumeration. Whitespace nodes represent "insignificant" white space—that is, white space that appears between markup elements and therefore contributes nothing to a document's content—and aren't counted among a document's nodes unless you set *XmlDocument*'s *PreserveWhitespace* property, which defaults to false, equal to true before calling *Load*.

XmlNodeType	**Example**
Attribute	<Guitar **Image="MySG.jpeg"**>
CDATA	<![CDATA["This is character data"]]>
Comment	<!-- This is a comment -->
Document	<Guitars>
DocumentType	<!DOCTYPE Guitars SYSTEM "Guitars.dtd">
Element	<Guitar>
Entity	<!ENTITY filename "Strats.xml">
EntityReference	&lt;

(continued)

XmlNodeType	Example
Notation	<!NOTATION GIF89a SYSTEM "gif">
ProcessingInstruction	<?xml-stylesheet type="text/xsl" href="Guitars.xsl"?>
Text	<Model>**Stratocaster**</Model>
Whitespace	<Make/>**\r\n**<Model/>
XmlDeclaration	<?xml version="1.0"?>

Observe that the preceding output contains no attribute nodes even though the input document contained two elements having attributes. That's because attributes get special treatment. A node's *ChildNodes* property doesn't include attributes, but its *Attributes* property does. Here's how you'd modify the *OutputNode* method to list attributes as well as other node types:

```
void OutputNode (XmlNode node)
{
    Console.WriteLine ("Type={0}\tName={1}\tValue={2}",
        node.NodeType, node.Name, node.Value);

    if (node.Attributes != null) {
        foreach (XmlAttribute attr in node.Attributes)
            Console.WriteLine ("Type={0}\tName={1}\tValue={2}",
                attr.NodeType, attr.Name, attr.Value);
    }

    if (node.HasChildNodes) {
        foreach (XmlNode child in node.ChildNodes)
            OutputNode (child);
    }
}
```

An *XmlNode* object's *NodeType*, *Name*, and *Value* properties expose the type, name, and value of the corresponding node. For some node types (for example, elements), *Name* is meaningful and *Value* is not. For others (text nodes, for instance), *Value* is meaningful but *Name* is not. And for still others—attributes being a great example—both *Name* and *Value* are meaningful. *Name* returns a node's qualified name, which includes a namespace prefix if a prefix is present (for example, *win:Guitar*). Use the *LocalName* property to retrieve names without prefixes.

You don't have to iterate through every node in a document to find a specific node or set of nodes. You can use *XmlDocument*'s *GetElementsByTag-Name*, *SelectNodes*, and *SelectSingleNode* methods to target particular nodes. The sample application in Figure 13-5 uses *GetElementsByTagName* to quickly create an *XmlNodeList* targeting all of the document's *Guitar* nodes. *SelectNodes* and *SelectSingleNode* execute XPath expressions. XPath is introduced later in this chapter.

XmlDocument can be used to write XML documents as well as read them. The following code sample opens Guitars.xml, deletes the first *Guitar* element, adds a new *Guitar* element, and saves the results back to Guitars.xml:

```
XmlDocument doc = new XmlDocument ();
doc.Load ("Guitars.xml");

// Delete the first Guitar element
XmlNode root = doc.DocumentElement;
root.RemoveChild (root.FirstChild);

// Create element nodes
XmlNode guitar = doc.CreateElement ("Guitar");
XmlNode elem1 = doc.CreateElement ("Make");
XmlNode elem2 = doc.CreateElement ("Model");
XmlNode elem3 = doc.CreateElement ("Year");
XmlNode elem4 = doc.CreateElement ("Color");
XmlNode elem5 = doc.CreateElement ("Neck");

// Create text nodes
XmlNode text1 = doc.CreateTextNode ("Gibson");
XmlNode text2 = doc.CreateTextNode ("Les Paul");
XmlNode text3 = doc.CreateTextNode ("1959");
XmlNode text4 = doc.CreateTextNode ("Gold");
XmlNode text5 = doc.CreateTextNode ("Rosewood");

// Attach the text nodes to the element nodes
elem1.AppendChild (text1);
elem2.AppendChild (text2);
elem3.AppendChild (text3);
elem4.AppendChild (text4);
elem5.AppendChild (text5);

// Attach the element nodes to the Guitar node
guitar.AppendChild (elem1);
guitar.AppendChild (elem2);
guitar.AppendChild (elem3);
guitar.AppendChild (elem4);
guitar.AppendChild (elem5);

// Attach the Guitar node to the document node
root.AppendChild (guitar);

// Save the modified document
doc.Save ("Guitars.xml");
```

Other *XmlDocument* methods that are useful for modifying document content include *PrependChild*, *InsertBefore*, *InsertAfter*, *RemoveAll*, and *Replace-Child*. As an alternative to manually creating text nodes and making them children of element nodes, you can assign text by writing to elements' *InnerText* properties. By the same token, reading an element node's *InnerText* property is a quick way to retrieve the text associated with an XML element.

XmlDocument is typically used by applications that read XML documents and care about the relationships between nodes. Figure 13-6 shows one such application. Called XmlView, it's a Windows Forms application that reads an XML document and displays it in a tree view control. Each item in the control represents one node in the document. Items are color-coded to reflect node types. Items without colored blocks represent attributes.

Figure 13-6   Windows Forms XML viewer.

XmlView's source code appears in Figure 13-7. Clicking the Load button activates *XmlViewForm.OnLoadDocument*, which loads an *XmlDocument* from the specified data source and calls a local method named *AddNodeAndChildren* to recursively navigate the document tree and populate the tree view control. The end result is a graphic depiction of the document's structure and a handy tool for digging around in XML files to see what they're made of. Xml-View is compiled slightly differently than the Windows Forms applications in Chapter 4. Here's the command to compile it:

```
csc /t:winexe /res:buttons.bmp,Buttons xmlview.cs
```

The /res switch embeds the contents of Buttons.bmp in XmlView.exe and assigns the resulting resource the name "Buttons". Buttons.bmp contains an image depicting the colored blocks used in the tree view control. The statement

```
NodeImages.Images.AddStrip (new Bitmap (GetType (), "Buttons"));
```

loads the image and uses it to initialize the *ImageList* named *NodeImages*. Packaging the image as an embedded resource makes the resulting executable self-contained.

```
XmlView.cs
using System;
using System.Drawing;
using System.Windows.Forms;
using System.Xml;

class XmlViewForm : Form
{
    GroupBox DocumentGB;
    TextBox Source;
    Button LoadButton;
    ImageList NodeImages;
    TreeView XmlView;

    public XmlViewForm ()
    {
        // Initialize the form's properties
        Text = "XML Viewer";
        ClientSize = new System.Drawing.Size (488, 422);

        // Instantiate the form's controls
        DocumentGB = new GroupBox ();
        Source = new TextBox ();
        LoadButton = new Button ();
        XmlView = new TreeView ();

        // Initialize the controls
        Source.Anchor =
            AnchorStyles.Top | AnchorStyles.Left | AnchorStyles.Right;
        Source.Location = new System.Drawing.Point (16, 24);
        Source.Size = new System.Drawing.Size (336, 24);
        Source.TabIndex = 0;
        Source.Name = "Source";

        LoadButton.Anchor = AnchorStyles.Top | AnchorStyles.Right;
        LoadButton.Location = new System.Drawing.Point (368, 24);
        LoadButton.Size = new System.Drawing.Size (72, 24);
        LoadButton.TabIndex = 1;
        LoadButton.Text = "Load";
        LoadButton.Click += new System.EventHandler (OnLoadDocument);

        DocumentGB.Anchor =
            AnchorStyles.Top | AnchorStyles.Left | AnchorStyles.Right;
        DocumentGB.Location = new Point (16, 16);
        DocumentGB.Size = new Size (456, 64);
```

Figure 13-7   Source code for XmlView.

```csharp
            DocumentGB.Text = "Document";
            DocumentGB.Controls.Add (Source);
            DocumentGB.Controls.Add (LoadButton);

            NodeImages = new ImageList ();
            NodeImages.ImageSize = new Size (12, 12);
            NodeImages.Images.AddStrip (new Bitmap (GetType(), "Buttons"));
            NodeImages.TransparentColor = Color.White;

            XmlView.Anchor = AnchorStyles.Top | AnchorStyles.Bottom |
                AnchorStyles.Left | AnchorStyles.Right;
            XmlView.Location = new System.Drawing.Point (16, 96);
            XmlView.Size = new System.Drawing.Size (456, 308);
            XmlView.ImageList = NodeImages;
            XmlView.TabIndex = 2;
            XmlView.Name = "XmlView";

            // Add the controls to the form
            Controls.Add (DocumentGB);
            Controls.Add (XmlView);
        }

        void OnLoadDocument (object sender, EventArgs e)
        {
            try {
                XmlDocument doc = new XmlDocument ();
                doc.Load (Source.Text);
                XmlView.Nodes.Clear ();
                AddNodeAndChildren (doc.DocumentElement, null);
            }
            catch (Exception ex) {
                MessageBox.Show (ex.Message);
            }
        }

        void AddNodeAndChildren (XmlNode xnode, TreeNode tnode)
        {
            TreeNode child = AddNode (xnode, tnode);

            if (xnode.Attributes != null) {
                foreach (XmlAttribute attribute in xnode.Attributes)
                    AddAttribute (attribute, child);
            }

            if (xnode.HasChildNodes) {
                foreach (XmlNode node in xnode.ChildNodes)
                    AddNodeAndChildren (node, child);
            }
```

```
}

TreeNode AddNode (XmlNode xnode, TreeNode tnode)
{
    string text = null;
    TreeNode child = null;

    TreeNodeCollection tnodes = (tnode == null) ?
        XmlView.Nodes : tnode.Nodes;

    switch (xnode.NodeType) {

    case XmlNodeType.Element:
    case XmlNodeType.Document:
        tnodes.Add (child = new TreeNode (xnode.Name, 0, 0));
        break;

    case XmlNodeType.Text:
        text = xnode.Value;
        if (text.Length > 128)
            text = text.Substring (0, 128) + "...";
        tnodes.Add (child = new TreeNode (text, 2, 2));
        break;

    case XmlNodeType.CDATA:
        text = xnode.Value;
        if (text.Length > 128)
            text = text.Substring (0, 128) + "...";
        text = String.Format ("<![CDATA[{0}]]>", text);
        tnodes.Add (child = new TreeNode (text, 3, 3));
        break;

    case XmlNodeType.Comment:
        text = String.Format ("<!--{0}-->", xnode.Value);
        tnodes.Add (child = new TreeNode (text, 4, 4));
        break;

    case XmlNodeType.XmlDeclaration:
    case XmlNodeType.ProcessingInstruction:
        text = String.Format ("<?{0} {1}?>", xnode.Name,
            xnode.Value);
        tnodes.Add (child = new TreeNode (text, 5, 5));
        break;

    case XmlNodeType.Entity:
        text = String.Format ("<!ENTITY {0}>", xnode.Value);
        tnodes.Add (child = new TreeNode (text, 6, 6));
        break;
```

(continued)

XmlView.cs *(continued)*

```
        case XmlNodeType.EntityReference:
            text = String.Format ("&{0};", xnode.Value);
            tnodes.Add (child = new TreeNode (text, 7, 7));
            break;

        case XmlNodeType.DocumentType:
            text = String.Format ("<!DOCTYPE {0}>", xnode.Value);
            tnodes.Add (child = new TreeNode (text, 8, 8));
            break;

        case XmlNodeType.Notation:
            text = String.Format ("<!NOTATION {0}>", xnode.Value);
            tnodes.Add (child = new TreeNode (text, 9, 9));
            break;

        default:
            tnodes.Add (child =
                new TreeNode (xnode.NodeType.ToString (), 1, 1));
            break;
        }
        return child;
    }

    void AddAttribute (XmlAttribute attribute, TreeNode tnode)
    {
        string text = String.Format ("{0}={1}", attribute.Name,
            attribute.Value);
        tnode.Nodes.Add (new TreeNode (text, 1, 1));
    }

    static void Main ()
    {
        Application.Run (new XmlViewForm ());
    }
}
```

Incidentally, the FCL includes a class named *XmlDataDocument* that's closely related to and, in fact, derives from *XmlDocument*. *XmlDataDocument* is a mechanism for treating relational data as XML data. You can wrap an *XmlDataDocument* around a *DataSet*, as shown here:

```
DataSet ds = new DataSet ();
// TODO: Initialize the DataSet with a database query
XmlDataDocument doc = new XmlDataDocument (ds);
```

This action layers an XML DOM over a *DataSet* and allows the *DataSet*'s contents to be read and written using *XmlDocument* semantics.

The *XmlTextReader* Class

XmlDocument is an efficient and easy-to-use mechanism for reading XML documents. It allows you to move backward, forward, and sideways within a document and even make changes to the document as you go. But if your intent is simply to read XML and you're less interested in the structure of the document than its contents, there's another way to go about it: the FCL's *XmlTextReader* class. *XmlTextReader*, which, like *XmlDocument*, belongs to the *System.Xml* namespace, provides a fast, forward-only, read-only interface to XML documents. It's stream-based like SAX. It's more memory-efficient than *XmlDocument*, especially for large documents, because it doesn't read an entire document into memory at once. And it makes it even easier than *XmlDocument* to read through a document searching for particular elements, attributes, or other content items.

Using *XmlTextReader* is simplicity itself. The basic idea is to create an *XmlTextReader* object from a file, URL, or other data source, and to call *XmlTextReader.Read* repeatedly until you find the content you're looking for or reach the end of the document. Each call to *Read* advances an imaginary cursor to the next node in the document. *XmlTextReader* properties such as *NodeType*, *Name*, *Value*, and *AttributeCount* expose information about the current node. Methods such as *GetAttribute*, *MoveToFirstAttribute*, and *MoveToNextAttribute* let you access the attributes, if any, attached to the current node.

The following code fragment wraps an *XmlTextReader* around Guitars.xml and reads through the entire file node by node:

```
XmlTextReader reader = null;

try {
    reader = new XmlTextReader ("Guitars.xml");
    reader.WhitespaceHandling = WhitespaceHandling.None;
    while (reader.Read ()) {
        Console.WriteLine ("Type={0}\tName={1}\tValue={2}",
            reader.NodeType, reader.Name, reader.Value);
    }
}
finally {
    if (reader != null)
        reader.Close ();
}
```

Running it against the XML document in Figure 13-3 produces the following output:

```
Type=XmlDeclaration      Name=xml         Value=version="1.0"
Type=Element      Name=Guitars      Value=
Type=Element      Name=Guitar      Value=
Type=Element      Name=Make      Value=
Type=Text      Name=    Value=Gibson
Type=EndElement Name=Make      Value=
Type=Element      Name=Model      Value=
Type=Text      Name=    Value=SG
Type=EndElement Name=Model      Value=
Type=Element      Name=Year      Value=
Type=Text      Name=    Value=1977
Type=EndElement Name=Year      Value=
Type=Element      Name=Color      Value=
Type=Text      Name=    Value=Tobacco Sunburst
Type=EndElement Name=Color      Value=
Type=Element      Name=Neck      Value=
Type=Text      Name=    Value=Rosewood
Type=EndElement Name=Neck      Value=
Type=EndElement Name=Guitar      Value=
Type=Element      Name=Guitar      Value=
Type=Element      Name=Make      Value=
Type=Text      Name=    Value=Fender
Type=EndElement Name=Make      Value=
Type=Element      Name=Model      Value=
Type=Text      Name=    Value=Stratocaster
Type=EndElement Name=Model      Value=
Type=Element      Name=Year      Value=
Type=Text      Name=    Value=1990
Type=EndElement Name=Year      Value=
Type=Element      Name=Color      Value=
Type=Text      Name=    Value=Black
Type=EndElement Name=Color      Value=
Type=Element      Name=Neck      Value=
Type=Text      Name=    Value=Maple
Type=EndElement Name=Neck      Value=
Type=EndElement Name=Guitar      Value=
Type=EndElement Name=Guitars      Value=
```

Note the *EndElement* nodes in the output. Unlike *XmlDocument*, *XmlText-Reader* counts an element's start and end tags as separate nodes. *XmlTextReader* also includes whitespace nodes in its output unless told to do otherwise. Setting its *WhitespaceHandling* property to *WhitespaceHandling.None* prevents a reader from returning whitespace nodes.

Like *XmlDocument*, *XmlTextReader* treats attributes differently than other nodes and doesn't return them as part of the normal iterative process. If you want to enumerate attribute nodes, you have to read them separately. Here's a revised code sample that outputs attribute nodes as well as other nodes:

```
XmlTextReader reader = null;

try {
    reader = new XmlTextReader ("Guitars.xml");
    reader.WhitespaceHandling = WhitespaceHandling.None;
    while (reader.Read ()) {
        Console.WriteLine ("Type={0}\tName={1}\tValue={2}",
            reader.NodeType, reader.Name, reader.Value);
        if (reader.AttributeCount > 0) {
            while (reader.MoveToNextAttribute ()) {
                Console.WriteLine ("Type={0}\tName={1}\tValue={2}",
                    reader.NodeType, reader.Name, reader.Value);
            }
        }
    }
}
finally {
    if (reader != null)
        reader.Close ();
}
```

A common use for *XmlTextReader* is parsing an XML document and extracting selected node values. The following code sample finds all the *Guitar* elements that are accompanied by *Image* attributes and echoes the attribute values to a console window:

```
XmlTextReader reader = null;

try {
    reader = new XmlTextReader ("Guitars.xml");
    reader.WhitespaceHandling = WhitespaceHandling.None;

    while (reader.Read ()) {
        if (reader.NodeType == XmlNodeType.Element &&
            reader.Name == "Guitar" &&
            reader.AttributeCount > 0) {
            while (reader.MoveToNextAttribute ()) {
                if (reader.Name == "Image") {
                    Console.WriteLine (reader.Value);
                    break;
                }
            }
        }
    }
}
finally {
    if (reader != null)
        reader.Close ();
}
```

Run against Guitars.xml (Figure 13-3), this sample produces the following output:

```
MySG.jpeg
MyStrat.jpeg
```

It's important to close an *XmlTextReader* when you're finished with it so that the reader, in turn, can close the underlying data source. That's why all the samples in this section call *Close* on their *XmlTextReader*s and do so in *finally* blocks.

The *XmlValidatingReader* Class

XmlValidatingReader is a derivative of *XmlTextReader*. It adds one important feature that *XmlTextReader* lacks: the ability to validate XML documents as it reads them. It supports three schema types: DTD, XSD, and XML-Data Reduced (XDR). Its *Schemas* property holds the schema (or schemas) that a document is validated against, and its *ValidationType* property specifies the schema type. *ValidationType* defaults to *ValidationType.Auto*, which allows *XmlValidating-Reader* to determine the schema type from the schema document provided to it. Setting *ValidationType* to *ValidationType.None* creates a nonvalidating reader—the equivalent of *XmlTextReader*.

XmlValidatingReader doesn't accept a file name or URL as input, but you can initialize an *XmlTextReader* with a file name or URL and wrap an *XmlValidatingReader* around it. The following statements create an *XmlValidatingReader* and initialize it with an XML document and a schema document:

```
XmlTextReader nvr = new XmlTextReader ("Guitars.xml");
XmlValidatingReader reader = new XmlValidatingReader (nvr);
reader.Schemas.Add ("", "Guitars.xsd");
```

The first parameter passed to *Add* identifies the target namespace, if any, specified in the schema document. An empty string means the schema defines no target namespace.

Validating a document is as simple as iterating through all its nodes with repeated calls to *XmlValidatingReader.Read*:

```
while (reader.Read ());
```

If the reader encounters well-formedness errors as it reads, it throws an *XmlException*. If it encounter validation errors, it fires *ValidationEventHandler* events. An application that uses an *XmlValidatingReader* can trap these events by registering an event handler:

```
reader.ValidationEventHandler +=
    new ValidationEventHandler (OnValidationError);
```

The event handler receives a *ValidationEventArgs* containing information about the validation error, including a textual description of it (in *Validation-EventArgs.Message*) and an *XmlSchemaException* (in *ValidationEvent-Args.Exception*). The latter contains additional information about the error such as the position in the source document where the error occurred.

Figure 13-8 lists the source code for a console app named Validate that validates XML documents against XSD schemas. To use it, type the command name followed by the name or URL of an XML document and the name or URL of a schema document, as in

```
validate guitars.xml guitars.xsd
```

As a convenience for users, Validate uses an *XmlTextReader* to parse the schema document for the target namespace that's needed to add the schema to the *Schemas* collection. (See the *GetTargetNamespace* method for details.) It takes advantage of the fact that XSDs, unlike DTDs, are XML documents themselves and can therefore be read using XML parsers.

```
Validate.cs
using System;
using System.Xml;
using System.Xml.Schema;

class MyApp
{
    static void Main (string[] args)
    {
        if (args.Length < 2) {
            Console.WriteLine ("Syntax: VALIDATE xmldoc schemadoc");
            return;
        }

        XmlValidatingReader reader = null;

        try {
            XmlTextReader nvr = new XmlTextReader (args[0]);
            nvr.WhitespaceHandling = WhitespaceHandling.None;

            reader = new XmlValidatingReader (nvr);
            reader.Schemas.Add (GetTargetNamespace (args[1]), args[1]);
            reader.ValidationEventHandler +=
                new ValidationEventHandler (OnValidationError);

            while (reader.Read ());
        }
        catch (Exception ex) {
```

Figure 13-8 Utility for validating XML documents.

Validate.cs *(continued)*

```
                Console.WriteLine (ex.Message);
        }
        finally {
            if (reader != null)
                reader.Close ();
        }
    }


    static void OnValidationError (object sender, ValidationEventArgs e)
    {
        Console.WriteLine (e.Message);
    }


    public static string GetTargetNamespace (string src)
    {
        XmlTextReader reader = null;

        try {
            reader = new XmlTextReader (src);
            reader.WhitespaceHandling = WhitespaceHandling.None;

            while (reader.Read ()) {
                if (reader.NodeType == XmlNodeType.Element &&
                    reader.LocalName == "schema") {
                    while (reader.MoveToNextAttribute ()) {
                        if (reader.Name == "targetNamespace")
                            return reader.Value;
                    }
                }
            }
            return "";
        }
        finally {
            if (reader != null)
                reader.Close ();
        }
    }
}
```

The *XmlTextWriter* Class

The FCL's *XmlDocument* class can be used to modify existing XML documents, but it can't be used to generate XML documents from scratch. *XmlTextWriter* can. It features an assortment of *Write* methods that emit various types of XML, including elements, attributes, comments, and more. The following example uses some of these methods to create an XML file named Guitars.xml containing a document element named *Guitars* and a subelement named *Guitar*:

```
XmlTextWriter writer = null;

try {
    writer = new XmlTextWriter ("Guitars.xml", System.Text.Encoding.Unicode);
    writer.Formatting = Formatting.Indented;

    writer.WriteStartDocument ();
    writer.WriteStartElement ("Guitars");
    writer.WriteStartElement ("Guitar");
    writer.WriteAttributeString ("Image", "MySG.jpeg");
    writer.WriteElementString ("Make", "Gibson");
    writer.WriteElementString ("Model", "SG");
    writer.WriteElementString ("Year", "1977");
    writer.WriteElementString ("Color", "Tobacco Sunburst");
    writer.WriteElementString ("Neck", "Rosewood");
    writer.WriteEndElement ();
    writer.WriteEndElement ();
}
finally {
    if (writer != null)
        writer.Close ();
}
```

Here's what the generated document looks like:

```
<?xml version="1.0" encoding="utf-16"?>
<Guitars>
  <Guitar Image="MySG.jpeg">
    <Make>Gibson</Make>
    <Model>SG</Model>
    <Year>1977</Year>
    <Color>Tobacco Sunburst</Color>
    <Neck>Rosewood</Neck>
  </Guitar>
</Guitars>
```

Setting an *XmlTextWriter*'s *Formatting* property to *Formatting.Indented* before writing begins produces the indentation seen in the sample. Skipping this step omits the indents and the line breaks too. The default indentation depth is 2, and the default indentation character is the space character. You can change the indentation depth and indentation character using *XmlTextWriter*'s *Indentation* and *IndentChar* properties.

XPath

XPath, which is short for *XML Path Language*, is a language for addressing parts of an XML document. Its name includes the word "path" because of the similarities between XML paths and file system paths. In a file system, for example, \Book\Chap13 identifies the Chap13 subdirectory of the root directory's Book subdirectory. In an XML document, /Guitars/Guitar identifies all elements named *Guitar* that are children of the root element *Guitars*. "/Guitars/Guitar" is an XPath expression. XPath expressions are fully described in the XPath specification found at *http://www.w3.org/TR/xpath*.

XPath can be put to work in a variety of ways. Later in this chapter, you'll learn about XSL Transformations (XSLT), which is a language for converting XML documents from one format to another. XSLT uses XPath expressions to identify nodes and node sets. Another common use for XPath is extracting data from XML documents. Used this way, XPath becomes a query language of sorts—the XML equivalent of SQL, if you will. The W3C is working on an official XML query language called XQuery (*http://www.w3.org/TR/xquery*), but for the moment, an XPath processor is the best way to extract information from XML documents without having to manually traverse DOM trees. The FCL comes with an XPath engine named *System.Xml.XPath.XPathNavigator*. Before we discuss it, let's briefly review XPath.

XPath Basics

Expressions are the building blocks of XPath. The most common type of expression is the *location path*. The following location path evaluates to all *Guitar* elements that are children of a root element named *Guitars*:

```
/Guitars/Guitar
```

This one evaluates to all attributes (not elements) named *Image* that belong to *Guitar* elements that in turn are children of the root element *Guitars*:

```
/Guitars/Guitar/@Image
```

The next expression evaluates to all *Guitar* elements anywhere in the document:

```
//Guitar
```

The // prefix is extremely useful for locating elements in a document regardless of where they're positioned.

XPath also supports wildcards. This expression selects all elements that are children of a root element named *Guitars*:

```
/Guitars/*
```

The next example selects all attributes belonging to *Guitar* elements anywhere in the document:

```
//Guitar/@*
```

Location paths can be absolute or relative. Paths that begin with / or // are absolute because they specify a location relative to the root. Paths that don't begin with / or // are relative paths. They specify a location relative to the current node, or *context node*, in an XPath document.

The components of a location path are called *location steps*. The following location path has two location steps:

```
/Guitars/Guitar
```

A location step consists of three parts: an axis, a node test, and zero or more predicates. The general format for a location step is as follows:

```
axis::node-test[predicate1][predicate2][...]
```

The axis describes a relationship between nodes. Supported values include *child*, *descendant*, *descendant-or-self*, *parent*, *ancestor*, and *ancestor-or-self*, among others. If you don't specify an axis, the default is *child*. Therefore, the expression

```
/Guitars/Guitar
```

could also be written

```
/child::Guitars/child::Guitar
```

Other axes can be used to qualify location paths in different ways. For example, this expression evaluates to all elements named *Guitar* that are descendants of the root element:

```
/descendant::Guitar
```

The next expression evaluates to all *Guitar* elements that are descendants of the root element or are themselves root elements:

```
/descendant-or-self::Guitar
```

In fact, // is shorthand for */descendant-or-self*. Thus, the expression

```
//Guitar
```

is equivalent to the one above. Similarly, @ is shorthand for *attribute*. The statement

```
//Guitar/@*
```

can also be written

```
//Guitar/attribute::*
```

Most developers prefer the abbreviated syntax, but both syntaxes are supported by XPath 1.0–compliant expression engines.

The predicate is the portion of the location path, if any, that appears in square brackets. Predicates are nothing more than filters. For example, the following expression evaluates to all *Guitar* elements in the document:

```
//Guitar
```

But this one uses a predicate to narrow down the selection to *Guitar* elements having attributes named *Image*:

```
//Guitar[@Image]
```

The next one evaluates to all *Guitar* elements that have attributes named *Image* whose value is "MyStrat.jpeg":

```
//Guitar[@Image = "MyStrat.jpeg"]
```

Predicates can include the following comparison operators: <, >, =, !=, <=, and >=. The following expression targets *Guitar* elements whose *Year* elements designate a year after 1980:

```
//Guitar[Year > 1980]
```

Predicates can also include *and* and *or* operators. This expression selects guitars manufactured after 1980 by Fender:

```
//Guitar[Year > 1980][Make = "Fender"]
```

The next expression does the same, but combines two predicates into one using the *and* operator:

```
//Guitar[Year > 1980 and Make = "Fender"]
```

Changing *and* to *or* identifies guitars that were manufactured by Fender *or* built after 1980:

```
//Guitar[Year > 1980 or Make = "Fender"]
```

XPath also supports a set of intrinsic functions that are often (but not always) used in predicates. The following expression evaluates to all *Guitar* elements having *Make* elements whose text begins with the letter G. The key is the *starts-with* function invoked in the predicate:

```
//Guitar[starts-with (Make, "G")]
```

The next expression uses the *text* function to return all text nodes associated with *Make* elements that are subelements of *Guitar* elements. Like DOM, XPath treats the text associated with an element as a separate node:

```
//Guitar/Make/text ()
```

The *starts-with* and *text* functions are but two of many that XPath supports. For a complete list, refer to the XPath specification.

When executed by an XPath processor, a location path returns a *node set*. XPath, like DOM, uses tree-structured node sets to represent XML content. Suppose you're given the XML document in Figure 13-3 and you execute the following location path against it:

```
//Guitar
```

The resulting node set contains two nodes, each representing a *Guitar* element. Each *Guitar* element is the root of a node tree containing *Make, Model, Year, Color,* and *Neck* subelement nodes (Figure 13-9). Each subelement node is the parent of a text node that holds the element's text. XPath node types are defined separately from DOM node types, although the two share many similarities. XPath defines fewer node types than DOM, which make XPath node types a functional subset of DOM node types.

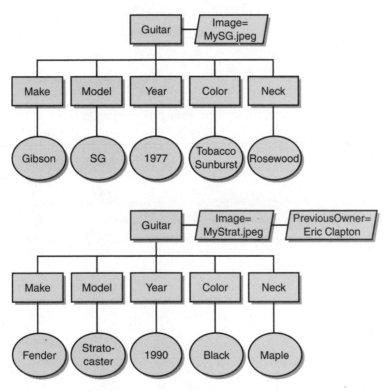

Figure 13-9   Node set resulting from an XPath expression.

XPathNavigator and Friends

The .NET Framework class library's *System.Xml.XPath* namespace contains classes for putting XPath to work in managed applications. Chief among those classes are *XPathDocument*, which represents XML documents that you want to query with XPath; *XPathNavigator*, which provides a mechanism for performing XPath queries; and *XPathNodeIterator,* which represents node sets generated by XPath queries and lets you iterate over them.

The first step in performing XPath queries on XML documents is to create an *XPathDocument* wrapping the XML document itself. *XPathDocument* features a variety of constructors capable of initializing an *XPathDocument* from a stream, a URL, a file, a *TextReader*, or an *XmlReader*. The following statement creates an *XPathDocument* object and initializes it with the content found in Guitars.xml:

```
XPathDocument doc = new XPathDocument ("Guitars.xml");
```

Step two is to create an *XPathNavigator* from the *XPathDocument. XPathDocument* features a method named *CreateNavigator* for just that purpose. The following statement creates an *XPathNavigator* object from the *XPathDocument* created in the previous step:

```
XPathNavigator nav = doc.CreateNavigator ();
```

The final step is actually executing the query. *XPathNavigator* features five methods for executing XPath queries. The two most important are *Evaluate* and *Select. Evaluate* executes any XPath expression. It returns a generic *Object* that can be a string, a float, a bool, or an *XPathNodeIterator*, depending on the expression and the type of data that it returns. *Select* works exclusively with expressions that return node sets and is therefore an ideal vehicle for evaluating location paths. It always returns an *XPathNodeIterator* representing an XPath node set. The following statement uses *Select* to create a node set representing all nodes that match the expression "//Guitar":

```
XPathNodeIterator iterator = nav.Select ("//Guitar");
```

XPathNodeIterator is a simple class that lets you iterate over the nodes returned in a node set. Its *Count* property tells you how many nodes were returned:

```
Console.WriteLine ("Select returned {0} nodes", iterator.Count);
```

XPathNodeIterator's MoveNext method lets you iterate over the node set a node at a time. As you iterate, *XPathNodeIterator's Current* property exposes an *XPathNavigator* object that represents the current node. The following code iterates over the node set, displaying the type, name, and value of each node:

```
while (iterator.MoveNext ()) {
    Console.WriteLine ("Type={0}, Name={1}, Value={2}",
        iterator.Current.NodeType,
        iterator.Current.Name,
        iterator.Current.Value);
}
```

The string returned by the *XPathNavigator*'s *Value* property depends on
the node's type and content. For example, if *Current* represents an attribute
node or an element node that contains simple text (as opposed to other elements), then *Value* returns the attribute's value or the text value of the element.
If, however, *Current* represents an element node that contains other elements,
Value returns the text of the subelements concatenated together into one long
string.

Each node in the node set that *Select* returns can be a single node or the
root of a tree of nodes. Traversing a tree of nodes encapsulated in an *XPath-
Navigator* is slightly different from traversing a tree of nodes in an *XmlDocument*. Here's how to perform a depth-first traversal of the node trees returned
by *XPathNavigator.Select*:

```
while (iterator.MoveNext ())
    OutputNode (iterator.Current);

    .

    .

    .

void OutputNode (XPathNavigator nav)
{
    Console.WriteLine ("Type={0}, Name={1}, Value={2}",
        nav.NodeType, nav.Name, nav.Value);

    if (nav.HasAttributes) {
        nav.MoveToFirstAttribute ();
        do {
            OutputNode (nav);
        } while (nav.MoveToNextAttribute ());
        nav.MoveToParent ();
    }

    if (nav.HasChildren) {
        nav.MoveToFirstChild ();
        do {
            OutputNode (nav);
        } while (nav.MoveToNext ());
        nav.MoveToParent ();
    }
}
```

XPathNavigator features a family of *Move* methods that you can call to move any direction—up, down, or sideways—in a tree of nodes. This sample uses five of them: *MoveToFirstAttribute*, *MoveToNextAttribute*, *MoveToParent*, *MoveToFirstChild*, and *MoveToNext*. Observe also that the *XPathNavigator* itself exposes the properties of the nodes that you iterate over, in much the same manner as *XmlTextReader*.

So how might you put this knowledge to work in a real application? Look again at Figure 13-5. The application listed there uses *XmlDocument* to extract content from an XML document. Content can also be extracted—often with less code—with XPath. To demonstrate, the application in Figure 13-10 is the functional equivalent of the one in Figure 13-5. Besides demonstrating the basic semantics of *XPathNavigator* usage, it shows that you can perform subqueries on node sets returned by XPath queries by calling *Select* on the *XPathNavigator* exposed through an iterator's *Current* property. XPathDemo first calls *Select* to create a node set representing all *Guitar* elements that are children of *Guitars*. Then it iterates through the node set, calling *Select* on each *Guitar* node to select the node's *Make* and *Model* child elements.

XPathDemo.cs
```csharp
using System;
using System.Xml.XPath;

class MyApp
{
    static void Main ()
    {
        XPathDocument doc = new XPathDocument ("Guitars.xml");
        XPathNavigator nav = doc.CreateNavigator ();
        XPathNodeIterator iterator = nav.Select ("/Guitars/Guitar");

        while (iterator.MoveNext ()) {
            XPathNodeIterator it = iterator.Current.Select ("Make");
            it.MoveNext ();
            string make = it.Current.Value;

            it = iterator.Current.Select ("Model");
            it.MoveNext ();
            string model = it.Current.Value;

            Console.WriteLine ("{0} {1}", make, model);
        }
    }
}
```

Figure 13-10 Utility that uses XPath to extract XML content.

A Do-It-Yourself XPath Expression Evaluator

To help you get acquainted with XPath, the application pictured in Figure 13-11 is a working XPath expression analyzer that evaluates XPath expressions against XML documents and displays the results. Like Microsoft SQL Server's query analyzer, which lets you test SQL commands, the XPath expression analyzer—Expressalyzer for short—lets you experiment with XPath queries. To try it out, type a file name or URL into the Document box and click Load to point Expressalyzer to an XML document. Then type a location path into the Expression box and click the Execute button. The results appear in the tree view control in the lower half of the window.

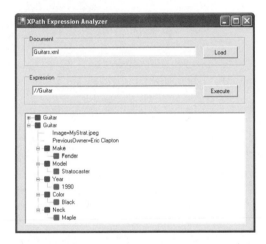

Figure 13-11   Windows Forms XPath expression analyzer.

Expressalyzer's source code appears in Figure 13-12. Expressalyzer is a Windows Forms application whose main form is an instance of *AnalyzerForm*. Clicking the Load button activates the form's *OnLoadDocument* method, which wraps an *XPathDocument* around the data source. Clicking the Execute button activates the *OnExecuteExpression* method, which executes the expression by calling *Select* on the *XPathDocument*. If you need more real estate, resize the Expressalyzer window and the controls inside it will resize too. That little piece of magic results from the *AnchorStyles* assigned to the controls' *Anchor* properties. For a review of Windows Forms anchoring, refer to Chapter 4.

Expressalyzer.cs

```csharp
using System;
using System.Drawing;
using System.Windows.Forms;
using System.Xml.XPath;

class AnalyzerForm : Form
{
    GroupBox DocumentGB;
    TextBox Source;
    Button LoadButton;
    GroupBox ExpressionGB;
    TextBox Expression;
    Button ExecuteButton;
    ImageList NodeImages;
    TreeView XmlView;

    XPathNavigator Navigator;

    public AnalyzerForm ()
    {
        // Initialize the form's properties
        Text = "XPath Expression Analyzer";
        ClientSize = new System.Drawing.Size (488, 422);

        // Instantiate the form's controls
        DocumentGB = new GroupBox ();
        Source = new TextBox ();
        LoadButton = new Button ();
        ExpressionGB = new GroupBox ();
        Expression = new TextBox ();
        ExecuteButton = new Button ();
        XmlView = new TreeView ();

        // Initialize the controls
        Source.Anchor =
            AnchorStyles.Top | AnchorStyles.Left | AnchorStyles.Right;
        Source.Location = new System.Drawing.Point (16, 24);
        Source.Size = new System.Drawing.Size (336, 24);
        Source.TabIndex = 0;
        Source.Name = "Source";

        LoadButton.Anchor = AnchorStyles.Top | AnchorStyles.Right;
        LoadButton.Location = new System.Drawing.Point (368, 24);
        LoadButton.Size = new System.Drawing.Size (72, 24);
        LoadButton.TabIndex = 1;
```

Figure 13-12   Source code for an XPath expression analyzer.

```
LoadButton.Text = "Load";
LoadButton.Click += new System.EventHandler (OnLoadDocument);


DocumentGB.Anchor =
    AnchorStyles.Top | AnchorStyles.Left | AnchorStyles.Right;
DocumentGB.Location = new Point (16, 16);
DocumentGB.Size = new Size (456, 64);
DocumentGB.Text = "Document";
DocumentGB.Controls.Add (Source);
DocumentGB.Controls.Add (LoadButton);


Expression.Anchor =
    AnchorStyles.Top | AnchorStyles.Left | AnchorStyles.Right;
Expression.Location = new System.Drawing.Point (16, 24);
Expression.Size = new System.Drawing.Size (336, 24);
Expression.TabIndex = 2;
Expression.Name = "Expression";


ExecuteButton.Anchor = AnchorStyles.Top | AnchorStyles.Right;
ExecuteButton.Location = new System.Drawing.Point (368, 24);
ExecuteButton.Size = new System.Drawing.Size (72, 24);
ExecuteButton.TabIndex = 3;
ExecuteButton.Text = "Execute";
ExecuteButton.Enabled = false;
ExecuteButton.Click +=
    new System.EventHandler (OnExecuteExpression);


ExpressionGB.Anchor =
    AnchorStyles.Top | AnchorStyles.Left | AnchorStyles.Right;
ExpressionGB.Location = new System.Drawing.Point (16, 96);
ExpressionGB.Name = "ExpressionGB";
ExpressionGB.Size = new System.Drawing.Size (456, 64);
ExpressionGB.Text = "Expression";
ExpressionGB.Controls.Add (Expression);
ExpressionGB.Controls.Add (ExecuteButton);


NodeImages = new ImageList ();
NodeImages.ImageSize = new Size (12, 12);
NodeImages.Images.AddStrip (new Bitmap (GetType (), "Buttons"));
NodeImages.TransparentColor = Color.White;


XmlView.Anchor = AnchorStyles.Top | AnchorStyles.Bottom |
    AnchorStyles.Left | AnchorStyles.Right;
XmlView.Location = new System.Drawing.Point (16, 176);
XmlView.Size = new System.Drawing.Size (456, 232);
XmlView.ImageList = NodeImages;
XmlView.TabIndex = 4;
XmlView.Name = "XmlView";
```

(continued)

Expressalyzer.cs *(continued)*

```csharp
        // Add the controls to the form
        Controls.Add (DocumentGB);
        Controls.Add (ExpressionGB);
        Controls.Add (XmlView);
    }

    void OnLoadDocument (object sender, EventArgs e)
    {
        try {
            XPathDocument doc = new XPathDocument (Source.Text);
            Navigator = doc.CreateNavigator ();
            ExecuteButton.Enabled = true;
        }
        catch (Exception ex) {
            MessageBox.Show (ex.Message);
        }
    }

    void OnExecuteExpression (object sender, EventArgs e)
    {
        try {
            XPathNodeIterator iterator =
                Navigator.Select (Expression.Text);
            XmlView.Nodes.Clear ();
            while (iterator.MoveNext ())
                AddNodeAndChildren (iterator.Current, null);
        }
        catch (Exception ex) {
            MessageBox.Show (ex.Message);
        }
    }

    void AddNodeAndChildren (XPathNavigator nav, TreeNode tnode)
    {
        TreeNode child = AddNode (nav, tnode);

        if (nav.HasAttributes) {
            nav.MoveToFirstAttribute ();
            do {
                AddAttribute (nav, child);
            } while (nav.MoveToNextAttribute ());
            nav.MoveToParent ();
        }

        if (nav.HasChildren) {
            nav.MoveToFirstChild ();
            do {
                AddNodeAndChildren (nav, child);
```

```
            } while (nav.MoveToNext ());
            nav.MoveToParent ();
        }
    }

    TreeNode AddNode (XPathNavigator nav, TreeNode tnode)
    {
        string text = null;
        TreeNode child = null;

        TreeNodeCollection tnodes = (tnode == null) ?
            XmlView.Nodes : tnode.Nodes;

        switch (nav.NodeType) {

        case XPathNodeType.Root:
        case XPathNodeType.Element:
            tnodes.Add (child = new TreeNode (nav.Name, 0, 0));
            break;

        case XPathNodeType.Attribute:
            text = String.Format ("{0}={1}", nav.Name, nav.Value);
            tnodes.Add (child = new TreeNode (text, 1, 1));
            break;

        case XPathNodeType.Text:
            text = nav.Value;
            if (text.Length > 128)
                text = text.Substring (0, 128) + "...";
            tnodes.Add (child = new TreeNode (text, 2, 2));
            break;

        case XPathNodeType.Comment:
            text = String.Format ("<!--{0}-->", nav.Value);
            tnodes.Add (child = new TreeNode (text, 4, 4));
            break;

        case XPathNodeType.ProcessingInstruction:
            text = String.Format ("<?{0} {1}?>", nav.Name, nav.Value);
            tnodes.Add (child = new TreeNode (text, 5, 5));
            break;
        }
        return child;
    }

    void AddAttribute (XPathNavigator nav, TreeNode tnode)
    {
        string text = String.Format ("{0}={1}", nav.Name, nav.Value);
        tnode.Nodes.Add (new TreeNode (text, 1, 1));
```

(continued)

Expressalyzer.cs   *(continued)*

```
    }

    static void Main ()
    {
        Application.Run (new AnalyzerForm ());
    }
}
```

XSL Transformations (XSLT)

For programmers laboring in the trenches with XML, XSLT is one of the brightest stars in the XML universe. XSLT stands for Extensible Stylesheet Language Transformations. It is a language for converting XML documents from one format to another. Although it can be applied in a variety of ways, XSLT enjoys two primary uses:

- Converting XML documents into HTML documents
- Converting XML documents into other XML documents

The first application—turning XML into HTML—is useful for building Web pages and other browser-based documents in XML. XML defines the content and structure of data, but it doesn't define the data's appearance. Using XSLT to generate HTML from XML is a fine way to separate content from appearance and to build generic documents that can be displayed however you want them displayed. You can also use cascading style sheets (CSS) to layer appearance over XML content, but XSLT is more versatile than CSS and provides substantially more control over the output.

XSLT is also used to convert XML document formats. Suppose company A expects XML invoices submitted by company B to conform to a particular format (that is, fit a particular schema), but company B already has an XML invoice format and doesn't want to change it to satisfy the whims of company A. Rather than lose company B's business, company A can use XSLT to convert invoices submitted by company B to company A's format. That way both companies are happy, and neither has to go to extraordinary lengths to work with the other. XML-to-XML XSLT conversions are the nucleus of middleware applications such as Microsoft BizTalk Server that automate business processes by orchestrating the flow of information.

Figure 13-13 illustrates the mechanics of XSLT. You feed a source document (the XML document to be transformed) and an XSL style sheet that describes how the document is to be transformed to an XSLT processor. The XSLT processor, in turn, generates the output document using the rules in the style sheet.

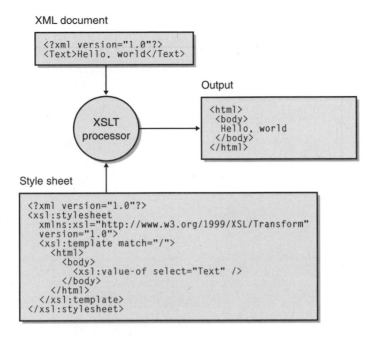

XML document

```
<?xml version="1.0"?>
<Text>Hello, world</Text>
```

Output

```
<html>
  <body>
    Hello, world
  </body>
</html>
```

XSLT processor

Style sheet

```
<?xml version="1.0"?>
<xsl:stylesheet
  xmlns:xsl="http://www.w3.org/1999/XSL/Transform"
  version="1.0">
  <xsl:template match="/">
    <html>
      <body>
        <xsl:value-of select="Text" />
      </body>
    </html>
  </xsl:template>
</xsl:stylesheet>
```

Figure 13-13   XSL Transformations.

MSXML is an XSLT processor. So is the *XslTransform* class located in the FCL's *System.Xml.Xsl* namespace. *XslTransform* is one of the coolest classes in the FCL. It's exceedingly simple to use, and it's an essential tool to have at your disposal when the need arises to programmatically convert XML documents from one format to another. The following sections describe how to put *Xsl-Transform* to work.

Converting XML to HTML on the Client

If you've never worked with XSLT before, a great way to get acquainted with it is to build a simple XML document and transform it to HTML using Internet Explorer (which, under the hood, relies on MSXML to perform XSL transformations). Here's how:

1. Copy Figure 13-16's Guitars.xml and Guitars.xsl to the directory of your choice.

2. Temporarily delete (or comment out) the following statement in Guitars.xml:

```
<?xml-stylesheet type="text/xsl" href="Guitars.xsl"?>
```

3. Open Guitars.xml in Internet Explorer. The file is displayed as XML (Figure 13-14).

4. Restore (or uncomment) the statement you deleted (or commented out) in step 2.

5. Open Guitars.xml again in Internet Explorer. This time, the file is displayed as HTML (Figure 13-15).

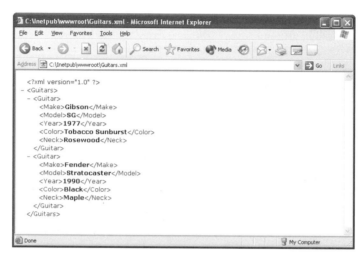

Figure 13-14   Guitars.xml displayed without XSLT.

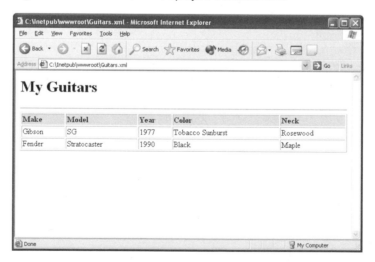

Figure 13-15   Guitars.xml displayed with XSLT.

Guitars.xml

```xml
<?xml version="1.0"?>
<?xml-stylesheet type="text/xsl" href="Guitars.xsl"?>
<Guitars>
  <Guitar>
    <Make>Gibson</Make>
    <Model>SG</Model>
    <Year>1977</Year>
    <Color>Tobacco Sunburst</Color>
    <Neck>Rosewood</Neck>
  </Guitar>
  <Guitar>
    <Make>Fender</Make>
    <Model>Stratocaster</Model>
    <Year>1990</Year>
    <Color>Black</Color>
    <Neck>Maple</Neck>
  </Guitar>
</Guitars>
```

Figure 13-16   XML file and an XSL style sheet for transforming it into HTML.

Guitars.xsl

```xml
<?xml version="1.0"?>
<xsl:stylesheet xmlns:xsl="http://www.w3.org/1999/XSL/Transform"
  version="1.0">
  <xsl:template match="/">
    <html>
      <body>
        <h1>My Guitars</h1>
        <hr />
        <table width="100%" border="1">
          <tr bgcolor="gainsboro">
            <td><b>Make</b></td>
            <td><b>Model</b></td>
            <td><b>Year</b></td>
            <td><b>Color</b></td>
            <td><b>Neck</b></td>
          </tr>
          <xsl:for-each select="Guitars/Guitar">
          <tr>
            <td><xsl:value-of select="Make" /></td>
            <td><xsl:value-of select="Model" /></td>
            <td><xsl:value-of select="Year" /></td>
            <td><xsl:value-of select="Color" /></td>
            <td><xsl:value-of select="Neck" /></td>
          </tr>
```

(continued)

Guitars.xsl   *(continued)*

```
        </xsl:for-each>
      </table>
    </body>
  </html>
  </xsl:template>
</xsl:stylesheet>
```

What happened? The statement

```
<?xml-stylesheet type="text/xsl" href="Guitars.xsl"?>
```

is a processing instruction informing Internet Explorer that Guitars.xsl is a style sheet containing instructions for converting the content found in Guitars.xml to another format. IE downloaded the style sheet and ran it against Guitars.xml, producing HTML.

Most XSL transformations are template-driven. In Guitars.xsl, the statement

```
<xsl:template match="/">
```

marks the beginning of a template that applies to the entire document. "/" is an XPath expression that signifies the root of the document. The first several statements inside the template output the beginnings of an HTML document that includes an HTML table. The *for-each* element iterates over all the *Guitar* elements that are subelements of *Guitars* (note the XPath expression "Guitar/Guitars" defining the selection). Each iteration adds another row to the table, and the *value-of* elements initialize the table's cells with the values of the corresponding XML elements.

Converting XML to HTML on the Server

That's one way to convert XML to HTML. One drawback to this approach is that the XML document must contain a processing directive pointing to the style sheet. Another drawback is that the transformation is performed on the client. It doesn't work in IE 4 and probably won't work in most third-party browsers because XSLT wasn't standardized until recently. Unless you can control the browsers that your clients use, it behooves you to perform the transformation on the server where you can be sure an up-to-date XSLT processor is available.

How do you perform XSL transformations on the server? With *XslTransform*, of course. The Web page in Figure 13-18—Quotes.aspx—demonstrates the mechanics. It contains no HTML; just a server-side script that generates HTML from an XML input document named Quotes.xml and a style sheet named Quotes.xsl. *XslTransform.Transform* performs the transformation. Its first parameter is an *XPathDocument* object wrapping the source document. The third parameter specifies the destination for the output, which in this example is the HTTP response. The second parameter, which is not used here, is an *XsltArgumentList* containing input arguments. Before calling *XslTransform.Transform*, Quotes.aspx calls another *XslTransform* method named *Load* to load the style sheet that governs the conversion. The resulting Web page is shown in Figure 13-17.

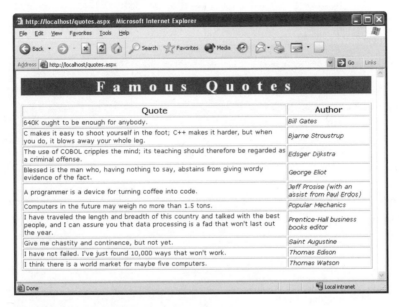

Figure 13-17   Output from Quotes.aspx.

Quotes.aspx

```
<%@ Page Language="C#" %>
<%@ Import Namespace="System.Xml.XPath" %>
<%@ Import Namespace="System.Xml.Xsl" %>

<%
  XPathDocument doc =
      new XPathDocument (Server.MapPath ("Quotes.xml"));
  XslTransform xsl = new XslTransform ();
  xsl.Load (Server.MapPath ("Quotes.xsl"));
  xsl.Transform (doc, null, Response.OutputStream);
%>
```

Figure 13-18   Web page that converts XML to HTML on the server.

Quotes.xml

```xml
<?xml version="1.0"?>
<Quotes>
  <Quote>
    <Text>Give me chastity and continence, but not yet.</Text>
    <Author>Saint Augustine</Author>
  </Quote>
  <Quote>
    <Text>The use of COBOL cripples the mind; its teaching should
      therefore be regarded as a criminal offense.</Text>
    <Author>Edsger Dijkstra</Author>
  </Quote>
  <Quote>
    <Text>C makes it easy to shoot yourself in the foot; C++ makes it
      harder, but when you do, it blows away your whole leg.</Text>
    <Author>Bjarne Stroustrup</Author>
  </Quote>
  <Quote>
    <Text>A programmer is a device for turning coffee into code.</Text>
    <Author>Jeff Prosise (with an assist from Paul Erdos)</Author>
  </Quote>
  <Quote>
    <Text>I have not failed. I&apos;ve just found 10,000 ways that
      won&apos;t work.</Text>
    <Author>Thomas Edison</Author>
  </Quote>
  <Quote>
    <Text>Blessed is the man who, having nothing to say, abstains from
      giving wordy evidence of the fact.</Text>
    <Author>George Eliot</Author>
  </Quote>
  <Quote>
    <Text>I think there is a world market for maybe five
      computers.</Text>
    <Author>Thomas Watson</Author>
  </Quote>
  <Quote>
    <Text>Computers in the future may weigh no more than 1.5
      tons.</Text>
    <Author>Popular Mechanics</Author>
  </Quote>
  <Quote>
    <Text>I have traveled the length and breadth of this country and
      talked with the best people, and I can assure you that data
      processing is a fad that won&apos;t last out the year.</Text>
    <Author>Prentice-Hall business books editor</Author>
  </Quote>
  <Quote>
```

```
      <Text>640K ought to be enough for anybody.</Text>
      <Author>Bill Gates</Author>
    </Quote>
</Quotes>
```

Quotes.xsl

```
<?xml version="1.0"?>
<xsl:stylesheet xmlns:xsl="http://www.w3.org/1999/XSL/Transform"
  version="1.0">
  <xsl:template match="/">
    <html>
      <body>
        <h1 style="background-color: teal; color: white;
          font-size: 24pt; text-align: center; letter-spacing: 1.0em">
          Famous Quotes
        </h1>
        <table border="1">
          <tr style="font-size: 12pt; font-family: verdana;
            font-weight: bold">
            <td style="text-align: center">Quote</td>
            <td style="text-align: center">Author</td>
          </tr>
          <xsl:for-each select="Quotes/Quote">
            <xsl:sort select="Author" />
            <tr style="font-size: 10pt; font-family: verdana">
              <td><xsl:value-of select="Text"/></td>
              <td><i><xsl:value-of select="Author"/></i></td>
            </tr>
          </xsl:for-each>
        </table>
      </body>
    </html>
  </xsl:template>
</xsl:stylesheet>
```

As you might guess, there's much more to XSLT than these examples demonstrate. In addition to supporting *for-each* and *value-of* elements, for example, XSLT supports *if* and *choose* elements for conditional branching, *variable* elements for declaring variables, *sort* elements for sorting (look closely and you'll see *sort* used in Quotes.xsl), and a whole lot more. For a complete list of elements and a summary of XSLT's syntax, refer to the XSLT specification at *http://www.w3.org/TR/xslt*.

Converting XML Document Formats

To put an exclamation point at the end of this chapter, Figure 13-19 contains the source code for a simple application that transforms an XML document using the specified XSL style sheet and writes the results to the host console window. It's a handy tool for debugging style sheets by previewing their output. The following command lists the HTML that's generated when Quotes.xml is transformed with Quotes.xsl:

```
transform quotes.xml quotes.xsl
```

As you can see, the *XslTransform* class makes such a utility exceedingly easy to write—just one more piece of evidence of how valuable and capable a tool the .NET Framework class library is for reading, writing, and manipulating XML documents.

```
Transform.cs
using System;
using System.Xml.XPath;
using System.Xml.Xsl;

class MyApp
{
    static void Main (string[] args)
    {
        if (args.Length < 2) {
            Console.WriteLine ("Syntax: TRANSFORM xmldoc xsldoc");
            return;
        }

        try {
            XPathDocument doc = new XPathDocument (args[0]);
            XslTransform xsl = new XslTransform ();
            xsl.Load (args[1]);
            xsl.Transform (doc, null, Console.Out);
        }
        catch (Exception ex) {
            Console.WriteLine (ex.Message);
        }
    }
}
```

Figure 13-19   Utility for previewing XSL transformations.

Summary

Classes in the .NET Framework class library's *System.Xml* namespace and its children vastly simplify the reading, writing, and manipulating of XML documents. Key members of those namespaces include *XmlDocument*, which provides a DOM interface to XML documents; *XmlTextReader* and *XmlValidatingReader*, which combine SAX's efficiency with an easy-to-use pull model for reading XML and optionally validating it too; *XmlTextWriter*, which writes XML documents; *XPathDocument*, *XPathNavigator*, and *XPathNodeIterator*, which enable you to perform XPath queries on XML documents and iterate over the results; and *XslTransform*, which performs XSL transformations on XML data. Working with XML is an inescapable fact of life in software development today. The FCL's XML classes make life with XML a great deal easier.

14

Multithreading

In the managed world of the common language runtime, the fundamental unit of execution is the thread. A managed application begins its life as a single thread but can spawn additional threads to help it carry out its appointed mission. Threads running concurrently share the CPU (or CPUs) by using scheduling algorithms provided by the system. To an observer, it appears as if all the threads are running at once. In reality, they simply share processor time—and do so very efficiently.

Why would an application spawn additional threads? Multithreading is a mechanism for performing two or more tasks concurrently. Tasks executed by threads running side by side on a single-CPU system don't execute any faster; CPU time is, after all, a finite resource. They do, however, execute asynchronously with respect to one another, allowing independent units of work to be performed in parallel. Multithreading is also a vehicle for taking advantage of multiple CPUs. A single-threaded application uses just one processor at a time. A multithreaded application can have different threads running on different processors—provided, of course, that the operating system supports it. Versions of Windows built on the NT kernel support multiple processors using a strategy called *symmetric multiprocessing* (SMP). Versions that derive from Windows 95 do not.

The canonical example for demonstrating the benefits of multithreading is a single-threaded GUI application that enters a lengthy computational loop. While the application's one and only thread is busy crunching numbers, it ignores the message queue that serves as the conduit for user input. Until the computation ends, the application's user interface is frozen. A multithreaded design can solve this problem by relegating the computational work to a background thread. With the primary thread free to service the message queue, the application remains responsive to user input even while the computation is going on. This chapter's first two sample programs model this very scenario.

Multithreading isn't for the faint of heart. Multithreaded applications are difficult to write and debug because the parallelism of concurrently running threads adds an extra layer of complexity to a program's code. If one thread can write to a data structure at the same time that another thread can read from it, for example, the threads probably need to be synchronized to prevent reads and writes from overlapping. What happens if they're not synchronized? Data could be corrupted or spurious exceptions could be thrown. The most difficult aspect of threading is that bugs in multithreaded code tend to be highly dependent on timing and therefore difficult to reproduce. Experienced developers know that you can never be entirely sure that a multithreaded program is bug-free. The inherent parallelism of multithreaded code, multiplied by the uncertainty of how much or how little processor time individual threads are allotted, yields a figure that is too high for the human mind to comprehend.

Aspersions aside, if you set out to create a multithreaded program, you'd better know what you're getting into. This chapter describes the .NET Framework's threading API. It begins with an overview of how to start, stop, and manipulate threads. It continues with a treatment of thread synchronization— why it's important and what devices the framework places at your disposal for coordinating the actions of concurrently running threads. All things considered, I think you'll agree that threading is one of the most interesting—and potentially useful—features of the CLR and the .NET Framework class library.

Threads

The .NET Framework's threading API is embodied in members of the *System.Threading* namespace. Chief among the namespace's members is the *Thread* class, which represents threads of execution. *Thread* implements a variety of properties and methods that enable developers to launch and manipulate concurrently running threads.

The following table lists some of *Thread*'s public properties. I won't detail all of them now because many are formally introduced later in the chapter. Scanning the list, however, provides a feel for the innate properties of a thread as the CLR sees it. *IsBackground*, for example, is a read/write property that determines whether a thread is a foreground or background thread, a concept that's described in the section entitled "Foreground Threads vs. Background Threads." *ThreadState* lets you determine the current state of a thread—is it running, for example, and if so, is it blocked on a synchronization object or is it executing code?—while *Name* allows you to assign human-readable names to the threads that you create.

Selected Public Properties of the *Thread* Class

Property	Description	Get	Set	Static
CurrentPrincipal	The security principal (identity) assigned to the calling thread	✓	✓	✓
CurrentThread	Returns a *Thread* reference representing the calling thread	✓		✓
IsAlive	Indicates whether the thread is alive—that is, has started but has not terminated	✓		
IsBackground	Indicates whether the thread is a foreground thread or a background thread (default = false)	✓	✓	
Name	The thread's human-readable name (default = null)	✓	✓	
Priority	The thread's priority (default = *Thread-Priority.Normal*)	✓	✓	
ThreadState	The thread's current state	✓		

CurrentThread is a static property that returns a *Thread* reference to the calling thread. It enables a thread to acquire information about itself and to change its own properties and call its own methods. If you create a thread and have a reference to it in a *Thread* object named *thread*, you can read the thread's name by invoking *Name* on the *thread* object:

```
string name = thread.Name;
```

If a thread wants to retrieve its own name, it can use *CurrentThread* to acquire the *Thread* reference that it needs:

```
string myname = Thread.CurrentThread.Name;
```

You'll use *CurrentThread* and other *Thread* properties extensively when implementing multithreaded applications.

Starting Threads

Starting a thread is simplicity itself. The following statements launch a new thread:

```
Thread thread = new Thread (new ThreadStart (ThreadFunc));
thread.Start ();
```

The first statement creates a *Thread* object representing the new thread and identifies a *thread method*—the method that the thread executes when it starts. The reference to the thread method is wrapped in a *ThreadStart* delegate—an instance of *System.Threading.ThreadStart*—to enable the new thread to call the thread method in a type-safe manner. The second statement starts the thread running. Once running—that is, once the thread's *Start* method is called—the thread becomes "alive" and remains alive until it terminates. You can determine whether a thread is alive at a given point in time by reading its *IsAlive* property. The following *if* clause suspends the thread represented by *thread* if the thread has started but has not terminated:

```
if (thread.IsAlive) {
    thread.Suspend ();
}
```

Note that calling *Start* on a *Thread* object does not guarantee that the thread will begin executing immediately. Technically, *Start* simply makes the thread eligible to be allotted CPU time. The system decides when the thread begins running and how often it's accorded processor time.

A thread method receives no parameters and returns void. It can be static or nonstatic and can be given any legal method name. Here's a thread method that counts from 1 to 1,000,000 and returns:

```
void ThreadFunc ()
{
    for (int i=1; i<=1000000; i++)
        ;
}
```

When a thread method returns, the corresponding thread ends. In this example, the thread ends following the *for* loop's final iteration. *IsAlive* returns true while the *for* loop is running and false after the *for* loop ends and *ThreadFunc* returns.

Foreground Threads vs. Background Threads

The common language runtime distinguishes between two types of threads: foreground threads and background threads. An application doesn't end until all of its foreground threads have ended. It can, however, end with background threads running. Background threads are automatically terminated when the application that hosts them ends.

Whether a thread is a foreground thread or a background thread is determined by a read/write *Thread* property named *IsBackground*. The *IsBackground* property defaults to false, which means that threads are foreground threads by default. Setting *IsBackground* to true makes a thread a background thread. In the following example, a console application launches 10 threads when it's started. Each thread loops for 5 seconds. Because the application doesn't set the threads' *IsBackground* property to true, it doesn't end until all 10 threads have run their course. This happens despite the fact that the application's primary thread—the one that was started when the application was started—ends immediately after launching the other threads:

```csharp
using System;
using System.Threading;

class MyApp
{
    static void Main ()
    {
        for (int i=0; i<10; i++) {
            Thread thread = new Thread (new ThreadStart (ThreadFunc));
            thread.Start ();
        }
    }

    static void ThreadFunc ()
    {
        DateTime start = DateTime.Now;
        while ((DateTime.Now - start).Seconds < 5)
            ;
    }
}
```

In the next example, however, the application ends almost as soon as it's started because it changes the auxiliary threads from foreground threads to background threads:

```csharp
using System;
using System.Threading;

class MyApp
{
    static void Main ()
    {
        for (int i=0; i<10; i++) {
            Thread thread = new Thread (new ThreadStart (ThreadFunc));
            thread.IsBackground = true;
            thread.Start ();
        }
    }

    static void ThreadFunc ()
    {
        DateTime start = DateTime.Now;
        while ((DateTime.Now - start).Seconds < 5)
            ;
    }
}
```

What determines whether a thread should be a foreground thread or a background thread? That's up to the application. Threads that perform work in the background and have no reason to continue running if the application shuts down should be background threads. If an application launches a thread that performs a lengthy computation, for example, making the thread a background thread enables the application to shut down while a computation is in progress without explicitly stopping the thread. Foreground threads are ideal for threads that make up the very fabric of an application. If you write a managed user interface shell and launch different threads to service the different windows that the shell displays, for example, you could use foreground threads to prevent the shell from shutting down when the thread that created the other threads ends.

Thread Priorities

Once a thread is started, the amount of processor time it's allotted is determined by the thread scheduler. When a managed application runs on a Windows machine, the thread scheduler is provided by Windows itself. On other platforms, the thread scheduler might be part of the operating system, or it might be part of the .NET Framework. Regardless of how the thread scheduler is physically implemented, you can influence how much or how little CPU time a thread receives relative to other threads in the same process by changing the thread's priority.

A thread's priority is controlled by the *Thread.Priority* property. Here are the priority values that the .NET Framework supports:

Priority	Meaning
ThreadPriority.Highest	Highest thread priority
ThreadPriority.AboveNormal	Higher than normal priority
ThreadPriority.Normal	Normal priority (the default)
ThreadPriority.BelowNormal	Lower than normal priority
ThreadPriority.Lowest	Lowest thread priority

A thread's default priority is *ThreadPriority.Normal*. All else being equal, n threads of equal priority receive roughly equal amounts of CPU time. (Note that many factors can make the distribution of CPU time uneven—for example, threads blocking on message queues or synchronization objects and priority boosting by the operating system. Conceptually, however, it's accurate to say that equal threads with equal priorities will receive, on average, about the same amount of CPU time.)

You can change a thread's priority by writing to its *Priority* property. The following statement boosts a thread's priority:

```
thread.Priority = ThreadPriority.AboveNormal;
```

The next statement lowers the thread's priority:

```
thread.Priority = ThreadPriority.BelowNormal;
```

Raising a thread's priority increases the likelihood (but does not guarantee) that the thread will receive a larger share of CPU time. Lowering the priority means the thread will probably receive less CPU time. You should never raise a thread's priority without a compelling reason for doing so. In theory, you could starve some threads of processor time by boosting the priorities of other threads too high. You could even affect threads in other applications if those applications share an application domain with yours. That's because thread priorities are relative to all threads in the host process, not just other threads in your application domain.

You can change a thread's priority at any time during the thread's lifetime—before the thread is started or after it's started—and you can change it as frequently and as many times as you like. Just remember that the effect of changing thread priorities is highly platform-dependent and that it might have no effect at all on non-Windows platforms.

Suspending and Resuming Threads

The *Thread* class features two methods for stopping a running thread and starting it again. *Thread.Suspend* temporarily suspends a running thread. *Thread.Resume* starts it running again. Unlike the Windows kernel, the .NET Framework doesn't maintain suspend counts for individual threads. The practical implication is that if you call *Suspend* on a thread 10 times, one call to *Resume* will get it running again.

Thread also provides a static method named *Sleep* that a thread can call to suspend itself for a specified number of milliseconds. The following example demonstrates how *Sleep* might be used to drive a slide show:

```
while (ContinueDrawing) {
    DrawNextSlide ();    // Draw another slide
    Thread.Sleep (5000); // Pause for 5 seconds and go again
}
```

A thread can call *Sleep* only on itself. Any thread, however, can call *Suspend* on another thread. If a thread calls *Suspend* on itself, another thread must call *Resume* on it to start it running again. (Think about it!)

Terminating Threads

Windows programmers have long lamented the fact that the Windows API provides no guaranteed way for one thread to cleanly terminate another. If thread A wants to terminate thread B, it typically does so by signaling thread B that it's time to end and having thread B respond to the signal by terminating itself. This means that a developer has to include logic in thread B that checks for and responds to the signal, which complicates development and means that the timeliness of thread B's termination depends on how often B checks for A's signal.

Good news: in managed code, a thread can cleanly terminate another—sort of (more on my equivocation in a moment). *Thread.Abort* terminates a running thread. The following statement terminates the thread represented by *thread*:

```
thread.Abort ();
```

How does *Abort* work? Since the CLR supervises the execution of managed threads, it can throw exceptions in them too. *Abort* throws a *ThreadAbortException* in the targeted thread, causing the thread to end. The thread might not end immediately; in fact, it's not guaranteed to end at all. If the thread has called out to unmanaged code, for example, and hasn't yet returned, it doesn't terminate until it begins executing managed code again. If the thread gets stuck in an infinite loop in unmanaged code outside the CLR's purview, it won't terminate at all. Hopefully, however, cases such as this will be the exception rather than the rule. In practice, calling *Abort* on a thread that executes only managed code kills the thread quickly.

The CLR does everything in its power to terminate an aborted thread cleanly. Sometimes, however, its best isn't good enough. Consider the case of a thread that uses a *SqlConnection* object to query a database. How can the thread close the connection if the CLR kills it prematurely? The answer is to close the connection in a *finally* block, as shown here:

```
SqlConnection conn = new SqlConnection
    ("server=localhost;database=pubs;uid=sa;pwd=");
try {
    conn.Open ();
        .
        .
        .
}
finally {
    conn.Close ();
}
```

When the CLR throws a *ThreadAbortException* to terminate the thread, the *finally* block executes before the thread ends. Closing the connection in a *finally* block is a good idea anyway because it ensures that the connection is closed if any kind of exception occurs. It's an especially good idea if the code is executed by a thread that might be terminated by another. Otherwise, the clean kill you intended to perform with *Abort* might not be so clean after all.

A thread can catch *ThreadAbortException*s with *catch* blocks. It cannot, however, "eat" the exception and prevent itself from being terminated. The CLR automatically throws another *ThreadAbortException* when the *catch* handler ends, effectively terminating the thread. A thread can prevent itself from being terminated with *Thread.ResetAbort*. The thread in the following example foils attempts to shut it down by calling *ResetAbort* in the *catch* block that executes when the CLR throws a *ThreadAbortException*:

```
try {

    .

    .

    .

}
catch (ThreadAbortException) {
    Thread.ResetAbort ();
}
```

Assuming the thread has sufficient privilege to overrule another thread's call to *Abort*, execution continues following the *catch* block.

In practice, a thread that terminates another thread often wants to pause until the other thread has terminated. The *Thread.Join* method lets it do just that. The following example requests the termination of another thread and waits until it ends:

```
thread.Abort (); // Ask the other thread to terminate
thread.Join ();  // Pause until it does
```

Because there's no ironclad guarantee that the other thread will terminate (it could, after all, get stuck in the never-never land of unmanaged code or become entangled in an infinite loop in a *finally* block), *Thread* offers an alternative form of *Join* that accepts a time-out value in milliseconds:

```
thread.Join (5000);  // Pause for up to 5 seconds
```

In this example, *Join* returns when *thread* ends or 5 seconds elapse, whichever comes first, and returns a Boolean indicating what happened. A return value equal to true means the thread ended, while false means the time-out interval elapsed first. The time-out interval can also be expressed as a *TimeSpan* value.

If It Sounds Too Good to Be True...

In version 1.0 of the CLR, the *ThreadAbortException* mechanism for terminating threads suffers from a potentially fatal flaw. If thread B is executing code in a *finally* block at the exact moment that thread A calls *Abort* on it, the resulting *ThreadAbortException* causes B to exit its *finally* block early, possibly skipping critical clean-up code. In other words, it's still not possible to guarantee a clean kill on another thread without that thread's cooperation unless the thread is kind enough to avoid using *finally* blocks.

As I write this, Microsoft is investigating ways to fix this problem in a future release of the .NET Framework. Hopefully, everything I said in the previous section will be true in the near future. Meanwhile, if you need to cleanly terminate one thread from another and you can't avoid *finally* blocks, do it the old-fashioned way: use a *ManualResetEvent* or some other type of synchronization object as a signaling mechanism and have the thread that you want to kill terminate itself when the signal is given.

The Sieve and MultiSieve Applications

The sample applications in this section demonstrate basic multithreading programming techniques as well as why multithreading is sometimes useful in the first place. The first application is pictured in Figure 14-1; its source code appears in Figure 14-2. Named Sieve, it's a single-threaded Windows Forms application that uses the famous Sieve of Eratosthenes algorithm to compute the number of prime numbers between 2 and a user-specified ceiling. Clicking the Start button starts the computation rolling. The results appear in the box in the center of the form. Depending on the value that you enter in the text box in the upper right, the computation can take a long time or a short time to complete.

Because the same thread that drives the application's user interface also performs the computation, Sieve is dead to user input while it counts prime numbers. Try it. Enter a fairly large value (say, 100,000,000) into the input box and click Start. Now try to move the window. It doesn't budge. Under the hood, your attempts to move the window place messages in the thread's message queue. The messages are ignored, however, while the computation proceeds because the thread responsible for retrieving them and dispatching them to the window is busy crunching numbers. Sieve doesn't even bother to enable the Cancel button because clicking it would do nothing. Button clicks produce messages. Those messages go unanswered if the message queue isn't being serviced.

Figure 14-1   The Sieve application.

Sieve.cs

```csharp
using System;
using System.Drawing;
using System.Windows.Forms;
using System.Collections;
using System.Threading;

class SieveForm : Form
{
    Label Label1;
    TextBox Input;
    TextBox Output;
    Button MyStartButton;
    Button MyCancelButton;

    SieveForm ()
    {
        // Initialize the form's properties
        Text = "Sieve";
        ClientSize = new System.Drawing.Size (292, 158);
        FormBorderStyle = FormBorderStyle.FixedDialog;
        MaximizeBox = false;

        // Instantiate the form's controls
        Label1 = new Label ();
        Input = new TextBox ();
        Output = new TextBox ();
        MyStartButton = new Button ();
        MyCancelButton = new Button ();

        // Initialize the controls
        Label1.Location = new Point (24, 28);
        Label1.Size = new Size (144, 16);
        Label1.Text = "Number of primes from 2 to";
```

Figure 14-2   Single-threaded Sieve application.

Sieve.cs   *(continued)*

```csharp
        Input.Location = new Point (168, 24);
        Input.Size = new Size (96, 20);
        Input.Name = "Input";
        Input.TabIndex = 0;

        Output.Location = new Point (24, 64);
        Output.Size = new Size (240, 20);
        Output.Name = "Output";
        Output.ReadOnly = true;
        Output.TabStop = false;

        MyStartButton.Location = new Point (24, 104);
        MyStartButton.Size = new Size (104, 32);
        MyStartButton.Text = "Start";
        MyStartButton.TabIndex = 1;
        MyStartButton.Click += new EventHandler (OnStart);

        MyCancelButton.Location = new Point (160, 104);
        MyCancelButton.Size = new Size (104, 32);
        MyCancelButton.Text = "Cancel";
        MyCancelButton.TabIndex = 2;
        MyCancelButton.Enabled = false;

        // Add the controls to the form
        Controls.Add (Label1);
        Controls.Add (Input);
        Controls.Add (Output);
        Controls.Add (MyStartButton);
        Controls.Add (MyCancelButton);
    }

    void OnStart (object sender, EventArgs e)
    {
        // Get the number that the user typed
        int MaxVal = 0;
        try {
            MaxVal = Convert.ToInt32 (Input.Text);
        }
        catch (FormatException) {
            MessageBox.Show ("Please enter a number greater than 2");
            return;
        }

        if (MaxVal < 3) {
            MessageBox.Show ("Please enter a number greater than 2");
            return;
        }
```

```
        // Prepare the UI
        MyStartButton.Enabled = false;
        Output.Text = "";
        Refresh ();

        // Perform the computation
        int count = CountPrimes (MaxVal);

        // Update the UI
        Output.Text = count.ToString ();
        MyStartButton.Enabled = true;
    }

    int CountPrimes (int max)
    {
        BitArray bits = new BitArray (max + 1, true);

        int limit = 2;
        while (limit * limit < max)
            limit++;

        for (int i=2; i<=limit; i++) {
            if (bits[i]) {
                for (int k=i + i; k<=max; k+=i)
                    bits[k] = false;
            }
        }

        int count = 0;
        for (int i=2; i<=max; i++) {
            if (bits[i])
                count++;
        }

        return count;
    }

    static void Main ()
    {
        Application.Run (new SieveForm ());
    }
}
```

The MultiSieve application listed in Figure 14-3 solves the user interface problem by spawning a separate thread to count primes. On the outside, the two applications are identical save for the names in their title bars. On the inside, they're very different. MultiSieve's Start button creates a thread, converts it into a background thread, and starts it running:

```
SieveThread = new Thread (new ThreadStart (ThreadFunc));
SieveThread.IsBackground = true;
SieveThread.Start ();
```

The new thread performs the prime number computation and displays the results in the window:

```
int count = CountPrimes (MaxVal);
Output.Text = count.ToString ();
```

See for yourself that this makes the program more responsive by dragging the window around the screen while the background thread counts primes. Dragging works because the application's primary thread is no longer tied up crunching numbers.

Clicking the Start button also causes the Cancel button to become enabled. If the user clicks Cancel while the computation is ongoing, *OnCancel* cancels the computation by aborting the background thread. Here's the relevant code:

```
SieveThread.Abort ();
```

OnCancel also calls *Thread.Join* to wait for the thread to terminate, even though no harm would occur if a new computation was started before the previous computation ends.

MultiSieve sets the computational thread's *IsBackground* property to true for a reason: to allow the user to close the application even if the computational thread is busy. If that thread were a foreground thread, additional logic would be required to shut down immediately if the close box in the window's upper right corner was clicked while the thread was running. As it is, no such logic is required because the background thread terminates automatically.

Calling a method from an auxiliary thread is one way to prevent an application's primary thread from blocking while waiting for a method call to return. But there's another way, too. You can use *asynchronous delegates* to call methods asynchronously—that is, without blocking the calling threads. An asynchronous call returns immediately; later, you make another call to "complete" the call and retrieve the results. Asynchronous delegates obviate the need to spin up background threads for the sole purpose of making method calls and are exceedingly easy to use. They work perfectly well with local objects, but the canonical use for them is to call remote objects—objects that live outside the caller's application domain (often on entirely different machines). Asynchronous delegates are introduced in Chapter 15.

MultiSieve.cs

```csharp
using System;
using System.Drawing;
using System.Windows.Forms;
using System.Collections;
using System.Threading;

class SieveForm : Form
{
    Label Label1;
    TextBox Input;
    TextBox Output;
    Button MyStartButton;
    Button MyCancelButton;
    Thread SieveThread;
    int MaxVal;

    SieveForm ()
    {
        // Initialize the form's properties
        Text = "MultiSieve";
        ClientSize = new System.Drawing.Size (292, 158);
        FormBorderStyle = FormBorderStyle.FixedDialog;
        MaximizeBox = false;

        // Instantiate the form's controls
        Label1 = new Label ();
        Input = new TextBox ();
        Output = new TextBox ();
        MyStartButton = new Button ();
        MyCancelButton = new Button ();

        // Initialize the controls
        Label1.Location = new Point (24, 28);
        Label1.Size = new Size (144, 16);
        Label1.Text = "Number of primes from 2 to";

        Input.Location = new Point (168, 24);
        Input.Size = new Size (96, 20);
        Input.Name = "Input";
        Input.TabIndex = 0;

        Output.Location = new Point (24, 64);
        Output.Size = new Size (240, 20);
```

Figure 14-3   Multithreaded Sieve application.

MultiSieve.cs   *(continued)*

```csharp
            Output.Name = "Output";
            Output.ReadOnly = true;
            Output.TabStop = false;

            MyStartButton.Location = new Point (24, 104);
            MyStartButton.Size = new Size (104, 32);
            MyStartButton.Text = "Start";
            MyStartButton.TabIndex = 1;
            MyStartButton.Click += new EventHandler (OnStart);

            MyCancelButton.Location = new Point (160, 104);
            MyCancelButton.Size = new Size (104, 32);
            MyCancelButton.Text = "Cancel";
            MyCancelButton.TabIndex = 2;
            MyCancelButton.Enabled = false;
            MyCancelButton.Click += new EventHandler (OnCancel);

            // Add the controls to the form
            Controls.Add (Label1);
            Controls.Add (Input);
            Controls.Add (Output);
            Controls.Add (MyStartButton);
            Controls.Add (MyCancelButton);
        }

        void OnStart (object sender, EventArgs e)
        {
            // Get the number that the user typed
            try {
                MaxVal = Convert.ToInt32 (Input.Text);
            }
            catch (FormatException) {
                MessageBox.Show ("Please enter a number greater than 2");
                return;
            }

            if (MaxVal < 3) {
                MessageBox.Show ("Please enter a number greater than 2");
                return;
            }

            // Prepare the UI
            MyStartButton.Enabled = false;
            MyCancelButton.Enabled = true;
            Output.Text = "";

            // Start a background thread to count prime numbers
            SieveThread = new Thread (new ThreadStart (ThreadFunc));
```

```csharp
        SieveThread.IsBackground = true;
        SieveThread.Start ();
}

void OnCancel (object sender, EventArgs e)
{
    if (SieveThread != null && SieveThread.IsAlive) {
        // Terminate the background thread
        SieveThread.Abort ();

        // Wait until the thread terminates
        SieveThread.Join ();

        // Restore the UI
        MyStartButton.Enabled = true;
        MyCancelButton.Enabled = false;
        SieveThread = null;
    }
}

int CountPrimes (int max)
{
    BitArray bits = new BitArray (max + 1, true);

    int limit = 2;
    while (limit * limit < max)
        limit++;

    for (int i=2; i<=limit; i++) {
        if (bits[i]) {
            for (int k=i + i; k<=max; k+=i)
                bits[k] = false;
        }
    }

    int count = 0;
    for (int i=2; i<=max; i++) {
        if (bits[i])
            count++;
    }

    return count;
}

void ThreadFunc ()
{
    // Do the computation
    int count = CountPrimes (MaxVal);
```

(continued)

MultiSieve.cs   *(continued)*

```
        // Update the UI
        Output.Text = count.ToString ();
        MyStartButton.Enabled = true;
        MyCancelButton.Enabled = false;
    }

    static void Main ()
    {
        Application.Run (new SieveForm ());
    }
}
```

Timer Threads

The *System.Threading* namespace's *Timer* class enables you to utilize *timer threads*—threads that call a specified method at specified intervals. To demonstrate, the console application in the following code listing uses a timer thread to alternately write "Tick" and "Tock" to the console window at 1-second intervals:

```
using System;
using System.Threading;

class MyApp
{
    static bool TickNext = true;

    static void Main ()
    {
        Console.WriteLine ("Press Enter to terminate...");
        TimerCallback callback = new TimerCallback (TickTock);
        Timer timer = new Timer (callback, null, 1000, 1000);
        Console.ReadLine ();
    }

    static void TickTock (object state)
    {
        Console.WriteLine (TickNext ? "Tick" : "Tock");
        TickNext = ! TickNext;
    }
}
```

In this example, the first callback comes after 1000 milliseconds have passed (the third parameter passed to *Timer*'s constructor); subsequent callbacks come at 1000-millisecond intervals (the fourth parameter). Callbacks come on threads created and owned by the system, so they execute asynchronously with respect to other threads in the application (including the primary thread). You can reprogram the callback intervals while a timer thread is running with a call to *Timer.Change*. You can also use the constructor's second parameter to pass data to the callback method. A reference provided there becomes the callback method's one and only parameter: *state*.

Don't expect the callback method to be called at *exactly* the intervals you specify. Windows is not a real-time operating system, nor is the CLR a real-time execution engine. Timer callbacks occur at *about* the intervals you specify, but because of the vagaries of thread scheduling, you can't count on millisecond accuracy. Nonetheless, timer threads are extraordinarily useful for performing tasks at (approximately) regular intervals and doing so asynchronously with respect to other threads. A classic use for timer threads in a GUI application is driving a simulated clock. Rather than advance the second hand one stop in each callback, the correct approach is to check the wall-clock time in each callback and update the on-screen clock accordingly. That way the precise timing of the callbacks is unimportant.

Thread Synchronization

Launching threads is easy; making them work cooperatively is not. The hard part of designing a multithreaded program is figuring out where concurrently running threads might clash and using thread synchronization logic to prevent clashes from occurring. You provide the logic; the .NET Framework provides the synchronization primitives.

Here's a list of the thread synchronization classes featured in the FCL. All are members of the *System.Threading* namespace:

Class	Description
AutoResetEvent	Blocks a thread until another thread sets the event
Interlocked	Enables simple operations such as incrementing and decrementing integers to be performed in a thread-safe manner
ManualResetEvent	Blocks one or more threads until another thread sets the event
Monitor	Prevents more than one thread at a time from accessing a resource
Mutex	Prevents more than one thread at a time from accessing a resource and has the ability to span application and process boundaries
ReaderWriterLock	Enables multiple threads to read a resource simultaneously but prevents overlapping reads and writes as well as overlapping writes

Each of these synchronization classes will be described in due time. But first, here's an example demonstrating why thread synchronization is so important.

Suppose you write an application that launches a background thread for the purpose of gathering data from a data source—perhaps an online connection to another server or a physical device on the host system. As data arrives, the background thread writes it to a linked list. Furthermore, suppose that other threads in the application read the linked list and process the data contained therein. Figure 14-4 illustrates what might happen if the threads that read and write the linked list aren't synchronized. Most of the time, you get lucky: reads and writes don't overlap and the code works fine. But if by chance a read and write occur at the same time, it's entirely possible that the reader thread will catch the linked list in an inconsistent state as it's being updated by the writer thread. The results are unpredictable. The reader thread might read invalid data, it might throw an exception, or it might suffer no ill effects whatsoever. The point is *you don't know*, and software should never be left to chance.

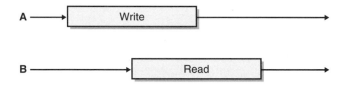

Figure 14-4 An overlapping read and write.

Figure 14-5 illustrates how a *Monitor* object can solve the problem by synchronizing access to the linked list. Each thread checks with a *Monitor* before accessing the linked list. The *Monitor* serializes access to the linked list, turning what would have been an overlapping read and write into a synchronized read and write. The linked list is now protected, and neither thread has to worry about interfering with the other.

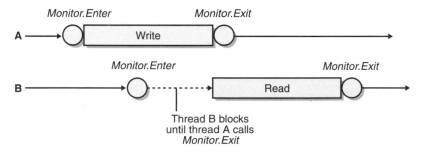

Figure 14-5 A synchronized read and write.

The Interlocked Class

The simplest way to synchronize threads is to use the *System.Threading.Interlocked* class. *Interlocked* has four static methods that you can use to perform simple operations on 32-bit and 64-bit values and do so in a thread-safe manner:

Method	Purpose
Increment	Increments a 32-bit or 64-bit value
Decrement	Decrements a 32-bit or 64-bit value
Exchange	Exchanges two 32-bit or 64-bit values
CompareExchange	Compares two 32-bit or 64-bit values and replaces one with a third if the two are equal

The following example increments a 32-bit integer named *count* in a thread-safe manner:

```
Interlocked.Increment (ref count);
```

The next example decrements the same integer:

```
Interlocked.Decrement (ref count);
```

Routing all accesses to a given variable through the *Interlocked* class ensures that two threads can't touch the variable at the same time, even if the threads are running on different CPUs.

Monitors

Monitors in the .NET Framework are similar to critical sections in Windows. They synchronize concurrent thread accesses so that an object, a linked list, or some other resource can be manipulated only by one thread at a time. In other words, they support mutually exclusive access to a guarded resource. Monitors are represented by the FCL's *Monitor* class.

Monitor's two most important methods are *Enter* and *Exit*. The former claims a lock on the resource that the monitor guards and is called prior to accessing the resource. If the lock is currently owned by another thread, the thread that calls *Enter* blocks—that is, is taken off the processor and placed in a very efficient wait state—until the lock comes free. *Exit* frees the lock after the access is complete so that other threads can access the resource.

As an aid in understanding how monitors are used and why they exist, consider the code in Figure 14-6. Called BadNews, it's a multithreaded console application. At startup, it initializes a buffer of bytes with the values 1 through 100. Then it launches a "writer" thread that for 10 seconds randomly swaps values in the buffer, and 10 "reader" threads that sum up all the values in the buffer. Because the sum of all the numbers from 1 to 100 is 5050, the reader threads should always come up with that sum. That's the theory, anyway. The problem is that the reader and writer threads aren't synchronized. Given enough iterations, it's highly likely that a reader thread will catch the buffer in an inconsistent state and arrive at the wrong sum. In this sample program, a reader thread writes an error message to the console window if it computes a sum other than 5050—proof positive that a synchronization error has occurred.

```
BadNews.cs
using System;
using System.Threading;

class MyApp
{
    static Random rng = new Random ();
    static byte[] buffer = new byte[100];
    static Thread writer;

    static void Main ()
    {
        // Initialize the buffer
        for (int i=0; i<100; i++)
            buffer[i] = (byte) (i + 1);

        // Start one writer thread
        writer = new Thread (new ThreadStart (WriterFunc));
        writer.Start ();

        // Start 10 reader threads
        Thread[] readers = new Thread[10];

        for (int i=0; i<10; i++) {
            readers[i] = new Thread (new ThreadStart (ReaderFunc));
            readers[i].Name = (i + 1).ToString ();
            readers[i].Start ();
        }
    }

    static void ReaderFunc ()
    {
        // Loop until the writer thread ends
        for (int i=0; writer.IsAlive; i++) {
            int sum = 0;
```

Figure 14-6   An application that demonstrates the ill effects of unsynchronized reads and writes.

```
        // Sum the values in the buffer
        for (int k=0; k<100; k++)
            sum += buffer[k];

        // Report an error if the sum is incorrect
        if (sum != 5050) {
            string message = String.Format ("Thread {0} " +
                "reports a corrupted read on iteration {1}",
                Thread.CurrentThread.Name, i + 1);
            Console.WriteLine (message);
            writer.Abort ();
            return;
        }
    }
}

static void WriterFunc ()
{
    DateTime start = DateTime.Now;

    // Loop for up to 10 seconds
    while ((DateTime.Now - start).Seconds < 10) {
        int j = rng.Next (0, 100);
        int k = rng.Next (0, 100);
        Swap (ref buffer[j], ref buffer[k]);
    }
}

static void Swap (ref byte a, ref byte b)
{
    byte tmp = a;
    a = b;
    b = tmp;
}
}
```

Give BadNews a try by running it a few times. The following command compiles the source code file into an EXE:

```
csc badnews.cs
```

And this command runs the resulting EXE:

```
badnews
```

In all likelihood, one or more reader threads will report an error, as shown in Figure 14-7. Once a reader thread encounters an error, it aborts the writer thread, causing all the other reader threads to shut down, too. Run the program

10 times and you'll get 10 different sets of results, graphically illustrating the unpredictability and hard-to-reproduce nature of thread synchronization errors.

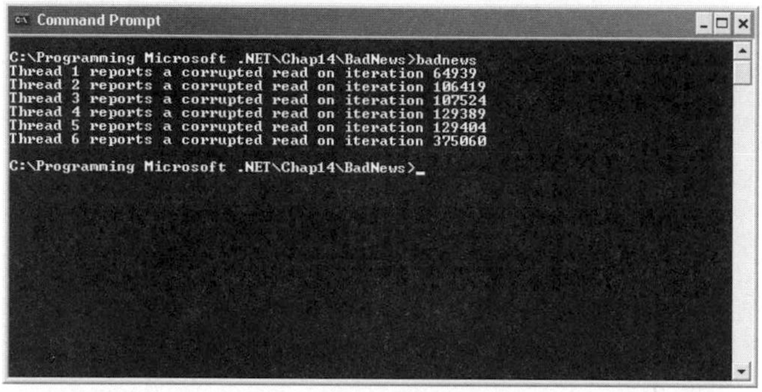

Figure 14-7   Synchronization errors reported by BadNews.exe.

Figure 14-8 contains a corrected version of BadNews.cs. Monitor.cs uses monitors to prevent reader and writer threads from accessing the buffer at the same time. It runs for the full 10 seconds without reporting any errors. Changes are highlighted in boldface type. Before accessing the buffer, Monitor.cs threads acquire a lock by calling *Monitor.Enter*:

```
Monitor.Enter (buffer);
```

After reading from or writing to the buffer, each thread releases the lock it acquired by calling *Monitor.Exit*:

```
Monitor.Exit (buffer);
```

Calls to *Exit* are enclosed in *finally* blocks to ensure that they're executed even in the face of inopportune exceptions. Always use *finally* blocks to exit monitors or else you run the risk of orphaning a lock and causing other threads to hang indefinitely.

Monitor.cs
```
using System;
using System.Threading;

class MyApp
{
    static Random rng = new Random ();
    static byte[] buffer = new byte[100];
    static Thread writer;
```

Figure 14-8   Using monitors to synchronize threads.

```csharp
static void Main ()
{
    // Initialize the buffer
    for (int i=0; i<100; i++)
        buffer[i] = (byte) (i + 1);

    // Start one writer thread
    writer = new Thread (new ThreadStart (WriterFunc));
    writer.Start ();

    // Start 10 reader threads
    Thread[] readers = new Thread[10];

    for (int i=0; i<10; i++) {
        readers[i] = new Thread (new ThreadStart (ReaderFunc));
        readers[i].Name = (i + 1).ToString ();
        readers[i].Start ();
    }
}

static void ReaderFunc ()
{
    // Loop until the writer thread ends
    for (int i=0; writer.IsAlive; i++) {
        int sum = 0;

        // Sum the values in the buffer
        Monitor.Enter (buffer);

        try {
            for (int k=0; k<100; k++)
                sum += buffer[k];
        }
        finally {
            Monitor.Exit (buffer);
        }

        // Report an error if the sum is incorrect
        if (sum != 5050) {
            string message = String.Format ("Thread {0} " +
                "reports a corrupted read on iteration {1}",
                Thread.CurrentThread.Name, i + 1);
            Console.WriteLine (message);
            writer.Abort ();
            return;
        }
    }
}
```

(continued)

Monitor.cs *(continued)*

```
    static void WriterFunc ()
    {
        DateTime start = DateTime.Now;

        // Loop for up to 10 seconds
        while ((DateTime.Now - start).Seconds < 10) {
            int j = rng.Next (0, 100);
            int k = rng.Next (0, 100);

            Monitor.Enter (buffer);

            try {
                Swap (ref buffer[j], ref buffer[k]);
            }
            finally {
                Monitor.Exit (buffer);
            }
        }
    }

    static void Swap (ref byte a, ref byte b)
    {
        byte tmp = a;
        a = b;
        b = tmp;
    }
}
```

The C# *lock* Keyword

The previous section shows one way to use monitors, but there's another way, too: C#'s *lock* keyword (in Visual Basic .NET, *SyncLock*). In C#, the statements

```
lock (buffer) {
  ...
}
```

are functionally equivalent to

```
Monitor.Enter (buffer);
try {
  ...
}
finally {
    Monitor.Exit (buffer);
}
```

The CIL generated by these two sets of statements are nearly identical. Figure 14-9 shows the code in Figure 14-8 rewritten to use *lock*. The *lock* keyword makes the code more concise and also ensures the presence of a *finally* block to make sure the lock is released. You don't see the *finally* block, but it's there. Check the CIL if you want to see for yourself.

Lock.cs
```
using System;
using System.Threading;

class MyApp
{
    static Random rng = new Random ();
    static byte[] buffer = new byte[100];
    static Thread writer;

    static void Main ()
    {
        // Initialize the buffer
        for (int i=0; i<100; i++)
            buffer[i] = (byte) (i + 1);

        // Start one writer thread
        writer = new Thread (new ThreadStart (WriterFunc));
        writer.Start ();

        // Start 10 reader threads
        Thread[] readers = new Thread[10];

        for (int i=0; i<10; i++) {
            readers[i] = new Thread (new ThreadStart (ReaderFunc));
            readers[i].Name = (i + 1).ToString ();
            readers[i].Start ();
        }
    }

    static void ReaderFunc ()
    {
        // Loop until the writer thread ends
        for (int i=0; writer.IsAlive; i++) {
            int sum = 0;

            // Sum the values in the buffer
            lock (buffer) {
                for (int k=0; k<100; k++)
```

Figure 14-9   Using C#'s *lock* keyword to synchronize threads.

Lock.cs   *(continued)*

```
                    sum += buffer[k];
            }

            // Report an error if the sum is incorrect
            if (sum != 5050) {
                string message = String.Format ("Thread {0} " +
                    "reports a corrupted read on iteration {1}",
                        Thread.CurrentThread.Name, i + 1);
                Console.WriteLine (message);
                writer.Abort ();
                return;
            }
        }
    }

    static void WriterFunc ()
    {
        DateTime start = DateTime.Now;

        // Loop for up to 10 seconds
        while ((DateTime.Now - start).Seconds < 10) {
            int j = rng.Next (0, 100);
            int k = rng.Next (0, 100);

            lock (buffer) {
                Swap (ref buffer[j], ref buffer[k]);
            }
        }
    }

    static void Swap (ref byte a, ref byte b)
    {
        byte tmp = a;
        a = b;
        b = tmp;
    }
}
```

Conditionally Acquiring a Lock

Preventing *Monitor.Enter* from blocking if the lock is owned by another thread is impossible. That's why *Monitor* includes a separate method named *TryEnter*. *TryEnter* returns, regardless of whether the lock is available. A return value equal to true means the caller acquired the lock and can safely access the resource guarded by the monitor. False means the lock is currently owned by another thread:

```
if (Monitor.TryEnter (buffer)) {
    // TODO: Acquired the lock; access the buffer
}
else {
    // TODO: Couldn't acquire the lock; try again later
}
```

The fact that *TryEnter*, unlike *Enter*, returns if the lock isn't free affords the caller the opportunity to attend to other matters rather than sit idle, waiting for a lock to come free.

   TryEnter comes in a version that accepts a time-out value and waits for up to the specified number of milliseconds to acquire the lock:

```
if (Monitor.TryEnter (buffer, 2000)) {
    // TODO: Acquired the lock; access the buffer
}
else {
    // TODO: Waited 2 seconds but couldn't acquire the lock;
    // try again later
}
```

TryEnter also accepts a *TimeSpan* value in lieu of a number of milliseconds.

Waiting and Pulsing

Monitor includes static methods named *Wait*, *Pulse*, and *PulseAll* that are functionally equivalent to Java's *Object.wait*, *Object.notify*, and *Object.notifyAll* methods. *Wait* temporarily relinquishes the lock held by the calling thread and blocks until the lock is reacquired. The *Pulse* and *PulseAll* methods notify threads blocking in *Wait* that a thread has updated the object guarded by the lock. *Pulse* queues up the next waiting thread and allows it to run when the thread that's currently executing releases the lock. *PulseAll* gives all waiting threads the opportunity to run.

   To picture how waiting and pulsing work, consider the following thread methods. The first one places items in a queue at half-second intervals and is executed by thread A:

```
static void WriterFunc ()
{
    string[] strings = new string[] { "One", "Two", "Three" };
    lock (queue) {
        foreach (string item in strings) {
            queue.Enqueue (item);
            Monitor.Pulse (queue);
            Monitor.Wait (queue);
            Thread.Sleep (500);
        }
    }
}
```

The second method reads items from the queue as they come available and is executed by thread B:

```
static void ReaderFunc ()
{
    lock (queue) {
        while (true) {
            if (queue.Count > 0) {
                while (queue.Count > 0) {
                    string item = (string) queue.Dequeue ();
                    Console.WriteLine (item);
                }
                Monitor.Pulse (queue);
            }
            Monitor.Wait (queue);
        }
    }
}
```

On the surface, it appears as if only one of these methods could execute at a time. After all, both attempt to acquire a lock on the same object. Nevertheless, the methods execute concurrently. Here's how.

Imagine that *ReaderFunc* (thread B) acquires the lock first. It finds that the queue contains no items and calls *Monitor.Wait*. *WriterFunc*, which executes on thread A, is currently blocking in the call to *Monitor.Enter* generated from the *lock* statement. It comes unblocked, adds an item to the queue, and calls *Monitor.Pulse*. That readies thread B for execution. Thread A then calls *Wait* itself, allowing thread B to awake from its call to *Monitor.Wait* and retrieve the item that thread A placed in the queue. Afterward, thread B calls *Monitor.Pulse* and *Monitor.Wait* and the whole process starts over again.

Personally, I don't find this architecture very exciting. There are other ways to synchronize threads on queues (*AutoResetEvents*, for example) that are easier to write and maintain and that don't rely on nested locks. *Wait*, *Pulse*, and *PulseAll* might be very useful, however, for porting Java code to the .NET Framework.

Monitor Internals

Curious to know how *Monitor* objects work? Here's a short synopsis—and one big reason why you should care.

Monitor's Enter and *Exit* methods accept a reference to an *Object* or an *Object*-derivative—in other words, the address of a reference type allocated on the garbage-collected (GC) heap. Every object on the GC heap has two overhead members associated with it:

■ A method table pointer containing the address of the object's method table

■ A SyncBlock index referencing a SyncBlock created by the .NET Framework.

The method table pointer serves the same purpose as a virtual function table, or "vtable," in C++. A SyncBlock is the moral equivalent of a Windows mutex or critical section and is the physical data structure that makes up the lock manipulated by *Monitor.Enter* and *Monitor.Exit*. SyncBlocks aren't created unless needed to avoid undue overhead on the system.

When you call *Monitor.Enter*, the framework checks the SyncBlock of the object identified in the method call. If the SyncBlock indicates that another thread owns the lock, the framework blocks the calling thread until the lock becomes available. *Monitor.Exit* frees the lock by updating the object's SyncBlock. The relationship between objects allocated on the GC heap and SyncBlocks is diagrammed in Figure 14-10.

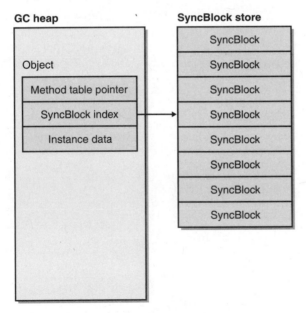

Figure 14-10   SyncBlocks and SyncBlock indexes.

Why is understanding how monitors work important? Because that knowledge can prevent you from committing a grievous error that is all too easy to make. Before I say more, can you spot the bug in the following code?

```
int a = 1;
   .
   .
   .
Monitor.Enter (a);
try {
    a *= 3;
}
finally {
    Monitor.Exit (a);
}
```

Check the CIL that the C# compiler generates from this code and you'll find that it contains two BOX instructions. *Monitor.Enter* and *Monitor.Exit* operate on reference types. Since variable *a* is a value type, it can't be passed directly to *Enter* and *Exit*; it must be boxed first. The C# compiler obligingly emits two BOX instructions—one to box the value type passed to *Enter*, and another to box the value type passed to *Exit*. The two boxing operations create two different objects on the heap, each containing the same value but each with its own SyncBlock index pointing to a different SyncBlock (Figure 14-11). See the problem? The code compiles just fine, but it throws an exception at run time because it calls *Exit* on a lock that hasn't been acquired. Be thankful for the exception, because otherwise the code might seem to work when in fact it provides no synchronization at all.

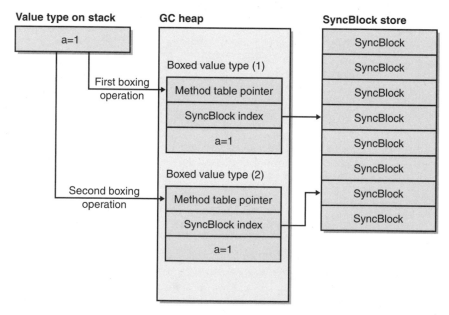

Figure 14-11   The effect of boxing a value type twice.

Is there a solution? You bet. Manually box the value type and pass the resultant object reference to both *Enter* and *Exit*:

```
int a;
object o = a;
    .

    .

    .
Monitor.Enter (o);
try {
    a *= 3;
}
finally {
    Monitor.Exit (o);
}
```

If you do this in multiple threads (and you will; otherwise you wouldn't be using a monitor in the first place), be sure to box the value type *one time* and use the resulting reference in calls to *Enter* and *Exit* in all threads. If the value type you're synchronizing access to is a field, declare a corresponding *Object* field and store the boxed reference there. Then use that field to acquire the reference passed to *Enter* and *Exit*. (Technically, the object reference you pass to *Enter* and *Exit* doesn't have to be a boxed version of the value type you're guarding. All that matters is that you pass the same reference to both methods.)

The fact that the C# compiler automatically boxes value types passed to *Monitor.Enter* and *Monitor.Exit* is another reason that using C#'s *lock* keyword is superior to calling *Monitor.Enter* and *Monitor.Exit* directly. The following code won't compile because the C# compiler knows that *a* is a value type and that boxing the value type won't yield the desired result:

```
lock (a) {
    a *= 3;
}
```

However, if *o* is an *Object* representing a boxed version of *a*, the code compiles just fine:

```
lock (o) {
    a *= 3;
}
```

An ounce of prevention is worth a pound of cure. Be aware that value types require special handling when used with monitors and you'll avoid one of the .NET Framework's nastiest traps.

Reader/Writer Locks

Reader/writer locks are similar to monitors in that they prevent concurrent threads from accessing a resource simultaneously. The difference is that reader/writer locks are a little smarter: they permit multiple threads to read concurrently, but they prevent overlapping reads and writes as well as overlapping writes. For situations in which reader threads outnumber writer threads, reader/writer locks frequently offer better performance than monitors. No harm can come, after all, from allowing several threads to read the same location in memory at the same time.

Windows lacks a reader/writer lock implementation, but the .NET Framework class library provides one in the class named *ReaderWriterLock*. To use it, set up one reader/writer lock for each resource that you want to guard. Have reader threads call *AcquireReaderLock* before accessing the resource and *ReleaseReaderLock* after the access is complete. Have writer threads call *AcquireWriterLock* before accessing the resource and *ReleaseWriterLock* afterward. *AcquireReaderLock* blocks if the lock is currently owned by a writer thread but not if it's owned by other reader threads. *AcquireWriterLock* blocks if the lock is owned by anyone. Consequently, multiple threads can read the resource concurrently, but only one thread at a time can write to it and it can't write if another thread is reading.

That's *ReaderWriterLock* in a nutshell. The application in Figure 14-12 demonstrates how these concepts translate to real-world code. It's the same basic application used in the monitor samples, but this time the buffer is protected by a reader/writer lock instead of a monitor. A reader/writer lock makes sense when reader threads outnumber writer threads 10 to 1 as they do in this sample.

Observe that calls to *ReleaseReaderLock* and *ReleaseWriterLock* are enclosed in *finally* blocks to be absolutely certain that they're executed. Also, the *Timeout.Infinite* passed to the *Acquire* methods indicate that the calling thread is willing to wait for the lock indefinitely. If you prefer, you can pass in a time-out value expressed in milliseconds or as a *TimeSpan* value, after which the call will return if the lock hasn't been acquired. Unfortunately, neither *AcquireReaderLock* nor *AcquireWriterLock* returns a value indicating whether the call returned because the lock was acquired or because the time-out period expired. For that, you must read the *ReaderWriterLock*'s *IsReaderLockHeld* or *IsWriterLockHeld* property. The former returns true if the calling thread holds a reader lock and false if it does not. The latter does the same for writer locks.

ReaderWriterLock.cs

```csharp
using System;
using System.Threading;

class MyApp
{
    static Random rng = new Random ();
    static byte[] buffer = new byte[100];
    static Thread writer;
    static ReaderWriterLock rwlock = new ReaderWriterLock ();

    static void Main ()
    {
        // Initialize the buffer
        for (int i=0; i<100; i++)
            buffer[i] = (byte) (i + 1);

        // Start one writer thread
        writer = new Thread (new ThreadStart (WriterFunc));
        writer.Start ();

        // Start 10 reader threads
        Thread[] readers = new Thread[10];

        for (int i=0; i<10; i++) {
            readers[i] = new Thread (new ThreadStart (ReaderFunc));
            readers[i].Name = (i + 1).ToString ();
            readers[i].Start ();
        }
    }

    static void ReaderFunc ()
    {
        // Loop until the writer thread ends
        for (int i=0; writer.IsAlive; i++) {
            int sum = 0;

            // Sum the values in the buffer
            rwlock.AcquireReaderLock (Timeout.Infinite);

            try {
                for (int k=0; k<100; k++)
                    sum += buffer[k];
            }
```

Figure 14-12   Using reader/writer locks to synchronize threads.

ReaderWriterLock.cs   *(continued)*

```
        finally {
            rwlock.ReleaseReaderLock ();
        }

        // Report an error if the sum is incorrect
        if (sum != 5050) {
            string message = String.Format ("Thread {0} " +
                "reports a corrupted read on iteration {1}",
                Thread.CurrentThread.Name, i + 1);
            Console.WriteLine (message);
            writer.Abort ();
            return;
        }
    }
}

static void WriterFunc ()
{
    DateTime start = DateTime.Now;

    // Loop for up to 10 seconds
    while ((DateTime.Now - start).Seconds < 10) {
        int j = rng.Next (0, 100);
        int k = rng.Next (0, 100);

        rwlock.AcquireWriterLock (Timeout.Infinite);

        try {
            Swap (ref buffer[j], ref buffer[k]);
        }
        finally {
            rwlock.ReleaseWriterLock ();
        }
    }
}

static void Swap (ref byte a, ref byte b)
{
    byte tmp = a;
    a = b;
    b = tmp;
}
}
```

A potential gotcha to watch out for regarding *ReaderWriterLock* has to do with threads that need writer locks while they hold reader locks. In the following example, a thread first acquires a reader lock and then later decides to grab a writer lock, too:

```
rwlock.AcquireReaderLock (Timeout.Infinite);
try {
    // TODO: Read from the resource guarded by the lock

       .

       .

       .

    // Oops! Need to do some writing, too
    rwlock.AcquireWriterLock (Timeout.Infinite);
    try {
        // TODO: Write to the resource guarded by the lock

          .

          .

          .

    }
    finally {
        rwlock.ReleaseWriterLock ();
    }
}
finally {
    rwlock.ReleaseReaderLock ();
}
```

The result? Deadlock. *ReaderWriterLock* supports nested calls, which means it's perfectly safe for the same thread to request a read lock or write lock as many times as it wants. That's essential for threads that call methods recursively. But if a thread holding a read lock requests a write lock, it locks alright—it locks forever. In this example, the call to *AcquireWriterLock* disappears into the framework and never returns.

The solution is a pair of *ReaderWriterLock* methods named *UpgradeToWriterLock* and *DowngradeFromWriterLock*, which allow a thread that holds a reader lock to temporarily convert it to a writer lock. Here's the proper way to nest reader and writer locks:

```
rwlock.AcquireReaderLock (Timeout.Infinite);
try {
    // TODO: Read from the resource guarded by the lock

       .

       .

       .

    LockCookie cookie = rwlock.UpgradeToWriterLock (Timeout.Infinite);
    try {
        // TODO: Write to the resource guarded by the lock

          .

          .

          .

    }
    finally {
        rwlock.DowngradeFromWriterLock (ref cookie);
```

```
    }
  }
finally {
    rwlock.ReleaseReaderLock ();
}
```

Now the code will work as intended, and it won't bother end users with pesky infinite loops.

There is some debate in the developer community about how efficient *ReaderWriterLock* is and whether it's vulnerable to locking out some threads entirely in extreme situations. Traditional reader/writer locks give writers precedence over readers and never deny a writer thread access, even if reader threads have been blocking longer. *ReaderWriterLock*, however, attempts to divide time more equitably between reader and writer threads. If one writer thread and several reader threads are waiting for the lock to come free, *ReaderWriterLock* may let one or more readers run before the writer. The jury is still out on whether this design is good or bad. Microsoft is actively investigating the implications and might change *ReaderWriterLock*'s behavior in future versions of the .NET Framework. Stay tuned for late-breaking news.

Mutexes

The word "mutex" is a contraction of the words "mutually exclusive." A mutex is a synchronization object that guards a resource and prevents it from being accessed by more than one thread at a time. It's similar to a monitor in that regard. Two fundamental differences, however, distinguish monitors and mutexes:

■ Mutexes have the power to synchronize threads belonging to different applications and processes; monitors do not.

■ If a thread acquires a mutex and terminates without freeing it, the system deems the mutex to be abandoned and automatically frees it. Monitors are not afforded the same protection.

The FCL's *System.Threading.Mutex* class represents mutexes. The following statement creates a *Mutex* instance:

```
Mutex mutex = new Mutex ();
```

These statements acquire the mutex prior to accessing the resource that it guards and release it once the access is complete:

```
mutex.WaitOne ();
try {

    .

    .

    .

}
finally {
    mutex.ReleaseMutex ();
}
```

As usual, the *finally* block ensures that the mutex is released even if an exception occurs while the mutex is held.

You could easily demonstrate mutexes at work by rewiring Monitor.cs or ReaderWriterLock.cs to use a mutex instead of a monitor or reader/writer lock. But to do so would be to misrepresent the purpose of mutexes. When used to synchronize threads in the same application, mutexes are orders of magnitude slower than monitors. The real power of mutexes lies in reaching across application boundaries. Suppose two different applications communicate with each other using shared memory. They can use a mutex to synchronize accesses to the memory that they share, even though the threads performing the accesses belong to different applications and probably to different processes as well. The secret is to have each application create a named mutex and for each to use the same name:

```
// Application A
Mutex mutex = new Mutex ("StevieRayVaughanRocks");

// Application B
Mutex mutex = new Mutex ("StevieRayVaughanRocks");
```

Even though two different *Mutex* objects are created in two different memory spaces, both refer to a common mutex object inside the operating system kernel. Therefore, if a thread in application A calls *WaitOne* on its mutex and the mutex kernel object is owned by a thread in application B, A's thread will block until the mutex comes free. You can't do that with a monitor, nor can you do it with a *ReaderWriterLock*.

Since *Mutex* wraps an unmanaged resource—a mutex kernel object—it also provides a *Close* method for closing the underlying handle representing the object. If you create and destroy *Mutex* objects on the fly, be sure to call *Close* on them the moment you're done with them to prevent objects from piling up unabated in the operating system kernel.

Events

When I speak about events at conferences and in classes, I like to describe them as "software triggers" or "thread triggers." Whereas monitors, mutexes, and reader/writer locks are used to guard access to resources, events are used to coordinate the actions of multiple threads in a more general way, ensuring that each thread does its thing in the proper sequence with regard to the other threads. As a simple example, suppose that thread A fills a buffer with data that it gathers and thread B is charged with the task of reading data from the buffer and doing something with it. Thread A doesn't want thread B to begin reading until the buffer is prepared, so it sets an event object when the buffer is ready. Thread B, meanwhile, blocks on the event waiting for it to become set. Until A sets the event, B blocks in an efficient wait state. The moment A sets the event, B comes out of its blocked state and begins reading from the buffer.

Windows supports two different types of events: auto-reset events and manual-reset events. The .NET Framework class library wraps these operating system kernel objects with classes named *AutoResetEvent* and *ManualResetEvent*. Both classes feature methods named *Set*, *Reset*, and *WaitOne* for setting an event, resetting an event, and blocking until an event becomes set, respectively. If called on an event that is currently reset, *WaitOne* blocks until another thread sets the event. If called on an event that is already set, *WaitOne* returns immediately. An event that is set is sometimes said to be *signaled*. The reset state is also called the *nonsignaled* state.

The difference between *AutoResetEvent* and *ManualResetEvent* is what happens following a call to *WaitOne*. The system automatically resets an *AutoResetEvent*, hence the name. The system doesn't automatically reset a *ManualResetEvent*; a thread must reset it manually by calling the event's *Reset* method. This seemingly minor behavioral difference has far-reaching implications for your code. *AutoResetEvent*s are generally used when just one thread calls *WaitOne*. Since an *AutoResetEvent* is reset before the call to *WaitOne* returns, it's only capable of signaling one thread at a time. One call to *Set* on a *ManualResetEvent*, by contrast, is sufficient to signal any number of threads that call *WaitOne*. For this reason, *ManualResetEvent* is typically used to trigger multiple threads.

To serve as an example of events at work, the console application in Figure 14-13 uses two threads to write alternating even and odd numbers to the console, beginning with 1 and ending with 100. One thread writes even numbers; the other writes odd numbers. Left unsynchronized, the threads would blow their output to the console window as quickly as possible and produce a random mix of even and odd numbers (or, more than likely, a long series of evens followed by a long series of odds, or vice versa, because one thread might run out its lifetime before the other gets a chance to execute). With a little help from a pair of *AutoResetEvents*, however, the threads can be coerced into working together.

Events.cs
```
using System;
using System.Threading;

class MyApp
{
    static AutoResetEvent are1 = new AutoResetEvent (false);
    static AutoResetEvent are2 = new AutoResetEvent (false);

    static void Main ()
    {
        try {
            // Create two threads
            Thread thread1 =
                new Thread (new ThreadStart (ThreadFuncOdd));
            Thread thread2 =
                new Thread (new ThreadStart (ThreadFuncEven));

            // Start the threads
            thread1.Start ();
            thread2.Start ();

            // Wait for the threads to end
            thread1.Join ();
            thread2.Join ();
        }
        finally {
            // Close the events
            are1.Close ();
            are2.Close ();
        }
    }

    static void ThreadFuncOdd ()
    {
        for (int i=1; i<=99; i+=2) {
            Console.WriteLine (i);   // Output the next odd number
            are1.Set ();             // Release the other thread
            are2.WaitOne ();         // Wait for the other thread
        }
    }
}
```

Figure 14-13 Using auto-reset events to synchronize threads.

Events.cs   *(continued)*

```
static void ThreadFuncEven ()
{
    for (int i=2; i<=100; i+=2) {
        are1.WaitOne ();        // Wait for the other thread
        Console.WriteLine (i);  // Output the next even number
        are2.Set ();            // Release the other thread
    }
}
}
```

Here's how the sample works. At startup, it launches two threads: one that outputs odd numbers and one that outputs even numbers. The "odd" thread writes a 1 to the console window. It then sets an *AutoResetEvent* object named *are1* and blocks on an *AutoResetEvent* object named *are2*:

```
Console.WriteLine (i);
are1.Set ();
are2.WaitOne ();
```

The "even" thread, meanwhile, blocks on *are1* right out of the gate. When *WaitOne* returns because the odd thread set *are1*, the even thread outputs a 2, sets *are2*, and loops back to call *WaitOne* again on *are1*:

```
are1.WaitOne ();
Console.WriteLine (i);
are2.Set ();
```

When the even thread sets *are2*, the odd thread comes out of its call to *WaitOne*, and the whole process repeats. The result is a perfect stream of numbers in the console window.

Though this sample borders on the trivial, it's entirely representative of how events are typically used in real applications. They're often used in pairs, and they're often used to sequence the actions of two or more threads.

Note the *finally* block in *Main* that calls *Close* on the *AutoResetEvent* objects. Events, like mutexes, wrap Windows kernel objects and should therefore be closed when they're no longer needed. Technically, the calls to *Close* are superfluous here because the events are automatically closed when the application ends, but I included them anyway to emphasize the importance of closing event objects.

Waiting on Multiple Synchronization Objects

Occasionally a thread needs to block on multiple synchronization objects. It might, for example, need to block on two or more *AutoResetEvent*s and come alive when any of the events becomes set to perform some action on behalf of the thread that did the setting. Or it could block on several *AutoResetEvent*s and want to remain blocked until *all* of the events become set. Both goals can be accomplished using *WaitHandle* methods named *WaitAny* and *WaitAll*.

WaitHandle is a *System.Threading* class that serves as a managed wrapper around Windows synchronization objects. *Mutex*, *AutoResetEvent*, and *Manual-ResetEvent* all derive from it. When you call *WaitOne* on an event or a mutex, you're calling a method inherited from *WaitHandle*. *WaitAny* and *WaitAll* are static methods that enable a thread to block on several (on most platforms, up to 64) mutexes and events at once. They expose the same functionality to managed applications that the Windows API function *WaitForMultipleObjects* exposes to unmanaged applications. In the following example, the calling thread blocks until one of the three *AutoResetEvent* objects in the *syncobjects* array becomes set:

```
AutoResetEvent are1 = new AutoResetEvent (false);
AutoResetEvent are2 = new AutoResetEvent (false);
AutoResetEvent are3 = new AutoResetEvent (false);
    .
    .
    .
WaitHandle[] syncobjects = new WaitHandle[3] { are1, are2, are3 };
WaitHandle.WaitAny (syncobjects);
```

Changing *WaitAny* to *WaitAll* blocks the calling thread until all of the *AutoResetEvent*s are set:

```
WaitHandle.WaitAll (syncobjects);
```

WaitAny and *WaitAll* also come in versions that accept time-out values. Time-outs can be expressed as integers (milliseconds) or *TimeSpan* values.

Should you ever need to interrupt a thread while it waits for one or more synchronization objects to become signaled, use the *Thread* class's *Interrupt* method. *Interrupt* throws a *ThreadInterruptedException* in the thread it's called on. It works only on threads that are waiting, sleeping, or suspended; call it on an unblocked thread and it interrupts the thread the next time the thread blocks. A common use for *Interrupt* is getting the attention of a thread that's blocking inside a call to *WaitAll* after the application has determined that one of the synchronization objects will never become signaled.

Serializing Access to Collections

The vast majority of the classes in the .NET Framework class library are not thread-safe. If you want to share an *ArrayList* between a reader thread and a writer thread, for example, it's important to synchronize access to the *ArrayList* so that one thread can't read from it while another thread writes to it.

One way to synchronize access to an *ArrayList* is to use a monitor, as demonstrated here:

```
// Create the ArrayList
ArrayList list = new ArrayList ();
    .
    .
    .
// Thread A
lock (list) {
    // Add an item to the ArrayList
    list.Add ("Fender Stratocaster");
}
    .
    .
    .
// Thread B
lock (list) {
    // Read the ArrayList's last item
    string item = (string) list[list.Count - 1];
}
```

However, there's an easier way. *ArrayList, Hashtable, Queue, Stack,* and selected other FCL classes implement a method named *Synchronized* that returns a thread-safe wrapper around the object passed to it. Here's the proper way to serialize reads and writes to an *ArrayList*:

```
// Create the ArrayList and a thread-safe wrapper for it
ArrayList list = new ArrayList ();
ArrayList safelist = ArrayList.Synchronized (list);
    .
    .
    .
// Thread A
safelist.Add ("Fender Stratocaster");
    .
    .
    .
// Thread B
string item = (string) safelist[safelist.Count - 1];
```

Using thread-safe wrappers created with the *Synchronized* method shifts the burden of synchronization from your code to the framework. It can also improve performance because a well-designed wrapper class can use its knowledge of the underlying class to lock only when necessary and for no longer than required.

Different collection classes implement different threading behaviors. For example, a *Hashtable* can safely be used by one writer thread and unlimited reader threads right out of the box. Synchronization is only required when there are two or more writer threads. A *Queue*, on the other hand, doesn't even support simultaneous reads because the very act of reading from a *Queue* modifies its contents and internal data structures. Therefore, you should use a synchronized wrapper whenever multiple threads access a *Queue*, regardless of whether the threads are readers or writers.

Thread-safe wrappers returned by *Synchronized* guarantee the atomicity of individual method calls but offer no such assurances for groups of method calls. In other words, if you create a thread-safe wrapper around an *ArrayList*, multiple threads can safely access the *ArrayList* through the wrapper. If, however, a reader thread iterates over an *ArrayList* while a writer thread writes to it, the *ArrayList*'s contents could change even as they're being enumerated.

Treating multiple reads and writes as atomic operations requires external synchronization. Here's the proper way to externally synchronize *ArrayLists* and other types that implement *ICollection*:

```
// Create the ArrayList
ArrayList list = new ArrayList ();
    .
    .
    .
// Thread A
lock (list.SyncRoot) {
    // Add two items to the ArrayList
    list.Add ("Fender Stratocaster");
    list.Add ("Gibson SG");
}
    .
    .
    .
// Thread B
lock (list.SyncRoot) {
    // Enumerate the ArrayList's items
    foreach (string item in list) {
      ...
    }
}
```

The argument passed to *lock* isn't the *ArrayList* itself but rather an *ArrayList* property named *SyncRoot*. *SyncRoot* is a member of the *ICollection* interface. If called on a raw collection class instance, *SyncRoot* returns *this*. If called on a thread-safe wrapper class created with *Synchronized*, *SyncRoot* returns a reference to the object that the wrapper wraps. That's important, because adding synchronization to an already synchronized object impedes performance. Synchronizing on *SyncRoot* makes your code generic and allows it to perform equally well with synchronized and unsynchronized objects.

Thread Synchronization via the *MethodImpl* Attribute

The .NET Framework offers a simple and easy-to-use means for synchronizing access to entire methods through the *MethodImplAttribute* class, which belongs to the *System.Runtime.CompilerServices* namespace. To prevent a method from being executed by more than one thread at a time, decorate it as shown here:

```
[MethodImpl (MethodImplOptions.Synchronized)]
byte[] TransformData (byte[] buffer)
{
  ...
}
```

Now the framework will serialize calls to *TransformData*. A method synchronized in this manner closely approximates the classic definition of a critical section—a section of code that can't be executed simultaneously by concurrent threads.

Thread Pooling

I'll close this chapter by briefly mentioning a handy *System.Threading* class named *ThreadPool* that provides a managed thread pooling API. The basic idea behind thread pooling is that instead of launching threads yourself, you pass requests to a thread pool manager. The thread pool manager maintains a pool of threads that's sized as needed to satisfy incoming requests. The following example demonstrates a very simple use of the *ThreadPool* class:

```
using System;
using System.Threading;

class MyApp
{
    static int count = 0;

    static void Main ()
    {
        WaitCallback callback = new WaitCallback (ProcessRequest);

        ThreadPool.QueueUserWorkItem (callback);
        ThreadPool.QueueUserWorkItem (callback);
        ThreadPool.QueueUserWorkItem (callback);
        ThreadPool.QueueUserWorkItem (callback);
        ThreadPool.QueueUserWorkItem (callback);
```

```
ThreadPool.QueueUserWorkItem (callback);
ThreadPool.QueueUserWorkItem (callback);
ThreadPool.QueueUserWorkItem (callback);
ThreadPool.QueueUserWorkItem (callback);
ThreadPool.QueueUserWorkItem (callback);

    Thread.Sleep (5000); // Give the requests a chance to execute
}

static void ProcessRequest (object state)
{
    int n = Interlocked.Increment (ref count);
    Console.WriteLine (n);
}
}
```

This application counts from 1 to 10 in a console window and uses background threads to do the writing. Rather than launch 10 threads itself, the application submits 10 requests to *ThreadPool* by calling *ThreadPool.QueueUserWorkItem*. Then *ThreadPool* determines how many threads are needed to handle the requests.

You can use an alternate form of *QueueUserWorkItem*—one that accepts an *Object* in its second parameter—to pass additional information in each request. The following example passes an array of five integers:

```
int[] vals = new int[5] { 1, 2, 3, 4, 5 };
ThreadPool.QueueUserWorkItem (callback, vals);
```

QueueUserWorkItem's second parameter is the first (and only) parameter to the callback method:

```
static void ProcessRequest (object state)
{
    int[] vals = (int[]) state;
    ...
}
```

A simple cast converts the *Object* reference to a strong type and gives the callback method access to the data provided by the requestor.

You must never terminate a pooled thread. The thread pool manager creates pooled threads, and it terminates them, too. You can use *Thread*'s *IsThreadPoolThread* property to determine whether a thread is a pooled thread. In the following example, the current thread terminates itself if and only if it's a nonpooled thread:

```
if (!Thread.CurrentThread.IsThreadPoolThread)
    Thread.CurrentThread.Abort ();
```

For server applications anticipating a high volume of requests that require concurrent processing, thread pooling simplifies thread management and increases performance. The performance increase comes because the thread pool manager maintains a pool of threads that it can use to service requests. It's far faster to transfer a call to an existing thread than it is to launch a whole new thread from scratch. Plus, divvying up requests among threads enables the system to take advantage of multiple CPUs if they're present. You do the easy part by handing requests off to *ThreadPool*. *ThreadPool* does the rest.

15

Remoting

ASP.NET is a giant step forward in the evolution of programming models because it vastly simplifies the development of Web applications. For companies seeking to build traditional thin-client applications—applications that rely on browsers to display HTML generated on servers—ASP.NET is the right tool for the job. Its benefits include shorter development cycles and software that is more scalable, more maintainable, and more robust.

Despite the importance of thin-client applications in today's market, there still exist applications that benefit from, and sometimes require, a tighter coupling of client and server. In recent years, literally thousands of companies have deployed distributed applications built on DCOM (Distributed Component Object Model), CORBA (Common Object Request Broker Architecture), Java RMI (Remote Method Invocation), and other remoting technologies. These types of applications won't go away anytime soon, nor will the advantages that they enjoy over thin-client applications. Closely coupled applications are better suited for two-way communication between clients and servers than are conventional Web applications. They also tend to utilize network bandwidth more efficiently because they can use lean binary protocols in lieu of HTTP. And close coupling facilitates stateful connections between clients and servers, which in turn simplifies the task of building stateful applications.

Many people feel that the sweet spot for intranet applications built with the .NET Framework in coming years won't be traditional thin-client applications but "rich-client" applications—applications that feature Windows forms on the client (better to overcome the limitations of HTML), managed components on the server, and pluggable protocol channels in between. One reason for this belief is that the .NET Framework includes a robust and easy-to-use remoting infrastructure that supports DCOM-style applications. This infrastructure is physically manifested as a set of types in the *System.Runtime.Remoting* namespace and its descendants. Get to know these types and you can be building closely coupled rich-client applications in no time. And you can do so without all the hassles that come with COM programming—apartments, IDL (Interface Definition Language), reference counting, lack of exception handling, incompatible languages and data types, and so on.

For an author who has spent the past several years of his life working with COM and helping companies overcome the problems and limitations thereof, it's fitting that the final chapter of this book be devoted to .NET remoting. In this writer's opinion, .NET remoting is a better COM than COM. Let's see if that assertion holds up.

Remoting Basics

Remoting begins with the class or classes you want to remote. A conventional class can be used only by clients running in the same application domain. A remotable class can be used by clients in other application domains, which can mean other application domains in the client's process, application domains in other processes, or application domains on other machines. How hard is it to write a remotable class? Not hard at all. All you have to do is derive from *System.MarshalByRefObject*.

The following class can be instantiated only in a client's own application domain:

```
public class LocalClass
{
  ...
}
```

The following class can be instantiated in a client's application domain or in a remote application domain:

```
public class RemotableClass : MarshalByRefObject
{
  ...
}
```

When a client creates a remote instance of *RemotableClass*, the .NET Framework creates a *proxy* in the client's application domain, as shown in Figure 15-1. The proxy looks and feels like the real object. Calls received by the proxy, however, are transmitted to the remote object through a channel connecting the two application domains. We say that an object served by a proxy has been *marshaled by reference* because the object isn't copied to the client's application domain; the client merely holds a reference to the object. That reference is the proxy.

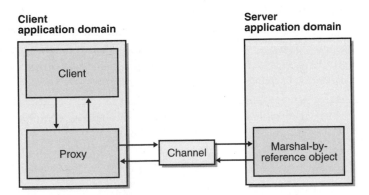

Figure 15-1   Marshal-by-reference remoting architecture.

The second step in remoting an object is to have a server process register the remotable class so that it can be activated from another application domain. Depending on how the object is to be activated, the server registers the remotable class by calling one of two static *System.Runtime.Remoting.RemotingConfiguration* methods: *RegisterActivatedServiceType* or *RegisterWellKnownServiceType*. The following statement uses *RegisterWellKnownServiceType* to register *RemotableClass* for remote activation:

```
RemotingConfiguration.RegisterWellKnownServiceType (
    typeof (RemotableClass),        // Remotable class
    "RemoteObject",                 // URI of remotable class
    WellKnownObjectMode.SingleCall // Activation mode
);
```

The first parameter identifies the remotable class. The second specifies the uniform resource identifier (URI) that the client will use to activate the object—that is, the URI that the client will use to tell the server to activate an instance of *RemotableClass*. The third and final parameter specifies the activation mode. The two possible choices are *WellKnownObjectMode.SingleCall*, which creates a new instance of *RemotableClass* for each and every call placed by a client, and *WellKnownObjectMode.Singleton*, which creates one instance of *RemotableClass* to process all calls from all clients.

To make *RemotableClass* available to remote clients, the server process must also create and register a *channel*. The channel provides a conduit for communication between an object and a remote client. The .NET Framework class library includes two channels for use on the server side: *System.Runtime.Remoting.Channels.Tcp.TcpServerChannel*, which accepts TCP connections from remote clients, and *System.Runtime.Remoting.Channels.Http.HttpServerChannel*, which accepts HTTP connections. The following statements create a *TcpServerChannel* that listens on port 1234 and register it with the .NET Framework:

```
TcpServerChannel channel = new TcpServerChannel (1234);
ChannelServices.RegisterChannel (channel);
```

These statements register an *HttpServerChannel* that listens on port 1234:

```
HttpServerChannel channel = new HttpServerChannel (1234);
ChannelServices.RegisterChannel (channel);
```

TcpServerChannel is the more efficient of the two because TCP is a leaner protocol than HTTP. *HttpServerChannel*, however, is the channel of choice for applications that use Internet Information Services (IIS) as a remote activation agent—a topic that's discussed later in this chapter.

A client application that wants to create a remote instance of *Remotable-Class* has to do some registration of its own. First it must register a client channel. The .NET Framework provides two client channel types: *TcpClientChannel* and *HttpClientChannel*. The former lets a client talk to a server that's listening with a *TcpServerChannel*; the latter enables it to communicate with a server listening with an *HttpServerChannel*. Second, if the client wants to use the *new* operator to instantiate the remote object, it must register the remote class in the local application domain. *RemotingConfiguration.RegisterWellKnownClient-Type* registers a class on the client that's registered with *RemotingConfiguration.RegisterWellKnownServiceType* on the server. The following statements create and register a client-side TCP channel. They also register *RemotableClass* as a valid type in the client's application domain:

```
TcpClientChannel channel = new TcpClientChannel ();
ChannelServices.RegisterChannel (channel);

RemotingConfiguration.RegisterWellKnownClientType (
    typeof (RemotableClass),              // Remotable class
    "tcp://localhost:1234/RemoteObject" // URL of remotable class
);
```

The second parameter passed to *RegisterWellKnownClientType* specifies the URL where the remote class is located. The protocol (*tcp* in this example) must match the protocol of the channels registered in the application domains. The machine identifier—*localhost*—identifies the server that exports *RemotableClass* and thus identifies the machine on which the object will be created. You can replace *localhost* with a machine name or an IP address. The port number following the machine identifier must match the port number that the server is listening on—that is, the port number that the server registered with *TcpServerChannel*. Finally, after the machine identifier and port number comes the object URI, which must match the URI that the server passed to *Register-WellKnownServiceType*.

Once both the client and server have performed the requisite registrations, all that remains is for the client to instantiate *RemotableClass* with the *new* operator:

```
RemotableClass rc = new RemotableClass ();
```

This action creates a proxy in the client's application domain and returns a *RemotableClass* reference that physically refers to the proxy but logically refers to the remote object. Let's prove that this works by testing it out in a real application.

Your First Remoting Application

The application in Figure 15-2 demonstrates the basic steps involved in activating an object in a remote application domain. It is centered on a remotable class named *Clock*. *Clock* has one public method—*GetCurrentTime*—that retrieves the current wall-clock time and returns it as a string. The application contains three constituent parts:

■   A DLL named ClockServer.dll that houses the *Clock* class

■   A server named TimeServer.exe that registers *Clock* for remote activation

■   A client named TimeClient.exe that activates *Clock* remotely

TimeServer and TimeClient are console applications. When executed, TimeClient displays the current time. It gets the time by instantiating a *Clock* object and calling *Clock.GetCurrentTime*.

ClockServer.cs
```
using System;

public class Clock : MarshalByRefObject
{
    public string GetCurrentTime ()
    {
        return DateTime.Now.ToLongTimeString ();
    }
}
```

Figure 15-2   A simple remoting application.

TimeServer.cs

```csharp
using System;
using System.Runtime.Remoting;
using System.Runtime.Remoting.Channels;
using System.Runtime.Remoting.Channels.Tcp;

class MyApp
{
    static void Main ()
    {
        TcpServerChannel channel = new TcpServerChannel (1234);
        ChannelServices.RegisterChannel (channel);

        RemotingConfiguration.RegisterWellKnownServiceType
            (typeof (Clock), "Clock", WellKnownObjectMode.SingleCall);

        Console.WriteLine ("Press Enter to terminate...");
        Console.ReadLine ();
    }
}
```

TimeClient.cs

```csharp
using System;
using System.Runtime.Remoting;
using System.Runtime.Remoting.Channels;
using System.Runtime.Remoting.Channels.Tcp;

class MyApp
{
    static void Main ()
    {
        TcpClientChannel channel = new TcpClientChannel ();
        ChannelServices.RegisterChannel (channel);

        RemotingConfiguration.RegisterWellKnownClientType
            (typeof (Clock), "tcp://localhost:1234/Clock");

        Clock clock = new Clock ();
        Console.WriteLine (clock.GetCurrentTime ());
    }
}
```

Here's a script for building and testing the application:

1. Use the commands below to build ClockServer.dll, TimeServer.exe, and TimeClient.exe, or simply copy them from the CD that comes with this book:

    ```
    csc /t:library clockserver.cs
    csc /r:clockserver.dll timeserver.cs
    csc /r:clockserver.dll timeclient.cs
    ```

2. Open a console window and start TimeServer. Do not press the Enter key to terminate the application.

3. Open a second console window and run TimeClient. The current time should be displayed in the window.

4. Terminate TimeServer by switching back to the first console window and pressing the Enter key.

TimeClient runs in one process, and TimeServer runs in another. Because *Clock* is instantiated in the application domain in which it is registered, calls from TimeClient cross process boundaries to TimeServer.

When most people hear the term "remoting," they think of calls going from machine to machine. With some minor tweaking, the application in Figure 15-2 can be modified to work across machines. To demonstrate, pick two computers on your network, one to act as the server (machine A), and the other to act as the client (machine B). Then do the following:

1. Copy TimeServer.exe and ClockServer.dll to a directory on machine A.

2. Replace *localhost* in the URL that TimeClient passes to *RemotingConfiguration.RegisterWellKnownClientType* with machine A's name or IP address.

3. Rebuild TimeClient.exe.

4. Copy the modified version of TimeClient.exe to a directory on machine B. Copy ClockServer.dll to the same directory.

5. Open a console window on machine A and start TimeServer.

6. Open a console window on machine B and run TimeClient. To prove that the time displayed on machine B came from machine A, temporarily change the clock on machine A and verify that Time-Client displays the modified time.

7. Terminate TimeServer on machine A.

Were you surprised by step 4—surprised that you had to copy Clock-Server.dll to the client machine? To create a proxy for a remote *Clock* object, the .NET Framework has to have metadata describing the *Clock* class. It gets that metadata from the DLL. If you don't copy the DLL to the client machine, the framework can't activate a remote *Clock* object because it can't create the proxy. You can prove it by temporarily deleting ClockServer.dll from machine B and running TimeClient again. This time, the .NET Framework throws an exception because it has no metadata describing *Clock*.

Programmatic vs. Declarative Configuration

TimeServer and TimeClient use information embedded in their source code to register channels and remotable classes. The drawback to performing registrations this way is that if any of the registration data changes (as it did when you modified TimeClient to point to a remote server), you have to modify the source code and rebuild the executables.

That's why the .NET Framework supports an alternate form of registration that is declarative rather than programmatic. Declarative registration takes information from CONFIG files and is enacted by calling the static *RemotingConfiguration.Configure* method.

Figure 15-3 contains modified versions of TimeServer and TimeClient that demonstrate how declarative configuration works. Functionally, this application is identical to the one in Figure 15-2. Internally, it's different. Rather than call *RegisterChannel*, *RegisterWellKnownServiceType*, and *RegisterWellKnown-ClientType*, the revised source code files call *RemotingConfiguration.Configure* and pass in the names of configuration files. Now modifying the client to activate a *Clock* object on another machine is a simple matter of using Notepad or the text editor of your choice to edit TimeClient.exe.config. No source code changes are required.

```
ClockServer.cs
using System;

public class Clock : MarshalByRefObject
{
    public string GetCurrentTime ()
    {
        return DateTime.Now.ToLongTimeString ();
    }
}
```

Figure 15-3   A remoting application that uses declarative configuration.

TimeServer.cs

```
using System;
using System.Runtime.Remoting;

class MyApp
{
    static void Main ()
    {
        RemotingConfiguration.Configure ("TimeServer.exe.config");
        Console.WriteLine ("Press Enter to terminate...");
        Console.ReadLine ();
    }
}
```

TimeServer.exe.config

```
<configuration>
  <system.runtime.remoting>
    <application>
      <service>
        <wellknown mode="SingleCall" type="Clock, ClockServer"
          objectUri="Clock" />
      </service>
      <channels>
        <channel ref="tcp server" port="1234" />
      </channels>
    </application>
  </system.runtime.remoting>
</configuration>
```

TimeClient.cs

```
using System;
using System.Runtime.Remoting;

class MyApp
{
    static void Main ()
    {
        RemotingConfiguration.Configure ("TimeClient.exe.config");
        Clock clock = new Clock ();
        Console.WriteLine (clock.GetCurrentTime ());
    }
}
```

```
TimeClient.exe.config
<configuration>
  <system.runtime.remoting>
    <application>
      <client>
        <wellknown type="Clock, ClockServer"
          url="tcp://localhost:1234/Clock" />
      </client>
      <channels>
        <channel ref="tcp client" />
      </channels>
    </application>
  </system.runtime.remoting>
</configuration>
```

Declarative registration has its drawbacks, too. Registration information embedded in an EXE isn't easily changed by an end user. Registration information encoded in a text file, however, can be modified by anyone savvy enough to run Notepad. It can also be deleted altogether. Choosing between declarative and programmatic registration means choosing which quality is more important to you: convenience or robustness. The right choice depends on the scenario and is ultimately left up to you.

Server Activation vs. Client Activation

The .NET Framework distinguishes between two types of remotable objects: server-activated objects and client-activated objects. Server-activated objects are registered with *RemotingConfiguration*'s *RegisterWellKnownServiceType* and *RegisterWellKnownClientType* methods. The applications in Figures 15-2 and 15-3 rely on server-activated objects. Client-activated objects are registered with *RegisterActivatedServiceType* and *RegisterActivatedClientType* instead. Server-activated objects are called "server activated" because when the client calls *new*, only a proxy is created. The objects themselves aren't created ("activated") until a method call is placed through the proxy. In other words, the server, not the client, decides when to physically create the objects. Client-activated objects, on the other hand, are created on the server the moment the client calls *new*. The differences between server-activated objects and client-activated objects, however, run deeper than these simple descriptions suggest.

A practical difference between server-activated objects and client-activated objects is that the latter can be activated with nondefault constructors (constructors that accept parameters), but the former can not. Server-activated objects don't support nondefault constructors because calls to *new* don't map 1-to-1 to object instantiations; *new* creates a proxy but doesn't create the corresponding object. Client-activated objects, on the other hand, can be activated with non-default constructors because *new* instantiates both the proxy and the object.

A more fundamental difference between server-activated objects and client-activated objects has to do with how clients and objects are paired together. When you register a server-activated object, you specify an *activation mode* that determines whether a new object instance is created to service every request or one object instance is created to service all requests. The two supported activation modes are

- *WellKnownObjectMode.SingleCall*, which creates a unique object instance for each request

- *WellKnownObjectMode.Singleton*, which creates one object instance and uses it to service all requests

Circumstances usually dictate which activation mode is appropriate. For example, if a remote object provides a "one-shot" service to its clients (such as the current time of day) and has no need to preserve state between method calls or to share state among its clients, then *SingleCall* is the right choice. A single-call object can't easily preserve state between method calls because if one client places 10 method calls through the same proxy, 10 different object instances are created to satisfy those calls. A single-call object can't easily share state among clients either, because if 10 different clients activate an instance of the same class and place one call each through their respective proxies, again the .NET Framework creates 10 different object instances to service the clients' requests.

By contrast, the .NET Framework creates a singleton object one time and uses it to service all requests from all clients. If 10 clients activate a singleton object and place 10 calls each to it through their proxies, just one object instance is created. That instance receives all 100 calls placed by the clients. Because a singleton object hangs around between method calls and is shared by all active clients, it's perfectly capable of retaining state between method calls and even of disbursing state among its clients. One client could pass some data to the object, for example, and the object could store the data in a field. Another client could then call the object and retrieve the data.

One nuance to be aware of regarding singleton objects is that the .NET Framework makes no attempts to synchronize calls placed to them. If two clients call a singleton at exactly the same time, the calls will arrive on two different threads and be processed concurrently. The implication? Unless you know beyond the shadow of a doubt that calls from clients will never overlap (you normally don't), the object had better be thread-safe. For a refresher on thread synchronization mechanisms supported by the .NET Framework, refer to Chapter 14.

Client-activated objects offer a third option that serves as a middle ground between single-call server-activated objects and singleton server-activated objects. Each call to *new* placed by a client creates a new instance of a client-activated object that serves that client and that client only. Client-activated objects can preserve state from one method call to the next because they don't get discarded following each request. They are not, however, suitable for sharing state between clients because every client that creates a client-activated object receives a brand new object instance that is unique to that client.

The combination of single-call server-activated objects, singleton server-activated objects, and client-activated objects gives you three different activation models to choose from. Which model is correct? That depends on the application and what it's designed to do. For applications such as the ones in Figures 15-2 and 15-3, single-call server-activated objects make sense because the application doesn't need to preserve state between method calls or share state among clients. For the distributed drawing application at the end of this chapter, however, singleton server-activated objects fit the bill nicely because the design of the application requires that all clients connect to a common object instance. For an application that doesn't require all clients to connect to the same object but that holds per-client state on the server, a client-activated object should be used instead.

The application shown in Figure 15-4 demonstrates how client activation works and why client-activated objects are sometimes appropriate in the first place. It publishes a remotable client-activated class named *Stopwatch*. *Stopwatch* has two methods: *Start* and *Stop*. Because *Stop* returns the number of milliseconds elapsed since the last call to *Start*, a client can implement a software stopwatch by calling *Start* and *Stop* in succession.

Start records the current time in a private field named *mark*. *Stop* subtracts *mark* from the current time and returns the difference in milliseconds. In this example, a single-call server-activated object wouldn't do because the call to *Start* would be processed by one *Stopwatch* instance and the call to *Stop* would be processed by another. A singleton server-activated object wouldn't fare any better. If two different clients were executed concurrently and one called *Start* right after the other, the value written to *mark* by the first would be overwritten by the second. Consequently, the first client would receive a bogus count from *Stop*. This is a great example of an application that benefits from a client-activated object because it needs to retain state between method calls but also needs to pair each client with a unique object instance.

To run the application, compile the three source code files and run StopwatchServer. (Be sure to compile Stopwatch.cs with a */t:library* switch first and include a */r:stopwatch.dll* switch when compiling StopwatchServer.cs and StopwatchClient.cs.) Then, in a separate console window, run StopwatchClient, wait a couple of seconds, and press Enter to display the elapsed time.

Stopwatch.cs

```csharp
using System;

public class Stopwatch : MarshalByRefObject
{
    DateTime mark = DateTime.Now;

    public void Start ()
    {
        mark = DateTime.Now;
    }

    public int Stop ()
    {
        return (int) ((DateTime.Now - mark).TotalMilliseconds);
    }
}
```

Figure 15-4   An application that uses a client-activated object.

StopwatchServer.cs

```csharp
using System;
using System.Runtime.Remoting;
using System.Runtime.Remoting.Channels;
using System.Runtime.Remoting.Channels.Tcp;

class MyApp
{
    static void Main ()
    {
        TcpServerChannel channel = new TcpServerChannel (1234);
        ChannelServices.RegisterChannel (channel);

        RemotingConfiguration.RegisterActivatedServiceType
            (typeof (Stopwatch));

        Console.WriteLine ("Press Enter to terminate...");
        Console.ReadLine ();
    }
}
```

```
StopwatchClient.cs
using System;
using System.Runtime.Remoting;
using System.Runtime.Remoting.Channels;
using System.Runtime.Remoting.Channels.Tcp;

class MyApp
{
    static void Main ()
    {
        TcpClientChannel channel = new TcpClientChannel ();
        ChannelServices.RegisterChannel (channel);

        RemotingConfiguration.RegisterActivatedClientType
            (typeof (Stopwatch), "tcp://localhost:1234");

        Stopwatch sw = new Stopwatch ();
        sw.Start ();

        Console.WriteLine ("Press Enter to show elapsed time...");
        Console.ReadLine ();

        Console.WriteLine (sw.Stop () + " millseconds");
    }
}
```

The *Activator.GetObject* and *Activator.CreateInstance* Methods

The *new* operator isn't the only way to activate remote objects. The .NET Framework offers alternative activation mechanisms in the form of static methods named *GetObject* and *CreateInstance*. Both are members of the *System.Activator* class. *GetObject* is used to activate server-activated objects, while *CreateInstance* is used to activate client-activated objects.

When you use *GetObject* or *CreateInstance* to activate remote objects, you no longer have to call *RegisterActivatedClientType* or *RegisterWellKnownClientType* to register remotable classes on the server. For example, rather than activate a server-activated object this way

```
RemotingConfiguration.RegisterWellKnownClientType
    (typeof (Clock), "tcp://localhost:1234/Clock");
Clock clock = new Clock ();
```

you can can activate the object this way:

```
Clock clock = (Clock) Activator.GetObject
    (typeof (Clock), "tcp://localhost:1234/Clock");
```

And rather than activate a client-activated object this way

```
RemotingConfiguration.RegisterActivatedClientType
    (typeof (Stopwatch), "tcp://localhost:1234");
Stopwatch sw = new Stopwatch ();
```

you can activate it this way:

```
object[] url = { new UrlAttribute ("tcp://localhost:1234") };
Stopwatch sw = (Stopwatch) Activator.CreateInstance
    (typeof (Stopwatch), null, url);
```

The big question is why? Why use *GetObject* or *CreateInstance* to activate a remote object when you could use *new* instead? Neither *GetObject* nor *CreateInstance* is intrinsically better than *new*, but both offer one option that *new* doesn't. *GetObject* and *CreateInstance* can be used to activate a remote type if you possess no knowledge of the type other than a URL and an interface that the type supports. For example, suppose you modify Figure 15-2's *Clock* class so that it implements an interface named *IClock*. With *GetObject*, you could activate a *Clock* object and get back an *IClock* interface without referencing the *Clock* type in your source code:

```
IClock ic = (IClock) Activator.GetObject
    (typeof (IClock), "tcp://localhost:1234/Clock");
```

Try the same thing with *new*, however, and the code won't compile because *new* won't accept an interface name:

```
// Won't compile!
RemotingConfiguration.RegisterWellKnownClientType
    (typeof (IClock), "tcp://localhost:1234/Clock");
IClock ic = new IClock ();
```

CreateInstance can be used in a similar manner to activate a remote client-activated object and return an interface—again, without having intimate knowledge of the type that implements the interface.

Outside the admittedly rare circumstances in which you have metadata describing an interface that a type implements but no metadata describing the type itself, you can use *new* and *GetObject* and *new* and *CreateInstance* interchangeably.

Object Lifetimes and Lifetime Leases

How long does a remote object live once it's activated? In DCOM, an object is destroyed (rather, the object destroys itself) when its reference count reaches 0—that is, when the last client calls *Release* on the last interface pointer. There is no reference counting in .NET remoting. A single-call server-activated object lives for the duration of exactly one method call. After that, it's marked for deletion by the garbage collector. Singleton server-activated objects and client-activated objects work differently. Their lifetimes are controlled by *leases* that can be manipulated declaratively or programmatically. Physically, a lease is an object that implements the *ILease* interface defined in the *System.Runtime.Remoting.Lifetime* namespace.

The following *ILease* properties govern the lifetime of the object with which a lease is associated:

Property	Description	Get	Set
InitialLeaseTime	Length of time following activation that the object lives if it receives no method calls	✓	✓
RenewOnCallTime	Minimum value that *CurrentLeaseTime* is set to each time the object receives a call	✓	✓
CurrentLeaseTime	Amount of time remaining before the object is deactivated if it doesn't receive a method call	✓	

The default lease assigned to singleton server-activated objects and client-activated objects has an *InitialLeaseTime* of 5 minutes, a *RenewOnCallTime* equal to 2 minutes, and a *CurrentLeaseTime* of 5 minutes. If the object receives no method calls, it's deactivated when *CurrentLeaseTime* ticks down to 0—that is, after 5 minutes. However, each method call that the object receives in the last 2 minutes of its life extends the lease by setting *CurrentLeaseTime* to 2 minutes. This effectively means that after an initial grace period whose duration equals *InitialLeaseTime*, the object must be called at intervals no greater than *RenewOnCallTime* or it will go away.

If the default *InitialLeaseTime* and *RenewOnCallTime* values aren't suitable for an application you're writing, you can change them in either of two ways. The first option is to specify lease times in a CONFIG file. Lease properties set this way affect all remote objects in the server process. The second option is to override *MarshalByRefObject.InitializeLifetimeService* in the remotable class. Lease properties set that way affect only instances of the overriding class and can be used to assign different lifetimes to different objects.

Here's an example demonstrating the first option. The following CONFIG file sets *InitialLeaseTime* and *RenewOnCallTime* to 20 minutes and 10 minutes, respectively, for all objects in the process:

```
<configuration>
  <system.runtime.remoting>
    <application>
      <lifetime leaseTime="20M" renewOnCallTime="10M" />
    </application>
  </system.runtime.remoting>
</configuration>
```

20M means 20 minutes. Other supported suffixes include D for days, H for hours, S for seconds, and MS for milliseconds. A number without a suffix is interpreted to mean seconds. In order for the policies outlined in the CONFIG file to take effect, the server process—the one that registers objects for remote activation—must register the file with *RemotingConfiguration.Configure*.

The alternative to setting lease options declaratively is to set them programmatically by overriding *InitializeLifetimeService*. Here's a remotable class that does just that:

```
using System;
using System.Runtime.Remoting.Lifetime;

public class RemotableClass : MarshalByRefObject
{
    public override object InitializeLifetimeService ()
    {
        // Get the default lease
        ILease lease = (ILease) base.InitializeLifetimeService ();

        // Modify it
        if (lease.CurrentState == LeaseState.Initial) {
            lease.InitialLeaseTime = TimeSpan.FromMinutes (20);
            lease.RenewOnCallTime = TimeSpan.FromMinutes (10);
        }
        return lease;
    }
    ...
}
```

A lease can be modified only if it hasn't been activated yet (that is, if the object has just been created). The *if* clause in this sample reads *ILease.CurrentState* to make absolutely sure that the lease hasn't been activated.

A remotable class can do away with leases altogether by overriding *InitializeLifetimeService* and returning null:

```
using System;

public class Foo : MarshalByRefObject
{
    public override object InitializeLifetimeService ()
    {
        return null;
    }
    ...
}
```

An object that does this won't be deleted by the .NET Framework and will continue to run as long as the application domain, process, and machine that host it are running.

A remotable object can acquire a reference to its own lease's *ILease* interface at any point during its lifetime by calling the *GetLifetimeService* method that it inherits from *MarshalByRefObject*. It can also call *ILease.CurrentLeaseTime* and *ILease.Renew* to find out how much time it has left and ask the system to extend the lease. Clients too can acquire *ILease* interfaces and use them to exert control over leases. The static *RemotingServices.GetLifetimeService* method takes a client-side object reference as input and returns an *ILease* interface. Here's an example demonstrating how to manipulate a lease from the client side:

```
RemotableClass rc = new RemotableClass ();
ILease lease = (ILease) RemotingServices.GetLifetimeService (rc);
TimeSpan remaining = lease.CurrentLeaseTime;
if (remaining.TotalMinutes < 1.0)
    lease.Renew (TimeSpan.FromMinutes (10));
```

In this example, the client renews the lease if *ILease.CurrentLeaseTime* reveals that the lease runs out in less than a minute. The *TimeSpan* value passed to *Renew* specifies the amount of time to add to the lease. If *CurrentLeaseTime* is greater than the value passed to *Renew*, *Renew* has no effect. But if *CurrentLeaseTime* is less than the value specified in *Renew*'s parameter list, *Renew* sets *CurrentLeaseTime* to the specified value.

ILease also has methods named *Register* and *Unregister* that register and unregister sponsors. A *sponsor* is an object that implements the *System.Runtime.Remoting.Lifetime.ISponsor* interface. When an object's lease expires, the .NET Framework doesn't mark the object for deletion immediately; first it checks with the application domain's lease manager to see whether any sponsors are registered. If the answer is yes, the lease manager calls the sponsors' *ISponsor.Renewal* methods to see whether any of the sponsors are willing to "sponsor" the object and extend its lease. Sponsors can be registered by clients and servers, and they provide a handy mechanism for controlling object lifetimes based on criteria that you define rather than on the passage of time and the frequency of incoming calls. The *ClientSponsor* class in the FCL's *System.Runtime.Remoting.Lifetime* namespace provides a canned implementation of sponsors that you can use without building sponsor classes of your own.

Because sponsors don't have to reside on the same machine as the objects they serve, the .NET Framework limits the length of time it waits for a response when it calls a sponsor's *Renewal* method. The default is 2 minutes. You can modify the time-out interval by setting a lease's *ILease.SponsorshipTimeout* property.

The .NET Framework's reliance on leases to control the lifetimes of remote objects has an important implication that requires some getting used to by COM programmers. COM objects don't disappear prematurely unless a buggy client releases one interface too many or the host process terminates. In .NET remoting, however, objects can go away without warning. What happens if a client calls an object that no longer exists? The framework throws a *RemotingException*. A client might respond to that exception by creating a new object instance and trying again. To the extent you can, try to avoid such errors by using leases with sufficiently high *InitialLeaseTime* and *RenewOnCallTime* values.

Advanced Remoting

The first half of this chapter imparted the fundamental knowledge you need to activate managed objects remotely. You learned how to make classes remotable, how to register them for remote activation, and how to activate them. You learned about the difference between server-activated objects and client-activated objects, and you learned about the two activation modes—single-call and singleton—supported by server-activated objects. You also learned about the role that channels play in remote activation and how leases control a remote object's lifetime.

The second half of this chapter builds on what you've learned and enriches your understanding of .NET remoting. In it, you'll learn:

■   How to use IIS as an activation agent in order to avoid having to manually start server processes running

■   How to combine HTTP channels with binary formatters to increase efficiency on the wire

■   How to use events and delegates with remotely activated objects

■   How to place asynchronous method calls to remote objects

This part of the chapter concludes with a distributed drawing application that ties together many of the concepts introduced in the following pages.

Using IIS as an Activation Agent

One of the most striking differences between .NET remoting and DCOM is that the former offers no support for automatically launching server processes. Someone has to start the server process running so that it can register classes for remote activation and listen for activation requests. This behavior contrasts starkly with that of DCOM, which starts new server processes on request when remote clients call *CoCreateInstanceEx* or other activation API functions.

.NET remoting offers two ways for you to avoid having to manually start server processes. Option number 1 is to implement the server application as a service. You can write a service by deriving from *System.ServiceProcess.Service-Base* and overriding key virtual methods such as *OnStart* and *OnStop*. The benefit to implementing a remoting server as a service is that you can configure a service to start automatically each time the system starts up. A service can also run absent a logged-on user, meaning that after auto-starting, it's always running and always available—even when no one is logged in at the server console.

Option number 2 is to use IIS as an activation agent. IIS is a service itself and is always up and running on most Web servers. Moreover, IIS is capable of responding to requests from remote clients who want to activate objects on the server using the .NET remoting infrastructure. Using IIS as an activation agent has several advantages:

- You don't have to write a server application to register remotable classes and listen for activation requests; IIS is the server application.

- You can use IIS to authenticate remote callers and also to safeguard data with Secure Sockets Layer (SSL).

- You can use IIS for port negotiation. If you deploy two conventional server applications on the same machine, it's up to you to ensure that the applications use different port numbers. With IIS as the host, however, IIS picks the port numbers, which simplifies deployment and administration.

IIS supports both server-activated objects and client-activated objects. Classes remoted with IIS's help can be registered programmatically (in Global.asax) or declaratively (in Web.config). The following Web.config file registers the *Clock* class in Figure 15-2 for remote activation using IIS:

```
<configuration>
  <system.runtime.remoting>
    <application>
      <service>
        <wellknown mode="SingleCall" type="Clock, ClockServer"
          objectUri="Clock.rem" />
      </service>
    </application>
  </system.runtime.remoting>
</configuration>
```

Note *Clock*'s URI: Clock.rem. URIs registered with IIS must end in .rem or .soap because both extensions are mapped to Aspnet_isapi.dll in the IIS metabase and to the .NET remoting subsystem in Machine.config. You can register additional extensions if you'd like, but these are the only two that work out of the box.

Objects activated with IIS always use HTTP channels to communicate with remote clients. Clients must also register HTTP channels. Here's how a client would create a *Clock* instance, assuming *Clock* resides in a virtual directory named MyClock on the local machine:

```
HttpClientChannel channel = new HttpClientChannel ();
ChannelServices.RegisterChannel (channel);
RemotingConfiguration.RegisterWellKnownClientType
    (typeof (Clock), "http://localhost/MyClock/Clock.rem");
Clock clock = new Clock ();
```

Notice that no port number is specified anywhere—neither on the client nor on the server. IIS picks the port numbers.

Client-activated objects are registered and activated differently. This Web.config file registers *Clock* as a client-activated object rather than a server-activated one:

```
<configuration>
  <system.runtime.remoting>
    <application>
      <service>
        <activated type="Clock, ClockServer" />
      </service>
    </application>
  </system.runtime.remoting>
</configuration>
```

And here's how a remote client would activate it, once more assuming *Clock* resides in a virtual directory named MyClock on the local machine:

```
HttpClientChannel channel = new HttpClientChannel ();
ChannelServices.RegisterChannel (channel);
RemotingConfiguration.RegisterActivatedClientType
    (typeof (Clock), "http://localhost/MyClock");
Clock clock = new Clock ();
```

Be aware that IIS client activation *requires* the remotable class to be hosted in a virtual directory other than wwwroot. You can't use IIS to activate a client-activated object by putting a Web.config file registering the class in wwwroot and the DLL that implements the class in wwwroot\bin. Instead, you must install Web.config in a separate virtual directory (for example, MyClock) and the DLL in the bin subdirectory (MyClock\bin). Only then will IIS activate a client-activated object.

HTTP Channels and Binary Formatters

One drawback to using IIS as an activation agent is that you have no choice but to use HTTP channels to link application domains. HTTP is a higher-level protocol than TCP and is also less efficient on the wire. Furthermore, HTTP channels encode calls as SOAP messages, which increases the verbosity of message traffic.

Fortunately, the .NET remoting infrastructure uses a pluggable channel architecture that lets you choose the channel type as well as the format in which messages are encoded by the chosen channel. IIS supports only HTTP channels, but it doesn't require the channel to encode calls as SOAP messages. HTTP channels use SOAP by default because they use formatters named *Soap-ClientFormatterSinkProvider* and *SoapServerFormatterSinkProvider* to serialize and deserialize messages. You can replace these formatters with instances of *BinaryClientFormatterSinkProvider* and *BinaryServerFormatterSinkProvider* and encode messages in a more compact binary format. Binary messages utilize network bandwidth more efficiently and still allow you to use IIS as the activation agent.

The following Web.config file registers *Clock* to be activated by IIS as a single-call server-activated object. It also replaces the default SOAP formatter with a binary formatter on the server side. Changes are highlighted in bold:

```
<configuration>
  <system.runtime.remoting>
    <application>
      <service>
        <wellknown mode="SingleCall" type="Clock, ClockServer"
          objectUri="Clock.rem" />
      </service>
      <channels>
        <channel ref="http server">
          <serverProviders>
            <formatter ref="binary" />
          </serverProviders>
        </channel>
      </channels>
    </application>
  </system.runtime.remoting>
</configuration>
```

A client that wants to activate instances of *Clock* that are registered in this way must pair a client-side HTTP channel with a binary formatter too. The following example demonstrates how a client can configure the channel programmatically and then activate a remote instance of *Clock*:

```
HttpClientChannel channel = new HttpClientChannel
    ("HttpBinary", new BinaryClientFormatterSinkProvider ());
ChannelServices.RegisterChannel (channel);
RemotingConfiguration.RegisterWellKnownClientType
    (typeof (Clock), "http://localhost/MyClock/Clock.rem");
Clock clock = new Clock ();
```

A client that prefers declarative configuration would do it this way instead:

```
RemotingConfiguration.Configure ("Client.exe.config");
Clock clock = new Clock ();
```

Here are the contents of Client.exe.config:

```
<configuration>
  <system.runtime.remoting>
    <application>
      <client>
        <wellknown type="Clock, ClockServer"
          url="http://localhost/MyClock/Clock.rem" />
      </client>
      <channels>
        <channel ref="http client">
          <clientProviders>
            <formatter ref="binary" />
          </clientProviders>
        </channel>
      </channels>
    </application>
  </system.runtime.remoting>
</configuration>
```

Combining HTTP channels with binary formatters lets you have your cake and eat it too. Using similar tactics, you could combine TCP channels with SOAP formatters to encode message traffic as SOAP messages. You can even build formatters of your own and plug them into existing channels. The modular nature of the .NET Framework's remoting infrastructure makes all sorts of interesting extensions possible without requiring you to write a ton of code or replace portions of the framework that you have no desire to replace.

Delegates and Events

One of the hallmarks of the .NET Framework's type system is that it elevates events to first-class type members along with methods, properties, and fields. Better still, the framework's event infrastructure works with remote objects as well as local objects. A client connects event handlers to events fired by remote objects using the very same syntax that it uses to connect handlers to events fired by local objects. The only catch is that the client must register a server channel as well as a client channel so that it can receive event callbacks. By the same token, the server, which normally registers only a server channel, must register a client channel too so that it can fire events to remote clients.

Suppose you built a *Clock* class that fires a *NewHour* event at the top of every hour. Here's how that class—and a delegate defining the signature of *NewHour* handlers—might be declared:

```
public delegate void NewHourHandler (int hour);

public class Clock : MarshalByRefObject
{
    public event NewHourHandler NewHour;
       ...
}
```

Here's a Web.config file that registers *Clock* for remote activation as a server-activated singleton using IIS:

```
<configuration>
  <system.runtime.remoting>
    <application>
      <service>
        <wellknown mode="Singleton" type="Clock, ClockServer"
          objectUri="Clock.rem" />
      </service>
      <channels>
        <channel ref="http" />
      </channels>
    </application>
  </system.runtime.remoting>
</configuration>
```

Note the *ref* attribute accompanying the *channel* element. The value "http" instantiates a two-way *HttpChannel* object instead of a one-way *HttpServer-Channel*. The two-way channel is necessary if *Clock* is to receive calls from remote clients and fire events to them as well.

Here's client code to create a *Clock* instance and register a handler for *NewHour* events:

```
RemotingConfiguration.Configure ("Client.exe.config");
Clock clock = new Clock ();
clock.NewHour += new NewHourHandler (OnNewHour);
   .

   .

   .
public void OnNewHour (int hour)
{
    // NewHour event received
}
```

And here's the CONFIG file referenced in the client's code, which assumes that *Clock* is deployed in a virtual directory named MyClock:

```
<configuration>
  <system.runtime.remoting>
    <application>
      <client>
        <wellknown type="Clock, ClockServer"
          url="http://localhost/MyClock/Clock.rem" />
      </client>
      <channels>
        <channel ref="http" port="0" />
      </channels>
    </application>
  </system.runtime.remoting>
</configuration>
```

The client also registers a two-way *HttpChannel*, and it specifies a port number of 0. The 0 configures the channel to listen for callbacks but permits the .NET Framework to pick the port number.

A client that receives events from remote objects must have access to metadata describing the objects. In addition, the objects must have metadata describing the client—at least the client components that contain the callback methods. The practical implication is that if you deploy clients on one machine and remote classes on another, you need to put the clients' binaries in the directory that holds the server components and vice versa.

Asynchronous Method Calls

By default, calls to remote objects are synchronous. A thread that places a synchronous call blocks until the call returns. If the call takes a long time to find its way to the recipient or the recipient takes a long time to process the call once it arrives, the caller waits for a long time as well.

That's why the .NET Framework supports asynchronous method calls. Asynchronous method calls aren't limited to remote objects; they work with local objects too. They're enacted through *asynchronous delegates*, which make placing asynchronous calls almost as easy as placing synchronous ones. Asynchronous calls return immediately, no matter how long they take to reach their recipients or how long the recipients take to process them.

Suppose a remote object has a *CountPrimes* method similar to the one in Figure 14-2. Counting primes is a CPU-intensive task that can take a long time to complete. Calling *CountPrimes* as in the following takes more than 10 seconds on my PC—a 1.4 GHz Pentium with 384 MB of memory:

```
int count = sieve.CountPrimes (100000000);
```

If called through an asynchronous delegate, however, *CountPrimes* returns immediately. To call *CountPrimes* asynchronously, you first declare a delegate whose signature matches *CountPrimes'* signature, as shown here:

```
delegate int CountPrimesDelegate (int max);
```

You then wrap an instance of the delegate around *CountPrimes* and call the delegate's *BeginInvoke* method:

```
CountPrimesDelegate del = new CountPrimesDelegate (sieve.CountPrimes);
IAsyncResult ar = del.BeginInvoke (100000000, null, null);
```

To retrieve the value that *CountPrimes* returns, you later complete the call by calling the delegate's *EndInvoke* method and passing in the *IAsyncResult* returned by *BeginInvoke*:

```
int count = del.EndInvoke (ar);
```

If *CountPrimes* hasn't returned when *EndInvoke* is called, *EndInvoke* blocks until it does. Calling *BeginInvoke* and *EndInvoke* in rapid succession is morally equivalent to calling *CountPrimes* synchronously.

Can a client determine whether an asynchronous call has completed before calling *EndInvoke*? You bet. The *IsCompleted* property of the *IAsyncResult* that *BeginInvoke* returns is true if the call has completed, false if it has not. The following code snippet calls *EndInvoke* if and only if the call has completed:

```
CountPrimesDelegate del = new CountPrimesDelegate (sieve.CountPrimes);
IAsyncResult ar = del.BeginInvoke (100000000, null, null);
    .
    .
    .
if (ar.IsCompleted) {
    int count = del.EndInvoke (ar);
}
else {
    // Try again later
}
```

A client can also use *IAsyncResult's* *AsyncWaitHandle* property to retrieve a synchronization handle. A thread that calls *WaitOne* on that handle blocks until the call completes.

A client can also ask to be notified when an asynchronous call completes. Completion notifications enable a client to learn when a call completes without polling *IsCompleted*. The basic strategy is to wrap a callback method in an instance of *System.AsyncCallback* and pass the resulting delegate to *BeginInvoke*. When the call completes, the callback method is called. Here's an example:

```
CountPrimesDelegate del = new CountPrimesDelegate (sieve.CountPrimes);
AsyncCallback ab = new AsyncCallback (PrimesCounted);
IAsyncResult ar = del.BeginInvoke (100000000, ab, null);
    .
    .
    .
void PrimesCounted (IAsyncResult ar)
{
    // CountPrimes completed
}
```

After the callback method is called, you still need to complete the call by calling *EndInvoke*. Only by calling *EndInvoke* can you get the results of the call and let the system clean up after itself following a successful asynchronous call. You can call *EndInvoke* from inside the callback method if you'd like.

One-Way Methods

The .NET remoting infrastructure supports a slightly different form of asynchronous method calls that rely on entities known as *one-way methods*. A one-way method has input parameters only—no *out* or *ref* parameters are allowed—or no parameters at all, and it returns void. You designate a method as a one-way method by tagging it with a *OneWay* attribute:

```
[OneWay]
public void LogError (string message)
{
  ...
}
```

OneWay is shorthand for *OneWayAttribute*, which is an attribute class defined in the *System.Runtime.Remoting.Messaging* namespace.

Calls to one-way methods execute asynchronously. You don't get any results back, and you aren't notified if the method throws an exception. You don't even know for sure that a one-way method call reached the recipient. One-way methods let you place calls using "fire-and-forget" semantics, which are appropriate when you want to fire off a method call, you don't want any results back, and the method's success or failure isn't critical to the integrity of the application as a whole. Sound intriguing? The application in the next section uses one-way methods to fire notifications to remote objects without affecting the liveliness of its user interface. As you work with .NET remoting, you'll probably find additional uses for one-way methods.

Putting It All Together: The NetDraw Application

Let's close with an application that assembles many of the concepts outlined in this chapter into one tidy package. The application is shown in Figure 15-5. It's a distributed drawing program that links clients together so that sketches drawn in one window appear in the other windows, too. Before you try it, you need to deploy it. Here's how:

1. Build the application's binaries. Here are the commands:

```
csc /t:library paperserver.cs
csc /t:winexe /r:paperserver.dll netdraw.cs
```

   These commands produce binaries named PaperServer.dll and NetDraw.exe. PaperServer.dll implements a remotable class named *Paper* and a utility class named *Stroke*. It also declares a delegate that clients can use to wrap handlers for the *NewStroke* events that *Paper* fires. NetDraw.exe is a Windows Forms application that serves as a remote client to *Paper* objects.

2. Create a virtual directory named NetDraw on your Web server. Copy Web.config to the NetDraw directory. Create a bin subdirectory in the NetDraw directory and copy both NetDraw.exe and PaperServer.dll to bin.

3. Create another directory somewhere on your Web server (it needn't be a virtual directory) and copy NetDraw.exe, NetDraw.exe.config, and PaperServer.dll to it.

Now start two instances of NetDraw.exe and scribble in one of them by moving the mouse with the left button held down. Each time you release the button, the stroke that you just drew should appear in the other NetDraw window. If you'd like to try it over a network, simply move NetDraw.exe, NetDraw.exe.config, and PaperServer.dll to another machine and modify the URL in NetDraw.exe.config to point to the remote server.

Figure 15-5   The NetDraw application.

NetDraw, whose source code appears in Figure 15-6, demonstrates several important principles of .NET remoting. Let's tackle the big picture first. At startup, the client—NetDraw.exe—instantiates a *Paper* object and registers a handler for the object's *NewStroke* events:

```
VirtualPaper = new Paper ();
NewStrokeHandler = new StrokeHandler (OnNewStroke);
VirtualPaper.NewStroke += NewStrokeHandler;
```

Upon completion of each new stroke drawn by the user (that is, when the mouse button comes up), NetDraw calls the *Paper* object's *DrawStroke* method and passes in a *Stroke* object containing a series of *x-y* coordinate pairs describing the stroke:

```
VirtualPaper.DrawStroke (CurrentStroke);
```

DrawStroke, in turn, fires a *NewStroke* event to all clients that registered handlers for *NewStroke* events. It passes the *Stroke* provided by the client in the event's parameter list:

```
public void DrawStroke (Stroke stroke)
{
    if (NewStroke != null)
        NewStroke (stroke);
}
```

The event activates each client's *OnNewStroke* method, which adds the *Stroke* to a collection of *Stroke* objects maintained by each individual client and draws the stroke on the screen. Because *Paper* is registered as a singleton, all clients that call *new* on it receive a reference to the same *Paper* object. Consequently, a stroke drawn in one client is reported immediately to the others.

That's the view from 10,000 feet. The meat, however, is in the details. Here are some highlights to look for as you peruse the source code:

■   Web.config registers the *Paper* class so that it can be activated remotely. Activation is performed by IIS. Web.config registers a two-way HTTP channel accompanied by binary formatters. The two-way channel enables *Paper* to receive calls from its clients and fire events to them as well. The binary formatters increase the channel's efficiency on the wire.

■   At startup, NetDraw registers a channel of its own and registers *Paper* in the local application domain using NetDraw.exe.config. That file contains the remote object's URL (*http://localhost/NetDraw/Paper.rem*). It also registers a two-way HTTP channel with binary formatters so that the client can place calls to remote *Paper* objects and receive events fired by those objects.

■   *Paper*'s *DrawStroke* method is a one-way method, enabling clients to fire off calls to it without waiting for the calls to return. Synchronous calls to *DrawStroke* would produce a sluggish user interface. Imagine 1000 instances of NetDraw connected over a slow network and you'll see what I mean.

■   Callbacks emanating from events fired by remote objects execute on threads provided by the .NET Framework. To make sure that its main thread can't access *Strokes* while *OnNewStroke* updates it (or vice versa), NetDraw uses C#'s *lock* keyword to synchronize access to *Strokes*.

■   *Stroke* objects accompany *DrawStroke* methods and *NewStroke* events as method parameters. So that instances of *Stroke* can travel between application domains (and, by extension, between machines), the *Stroke* class includes a *Serializable* attribute. That enables the .NET Framework to serialize a *Stroke* into the channel and rehydrate it on the other side. *Stroke* is a *marshal-by-value* (MBV) class, whereas *Paper* is marshal-by-reference. MBV means no proxies are created; instead, the object is copied to the destination.

■   The *Paper* class overrides *InitializeLifetimeService* and returns null so that *Paper* objects won't disappear if clients go for 5 minutes without calling them. As an alternative, *Paper* could simply set its lease's *RenewOnCallTime* property to something greater than 5 minutes—say, an hour.

If NetDraw.cs looks familiar to you, that's because it's almost identical to Chapter 4's NetDraw.cs. With a little help from .NET remoting, it didn't take much to turn a stand-alone application into a distributed application. You provide client and server components; the framework provides the plumbing that connects them. That's what .NET remoting is all about.

PaperServer.cs

```
using System;
using System.Drawing;
using System.Drawing.Drawing2D;
using System.Runtime.Remoting.Messaging;
using System.Collections;

public delegate void StrokeHandler (Stroke stroke);

public class Paper : MarshalByRefObject
{
    public event StrokeHandler NewStroke;

    public override object InitializeLifetimeService ()
    {
        return null;
    }

    [OneWay]
    public void DrawStroke (Stroke stroke)
    {
        if (NewStroke != null)
            NewStroke (stroke);
    }
}

[Serializable]
public class Stroke
{
    ArrayList Points = new ArrayList ();

    public int Count
    {
        get { return Points.Count; }
    }

    public Stroke (int x, int y)
    {
        Points.Add (new Point (x, y));
    }
```

Figure 15-6   Source code for a distributed drawing application.

PaperServer.cs   *(continued)*

```csharp
    public void Add (int x, int y)
    {
        Points.Add (new Point (x, y));
    }

    public void Draw (Graphics g)
    {
        Pen pen = new Pen (Color.Black, 8);
        pen.EndCap = LineCap.Round;
        for (int i=0; i<Points.Count - 1; i++)
            g.DrawLine (pen, (Point) Points[i], (Point) Points[i + 1]);
        pen.Dispose ();
    }

    public void DrawLastSegment (Graphics g)
    {
        Point p1 = (Point) Points[Points.Count - 2];
        Point p2 = (Point) Points[Points.Count - 1];
        Pen pen = new Pen (Color.Black, 8);
        pen.EndCap = LineCap.Round;
        g.DrawLine (pen, p1, p2);
        pen.Dispose ();
    }
}
```

Web.config

```xml
<configuration>
  <system.runtime.remoting>
    <application>
      <service>
        <wellknown mode="Singleton" type="Paper, PaperServer"
          objectUri="Paper.rem" />
      </service>
      <channels>
        <channel ref="http">
          <clientProviders>
            <formatter ref="binary"/>
          </clientProviders>
          <serverProviders>
            <formatter ref="binary"/>
          </serverProviders>
        </channel>
      </channels>
    </application>
  </system.runtime.remoting>
</configuration>
```

NetDraw.cs

```
using System;
using System.Collections;
using System.Windows.Forms;
using System.Drawing;
using System.Drawing.Drawing2D;
using System.Runtime.Remoting;
using System.ComponentModel;

class MyForm : Form
{
    Paper VirtualPaper;
    Stroke CurrentStroke = null;
    ArrayList Strokes = new ArrayList ();
    StrokeHandler NewStrokeHandler;

    MyForm ()
    {
        Text = "NetDraw";

        try {
            // Configure the remoting infrastructure
            RemotingConfiguration.Configure ("NetDraw.exe.config");

            // Create a remote Paper object
            VirtualPaper = new Paper ();

            // Connect a handler to the object's NewStroke events
            NewStrokeHandler = new StrokeHandler (OnNewStroke);
            VirtualPaper.NewStroke += NewStrokeHandler;
        }
        catch (Exception ex) {
            MessageBox.Show (ex.Message);
            Close ();
        }
    }

    protected override void OnPaint (PaintEventArgs e)
    {
        lock (Strokes.SyncRoot) {
            // Draw all currently recorded strokes
            foreach (Stroke stroke in Strokes)
                stroke.Draw (e.Graphics);
        }
    }

    protected override void OnMouseDown (MouseEventArgs e)
    {
```

(continued)

NetDraw.cs   *(continued)*

```csharp
        if (e.Button == MouseButtons.Left) {
            // Create a new Stroke and assign it to CurrentStroke
            CurrentStroke = new Stroke (e.X, e.Y);
        }
    }

    protected override void OnMouseMove (MouseEventArgs e)
    {
        if ((e.Button & MouseButtons.Left) != 0 &&
            CurrentStroke != null) {
            // Add a new segment to the current stroke
            CurrentStroke.Add (e.X, e.Y);
            Graphics g = Graphics.FromHwnd (Handle);
            CurrentStroke.DrawLastSegment (g);
            g.Dispose ();
        }
    }

    protected override void OnMouseUp (MouseEventArgs e)
    {
        if (e.Button == MouseButtons.Left && CurrentStroke != null) {
            // Complete the current stroke
            if (CurrentStroke.Count > 1) {
                // Let other clients know about it, too
                VirtualPaper.DrawStroke (CurrentStroke);
            }
            CurrentStroke = null;
        }
    }

    protected override void OnKeyDown (KeyEventArgs e)
    {
        if (e.KeyCode == Keys.Delete) {
            // Delete all strokes and repaint
            lock (Strokes.SyncRoot) {
                Strokes.Clear ();
            }
            Invalidate ();
        }
    }

    protected override void OnClosing (CancelEventArgs e)
    {
        // Disconnect event handler before closing
        base.OnClosing (e);
        VirtualPaper.NewStroke -= NewStrokeHandler;
    }
```

```
    public void OnNewStroke (Stroke stroke)
    {
        // Record and display a stroke drawn in a remote client
        lock (Strokes.SyncRoot) {
            Strokes.Add (stroke);
        }
        Graphics g = Graphics.FromHwnd (Handle);
        stroke.Draw (g);
        g.Dispose ();
    }

    static void Main ()
    {
        Application.Run (new MyForm ());
    }
}
```

NetDraw.exe.config

```
<configuration>
  <system.runtime.remoting>
    <application>
      <client>
        <wellknown type="Paper, PaperServer"
          url="http://localhost/NetDraw/Paper.rem" />
      </client>
      <channels>
        <channel ref="http" port="0">
          <clientProviders>
            <formatter ref="binary" />
          </clientProviders>
          <serverProviders>
            <formatter ref="binary" />
          </serverProviders>
        </channel>
      </channels>
    </application>
  </system.runtime.remoting>
</configuration>
```

Microsoft .NET: A Whole New Ball Game

That does it for .NET remoting. That does it for this book, too; you've reached the end. You've seen up close and personal what programming with the .NET Framework is like. If there's one thing that should be apparent to you, it's that Microsoft .NET changes the rules of the game and provides a whole new paradigm for writing and executing code. The old ways have passed away. New ways have taken their place.

As you embark upon your new career as a Microsoft .NET programmer, keep in mind that the .NET Framework isn't standing still. As you read this, programmers in Redmond, Washington, are busy adding new features and figuring out what the framework must do to adapt to the needs not only of today's developers, but also of tomorrow's. Keep an eye on the Microsoft .NET home page—*http://www.microsoft.com/net*—for late-breaking news.

Index

Jeff Prosise

Jeff Prosise makes his living programming Microsoft .NET and teaching others how to do the same. A former mechanical engineer who began writing software for PCs in 1983, Jeff has since written nine books and countless magazine articles about computers and computer programming, including the award-winning *Programming Windows with MFC, Second Edition* (Microsoft Press, 1999), and he currently serves as a contributing editor to *MSDN Magazine*. In 2000, Jeff cofounded Wintellect, a software consulting and  education firm based in Knoxville, Tennessee. After nearly two decades in the business, Jeff has developed a reputation for making complex technical topics understandable to developers of all skill levels.

Spring Scale

Reptiles, fish, and some insects have them. A series of musical notes can be one. But let's discuss another kind of scale-the kind commonly used in households, scientific laboratories, businesses, and industry to measure weight or mass. In a spring scale, a platform connected to a spring stretches or compresses according to the load placed on the platform. A needle shows how much the spring stretches or compresses to indicate the weight of the load. Many bathroom scales are spring scales. Spring scales are fairly inexpensive to manufacture for one simple reason-economies of scale.*

At Microsoft Press, we use tools to illustrate our books for software developers and IT professionals. Tools are an elegant symbol of human inventiveness and a powerful metaphor for how people can extend their capabilities, precision, and reach. From basic calipers and pliers to digital micrometers and lasers, our stylized illustrations of tools give each book a visual identity and each book series a personality. With tools and knowledge, there are no limits to creativity and innovation. Our tag line says it all: *The tools you need to put technology to work.*

The manuscript for this book was prepared and galleyed using Microsoft Word. Pages were composed by Microsoft Press using Adobe FrameMaker+SGML for Windows, with text in Garamond and display type in Helvetica Condensed. Composed pages were delivered to the printer as electronic prepress files.

Cover Designer:	Methodologie, Inc.
Interior Graphic Designer:	James D. Kramer
Principal Compositor:	Kerri DeVault
Interior Artist:	Joel Panchot
Principal Copy Editors:	Melissa Bryan, Patricia Masserman
Indexer:	Bill Meyers

Got .NET?

You will with this updated, witty overview—now based on final release code!

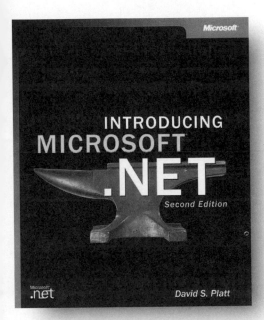

Introducing Microsoft® .NET, Second Edition
U.S.A. $29.99
Canada $43.99
ISBN: 0-7356-1571-3

What problems can Microsoft .NET solve? What architectural approaches does it take to solve them? How do you start using .NET, and how do you profit from it? Get the answers to these questions and more in the entertaining second edition of this book—now expanded with **seven new chapters** based on final release code for the .NET Framework. Its organization makes it easy to choose how deep you want to go technically. The well-known author and consultant expertly covers a single topic from the top down in each chapter, introducing simpler concepts first and then progressing into greater technical detail. He makes his points with a minimum of jargon, a maximum of wit, a multitude of diagrams, and a wealth of meaningful analogies and clear explanations. By the end of this illuminating .NET walkthrough, you'll know enough about this revolutionary platform to plan for the future of software as a Web service.

microsoft.com/mspress

Discover how to
develop and deploy
.NET My Services today!

Introducing Microsoft® .NET My Services
U.S.A. **$29.99**
Canada $43.99
ISBN: 0-7356-1558-6

Microsoft .NET My Services—an innovative set of user-centric XML Web services—empowers users and businesses to collaborate in exciting new ways by making communication among different devices and platforms seamless. Find out how to take full advantage of these services today with this expertly written technical treatise. This introduction details the architecture behind .NET My Services and provides real-world examples of how it benefits everyday users. Then it drills down into how to develop applications that consume .NET My Services. You'll explore the building blocks behind .NET My Services and examine the built-in support for it in Microsoft Visual Studio® .NET. You'll even build an application with Microsoft Visual C#™ .NET and tackle advanced design scenarios such as integrating .NET My Services functionality in a client-side application.

microsoft.com/mspress

Get the *expert guidance* you need to succeed *in .NET Framework development.*

U.S.A. **$49.99**
Canada $72.99
ISBN: 0-7356-1422-9

The Microsoft® .NET Framework allows developers to quickly build robust, secure ASP.NET Web Forms and XML Web service applications, Windows® Forms applications, tools, and types. Find out all about its common language runtime and learn how to leverage its power to build, package, and deploy any kind of application or component. APPLIED MICROSOFT .NET FRAMEWORK PROGRAMMING is ideal for anyone who understands object-oriented programming concepts such as data abstraction, inheritance, and polymorphism. The book carefully explains the extensible type system of the .NET Framework, examines how the runtime manages the behavior of types, and explores how an application manipulates types. While focusing on C#, the concepts presented apply to all programming languages that target the .NET Framework

microsoft.com/mspress

Programming ASP.NET
Starring Jeff Prosise

Learn to write cutting-edge Web applications and Web services by combining the richness of the .NET Framework with the easy-to-use programming model of ASP.NET.

Who should attend: Developers new .NET whose primary focus is writing applications that run on the Web; ASP developers migrating to ASP.NET.

Topics: Essential Web programming concepts; C# and the Common Language Runtime; the .NET Framework Class Library; Web Forms; Web controls; user controls; custom controls; ADO.NET; XML; ASP.NET application architecture; ASP.NET security; Web services; error handling and debugging; scalability and performance.

Prerequisites: Reading knowledge of HTML; understanding of basic object-oriented programming concepts.

Length: 5 days.

Wintellect.com

For the latest in .NET articles and code samples as well as tips, newsletters and course materials, check out our website at www.wintellect.com.

Programming the .NET Framework with C#

Starring Jeffrey Richter

A highly detailed, no-holds-barred introduction to the platform and its programming models, with special emphasis on understanding the Common and Language Runtime and .NET Framework Class Library -- all in C#.

Who should attend: Developers looking for a broad but detailed overview of .NET who wish to explore its architecture, learn about the types of applications that it supports, and get first-hand experience programming the new platform.

Topics: Platform architecture; assemblies; types and type members; automatic memory management (garbage collection); the .NET Framework Class Library; reflection; threading; Web Forms; Windows Forms; Web servers; interoperability.

Prerequisites: Understanding of basic object-oriented programming concepts.

Length: 5 days.

Programming Visual Basic.NET

Starring Francesco Balena

Everything new and experienced VB developers need to know to leverage the power of Visual Basic.NET and ease the transition from previous versions.

Who should attend: Visual Basic 6.0 developers migrating to Visual Basic.NET; programmers who never used Visual Basic but wish to learn Visual Basic.NET.

Topics: Language syntax changes; object-oriented programming; working with data; advanced language features; threading; regular expressions; assemblies; reflection; interoperability; Windows Forms; ADO.NET; Web Forms; Web services.

Prerequisites: Working knowledge of the BASIC language and its syntax.

Length: 5 days.

Programming ADO.NET

Starring Dino Esposito

An in-depth look at data access in the world of .NET.

Who should attend: Developers new to the platform whose applications will interact with back-end databases such as Microsoft SQL Serve experienced .NET developers who wish to enrich their knowledge of ADO.NET.

Topics: ADO.NET architecture; reading and viewing data; managed providers; updating data server-side data binding; advanced DataGrids; XML and DataSets; XML navigation and transformation; Web services; exposing data to clients.

Prerequisites: Understanding of basic object-oriented programming concepts; familiari with database design fundamentals.

Length: 4 days.

Debugging .NET Applications

Starring John Robbins

Write managed code that works right the first time, brought to you by the Bugslayer himself.

Who should attend: Developers with 6 months or more of .NET experience who wish to enrich their knowledge of the Framework and use that knowledge to become expert debuggers.

Topics: Platform architecture; exception handling; .NET debuggers; debugging with Visual Studio.NET; advanced debugging concepts and practices; debugging ASP.NET Web applications and Web services; debugging multithreaded .NET applications; performance tuning.

Prerequisites: Working knowledge of the .NET Common Language Runtime.

Length: 3 days.

Get a **Free**
e-mail newsletter, updates,
special offers, links to related books,
and more when you

register on line!

Register your Microsoft Press® title on our Web site and you'll get
a FREE subscription to our e-mail newsletter, *Microsoft Press
Book Connections*. You'll find out about newly released and upcoming
books and learning tools, online events, software downloads, special
offers and coupons for Microsoft Press customers, and information
about major Microsoft® product releases. You can also read useful
additional information about all the titles we publish, such as detailed book descriptions, tables of contents and indexes, sample
chapters, links to related books and book series, author biographies,
and reviews by other customers.

Registration is easy. Just visit this Web page and fill in your information:

http://www.microsoft.com/mspress/register

Microsoft®

- -

MICROSOFT LICENSE AGREEMENT

Book Companion CD

IMPORTANT—READ CAREFULLY: This Microsoft End-User License Agreement ("EULA") is a legal agreement between you (either an individual or an entity) and Microsoft Corporation for the Microsoft product identified above, which includes computer software and may include associated media, printed materials, and "online" or electronic documentation ("SOFTWARE PRODUCT"). Any component included within the SOFTWARE PRODUCT that is accompanied by a separate End-User License Agreement shall be governed by such agreement and not the terms set forth below. By installing, copying, or otherwise using the SOFTWARE PRODUCT, you agree to be bound by the terms of this EULA. If you do not agree to the terms of this EULA, you are not authorized to install, copy, or otherwise use the SOFTWARE PRODUCT; you may, however, return the SOFTWARE PRODUCT, along with all printed materials and other items that form a part of the Microsoft product that includes the SOFTWARE PRODUCT, to the place you obtained them for a full refund.

SOFTWARE PRODUCT LICENSE

The SOFTWARE PRODUCT is protected by United States copyright laws and international copyright treaties, as well as other intellectual property laws and treaties. The SOFTWARE PRODUCT is licensed, not sold.

1. **GRANT OF LICENSE.** This EULA grants you the following rights:

   a. **Software Product.** You may install and use one copy of the SOFTWARE PRODUCT on a single computer. The primary user of the computer on which the SOFTWARE PRODUCT is installed may make a second copy for his or her exclusive use on a portable computer.

   b. **Storage/Network Use.** You may also store or install a copy of the SOFTWARE PRODUCT on a storage device, such as a network server, used only to install or run the SOFTWARE PRODUCT on your other computers over an internal network; however, you must acquire and dedicate a license for each separate computer on which the SOFTWARE PRODUCT is installed or run from the storage device. A license for the SOFTWARE PRODUCT may not be shared or used concurrently on different computers.

   c. **License Pak.** If you have acquired this EULA in a Microsoft License Pak, you may make the number of additional copies of the computer software portion of the SOFTWARE PRODUCT authorized on the printed copy of this EULA, and you may use each copy in the manner specified above. You are also entitled to make a corresponding number of secondary copies for portable computer use as specified above.

   d. **Sample Code.** Solely with respect to portions, if any, of the SOFTWARE PRODUCT that are identified within the SOFTWARE PRODUCT as sample code (the "SAMPLE CODE"):

      i. **Use and Modification.** Microsoft grants you the right to use and modify the source code version of the SAMPLE CODE, *provided* you comply with subsection (d)(iii) below. You may not distribute the SAMPLE CODE, or any modified version of the SAMPLE CODE, in source code form.

      ii. **Redistributable Files.** Provided you comply with subsection (d)(iii) below, Microsoft grants you a nonexclusive, royalty-free right to reproduce and distribute the object code version of the SAMPLE CODE and of any modified SAMPLE CODE, other than SAMPLE CODE, or any modified version thereof, designated as not redistributable in the Readme file that forms a part of the SOFTWARE PRODUCT (the "Non-Redistributable Sample Code"). All SAMPLE CODE other than the Non-Redistributable Sample Code is collectively referred to as the "REDISTRIBUTABLES."

      iii. **Redistribution Requirements.** If you redistribute the REDISTRIBUTABLES, you agree to: (i) distribute the REDISTRIBUTABLES in object code form only in conjunction with and as a part of your software application product; (ii) not use Microsoft's name, logo, or trademarks to market your software application product; (iii) include a valid copyright notice on your software application product; (iv) indemnify, hold harmless, and defend Microsoft from and against any claims or lawsuits, including attorney's fees, that arise or result from the use or distribution of your software application product; and (v) not permit further distribution of the REDISTRIBUTABLES by your end user. Contact Microsoft for the applicable royalties due and other licensing terms for all other uses and/or distribution of the REDISTRIBUTABLES.

2. **DESCRIPTION OF OTHER RIGHTS AND LIMITATIONS.**

   - **Limitations on Reverse Engineering, Decompilation, and Disassembly.** You may not reverse engineer, decompile, or disassemble the SOFTWARE PRODUCT, except and only to the extent that such activity is expressly permitted by applicable law notwithstanding this limitation.

   - **Separation of Components.** The SOFTWARE PRODUCT is licensed as a single product. Its component parts may not be separated for use on more than one computer.

   - **Rental.** You may not rent, lease, or lend the SOFTWARE PRODUCT.

   - **Support Services.** Microsoft may, but is not obligated to, provide you with support services related to the SOFTWARE PRODUCT ("Support Services"). Use of Support Services is governed by the Microsoft policies and programs described in the user manual, in "online" documentation, and/or in other Microsoft-provided materials. Any supplemental software code provided to you as part of the Support Services shall be considered part of the SOFTWARE PRODUCT and subject to the terms and conditions of this EULA. With respect to technical information you provide to Microsoft as part of the Support Services, Microsoft may use such information for its business purposes, including for product support and development. Microsoft will not utilize such technical information in a form that personally identifies you.

- **Software Transfer.** You may permanently transfer all of your rights under this EULA, provided you retain no copies, you transfer all of the SOFTWARE PRODUCT (including all component parts, the media and printed materials, any upgrades, this EULA, and, if applicable, the Certificate of Authenticity), **and** the recipient agrees to the terms of this EULA.

- **Termination.** Without prejudice to any other rights, Microsoft may terminate this EULA if you fail to comply with the terms and conditions of this EULA. In such event, you must destroy all copies of the SOFTWARE PRODUCT and all of its component parts.

3. COPYRIGHT. All title and copyrights in and to the SOFTWARE PRODUCT (including but not limited to any images, photographs, animations, video, audio, music, text, SAMPLE CODE, REDISTRIBUTABLES, and "applets" incorporated into the SOFTWARE PRODUCT) and any copies of the SOFTWARE PRODUCT are owned by Microsoft or its suppliers. The SOFTWARE PRODUCT is protected by copyright laws and international treaty provisions. Therefore, you must treat the SOFTWARE PRODUCT like any other copyrighted material **except** that you may install the SOFTWARE PRODUCT on a single computer provided you keep the original solely for backup or archival purposes. You may not copy the printed materials accompanying the SOFTWARE PRODUCT.

4. U.S. GOVERNMENT RESTRICTED RIGHTS. The SOFTWARE PRODUCT and documentation are provided with RESTRICTED RIGHTS. Use, duplication, or disclosure by the Government is subject to restrictions as set forth in subparagraph (c)(1)(ii) of the Rights in Technical Data and Computer Software clause at DFARS 252.227-7013 or subparagraphs (c)(1) and (2) of the Commercial Computer Software—Restricted Rights at 48 CFR 52.227-19, as applicable. Manufacturer is Microsoft Corporation/One Microsoft Way/Redmond, WA 98052-6399.

5. EXPORT RESTRICTIONS. You agree that you will not export or re-export the SOFTWARE PRODUCT, any part thereof, or any process or service that is the direct product of the SOFTWARE PRODUCT (the foregoing collectively referred to as the "Restricted Components"), to any country, person, entity, or end user subject to U.S. export restrictions. You specifically agree not to export or re-export any of the Restricted Components (i) to any country to which the U.S. has embargoed or restricted the export of goods or services, which currently include, but are not necessarily limited to, Cuba, Iran, Iraq, Libya, North Korea, Sudan, and Syria, or to any national of any such country, wherever located, who intends to transmit or transport the Restricted Components back to such country; (ii) to any end user who you know or have reason to know will utilize the Restricted Components in the design, development, or production of nuclear, chemical, or biological weapons; or (iii) to any end user who has been prohibited from participating in U.S. export transactions by any federal agency of the U.S. government. You warrant and represent that neither the BXA nor any other U.S. federal agency has suspended, revoked, or denied your export privileges.

DISCLAIMER OF WARRANTY

NO WARRANTIES OR CONDITIONS. MICROSOFT EXPRESSLY DISCLAIMS ANY WARRANTY OR CONDITION FOR THE SOFTWARE PRODUCT. THE SOFTWARE PRODUCT AND ANY RELATED DOCUMENTATION ARE PROVIDED "AS IS" WITHOUT WARRANTY OR CONDITION OF ANY KIND, EITHER EXPRESS OR IMPLIED, INCLUDING, WITHOUT LIMITATION, THE IMPLIED WARRANTIES OF MERCHANTABILITY, FITNESS FOR A PARTICULAR PURPOSE, OR NONINFRINGEMENT. THE ENTIRE RISK ARISING OUT OF USE OR PERFORMANCE OF THE SOFTWARE PRODUCT REMAINS WITH YOU.

LIMITATION OF LIABILITY. TO THE MAXIMUM EXTENT PERMITTED BY APPLICABLE LAW, IN NO EVENT SHALL MICROSOFT OR ITS SUPPLIERS BE LIABLE FOR ANY SPECIAL, INCIDENTAL, INDIRECT, OR CONSEQUENTIAL DAMAGES WHATSOEVER (INCLUDING, WITHOUT LIMITATION, DAMAGES FOR LOSS OF BUSINESS PROFITS, BUSINESS INTERRUPTION, LOSS OF BUSINESS INFORMATION, OR ANY OTHER PECUNIARY LOSS) ARISING OUT OF THE USE OF OR INABILITY TO USE THE SOFTWARE PRODUCT OR THE PROVISION OF OR FAILURE TO PROVIDE SUPPORT SERVICES, EVEN IF MICROSOFT HAS BEEN ADVISED OF THE POSSIBILITY OF SUCH DAMAGES. IN ANY CASE, MICROSOFT'S ENTIRE LIABILITY UNDER ANY PROVISION OF THIS EULA SHALL BE LIMITED TO THE GREATER OF THE AMOUNT ACTUALLY PAID BY YOU FOR THE SOFTWARE PRODUCT OR US$5.00; PROVIDED, HOWEVER, IF YOU HAVE ENTERED INTO A MICROSOFT SUPPORT SERVICES AGREEMENT, MICROSOFT'S ENTIRE LIABILITY REGARDING SUPPORT SERVICES SHALL BE GOVERNED BY THE TERMS OF THAT AGREEMENT. BECAUSE SOME STATES AND JURISDICTIONS DO NOT ALLOW THE EXCLUSION OR LIMITATION OF LIABILITY, THE ABOVE LIMITATION MAY NOT APPLY TO YOU.

MISCELLANEOUS

This EULA is governed by the laws of the State of Washington USA, except and only to the extent that applicable law mandates governing law of a different jurisdiction.

Should you have any questions concerning this EULA, or if you desire to contact Microsoft for any reason, please contact the Microsoft subsidiary serving your country, or write: Microsoft Sales Information Center/One Microsoft Way/Redmond, WA 98052-6399.